1 MONTH OF
FREE
READING

at

www.ForgottenBooks.com

By purchasing this book you are eligible for one month membership to ForgottenBooks.com, giving you unlimited access to our entire collection of over 1,000,000 titles via our web site and mobile apps.

To claim your free month visit:

www.forgottenbooks.com/free1304435

ISBN 978-0-428-70705-7
PIBN 11304435

TIMBER RESOURCE
STATISTICS
for
MIDSOUTH COUNTIES,
1971

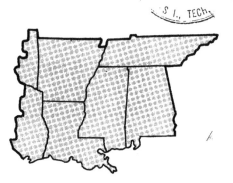

Resource Bulletin SO-31

SOUTHERN FOREST EXPERIMENT STATION

FOREST SERVICE, U. S. DEPARTMENT OF AGRICULTURE

1971

ER RESOURCE STATISTICS
MIDSOUTH COUNTIES, 1971

. Beltz

F. Bertelson

U. S. DEPARTMENT OF AGRICULTURE
FOREST SERVICE

SOUTHERN FOREST EXPERIMENT STATION
New Orleans, Louisiana

1971

Figure 1. Forest Resource regions in the Midsouth.

——————— FOREST RESOURCE REGION BOUNDARY

TIMBER RESOURCE STATISTICS FOR MIDSOUTH COUNTIES, 1971

Roy C. Beltz and Daniel F. Bertelson

Southern forests are changing constantly and rapidly. Though fast-growing, they are subject to heavy cutting for timber and, in some parts, to extensive clearing. Growth and change in industries drawing upon the forests are also rapid. To gage these changes and their effect upon the resource, the Forest Resources Research Unit of the Southern Forest Experiment Station makes on-the-ground surveys at 10-year intervals. The surveys are conducted continuously, one State after another. Hence the information for each State is from a different year; the dates of the most recent surveys are as follows:

Alabama	1963
Arkansas	1969
Louisiana	1964
Mississippi	1967
Oklahoma	1966
Tennessee	1971
Texas	1965

The resource statistics provided by the surveys are the basis for many decisions about the management of both public and private forest land. Because of the interval between surveys, decisions have often been made with information that was neither current nor detailed enough for local needs. To remedy this shortcoming, Forest Resources Research has developed a computerized system for annually updating the basic field data. In this report the method has been applied to produce current resource and production statistics for counties of six States. It is the first such report to become available for the Midsouth—or for any other forest region of comparable size.

In general, Midsouth forest inventories have been trending upward for some time. State or regional totals, however, often mask localized situations in which timber is becoming exceptionally abundant or where the harvest is making inroads upon the growing stock. Current, county-level information enables resource managers to identify such situations in early stages of development.

The basic procedure for updating field survey data was developed and programmed for Mississippi.[1] Now it has not only been expanded to other States but has also been constrained to conform with results of the TRAS program[2] used by the USDA Forest Service to make appraisals on the national and State levels. Hence the present data agree with national statistics and yet provide information for individual counties.

Fundamentally, the procedure is one of updating resource statistics by applying current information about rate of use. The beginning point is always the inventory and growth rates determined by the field surveys, but the information about current change varies by States. Severance tax data provide trend information in Mississippi, Louisiana, Arkansas, and Alabama. The Texas Forest Service makes a yearly census of lumber production. The annual pulpwood production estimates compiled by Forest Resources Research are also valuable sources.

Product output, timber removals, and growth are shown for calendar year 1970. The resultant inventory is estimated as of January 1, 1971. The information for Tennessee is a reproduction of results from the 1971 survey. Alabama has been omitted, as data from a new field survey will be available in 1972.

[2] Larson, R. W., and Goforth, M. H. TRAS—a computer program for the projection of timber volume. USDA Agric. Handb. 377, 24 p. 1970.

[1] Beltz, R. C., and Christopher, J. F. Computer program for updating timber resource statistics by county, with tables for Mississippi. USDA Forest Serv. Resour. Bull. SO-23, 22 p. South. Forest Exp. Stn., New Orleans, La. 1970.

In the tables of product output, zeros may indicate either no production or lack of information to update survey data. Updated product output is the basis for estimating timber cut; when current product information was lacking the survey data for timber cut were either held constant or adjusted in the light of previous trends. Adjustments were made for removals occasioned by harvest for minor products, by timber stand improvement, and by land clearing in the Louisiana Delta. Allowances were also made for the effects of Hurricane Camille in the southern counties of Mississippi.

Users of the updated statistics should be cognizant of some inherent limitations. The precision of the estimates hinges not only about the accuracy of the field survey but also upon the data available to indicate change. While there is substantial information about product output for most States, only pulpwood data are available for Oklahoma and Tennessee. Perhaps in the interim between this and succeeding estimates additional information will become available in these States.

Even at the time of field survey, county estimates are subject to high sampling errors. Combining county estimates into groups of at least five markedly improves reliability.

Table 1. *Arkansas: Timber products output by county, 1970*

County	Saw logs		Posts	Poles and piling	Other		Pulpwood		All products total
	Softwood	Hardwood			Softwood	Hardwood	Softwood	Hardwood	
									Thousand cubic feet
1 ARKANSAS	19.1	1778.8	0.0	0.0	4.2	403.4	0.0	C.0	2205.5
2 ASHLEY	17206.8	321.3	0.0	18.4	4.0	542.3	4698.8	2107.5	24899.1
3 BAXTER	363.8	5.9	8.9	0.0	7.1	613.9	0.0	28.1	1027.7
4 BENTON	0.0	480.0	0.0	65.5	16.6	1201.4	0.0	76.6	1840.1
5 BOONE	9.6	501.3	44.4	9.2	15.1	1123.6	0.0	997.1	2700.3
6 BRADLEY	7947.9	8641.1	0.0	12.9	2.8	351.7	779.9	724.5	18460.8
7 CALHOUN	12367.3	198.5	0.0	141.2	1.7	345.1	3012.5	1527.0	17593.3
8 CARROLL	97.4	286.3	2.2	0.0	14.3	1587.4	0.0	562.1	2549.7
9 CHICOT	0.0	290.0	0.0	0.0	5.0	397.3	0.0	1045.1	1737.4
10 CLARK	9391.6	2315.1	0.0	0.0	1325.4	471.7	4204.5	1846.9	19555.2
11 CLAY	1.0	578.7	0.0	0.0	6.2	649.2	0.0	C.0	1235.1
12 CLEBURNE	644.6	489.0	112.2	4.9	6.0	335.7	1940.6	300.9	3833.9
13 CLEVELAND	5884.8	1687.0	104.1	433.5	3.8	394.0	1736.6	1220.0	11463.8
14 COLUMBIA	1709.6	693.3	0.0	0.0	5.8	558.2	4381.4	1243.8	8592.1
15 CONWAY	771.3	334.3	0.8	0.0	9.1	386.7	2183.8	307.8	3993.8
16 CRAIGHEAD	116.4	360.2	0.0	0.0	5.1	1007.0	0.0	200.3	1695.0
17 CRAWFORD	47.2	167.6	0.0	0.0	7.7	542.3	51.1	214.1	1030.0
18 CRITTENDEN	12.7	261.1	0.0	0.0	4.4	1067.7	0.0	49.2	1395.1
19 CROSS	10.4	297.0	0.0	0.0	2.7	530.5	0.0	19.5	860.1
20 DALLAS	14795.6	2552.5	0.0	287.9	21.3	378.3	4403.8	2815.1	25254.5
21 DESHA	95.4	663.0	0.0	0.0	3.5	477.6	0.3	629.0	1868.8
22 DREW	3689.6	1668.6	0.0	0.0	5.2	429.4	3926.8	3003.4	12723.0
23 FAULKNER	7.4	299.8	0.0	0.0	11.7	569.9	0.0	17.2	906.0
24 FRANKLIN	240.5	236.4	1.1	0.0	12.2	1119.6	85.1	249.2	1944.1
25 FULTON	20.5	31.2	32.1	0.0	9.8	298.2	0.0	2.6	394.4
26 GARLAND	6448.6	992.0	490.0	2869.3	9.9	760.9	899.3	283.2	12753.2
27 GRANT	14406.0	306.3	0.0	262.0	21.4	441.0	6386.4	4819.9	26643.0
28 GREENE	51.9	132.7	0.0	0.0	4.7	588.6	0.0	11.8	789.7
29 HEMPSTEAD	1473.2	409.8	0.0	0.0	12.3	438.3	2795.8	922.9	6052.3
30 HOT SPRING	3199.2	367.5	0.0	229.1	88.3	466.5	2783.5	1497.8	8631.9
31 HOWARD	8406.9	593.1	551.5	694.7	45.8	283.4	1648.2	736.9	12960.5
32 INDEPENDENCE	130.7	350.9	0.0	0.0	11.7	529.1	396.3	581.3	2000.0
33 IZARD	260.1	468.1	89.1	0.7	10.8	282.2	285.4	70.9	1467.3
34 JACKSON	24.3	315.8	0.0	0.0	4.8	543.8	3.3	50.6	942.6
35 JEFFERSON	2856.1	1293.6	0.0	26.1	7.1	1192.1	1604.1	1576.1	8555.2
36 JOHNSON	844.9	448.8	144.4	55.3	6.0	588.6	832.7	1060.9	3981.6
37 LAFAYETTE	4483.9	195.4	0.0	41.4	6.0	311.0	2411.4	1189.6	8638.7
38 LAWRENCE	31.1	600.2	0.0	0.0	6.7	520.2	0.0	0.3	1158.5
39 LEE	73.5	1262.8	0.0	0.0	3.9	543.5	12.0	351.4	2247.1
40 LINCOLN	19.4	1689.1	0.0	0.0	4.7	506.9	227.4	398.2	2845.7
41 LITTLE RIVER	3131.8	731.3	134.1	185.7	8.8	261.3	2212.7	882.3	7548.0
42 LOGAN	1082.9	255.8	0.0	0.0	15.9	971.8	869.7	928.2	4124.3
43 LONOKE	2.0	3.1	0.0	0.0	7.5	810.7	21.5	503.2	1348.0
44 MADISON	14.9	1316.1	0.0	0.0	11.0	790.8	0.0	36.6	2169.4
45 MARION	0.3	32.8	13.4	0.0	8.7	285.0	0.0	C.0	340.2
46 MILLER	825.4	255.9	52.5	0.0	10.3	567.8	1164.7	632.2	3508.8
47 MISSISSIPPI	9.6	86.9	0.0	0.0	5.9	1442.7	0.0	123.0	1668.1
48 MONROE	63.6	5787.0	0.0	0.0	2.5	727.4	6.5	13.5	6600.5
49 MONTGOMERY	1952.7	18.4	15.6	0.0	4.6	242.4	1416.6	437.4	4087.7
50 NEVADA	1.6	1306.7	7.6	0.0	5.8	267.5	4841.9	1338.8	7769.9
51 NEWTON	0.8	522.8	18.1	0.0	4.7	1223.1	1.0	249.7	2020.2
52 OUACHITA	7239.2	4043.7	0.0	131.9	4.9	642.1	2681.7	995.4	15738.9
53 PERRY	3070.5	159.6	0.0	0.0	3.6	201.2	452.3	50.6	3937.8
54 PHILLIPS	146.1	1310.1	0.0	0.0	3.8	1215.0	0.0	914.8	3589.8
55 PIKE	10016.6	1309.6	94.9	303.6	3.9	444.5	3116.6	657.6	15947.3
56 POINSETT	2.8	611.3	0.0	0.0	3.6	876.5	0.0	C.0	1494.2
57 POLK	2527.0	1749.4	703.9	776.6	6.9	315.2	1898.6	354.0	8331.6
58 POPE	2215.3	370.8	8.0	0.0	9.4	479.1	1168.6	258.2	4509.4
59 PRAIRIE	0.0	1693.7	0.0	0.0	4.2	940.2	0.4	160.6	2799.1
60 PULASKI	696.7	990.7	0.0	0.0	163.6	1654.1	1917.4	592.2	6014.7
61 RANDOLPH	17.6	390.7	0.0	0.0	9.0	1074.3	0.0	293.4	1785.0
62 ST. FRANCIS	105.2	881.9	0.0	0.0	4.6	796.0	11.7	98.9	1898.3
63 SALINE	7401.7	1110.7	0.0	0.0	5.2	684.8	3004.1	1648.2	13854.7
64 SCOTT	4179.0	27.5	97.7	64.6	10.5	746.7	975.7	634.8	6736.5
65 SEARCY	51.7	909.5	51.1	2.1	8.9	482.3	0.0	264.3	1769.9
66 SEBASTIAN	105.6	98.0	5.7	0.9	12.4	558.4	17.0	2.4	800.4
67 SEVIER	1825.4	4103.5	296.7	409.0	5.8	276.7	2095.9	1444.0	10457.0
68 SHARP	12.9	609.7	0.0	0.0	8.8	284.1	0.0	C.0	915.5
69 STONE	134.5	4.0	0.8	0.0	5.8	346.2	85.1	139.9	616.3
70 UNION	10688.0	1395.5	3.8	46.2	5.8	1008.2	7442.2	2159.9	22749.6
71 VAN BUREN	212.5	750.0	120.8	27.6	6.8	303.7	1358.0	79.1	2858.5
72 WASHINGTON	0.0	1293.3	0.0	0.0	15.9	1248.4	0.0	12.5	2570.1
73 WHITE	62.9	4313.7	0.0	0.0	15.0	1190.8	200.2	646.9	6429.5
74 WOODRUFF	37.0	46.1	0.0	0.0	2.7	501.5	0.0	65.9	653.2
75 YELL	5090.5	604.5	421.6	314.3	9.3	470.1	2283.0	639.7	9833.0
STATE TOTAL	181084.5	73658.4	3627.1	7414.6	2170.9	48108.8	90934.1	49903.0	456901.4

3

Table 2. Arkansas: *Growing stock and sawtimber volume by county, 1971*

County	Growing stock			Sawtimber		
	Total	Softwood	Hardwood	Total	Softwood	Hardwood
	------ Million cubic feet ------			------ Million board feet ------		
1 ARKANSAS	254.6	20.3	234.3	922.7	115.5	807.2
2 ASHLEY	417.1	285.1	132.0	1773.5	1404.0	369.5
3 BAXTER	113.6	13.2	100.4	267.2	32.3	234.9
4 BENTON	139.3	0.4	138.9	331.6	....	331.6
5 BOONE	104.9	0.8	104.1	235.2	....	235.2
6 BRADLEY	386.5	227.2	159.3	1450.5	1001.1	449.4
7 CALHOUN	328.7	169.3	159.4	1163.3	697.0	466.3
8 CARROLL	153.3	43.4	109.9	442.4	163.2	279.2
9 CHICOT	74.7	....	74.7	285.5	....	285.5
10 CLARK	513.3	271.9	241.4	1759.5	1189.7	569.8
11 CLAY	64.9	....	64.9	166.6	....	166.6
12 CLEBURNE	131.6	46.8	84.8	255.9	106.0	149.9
13 CLEVELAND	347.3	152.7	194.6	1203.2	623.1	580.1
14 COLUMBIA	339.7	191.6	148.1	1119.5	738.3	381.2
15 CONWAY	55.6	19.8	35.8	113.1	44.5	68.6
16 CRAIGHEAD	23.3	4.0	19.3	65.8	18.5	47.3
17 CRAWFORD	136.6	23.8	112.8	379.2	96.0	283.2
18 CRITTENDEN	42.1	....	42.1	139.2	....	139.2
19 CROSS	30.9	0.3	30.6	92.5	....	92.5
20 DALLAS	374.6	214.3	160.3	1322.8	1007.9	314.9
21 DESHA	172.4	15.9	156.5	671.6	95.1	576.5
22 DREW	329.4	162.1	167.3	1115.8	706.5	409.3
23 FAULKNER	44.9	1.9	43.0	97.9	7.0	90.9
24 FRANKLIN	151.1	24.1	127.0	413.3	105.6	307.7
25 FULTON	72.5	21.1	51.4	108.9	3.4	105.5
26 GARLAND	349.1	241.5	107.6	1079.6	909.6	170.0
27 GRANT	417.4	160.6	256.8	1401.8	723.0	678.8
28 GREENE	42.2	4.8	37.4	123.9	21.1	102.8
29 HEMPSTEAD	340.4	183.7	156.7	1053.9	649.7	404.2
30 HOT SPRING	320.3	185.8	134.5	950.4	730.4	220.0
31 HOWARD	307.9	226.4	81.5	991.2	885.1	106.1
32 INDEPENDENCE	124.4	14.9	109.5	284.0	34.7	249.3
33 IZARD	67.4	13.9	53.5	143.3	20.3	123.0
34 JACKSON	27.9	....	27.9	74.5	....	74.5
35 JEFFERSON	153.0	50.0	103.0	419.8	196.3	223.5
36 JOHNSON	242.4	62.7	179.7	689.3	263.7	425.6
37 LAFAYETTE	206.3	119.8	86.5	621.2	416.9	204.3
38 LAWRENCE	47.0	0.5	46.5	91.2	....	91.2
39 LEE	146.4	2.2	144.2	531.7	11.5	520.2
40 LINCOLN	122.6	32.3	90.3	348.3	102.6	245.7
41 LITTLE RIVER	185.3	120.0	65.3	570.0	475.0	95.0
42 LOGAN	167.9	104.3	63.6	489.3	359.9	129.4
43 LONOKE	73.9	1.9	72.0	214.9	11.9	203.0
44 MADISON	218.2	8.9	209.3	405.7	12.0	393.7
45 MARION	152.9	7.3	145.6	311.0	7.7	303.3
46 MILLER	225.1	113.4	111.7	711.2	415.1	296.1
47 MISSISSIPPI	40.2	5.1	35.1	104.5	28.9	75.6
48 MONROE	164.2	20.7	143.5	524.8	108.9	415.9
49 MONTGOMERY	504.1	369.7	134.4	1547.2	1316.3	230.9
50 NEVADA	313.3	156.4	156.9	892.3	540.0	352.3
51 NEWTON	322.7	42.8	279.9	682.7	121.9	560.8
52 OUACHITA	456.0	189.6	266.4	1381.3	750.4	630.9
53 PERRY	277.3	211.6	65.7	865.5	772.5	93.0
54 PHILLIPS	78.8	0.1	78.7	153.2	0.7	152.5
55 PIKE	361.7	255.3	106.4	1183.0	1056.2	126.8
56 POINSETT	52.1	1.5	50.6	149.3	8.3	141.0
57 POLK	346.6	237.7	108.9	1052.3	887.5	164.8
58 POPE	289.5	91.5	198.0	710.0	299.1	410.9
59 PRAIRIE	163.6	6.0	157.6	595.2	30.9	564.3
60 PULASKI	166.7	79.3	87.4	371.4	232.1	139.3
61 RANDOLPH	100.4	0.9	99.5	210.3	3.6	206.7
62 ST. FRANCIS	55.9	3.0	52.9	173.3	17.8	155.5
63 SALINE	349.0	177.8	171.2	898.1	558.8	339.3
64 SCOTT	443.1	332.2	110.9	1235.4	1057.8	177.6
65 SEARCY	163.3	23.3	140.0	327.7	91.0	236.7
66 SEBASTION	26.4	9.7	16.7	47.0	21.9	25.1
67 SEVIER	319.9	163.4	156.5	1134.4	802.6	331.8
68 SHARP	88.2	14.5	73.7	129.5	27.4	102.1
69 STONE	175.0	41.0	134.0	437.7	161.8	275.9
70 UNION	626.7	333.1	293.6	2077.1	1296.2	780.9
71 VAN BUREN	165.2	44.2	121.0	294.7	116.1	178.6
72 WASHINGTON	121.6	9.1	112.5	165.9	22.0	143.9
73 WHITE	118.6	5.8	112.8	295.7	16.5	279.2
74 WOODRUFF	84.2	5.6	78.6	240.8	23.9	216.9
75 YELL	389.1	246.6	142.5	1116.6	818.3	298.3
STATE TOTAL	15504.3	6642.4	8861.9	46399.8	25590.6	20809.2

4

Table 3. *Arkansas: Net growth of growing stock and sawtimber by county, 1970*

County	Growing stock			Sawtimber		
	Total	Softwood	Hardwood	Total	Softwood	Hardwood
	----- Million cubic feet -----			----- Million board feet -----		
1 ARKANSAS	10.1	0.2	9.9	33.3	1.4	31.9
2 ASHLEY	23.3	16.7	6.6	103.5	89.5	14.0
3 BAXTER	2.5	0.7	1.8	5.5	2.0	3.5
4 BENTON	4.4	....	4.4	8.1	....'	8.1
5 BOONE	3.2	0.1	3.1	7.5	....	7.5
6 BRADLEY	23.8	16.0	7.8	99.1	70.8	28.3
7 CALHOUN	21.0	13.0	8.0	65.5	43.1	22.4
8 CARROLL	4.5	2.0	2.5	16.6	7.3	9.3
9 CHICOT	2.9	....	2.9	8.1	....	8.1
10 CLARK	29.1	17.0	12.1	112.6	83.3	29.3
11 CLAY	3.4	....	3.4	10.4	....	10.4
12 CLEBURNE	5.3	3.3	2.0	14.8	12.2	2.6
13 CLEVELAND	20.3	11.7	8.6	63.8	42.0	21.8
14 COLUMBIA	22.5	15.5	7.0	82.5	66.4	16.1
15 CONWAY	3.6	1.9	1.7	4.2	2.7	1.5
16 CRAIGHEAD	1.4	0.2	1.2	4.0	1.2	2.8
17 CRAWFORD	4.3	1.3	3.0	15.3	4.0	11.3
18 CRITTENDEN	1.6	....	1.6	5.5	....	5.5
19 CROSS	1.2	....	1.2	3.6	....	3.6
20 DALLAS	22.0	13.4	8.6	85.5	66.9	18.6
21 DESHA	6.4	0.1	6.3	22.4	0.9	21.5
22 DREW	18.1	11.1	7.0	64.1	46.4	17.7
23 FAULKNER	1.6	0.1	1.5	1.6	0.3	1.3
24 FRANKLIN	5.4	1.0	4.4	14.5	4.6	9.9
25 FULTON	3.2	2.3	0.9	2.0	0.4	1.6
26 GARLAND	15.2	10.3	4.9	70.4	60.6	9.8
27 GRANT	24.7	11.4	13.3	90.4	52.7	37.7
28 GREENE	1.8	0.3	1.5	8.5	2.2	6.3
29 HEMPSTEAD	22.5	15.6	6.9	64.7	47.3	17.4
30 HOT SPRING	19.4	11.8	7.6	77.0	59.1	17.9
31 HOWARD	16.1	12.6	3.5	64.9	56.9	8.0
32 INDEPENDENCE	4.7	0.9	3.8	8.5	2.4	6.1
33 IZARD	2.7	1.0	1.7	4.2	1.9	2.3
34 JACKSON	2.1	....	2.1	6.3	....	6.3
35 JEFFERSON	10.8	3.6	7.2	32.8	15.1	17.7
36 JOHNSON	8.2	2.9	5.3	19.9	12.4	7.5
37 LAFAYETTE	14.9	10.7	4.2	37.1	29.5	7.6
38 LAWRENCE	3.0	0.1	2.9	4.1	....	4.1
39 LEE	6.2	0.1	6.1	23.3	0.4	22.9
40 LINCOLN	7.4	2.5	4.9	21.6	8.9	12.7
41 LITTLE RIVER	13.0	8.7	4.3	39.5	32.8	6.7
42 LOGAN	7.8	4.9	2.9	28.5	23.0	5.5
43 LONOKE	3.7	....	3.7	11.1	0.2	10.9
44 MADISON	6.5	0.6	5.9	16.2	1.1	15.1
45 MARION	3.3	0.6	2.7	4.5	0.2	4.3
46 MILLER	12.2	7.1	5.1	34.0	24.4	9.6
47 MISSISSIPPI	2.1	0.1	2.0	3.8	0.8	3.0
48 MONROE	8.0	0.7	7.3	27.9	3.0	24.9
49 MONTGOMERY	22.8	15.9	6.9	80.8	73.3	7.5
50 NEVADA	21.2	12.9	8.3	62.5	45.4	17.1
51 NEWTON	9.8	2.7	7.1	22.6	5.5	17.1
52 OUACHITA	26.5	12.6	13.9	89.3	50.5	38.8
53 PERRY	13.9	9.0	4.9	45.8	43.3	2.5
54 PHILLIPS	5.2	....	5.2	10.3	0.1	10.2
55 PIKE	22.4	16.2	6.2	95.0	86.6	8.4
56 POINSETT	2.5	0.1	2.4	6.7	0.4	6.3
57 POLK	16.5	10.8	5.7	63.8	57.9	5.9
58 POPE	10.6	5.2	5.4	24.5	17.0	7.5
59 PRAIRIE	6.3	0.1	6.2	32.7	0.7	32.0
60 PULASKI	9.0	5.0	4.0	20.8	14.7	6.1
61 RANDOLPH	3.6	....	3.6	5.3	0.3	5.0
62 ST. FRANCIS	3.3	0.1	3.2	10.9	0.4	10.5
63 SALINE	17.0	9.4	7.6	54.0	40.9	13.1
64 SCOTT	20.7	16.0	4.7	80.2	71.9	8.3
65 SEARCY	4.7	1.0	3.7	11.3	4.7	6.6
66 SEBASTION	1.5	0.6	0.9	2.0	0.9	1.1
67 SEVIER	16.0	8.4	7.6	69.0	52.1	16.9
68 SHARP	2.5	0.8	1.7	3.0	1.4	1.6
69 STONE	5.5	2.2	3.3	19.3	7.5	11.8
70 UNION	37.7	23.9	13.8	135.7	101.2	34.5
71 VAN BUREN	6.7	2.8	3.9	16.8	8.0	8.8
72 WASHINGTON	4.2	0.4	3.8	3.8	1.3	2.5
73 WHITE	3.9	0.3	3.6	10.4	1.0	9.4
74 WOODRUFF	4.4	0.3	4.1	10.3	1.1	9.2
75 YELL	18.8	12.2	6.6	63.6	45.5	18.1
STATE TOTAL	778.6	403.0	375.6	2603.6	1713.9	889.7

5

Table 4. Arkansas: Removals of growing stock and sawtimber by county, 1970

County	Growing stock			Sawtimber		
	Total	Softwood	Hardwood	Total	Softwood	Hardwood
	------ Million cubic feet ------			------ Million board feet ------		
1 ARKANSAS	7.2	....	7.2	30.4	0.1	30.3
2 ASHLEY	30.2	23.5	6.7	133.9	117.3	16.6
3 BAXTER	4.1	0.4	3.7	14.5	2.2	12.3
4 BENTON	2.7	0.1	2.6	9.8	0.4	9.4
5 BOONE	4.7	0.1	4.6	13.7	0.1	13.6
6 BRADLEY	26.0	9.5	16.5	133.4	50.6	82.8
7 CALHOUN	22.4	16.7	5.7	96.6	84.1	12.5
8 CARROLL	3.0	0.1	2.9	8.4	0.6	7.8
9 CHICOT	2.1	....	2.1	6.1	....	6.1
10 CLARK	21.8	15.6	6.2	96.1	70.1	26.0
11 CLAY	1.5	....	1.5	5.4	....	5.4
12 CLEBURNE	4.1	2.7	1.4	14.1	9.0	5.1
13 CLEVELAND	14.1	8.7	5.4	63.6	42.8	20.8
14 COLUMBIA	9.0	6.1	2.9	31.2	21.7	9.5
15 CONWAY	10.7	3.0	7.7	30.3	10.4	19.9
16 CRAIGHEAD	1.9	0.1	1.8	5.4	0.7	4.7
17 CRAWFORD	1.1	0.1	1.0	2.8	0.4	2.4
18 CRITTENDEN	1.6	....	1.6	3.5	0.1	3.4
19 CROSS	1.2	....	1.2	3.3	0.1	3.2
20 DALLAS	29.1	20.9	8.2	135.5	103.5	32.0
21 DESHA	8.2	0.1	8.1	39.4	0.6	38.8
22 DREW	16.5	7.8	8.7	60.5	32.7	27.8
23 FAULKNER	2.1	....	2.1	3.3	0.1	3.2
24 FRANKLIN	2.8	0.4	2.4	6.9	1.7	5.2
25 FULTON	0.5	0.1	0.4	0.8	0.1	0.7
26 GARLAND	17.5	8.6	8.9	78.7	41.7	37.0
27 GRANT	29.9	22.4	7.5	125.3	106.0	19.3
28 GREENE	0.9	0.1	0.8	2.3	0.3	2.0
29 HEMPSTEAD	7.8	4.3	3.5	26.3	16.2	10.1
30 HOT SPRING	9.8	6.6	3.2	39.4	28.4	11.0
31 HOWARD	16.9	12.2	4.7	77.1	59.5	17.6
32 INDEPENDENCE	2.1	0.5	1.6	6.6	1.8	4.8
33 IZARD	8.0	0.7	7.3	14.7	2.3	12.4
34 JACKSON	1.0	....	1.0	3.2	0.2	3.0
35 JEFFERSON	14.2	4.7	9.5	57.7	21.7	36.0
36 JOHNSON	5.6	1.9	3.7	18.6	7.6	11.0
37 LAFAYETTE	9.4	7.3	2.1	39.6	33.8	5.8
38 LAWRENCE	1.5	....	1.5	5.9	0.2	5.7
39 LEE	3.0	0.1	2.9	12.5	0.5	12.0
40 LINCOLN	5.4	0.2	5.2	22.9	0.7	22.2
41 LITTLE RIVER	13.4	6.2	7.2	50.5	27.1	23.4
42 LOGAN	4.2	2.0	2.2	14.1	8.9	5.2
43 LONOKE	4.2	....	4.2	10.9	0.1	10.8
44 MADISON	2.9	....	2.9	12.5	0.1	12.4
45 MARION	0.3	....	0.3	0.6	....	0.6
46 MILLER	3.9	2.1	1.8	13.6	8.1	5.5
47 MISSISSIPPI	1.5	....	1.5	1.5	0.1	1.4
48 MONROE	18.8	0.1	18.7	88.3	0.4	87.9
49 MONTGOMERY	5.2	3.5	1.7	20.1	15.6	4.5
50 NEVADA	8.8	4.7	4.1	27.8	12.5	15.3
51 NEWTON	4.5	....	4.5	13.3	....	13.3
52 OUACHITA	19.2	10.7	8.5	91.2	51.9	39.3
53 PERRY	5.2	3.8	1.4	22.4	19.9	2.5
54 PHILLIPS	13.7	0.1	13.6	65.0	0.6	64.4
55 PIKE	18.2	14.4	3.8	85.9	70.9	15.0
56 POINSETT	1.8	....	1.8	6.0	....	6.0
57 POLK	11.1	7.3	3.8	45.2	28.5	16.7
58 POPE	5.6	3.6	2.0	21.0	16.6	4.4
59 PRAIRIE	8.4	....	8.4	33.7	....	33.7
60 PULASKI	6.6	2.6	4.0	20.8	9.6	11.2
61 RANDOLPH	10.3	....	10.3	12.5	0.1	12.4
62 ST. FRANCIS	2.3	0.1	2.2	9.1	0.7	8.4
63 SALINE	15.8	11.3	4.5	68.6	53.7	14.9
64 SCOTT	7.7	5.7	2.0	32.0	28.4	3.6
65 SEARCY	2.6	0.1	2.5	11.2	0.3	10.9
66 SEBASTION	1.7	0.2	1.5	2.2	0.7	1.5
67 SEVIER	13.4	4.8	8.6	59.2	18.8	40.4
68 SHARP	1.6	....	1.6	5.8	0.1	5.7
69 STONE	6.0	0.2	5.8	24.2	1.0	23.2
70 UNION	25.2	19.0	6.2	105.7	84.7	21.0
71 VAN BUREN	4.6	2.5	2.1	13.3	6.1	7.2
72 WASHINGTON	3.8	....	3.8	15.8	....	15.8
73 WHITE	13.2	0.3	12.9	54.8	0.9	53.9
74 WOODRUFF	0.6	....	0.6	1.2	0.2	1.0
75 YELL	12.1	8.8	3.3	50.4	38.7	11.7
STATE TOTAL	640.0	299.7	340.3	2590.1	1375.6	1214.5

6

Table 5. *Arkansas: Growing stock and sawtimber volume by resource regions, 1971*

Region	Growing stock			Sawtimber		
	Total	Softwood	Hardwood	Total	Softwood	Hardwood
	- - - - - - Million cubic feet - - - - - -			- - - - - - Million board feet - - - - - -		
1 SOUTH DELTA	1404.1	149.3	1254.8	4667.9	673.5	3994.4
1 NORTH DELTA	511.0	25.0	486.0	1421.8	118.6	1303.2
3 SOUTHWEST	7116.6	3881.6	3235.0	23875.9	16108.1	7767.8
3 OUACHITA	3019.4	2010.4	1009.0	8702.2	6934.5	1767.7
5 OZARK	3453.2	575.9	2877.3	7732.3	1756.0	5976.3
STATE TOTAL	15504.3	6642.2	8862.1	46400.1	25590.7	20809.4

Table 6. *Arkansas: Net growth of growing stock and sawtimber by resource regions, 1970*

Region	Growing stock			Sawtimber		
	Total	Softwood	Hardwood	Total	Softwood	Hardwood
	- - - - - - Million cubic feet - - - - - -			- - - - - - Million board feet - - - - - -		
1 SOUTH DELTA	67.1	7.3	59.8	223.4	30.6	192.8
1 NORTH DELTA	26.8	1.2	25.6	74.1	6.2	67.9
3 SOUTHWEST	426.8	266.3	160.5	1535.6	1147.0	388.6
3 OUACHITA	143.1	94.1	49.0	510.0	432.1	77.9
5 OZARK	115.0	34.1	80.9	260.5	98.2	162.3
STATE TOTAL	778.8	403.0	375.8	2603.6	1714.1	889.5

Table 7. *Arkansas: Removals of growing stock and sawtimber by resource regions, 1970*

Region	Growing stock			Sawtimber		
	Total	Softwood	Hardwood	Total	Softwood	Hardwood
	- - - - - - Million cubic feet - - - - - -			- - - - - - Million board feet - - - - - -		
1 SOUTH DELTA	85.3	5.4	79.9	367.0	24.8	342.2
1 NORTH DELTA	16.0	0.5	15.5	46.9	2.6	44.3
3 SOUTHWEST	345.1	223.4	121.7	1492.5	1040.8	451.7
3 OUACHITA	87.0	53.8	33.2	354.7	245.8	108.9
5 OZARK	106.9	16.8	90.1	329.7	62.2	267.5
STATE TOTAL	640.3	299.9	340.4	2590.8	1376.2	1214.6

Table 8. *Louisiana: Timber products output by parish, 1970*

Parish	Saw logs		Posts	Poles and piling	Other		Pulpwood		All products total
	Softwood	Hardwood			Softwood	Hardwood	Softwood	Hardwood	
				- - - - - - - Thousand cubic feet - - - - - - -					
1 ACADIA	2243.5	97.0	0.0	0.0	0.0	5.0	1429.2	11.4	3786.1
2 ALLEN	7277.3	719.9	0.0	0.0	20.0	148.0	6584.8	310.3	15060.3
3 ASCENSION	5.7	93.5	0.0	0.0	0.C	0.0	381.9	1636.1	2117.2
4 ASSUMPTION	34.2	275.1	0.0	0.0	0.0	0.0	0.0	0.0	309.3
5 AVOYELLES	696.6	2075.7	0.0	0.0	0.0	870.0	424.1	2005.0	6071.4
6 BEAUREGARD	5233.3	511.4	0.0	0.0	0.0	8.0	13230.8	510.5	19494.0
7 BIENVILLE	9155.1	585.9	0.0	0.0	0.C	0.0	10722.1	2560.3	23023.4
8 BOSSIER	2537.3	392.9	0.0	0.0	0.C	0.0	4694.8	1238.9	8863.9
9 CADDO	514.0	386.6	0.0	0.0	0.0	0.0	2770.0	567.7	4238.3
10 CALCASIEU	1274.7	703.7	0.0	0.0	0.C	0.0	3344.2	200.6	5523.2
11 CALDWELL	7761.8	1035.4	0.0	0.0	0.0	368.0	3760.3	1095.0	14020.5
12 CAMERON	0.0	0.0	0.0	0.0	0.0	0.0	10.7	0.0	10.7
13 CATAHOULA	1148.5	2522.4	0.0	0.0	0.C	153.0	1794.5	2288.8	7907.2
14 CLAIBORNE	1747.8	215.8	0.0	0.0	0.C	7.0	4929.1	815.7	7715.4
15 CONCORDIA	221.4	14596.0	0.0	0.0	0.C	1127.0	0.5	2933.9	18878.8
16 DE SOTO	4748.0	529.8	0.0	0.0	0.0	0.0	7971.3	564.9	13814.0
17 E BATON ROUGE	16.7	260.8	0.0	0.0	0.0	11.0	26.5	379.2	694.2
18 EAST CARROLL	7.0	994.9	0.0	0.0	0.0	36.0	0.0	1112.3	2150.2
19 E FELICIANA	3178.3	913.5	0.0	0.0	0.0	0.0	1648.3	723.2	6463.3
20 EVANGELINE	1341.5	300.3	0.0	0.0	0.0	68.0	1769.0	489.9	3968.7
21 FRANKLIN	48.4	190.6	0.0	0.0	0.0	51.0	57.9	40.0	387.9
22 GRANT	7185.9	960.8	0.0	0.0	0.0	145.0	4305.5	1958.3	14555.5
23 IBERIA	0.0	0.0	0.0	0.0	0.C	0.0	0.0	1.8	1.8
24 IBERVILLE	105.1	1019.0	0.0	0.0	0.0	7.0	0.0	276.9	1408.0
25 JACKSON	9201.5	1095.1	0.0	0.0	0.0	0.0	6037.1	1643.6	17977.9
26 JEFFERSON	0.0	0.0	0.0	0.0	0.0	0.0	0.0	0.0	0.0
27 JEFF DAVIS	344.2	73.6	0.0	0.0	0.C	0.0	749.3	21.9	1189.0
28 LAFAYETTE	0.0	0.0	0.0	0.0	0.0	0.0	0.0	0.0	0.0
29 LAFOURCHE	163.1	336.9	0.0	0.0	0.0	0.0	0.0	0.0	500.0
30 LA SALLE	9162.6	1105.9	0.0	0.0	0.0	119.0	6567.8	1216.8	18172.1
31 LINCOLN	2293.5	436.3	0.0	0.0	0.0	0.0	4467.7	1054.5	8252.0
32 LIVINGSTON	17030.5	1944.2	0.0	0.0	0.0	11.0	4977.6	1242.5	25205.8
33 MADISON	0.0	2112.8	0.0	0.0	0.0	0.0	1.4	1942.0	4056.2
34 MOREHOUSE	4033.2	276.1	0.0	0.0	0.0	1322.0	2739.7	2181.9	10552.9
35 NATCHITOCHES	7106.4	878.9	0.0	0.0	0.C	0.0	5632.3	870.2	14487.8
36 ORLEANS	0.0	0.0	0.0	0.0	0.0	0.0	0.0	0.0	1.1
37 OUACHITA	1725.5	728.9	0.0	0.0	0.0	54.0	2886.4	1541.7	6936.5
38 PLAQUEMINES	0.0	0.0	0.0	0.0	0.0	0.0	0.0	0.0	0.0
39 POINTE COUPEE	27.3	880.5	0.0	0.0	0.0	33.0	0.0	3615.0	4555.8
40 RAPIDES	8681.9	2695.9	0.0	0.0	0.0	145.0	9665.9	3666.2	24854.9
41 RED RIVER	2296.1	181.2	0.0	0.0	0.0	0.0	1962.0	459.6	4898.9
42 RICHLAND	36.2	305.9	0.0	0.0	0.0	0.0	13.9	20.6	376.6
43 SABINE	15842.7	1028.6	0.0	0.0	0.0	0.0	13118.0	1560.2	31549.5
44 ST BERNARD	0.0	0.0	0.0	0.0	0.0	0.0	0.0	0.0	0.0
45 ST CHARLES	0.0	0.0	0.0	0.0	0.0	0.0	0.0	0.0	0.0
46 ST HELENA	7907.4	301.1	0.0	0.0	0.0	0.0	3805.8	1184.2	13198.5
47 ST JAMES	1.7	18.8	0.0	0.0	0.0	0.0	0.0	0.0	20.5
48 ST JOHN	25.2	15.1	0.0	0.0	0.0	0.0	0.0	0.0	40.3
49 ST LANDRY	115.9	1476.7	0.0	0.0	0.0	105.0	266.4	1727.4	3691.4
50 ST MARTIN	71.7	1040.9	0.0	0.0	0.0	0.0	0.0	68.0	1180.6
51 ST MARY	21.7	44.6	0.0	0.0	0.0	0.0	0.0	0.0	66.3
52 ST TAMMANY	3363.7	224.6	0.0	0.0	0.0	0.0	3031.3	118.5	6738.1
53 TANGIPAHOA	4702.8	523.8	0.0	0.0	0.0	0.0	3381.1	863.7	9471.4
54 TENSAS	54.7	2577.8	0.0	0.0	0.0	1.0	0.6	935.0	3569.1
55 TERREBONNE	143.9	372.4	0.0	0.0	0.0	0.0	0.6	0.0	516.9
56 UNION	8955.7	2368.3	0.0	0.0	0.0	7.0	10663.2	5052.4	27046.6
57 VERMILION	8.2	14.1	0.0	0.0	0.0	0.0	2.1	0.3	24.7
58 VERNON	10943.1	2307.4	0.0	0.0	0.C	2.0	14316.6	1001.1	28570.2
59 WASHINGTON	6744.3	403.2	0.0	0.0	0.C	0.0	10100.3	2546.2	19794.0
60 WEBSTER	2548.0	463.5	0.0	0.0	0.0	46.0	3189.1	552.4	6799.0
61 W BATON ROUGE	3.2	382.0	0.0	0.0	0.0	11.0	0.0	311.9	708.1
62 WEST CARROLL	0.0	68.1	0.0	0.0	0.C	12.0	0.0	4.2	84.3
63 W FELICIANA	545.7	1801.8	0.0	0.0	0.0	0.0	183.5	604.1	3135.1
64 WINN	21613.5	3275.5	0.0	0.0	0.0	318.0	4498.5	1562.4	31267.9
STATE TOTAL	202197.2	61142.1	0.0	0.0	20.0	5190.0	182113.7	59290.3	509953.2

8

Table 9. *Louisiana: Growing stock and sawtimber volume by parish, 1971*

	Parish	Growing stock			Sawtimber		
		Total	Softwood	Hardwood	Total	Softwood	Hardwood
		------ Million cubic feet ------			------ Million board feet ------		
1	ACADIA	107.8	16.2	91.6	416.0	83.7	332.3
2	ALLEN	337.3	265.8	71.5	1768.0	1498.8	269.2
3	ASCENSION	92.1	28.0	64.1	291.5	137.7	153.8
4	ASSUMPTION	315.4	152.9	162.5	1195.7	772.2	423.5
5	AVOYELLES	164.7	51.1	113.6	637.2	208.7	428.5
6	BEAUREGARD	328.1	218.2	109.9	1340.1	983.8	356.3
7	BIENVILLE	391.8	341.2	50.6	1946.4	1722.5	223.9
8	BOSSIER	261.9	194.2	67.7	1016.4	848.5	167.9
9	CADDO	178.6	106.3	72.3	688.1	446.4	241.7
10	CALCASIEU	135.0	94.7	40.3	583.7	441.3	142.4
11	CALDWELL	367.9	205.3	162.6	1640.7	1097.8	542.9
12	CAMERON	....	....	....	....	....	....
13	CATAHOULA	167.7	52.5	115.2	734.6	292.8	441.8
14	CLAIBORNE	278.6	228.2	50.4	994.6	873.1	121.5
15	CONCORDIA	185.9	3.6	182.3	744.2	31.1	713.1
16	DE SOTO	426.6	349.2	77.4	1437.9	1220.6	217.3
17	E BATON ROUGE	89.0	8.7	80.3	284.3	46.7	237.6
18	EAST CARROLL	70.6	0.8	69.8	196.4	3.2	193.2
19	E FELICIANA	109.9	71.5	38.4	463.0	321.9	141.1
20	EVANGELINE	123.1	81.1	42.0	473.2	337.5	135.7
21	FRANKLIN	45.4	10.1	35.3	163.5	41.1	122.4
22	GRANT	458.8	329.6	129.2	2239.6	1807.6	432.0
23	IBERIA	116.7	47.1	69.6	413.2	199.7	213.5
24	IBERVILLE	340.8	74.6	266.2	1367.8	401.4	966.4
25	JACKSON	400.9	306.5	94.4	1544.4	1308.8	235.6
26	JEFFERSON	....	....	....	....	....	....
27	JEFF DAVIS	81.9	58.9	23.0	315.4	237.8	77.6
28	LAFAYETTE	....	....	....	....	....	....
29	LAFOURCHE	216.4	95.4	121.0	849.5	516.3	333.2
30	LA SALLE	274.9	178.7	96.2	1247.7	921.2	326.5
31	LINCOLN	65.5	40.6	24.9	234.2	183.4	50.8
32	LIVINGSTON	544.5	346.8	197.7	2412.7	1792.6	620.1
33	MADISON	201.5	....	201.5	712.7	....	712.7
34	MOREHOUSE	104.7	34.9	69.8	326.7	121.5	205.2
35	NATCHITOCHES	625.4	459.5	165.9	2333.4	1909.6	423.8
36	ORLEANS	....	....	....	....	....	....
37	OUACHITA	280.3	125.6	154.7	896.1	526.4	369.7
38	PLAQUEMINES	....	....	....	....	....	....
39	POINTE COUPEE	154.1	4.5	149.6	632.5	26.8	605.7
40	RAPIDES	495.6	282.9	212.7	1926.7	1260.0	666.7
41	RED RIVER	110.3	47.9	62.4	378.6	209.6	169.0
42	RICHLAND	52.9	5.9	47.0	121.8	28.1	93.7
43	SABINE	585.1	420.4	164.7	2030.7	1703.2	327.5
44	ST BERNARD	....	....	....	....	....	....
45	ST CHARLES	76.3	33.0	43.3	331.9	175.6	156.3
46	ST HELENA	169.7	143.3	26.4	835.7	779.4	56.3
47	ST JAMES	146.9	67.1	79.8	591.6	362.4	229.2
48	ST JOHN	174.5	76.8	97.7	693.4	402.0	291.4
49	ST LANDRY	196.5	41.7	154.8	776.1	226.1	550.0
50	ST MARTIN	264.4	79.5	184.9	980.8	412.6	568.2
51	ST MARY	162.2	60.4	101.8	584.6	262.1	322.5
52	ST TAMMANY	280.3	170.4	109.9	1109.4	786.4	323.0
53	TANGIPAHOA	164.4	80.8	83.6	608.9	358.4	250.5
54	TENSAS	145.3	....	145.3	468.3	....	468.3
55	TERREBONNE	196.2	91.0	105.2	884.8	464.3	420.5
56	UNION	357.1	206.7	150.4	1076.5	653.4	423.1
57	VERMILION	....	....	....	....	....	....
58	VERNON	433.4	308.9	124.5	1542.3	1226.8	315.5
59	WASHINGTON	190.3	145.9	44.4	848.6	694.5	154.1
60	WEBSTER	212.9	160.4	52.5	719.0	581.3	137.7
61	W BATON ROUGE	159.8	3.0	156.8	597.6	20.0	577.6
62	WEST CARROLL	24.2	....	24.2	69.4	....	69.4
63	W FELICIANA	155.0	57.2	97.8	662.7	306.0	356.7
64	WINN	828.6	611.9	216.7	3746.8	3124.2	622.6
	STATE TOTAL	13625.7	7677.4	5948.3	54127.6	35398.9	18728.7

9

Table 10. *Louisiana: Net growth of growing stock and sawtimber by parish, 1970*

Parish	Growing stock			Sawtimber		
	Total	Softwood	Hardwood	Total	Softwood	Hardwood
	— — — — — *Million cubic feet* — — — — —			— — — — — *Million board feet* — — — — —		
1 ACADIA	2.6	0.7	1.9	12.0	3.8	8.2
2 ALLEN	23.9	22.3	1.6	125.2	120.2	5.0
3 ASCENSION	2.4	1.0	1.4	9.1	5.3	3.8
4 ASSUMPTION	8.7	5.3	3.4	40.2	29.8	10.4
5 AVOYELLES	4.2	1.8	2.4	19.0	8.2	10.8
6 BEAUREGARD	21.2	18.7	2.5	87.2	80.6	6.6
7 BIENVILLE	32.5	30.9	1.6	157.0	152.4	4.6
8 BOSSIER	19.3	17.3	2.0	77.6	74.2	3.4
9 CADDO	11.5	9.4	2.1	43.6	38.7	4.9
10 CALCASIEU	8.8	7.9	0.9	38.1	35.4	2.7
11 CALDWELL	23.4	18.6	4.8	108.4	97.4	11.0
12 CAMERON	....	....	....	....	....	....
13 CATAHOULA	4.9	2.9	2.0	23.3	14.9	8.4
14 CLAIBORNE	21.7	20.2	1.5	78.5	76.0	2.5
15 CONCORDIA	3.5	0.2	3.3	15.6	1.6	14.0
16 DE SOTO	33.4	31.1	2.3	111.9	107.5	4.4
17 E BATON ROUGE	2.8	0.6	2.2	10.2	3.6	6.6
18 EAST CARROLL	1.2	....	1.2	3.9	0.2	3.7
19 E FELICIANA	6.6	5.5	1.1	30.0	26.0	4.0
20 EVANGELINE	7.7	6.7	1.0	29.5	27.0	2.5
21 FRANKLIN	1.2	0.6	0.6	4.4	2.1	2.3
22 GRANT	30.3	27.3	3.0	152.1	144.0	8.1
23 IBERIA	3.0	1.6	1.4	13.0	7.7	5.3
24 IBERVILLE	8.2	2.6	5.6	39.3	15.5	23.8
25 JACKSON	30.4	27.6	2.8	121.3	116.5	4.8
26 JEFFERSON	....	....	....	....	....	....
27 JEFF DAVIS	5.3	4.8	0.5	20.1	18.7	1.4
28 LAFAYETTE	....	....	....	....	....	....
29 LAFOURCHE	5.8	3.3	2.5	28.1	19.9	8.2
30 LA SALLE	17.6	15.4	2.2	82.1	76.0	6.1
31 LINCOLN	4.8	4.0	0.8	18.5	17.4	1.1
32 LIVINGSTON	31.9	26.4	5.5	160.5	143.2	17.3
33 MADISON	3.4	....	3.4	13.4	....	13.4
34 MOREHOUSE	3.4	2.2	1.2	11.1	7.2	3.9
35 NATCHITOCHES	41.6	37.8	3.8	159.9	151.9	8.0
36 ORLEANS	....	....	....	....	....	....
37 OUACHITA	15.8	11.2	4.6	53.6	46.1	7.5
38 PLAQUEMINES	....	....	....	....	....	....
39 POINTE COUPEE	3.4	0.2	3.2	16.0	1.0	15.0
40 RAPIDES	28.8	23.9	4.9	115.3	102.8	12.5
41 RED RIVER	6.3	4.5	1.8	22.7	19.3	3.4
42 RICHLAND	1.1	0.3	0.8	3.7	1.4	2.3
43 SABINE	39.4	35.6	3.8	146.5	140.3	6.2
44 ST BERNARD	....	....	....	....	....	....
45 ST CHARLES	2.0	1.1	0.9	10.6	6.8	3.8
46 ST HELENA	11.9	11.1	0.8	64.4	62.8	1.6
47 ST JAMES	4.0	2.3	1.7	19.6	14.0	5.6
48 ST JOHN	4.7	2.7	2.0	22.7	15.5	7.2
49 ST LANDRY	4.8	1.5	3.3	22.4	8.7	13.7
50 ST MARTIN	6.7	2.8	3.9	29.9	15.9	14.0
51 ST MARY	4.2	2.1	2.1	18.0	10.1	7.9
52 ST TAMMANY	15.8	12.8	3.0	71.0	62.1	8.9
53 TANGIPAHOA	8.8	6.5	2.3	37.5	30.5	7.0
54 TENSAS	2.5	....	2.5	8.8	....	8.8
55 TERREBONNE	5.4	3.2	2.2	28.3	17.9	10.4
56 UNION	23.7	19.2	4.5	70.0	61.3	8.7
57 VERMILION	....	....	....	....	....	....
58 VERNON	29.3	26.4	2.9	107.7	101.7	6.0
59 WASHINGTON	12.8	11.5	1.3	61.2	56.9	4.3
60 WEBSTER	15.9	14.3	1.6	54.0	51.2	2.8
61 W BATON ROUGE	3.4	0.1	3.3	15.0	0.8	14.2
62 WEST CARROLL	0.4	....	0.4	1.3	....	1.3
63 W FELICIANA	4.1	2.0	2.1	20.8	11.9	8.9
64 WINN	61.3	54.8	6.5	288.7	276.0	12.7
STATE TOTAL	743.7	604.8	138.9	3153.8	2737.9	415.9

10

Table 11. *Louisiana: Removals of growing stock and sawtimber by parish, 1970*

Parish	Growing stock			Sawtimber		
	Total	Softwood	Hardwood	Total	Softwood	Hardwood
	----- Million cubic feet -----			----- Million board feet -----		
2 ALLEN	21.1	18.5	2.6	88.6	82.9	5.7
3 ASCENSION	2.7	0.5	2.2	6.7	1.3	5.4
4 ASSUMPTION	1.4	0.1	1.3	3.1	1.0	2.1
5 AVOYELLES	8.4	1.6	6.8	37.1	7.2	29.9
6 BEAUREGARD	25.3	24.0	1.3	94.5	90.7	3.8
7 BIENVILLE	30.5	25.7	4.8	118.0	110.5	7.5
8 BOSSIER	11.7	9.5	2.2	42.1	37.7	4.4
9 CADDO	6.0	4.3	1.7	17.6	14.1	3.5
10 CALCASIEU	8.6	6.7	1.9	31.7	25.7	6.0
11 CALDWELL	19.0	15.3	3.7	86.0	75.6	10.4
12 CAMERON	0.1	....	0.1	0.2	0.1	0.1
13 CATAHOULA	11.4	3.7	7.7	37.4	15.2	22.2
14 CLAIBORNE	9.7	8.6	1.1	34.4	31.7	2.7
15 CONCORDIA	28.0	0.3	27.7	109.0	1.8	107.2
16 DE SOTO	20.0	16.8	3.2	74.3	67.7	6.6
17 E BATON ROUGE	1.9	0.2	1.7	6.0	0.6	5.4
18 EAST CARROLL	3.5	....	3.5	10.5	0.1	10.4
19 E FELICIANA	9.0	7.0	2.0	39.6	33.2	6.4
20 EVANGELINE	5.7	4.4	1.3	21.6	18.2	3.4
21 FRANKLIN	1.3	0.1	1.2	4.2	0.6	3.6
22 GRANT	20.1	16.7	3.4	90.7	80.9	9.8
23 IBERIA	0.4	....	0.4	0.8	....	0.8
24 IBERVILLE	3.3	0.2	3.1	12.1	0.9	11.2
25 JACKSON	26.0	20.5	5.5	109.6	96.7	12.9
26 JEFFERSON	....	....	....	....	....	....
27 JEFF DAVIS	1.8	1.5	0.3	6.0	5.4	0.6
28 LAFAYETTE	0.6	....	0.6	0.5	....	0.5
29 LAFOURCHE	1.4	0.2	1.2	4.3	1.3	3.0
30 LA SALLE	24.2	20.9	3.3	107.3	97.3	10.0
31 LINCOLN	10.4	8.7	1.7	38.4	34.2	4.2
32 LIVINGSTON	34.9	30.1	4.8	174.0	156.6	17.4
33 MADISON	6.5	....	6.5	22.3	....	22.3
34 MOREHOUSE	15.4	8.8	6.6	60.1	41.3	18.8
35 NATCHITOCHES	22.2	18.1	4.1	95.0	81.4	13.6
36 ORLEANS	....	....	....	....	....	....
37 OUACHITA	8.7	6.1	2.6	31.5	24.4	7.1
38 PLAQUEMINES	....	....	....	....	....	....
39 POINTE COUPEE	5.5	0.1	5.4	13.8	0.3	13.5
40 RAPIDES	32.7	25.0	7.7	131.6	108.4	23.2
41 RED RIVER	6.8	6.1	0.7	29.5	27.7	1.8
42 RICHLAND	3.0	0.1	2.9	70.0	0.3	69.7
43 SABINE	44.6	38.4	6.2	193.3	175.0	18.3
44 ST BERNARD	....	....	....	....	....	....
45 ST CHARLES	0.4	....	0.4	0.3	....	0.3
46 ST HELENA	18.2	16.2	2.0	85.7	79.9	5.8
47 ST JAMES	0.4	....	0.4	0.4	....	0.4
48 ST JOHN	0.5	....	0.5	1.4	0.2	1.2
49 ST LANDRY	8.6	0.5	8.1	25.8	1.9	23.9
50 ST MARTIN	2.4	0.1	2.3	8.8	0.6	8.2
51 ST MARY	0.5	....	0.5	1.3	0.2	1.1
52 ST TAMMANY	12.3	11.2	1.1	56.7	53.2	3.5
53 TANGIPAHOA	17.5	15.4	2.1	77.8	72.2	5.6
54 TENSAS	5.2	0.1	5.1	19.6	0.3	19.3
55 TERREBONNE	1.3	0.2	1.1	4.4	1.2	3.2
56 UNION	33.5	25.8	7.7	132.2	110.1	22.1
57 VERMILION	0.4	....	0.4	0.5	0.1	0.4
58 VERNON	37.2	32.9	4.3	154.7	139.0	15.7
59 WASHINGTON	24.9	22.0	2.9	97.3	90.6	6.7
60 WEBSTER	9.1	7.7	1.4	36.6	32.6	4.0
61 W BATON ROUGE	1.2	....	1.2	3.8	....	3.8
62 WEST CARROLL	1.2	....	1.2	2.9	....	2.9
63 W FELICIANA	4.1	1.0	3.1	16.5	5.0	11.5
64 WINN	43.4	36.1	7.3	220.8	192.8	28.0
STATE TOTAL	721.5	522.9	198.6	3024.6	2350.6	674.0

11

Table 12. *Louisiana: Growing stock and sawtimber volume by resource regions, 1971*

Region	Growing stock			Sawtimber		
	Total	Softwood	Hardwood	Total	Softwood	Hardwood
	— — — — — Million cubic feet — — — — —			— — — — — Million board feet — — — — —		
1 NORTH DELTA	998.1	107.7	890.4	3537.6	517.8	3019.8
2 SOUTH DELTA	3039.8	979.6	2060.2	11906.9	4977.6	6929.3
3 SOUTHWEST	3878.9	2699.0	1179.9	15801.0	12327.8	3473.2
4 SOUTHEAST	1548.0	967.3	580.7	6562.7	4780.0	1782.7
5 NORTHWEST	4160.9	2924.0	1236.9	16319.9	12796.1	3523.8
STATE TOTAL	13625.7	7677.6	5948.1	54128.1	35399.3	18728.8

Table 13. *Louisiana: Net growth of growing stock and sawtimber by resource regions, 1970*

Region	Growing stock			Sawtimber		
	Total	Softwood	Hardwood	Total	Softwood	Hardwood
	— — — — — Million cubic feet — — — — —			— — — — — Million board feet — — — — —		
1 NORTH DELTA	21.7	6.2	15.5	85.5	27.4	58.1
2 SOUTH DELTA	77.2	34.1	43.1	363.9	192.6	171.3
3 SOUTHWEST	254.0	226.9	27.1	1064.0	998.8	65.2
4 SOUTHEAST	90.5	74.3	16.2	434.7	385.0	49.7
5 NORTHWEST	299.9	263.0	36.9	1205.6	1134.0	71.6
STATE TOTAL	743.3	604.5	138.8	3153.7	2737.8	415.9

Table 14. *Louisiana: Removals of growing stock and sawtimber by resource regions, 1970*

Region	Growing stock			Sawtimber		
	Total	Softwood	Hardwood	Total	Softwood	Hardwood
	— — — — — Million cubic feet — — — — —			— — — — — Million board feet — — — — —		
1 NORTH DELTA	75.6	13.1	62.5	335.8	59.5	276.3
2 SOUTH DELTA	48.8	9.3	39.5	165.3	43.9	121.4
3 SOUTHWEST	243.2	207.1	36.1	1015.1	905.0	110.1
4 SOUTHEAST	118.6	102.0	16.6	537.2	486.4	50.8
5 NORTHWEST	234.9	191.1	43.8	971.1	855.9	115.2
STATE TOTAL	721.1	522.6	198.5	3024.5	2350.7	673.8

Table 15. *Mississippi: Timber products output by county, 1970*

County	Saw logs Softwood	Saw logs Hardwood	Posts	Poles and piling	Other Softwood	Other Hardwood	Pulpwood Softwood	Pulpwood Hardwood	All products total
					Thousand cubic feet				
1 ADAMS	541.1	1949.9	0.0	0.0	0.0	1.0	248.7	2579.4	5320.1
2 ALCORN	4.0	429.9	0.0	0.0	0.0	25.0	1156.1	143.0	1758.0
3 AMITE	3589.9	1062.2	0.0	117.1	0.0	1.0	5611.8	841.8	11223.8
4 ATTALA	1587.7	1476.3	0.0	4.4	0.0	113.6	6091.2	1809.1	11082.3
5 BENTON	502.0	758.1	0.0	0.0	0.0	44.0	993.5	328.6	2626.2
6 BOLIVAR	5.3	672.5	0.0	0.0	0.0	0.0	117.0	850.9	1645.7
7 CALHOUN	555.1	1320.2	0.0	0.0	0.0	626.0	1395.1	281.0	4177.4
8 CARROLL	891.6	1577.0	0.0	0.0	0.0	31.0	684.9	377.9	3562.4
9 CHICKASAW	347.4	321.9	0.0	0.0	0.0	179.0	1619.4	416.6	2884.3
10 CHOCTAW	159.4	484.3	0.0	0.2	0.0	13.0	1743.8	1112.2	3512.9
11 CLAIBORNE	637.4	3102.8	0.0	9.9	0.0	0.0	1206.7	2687.9	7644.7
12 CLARKE	5278.1	862.7	0.0	48.9	0.0	4.0	12284.4	4488.4	22966.5
13 CLAY	98.2	716.1	0.0	0.0	0.0	210.0	563.1	116.9	1704.3
14 COAHOMA	8.8	348.2	0.0	0.0	0.0	32.0	6.2	104.5	499.7
15 COPIAH	6751.5	1523.3	0.0	537.5	110.0	0.0	6354.3	2888.6	18165.2
16 COVINGTON	2119.0	934.6	0.0	28.1	0.0	0.0	5158.8	1358.7	9599.2
17 DE SOTO	19.5	105.1	0.0	0.0	0.0	78.0	0.2	17.8	220.6
18 FORREST	1767.5	273.1	0.0	902.5	0.0	6.0	3901.4	569.6	7420.1
19 FRANKLIN	3479.8	1811.1	0.0	108.5	0.0	1.0	2771.2	1837.3	10008.9
20 GEORGE	1613.7	135.8	0.0	187.5	0.0	12.0	2759.8	682.6	5391.4
21 GREENE	4214.3	397.9	0.0	560.6	0.0	3.0	6978.1	2519.0	14672.9
22 GRENADA	112.9	560.9	0.0	0.0	0.0	223.0	194.3	123.4	1214.5
23 HANCOCK	681.2	43.5	0.0	291.7	0.0	0.0	741.5	185.8	1943.7
24 HARRISON	1600.0	26.4	0.0	1089.1	0.0	0.0	10935.1	272.1	13922.7
25 HINDS	202.8	746.6	0.0	11.5	258.0	0.0	1289.0	1720.9	4228.8
26 HOLMES	351.3	605.2	0.0	0.0	0.0	26.0	2110.1	1887.8	4980.4
27 HUMPHREYS	2.4	896.9	0.0	0.0	0.0	4.0	1.9	640.4	1545.6
28 ISSAQUENA	9.6	1185.8	0.0	0.0	0.0	41.0	246.6	1057.2	2540.2
29 ITAWAMBA	932.1	1367.9	0.0	0.0	0.0	1.0	2402.8	107.5	4811.3
30 JACKSON	1443.1	31.1	0.0	197.5	0.0	5.0	4931.1	409.7	7017.5
31 JASPER	3569.4	1025.9	0.0	44.5	0.0	17.0	7661.6	2167.0	14485.4
32 JEFFERSON	3877.0	1182.4	0.0	24.7	0.0	0.0	3346.4	3412.3	11842.8
33 JEFF DAVIS	1108.0	375.0	0.0	71.2	0.0	0.0	2140.0	432.2	4126.4
34 JONES	5040.3	1335.9	0.0	81.5	0.0	18.0	6160.5	3349.9	15986.1
35 KEMPER	8985.5	1724.7	0.0	11.4	0.0	15.0	4686.9	1938.2	17361.7
36 LAFAYETTE	757.9	677.4	0.0	110.5	0.0	56.0	999.5	962.6	3563.9
37 LAMAR	2700.7	351.3	0.0	1576.5	0.0	0.0	926.9	1249.9	6805.3
38 LAUDERDALE	4780.5	490.6	0.0	51.5	0.0	110.0	6222.2	2769.5	14424.3
39 LAWRENCE	2001.5	696.1	0.0	25.1	0.0	0.0	4863.9	354.5	7941.1
40 LEAKE	1932.1	738.1	0.0	32.9	0.0	30.0	5004.5	899.4	8637.0
41 LEE	51.6	11.9	0.0	0.0	0.0	0.0	510.7	1.0	575.2
42 LEFLORE	4.2	565.7	0.0	0.0	0.0	203.0	48.4	225.2	1046.5
43 LINCOLN	2988.1	1531.5	0.0	98.8	0.0	0.0	6541.6	1355.9	12518.9
44 LOWNDES	112.1	988.9	0.0	0.0	0.0	14.0	855.4	116.4	2086.8
45 MADISON	704.0	815.5	0.0	21.1	0.0	30.0	2111.4	1318.2	5000.2
46 MARION	2612.5	633.7	0.0	44.0	0.0	0.0	6623.4	1323.7	11237.3
47 MARSHALL	2.1	733.7	0.0	0.0	0.0	152.0	889.8	441.6	2219.2
48 MONROE	1294.8	1001.9	0.0	12.6	0.0	6.0	1129.9	221.7	3666.9
49 MONTGOMERY	157.9	821.1	0.0	66.4	0.0	73.0	2634.8	627.9	4381.1
50 NESHOBA	1207.6	117.6	0.0	24.7	0.0	54.0	3822.8	1347.7	6574.4
51 NEWTON	2734.6	1625.9	0.0	22.0	0.0	18.0	5876.6	2106.7	12383.8
52 NOXUBEE	2325.0	1435.5	0.0	1.4	0.0	41.0	2585.7	1159.2	7547.8
53 OKTIBBEHA	290.9	999.3	0.0	3.5	0.0	58.0	1262.3	445.4	3059.4
54 PANOLA	44.2	809.4	0.0	0.0	0.0	40.0	166.4	844.2	1906.2
55 PEARL RIVER	2270.7	502.5	0.0	568.5	0.0	0.0	6752.8	1716.0	11810.5
56 PERRY	4051.9	246.0	0.0	1059.7	0.0	3.0	5789.9	1512.7	12663.2
57 PIKE	847.2	162.8	0.0	147.7	0.0	1.0	3882.9	929.7	5971.3
58 PONTOTOC	113.6	1021.1	0.0	0.0	0.0	104.0	1662.4	194.6	3095.7
59 PRENTISS	185.2	473.5	0.0	0.0	0.0	42.0	1186.6	108.7	1996.0
60 QUITMAN	21.9	16.9	0.0	0.0	0.0	214.0	32.2	0.3	285.3
61 RANKIN	1990.9	313.4	0.0	53.6	0.0	88.0	5310.9	2618.6	10375.4
62 SCOTT	2855.2	1192.2	0.0	5.5	0.0	105.0	3839.6	1097.8	9095.3
63 SHARKEY	16.0	1091.3	0.0	0.0	0.0	0.0	5.6	708.9	1821.8
64 SIMPSON	3202.4	812.2	0.0	16.5	0.0	0.0	4636.7	1089.2	9757.0
65 SMITH	5199.4	422.2	0.0	26.9	0.0	17.0	2327.0	1387.1	9379.6
66 STONE	2166.4	224.4	0.0	700.6	0.0	12.0	4588.5	1164.1	8856.0
67 SUNFLOWER	51.3	23.0	0.0	0.0	0.0	0.0	0.0	0.0	74.3
68 TALLAHATCHIE	56.2	1267.4	0.0	0.0	0.0	215.0	34.5	171.9	1745.0
69 TATE	0.0	157.7	0.0	0.0	0.0	13.0	53.0	435.3	659.0
70 TIPPAH	279.4	684.8	0.0	0.0	0.0	24.0	1491.9	516.2	2996.3
71 TISHOMINGO	241.3	767.5	0.0	0.0	0.0	39.0	2156.1	568.9	3772.8
72 TUNICA	72.3	2089.6	0.0	0.0	0.0	201.0	0.0	572.6	2935.5
73 UNION	73.0	288.8	0.0	0.0	0.0	31.0	897.7	161.6	1452.1
74 WALTHALL	1077.5	199.3	0.0	60.0	0.0	1.0	4148.7	586.2	6072.7
75 WARREN	281.4	2790.2	0.0	0.0	0.0	290.0	74.8	1054.3	4490.7
76 WASHINGTON	0.4	678.5	0.0	0.0	0.0	23.0	1.9	940.1	1643.9
77 WAYNE	4208.3	627.9	0.0	15.5	0.0	12.0	7821.8	1902.3	14587.8
78 WEBSTER	338.1	966.6	0.0	2.4	0.0	70.0	3221.1	503.3	5101.5
79 WILKINSON	6711.3	2700.9	0.0	268.6	0.0	142.0	2447.3	3283.6	15553.7
80 WINSTON	4360.3	2472.4	0.0	21.5	0.0	165.0	3320.6	1012.1	11351.9
81 YALOBUSHA	24.3	1080.8	0.0	0.0	0.0	33.0	1251.1	1060.4	3449.6
82 YAZOO	42.3	5355.2	0.0	0.0	0.0	10.0	81.3	1366.4	6855.2
STATE TOTAL	129527.4	75045.4	0.0	9366.3	368.0	4469.6	228589.5	88151.8	535518.0

13

Table 16. *Mississippi: Growing stock and sawtimber volume by county, 1971*

County	Growing stock			Sawtimber		
	Total	Softwood	Hardwood	Total	Softwood	Hardwood
	------ Million cubic feet ------			------ Million board feet ------		
1 ADAMS	153.8	48.4	105.4	573.2	257.7	315.5
2 ALCORN	76.7	20.0	56.7	173.8	50.2	123.6
3 AMITE	364.2	261.5	102.7	1201.6	960.6	241.0
4 ATTALA	253.9	122.0	131.9	595.0	348.4	246.6
5 BENTON	175.7	53.0	122.7	445.2	156.4	288.8
6 BOLIVAR	105.9	3.0	102.9	371.1	23.6	347.5
7 CALHOUN	165.7	128.2	37.5	428.2	401.1	27.1
8 CARROLL	110.9	27.4	83.5	254.2	34.8	219.4
9 CHICKASAW	98.6	31.4	67.2	220.6	91.7	128.9
10 CHOCTAW	146.0	85.7	60.3	372.9	291.5	81.4
11 CLAIBORNE	203.2	51.6	151.6	578.3	182.7	395.6
12 CLARKE	326.8	198.1	128.7	971.8	726.9	244.9
13 CLAY	86.8	8.3	78.5	254.8	41.7	213.1
14 COAHOMA	58.0	5.2	52.8	207.7	28.8	178.9
15 COPIAH	349.8	193.4	156.4	1218.5	801.5	417.0
16 COVINGTON	134.0	55.2	78.8	457.0	256.8	200.2
17 DE SOTO	67.0	2.6	64.4	160.5	14.5	146.0
18 FORREST	139.3	123.8	15.5	513.2	474.7	38.5
19 FRANKLIN	454.3	369.7	84.6	2080.3	1884.4	195.9
20 GEORGE	163.7	107.9	55.8	596.2	436.5	159.7
21 GREENE	246.9	161.1	85.8	832.9	629.7	203.2
22 GRENADA	108.4	30.7	77.7	252.9	66.6	186.3
23 HANCOCK	117.1	89.4	27.7	406.0	343.4	62.6
24 HARRISON	232.0	189.8	42.2	797.2	700.2	97.0
25 HINDS	133.2	49.3	83.9	357.0	172.5	184.5
26 HOLMES	75.8	24.4	51.4	126.9	75.4	51.5
27 HUMPHREYS	39.5	....	39.5	124.6	....	124.6
28 ISSAQUENA	115.1	2.0	113.1	477.4	19.0	458.4
29 ITAWAMBA	159.8	61.7	98.1	318.5	116.6	201.9
30 JACKSON	327.4	188.2	139.2	1038.5	688.4	350.1
31 JASPER	313.3	205.4	107.9	1057.0	848.1	208.9
32 JEFFERSON	232.3	138.3	94.0	1004.0	768.9	235.1
33 JEFF DAVIS	107.2	69.4	37.8	347.0	266.2	80.8
34 JONES	291.7	225.0	66.7	1315.7	1115.7	200.0
35 KEMPER	322.8	180.3	142.5	781.7	559.8	221.9
36 LAFAYETTE	162.8	67.8	95.0	533.4	303.7	229.7
37 LAMAR	96.2	72.7	23.5	446.6	357.0	89.6
38 LAUDERDALE	405.9	246.7	159.2	1241.6	929.7	311.9
39 LAWRENCE	173.2	114.4	58.8	614.2	445.3	168.9
40 LEAKE	270.0	148.4	121.6	826.2	510.1	316.1
41 LEE	27.9	4.8	23.1	43.3	11.2	32.1
42 LEFLORE	60.9	....	60.9	105.9	....	105.9
43 LINCOLN	229.7	143.8	85.9	725.3	468.7	256.6
44 LOWNDES	80.3	20.7	59.6	148.0	78.0	70.0
45 MADISON	142.0	56.3	85.7	368.4	188.1	180.3
46 MARION	137.2	68.9	68.3	528.9	334.9	194.0
47 MARSHALL	121.9	33.9	88.0	257.0	92.8	164.2
48 MONROE	192.1	62.5	129.6	395.7	174.5	221.2
49 MONTGOMERY	127.4	63.8	63.6	354.9	163.6	191.3
50 NESHOBA	250.0	136.6	113.4	796.1	566.2	229.9
51 NEWTON	226.2	115.6	110.6	693.2	384.5	308.7
52 NOXUBEE	209.5	97.4	112.1	680.4	466.4	214.0
53 OKTIBBEHA	112.6	46.9	65.7	332.0	153.8	178.2
54 PANOLA	72.4	3.9	68.5	100.7	1.3	99.4
55 PEARL RIVER	164.4	104.5	59.9	520.0	403.5	116.5
56 PERRY	267.1	199.7	67.4	1084.1	932.5	151.6
57 PIKE	102.3	48.5	53.8	367.4	208.5	158.9
58 PONTOTOC	97.6	44.5	53.1	240.4	161.4	79.0
59 PRENTISS	88.6	36.5	52.1	172.8	67.7	105.1
60 QUITMAN	24.6	0.2	24.4	20.6	0.9	19.7
61 RANKIN	398.2	226.4	171.8	1171.2	746.4	424.8
62 SCOTT	268.7	174.0	94.7	948.6	673.1	275.5
63 SHARKEY	83.3	0.1	83.2	394.3	3.2	391.1
64 SIMPSON	192.2	110.1	82.1	507.2	329.1	178.1
65 SMITH	377.2	256.3	120.9	1391.6	1156.1	235.5
66 STONE	183.8	141.0	42.8	695.9	569.1	126.8
67 SUNFLOWER	40.7	10.7	30.0	140.2	70.2	70.0
68 TALLAHATCHIE	112.6	21.2	91.4	227.4	27.8	199.6
69 TATE	75.8	....	75.8	116.6	0.1	116.5
70 TIPPAH	104.8	31.5	73.3	200.6	59.7	140.9
71 TISHOMINGO	142.9	72.3	70.6	296.9	189.6	107.3
72 TUNICA	42.2	0.4	41.8	165.8	3.7	162.1
73 UNION	72.3	19.9	52.4	119.8	28.0	91.8
74 WALTHALL	108.2	44.2	64.0	420.5	200.2	220.3
75 WARREN	198.3	3.0	195.3	779.8	22.2	757.6
76 WASHINGTON	29.2	....	29.2	81.8	....	81.8
77 WAYNE	362.3	241.3	121.0	1403.4	1103.9	299.5
78 WEBSTER	148.8	81.4	67.4	378.9	219.6	159.3
79 WILKINSON	367.5	254.0	113.5	1875.0	1457.2	417.8
80 WINSTON	209.7	121.4	88.3	586.8	371.5	215.3
81 YALOBUSHA	110.9	56.9	54.0	258.7	127.4	131.3
82 YAZOO	169.4	2.5	166.9	534.5	3.7	530.8
STATE TOTAL	14098.6	7319.0	6779.6	45204.0	28601.1	16602.9

14

Table 17. *Mississippi: Net growth of growing stock and sawtimber by county, 1970*

County	Growing stock			Sawtimber		
	Total	Softwood	Hardwood	Total	Softwood	Hardwood
	------ Million cubic feet ------			------ Million board feet ------		
1 ADAMS	8.0	2.5	5.5	32.2	15.0	17.2
2 ALCORN	5.4	1.8	3.6	16.5	5.8	10.7
3 AMITE	29.5	24.1	5.4	90.8	81.8	9.0
4 ATTALA	20.7	12.0	8.7	50.3	31.8	18.5
5 BENTON	11.3	5.1	6.2	24.4	11.2	13.2
6 BOLIVAR	5.9	0.1	5.8	19.3	0.5	18.8
7 CALHOUN	11.3	9.4	1.9	35.2	32.9	2.3
8 CARROLL	7.5	3.2	4.3	12.8	4.5	8.3
9 CHICKASAW	7.8	3.3	4.5	13.3	7.2	6.1
10 CHOCTAW	11.3	7.3	4.0	28.7	23.9	4.8
11 CLAIBORNE	12.0	4.8	7.2	28.7	14.8	13.9
12 CLARKE	24.2	17.5	6.7	67.8	56.1	11.7
13 CLAY	4.9	0.6	4.3	14.8	3.8	11.0
14 COAHOMA	3.1	0.1	3.0	9.3	0.7	8.6
15 COPIAH	22.1	14.7	7.4	78.2	60.5	17.7
16 COVINGTON	8.1	4.5	3.6	28.0	20.3	7.7
17 DE SOTO	3.6	0.1	3.5	6.7	0.7	6.0
18 FORREST	10.4	9.7	0.7	48.9	47.7	1.2
19 FRANKLIN	31.3	26.0	5.3	144.1	137.8	6.3
20 GEORGE	10.7	8.4	2.3	43.2	36.4	6.8
21 GREENE	16.9	12.4	4.5	49.9	40.3	9.6
22 GRENADA	7.4	2.8	4.6	12.4	5.1	7.3
23 HANCOCK	7.6	6.3	1.3	27.5	25.9	1.6
24 HARRISON	16.1	14.0	2.1	66.8	60.7	6.1
25 HINDS	10.3	4.9	5.4	36.8	15.9	20.9
26 HOLMES	7.0	2.4	4.6	10.8	7.6	3.2
27 HUMPHREYS	2.7	....	2.7	5.0	....	5.0
28 ISSAQUENA	5.5	....	5.5	20.7	0.3	20.4
29 ITAWAMBA	12.3	6.9	5.4	26.7	14.8	11.9
30 JACKSON	18.7	14.1	4.6	60.2	51.7	8.5
31 JASPER	22.1	16.6	5.5	83.4	71.9	11.5
32 JEFFERSON	13.7	8.3	5.4	55.8	45.0	10.8
33 JEFF DAVIS	8.1	5.8	2.3	21.3	17.0	4.3
34 JONES	18.3	15.1	3.2	86.9	75.5	11.4
35 KEMPER	23.3	14.8	8.5	59.7	47.6	12.1
36 LAFAYETTE	9.7	4.2	5.5	38.2	21.8	16.4
37 LAMAR	5.9	4.7	1.2	40.1	35.1	5.0
38 LAUDERDALE	28.8	19.5	9.3	97.0	79.7	17.3
39 LAWRENCE	12.3	9.5	2.8	44.1	34.4	9.7
40 LEAKE	19.4	12.7	6.7	63.1	50.1	13.0
41 LEE	2.5	0.6	1.9	2.4	1.4	1.0
42 LEFLORE	5.4	....	5.4	8.6	....	8.6
43 LINCOLN	18.2	13.8	4.4	53.5	39.6	13.9
44 LOWNDES	5.9	1.5	4.4	11.9	4.9	7.0
45 MADISON	11.0	5.9	5.1	26.5	16.9	9.6
46 MARION	8.4	5.0	3.4	32.6	23.6	9.0
47 MARSHALL	7.9	2.7	5.2	17.9	8.1	9.8
48 MONROE	13.1	5.8	7.3	40.2	21.5	18.7
49 MONTGOMERY	9.0	5.7	3.3	24.1	11.8	12.3
50 NESHOBA	18.2	11.3	6.9	53.9	45.7	8.2
51 NEWTON	16.0	11.0	5.0	50.7	38.7	12.0
52 NOXUBEE	12.5	7.2	5.3	46.0	39.0	7.0
53 OKTIBBEHA	7.6	4.4	3.2	22.0	13.0	9.0
54 PANOLA	4.4	0.5	3.9	5.4	0.1	5.3
55 PEARL RIVER	10.1	7.9	2.2	34.9	31.1	3.8
56 PERRY	15.5	12.7	2.8	78.7	74.5	4.2
57 PIKE	7.0	4.6	2.4	26.8	22.1	4.7
58 PONTOTOC	7.0	3.5	3.5	22.7	16.1	6.6
59 PRENTISS	7.3	4.0	3.3	14.1	6.6	7.5
60 QUITMAN	2.4	....	2.4	2.0	0.1	1.9
61 RANKIN	32.4	22.2	10.2	82.4	63.4	19.0
62 SCOTT	21.2	15.8	5.4	94.2	76.3	17.9
63 SHARKEY	3.0	....	3.0	15.0	0.1	14.9
64 SIMPSON	16.0	11.2	4.8	43.9	31.2	12.7
65 SMITH	27.4	20.1	7.3	119.4	106.8	12.6
66 STONE	11.3	9.2	2.1	54.2	43.3	10.9
67 SUNFLOWER	3.7	0.3	3.4	5.6	2.4	3.2
68 TALLAHATCHIE	7.6	1.5	6.1	18.1	1.9	16.2
69 TATE	6.0	....	6.0	6.0	....	6.0
70 TIPPAH	8.1	3.1	5.0	21.7	7.5	14.2
71 TISHOMINGO	11.6	6.9	4.7	18.8	14.5	4.3
72 TUNICA	2.2	....	2.2	7.0	0.1	6.9
73 UNION	5.7	2.2	3.5	10.6	3.3	7.3
74 WALTHALL	5.0	3.3	1.7	20.8	16.5	4.3
75 WARREN	9.9	0.1	9.8	56.7	1.0	55.7
76 WASHINGTON	1.9	....	1.9	4.4	....	4.4
77 WAYNE	22.1	16.9	5.2	105.2	86.7	18.5
78 WEBSTER	10.5	7.2	3.3	28.0	21.5	6.5
79 WILKINSON	21.8	16.0	5.8	145.3	120.8	24.5
80 WINSTON	16.3	11.8	4.5	43.6	32.9	10.7
81 YALOBUSHA	9.3	5.5	3.8	16.5	7.5	9.0
82 YAZOO	9.3	0.2	9.1	36.4	0.2	36.2
STATE TOTAL	966.9	591.8	375.1	3228.3	2346.5	881.8

Table 18. *Mississippi: Removals of growing stock and sawtimber by county, 1970*

County	Growing stock			Sawtimber		
	Total	Softwood	Hardwood	Total	Softwood	Hardwood
	— — — — — Million cubic feet — — — — — —			— — — — — — Million board feet — — — — — —		
1 ADAMS	6.7	1.1	5.6	25.1	5.1	20.0
2 ALCORN	2.5	1.4	1.1	7.6	3.9	3.7
3 AMITE	14.7	11.8	2.9	57.2	47.6	9.6
4 ATTALA	13.6	9.4	4.2	46.9	32.3	14.6
5 BENTON	3.5	1.9	1.6	13.6	7.2	6.4
6 BOLIVAR	2.9	0.3	2.6	7.5	0.5	7.0
7 CALHOUN	5.8	2.4	3.4	21.5	8.9	12.6
8 CARROLL	8.3	2.1	6.2	33.2	9.2	24.0
9 CHICKASAW	3.9	2.4	1.5	13.0	8.1	4.9
10 CHOCTAW	4.2	2.3	1.9	12.8	7.0	5.8
11 CLAIBORNE	9.2	2.3	6.9	35.6	9.0	26.6
12 CLARKE	28.0	21.7	6.3	98.1	81.5	16.6
13 CLAY	2.6	0.8	1.8	9.9	2.7	7.2
14 COAHOMA	2.5	0.1	2.4	5.1	0.2	4.9
15 COPIAH	22.8	17.6	5.2	94.5	78.0	16.5
16 COVINGTON	11.9	9.0	2.9	42.8	33.5	9.3
17 DE SOTO	1.0	0.1	0.9	2.2	0.3	1.9
18 FORREST	9.5	8.3	1.2	35.9	32.7	3.2
19 FRANKLIN	12.9	8.3	4.6	54.0	37.5	16.5
20 GEORGE	6.8	5.7	1.1	25.3	22.8	2.5
21 GREENE	17.7	14.7	3.0	67.1	59.3	7.8
22 GRENADA	1.9	0.4	1.5	7.7	1.6	6.1
23 HANCOCK	2.6	2.2	0.4	10.7	9.9	0.8
24 HARRISON	17.5	16.6	0.9	57.0	55.8	1.2
25 HINDS	5.8	2.3	3.5	16.1	6.8	9.3
26 HOLMES	8.5	3.0	5.5	28.2	9.7	18.5
27 HUMPHREYS	4.4	....	4.4	15.0	0.1	14.9
28 ISSAQUENA	11.4	0.3	11.1	42.8	0.9	41.9
29 ITAWAMBA	6.9	4.1	2.8	25.6	15.1	10.5
30 JACKSON	9.0	8.1	0.9	30.2	28.8	1.4
31 JASPER	17.9	14.0	3.9	64.9	53.1	11.8
32 JEFFERSON	14.7	9.3	5.4	56.5	41.5	15.0
33 JEFF DAVIS	5.6	4.2	1.4	19.8	16.1	3.7
34 JONES	19.8	14.2	5.6	77.1	59.9	17.2
35 KEMPER	22.8	17.7	5.1	101.2	85.0	16.2
36 LAFAYETTE	4.8	2.4	2.4	17.9	10.0	7.9
37 LAMAR	9.4	6.9	2.5	40.1	34.7	5.4
38 LAUDERDALE	17.7	13.9	3.8	67.9	57.8	10.1
39 LAWRENCE	10.1	8.5	1.6	37.4	31.7	5.7
40 LEAKE	11.2	8.6	2.6	39.4	31.7	7.7
41 LEE	1.3	0.7	0.6	2.8	2.2	0.6
42 LEFLORE	2.1	0.1	2.0	6.7	0.2	6.5
43 LINCOLN	15.7	12.0	3.7	59.2	45.7	13.5
44 LOWNDES	3.2	1.2	2.0	11.4	3.8	7.6
45 MADISON	6.5	3.6	2.9	21.5	12.6	8.9
46 MARION	14.0	11.4	2.6	49.6	42.3	7.3
47 MARSHALL	3.6	1.1	2.5	10.8	3.0	7.8
48 MONROE	5.8	3.2	2.6	21.9	13.9	8.0
49 MONTGOMERY	6.2	3.4	2.8	17.5	9.9	7.6
50 NESHOBA	8.1	6.2	1.9	30.6	22.1	8.5
51 NEWTON	15.5	10.7	4.8	57.0	40.6	16.4
52 NOXUBEE	10.0	6.3	3.7	39.5	26.6	12.9
53 OKTIBBEHA	5.3	2.0	3.3	15.3	6.5	8.8
54 PANOLA	3.0	0.4	2.6	9.1	1.0	8.1
55 PEARL RIVER	14.4	11.8	2.6	50.9	43.8	7.1
56 PERRY	15.7	13.8	1.9	62.4	57.6	4.8
57 PIKE	7.6	6.0	1.6	24.3	20.4	3.9
58 PONTOTOC	4.4	2.2	2.2	14.5	6.4	8.1
59 PRENTISS	3.6	1.7	1.9	11.9	5.4	6.5
60 QUITMAN	3.2	0.1	3.1	13.9	0.3	13.6
61 RANKIN	13.6	9.2	4.4	42.8	33.7	9.1
62 SCOTT	11.8	8.4	3.4	45.8	34.8	11.0
63 SHARKEY	2.5	0.1	2.4	9.2	0.2	9.0
64 SIMPSON	13.3	9.9	3.4	50.2	40.2	10.0
65 SMITH	12.4	9.8	2.6	54.9	48.2	6.7
66 STONE	11.1	9.3	1.8	40.6	36.7	3.9
67 SUNFLOWER	1.1	0.2	0.9	1.4	0.5	0.9
68 TALLAHATCHIE	6.7	0.2	6.5	21.9	0.6	21.3
69 TATE	1.0	....	1.0	2.6	0.2	2.4
70 TIPPAH	4.0	2.2	1.8	13.3	7.1	6.2
71 TISHOMINGO	4.9	2.9	2.0	16.2	9.0	7.2
72 TUNICA	5.3	0.1	5.2	23.2	0.6	22.6
73 UNION	2.1	1.2	0.9	6.5	3.6	2.9
74 WALTHALL	7.6	6.5	1.1	25.2	22.4	2.8
75 WARREN	8.6	0.5	8.1	39.0	2.5	36.5
76 WASHINGTON	5.4	0.1	5.3	18.6	0.1	18.5
77 WAYNE	17.8	14.9	2.9	66.7	58.4	8.3
78 WEBSTER	6.5	4.3	2.2	21.6	13.2	8.4
79 WILKINSON	24.7	12.3	12.4	92.2	62.0	30.2
80 WINSTON	15.5	9.9	5.6	66.5	44.9	21.6
81 YALOBUSHA	5.2	1.5	3.7	15.8	4.3	11.5
82 YAZOO	22.9	0.2	22.7	87.9	0.7	87.2
STATE TOTAL	746.2	462.0	284.2	2757.3	1825.7	931.6

16

Table 19. *Mississippi: Growing stock and sawtimber volume by resource regions, 1971*

Region	Growing stock			Sawtimber		
	Total	Softwood	Hardwood	Total	Softwood	Hardwood
	— — — — — Million cubic feet — — — — —			— — — — Million board feet — — — — —		
1 DELTA	1155.6	72.7	1082.9	3758.0	278.5	3479.5
2 NORTH	2934.5	1096.3	1838.2	6831.0	3097.5	3733.5
3 CENTRAL	4024.2	2338.4	1685.8	12248.3	8616.2	3632.1
4 SOUTH	3251.6	2196.5	1055.1	12017.2	9257.7	2759.5
5 SOUTHWEST	2732.4	1614.8	1117.6	10349.1	7350.9	2998.2
STATE TOTAL	14098.3	7318.7	6779.6	45203.6	28600.8	16602.8

Table 20. *Mississippi: Net growth of growing stock and sawtimber by resource regions, 1970*

Region	Growing stock			Sawtimber		
	Total	Softwood	Hardwood	Total	Softwood	Hardwood
	— — — — — Million cubic feet — — — — —			— — — — — Million board feet — — — — —		
1 DELTA	69.4	4.7	64.7	219.0	14.9	204.1
2 NORTH	208.3	98.1	110.2	491.8	269.5	222.3
3 CENTRAL	298.3	203.6	94.7	955.7	771.4	184.3
4 SOUTH	205.5	159.7	45.8	843.2	720.6	122.6
5 SOUTHWEST	184.7	125.5	59.2	718.7	570.4	148.3
STATE TOTAL	966.2	591.6	374.6	3228.4	2346.8	881.6

Table 21. *Mississippi: Removals of growing stock and sawtimber by resource regions, 1970*

Region	Growing stock			Sawtimber		
	Total	Softwood	Hardwood	Total	Softwood	Hardwood
	— — — — — Million cubic feet — — — — —			— — — — — Million board feet — — — — —		
1 DELTA	87.6	5.4	82.2	320.5	17.2	303.3
2 NORTH	105.6	48.4	57.2	355.9	163.3	192.6
3 CENTRAL	211.1	155.6	55.5	805.7	632.5	173.2
4 SOUTH	200.5	166.2	34.3	738.9	646.4	92.5
5 SOUTHWEST	141.3	86.5	54.8	536.1	366.2	169.9
STATE TOTAL	746.1	462.1	284.0	2757.1	1825.6	931.5

Table 22. Oklahoma: Timber products output by county, 1970

County	Saw logs Softwood	Saw logs Hardwood	Posts	Poles and piling	Other Softwood	Other Hardwood	Pulpwood Softwood	Pulpwood Hardwood	All products total
	- Thousand cubic feet -								
1 ADAIR	0.0	0.0	0.0	0.0	0.0	172.0	0.0	0.0	172.0
2 ATOKA	0.0	0.0	0.0	0.0	0.0	52.0	0.0	0.0	52.0
3 CHEROKEE	0.0	0.0	0.0	0.0	0.0	92.0	0.0	0.0	92.0
4 CHOCTAW	0.0	0.0	0.0	0.0	0.C	15.0	198.5	93.7	307.2
5 COAL	0.0	0.0	0.0	0.0	0.0	70.0	0.0	0.0	70.0
6 DELAWARE	0.0	0.0	0.0	0.0	0.C	219.0	0.0	0.0	219.0
7 HASKELL	0.0	0.0	0.0	0.0	0.0	2.0	0.0	179.5	181.5
8 LATIMER	0.0	0.0	0.0	0.0	0.0	426.0	52.2	0.0	478.2
9 LE FLORE	0.0	0.0	0.0	0.0	0.0	1039.0	698.9	29.1	1767.0
10 MC CURTAIN	0.0	0.0	0.0	0.0	0.C	0.0	2209.7	1003.1	3212.8
11 MC INTOSH	0.0	0.0	0.0	0.0	0.0	6.0	0.0	0.0	6.0
12 MAYES	0.0	0.0	0.0	0.0	0.0	29.0	0.0	117.6	146.6
13 MUSKOGEE	0.0	0.0	0.0	0.0	0.0	3.0	0.0	146.6	149.6
14 OTTAWA	0.0	0.0	0.0	0.0	0.0	59.0	0.0	123.8	182.8
15 PITTSBURG	0.0	0.0	0.0	0.0	0.0	2.0	0.0	0.0	2.0
16 PUSHMATAHA	0.0	0.0	0.0	0.0	0.0	15.0	844.5	154.2	1013.7
17 SEQUOYAH	0.0	0.0	0.0	0.0	0.0	152.0	0.0	60.6	212.6
STATE TOTAL	0.0	0.0	0.0	0.0	0.0	2353.0	4003.8	1908.2	8265.0

Table 23. Oklahoma: Growing stock and sawtimber volume by county, 1971

County	Growing stock Total	Growing stock Softwood	Growing stock Hardwood	Sawtimber Total	Sawtimber Softwood	Sawtimber Hardwood
	- - - - - Million cubic feet - - - - -			- - - - - Million board feet - - - - -		
1 ADAIR	56.5	6.2	50.3	77.4	17.0	60.4
2 ATOKA	56.9	16.8	40.1	136.9	40.1	96.8
3 CHEROKEE	61.2	3.6	57.6	149.6	10.5	139.1
4 CHOCTAW	74.9	1.7	73.2	186.8	4.0	182.8
5 COAL	25.6	....	25.6	94.4	....	94.4
6 DELAWARE	43.3	0.9	42.4	106.8	5.0	101.8
7 HASKELL	42.1	4.3	37.8	97.9	8.7	89.2
8 LATIMER	56.6	38.1	18.5	115.5	82.0	33.5
9 LE FLORE	226.5	147.3	79.2	609.9	494.3	115.6
10 MC CURTAIN	632.1	438.5	193.6	1897.4	1540.1	357.3
11 MC INTOSH	8.0	....	8.0	31.9	....	31.9
12 MAYES	28.2	4.1	24.1	80.4	16.3	64.1
13 MUSKOGEE	10.6	0.2	10.6	8.0	1.3	6.7
14 OTTAWA	21.6	....	21.6	49.6	....	49.6
15 PITTSBURG	31.0	5.4	25.6	83.8	9.7	74.1
16 PUSHMATAHA	271.5	197.3	74.2	726.5	575.4	151.1
17 SEQUOYAH	20.0	12.2	7.8	39.9	39.2	0.7
STATE TOTAL	1666.8	876.6	790.2	4492.7	2843.6	1649.1

Table 24. Oklahoma: Net growth of growing stock and sawtimber by county, 1970

County	Growing stock Total	Growing stock Softwood	Growing stock Hardwood	Sawtimber Total	Sawtimber Softwood	Sawtimber Hardwood
	- - - - - Million cubic feet - - - - -			- - - - - Million board feet - - - - -		
1 ADAIR	2.0	0.1	1.9	2.5	0.7	1.8
2 ATOKA	1.8	0.9	0.9	4.0	2.2	1.8
3 CHEROKEE	2.3	0.1	2.2	4.5	0.4	4.1
4 CHOCTAW	1.8	0.1	1.7	3.5	0.2	3.3
5 COAL	0.6	....	0.6	1.7	....	1.7
6 DELAWARE	1.6	....	1.6	3.2	0.2	3.0
7 HASKELL	1.1	0.2	0.9	2.1	0.5	1.6
8 LATIMER	2.5	2.1	0.4	5.1	4.5	0.6
9 LE FLORE	10.1	8.3	1.8	29.4	27.2	2.2
10 MC CURTAIN	29.4	24.9	4.5	92.7	86.0	6.7
11 MC INTOSH	0.3	....	0.3	0.9	....	0.9
12 MAYES	1.0	0.1	0.9	2.5	0.6	1.9
13 MUSKOGEE	0.4	....	0.4	0.3	0.1	0.2
14 OTTAWA	0.8	....	0.8	1.5	....	1.5
15 PITTSBURG	0.9	0.3	0.6	1.8	0.5	1.3
16 PUSHMATAHA	12.9	11.2	1.7	34.8	32.1	2.7
17 SEQUOYAH	0.5	0.2	0.3	1.6	1.5	0.1
STATE TOTAL	70.0	48.5	21.5	192.1	156.7	35.4

18

Table 25. *Oklahoma: Removals of growing stock and sawtimber by co unty, 1970*

County		Growing stock			Sawtimber		
		Total	Softwood	Hardwood	Total	Softwood	Hardwood
		----- Million cubic feet -----			----- Million board feet -----		
1	ADAIR	0.6	....	0.6	1.4	....	1.4
2	ATOKA	1.7	0.2	1.5	5.8	0.8	5.0
3	CHEROKEE	1.9	....	1.9	4.6	....	4.6
4	CHOCTAW	1.8	0.4	1.4	5.2	0.9	4.3
5	COAL	0.6	....	0.6	2.7	....	2.7
6	DELAWARE	1.2	....	1.2	4.1	....	4.1
·7	HASKELL	0.7	....	0.7	2.7	....	2.7
8	LATIMER	1.3	0.1	1.2	2.0	0.3	1.7
9	LE FLORE	6.8	2.8	4.0	18.6	8.4	10.2
10	MC CURTAIN	22.4	13.7	8.7	98.8	66.4	32.4
11	MC INTOSH	0.8	....	0.8	0.6	....	0.6
12	MAYES	0.6	....	0.6	2.0	....	2.0
13	MUSKOGEE	1.0	....	1.0	2.0	....	2.0
14	OTTAWA	1.1	....	1.1	3.3	....	3.3
15	PITTSBURG	1.0	0.1	0.9	1.6	0.4	1.2
16	PUSHMATAHA	7.7	5.2	2.5	31.1	24.6	6.5
17	SEQUOYAH	0.8	....	0.8	2.3	....	2.3
	STATE TOTAL	52.0	22.5	29.5	188.8	101.8	87.0

Table 26. *Oklahoma: Growing stock and sawtimber volume by resource regions, 1971*

Region	Growing stock			Sawtimber		
	Total	Softwood	Hardwood	Total	Softwood	Hardwood
	----- Million cubic feet -----			----- Million board feet -----		
1 SOUTHEAST	1417.3	849.5	567.8	3949.0	2754.3	1194.7
2 NORTHEAST	249.7	27.2	222.5	543.6	89.3	454.3
STATE TOTAL	1667.0	876.7	790.3	4492.6	2843.6	1649.0

Table 27. *Oklahoma: Net growth of growing stock and sawtimber by resource regions, 1970*

Region	Growing stock			Sawtimber		
	Total	Softwood	Hardwood	Total	Softwood	Hardwood
	----- Million cubic feet -----			----- Million board feet -----		
1 SOUTHEAST	61.2	48.0	13.2	175.1	153.3	21.8
2 NORTHEAST	9.0	0.5	8.5	16.8	3.4	13.4
STATE TOTAL	70.2	48.5	21.7	191.9	156.7	35.2

Table 28. *Oklahoma: Removals of growing stock and sawtimber by resource regions, 1970*

Region	Growing stock			Sawtimber		
	Total	Softwood	Hardwood	Total	Softwood	Hardwood
	----- Million cubic feet -----			----- Million board feet -----		
1 SOUTHEAST	44.0	22.5	21.5	168.7	101.8	66.9
2 NORTHEAST	7.9	....	7.9	20.3	....	20.3
STATE TOTAL	51.9	22.5	29.4	189.0	101.8	87.2

Table 29. Tennessee: Timber products output by county, 1970

County	Saw logs		Posts	Poles and piling	Other		Pulpwood		All products total
	Softwood	Hardwood			Softwood	Hardwood	Softwood	Hardwood	
				Thousand cubic feet					
1 ANDERSON	36.2	1771.7	0.0	0.0	0.C	34.7	193.1	289.9	2325.6
2 BEDFORD	79.9	231.9	0.0	0.0	0.C	65.7	C.0	C.C	377.5
3 BENTON	3.4	1031.4	0.0	0.0	C.C	3.8	35.2	456.0	1529.8
4 BLEDSOE	135.4	686.8	0.0	C.C	18.7	90.C	556.9	221.7	1709.5
5 BLOUNT	164.8	189.5	0.0	C.C	C.C	15.4	713.2	255.0	1337.9
6 BRADLEY	274.4	204.5	0.0	0.0	C.C	15.1	1189.2	160.6	1843.8
7 CAMPBELL	138.6	822.7	0.0	0.0	C.C	27.1	219.6	424.9	1632.9
8 CANNON	45.7	571.4	C.0	C.0	C.C	2.8	C.0	C.C	619.9
9 CARROLL	23.7	1722.8	296.0	2.7	0.C	135.1	18.9	228.7	2427.9
10 CARTER	305.7	150.3	0.0	0.0	C.C	0.0	9.2	278.2	743.4
11 CHEATHAM	6.9	897.7	C.0	0.0	C.C	1.3	C.C	C.C	905.9
12 CHESTER	18.7	626.2	0.0	0.0	C.C	25.8	84.2	51.1	806.0
13 CLAIBORNE	139.6	1081.6	C.0	C.0	C.C	25.0	0.0	19.4	1265.6
14 CLAY	0.7	691.9	0.0	0.C	C.C	58.0	0.0	C.0	750.6
15 COCKE	377.9	359.4	0.0	0.0	9.2	27.2	412.9	271.9	1458.5
16 COFFEE	47.3	1708.9	1.2	C.C	C.C	31.8	207.6	C.0	1996.8
17 CROCKETT	0.0	294.2	0.0	C.C	C.C	0.C	C.0	C.0	294.2
18 CUMBERLAND	93.9	496.3	0.0	C.0	C.C	287.7	5C7.9	1138.3	2524.1
19 DAVIDSON	37.5	255.8	0.0	C.0	C.C	33.5	0.0	C.0	326.8
20 DECATUR	28.6	1482.5	C.0	C.0	C.C	164.3	69.3	C.0	1744.7
21 DEKALB	69.6	706.0	C.0	C.0	C.C	11.8	0.0	C.0	787.4
22 DICKSON	32.2	1293.8	C.0	C.0	C.C	139.8	C.0	221.C	1686.8
23 DYER	101.3	1576.5	C.0	C.0	C.C	0.C	C.0	C.0	1677.8
24 FAYETTE	0.0	886.1	C.0	0.0	C.C	75.3	13.5	0.2	975.1
25 FENTRESS	333.6	1134.6	0.0	0.0	C.C	336.7	320.0	142.2	2267.1
26 FRANKLIN	39.1	1107.0	0.0	C.0	4.C	242.0	C.0	C.0	1392.1
27 GIBSON	17.5	599.1	0.0	C.0	0.C	0.C	C.2	13.0	649.8
28 GILES	105.7	715.2	74.3	0.4	C.C	76.4	3.4	C.0	975.4
29 GRAINGER	49.2	321.5	C.0	C.C	0.C	1455.C	0.0	29.3	1855.0
30 GREENE	82.3	512.5	C.0	C.C	9.2	47.8	46.4	168.3	866.5
31 GRUNDY	221.2	1090.1	C.0	C.0	C.C	283.6	212.0	C.0	1806.9
32 HAMBLEN	37.9	538.7	C.0	0.0	0.C	1460.7	7.7	2.9	2047.9
33 HAMILTON	363.5	282.6	C.0	C.0	0.C	6.1	578.5	427.2	1657.9
34 HANCOCK	16.5	277.2	0.0	0.0	C.C	0.C	C.0	54.2	348.4
35 HARDEMAN	105.5	2160.9	C.0	0.0	C.C	86.6	727.0	51.2	3131.2
36 HARDIN	116.4	2101.3	C.0	0.C	0.C	201.9	762.4	1024.6	4206.6
37 HAWKINS	55.4	502.5	0.0	0.C	C.C	0.0	0.0	281.2	839.1
38 HAYWOOD	36.8	1589.8	0.0	C.C	0.C	5.6	39.4	C.2	1671.8
39 HENDERSON	5.7	1470.8	73.7	0.4	C.C	71.4	129.9	2.0	1753.9
40 HENRY	24.8	1174.7	49.3	C.4	0.C	42.4	26.2	849.5	2167.3
41 HICKMAN	33.6	1409.6	C.5	C.C	C.C	39.4	2.5	908.C	2393.6
42 HOUSTON	0.0	816.0	C.0	0.0	C.C	0.C	C.0	47.2	863.2
43 HUMPHREYS	0.0	1035.7	5.1	0.0	C.C	30.7	C.0	1752.9	2824.4
44 JACKSON	0.0	572.7	C.0	C.C	C.C	17.6	C.0	C.0	590.3
45 JEFFERSON	33.2	194.1	0.0	C.0	0.C	1466.3	5.7	7.8	1707.1
46 JOHNSON	414.4	496.9	0.0	0.0	C.C	0.0	0.0	305.3	1216.6
47 KNOX	77.0	188.1	0.0	0.0	C.C	46.5	285.1	138.7	735.4
48 LAKE	111.7	541.5	0.0	0.C	0.C	0.0	0.0	0.0	653.2
49 LAUDERDALE	205.0	3326.0	0.0	C.C	0.C	181.3	C.0	0.0	3712.3
50 LAWRENCE	0.0	1335.6	0.0	0.0	C.C	148.5	26.7	2.7	1513.5
51 LEWIS	53.5	723.5	0.0	C.0	C.C	19.8	C.9	454.1	1251.8
52 LINCOLN	120.5	797.0	0.0	C.0	C.C	48.2	C.0	C.C	965.7
53 LOUDON	32.4	38.5	C.0	0.0	0.C	27.8	154.5	396.6	649.8
54 MCMINN	205.5	266.6	C.3	85.8	0.C	53.9	1683.3	316.7	2612.1
55 MCNAIRY	103.4	2667.0	0.0	0.0	0.C	115.3	604.8	116.6	3607.1
56 MACON	4.8	1158.8	C.0	0.0	0.C	126.8	C.0	0.0	1290.4
57 MADISON	99.0	1342.0	C.7	31.0	0.C	30.C	32.4	23.2	1558.3
58 MARION	240.2	744.2	C.0	C.0	C.C	117.1	C.0	0.0	1102.5
59 MARSHALL	68.4	170.7	C.0	0.0	243.C	147.4	C.0	0.0	629.5
60 MAURY	41.6	603.8	0.0	0.0	0.C	173.2	C.0	C.0	818.6
61 MEIGS	117.5	128.5	C.3	85.8	0.C	12.7	522.0	496.4	1363.2
62 MONROE	1703.7	579.6	0.2	57.4	0.C	114.C	116C.8	698.8	4312.5
63 MONTGOMERY	6.9	1245.8	0.0	0.0	0.C	17.7	0.0	C.0	1270.4
64 MOORE	103.4	386.7	0.0	C.U	0.C	60.C	0.0	0.0	550.1
65 MORGAN	251.7	588.3	C.0	C.C	0.C	36.9	473.0	1146.6	2496.5
66 OBION	108.0	1817.3	C.0	C.C	0.C	13.6	C.6	42.8	1982.3
67 OVERTON	16.8	925.5	C.0	C.C	0.C	370.5	0.0	C.C	1312.8
68 PERRY	0.2	1657.4	C.0	C.C	0.C	23.3	2.2	454.C	2137.1
69 PICKETT	0.0	362.9	0.0	C.0	0.C	315.1	C.0	C.0	678.0
70 POLK	1810.0	608.3	0.0	C.0	0.C	9.4	571.4	277.9	3277.0
71 PUTNAM	0.0	1329.3	0.0	C.0	0.C	59.7	426.2	76C.9	2576.1
72 RHEA	39.4	59.3	0.9	57.4	0.C	0.C	615.2	1046.2	1818.4
73 ROANE	142.8	199.3	C.0	C.0	0.C	21.7	718.7	360.7	1443.2
74 ROBERTSON	0.0	1005.1	0.0	0.C	C.C	62.8	C.0	C.0	1067.9
75 RUTHERFORD	70.0	133.9	0.0	0.0	0.C	143.3	C.0	C.0	347.2
76 SCOTT	161.4	2678.C	0.0	C.0	0.C	217.5	358.3	877.C	4292.6
77 SEQUATCHIE	40.8	383.4	C.0	C.C	0.C	40.0	109.2	138.5	711.9
78 SEVIER	89.4	82.7	0.0	0.0	0.C	11.3	101.5	9.1	294.0
79 SHELBY	4.2	406.7	0.0	0.0	0.C	75.7	0.0	C.0	486.6
80 SMITH	61.6	478.8	0.0	0.0	0.C	20.4	C.0	C.0	560.8
81 STEWART	0.0	1188.0	C.0	0.0	0.C	0.0	0.1	3.1	1191.2
82 SULLIVAN	15.2	218.7	C.0	0.0	0.C	0.C	0.0	791.4	1025.3
83 SUMNER	33.6	422.0	0.0	0.0	0.C	129.7	C.0	C.0	585.3
84 TIPTON	31.5	695.9	0.0	0.0	0.C	75.5	C.C	15.8	818.7
85 TROUSDALE	5.9	20.9	0.0	0.0	0.C	27.1	0.0	C.0	53.9
86 UNICOI	290.8	115.5	0.0	0.0	C.C	0.C	9.2	566.8	982.3
87 UNION	101.9	385.2	0.0	0.0	C.C	5.7	97.4	133.0	723.2
88 VAN BUREN	98.6	678.5	0.0	0.0	C.C	17.2	0.0	C.0	794.3
89 WARREN	62.5	793.1	C.0	0.0	0.C	300.5	111.0	7.2	1274.3
90 WASHINGTON	27.7	369.6	0.0	0.0	0.C	0.C	18.4	183.4	599.1
91 WAYNE	194.6	1527.0	C.0	0.0	0.C	52.7	208.7	35.5	2018.5
92 WEAKLEY	58.8	1688.7	C.0	C.0	0.C	30.1	14.9	171.0	1963.5
93 WHITE	22.4	1124.4	0.0	C.C	C.C	93.9	0.0	C.0	1240.7
94 WILLIAMSON	35.9	438.4	0.0	C.0	C.C	15.5	C.0	C.0	589.8
95 WILSON	53.5	180.4	0.0	0.C	C.C	93.7	C.0	C.0	327.6
STATE TOTAL	11398.0	78650.3	5C2.5	321.3	285.1	10944.8	15398.5	19746.6	137247.1

20

Table 30. *Tennessee. Growing stock and sawtimber volume by county, 1971*

County		Growing stock			Sawtimber		
		Total	Softwood	Hardwood	Total	Softwood	Hardwood
		- - - - - - Million cubic feet - - - - - -			- - - - - - Million board feet - - - - - -		
1	ANDERSON	103.4	23.3	80.1	273.8	73.5	200.3
2	BEDFORD	32.2	0.8	31.4	64.3	....	64.3
3	BENTON	121.5	5.8	115.7	219.4	13.8	205.6
4	BLEDSOE	69.9	15.6	54.3	125.9	34.6	91.3
5	BLOUNT	143.0	65.4	77.6	415.1	187.0	228.1
6	BRADLEY	100.2	64.9	35.3	126.5	63.3	63.2
7	CAMPBELL	246.4	62.2	184.2	716.9	169.4	547.5
8	CANNON	28.3	1.3	27.0	31.3	....	31.3
9	CARROLL	131.1	14.1	117.0	310.4	29.7	280.7
10	CARTER	168.1	37.2	130.9	439.0	143.0	296.0
11	CHEATHAM	84.1	1.5	82.6	243.6	....	243.6
12	CHESTER	75.8	19.9	55.9	178.4	58.8	119.6
13	CLAIBORNE	112.1	17.8	94.3	264.6	38.0	226.6
14	CLAY	69.3	1.8	67.5	190.3	7.0	183.3
15	COCKE	169.2	39.1	130.1	447.7	141.3	306.4
16	COFFEE	98.0	....	98.0	263.0	....	263.0
17	CROCKETT	16.5	1.1	15.4	60.0	5.6	54.4
18	CUMBERLAND	247.3	66.3	181.0	595.9	203.4	392.5
19	DAVIDSON	66.5	....	66.5	184.3	....	184.3
20	DECATUR	126.8	10.4	116.4	296.8	11.4	285.4
21	DEKALB	53.3	5.4	47.9	129.2	1.5	127.7
22	DICKSON	168.6	0.2	168.4	415.2	....	415.2
23	DYER	86.4	....	86.4	343.7	....	343.7
24	FAYETTE	58.9	3.0	55.9	163.7	4.6	159.1
25	FENTRESS	199.3	75.9	123.4	540.2	225.8	314.4
26	FRANKLIN	172.7	4.4	168.3	509.7	1.4	508.3
27	GIBSON	49.4	....	49.4	129.4	....	129.4
28	GILES	69.8	1.2	68.6	142.4	....	142.4
29	GRAINGER	84.5	12.0	72.5	233.2	30.1	203.1
30	GREENE	100.1	18.2	81.9	307.8	52.6	255.2
31	GRUNDY	127.5	14.8	112.7	333.6	33.3	300.3
32	HAMBLEN	31.6	6.6	25.0	72.2	5.3	66.9
33	HAMILTON	150.1	66.1	84.0	450.8	217.7	233.1
34	HANCOCK	61.9	2.4	59.5	175.9	8.9	167.0
35	HARDEMAN	181.8	27.3	154.5	425.9	73.2	352.7
36	HARDIN	184.6	38.4	146.2	429.3	81.8	347.5
37	HAWKINS	144.4	26.8	117.6	357.0	43.0	314.0
38	HAYWOOD	88.9	....	88.9	286.7	....	286.7
39	HENDERSON	151.1	26.6	124.5	397.2	66.2	331.0
40	HENRY	110.7	....	110.7	259.1	....	259.1
41	HICKMAN	204.1	3.0	201.1	399.4	6.7	392.7
42	HOUSTON	80.4	0.6	79.8	176.4	1.8	174.6
43	HUMPHREYS	168.2	1.6	166.6	286.6	3.1	283.5
44	JACKSON	71.5	5.8	65.7	201.1	1.1	200.0
45	JEFFERSON	40.0	5.8	34.2	125.0	10.4	114.6
46	JOHNSON	123.4	19.1	104.3	295.5	73.4	222.1
47	KNOX	91.9	29.4	62.5	287.0	59.2	227.8
48	LAKE	31.0	....	31.0	132.0	....	132.0
49	LAUDERDALE	173.0	....	173.0	700.0	....	700.0
50	LAWRENCE	123.9	....	123.9	274.3	....	274.3
51	LEWIS	114.2	3.5	110.7	197.3	11.5	185.8
52	LINCOLN	45.4	4.3	41.1	72.2	....	72.2
53	LOUDON	43.0	15.9	27.1	110.9	23.2	87.7
54	MCMINN	120.0	53.7	66.3	275.1	110.2	164.9
55	MCNAIRY	118.6	31.7	86.9	255.3	94.1	161.2
56	MACON	57.1	....	57.1	99.5	....	99.5
57	MADISON	105.7	1.2	104.5	348.0	2.0	346.0
58	MARION	187.3	24.9	162.4	553.8	83.8	470.0
59	MARSHALL	33.1	2.3	30.8	94.6	2.7	91.9
60	MAURY	67.5	....	67.5	173.1	....	173.1
61	MEIGS	64.0	30.3	33.7	136.2	53.5	82.7
62	MONROE	320.6	153.6	167.0	885.5	429.2	456.3
63	MONTGOMERY	69.3	1.7	67.6	149.6	....	149.6
64	MOORE	31.7	1.9	29.8	82.8	6.4	76.4
65	MORGAN	207.7	37.7	170.0	552.8	122.0	430.8
66	OBION	66.6	17.3	49.3	234.3	87.0	147.3
67	OVERTON	176.0	20.7	155.3	441.7	88.8	352.9
68	PERRY	174.4	1.7	172.7	304.7	2.0	302.7
69	PICKETT	52.6	4.6	48.0	129.4	3.1	126.3
70	POLK	274.0	160.8	113.2	764.5	471.0	293.5
71	PUTNAM	134.3	8.5	125.8	313.2	25.1	288.1
72	RHEA	93.3	16.4	76.9	224.7	44.8	179.9
73	ROANE	89.9	23.4	66.5	183.1	35.0	148.1
74	ROBERTSON	55.0	....	55.0	176.7	....	176.7
75	RUTHERFORD	31.2	5.6	25.6	17.9	....	17.9
76	SCOTT	321.1	78.6	242.5	854.9	230.7	624.2
77	SEQUATCHIE	91.1	28.8	62.3	247.5	92.8	154.7
78	SEVIER	127.5	48.3	79.2	303.4	106.9	196.5
79	SHELBY	59.6	1.0	58.6	173.7	4.0	169.7
80	SMITH	39.6	2.3	37.3	60.4	0.5	59.9
81	STEWART	205.2	4.0	201.2	526.3	17.0	509.3
82	SULLIVAN	72.2	17.2	55.0	156.3	46.1	110.2
83	SUMNER	52.7	1.2	51.5	177.3	2.6	174.7
84	TIPTON	36.0	....	36.0	105.7	....	105.7
85	TROUSDALE	5.9	0.4	5.5	7.4	....	7.4
86	UNICOI	91.2	26.1	65.1	259.8	98.6	161.2
87	UNION	77.1	22.4	54.7	178.6	27.3	151.3
88	VAN BUREN	73.0	16.6	56.4	195.2	41.3	153.9
89	WARREN	93.5	6.0	87.5	205.7	7.1	198.6
90	WASHINGTON	69.2	20.6	48.6	181.6	64.4	117.2
91	WAYNE	315.1	39.0	276.1	525.3	52.4	472.9
92	WEAKLEY	98.7	12.3	86.4	361.9	24.9	337.0
93	WHITE	123.9	1.9	122.0	340.5	0.8	339.7
94	WILLIAMSON	85.5	4.8	80.7	217.4	4.8	212.6
95	WILSON	32.5	3.5	29.0	57.7	0.6	57.1
	STATE TOTAL	10395.8	1799.8	8596.0	26340.2	4699.1	21641.1

County	Growing stock			Sawtimber		
	Total	Softwood	Hardwood	Total	Softwood	Hardwood
	- - - - - Million cubic feet - - - - -			- - - - - Million board feet - - - - -		
1 ANDERSON	5.1	1.3	3.8	15.0	3.5	11.5
2 BEDFORD	2.2	0.2	2.0	4.7	....	4.7
3 BENTON	6.3	0.3	6.0	19.2	2.2	17.0
4 BLEDSOE	4.5	1.0	3.5	5.1	1.6	3.5
5 BLOUNT	7.3	3.3	4.0	23.7	12.3	11.4
6 BRADLEY	6.1	3.8	2.3	10.9	3.3	7.6
7 CAMPBELL	11.0	2.9	8.1	40.4	13.8	26.6
8 CANNON	2.4	0.3	2.1	1.3	....	1.3
9 CARROLL	7.6	0.8	6.8	22.5	3.1	19.4
10 CARTER	7.2	1.0	6.2	19.0	5.8	13.2
11 CHEATHAM	3.7	0.8	2.9	7.1	....	7.1
12 CHESTER	3.8	0.9	2.9	11.8	3.2	8.6
13 CLAIBORNE	5.4	1.4	4.0	11.9	1.6	10.3
14 CLAY	2.9	0.1	2.8	7.0	0.4	6.6
15 COCKE	7.8	1.2	6.6	21.0	4.3	16.7
16 COFFEE	4.7	....	4.7	10.1	....	10.1
17 CROCKETT	0.6	....	0.6	1.9	0.1	1.8
18 CUMBERLAND	10.8	3.4	7.4	35.4	12.5	22.9
19 DAVIDSON	2.4	....	2.4	6.6	....	6.6
20 DECATUR	5.4	0.9	4.5	17.4	1.7	15.7
21 DEKALB	2.7	0.2	2.5	5.6	0.1	5.5
22 DICKSON	9.0	....	9.0	22.0	....	22.0
23 DYER	3.2	....	3.2	15.2	....	15.2
24 FAYETTE	3.4	0.1	3.3	6.1	0.1	6.0
25 FENTRESS	10.1	5.3	4.8	29.6	20.6	9.0
26 FRANKLIN	6.9	0.5	6.4	20.4	0.1	20.3
27 GIBSON	3.2	....	3.2	5.0	....	5.0
28 GILES	4.3	....	4.3	9.5	....	9.5
29 GRAINGER	4.1	0.5	3.6	11.3	1.4	9.9
30 GREENE	5.1	1.3	3.8	15.3	3.7	11.6
31 GRUNDY	6.4	0.8	5.6	17.2	4.3	12.9
32 HAMBLEN	1.9	0.7	1.2	5.1	0.8	4.3
33 HAMILTON	7.2	3.6	3.6	28.8	18.1	10.7
34 HANCOCK	2.2	0.1	2.1	16.1	0.3	15.8
35 HARDEMAN	9.5	1.9	7.6	26.2	5.3	20.9
36 HARDIN	10.9	3.4	7.5	30.8	8.2	22.6
37 HAWKINS	7.6	1.6	6.0	16.4	4.6	11.8
38 HAYWOOD	4.4	....	4.4	19.9	....	19.9
39 HENDERSON	7.7	2.0	5.7	19.8	5.9	13.9
40 HENRY	5.2	....	5.2	14.4	....	14.4
41 HICKMAN	12.0	0.2	11.8	27.6	0.6	27.0
42 HOUSTON	3.9	....	3.9	18.6	....	18.6
43 HUMPHREYS	8.8	0.1	8.7	19.8	0.1	19.7
44 JACKSON	3.7	0.5	3.2	13.3	0.1	13.2
45 JEFFERSON	1.8	0.3	1.5	5.1	0.5	4.6
46 JOHNSON	6.0	0.8	5.2	13.2	1.9	11.3
47 KNOX	4.4	2.1	2.3	10.8	4.4	6.4
48 LAKE	1.2	....	1.2	7.7	....	7.7
49 LAUDERDALE	6.7	....	6.7	34.8	....	34.8
50 LAWRENCE	6.1	....	6.1	11.8	....	11.8
51 LEWIS	6.7	0.4	6.3	12.1	0.7	11.4
52 LINCOLN	2.7	0.5	2.2	4.1	....	4.1
53 LOUDON	2.0	1.1	0.9	4.6	1.7	2.9
54 MCMINN	7.1	4.0	3.1	13.7	7.2	6.5
55 MCNAIRY	7.4	2.1	5.3	13.0	3.2	9.8
56 MACON	2.7	....	2.7	5.7	....	5.7
57 MADISON	4.5	0.1	4.4	18.8	0.1	18.7
58 MARION	7.3	1.2	6.1	39.3	6.0	33.3
59 MARSHALL	1.6	0.3	1.3	5.1	0.1	5.0
60 MAURY	3.5	....	3.5	14.5	....	14.5
61 MEIGS	3.2	1.6	1.6	7.3	2.4	4.9
62 MONROE	16.0	8.2	7.8	48.0	28.1	19.9
63 MONTGOMERY	4.4	0.1	4.3	10.7	....	10.7
64 MOORE	1.4	0.1	1.3	5.2	0.2	5.0
65 MORGAN	8.7	2.1	6.6	25.9	9.0	16.9
66 OBION	3.0	0.4	2.6	11.3	1.9	9.4
67 OVERTON	7.4	0.7	6.7	22.5	4.1	18.4
68 PERRY	8.3	0.3	8.0	19.3	0.1	19.2
69 PICKETT	2.9	0.3	2.6	8.1	0.9	7.2
70 POLK	12.1	7.2	4.9	43.6	25.2	18.4
71 PUTNAM	5.7	0.5	5.2	14.3	1.0	13.3
72 RHEA	5.0	1.4	3.6	16.4	5.4	11.0
73 ROANE	5.3	1.7	3.6	12.8	4.9	7.9
74 ROBERTSON	1.8	....	1.8	5.7	....	5.7
75 RUTHERFORD	2.0	0.3	1.7	3.5	....	3.5
76 SCOTT	15.3	4.3	11.0	47.2	22.7	24.5
77 SEQUATCHIE	4.1	1.5	2.6	9.7	5.8	3.9
78 SEVIER	7.0	2.8	4.2	12.8	5.9	6.9
79 SHELBY	3.1	....	3.1	9.3	0.2	9.1
80 SMITH	2.6	0.1	2.5	4.6	....	4.6
81 STEWART	9.1	0.2	8.9	23.9	1.2	22.7
82 SULLIVAN	3.9	0.9	3.0	8.0	3.4	4.6
83 SUMNER	2.2	0.6	1.6	5.5	....	5.5
84 TIPTON	1.5	....	1.5	7.2	....	7.2
85 TROUSDALE	0.3	....	0.3	2.2	....	2.2
86 UNICOI	4.1	0.9	3.2	9.7	4.7	5.0
87 UNION	4.3	1.7	2.6	6.6	2.1	4.5
88 VAN BUREN	4.0	1.2	2.8	9.2	2.5	6.7
89 WARREN	4.1	0.4	3.7	10.3	0.4	9.9
90 WASHINGTON	3.0	0.7	2.3	7.1	2.1	5.0
91 WAYNE	15.9	2.5	13.4	32.6	3.7	28.9
92 WEAKLEY	3.8	0.6	3.2	20.0	1.5	18.5
93 WHITE	5.3	0.1	5.2	14.5	....	14.5
94 WILLIAMSON	3.8	0.1	3.7	10.9	0.1	10.8
95 WILSON	2.2	0.1	2.1	2.0	....	2.0
STATE TOTAL	509.1	102.9	406.2	1428.2	309.0	1119.2

Table 32. *Tennessee: Removals of growing stock and sawtimber by county, 1970*

County	Growing stock			Sawtimber		
	Total	Softwood	Hardwood	Total	Softwood	Hardwood
	- - - - - - Million cubic feet - - - - - -			- - - - - - Million board feet - - - - - -		
1 ANDERSON	3.1	0.2	2.9	13.1	0.7	12.4
2 BEDFORD	1.3	0.1	1.2	4.6	....	4.6
3 BENTON	2.0	....	2.0	8.2	0.1	8.1
4 BLEDSOE	3.1	0.7	2.4	9.2	2.5	6.7
5 BLOUNT	2.4	0.9	1.5	7.3	2.9	4.4
6 BRADLEY	3.6	2.5	1.1	9.0	6.8	2.2
7 CAMPBELL	3.1	0.5	2.6	11.1	1.9	9.2
8 CANNON	1.2	0.3	0.9	3.9	....	3.9
9 CARROLL	3.6	0.3	3.3	13.7	0.2	13.5
10 CARTER	1.1	0.4	0.7	4.0	1.9	2.1
11 CHEATHAM	1.3	....	1.3	5.9	....	5.9
12 CHESTER	3.4	0.4	3.0	7.6	1.5	6.1
13 CLAIBORNE	2.2	0.2	2.0	9.0	0.9	8.1
14 CLAY	1.2	....	1.2	5.0	....	5.0
15 COCKE	1.7	0.8	0.9	6.9	3.5	3.4
16 COFFEE	3.7	....	3.7	12.8	....	12.8
17 CROCKETT	0.6	0.1	0.5	2.5	0.3	2.2
18 CUMBERLAND	3.2	0.6	2.6	10.5	1.9	8.6
19 DAVIDSON	0.9	....	0.9	2.9	....	2.9
20 DECATUR	2.5	0.1	2.4	11.6	0.4	11.2
21 DEKALB	1.2	0.1	1.1	5.6	0.8	4.8
22 DICKSON	2.3	....	2.3	10.3	....	10.3
23 DYER	3.5	....	3.5	14.3	....	14.3
24 FAYETTE	2.4	....	2.4	8.7	0.1	8.6
25 FENTRESS	3.6	0.7	2.9	12.9	3.0	9.9
26 FRANKLIN	3.5	0.1	3.4	14.7	0.3	14.4
27 GIBSON	1.1	....	1.1	4.4	....	4.4
28 GILES	1.8	0.2	1.6	6.1	....	6.1
29 GRAINGER	2.2	0.1	2.1	7.2	0.3	6.9
30 GREENE	1.4	0.2	1.2	5.3	0.7	4.6
31 GRUNDY	2.7	0.5	2.2	11.3	1.9	9.4
32 HAMBLEN	2.6	0.1	2.5	8.5	0.3	8.2
33 HAMILTON	2.3	1.0	1.3	7.4	3.8	3.6
34 HANCOCK	0.5	....	0.5	2.1	0.1	2.0
35 HARDEMAN	4.3	1.0	3.3	18.0	2.9	15.1
36 HARDIN	5.4	0.9	4.5	20.6	2.8	17.8
37 HAWKINS	1.3	0.1	1.2	4.7	0.4	4.3
38 HAYWOOD	2.3	....	2.3	10.6	....	10.6
39 HENDERSON	3.0	0.2	2.8	12.3	0.4	11.9
40 HENRY	2.5	....	2.5	9.7	....	9.7
41 HICKMAN	3.1	....	3.1	12.0	0.2	11.8
42 HOUSTON	1.2	....	1.2	5.4	....	5.4
43 HUMPHREYS	3.0	....	3.0	10.3	....	10.3
44 JACKSON	0.9	....	0.9	4.0	....	4.0
45 JEFFERSON	2.0	....	2.0	6.4	0.2	6.2
46 JOHNSON	1.5	0.5	1.0	6.6	2.6	4.0
47 KNOX	1.6	0.4	1.2	4.7	1.3	3.4
48 LAKE	0.8	....	0.8	3.7	....	3.7
49 LAUDERDALE	4.7	....	4.7	21.8	....	21.8
50 LAWRENCE	4.2	....	4.2	15.0	....	15.0
51 LEWIS	2.0	0.1	1.9	7.4	0.3	7.1
52 LINCOLN	1.6	0.2	1.4	5.9	....	5.9
53 LOUDON	1.2	0.2	1.0	3.5	0.6	2.9
54 MCMINN	2.9	2.0	0.9	9.3	6.2	3.1
55 MCNAIRY	4.8	0.7	4.1	19.7	1.1	18.6
56 MACON	1.8	....	1.8	7.9	....	7.9
57 MADISON	3.5	0.3	3.2	13.4	1.4	12.0
58 MARION	2.1	0.3	1.8	8.0	1.5	6.5
59 MARSHALL	1.1	0.3	0.8	4.7	2.3	2.4
60 MAURY	1.4	....	1.4	5.6	....	5.6
61 MEIGS	1.4	0.7	0.7	4.6	2.6	2.0
62 MONROE	4.9	3.1	1.8	20.5	14.1	6.4
63 MONTGOMERY	2.4	....	2.4	8.7	....	8.7
64 MOORE	0.8	0.1	0.7	4.9	2.0	2.9
65 MORGAN	2.7	0.7	2.0	9.2	2.8	6.4
66 OBION	6.0	0.7	5.3	19.6	3.9	15.7
67 OVERTON	1.9	....	1.9	8.3	0.1	8.2
68 PERRY	2.7	....	2.7	11.7	....	11.7
69 PICKETT	1.1	....	1.1	4.6	....	4.6
70 POLK	3.7	2.5	1.2	17.6	12.9	4.7
71 PUTNAM	3.1	0.4	2.7	11.9	1.1	10.8
72 RHEA	3.2	1.4	1.8	9.3	5.3	4.0
73 ROANE	1.8	0.9	0.9	5.4	2.8	2.6
74 ROBERTSON	1.8	....	1.8	7.4	....	7.4
75 RUTHERFORD	1.6	0.7	0.9	3.3	....	3.3
76 SCOTT	5.2	0.5	4.7	22.0	2.0	20.0
77 SEQUATCHIE	1.8	0.2	1.6	5.0	0.5	4.5
78 SEVIER	0.8	0.4	0.4	2.0	0.9	1.1
79 SHELBY	3.2	0.3	2.9	11.4	1.5	9.9
80 SMITH	1.0	0.1	0.9	3.9	0.4	3.5
81 STEWART	1.7	....	1.7	7.8	....	7.8
82 SULLIVAN	1.9	....	1.9	5.7	0.1	5.6
83 SUMNER	1.2	0.1	1.1	4.5	0.3	4.2
84 TIPTON	1.3	....	1.3	5.5	....	5.5
85 TROUSDALE	0.1	....	0.1	0.3	....	0.3
86 UNICOI	1.5	0.3	1.2	6.1	1.8	4.3
87 UNION	0.9	0.2	0.7	3.8	0.9	2.9
88 VAN BUREN	1.1	0.1	1.0	5.4	0.6	4.8
89 WARREN	2.2	0.3	1.9	8.6	0.7	7.9
90 WASHINGTON	1.1	0.1	1.0	3.6	0.2	3.4
91 WAYNE	3.8	0.5	3.3	14.8	1.9	12.9
92 WEAKLEY	2.9	0.3	2.6	12.5	0.7	11.8
93 WHITE	2.9	....	2.9	11.8	0.2	11.6
94 WILLIAMSON	1.2	0.2	1.0	6.4	2.3	4.1
95 WILSON	1.0	0.1	0.9	2.7	0.4	2.3
STATE TOTAL	216.4	33.2	183.2	819.6	124.0	695.6

23

Table 31 *Tennessee· Net growth of growing stock and sawtimber by county, 1970*

Table 33. *Tennessee: Growing stock and sawtimber volume by resource regions, 1971*

Region	Growing stock			Sawtimber		
	Total	Softwood	Hardwood	Total	Softwood	Hardwood
	— — — — — Million cubic feet — — — — —			— — — — — Million board feet — — — — —		
1 WEST	1639.8	155.5	1484.3	4865.4	450.1	4415.3
2 WEST CENTRAL	1818.4	108.C	1710.4	3635.8	2C1.5	3434.3
3 CENTRAL	1348.1	46.C	13C2.1	3251.3	27.2	3224.1
4 PLATEAU	2523.6	467.5	2056.1	6656.9	1363.4	5293.5
5 EAST	3065.9	1C22.8	2043.1	7930.8	2656.9	5273.9
STATE TOTAL	10395.8	1799.8	8596.0	26340.2	4699.1	21641.1

Table 34. *Tennessee: Net growth of growing stock and sawtimber by resource regions, 1970*

Region	Growing stock			Sawtimber		
	Total	Softwood	Hardwood	Total	Softwood	Hardwood
	— — — — — Million cubic feet — — — — —			— — — — — Million board feet — — — — —		
1 WEST	79.8	8.9	70.9	264.9	24.6	240.3
2 WEST CENTRAL	93.4	8.3	85.1	233.1	18.5	214.6
3 CENTRAL	69.2	4.3	64.9	166.9	1.0	165.9
4 PLATEAU	114.5	26.2	88.3	349.1	1C5.3	243.8
5 EAST	152.2	55.2	97.0	414.2	159.6	254.6
STATE TOTAL	509.1	1C2.9	406.2	1428.2	3C9.0	1119.2

Table 35. *Tennessee: Removals of growing stock and sawtimber by resource regions, 1970*

Region	Growing stock			Sawtimber		
	Total	Softwood	Hardwood	Total	Softwood	Hardwood
	— — — — — Million cubic feet — — — — —			— — — — — Million board feet — — — — —		
1 WEST	53.9	4.3	49.6	209.4	14.0	195.4
2 WEST CENTRAL	31.6	1.6	30.0	124.8	5.7	119.1
3 CENTRAL	32.8	2.5	30.3	127.3	8.5	118.8
4 PLATEAU	43.3	5.6	37.7	164.5	21.0	143.5
5 EAST	54.8	19.2	35.6	193.6	74.8	118.8
STATE TOTAL	216.4	33.2	183.2	819.6	124.0	695.6

Table 36. *Texas: Timber products output by county, 1970*

	County	Saw logs		Posts	Poles and piling	Other		Pulpwood		All products total
		Softwood	Hardwood			Softwood	Hardwood	Softwood	Hardwood	
						Thousand cubic feet				
1	ANDERSON	3676.6	1463.4	0.0	0.0	29.3	297.0	1898.2	82.3	7446.8
2	ANGELINA	9739.7	111.5	0.0	0.0	34.3	317.0	5754.5	270.3	16227.3
3	BOWIE	24.7	89.8	0.0	0.0	45.4	358.0	2563.6	285.0	3366.5
4	CAMP	60.1	111.8	0.0	0.0	8.1	54.0	776.5	5.9	1016.4
5	CASS	1834.9	27.7	0.0	0.0	35.3	270.0	4250.0	380.0	6797.9
6	CHAMBERS	159.5	0.0	0.0	0.0	20.2	138.0	156.7	25.0	499.4
7	CHEROKEE	3435.5	1915.1	0.0	0.0	114.1	272.0	3634.2	510.6	9881.5
8	FRANKLIN	0.0	50.3	0.0	0.0	9.1	64.0	857.1	266.0	1246.5
9	GREGG	688.9	146.8	0.0	0.0	28.3	208.0	2521.4	92.2	3685.6
10	HARDIN	10494.0	2608.3	0.0	0.0	31.3	227.0	6982.2	1684.4	22027.2
11	HARRIS	113.8	9.9	0.0	0.0	117.1	842.0	1950.6	690.1	3723.5
12	HARRISON	1439.1	431.3	0.0	0.0	39.4	282.0	4251.1	43.9	6486.8
13	HOUSTON	8043.4	622.3	0.0	0.0	212.0	196.0	4587.8	277.7	13939.2
14	JASPER	13000.2	1967.7	0.0	0.0	29.3	247.0	9393.1	2285.4	26922.7
15	JEFFERSON	13.9	31.4	0.0	0.0	20.2	137.0	135.5	78.1	416.1
16	LIBERTY	2546.9	2038.3	0.0	0.0	31.3	261.0	1955.8	1553.7	8387.0
17	MARION	211.7	523.8	0.0	0.0	9.1	65.0	3429.3	241.8	4480.7
18	MONTGOMERY	6811.8	394.4	0.0	0.0	32.3	227.0	5317.5	988.7	13771.7
19	MORRIS	48.5	238.3	0.0	0.0	18.2	151.0	1129.1	54.6	1639.7
20	NACOGDOCHES	5286.1	246.5	0.0	0.0	213.0	222.0	8697.6	1054.6	15719.8
21	NEWTON	9127.9	641.6	0.0	0.0	18.2	152.0	6892.4	2390.1	19222.2
22	ORANGE	2498.6	60.8	0.0	0.0	33.3	246.0	1029.2	171.9	4039.8
23	PANOLA	1332.8	714.8	0.0	0.0	24.2	164.0	7704.7	284.0	10224.5
24	POLK	22011.2	1276.0	0.0	0.0	20.2	156.0	9407.4	1715.4	34586.2
25	RED RIVER	60.8	237.5	0.0	0.0	305.9	191.0	208.3	0.0	1003.5
26	RUSK	2390.4	1452.5	0.0	0.0	77.7	325.0	3956.7	61.6	8263.9
27	SABINE	13697.4	246.5	0.0	0.0	13.1	113.0	3297.5	438.7	17806.2
28	SAN AUGUSTINE	2006.4	608.0	0.0	0.0	9.1	99.0	6112.8	470.7	9306.0
29	SAN JACINTO	19.3	1109.8	0.0	0.0	12.1	81.0	3933.4	553.7	5709.3
30	SHELBY	3367.2	945.6	0.0	0.0	61.6	249.0	8628.9	546.7	13799.0
31	SMITH	41.3	61.6	0.0	0.0	92.9	452.0	1800.7	0.0	2448.5
32	TITUS	86.8	37.0	0.0	0.0	16.2	147.0	770.6	0.7	1058.3
33	TRINITY	2482.5	903.2	0.0	0.0	59.6	156.0	7747.4	604.9	11953.6
34	TYLER	3086.7	2572.5	0.0	0.0	18.2	157.0	5937.3	2624.9	14396.6
35	UPSHUR	453.4	261.9	0.0	0.0	26.2	192.0	4165.3	109.2	5208.0
36	WALKER	2972.9	70.5	0.0	0.0	18.2	129.0	3139.6	797.0	7127.2
37	WOOD	96.8	94.9	0.0	0.0	23.2	161.0	603.4	11.9	991.2
	STATE TOTAL	133361.7	24323.3	0.0	0.0	1907.2	8005.0	145577.4	21651.7	334826.2

Table 37. *Texas: Growing stock and sawtimber volume by county, 1971*

	County	Growing stock			Sawtimber		
		Total	Softwood	Hardwood	Total	Softwood	Hardwood
		Million cubic feet			*Million board feet*		
1	ANDERSON	212.8	125.9	86.9	667.0	486.9	180.1
2	ANGELINA	480.1	426.1	54.0	2228.0	2111.9	116.1
3	BOWIE	231.4	98.9	132.5	697.3	357.8	339.5
4	CAMP	54.7	29.7	25.0	182.0	94.7	87.3
5	CASS	232.6	91.5	141.1	586.6	251.4	335.2
6	CHAMBERS	23.6	23.6	....	62.0	61.8	0.2
7	CHEROKEE	287.5	203.2	84.3	876.9	762.3	114.6
8	FRANKLIN	23.7	7.4	16.3	69.9	23.3	46.6
9	GREGG	22.7	1.7	21.0	66.5	4.0	62.5
10	HARDIN	456.7	312.5	144.2	1717.2	1511.4	205.8
11	HARRIS	105.3	63.7	41.6	361.8	232.1	129.7
12	HARRISON	198.8	117.6	81.2	418.5	235.6	182.9
13	HOUSTON	413.1	318.5	94.6	1666.5	1424.4	242.1
14	JASPER	431.6	338.2	93.4	1657.6	1397.9	259.7
15	JEFFERSON	59.9	21.5	38.4	174.5	74.2	100.3
16	LIBERTY	384.3	228.0	156.3	1597.0	1220.0	377.0
17	MARION	148.2	111.0	37.2	551.0	456.9	94.1
18	MONTGOMERY	593.2	500.0	93.2	2050.2	1874.6	175.6
19	MORRIS	27.9	9.2	18.7	88.3	21.7	66.6
20	NACOGDOCHES	354.0	267.2	86.8	1162.0	1025.0	137.0
21	NEWTON	595.2	426.2	169.0	2215.7	1743.6	472.1
22	ORANGE	160.0	101.3	58.7	658.0	508.6	149.4
23	PANOLA	346.1	260.3	85.8	1118.5	903.0	215.5
24	POLK	651.7	567.8	83.9	2504.0	2290.3	213.7
25	RED RIVER	176.0	54.4	121.6	452.3	178.2	274.1
26	RUSK	210.8	176.9	33.9	431.3	431.2	0.1
27	SABINE	338.9	263.1	75.8	1242.6	1090.2	152.4
28	SAN AUGUSTINE	331.4	255.7	75.7	1351.6	1151.9	199.7
29	SAN JACINTO	379.9	340.6	39.3	1508.4	1421.1	87.3
30	SHELBY	299.2	219.8	79.4	1149.1	980.7	168.4
31	SMITH	138.8	68.7	70.1	504.8	319.7	185.1
32	TITUS	35.8	3.4	32.4	93.3	2.6	90.7
33	TRINITY	364.1	350.6	13.5	1677.2	1633.6	43.6
34	TYLER	726.1	559.2	166.9	3130.0	2670.6	459.4
35	UPSHUR	97.8	71.2	26.6	355.5	287.9	67.6
36	WALKER	379.9	322.5	57.4	1521.1	1335.8	185.3
37	WOOD	93.0	47.2	45.8	314.1	191.2	122.9
	STATE TOTAL	10066.8	7384.3	2682.5	37108.3	30768.1	6340.2

25

County	Growing stock			Sawtimber		
	Total	Softwood	Hardwood	Total	Softwood	Hardwood
	------ Million cubic feet ------			------ Million board feet ------		
1 ANDERSON	13.9	10.5	3.4	50.2	44.3	5.9
2 ANGELINA	25.4	23.6	1.8	129.1	125.6	3.5
3 BOWIE	13.3	8.2	5.1	42.3	32.0	10.3
4 CAMP	3.5	2.5	1.0	11.2	8.5	2.7
5 CASS	13.1	7.7	5.4	33.6	23.4	10.2
6 CHAMBERS	1.3	1.3	....	3.6	3.6	....
7 CHEROKEE	20.2	16.8	3.4	72.9	68.8	4.1
8 FRANKLIN	1.2	0.6	0.6	3.6	2.2	1.4
9 GREGG	1.0	0.2	0.8	2.5	0.6	1.9
10 HARDIN	22.2	17.5	4.7	97.5	91.0	6.5
11 HARRIS	4.8	3.5	1.3	17.3	13.7	3.6
12 HARRISON	12.9	9.8	3.1	27.6	21.9	5.7
13 HOUSTON	20.7	17.7	3.0	92.0	85.2	6.8
14 JASPER	22.2	19.1	3.1	93.0	85.3	7.7
15 JEFFERSON	2.4	1.2	1.2	7.0	4.3	2.7
16 LIBERTY	17.5	12.5	5.0	82.7	71.8	10.9
17 MARION	10.7	9.2	1.5	43.8	40.8	3.0
18 MONTGOMERY	30.5	27.5	3.0	116.0	111.1	4.9
19 MORRIS	1.5	0.8	0.7	4.2	2.1	2.1
20 NACOGDOCHES	25.8	22.4	3.4	97.5	93.2	4.3
21 NEWTON	28.9	23.6	5.3	117.5	104.3	13.2
22 ORANGE	7.4	5.6	1.8	34.4	30.3	4.1
23 PANOLA	24.8	21.5	3.3	87.7	81.0	6.7
24 POLK	34.5	31.8	2.7	145.4	139.1	6.3
25 RED RIVER	9.0	4.4	4.6	24.2	15.8	8.4
26 RUSK	16.1	14.7	1.4	39.4	39.3	0.1
27 SABINE	17.3	14.9	2.4	71.2	67.0	4.2
28 SAN AUGUSTINE	16.5	14.1	2.4	73.7	68.1	5.6
29 SAN JACINTO	19.8	18.5	1.3	85.9	83.1	2.8
30 SHELBY	21.5	18.4	3.1	94.1	88.7	5.4
31 SMITH	8.4	5.7	2.7	34.0	28.4	5.6
32 TITUS	1.5	0.3	1.2	3.2	0.4	2.8
33 TRINITY	19.8	19.3	0.5	97.8	96.3	1.5
34 TYLER	36.0	30.6	5.4	170.1	156.8	13.3
35 UPSHUR	7.0	6.0	1.0	28.2	26.1	2.1
36 WALKER	19.4	17.6	1.8	83.9	78.7	5.2
37 WOOD	5.6	3.9	1.7	20.7	17.0	3.7
STATE TOTAL	557.6	463.5	94.1	2239.0	2049.8	189.2

Table 39. *Texas: Removals of growing stock and sawtimber by county, 1970*

County	Growing stock			Sawtimber		
	Total	Softwood	Hardwood	Total	Softwood	Hardwood
	------ Million cubic feet ------			------ Million board feet ------		
1 ANDERSON	10.8	6.7	4.1	52.1	31.5	20.6
2 ANGELINA	25.9	18.4	7.5	100.8	85.4	15.4
3 BOWIE	6.0	3.6	2.4	14.2	11.0	3.2
4 CAMP	1.3	1.0	0.3	4.6	3.1	1.5
5 CASS	8.3	7.3	1.0	29.3	27.0	2.3
6 CHAMBERS	0.4	0.4	....	1.9	1.6	0.3
7 CHEROKEE	14.3	8.4	5.9	62.2	35.6	26.6
8 FRANKLIN	1.5	0.9	0.6	4.1	2.5	1.6
9 GREGG	2.5	1.8	0.7	6.8	4.4	2.4
10 HARDIN	30.6	20.8	9.8	140.3	94.7	45.6
11 HARRIS	4.3	2.3	2.0	10.3	6.7	3.6
12 HARRISON	8.1	6.7	1.4	29.7	23.7	6.0
13 HOUSTON	17.9	15.2	2.7	80.3	71.0	9.3
14 JASPER	35.8	27.5	8.3	158.6	124.3	34.3
15 JEFFERSON	0.5	0.2	0.3	1.4	0.5	0.9
16 LIBERTY	12.9	5.5	7.4	57.1	24.4	32.7
17 MARION	6.3	4.2	2.1	19.9	12.3	7.6
18 MONTGOMERY	18.0	14.8	3.2	73.3	64.4	8.9
19 MORRIS	2.3	1.4	0.9	7.6	3.9	3.7
20 NACOGDOCHES	18.9	16.5	2.4	71.3	63.9	7.4
21 NEWTON	25.1	19.9	5.2	106.7	89.2	17.5
22 ORANGE	5.0	4.3	0.7	22.3	20.6	1.7
23 PANOLA	13.8	10.3	3.5	43.2	32.9	10.3
24 POLK	44.6	37.8	6.8	209.6	182.8	26.8
25 RED RIVER	1.6	0.7	0.9	7.1	3.1	4.0
26 RUSK	11.2	7.4	3.8	32.4	28.7	3.7
27 SABINE	24.0	21.7	2.3	115.0	109.7	5.3
28 SAN AUGUSTINE	12.6	9.6	3.0	44.1	34.1	10.0
29 SAN JACINTO	9.8	4.5	5.3	32.4	12.3	20.1
30 SHELBY	17.6	13.9	3.7	65.4	50.5	14.9
31 SMITH	2.8	2.1	0.7	7.3	5.9	1.4
32 TITUS	1.3	1.0	0.3	3.9	2.9	1.0
33 TRINITY	16.9	11.6	5.3	54.8	40.5	14.3
34 TYLER	22.3	11.8	10.5	88.3	45.3	43.0
35 UPSHUR	6.4	5.4	1.0	20.6	16.6	4.0
36 WALKER	10.1	7.3	2.8	38.5	30.7	7.8
37 WOOD	1.5	1.1	0.4	5.2	3.7	1.5
STATE TOTAL	453.2	334.0	119.2	1822.6	1401.4	421.2

Table 40. *Texas: Growing stock and sawtimber volume by resource regions, 1971*

Region	Growing stock			Sawtimber		
	Total	Softwood	Hardwood	Total	Softwood	Hardwood
	------ Million cubic feet ------			------ Million board feet ------		
1 SOUTHEAST	6874.9	5419.1	1455.8	27323.6	23754.1	3569.5
2 NORTHEAST	3191.7	1965.2	1226.5	9785.1	7014.2	2770.9
STATE TOTAL	10066.6	7384.3	2682.3	37108.7	30768.3	6340.4

Table 41. *Texas: Net growth of growing stock and sawtimber by resource regions, 1970*

Region	Growing stock			Sawtimber		
	Total	Softwood	Hardwood	Total	Softwood	Hardwood
	------ Million cubic feet ------			------ Million board feet ------		
1 SOUTHEAST	346.7	299.8	46.9	1518.1	1415.3	102.8
2 NORTHEAST	211.2	163.7	47.5	720.9	634.4	86.5
STATE TOTAL	557.9	463.5	94.4	2239.0	2049.7	189.3

Table 42. *Texas: Removals of growing stock and sawtimber by resource regions, 1970*

Region	Growing stock			Sawtimber		
	Total	Softwood	Hardwood	Total	Softwood	Hardwood
	------ Million cubic feet ------			------ Million board feet ------		
1 SOUTHEAST	316.8	233.6	83.2	1336.1	1038.5	297.6
2 NORTHEAST	136.4	100.5	35.9	486.8	363.1	123.7
STATE TOTAL	453.2	334.1	119.1	1822.9	1461.6	421.3

Acknowledgments

Generous assistance from public and private organizations made it possible to keep the field work for the latest forest inventory of Tennessee ahead of the schedule that could have been maintained with regularly allotted funds. The very material aid of the organizations listed below, and of the individuals in them, is gratefully acknowledged:

Tennessee Department of Conservation

Tennessee Valley Authority

Ashby Veneer & Lumber Company

Hiwassee Land Company

Tennessee River Pulp & Paper Company

U. S. Plywood-Champion Papers, Inc.

Westvaco Corporation

Forest Statistics
for
Tennessee Counties

Arnold Hedlund

and

J. M. Earles

Southern Forest Experiment Station
New Orleans, Louisiana
Forest Service, U. S. Department of Agriculture

:

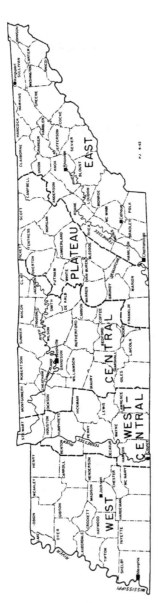

Forest Resource regions in Tennessee.

Forest Statistics
for
Tennessee Counties

This report tabulates information from a new forest survey of Tennessee, completed in 1971 by the Forest Resources Research Unit of the Southern Forest Experiment Station The tables are intended for use as source data in compiling estimates for groups of counties. Because the sampling procedure is intended primarily to furnish inventory data for the State as a whole, estimates for individual counties have limited and variable accuracy.

The data on forest acreage and timber volume were secured by a systematic sampling method involving a forest-nonforest classification on aerial photographs and on-the-ground measurements of trees at sample locations. The sample locations were at the intersections of a grid of lines spaced 3 miles apart. At each forested location, 10 small plots were uniformly distributed on an area of about 1 acre.

The sampling errors to which the State area and volume totals are liable (on a probability of two chances out of three) are indicated in table 1.

Detailed sampling errors are shown in tables 33-37. An approximation of sampling errors for groups of counties may be obtained from the formula:

$$e = \frac{(SE) \sqrt{(\text{Specified volume or area})}}{\sqrt{(\text{Volume or area total in question})}}$$

Where: e = Estimated sampling error of the volume or area total in question

   SE = Specified sampling error for the State.

Table 1. *Sampling errors for forest land and volume estimates*

Item	Sampling error
	Percent
Commercial forest land	0.3
Growing-stock volume	1.7
Sawtimber volume [1]	2.7
Growth on growing stock	2.4
Growth on sawtimber [1]	3.8
Removals from growing stock	3.2
Removals from sawtimber [1]	3.0

[1]International ¼-inch rule.

When data for two or more counties are grouped the error decreases. Conversely, as data for individual counties are broken down by various subdivisions, the possibility of error increases and is greatest for the smallest items.

Because of differences in standards of tree measurement, meaningful comparisons cannot be made between the volume estimates in this report and those from a prior inventory in 1961. In table 2, changes between the two surveys are summarized in terms of 1971 measurement standards. A statewide interpretive report, now in preparation, will include an evaluation of timber trends since the 1961 survey.

In the tables that follow, sawtimber volume is shown in International ¼-inch rule except when Doyle or Scribner rule is indicated.

Table 2. *Commercial forest land, growing-stock, and sawtimber volume, 1971, and change since 1961*

Resource region	Commercial forest		Growing stock				Sawtimber			
			Softwood		Hardwood		Softwood		Hardwood	
	Area	Change	Volume	Change [1]	Volume	Change [1]	Volume	Change [1]	Volume	Change [1]
	Thousand acres	*Percent*	*Million cu. ft.*	*Percent*	*Million cu. ft.*	*Percent*	*Million bd. ft.*	*Percent*	*Million bd. ft.*	*Percent*
West	1,768.5	− 7	155.5	+58	1,484.3	+ 3	450.1	+40	4,415.3	+ 5
West central	2,290.9	− 1	108.0	+62	1,710.4	+18	201.5	+80	3,434.3	+27
Central	2,276.3	−12	46.0	+65	1,302.1	+ 8	27.2	+28	3,224.1	+ 9
Plateau	3,077.0	− 3	467.5	+ 7	2,056.1	+ 7	1,363.4	+24	5,293.5	+12
East	3,407.1	− 2	1,022.8	+28	2,043.1	+20	2,656.9	+15	5,273.9	+18
All regions	12,819.8	− 5	1,799.8	+26	8,596.0	+11	4,699.1	+22	21,641.1	+14

[1] Based on 1971 measurement standards.

DEFINITIONS OF TERMS

Acceptable trees.—Growing-stock trees of commercial species that meet specified standards of size and quality but do not qualify as desirable trees.

Commercial forest land.—Forest land producing or capable of producing crops of industrial wood and not withdrawn from timber utilization.

Desirable trees.—Growing-stock trees that are of commercial species, have no defects in quality for timber products, are of relatively high vigor, and contain no pathogens that may result in death or serious deterioration before rotation age.

Forest type.—A classification of forest land based upon the species forming a plurality of live-tree stocking.

Growing-stock trees.—Live trees that are of commercial species and qualify as desirable or acceptable trees.

Growing-stock volume.—Net volume in cubic feet of growing-stock trees at least 5.0 inches in diameter at breast height, from a 1-foot stump to a minimum 4.0-inch top diameter outside bark of the central stem, or to the point where the central stem breaks into limbs.

Mortality.—Sound-wood volume of live trees dying from natural causes during a specified period.

Net annual growth.—The increase in volume of a specified size class for a specific year.

Poletimber trees.—Growing-stock trees of commercial species at least 5.0 inches in diameter at breast height, but smaller than sawtimber size.

Sawtimber trees.—Live trees that are of commercial species, contain at least a 12-foot saw log, and meet regional specifications for freedom from defect. Softwoods must be at least 9.0 inches in diameter at breast height and hardwoods at least 11.0 inches.

Sawtimber volume.—Net volume of the saw-log portion of live sawtimber in board feet, International ¼-inch rule, unless otherwise indicated.

Site class.—A classification of forest land in terms of inherent capacity to grow crops of industrial wood.

Stand-size class.—A classification of forest land based on the size class of growing-stock trees on the area; that is, sawtimber, poletimber, or seedling and saplings.

Timber removals.—The net volume of growing-stock trees removed from the inventory by harvesting, cultural operations such as timber-stand improvement, land clearing, or changs in land use.

Table 3. *Total area, commercial forest land and proportion of total area, 1971, and change since 1961*

County	Total area [1]	Commercial forest			County	Total area [1]	Commercial forest		
		Area	Pro- portion	Change since 1961			Area	Pro- portion	Change since 1961
	Thousand acres	*Thousand acres*	*− Percent −*			*Thousand acres*	*Thousand acres*	*− Percent −*	
Anderson	218.2	140.3	64	− 3	Lauderdale	325.8	88.5	27	−21
Bedford	308.5	76.0	25	− 8	Lawrence	405.8	182.7	45	− 4
Benton	279.0	168.2	60	+ 3	Lewis	182.4	144.9	79	− 5
Bledsoe	258.6	173.6	67	−10	Lincoln	371.2	116.6	31	−18
Blount	373.8	125.6	34	+16	Loudon	159.4	53.3	33	(²)
Bradley	216.3	107.2	50	−16	McMinn	278.4	145.5	52	+ 9
Campbell	299.5	225.5	75	+ 2	McNairy	364.2	197.6	54	+ 2
Cannon	173.4	86.4	50	− 6	Macon	194.6	73.6	38	−15
Carroll	381.4	153.0	40	+ 1	Madison	358.4	112.8	31	+ 2
Carter	227.2	145.0	64	− 3	Marion	329.6	247.5	75	− 2
Cheatham	197.1	108.8	55	−10	Marshall	241.3	78.1	32	−10
Chester	182.4	97.2	53	+ 5	Maury	393.0	126.0	32	−12
Claiborne	291.2	166.4	57	− 2	Meigs	139.5	80.6	58	+ 4
Clay	169.0	99.0	59	− 4	Monroe	424.9	295.8	70	+ 1
Cocke	278.4	168.0	60	+ 7	Montgomery	347.5	116.2	33	−18
Coffee	278.4	117.6	42	−16	Moore	79.4	30.8	39	−26
Crockett	172.2	12.4	7	−50	Morgan	345.0	291.6	85	− 2
Cumberland	434.5	324.5	75	− 8	Obion	359.0	72.8	20	−11
Davidson	341.1	104.0	30	−13	Overton	282.9	174.2	62	− 2
Decatur	225.3	149.1	66	+10	Perry	270.7	212.8	79	− 2
De Kalb	202.9	88.2	43	− 4	Pickett	111.4	67.0	60	− 6
Dickson	311.0	160.0	51	−15	Polk	281.0	227.7	81	(²)
Dyer	345.6	65.5	19	−31	Putnam	261.1	140.3	54	− 6
Fayette	450.5	108.0	24	− 5	Rhea	217.6	134.6	62	− 4
Fentress	319.4	246.4	77	− 2	Roane	248.3	131.2	53	−11
Franklin	358.4	187.0	52	− 6	Robertson	304.6	59.0	19	−19
Gibson	388.5	49.0	13	−25	Rutherford	403.2	117.6	29	−15
Giles	396.1	160.0	40	− 2	Scott	351.4	308.0	88	(²)
Grainger	199.7	94.6	47	− 7	Sequatchie	174.7	140.0	80	− 1
Greene	396.1	135.2	34	(²)	Sevier	387.2	159.2	41	(²)
Grundy	229.1	186.0	81	− 4	Shelby	492.1	73.0	15	−23
Hamblen	111.4	25.2	23	−19	Smith	208.0	72.0	35	− 8
Hamilton	375.7	180.2	48	−14	Stewart	314.9	221.1	70	− 5
Hancock	147.2	85.4	58	− 2	Sullivan	273.9	109.2	40	+ 2
Hardeman	419.8	222.0	53	+11	Sumner	351.4	98.1	28	− 4
Hardin	386.6	225.6	58	+ 1	Tipton	303.4	55.8	18	− 2
Hawkins	316.2	167.4	53	+ 6	Trousdale	74.2	23.8	32	− 2
Haywood	332.2	73.6	22	−22	Unicoi	118.4	94.4	80	− 2
Henderson	329.6	170.5	52	+ 7	Union	154.2	84.6	55	− 2
Henry	384.0	124.3	32	−12	Van Buren	163.2	124.2	76	− 8
Hickman	392.3	269.5	69	− 5	Warren	283.5	114.0	40	+ 4
Houston	133.1	91.0	68	−10	Washington	209.3	61.6	29	+ 7
Humphreys	357.8	248.0	69	+ 4	Wayne	474.2	378.0	80	+ 5
Jackson	209.3	110.5	53	−17	Weakley	368.6	76.5	21	− 7
Jefferson	206.1	58.5	28	+ 1	White	246.4	127.2	52	+ 1
Johnson	191.4	124.2	65	− 7	Williamson	379.5	145.0	38	− 8
Knox	337.9	106.2	31	(²)	Wilson	371.2	109.0	29	−15
Lake	122.9	16.0	13	−43	All counties	27,036.2	12,819.8	47	− 5

[1] Source: United States Bureau of the Census, Land and Water Area of the United States, 1960.
[2] Negligible.

Table 4. *Commercial forest land by ownership class, 1971*

County	All ownerships	National forest	Other public	Forest industry	Farmer	Misc. private
			--- Thousand acres ---			
Anderson	140.3	...	10.1	...	30.3	99.9
Bedford	76.0		(¹)	...	60.0	16.0
Benton	168.2	...	14.9	...	69.5	83.8
Bledsoe	173.6		5.8	47.4	35.5	84.9
Blount	125.6	...	.2	17.9	94.9	12.6
Bradley	107.2		.2	26.6	39.9	40.5
Campbell	225.5		12.9	33.7	16.9	162.0
Cannon	86.4	...	(¹)	...	56.8	29.6
Carroll	153.0	...	19.5	...	85.6	47.9
Carter	145.0	78.9	(¹)	...	23.0	43.1
Cheatham	108.8	...	21.2	...	13.4	74.2
Chester	97.2		6.3	...	32.0	58.9
Claiborne	166.4	...	6.4	...	95.3	64.7
Clay	99.0	...	9.8	...	16.3	72.9
Cocke	168.0	42.2	.1	...	72.3	53.4
Coffee	117.6	...	22.2	9.7	67.7	18.0
Crockett	12.4		...	...	12.4	...
Cumberland	324.5	...	49.9	39.3	106.8	128.5
Davidson	104.0		6.1	...	20.5	77.4
Decatur	149.1		3.4	11.4	74.0	60.3
De Kalb	88.2	...	17.6	...	12.4	58.2
Dickson	160.0		.3	...	74.0	85.7
Dyer	65.5		6.3	12.8	13.0	33.4
Fayette	108.0	...	9.0	...	66.8	32.2
Fentress	246.4		3.8	74.4	34.3	133.9
Franklin	187.0	...	13.8	5.6	50.6	117.0
Gibson	49.0		3.4	...	45.6	...
Giles	160.0	...	.1	4.9	88.8	66.2
Grainger	94.6	...	3.4	4.3	81.1	5.8
Greene	135.2	35.7	.1	...	92.9	6.5
Grundy	186.0	...	.7	19.0	19.0	147.3
Hamblen	25.2		1.9	...	18.8	4.5
Hamilton	180.2		13.8	5.3	57.9	103.2
Hancock	85.4		...	...	84.8	.6
Hardeman	222.0		5.5	5.9	77.1	133.5
Hardin	225.6		2.9	38.3	91.1	93.3
Hawkins	167.4		6.4	5.4	118.0	37.6
Haywood	73.6		8.2	...	27.3	38.1
Henderson	170.5	..	24.2	...	73.3	73.0
Henry	124.3	..	20.0	...	78.2	26.1
Hickman	269.5		...	83.2	117.5	68.8
Houston	91.0		.9	13.0	38.9	38.2
Humphreys	248.0		7.3	24.8	86.7	129.2
Jackson	110.5	...	3.0	...	83.8	23.7
Jefferson	58.5	...	.9	...	49.1	8.5
Johnson	124.2	49.0	.1	...	32.2	42.9
Knox	106.2		1.7	...	41.0	63.5
Lake	16.0	...	6.6	...	9.4	...

4

Table 4. *Commercial forest land by ownership class, 1971* (Continued)

County	All ownerships	National forest	Other public	Forest industry	Farmer	Misc. private
			— — — — — — — — — Thousand acres — — — — — — — — —			
Lauderdale	88.5		.2	51.9	...	36.4
Lawrence	182.7	...	12.6	6.3	100.6	63.2
Lewis	144.9	...	1.4	25.2	25.2	93.1
Lincoln	116.6		...	...	62.7	53.9
Loudon	53.3	...	1.0	4.1	28.5	19.7
McMinn	145.5	2.1	.5	22.2	55.6	65.1
McNairy	197.6	...	2.1	25.4	77.1	93.0
Macon	73.6		...	...	54.4	19.2
Madison	112.8		(¹)	...	102.2	10.6
Marion	247.5	...	34.9	28.1	28.1	156.4
Marshall	78.1		(¹)	...	42.0	36.1
Maury	126.0	...	...	...	65.1	60.9
Meigs	80.6	...	1.6	12.3	43.1	23.6
Monroe	295.8	138.1	.8	17.3	86.4	53.2
Montgomery	116.2	...	21.2	...	40.9	54.1
Moore	30.8		...	...	30.4	.4
Morgan	291.6	...	44.3	11.0	82.7	153.6
Obion	72.8		9.6	10.2	41.1	11.9
Overton	174.2		9.1	6.8	89.0	69.3
Perry	212.8	...	2.5	39.1	111.8	59.4
Pickett	67.0	...	14.5	...	13.7	38.8
Polk	227.7	148.8	2.3	5.4	21.7	49.5
Putnam	140.3	...	1.1	6.2	37.4	95.6
Rhea	134.6	...	...	36.1	71.8	26.7
Roane	131.2	...	27.7	...	73.3	30.2
Robertson	59.0		...		11.6	47.4
Rutherford	117.6		4.5	...	87.0	26.1
Scott	308.0		5.5	17.2	91.5	193.8
Sequatchie	140.0		.1	28.6	5.7	105.6
Sevier	159.2	...	.8	...	70.9	87.5
Shelby	73.0		5.5	...	21.7	45.8
Smith	72.0	...	1.8	...	35.5	34.7
Stewart	221.1	...	86.2	40.1	53.5	41.3
Sullivan	109.2	36.9	2.9	...	29.2	40.2
Sumner	98.1	...	1.3	...	43.0	53.8
Tipton	55.8		...	...	55.2	.6
Trousdale	23.8	...	.3	...	11.7	11.8
Unicoi	94.4	51.5	.1	11.8	...	31.0
Union	84.6	...	28.5	...	23.3	32.8
Van Buren	124.2		.4	93.8	11.0	19.0
Warren	114.0	...	...	...	58.2	55.8
Washington	61.6	16.5	(¹)	...	33.4	11.7
Wayne	378.0	...	.2	106.9	138.4	132.5
Weakley	76.5		(¹)	...	30.3	46.2
White	127.2		1.2	32.5	32.5	61.0
Williamson	145.0	...	.6	...	88.8	55.6
Wilson	109.0	...	8.3	...	75.2	25.5
All counties	12,819.8	599.7	686.5	1,121.4	5,079.1	5,333.1

¹ Negligible.

5

Table 5. *Commercial forest land by forest type, 1971*

County	All types	White pine	Loblolly-shortleaf pine	Oak-pine	Cedar	Oak-hickory	Maple-beech-birch	Elm-ash-cotton-wood	Oak-gum-cypress
					– – Thousand acres – –				
Anderson	140.3	...	6.1	18.3	12.2	103.7	...	...	...
Bedford	76.0	...	...	...	30.4	38.0	...	...	7.6
Benton	168.2	...	11.6	5.8	11.6	121.8	...	...	17.4
Bledsoe	173.6	...	23.1	17.4	...	133.1	...	...	...
Blount	125.6	6.0	12.0	47.8	...	59.8	...	...	...
Bradley	107.2	...	67.0	...	...	40.2	...	...	...
Campbell	225.5	...	38.5	16.5	...	170.5	...	...	...
Cannon	86.4	...	...	9.6	9.6	67.2	...	...	...
Carroll	153.0	...	10.2	5.1	5.1	102.0	...	5.1	25.5
Carter	145.0	5.8	11.6	11.6	...	110.2	5.8	...	...
Cheatham	108.8	...	...	...	13.6	95.2	...	...	...
Chester	97.2	...	10.8	16.2	...	59.4	...	...	10.8
Claiborne	166.4	...	6.4	12.8	12.8	128.0	6.4	...	...
Clay	99.0	...	...	...	16.5	82.5	...	...	...
Cocke	168.0	...	11.2	39.2	...	112.0	5.6	...	...
Coffee	117.6	...	...	...	9.8	98.0	...	...	9.8
Crockett	12.4	...	...	...	...	...	...	...	12.4
Cumberland	324.5	...	27.5	71.5	...	225.5	...	...	...
Davidson	104.0	...	...	...	10.4	93.6	...	...	...
Decatur	149.1	...	5.8	5.7	5.8	131.8	...	...	...
De Kalb	88.2	...	...	...	31.5	50.4	...	...	6.3
Dickson	160.0	...	...	...	...	160.0	...	...	...
Dyer	65.5	...	...	...	...	26.2	...	13.1	26.2
Fayette	108.0	...	13.5	...	...	81.0	...	...	13.5
Fentress	246.4	...	39.2	50.4	5.6	145.6	5.6	...	...
Franklin	187.0	...	...	...	5.5	176.0	5.5	...	...
Gibson	49.0	...	...	...	...	39.2	...	...	9.8
Giles	160.0	...	...	5.0	...	150.0	...	...	5.0
Grainger	94.6	...	...	...	8.6	86.0	...	...	...
Greene	135.2	...	5.2	10.4	10.4	109.2	...	...	...
Grundy	186.0	...	12.4	24.8	...	148.8	...	...	...
Hamblen	25.2	...	6.3	...	6.3	12.6	...	...	...
Hamilton	180.2	...	21.2	58.3	...	100.7	...	...	...
Hancock	85.4	...	...	...	...	85.4	...	...	...
Hardeman	222.0	...	30.0	...	...	156.0	...	6.0	30.0
Hardin	225.6	...	28.8	43.2	...	115.2	...	...	38.4
Hawkins	167.4	...	21.6	16.2	10.8	118.8	...	...	...
Haywood	73.6	...	...	...	9.2	9.2	...	9.2	46.0
Henderson	170.5	...	22.7	5.7	17.1	108.0	...	...	17.0
Henry	124.3	...	...	...	...	79.1	...	...	45.2
Hickman	269.5	...	4.9	...	...	264.6	...	...	...
Houston	91.0	...	...	...	6.5	84.5	...	...	...
Humphreys	248.0	...	...	...	12.4	235.6	...	...	...
Jackson	110.5	...	...	...	25.5	85.0	...	...	...
Jefferson	58.5	...	13.5	4.5	13.5	27.0	...	...	...
Johnson	124.2	...	...	16.2	...	102.6	5.4	...	...
Knox	106.2	...	11.8	17.7	11.8	64.9	...	...	...
Lake	16.0	...	...	...	...	...	...	8.0	8.0

6

Table 5. *Commercial forest land by forest type, 1971* (Continued)

County	All types	White pine	Loblolly-shortleaf pine	Oak-pine	Cedar	Oak-hickory	Maple-beech-birch	Elm-ash-cottonwood	Oak-gum-cypress
						Thousand acres			
Lauderdale	88.5	...	...	...	...	17.7	...	17.7	53.1
Lawrence	182.7	...	...	...	...	176.4	...	6.3	...
Lewis	144.9	...	...	6.3	...	138.6	...	...	...
Lincoln	116.6	...	...	...	53.0	42.4	...	10.6	10.6
Loudon	53.3	...	12.3	12.3	4.1	24.6	...	...	...
McMinn	145.5	...	56.0	22.3	5.6	61.6	...	...	...
McNairy	197.6	...	31.2	26.0	...	124.8	...	...	15.6
Macon	73.6	...	...	...	...	73.6	...	...	...
Madison	112.8	...	...	...	9.4	75.2	...	9.4	18.8
Marion	247.5	...	5.5	55.0	...	176.0	5.5	5.5	...
Marshall	78.1	...	...	...	28.4	49.7	...	...	...
Maury	126.0	...	...	...	6.0	114.0	...	...	6.0
Meigs	80.6	...	12.4	31.0	.	37.2	...	...	...
Monroe	295.8	5.8	92.8	58.0	5.8	121.8	11.6	...	...
Montgomery	116.2	...	...	8.3	8.3	74.7	...	...	24.9
Moore	30.8	...	...	...	...	30.8	...	...	...
Morgan	291.6	...	10.8	48.6	...	232.2	...	...	...
Obion	72.8	...	...	...	...	31.2	...	10.4	31.2
Overton	174.2	...	6.7	13.4	...	154.1	...	...	...
Perry	212.8	...	...	...	11.2	196.0	...	...	5.6
Pickett	67.0	...	6.7	6.7	...	53.6	...	...	...
Polk	227.7	...	92.3	70.6	...	64.8	...	...	...
Putnam	140.3	...	...	6.1	6.1	122.0	6.1	...	...
Rhea	134.6	...	15.5	36.3	.	82.8	...	...	...
Roane	131.2	...	16.4	16.4	8.2	90.2	...	...	...
Robertson	59.0	...	...	...	...	59.0	...	...	...
Rutherford	117.6	...	...	...	68.6	49.0	...	...	...
Scott	308.0	11.2	28.0	28.0	...	224.0	16.8	...	...
Sequatchie	140.0	...	16.8	44.8	...	78.4	...	...	...
Sevier	159.2	...	36.0	41.0	...	82.2	...	...	...
Shelby	73.0	.	...	...	...	29.2	...	21.9	21.9
Smith	72.0	...	...	...	18.0	54.0	...	...	...
Stewart	221.1	...	...	.	6.7	214.4	...	...	...
Sullivan	109.2	4.2	16.8	4.2	4.2	75.6	4.2	...	...
Sumner	98.1	...	...	...	10.9	76.3	...	10.9	...
Tipton	55.8	...	...	...	...	55.8	...	...	...
Trousdale	23.8	...	...	...	...	23.8	...	...	...
Unicoi	94.4	5.9	...	23.6	...	59.0	5.9	...	...
Union	84.6	...	9.4	23.5	14.1	37.6	...	...	...
Van Buren	124.2	...	10.8	32.4	...	81.0	...	...	...
Warren	114.0	...	5.7	...	5.7	102.6	...	...	...
Washington	61.6	...	...	16.8	...	44.8	...	...	...
Wayne	378.0	...	12.6	31.5	6.3	321.3	...	6.3	...
Weakley	76.5	...	15.3	...	...	30.6	...	...	30.6
White	127.2	...	15.9	...	5.3	100.7	...	5.3	...
Williamson	145.0	...	...	5.0	30.0	105.0	...	5.0	...
Wilson	109.0	...	...	...	65.4	43.6	...	...	...
All counties	12,819.8	38.9	998.8	1,198.0	693.8	9,108.0	84.4	150.7	547.2

Table 6. *Commercial forest land by stand-size class, 1971*

County	All classes	Saw-timber	Pole-timber	Sapling and seedling	Non-stocked areas
			— — — — — — — — Thousand acres — — — — — — — — —		
Anderson	140.3	36.6	42.7	61.0	
Bedford	76.0	15.2	7.6	53.2	
Benton	168.2	23.2	92.8	52.2	
Bledsoe	173.6	5.8	57.8	110.0	
Blount	125.6	36.0	47.8	41.8	
Bradley	107.2	13.4	80.4	13.4	
Campbell	225.5	88.0	110.0	27.5	
Cannon	86.4	9.6	48.0	28.8	
Carroll	153.0	35.7	81.6	35.7	
Carter	145.0	75.4	52.2	17.4	
Cheatham	108.8	40.8	40.8	27.2	...
Chester	97.2	27.0	37.8	32.4	...
Claiborne	166.4	38.4	51.2	70.4	6.4
Clay	99.0	33.0	49.5	16.5	...
Cocke	168.0	50.4	72.8	44.8	
Coffee	117.6	39.2	58.8	19.6	
Crockett	12.4	12.4	...	...	
Cumberland	324.5	93.5	126.5	104.5	
Davidson	104.0	20.8	31.2	52.0	
Decatur	149.1	51.6	63.1	34.4	
De Kalb	88.2	12.6	18.9	56.7	
Dickson	160.0	60.0	70.0	30.0	
Dyer	65.5	65.5	...	...	
Fayette	108.0	13.5	27.0	67.5	
Fentress	246.4	78.4	78.4	89.6	
Franklin	187.0	82.5	60.5	44.0	
Gibson	49.0	19.6	19.6	9.8	...
Giles	160.0	20.0	60.0	75.0	5.0
Grainger	94.6	30.1	21.5	43.0	...
Greene	135.2	26.0	20.8	88.4	
Grundy	186.0	49.6	49.6	86.8	
Hamblen	25.2	6.3	12.6	6.3	
Hamilton	180.2	58.3	31.8	90.1	
Hancock	85.4	18.3	30.5	36.6	
Hardeman	222.0	54.0	114.0	54.0	
Hardin	225.6	62.4	91.2	72.0	
Hawkins	167.4	27.0	81.0	59.4	
Haywood	73.6	46.0	18.4	9.2	...
Henderson	170.5	28.4	79.5	62.6	...
Henry	124.3	33.9	67.8	11.3	11.3
Hickman	269.5	44.1	127.4	98.0	...
Houston	91.0	32.5	32.5	26.0	
Humphreys	248.0	31.0	130.2	86.8	
Jackson	110.5	17.0	59.5	34.0	
Jefferson	58.5	13.5	9.0	36.0	
Johnson	124.2	32.4	64.8	27.0	
Knox	106.2	29.5	17.7	59.0	
Lake	16.0	16.0	...	...	...

Table 6. *Commercial forest land by stand-size class, 1971* (Continued)

County	All classes	Saw-timber	Pole-timber	Sapling and seedling	Non-stocked areas
	- - - - - - - - Thousand acres - - - - - - - -				
Lauderdale	88.5	70.8	17.7	...	
Lawrence	182.7	31.5	69.3	81.9	
Lewis	144.9	25.2	75.6	44.1	
Lincoln	116.6	10.6	42.4	63.6	
Loudon	53.3	16.4	16.4	20.5	
McMinn	145.5	33.6	44.8	67.1	
McNairy	197.6	20.8	78.0	98.8	
Macon	73.6	9.2	55.2	9.2	
Madison	112.8	47.0	37.6	28.2	
Marion	247.5	77.0	71.5	99.0	
Marshall	78.1	14.2	14.2	49.7	...
Maury	126.0	24.0	36.0	66.0	
Meigs	80.6	6.2	37.2	37.2	
Monroe	295.8	81.2	98.6	116.0	
Montgomery	116.2	24.9	24.9	66.4	
Moore	30.8	7.7	23.1	...	...
Morgan	291.6	102.6	75.6	113.4	
Obion	72.8	31.2	10.4	31.2	
Overton	174.2	40.2	87.1	46.9	
Perry	212.8	33.6	128.8	50.4	
Pickett	67.0	13.4	33.5	20.1	
Polk	227.7	102.7	76.1	48.9	
Putnam	140.3	48.8	61.0	30.5	
Rhea	134.6	15.5	51.9	67.2	
Roane	131.2	20.5	36.9	73.8	...
Robertson	59.0	23.6	11.8	23.6	...
Rutherford	117.6	...	49.0	58.8	9.8
Scott	308.0	89.6	123.2	95.2	
Sequatchie	140.0	22.4	50.4	67.2	
Sevier	159.2	36.0	51.3	71.9	
Shelby	73.0	21.9	29.2	21.9	
Smith	72.0	...	36.0	36.0	
Stewart	221.1	87.1	87.1	46.9	
Sullivan	109.2	29.4	29.4	50.4	
Sumner	98.1	32.7	...	65.4	
Tipton	55.8	18.6	...	37.2	
Trousdale	23.8	...	11.9	11.9	
Unicoi	94.4	47.2	17.7	29.5	
Union	84.6	28.2	37.6	18.8	
Van Buren	124.2	21.6	32.4	70.2	
Warren	114.0	22.8	51.3	39.9	
Washington	61.6	28.0	16.8	16.8	
Wayne	378.0	37.8	277.2	63.0	
Weakley	76.5	15.3	30.6	30.6	
White	127.2	42.4	42.4	42.4	
Williamson	145.0	30.0	25.0	90.0	...
Wilson	109.0	...	32.7	76.3	...
All counties	12,819.8	3,297.8	4,893.6	4,595.9	32.5

Table 7. *Commercial forest land by site class, 1971*

County	All classes	165 cu. ft. or more	120-165 cu. ft.	85-120 cu. ft.	50-85 cu. ft.	Less than 50 cu. ft.
			— — Thousand acres — —			
Anderson	140.3	...	12.2	24.4	67.1	36.6
Bedford	76.0		...	7.6	22.8	45.6
Benton	168.2	...	...	29.0	63.8	75.4
Bledsoe	173.6	...	...	11.6	98.3	63.7
Blount	125.6	12.0	12.0	11.9	71.7	18.0
Bradley	107.2	...	...	13.4	67.0	26.8
Campbell	225.5	11.0	11.0	77.0	110.0	16.5
Cannon	86.4	...	...	...	38.4	48.0
Carroll	153.0	...	10.2	40.8	76.5	25.5
Carter	145.0	...	...	23.2	63.8	58.0
Cheatham	108.8	...	...	13.6	81.6	13.6
Chester	97.2	5.4	16.2	43.2	21.6	10.8
Claiborne	166.4	...	...	51.2	76.8	38.4
Clay	99.0		...	49.5	...	49.5
Cocke	168.0		5.6	28.0	95.2	39.2
Coffee	117.6		...	19.6	58.8	39.2
Crockett	12.4		...	12.4	...	...
Cumberland	324.5		5.5	22.0	148.5	148.5
Davidson	104.0		...	...	62.4	41.6
Decatur	149.1	...	40.3	28.6	74.5	5.7
De Kalb	88.2		...	18.9	25.2	44.1
Dickson	160.0		...	30.0	85.0	45.0
Dyer	65.5	...	13.1	26.2	26.2	...
Fayette	108.0	...	...	40.5	40.5	27.0
Franklin	187.0	...	...	16.5	77.0	93.5
Fentress	246.4	5.6	5.6	67.2	128.8	39.2
Gibson	49.0		9.8	...	39.2	...
Giles	160.0		...	40.0	90.0	30.0
Grainger	94.6		4.3	25.8	25.8	38.7
Greene	135.2	...	10.4	15.6	57.2	52.0
Grundy	186.0		...	31.0	86.8	68.2
Hamblen	25.2			6.3	18.9	...
Hamilton	180.2		...	26.5	121.9	31.8
Hancock	85.4		...	18.3	48.8	18.3
Hardeman	222.0		...	30.0	168.0	24.0
Hardin	225.6	...	28.8	52.8	110.4	33.6
Hawkins	167.4	...	10.8	16.2	86.4	54.0
Haywood	73.6	...	9.2	27.6	36.8	...
Henderson	170.5	5.7	22.7	85.1	51.3	5.7
Henry	124.3	...	...	45.2	33.9	45.2
Hickman	269.5	...	4.9	24.5	181.3	58.8
Houston	91.0		...	19.5	58.5	13.0
Humphreys	248.0		...	49.6	80.6	117.8
Jackson	110.5		...	25.5	51.0	34.0
Jefferson	58.5	...	...	13.5	18.0	27.0
Johnson	124.2		...	16.2	81.0	27.0
Knox	106.2	...	11.8	29.5	47.2	17.7
Lake	16.0	8.0	...	...	8.0	...

10

Table 7. *Commercial forest land by site class, 1971* (Continued)

County	All classes	165 cu. ft. or more	120-165 cu. ft.	85-120 cu. ft.	50-85 cu. ft.	Less than 50 cu. ft.
			— Thousand acres —			
Lauderdale	88.5	53.1	17.7	...	17.7	...
Lawrence	182.7	...	...	31.5	88.2	63.0
Lewis	144.9		...	...	94.5	50.4
Lincoln	116.6		...	10.6	74.2	31.8
Loudon	53.3		4.1	4.1	36.9	8.2
McMinn	145.5	...	11.2	33.6	78.3	22.4
McNairy	197.6	...	...	31.2	109.2	57.2
Macon	73.6	...	...	18.4	55.2	...
Madison	112.8	9.4	...	37.6	47.0	18.8
Marion	247.5	...	11.0	11.0	154.0	71.5
Marshall	78.1		...	...	42.6	35.5
Maury	126.0	...	...	42.0	42.0	42.0
Meigs	80.6	...	6.2	6.2	62.0	6.2
Monroe	295.8	5.8	11.6	75.4	127.6	75.4
Montgomery	116.2	8.3	...	49.8	49.8	8.3
Moore	30.8	...		...	23.1	7.7
Morgan	291.6	...	...	75.6	167.4	48.6
Obion	72.8	10.4	...	20.8	20.8	20.8
Overton	174.2	...	...	20.1	127.3	26.8
Perry	212.8	...	...	11.2	128.8	72.8
Pickett	67.0	...	6.7	33.5	13.4	13.4
Polk	227.7	5.4	16.4	64.9	103.1	37.9
Putnam	140.3	...	...	12.2	103.7	24.4
Rhea	134.6		...	30.8	62.2	41.6
Roane	131.2		...	32.8	86.1	12.3
Robertson	59.0			...	59.0	...
Rutherford	117.6		...	...	19.6	98.0
Scott	308.0	...	11.2	84.0	168.0	44.8
Sequatchie	140.0	...	...	11.2	112.0	16.8
Sevier	159.2	...	...	20.5	66.9	71.8
Shelby	73.0	14.6	...	36.5	21.9	...
Smith	72.0	...		9.0	54.0	9.0
Stewart	221.1	...	...	20.1	140.7	60.3
Sullivan	109.2	4.2	...	16.8	50.4	37.8
Sumner	98.1	...	...	10.9	65.4	21.8
Tipton	55.8	...	18.6	18.6	18.6	
Trousdale	23.8		...	...	23.8	...
Unicoi	94.4		...	29.5	53.1	11.8
Union	84.6		...	28.2	37.6	18.8
Van Buren	124.2	...	...	27.0	64.8	32.4
Warren	114.0	...	...	28.5	51.3	34.2
Washington	61.6	...	...	16.8	28.0	16.8
Wayne	378.0	6.3	...	63.0	144.9	163.8
Weakley	76.5	...	15.3	15.3	15.3	30.6
White	127.2		5.3	10.6	84.8	26.5
Williamson	145.0	...	...	50.0	65.0	30.0
Wilson	109.0	...	...	10.9	54.5	43.6
All counties	12,819.8	165.2	379.7	2,465.7	6,497.2	3,312.0

11

Table 8. *Cordage of growing stock on commercial forest land by species group, 1971*

County	All species	Softwood			Hardwood			
		Total	Southern pine	Other	Total	Oak	Gum	Other
					— — — Thousand cords — — —			
Anderson	1,507	311	242	69	1,196	645	43	508
Bedford	480	11	...	11	469	108	...	361
Benton	1,804	77	77	...	1,727	1,199	134	394
Bledsoe	1,018	208	197	11	810	613	10	187
Blount	2,030	872	773	99	1,158	725	15	418
Bradley	1,392	865	834	31	527	236	31	260
Campbell	3,578	829	803	26	2,749	1,375	110	1,264
Cannon	420	17	10	7	403	90	19	294
Carroll	1,934	188	171	17	1,746	767	348	631
Carter	2,450	496	119	377	1,954	1,058	30	866
Cheatham	1,253	20	...	20	1,233	615	103	515
Chester	1,099	265	260	5	834	376	148	310
Claiborne	1,644	237	234	3	1,407	654	48	705
Clay	1,031	24	17	7	1,007	616	12	379
Cocke	2,463	521	313	208	1,942	1,133	12	797
Coffee	1,463	...	...	...	1,463	911	19	533
Crockett	245	15	...	15	230	122	52	56
Cumberland	3,585	884	763	121	2,701	1,770	151	780
Davidson	993	...	...	...	993	555	...	438
Decatur	1,876	139	113	26	1,737	1,022	105	610
De Kalb	787	72	...	72	715	190	85	440
Dickson	2,516	3	...	3	2,513	1,534	75	904
Dyer	1,290	...	...	...	1,290	639	124	527
Fayette	874	40	...	40	834	633	60	141
Fentress	2,854	1,012	889	123	1,842	1,136	57	649
Franklin	2,571	59	12	47	2,512	1,594	25	893
Gibson	737	...	...	...	737	294	139	304
Giles	1,040	16	8	8	1,024	373	69	582
Grainger	1,242	160	123	37	1,082	503	46	533
Greene	1,465	243	176	67	1,222	594	15	613
Grundy	1,879	197	189	8	1,682	782	81	819
Hamblen	461	88	60	28	373	266	...	107
Hamilton	2,135	881	881	...	1,254	827	22	405
Hancock	920	32	25	7	888	304	18	566
Hardeman	2,670	364	315	49	2,306	1,272	467	567
Hardin	2,694	512	477	35	2,182	1,031	241	910
Hawkins	2,112	357	340	17	1,755	982	33	740
Haywood	1,327	...	...	...	1,327	770	167	390
Henderson	2,213	355	311	44	1,858	684	521	653
Henry	1,652	...	...	...	1,652	460	288	904
Hickman	3,041	40	31	9	3,001	1,988	73	940
Houston	1,199	8	...	8	1,191	696	40	455
Humphreys	2,508	21	4	17	2,487	1,727	170	590
Jackson	1,058	77	...	77	981	219	...	762
Jefferson	587	77	49	28	510	248	19	243
Johnson	1,812	255	67	188	1,557	866	28	663
Knox	1,325	392	377	15	933	470	31	432
Lake	463	...	...	...	463	...	...	463

Table 8. *Cordage of growing stock on commercial forest land by species group, 1971* (Continued)

County	All species	Softwood			Hardwood			
		Total	Southern pine	Other	Total	Oak	Gum	Other
				— — Thousand cords — —				
Lauderdale	2,582	. . .	. . .	. . .	2,582	284	416	1,882
Lawrence	1,849	. .	. . .	. . .	1,849	1,031	170	648
Lewis	1,699	47	47	. . .	1,652	1,361	13	278
Lincoln	670	57	. . .	57	613	171	9	433
Loudon	616	212	195	17	404	291	12	101
McMinn	1,706	716	696	20	990	437	82	471
McNairy	1,720	423	407	16	1,297	725	130	442
Macon	852	. . .	. . .	. .	852	158	6	688
Madison	1,576	16	. . .	16	1,560	703	167	690
Marion	2,756	332	272	60	2,424	1,375	64	985
Marshall	491	31	. . .	31	460	145		315
Maury	1,007	. . .	. . .	. . .	1,007	267	31	709
Meigs	907	404	391	13	503	285	68	150
Monroe	4,541	2,048	1,873	175	2,493	1,339	96	1,058
Montgomery	1,032	23	. . .	23	1,009	379	52	578
Moore	470	25	. . .	25	445	178	4	263
Morgan	3,040	503	387	116	2,537	1,394	85	1,058
Obion	967	231	11	220	736	106	154	476
Overton	2,594	276	260	16	2,318	767	67	1,484
Perry	2,601	23	4	19	2,578	1,751	61	766
Pickett	778	62	47	15	716	251	12	453
Polk	3,834	2,144	1,829	315	1,690	1,095	65	530
Putnam	1,991	113	103	10	1,878	561	62	1,255
Rhea	1,367	219	167	52	1,148	677	120	351
Roane	1,304	312	295	17	992	579	76	337
Robertson	821	. . .	. . .	. . .	821	416	57	348
Rutherford	457	75	. . .	75	382	107	. . .	275
Scott	4,668	1,049	914	135	3,619	1,890	85	1,644
Sequatchie	1,314	384	345	39	930	543	66	321
Sevier	1,826	644	613	31	1,182	667	33	482
Shelby	888	13	. . .	13	875	101	250	524
Smith	588	31	. . .	31	557	204		353
Stewart	3,056	53	. . .	53	3,003	1,770	223	1,010
Sullivan	1,050	229	112	117	821	489	4	328
Sumner	785	16	. . .	16	769	364	99	306
Tipton	537	. . .	. . .	. .	537	34	18	485
Trousdale	87	5	. . .	5	82	12	. . .	70
Unicoi	1,320	348	71	277	972	397	16	559
Union	1,115	299	275	24	816	424	22	370
Van Buren	1,063	221	149	72	842	358	55	429
Warren	1,386	80	60	20	1,306	455	49	802
Washington	1,000	275	104	171	725	467	18	240
Wayne	4,641	520	499	21	4,121	2,678	131	1,312
Weakley	1,454	164	83	81	1,290	581	382	327
White	1,846	25	16	9	1,821	625	93	1,103
Williamson	1,268	64	. . .	64	1,204	407	61	736
Wilson	480	47	. . .	47	433	148		285
All counties	152,297	23,999	19,485	4,514	128,298	65,119	7,968	55,211

13

Table 9. *Growing-stock volume on commercial forest land by species group, 1971* [1]

County	All species	Softwood			Hardwood			
		Total	Southern pine	Other	Total	Oak	Gum	Other
				Million cubic feet				
Anderson	103.4	23.3	18.1	5.2	80.1	43.2	2.9	34.0
Bedford	32.2	.8	. .	.8	31.4	7.2	. . .	24.2
Benton	121.5	5.8	5.8	. . .	115.7	80.3	9.0	26.4
Bledsoe	69.9	15.6	14.8	.8	54.3	41.1	.7	12.5
Blount	143.0	65.4	58.0	7.4	77.6	48.6	1.0	28.0
Bradley	100.2	64.9	62.6	2.3	35.3	15.8	2.1	17.4
Campbell	246.4	62.2	60.2	2.0	184.2	92.1	7.4	84.7
Cannon	28.3	1.3	.8	.5	27.0	6.0	1.3	19.7
Carroll	131.1	14.1	12.8	1.3	117.0	51.4	23.3	42.3
Carter	168.1	37.2	8.9	28.3	130.9	70.9	2.0	58.0
Cheatham	84.1	1.5	. . .	1.5	82.6	41.2	6.9	34.5
Chester	75.8	19.9	19.5	.4	55.9	25.2	9.9	20.8
Claiborne	112.1	17.8	17.6	.2	94.3	43.8	3.2	47.3
Clay	69.3	1.8	1.3	.5	67.5	41.3	.8	25.4
Cocke	169.2	39.1	23.5	15.6	130.1	75.9	.8	53.4
Coffee	98.0	. . .	. .	. . .	98.0	61.0	1.3	35.7
Crockett	16.5	1.1	. . .	1.1	15.4	8.2	3.5	3.7
Cumberland	247.3	66.3	57.2	9.1	181.0	118.6	10.1	52.3
Davidson	66.5	. . .	. . .	. . .	66.5	37.2	. . .	29.3
Decatur	126.8	10.4	8.5	1.9	116.4	68.5	7.0	40.9
De Kalb	53.3	5.4	. .	5.4	47.9	12.7	5.7	29.5
Dickson	168.6	.2	. .	.2	168.4	102.8	5.0	60.6
Dyer	86.4	. .	. . .	. . .	86.4	42.8	8.3	35.3
Fayette	58.9	3.0	.	3.0	55.9	42.4	4.0	9.5
Fentress	199.3	75.9	66.7	9.2	123.4	76.1	3.8	43.5
Franklin	172.7	4.4	.9	3.5	168.3	106.8	1.7	59.8
Gibson	49.4	. . .	. .	. . .	49.4	19.7	9.3	20.4
Giles	69.8	1.2	.6	.6	68.6	25.0	4.6	39.0
Grainger	84.5	12.0	9.2	2.8	72.5	33.7	3.1	35.7
Greene	100.1	18.2	13.2	5.0	81.9	39.8	1.0	41.1
Grundy	127.5	14.8	14.2	.6	112.7	52.4	5.4	54.9
Hamblen	31.6	6.6	4.5	2.1	25.0	17.8	. .	7.2
Hamilton	150.1	66.1	66.1	. . .	84.0	55.4	1.5	27.1
Hancock	61.9	2.4	1.9	.5	59.5	20.4	1.2	37.9
Hardeman	181.8	27.3	23.6	3.7	154.5	85.2	31.3	38.0
Hardin	184.6	38.4	35.8	2.6	146.2	69.1	16.1	61.0
Hawkins	144.4	26.8	25.5	1.3	117.6	65.8	2.2	49.6
Haywood	88.9	. .	. . .	. . .	88.9	51.6	11.2	26.1
Henderson	151.1	26.6	23.3	3.3	124.5	45.8	34.9	43.8
Henry	110.7	. . .	. .	. .	110.7	30.8	19.3	60.6
Hickman	204.1	3.0	2.3	.7	201.1	133.2	4.9	63.0
Houston	80.4	.6	. . .	.6	79.8	46.6	2.7	30.5
Humphreys	168.2	1.6	.3	1.3	166.6	115.7	11.4	39.5
Jackson	71.5	5.8	. . .	5.8	65.7	14.7	. .	51.0
Jefferson	40.0	5.8	3.7	2.1	34.2	16.6	1.3	16.3
Johnson	123.4	19.1	5.0	14.1	104.3	58.0	1.9	44.4
Knox	91.9	29.4	28.3	1.1	62.5	31.5	2.1	28.9
Lake	31.0	. .	. . .	. . .	31.0	. .	. . .	31.0

14

Table 9. *Growing-stock volume on commercial forest land by species group, 1971* [1] (Continued)

County	All species	Softwood			Hardwood			
		Total	Southern pine	Other	Total	Oak	Gum	Other
				— Million cubic feet —				
Lauderdale	173.0	..	..	..	173.0	19.0	27.9	126.1
Lawrence	123.9	..	..	..	123.9	69.1	11.4	43.4
Lewis	114.2	3.5	3.5	..	110.7	91.2	.9	18.6
Lincoln	45.4	4.3	.	4.3	41.1	11.5	.6	29.0
Loudon	43.0	15.9	14.6	1.3	27.1	19.5	.8	6.8
McMinn	120.0	53.7	52.2	1.5	66.3	29.3	5.5	31.5
McNairy	118.6	31.7	30.5	1.2	86.9	48.6	8.7	29.6
Macon	57.1	..	..	..	57.1	10.6	.4	46.1
Madison	105.7	1.2	..	1.2	104.5	47.1	11.2	46.2
Marion	187.3	24.9	20.4	4.5	162.4	92.1	4.3	66.0
Marshall	33.1	2.3	..	2.3	30.8	9.7	..	21.1
Maury	67.5	..	..	..	67.5	17.9	2.1	47.5
Meigs	64.0	30.3	29.3	1.0	33.7	19.1	4.5	10.1
Monroe	320.6	153.6	140.5	13.1	167.0	89.7	6.4	70.9
Montgomery	69.3	1.7	..	1.7	67.6	25.4	3.5	38.7
Moore	31.7	1.9	..	1.9	29.8	11.9	.3	17.6
Morgan	207.7	37.7	29.0	8.7	170.0	93.4	5.7	70.9
Obion	66.6	17.3	.8	16.5	49.3	7.1	10.3	31.9
Overton	176.0	20.7	19.5	1.2	155.3	51.4	4.5	99.4
Perry	174.4	1.7	.3	1.4	172.7	117.3	4.1	51.3
Pickett	52.6	4.6	3.5	1.1	48.0	16.8	.8	30.4
Polk	274.0	160.8	137.2	23.6	113.2	73.4	4.3	35.5
Putnam	134.3	8.5	7.7	.8	125.8	37.6	4.1	84.1
Rhea	93.3	16.4	12.5	3.9	76.9	45.4	8.0	23.5
Roane	89.9	23.4	22.1	1.3	66.5	38.8	5.1	22.6
Robertson	55.0	..	..	..	55.0	27.9	3.8	23.3
Rutherford	31.2	5.6	..	5.6	25.6	7.2	..	18.4
Scott	321.1	78.6	68.5	10.1	242.5	126.6	5.7	110.2
Sequatchie	91.1	28.8	25.9	2.9	62.3	36.4	4.4	21.5
Sevier	127.5	48.3	46.0	2.3	79.2	44.7	2.2	32.3
Shelby	59.6	1.0	..	1.0	58.6	6.8	16.7	35.1
Smith	39.6	2.3	..	2.3	37.3	13.7	..	23.6
Stewart	205.2	4.0	..	4.0	201.2	118.6	14.9	67.7
Sullivan	72.2	17.2	8.4	8.8	55.0	32.7	.3	22.0
Sumner	52.7	1.2	..	1.2	51.5	24.4	6.6	20.5
Tipton	36.0	..	..	..	36.0	2.3	1.2	32.5
Trousdale	5.9	.4	..	.4	5.5	.8	..	4.7
Unicoi	91.2	26.1	5.3	20.8	65.1	26.6	1.1	37.4
Union	77.1	22.4	20.6	1.8	54.7	28.4	1.5	24.8
Van Buren	73.0	16.6	11.2	5.4	56.4	24.0	3.7	28.7
Warren	93.5	6.0	4.5	1.5	87.5	30.5	3.3	53.7
Washington	69.2	20.6	7.8	12.8	48.6	31.3	1.2	16.1
Wayne	315.1	39.0	37.4	1.6	276.1	179.4	8.8	87.9
Weakley	98.7	12.3	6.2	6.1	86.4	38.9	25.6	21.9
White	123.9	1.9	1.2	.7	122.0	41.9	6.2	73.9
Williamson	85.5	4.8	..	4.8	80.7	27.3	4.1	49.3
Wilson	32.5	3.5	..	3.5	29.0	9.9	..	19.1
All counties	10,395.8	1,799.8	1,461.3	338.5	8,596.0	4,363.1	533.8	3,699.1

[1] Detailed county statistics by species and diameter class are available upon request.

15

Table 10. *Sawtimber volume on commercial forest land by species group, 1971* [1]

County	All species	Softwood			Hardwood			
		Total	Southern pine	Other	Total	Oak	Gum	Other
					— Million board feet —			
Anderson	273.8	73.5	58.0	15.5	200.3	112.8	9.0	78.5
Bedford	64.3	...	...	...	64.3	29.2	..	35.1
Benton	219.4	13.8	13.8	...	205.6	158.7	17.2	29.7
Bledsoe	125.9	34.6	33.0	1.6	91.3	67.6	1.0	22.7
Blount	415.1	187.0	160.7	26.3	228.1	163.8	...	64.3
Bradley	126.5	63.3	59.5	3.8	63.2	27.4	...	35.8
Campbell	716.9	169.4	166.4	3.0	547.5	280.6	27.7	239.2
Cannon	31.3	..	..	.	31.3	11.2	2.1	18.0
Carroll	310.4	29.7	29.1	.6	280.7	145.0	43.0	92.7
Carter	439.0	143.0	11.4	131.6	296.0	173.5	7.2	115.3
Cheatham	243.6	...	...	...	243.6	112.4	36.4	94.8
Chester	178.4	58.8	58.8	..	119.6	63.9	12.9	42.8
Claiborne	264.6	38.0	37.3	.7	226.6	108.0	6.2	112.4
Clay	190.3	7.0	7.0	..	183.3	128.8	...	54.5
Cocke	447.7	141.3	68.2	73.1	306.4	186.4	1.8	118.2
Coffee	263.0	...	...	...	263.0	181.4	3.1	78.5
Crockett	60.0	5.6	...	5.6	54.4	35.9	4.2	14.3
Cumberland	595.9	203.4	169.6	33.8	392.5	263.5	15.6	113.4
Davidson	184.3	...	...	...	184.3	117.7	...	66.6
Decatur	296.8	11.4	8.6	2.8	285.4	170.6	14.6	100.2
De Kalb	129.2	1.5	...	1.5	127.7	37.5	16.5	73.7
Dickson	415.2	...	...	...	415.2	301.4	.7	113.1
Dyer	343.7	...	...	...	343.7	152.1	34.2	157.4
Fayette	163.7	4.6	...	4.6	159.1	124.1	3.2	31.8
Fentress	540.2	225.8	188.9	36.9	314.4	180.4	15.8	118.2
Franklin	509.7	1.4	...	1.4	508.3	344.9	4.4	159.0
Gibson	129.4	...	...	...	129.4	57.6	31.5	40.3
Giles	142.4	...	...	...	142.4	77.0	10.1	55.3
Grainger	233.2	30.1	29.1	1.0	203.1	104.8	5.6	92.7
Greene	307.8	52.6	35.2	17.4	255.2	138.8	2.4	114.0
Grundy	333.6	33.3	31.5	1.8	300.3	115.1	14.9	170.3
Hamblen	72.2	5.3	2.4	2.9	66.9	54.3	...	12.6
Hamilton	450.8	217.7	217.7	...	233.1	163.1	3.6	66.4
Hancock	175.9	8.9	7.6	1.3	167.0	71.7	1.5	93.8
Hardeman	425.9	73.2	61.2	12.0	352.7	168.4	80.5	103.8
Hardin	429.3	81.8	79.8	2.0	347.5	191.8	31.2	124.5
Hawkins	357.0	43.0	43.0	...	314.0	213.3	2.3	98.4
Haywood	286.7	...	...	..	286.7	171.1	41.1	74.5
Henderson	397.2	66.2	63.3	2.9	331.0	145.9	81.4	103.7
Henry	259.1	...	...	...	259.1	92.7	53.3	113.1
Hickman	399.4	6.7	4.0	2.7	392.7	265.9	5.4	121.4
Houston	176.4	1.8	...	1.8	174.6	112.9	4.4	57.3
Humphreys	286.6	3.1	.5	2.6	283.5	204.6	1.8	77.1
Jackson	201.1	1.1	...	1.1	200.0	43.6	...	156.4
Jefferson	125.0	10.4	8.5	1.9	114.6	64.7	4.2	45.7
Johnson	295.5	73.4	17.3	56.1	222.1	124.2	3.6	94.3
Knox	287.0	59.2	58.5	.7	227.8	126.7	6.6	94.5
Lake	132.0	...	...	...	132.0	...	...	132.0

County	All species	Softwood			Hardwood			
		Total	Southern pine	Other	Total	Oak	Gum	Other
				— — — — — Million board feet — — — — — — —				
Lauderdale	700.0	...	...	...	700.0	50.9	93.1	556.0
Lawrence	274.3	...	...	..	274.3	168.3	11.5	94.5
Lewis	197.3	11.5	11.5	...	185.8	152.5	...	33.3
Lincoln	72.2	...	...	...	72.2	17.7	..	54.5
Loudon	110.9	23.2	20.1	3.1	87.7	66.9	1.0	19.8
McMinn	275.1	110.2	110.2	...	164.9	87.6	1.3	76.0
McNairy	255.3	94.1	88.9	5.2	161.2	91.0	20.8	49.4
Macon	99.5	...	...	...	99.5	27.3	...	72.2
Madison	348.0	2.0	...	2.0	346.0	108.9	43.1	194.0
Marion	553.8	83.8	59.5	24.3	470.0	263.5	11.7	194.8
Marshall	94.6	2.7	...	2.7	91.9	29.0	...	62.9
Maury	173.1	...	...	...	173.1	53.9	6.3	112.9
Meigs	136.2	53.5	50.8	2.7	82.7	42.7	7.5	32.5
Monroe	885.5	429.2	390.0	39.2	456.3	225.2	8.4	222.7
Montgomery	149.6	...	...	...	149.6	59.2	5.2	85.2
Moore	82.8	6.4	...	6.4	76.4	47.9	...	28.5
Morgan	552.8	122.0	86.7	35.3	430.8	235.6	13.0	182.2
Obion	234.3	87.0	4.1	82.9	147.3	24.2	25.4	97.7
Overton	441.7	88.8	86.7	2.1	352.9	133.6	8.4	210.9
Perry	304.7	2.0	.8	1.2	302.7	212.9	2.2	87.6
Pickett	129.4	3.1	2.6	.5	126.3	57.3	1.3	67.7
Polk	764.5	471.0	388.2	82.8	293.5	203.2	8.2	82.1
Putnam	313.2	25.1	25.1	...	288.1	81.3	9.3	197.5
Rhea	224.7	44.8	32.4	12.4	179.9	115.6	20.0	44.3
Roane	183.1	35.0	32.6	2.4	148.1	86.6	11.4	50.1
Robertson	176.7	...	...	..	176.7	110.0	8.6	58.1
Rutherford	17.9	...	...	...	17.9	6.4	...	11.5
Scott	854.9	230.7	191.4	39.3	624.2	349.4	14.5	260.3
Sequatchie	247.5	92.8	79.2	13.6	154.7	93.0	11.2	50.5
Sevier	303.4	106.9	99.1	7.8	196.5	127.7	2.5	66.3
Shelby	173.7	4.0	...	4.0	169.7	12.6	54.9	102.2
Smith	60.4	.5	...	.5	59.9	19.1	...	40.8
Stewart	526.3	17.0	...	17.0	509.3	334.1	16.7	158.5
Sullivan	156.3	46.1	16.3	29.8	110.2	73.1	...	37.1
Sumner	177.3	2.6	...	2.6	174.7	99.2	13.4	62.1
Tipton	105.7	..	..	...	105.7	5.0	...	100.7
Trousdale	7.4	...	..	...	7.4	2.4	...	5.0
Unicoi	259.8	98.6	19.5	79.1	161.2	83.2	1.9	76.1
Union	178.6	27.3	24.7	2.6	151.3	89.6	5.9	55.8
Van Buren	195.2	41.3	17.2	24.1	153.9	64.3	6.7	82.9
Warren	205.7	7.1	5.3	1.8	198.6	72.9	8.0	117.7
Washington	181.6	64.4	10.9	53.5	117.2	84.4	3.7	29.1
Wayne	525.3	52.4	52.4	...	472.9	326.8	8.4	137.7
Weakley	361.9	24.9	3.3	21.6	337.0	180.6	97.3	59.1
White	340.5	.8	.5	.3	339.7	118.7	13.7	207.3
Williamson	217.4	4.8	...	4.8	212.6	72.0	12.0	128.6
Wilson	57.7	.6	...	.6	57.1	20.3	...	36.8
All counties	26,340.2	4,699.1	3,639.9	1,059.2	21,641.1	11,374.6	1,250.7	9,015.8

[1] Detailed county statistics by species and diameter class are available upon request.

Table 11. *Sawtimber volume on commercial forest land by species group and diameter class, 1971*

County	All species	Softwood			Hardwood		
		Total	9.0-14.9 inches	15.0 inches and up	Total	11.0-14.9 inches	15.0 inches and up
				Million board feet			
Anderson	273.8	73.5	67.5	6.0	200.3	84.9	115.4
Bedford	64.3	...	...	...	64.3	45.0	19.3
Benton	219.4	13.8	13.8	...	205.6	140.6	65.0
Bledsoe	125.9	34.6	32.9	1.7	91.3	65.8	25.5
Blount	415.1	187.0	166.1	20.9	228.1	114.4	113.7
Bradley	126.5	63.3	63.3	...	63.2	32.7	30.5
Campbell	716.9	169.4	140.4	29.0	547.5	249.5	298.0
Cannon	31.3	...	...	...	31.3	21.3	10.0
Carroll	310.4	29.7	27.2	2.5	280.7	154.0	126.7
Carter	439.0	143.0	44.6	98.4	296.0	149.4	146.6
Cheatham	243.6	...	...	...	243.6	91.3	152.3
Chester	178.4	58.8	56.1	2.7	119.6	77.4	42.2
Claiborne	264.6	38.0	36.3	1.7	226.6	146.9	79.7
Clay	190.3	7.0	7.0	...	183.3	119.4	63.9
Cocke	447.7	141.3	69.6	71.7	306.4	130.5	175.9
Coffee	263.0	...	...	...	263.0	114.7	148.3
Crockett	60.0	5.6	...	5.6	54.4	9.8	44.6
Cumberland	595.9	203.4	154.3	49.1	392.5	213.5	179.0
Davidson	184.3	...	...	...	184.3	88.4	95.9
Decatur	296.8	11.4	10.0	1.4	285.4	183.9	101.5
De Kalb	129.2	1.5	1.5	...	127.7	50.5	77.2
Dickson	415.2	...	...	..	415.2	238.3	176.9
Dyer	343.7	..	..	...	343.7	93.3	250.4
Fayette	163.7	4.6	4.6	...	159.1	49.5	109.6
Fentress	540.2	225.8	175.2	50.6	314.4	170.6	143.8
Franklin	509.7	1.4	1.4	...	508.3	260.2	248.1
Gibson	129.4	...	...	...	129.4	61.3	68.1
Giles	142.4	...	...	...	142.4	74.4	68.0
Grainger	233.2	30.1	25.8	4.3	203.1	86.7	116.4
Greene	307.8	52.6	31.5	21.1	255.2	87.9	167.3
Grundy	333.6	33.3	29.2	4.1	300.3	140.3	160.0
Hamblen	72.2	5.3	5.3	...	66.9	35.7	31.2
Hamilton	450.8	217.7	158.4	59.3	233.1	107.9	125.2
Hancock	175.9	8.9	5.8	3.1	167.0	79.0	88.0
Hardeman	425.9	73.2	62.7	10.5	352.7	216.7	136.0
Hardin	429.3	81.8	73.1	8.7	347.5	193.7	153.8
Hawkins	357.0	43.0	41.1	1.9	314.0	115.8	198.2
Haywood	286.7	...	...	...	286.7	71.8	214.9
Henderson	397.2	66.2	66.2	...	331.0	206.2	124.8
Henry	259.1	...	...	...	259.1	136.7	122.4
Hickman	399.4	6.7	4.0	2.7	392.7	257.0	135.7
Houston	176.4	1.8	...	1.8	174.6	98.8	75.8
Humphreys	286.6	3.1	1.6	1.5	283.5	198.3	85.2
Jackson	201.1	1.1	1.1	...	200.0	86.8	113.2
Jefferson	125.0	10.4	10.4	...	114.6	53.6	61.0
Johnson	295.5	73.4	27.6	45.8	222.1	111.3	110.8
Knox	287.0	59.2	48.9	10.3	227.8	52.4	175.4
Lake	132.0	...	...	...	132.0	13.2	118.8

18

County	All species	Softwood			Hardwood		
		Total	9.0-14.9 inches	15.0 inches and up	Total	11.0-14.9 inches	15.0 inches and up
				— Million board feet —			
Lauderdale	700.0	..	..	..	700.0	123.9	576.1
Lawrence	274.3	..	..	...	274.3	160.3	114.0
Lewis	197.3	11.5	11.5	..	185.8	143.6	42.2
Lincoln	72.2	...	...	...	72.2	48.9	23.3
Loudon	110.9	23.2	21.3	1.9	87.7	32.1	55.6
McMinn	275.1	110.2	78.7	31.5	164.9	83.4	81.5
McNairy	255.3	94.1	70.8	23.3	161.2	117.7	43.5
Macon	99.5	...	...	...	99.5	63.5	36.0
Madison	348.0	2.0	2.0	...	346.0	115.6	230.4
Marion	553.8	83.8	57.1	26.7	470.0	255.4	214.6
Marshall	94.6	2.7	2.7	...	91.9	38.7	53.2
Maury	173.1	...	...	...	173.1	89.1	84.0
Meigs	136.2	53.5	51.7	1.8	82.7	45.0	37.7
Monroe	885.5	429.2	310.6	118.6	456.3	208.9	247.4
Montgomery	149.6	...	...	...	149.6	62.6	87.0
Moore	82.8	6.4	6.4	...	76.4	29.7	46.7
Morgan	552.8	122.0	103.0	19.0	430.8	227.9	202.9
Obion	234.3	87.0	9.3	77.7	147.3	52.0	95.3
Overton	441.7	88.8	69.9	18.9	352.9	228.3	124.6
Perry	304.7	2.0	2.0	...	302.7	240.9	61.8
Pickett	129.4	3.1	3.1	...	126.3	56.5	69.8
Polk	764.5	471.0	394.4	76.6	293.5	155.4	138.1
Putnam	313.2	25.1	19.4	5.7	288.1	145.9	142.2
Rhea	224.7	44.8	33.0	11.8	179.9	94.6	85.3
Roane	183.1	35.0	31.8	3.2	148.1	74.1	74.0
Robertson	176.7	...	...	...	176.7	41.4	135.3
Rutherford	17.9	...	...	...	17.9	15.7	2.2
Scott	854.9	230.7	207.4	23.3	624.2	365.9	258.3
Sequatchie	247.5	92.8	78.6	14.2	154.7	84.0	70.7
Sevier	303.4	106.9	90.9	16.0	196.5	83.4	113.1
Shelby	173.7	4.0	4.0	...	169.7	46.1	123.6
Smith	60.4	.5	.5	...	59.9	16.3	43.6
Stewart	526.3	17.0	17.0	...	509.3	251.1	258.2
Sullivan	156.3	46.1	28.5	17.6	110.2	62.6	47.6
Sumner	177.3	2.6	...	2.6	174.7	49.6	125.1
Tipton	105.7	...	...	..	105.7	48.6	57.1
Trousdale	7.4	..	..	...	7.4	7.4	..
Unicoi	259.8	98.6	61.1	37.5	161.2	64.5	96.7
Union	178.6	27.3	23.2	4.1	151.3	54.8	96.5
Van Buren	195.2	41.3	34.2	7.1	153.9	90.5	63.4
Warren	205.7	7.1	7.1	...	198.6	90.9	107.7
Washington	181.6	64.4	37.7	26.7	117.2	39.5	77.7
Wayne	525.3	52.4	52.4	...	472.9	351.8	121.1
Weakley	361.9	24.9	17.3	7.6	337.0	96.1	240.9
White	340.5	.8	.3	.5	339.7	150.4	189.3
Williamson	217.4	4.8	1.7	3.1	212.6	101.4	111.2
Wilson	57.7	.6	.6	...	57.1	31.1	26.0
All counties	26,340.2	4,699.1	3,605.7	1,093.4	21,641.1	10,618.4	11,022.7

19

Table 12. *Sawtimber volume in Scribner rule on commercial forest land by species, 1971*

County	All species	Softwood			Hardwood			
		Total	Southern pine	Other	Total	Oak	Gum	Other
				— Million board feet —				
Anderson	234.5	59.1	46.0	13.1	175.4	98.0	7.9	69.5
Bedford	55.6	...	...	...	55.6	25.5	...	30.1
Benton	186.4	11.0	11.0	...	175.4	135.7	14.8	24.9
Bledsoe	103.5	26.4	25.3	1.1	77.1	56.9	.8	19.4
Blount	359.0	155.7	133.6	22.1	203.3	146.4	...	56.9
Bradley	104.8	51.0	47.9	3.1	53.8	22.7	...	31.1
Campbell	631.9	142.2	139.6	2.6	489.7	251.5	25.2	213.0
Cannon	26.4	...	...	...	26.4	9.6	1.6	15.2
Carroll	270.0	24.8	24.4	.4	245.2	128.0	36.9	80.3
Carter	384.6	124.2	9.1	115.1	260.4	153.9	6.2	100.3
Cheatham	215.4	...	...	...	215.4	101.2	32.1	82.1
Chester	152.2	48.0	48.0	...	104.2	55.5	11.2	37.5
Claiborne	227.3	31.0	30.5	.5	196.3	94.0	5.1	97.2
Clay	169.3	6.2	6.2	...	163.1	116.0	...	47.1
Cocke	391.8	120.3	56.9	63.4	271.5	165.4	1.5	104.6
Coffee	231.7	...	...	...	231.7	160.0	2.6	69.1
Crockett	54.6	5.1	...	5.1	49.5	33.1	3.2	13.2
Cumberland	507.3	166.9	138.1	28.8	340.4	227.4	13.1	99.9
Davidson	163.4	...	...	...	163.4	104.7	...	58.7
Decatur	256.3	10.0	7.4	2.6	246.3	146.6	12.3	87.4
De Kalb	114.6	2.3	...	2.3	112.3	32.7	14.1	65.5
Dickson	363.8	...	...	...	363.8	264.6	.6	98.6
Dyer	303.7	...	...	...	303.7	133.2	30.1	140.4
Fayette	146.8	3.6	...	3.6	143.2	112.3	2.7	28.2
Fentress	469.9	190.0	159.4	30.6	279.9	160.3	13.9	105.7
Franklin	448.5	1.1	...	1.1	447.4	302.1	3.8	141.5
Gibson	113.5	...	...	...	113.5	51.2	27.1	35.2
Giles	124.7	...	...	...	124.7	67.8	8.9	48.0
Grainger	205.8	25.2	24.5	.7	180.6	94.0	4.8	81.8
Greene	273.3	44.8	29.7	15.1	228.5	125.6	2.2	100.7
Grundy	292.5	27.4	26.0	1.4	265.1	100.6	13.3	151.2
Hamblen	64.3	4.6	2.3	2.3	59.7	48.8	...	10.9
Hamilton	386.9	182.1	182.1	...	204.8	143.9	3.3	57.6
Hancock	154.3	7.1	6.2	.9	147.2	63.4	1.3	82.5
Hardeman	370.1	60.6	50.3	10.3	309.5	146.2	71.4	91.9
Hardin	371.3	66.8	65.2	1.6	304.5	168.3	27.1	109.1
Hawkins	318.0	36.2	36.2	...	281.8	192.5	1.7	87.6
Haywood	255.4	...	...	...	255.4	153.8	35.7	65.9
Henderson	341.6	53.4	51.2	2.2	288.2	128.3	69.8	90.1
Henry	223.8	...	...	...	223.8	80.9	45.7	97.2
Hickman	348.8	5.5	3.2	2.3	343.3	232.0	4.8	106.5
Houston	154.0	1.6	...	1.6	152.4	99.1	3.6	49.7
Humphreys	247.0	2.6	.4	2.2	244.4	176.2	1.6	66.6
Jackson	177.3	1.4	...	1.4	175.9	38.2	...	137.7
Jefferson	110.6	8.5	7.2	1.3	102.1	57.7	3.6	40.8
Johnson	259.6	63.6	14.1	49.5	196.0	110.4	3.2	82.4
Knox	253.3	49.7	49.2	.5	203.6	113.9	6.1	83.6
Lake	118.0	...	...	...	118.0	...	...	118.0

Table 12. *Sawtimber volume in Scribner rule on commercial forest land by species, 1971* (Continued)

County	All species	Softwood			Hardwood			
		Total	Southern pine	Other	Total	Oak	Gum	Other
				Million board feet				
Lauderdale	621.6	...	...	...	621.6	46.6	82.1	492.9
Lawrence	240.3	...	...	...	240.3	147.6	9.7	83.0
Lewis	169.1	9.1	9.1	...	160.0	131.4	...	28.6
Lincoln	59.5	...	..	...	59.5	14.3	...	45.2
Loudon	96.9	19.2	16.5	2.7	77.7	59.4	.8	17.5
McMinn	237.2	91.1	91.1	...	146.1	77.9	1.1	67.1
McNairy	215.9	77.1	72.4	4.7	138.8	77.7	18.1	43.0
Macon	85.0	...	...	...	85.0	23.3	...	61.7
Madison	311.0	1.6	...	1.6	309.4	94.6	38.9	175.9
Marion	483.4	69.7	48.6	21.1	413.7	232.7	9.9	171.1
Marshall	82.3	1.9	...	1.9	80.4	25.4	...	55.0
Maury	153.2	...	...	...	153.2	48.1	5.7	99.4
Meigs	117.2	43.9	41.8	2.1	73.3	37.5	6.6	29.2
Monroe	765.9	362.2	327.4	34.8	403.7	198.4	7.2	198.1
Montgomery	131.0	...	...	...	131.0	51.6	4.6	74.8
Moore	72.9	5.2	...	5.2	67.7	43.0	...	24.7
Morgan	479.5	100.3	70.3	30.0	379.2	208.1	11.4	159.7
Obion	208.5	77.2	3.4	73.8	131.3	21.0	23.0	87.3
Overton	381.5	74.0	72.3	1.7	307.5	116.7	6.7	184.1
Perry	263.0	1.3	.5	.8	261.7	183.9	1.8	76.0
Pickett	114.7	2.7	2.2	.5	112.0	50.7	1.0	60.3
Polk	656.1	394.9	325.3	69.6	261.2	180.5	7.2	73.5
Putnam	273.5	21.2	21.2	...	252.3	70.7	8.0	173.6
Rhea	195.5	38.0	27.5	10.5	157.5	101.3	17.3	38.9
Roane	158.1	27.8	26.0	1.8	130.3	76.4	9.9	44.0
Robertson	157.6	...	...	...	157.6	98.4	7.6	51.6
Rutherford	15.2	...	...	...	15.2	5.3	...	9.9
Scott	745.7	190.7	157.7	33.0	555.0	310.4	13.0	231.6
Sequatchie	212.9	77.0	65.8	11.2	135.9	82.1	9.1	44.7
Sevier	263.4	88.8	82.2	6.6	174.6	113.1	2.2	59.3
Shelby	154.5	3.2	...	3.2	151.3	10.9	50.5	89.9
Smith	54.3	.9	...	.9	53.4	16.8	...	36.6
Stewart	460.7	13.3	...	13.3	447.4	293.5	14.4	139.5
Sullivan	135.0	38.4	12.7	25.7	96.6	64.3	...	32.3
Sumner	157.8	2.1	...	2.1	155.7	89.3	11.6	54.8
Tipton	90.2	...	...	...	90.2	4.2	...	86.0
Trousdale	5.3	...	...	...	5.3	1.7	...	3.6
Unicoi	225.5	82.6	16.3	66.3	142.9	74.3	1.5	67.1
Union	154.0	21.8	19.7	2.1	132.2	78.9	5.0	48.3
Van Buren	167.7	33.9	13.6	20.3	133.8	55.6	6.0	72.2
Warren	177.5	5.6	4.1	1.5	171.9	63.5	6.9	101.5
Washington	158.2	53.8	8.2	45.6	104.4	75.8	3.2	25.4
Wayne	456.4	42.4	42.4	...	414.0	287.3	7.2	119.5
Weakley	328.7	23.7	5.4	18.3	305.0	166.4	86.2	52.4
White	300.9	.7	.4	.3	300.2	105.9	11.5	182.8
Williamson	192.5	3.7	...	3.7	188.8	63.5	10.6	114.7
Wilson	51.0	1.0	...	1.0	50.0	17.6	...	32.4
All counties	22,975.2	3,922.0	3,015.3	906.7	19.053.2	10.027.7	1,092.4	7,933.1

21

Table 13. *Sawtimber volume in Scribner rule on commercial forest land by species group and diameter class, 1971*

County	All species	Softwood			Hardwood		
		Total	9.0-14.9 inches	15.0 inches and up	Total	11.0-14.9 inches	15.0 inches and up
				— — — — — — — — — — — — — Million board feet — — — — — — — — — — — — —			
Anderson	234.5	59.1	53.7	5.4	175.4	72.1	103.3
Bedford	55.6	...	...	...	55.6	38.4	17.2
Benton	186.4	11.0	11.0	...	175.4	117.8	57.6
Bledsoe	103.5	26.4	25.1	1.3	77.1	54.3	22.8
Blount	359.0	155.7	137.6	18.1	203.3	100.2	103.1
Bradley	104.8	51.0	51.0	...	53.8	26.6	27.2
Campbell	631.9	142.2	116.5	25.7	489.7	217.2	272.5
Cannon	26.4	...	.	...	26.4	17.6	8.8
Carroll	270.0	24.8	22.6	2.2	245.2	130.3	114.9
Carter	384.6	124.2	36.3	87.9	260.4	128.0	132.4
Cheatham	215.4	...	.	...	215.4	77.6	137.8
Chester	152.2	48.0	45.7	2.3	104.2	66.2	38.0
Claiborne	227.3	31.0	29.6	1.4	196.3	124.8	71.5
Clay	169.3	6.2	6.2	...	163.1	104.8	58.3
Cocke	391.8	120.3	56.9	63.4	271.5	111.7	159.8
Coffee	231.7	...	...	...	231.7	97.3	134.4
Crockett	54.6	5.1	...	5.1	49.5	8.3	41.2
Cumberland	507.3	166.9	124.0	42.9	340.4	179.2	161.2
Davidson	163.4	...	...	...	163.4	76.2	87.2
Decatur	256.3	10.0	8.8	1.2	246.3	155.2	91.1
De Kalb	114.6	2.3	2.3	...	112.3	42.8	69.5
Dickson	363.8	...	...	...	363.8	203.0	160.8
Dyer	303.7	...	...	...	303.7	78.7	225.0
Fayette	146.8	3.6	3.6	...	143.2	41.8	101.4
Fentress	469.9	190.0	144.7	45.3	279.9	149.1	130.8
Franklin	448.5	1.1	1.1	...	447.4	224.0	223.4
Gibson	113.5	...	...	...	113.5	52.3	61.2
Giles	124.7	...	...	...	124.7	63.4	61.3
Grainger	205.8	25.2	21.4	3.8	180.6	74.5	106.1
Greene	273.3	44.8	25.8	19.0	228.5	76.8	151.7
Grundy	292.5	27.4	23.9	3.5	265.1	119.3	145.8
Hamblen	64.3	4.6	4.6	...	59.7	31.3	28.4
Hamilton	386.9	182.1	129.9	52.2	204.8	91.8	113.0
Hancock	154.3	7.1	4.4	2.7	147.2	68.3	78.9
Hardeman	370.1	60.6	51.3	9.3	309.5	185.5	124.0
Hardin	371.3	66.8	59.2	7.6	304.5	164.6	139.9
Hawkins	318.0	36.2	34.6	1.6	281.8	100.0	181.8
Haywood	255.4	...	...	...	255.4	60.7	194.7
Henderson	341.6	53.4	53.4	..	288.2	176.0	112.2
Henry	223.8	...	...	...	223.8	115.1	108.7
Hickman	348.8	5.5	3.2	2.3	343.3	220.8	122.5
Houston	154.0	1.6	...	1.6	152.4	83.9	68.5
Humphreys	247.0	2.6	1.3	1.3	244.4	167.6	76.8
Jackson	177.3	1.4	1.4	...	175.9	73.8	102.1
Jefferson	110.6	8.5	8.5	...	102.1	46.4	55.7
Johnson	259.6	63.6	22.6	41.0	196.0	95.8	100.2
Knox	253.3	49.7	40.6	9.1	203.6	44.5	159.1
Lake	118.0	...	...	..	118.0	10.8	107.2

22

Table 13. *Sawtimber volume in Scribner rule on commercial forest land by species group and diameter class, 1971* (Continued)

County	All species	Softwood			Hardwood		
		Total	9.0-14.9 inches	15.0 inches and up	Total	11.0-14.9 inches	15.0 inches and up
				Million board feet			
Lauderdale	621.6	...	...	...	621.6	106.6	515.0
Lawrence	240.3	...	...	...	240.3	136.1	104.2
Lewis	169.1	9.1	9.1	...	160.0	122.3	37.7
Lincoln	59.5	...	...	...	59.5	39.3	20.2
Loudon	96.9	19.2	17.5	1.7	77.7	26.9	50.8
McMinn	237.2	91.1	63.2	27.9	146.1	71.7	74.4
McNairy	215.9	77.1	56.2	20.9	138.8	99.1	39.7
Macon	85.0	...	...	...	85.0	52.9	32.1
Madison	311.0	1.6	1.6	...	309.4	98.6	210.8
Marion	483.4	69.7	45.9	23.8	413.7	220.3	193.4
Marshall	82.3	1.9	1.9	...	80.4	32.6	47.8
Maury	153.2	...	...	...	153.2	77.3	75.9
Meigs	117.2	43.9	42.3	1.6	73.3	39.2	34.1
Monroe	765.9	362.2	256.5	105.7	403.7	178.9	224.8
Montgomery	131.0	...	...	...	131.0	52.5	78.5
Moore	72.9	5.2	5.2	...	67.7	25.8	41.9
Morgan	479.5	100.3	83.7	16.6	379.2	196.0	183.2
Obion	208.5	77.2	8.4	68.8	131.3	44.6	86.7
Overton	381.5	74.0	57.4	16.6	307.5	195.8	111.7
Perry	263.0	1.3	1.3	...	261.7	206.2	55.5
Pickett	114.7	2.7	2.7	...	112.0	48.2	63.8
Polk	656.1	394.9	327.4	67.5	261.2	134.5	126.7
Putnam	273.5	21.2	16.2	5.0	252.3	123.5	128.8
Rhea	195.5	38.0	27.5	10.5	157.5	80.0	77.5
Roane	158.1	27.8	25.0	2.8	130.3	63.1	67.2
Robertson	157.6	...	...	...	157.6	35.2	122.4
Rutherford	15.2	...	...	...	15.2	13.2	2.0
Scott	745.7	190.7	170.5	20.2	555.0	319.2	235.8
Sequatchie	212.9	77.0	64.5	12.5	135.9	71.5	64.4
Sevier	263.4	88.8	74.6	14.2	174.6	71.1	103.5
Shelby	154.5	3.2	3.2	...	151.3	38.8	112.5
Smith	54.3	.9	.9	...	53.4	13.2	40.2
Stewart	460.7	13.3	13.3	...	447.4	213.1	234.3
Sullivan	135.0	38.4	22.5	15.9	96.6	53.7	42.9
Sumner	157.8	2.1	..	2.1	155.7	42.3	113.4
Tipton	90.2	...	...	...	90.2	41.2	49.0
Trousdale	5.3	...	...	...	5.3	5.3	...
Unicoi	225.5	82.6	49.5	33.1	142.9	55.0	87.9
Union	154.0	21.8	18.3	3.5	132.2	44.9	87.3
Van Buren	167.7	33.9	27.7	6.2	133.8	77.1	56.7
Warren	177.5	5.6	5.6	...	171.9	76.2	95.7
Washington	158.2	53.8	30.1	23.7	104.4	33.8	70.6
Wayne	456.4	42.4	42.4	...	414.0	304.1	109.9
Weakley	328.7	23.7	17.2	6.5	305.0	83.0	222.0
White	300.9	.7	.3	.4	300.2	129.0	171.2
Williamson	192.5	3.7	1.2	2.5	188.8	87.4	101.4
Wilson	51.0	1.0	1.0	...	50.0	26.3	23.7
All counties	22,975.2	3,992.0	2,954.6	967.4	19,053.2	9,073.0	9,980.2

23

Table 14. *Sawtimber volume in Doyle rule on commercial forest land by species group, 1971*

County	All species	Softwood			Hardwood			
		Total	Southern pine	Other	Total	Oak	Gum	Other
				— Million board feet —				
Anderson	170.4	42.5	32.7	9.8	127.9	70.7	5.8	51.4
Bedford	37.8	...	...	...	37.8	17.8	...	20.0
Benton	128.3	8.1	8.1	...	120.2	94.2	10.2	15.8
Bledsoe	68.7	18.5	17.4	1.1	50.2	37.2	.5	12.5
Blount	269.1	113.7	97.7	16.0	155.4	113.0	...	42.4
Bradley	74.9	37.8	35.3	2.5	37.1	14.5	...	22.6
Campbell	488.7	105.8	103.6	2.2	382.9	196.8	21.3	164.8
Cannon	15.1	...	...	...	15.1	5.9	.7	8.5
Carroll	195.7	17.9	17.5	.4	177.8	98.5	24.2	55.1
Carter	287.8	96.1	6.5	89.6	191.7	117.3	4.3	70.1
Cheatham	162.1	...	...	...	162.1	81.1	23.9	57.1
Chester	109.5	35.1	35.1	...	74.4	40.3	7.5	26.6
Claiborne	161.9	23.0	22.5	.5	138.9	65.0	3.2	70.7
Clay	128.9	5.0	5.0	...	123.9	92.4	...	31.5
Cocke	294.7	89.5	41.5	48.0	205.2	125.9	.9	78.4
Coffee	173.4	...	...	...	173.4	121.1	1.4	50.9
Crockett	45.6	4.2	...	4.2	41.4	28.8	1.6	11.0
Cumberland	361.6	119.0	99.3	19.7	242.6	160.1	7.7	74.8
Davidson	122.4	...	...	...	122.4	78.9	...	43.5
Decatur	181.1	7.6	5.4	2.2	173.5	103.6	7.8	62.1
De Kalb	85.7	2.3	...	2.3	83.4	25.0	9.1	49.3
Dickson	267.3	...	...	...	267.3	196.4	.2	70.7
Dyer	230.4	...	...	...	230.4	99.1	21.9	109.4
Fayette	117.0	3.3	...	3.3	113.7	90.4	1.9	21.4
Fentress	358.4	143.2	120.5	22.7	215.2	122.0	10.7	82.5
Franklin	335.0	1.1	...	1.1	333.9	222.1	2.7	109.1
Gibson	80.9	...	...	...	80.9	38.2	18.1	24.6
Giles	92.1	...	...	...	92.1	53.0	6.2	32.9
Grainger	156.9	18.1	17.5	.6	138.8	73.5	3.1	62.2
Greene	210.8	34.6	23.0	11.6	176.2	100.9	1.8	73.5
Grundy	219.7	20.5	19.5	1.0	199.2	74.8	10.1	114.3
Hamblen	49.9	3.7	1.7	2.0	46.2	38.6	...	7.6
Hamilton	289.6	135.4	135.4	...	154.2	109.3	2.5	42.4
Hancock	113.4	5.5	4.7	.8	107.9	47.1	1.0	59.8
Hardeman	273.1	43.7	35.9	7.8	229.4	105.7	54.5	69.2
Hardin	273.8	49.1	47.5	1.6	224.7	125.2	19.3	80.2
Hawkins	251.6	28.2	28.2	...	223.4	155.9	.9	66.6
Haywood	199.7	...	...	...	199.7	123.2	25.6	50.9
Henderson	244.8	37.6	36.0	1.6	207.2	96.0	47.2	64.0
Henry	156.2	...	...	...	156.2	57.4	30.5	68.3
Hickman	253.5	3.9	2.5	1.4	249.6	167.2	3.9	78.5
Houston	112.9	1.1	...	1.1	111.8	73.8	2.2	35.8
Humphreys	170.9	2.0	.4	1.6	168.9	121.2	1.2	46.5
Jackson	131.7	1.4	...	1.4	130.3	28.6	...	101.7
Jefferson	85.6	7.0	5.7	1.3	78.6	45.1	2.4	31.7
Johnson	193.8	47.8	9.1	38.7	146.0	83.9	2.1	60.0
Knox	198.9	38.5	38.0	.5	160.4	91.7	5.0	63.7
Lake	93.7	...	...	...	93.7	...	...	93.7

Table 14. *Sawtimber volume in Doyle rule on commercial forest land by species group, 1971* (Continued)

County	All species	Softwood			Hardwood			
		Total	Southern pine	Other	Total	Oak	Gum	Other
		-------------			Million board feet		-------------	
Lauderdale	470.0	...	.	...	470.0	39.2	61.4	369.4
Lawrence	175.6	..	...	...	175.6	109.6	5.8	60.2
Lewis	116.8	6.8	6.8	.	110.0	90.2	..	19.8
Lincoln	36.0	...	...	...	36.0	8.6	...	27.4
Loudon	73.7	14.0	11.5	2.5	59.7	45.9	.5	13.3
McMinn	178.8	68.2	68.2	...	110.6	59.5	.5	50.6
McNairy	151.2	56.6	52.9	3.7	94.6	52.0	12.1	30.5
Macon	56.7	...	...	...	56.7	15.7	...	41.0
Madison	246.4	1.5	...	1.5	244.9	68.9	31.9	144.1
Marion	357.4	52.8	36.0	16.8	304.6	172.4	6.4	125.8
Marshall	59.8	1.6	...	1.6	58.2	18.7	..	39.5
Maury	117.1	..	,.	..	117.1	37.6	4.9	74.6
Meigs	86.7	31.7	30.5	1.2	55.0	28.0	4.7	22.3
Monroe	582.8	274.9	247.3	27.6	307.9	150.7	4.8	152.4
Montgomery	96.8	...	...	...	96.8	37.3	3.7	55.8
Moore	55.0	3.6	..	3.6	51.4	34.2	...	17.2
Morgan	353.5	70.4	48.3	22.1	283.1	157.5	8.1	117.5
Obion	158.3	57.8	2.3	55.5	100.5	15.0	18.6	66.9
Overton	271.8	52.2	51.0	1.2	219.6	84.4	3.5	131.7
Perry	183.4	1.2	.5	.7	182.2	128.7	.8	52.7
Pickett	87.1	2.5	2.0	.5	84.6	38.0	.5	46.1
Polk	483.2	284.0	234.5	49.5	199.2	137.1	5.3	56.8
Putnam	199.4	15.7	15.7	..	183.7	51.5	5.2	127.0
Rhea	144.9	28.7	21.1	7.6	116.2	75.0	12.6	28.6
Roane	116.2	19.8	18.5	1.3	96.4	57.6	6.7	32.1
Robertson	123.0	...	...	,..	123.0	77.8	5.6	39.6
Rutherford	11.0	...	...	...	11.0	4.0	...	7.0
Scott	561.9	137.5	114.1	23.4	424.4	237.9	10.3	176.2
Sequatchie	153.5	56.0	48.9	7.1	97.5	59.6	4.9	33.0
Sevier	198.9	65.1	60.9	4.2	133.8	86.0	1.8	46.0
Shelby	120.3	2.0	.	2.0	118.3	8.1	43.0	67.2
Smith	43.9	.9	...	.9	43.0	13.9	...	29.1
Stewart	345.3	10.2	...	10.2	335.1	217.6	10.4	107.1
Sullivan	98.3	29.6	8.5	21.1	68.7	45.6	...	23.1
Sumner	121.4	1.1	...	1.1	120.3	71.6	8.2	40.5
Tipton	59.8	..	..	...	59.8	2.8	...	57.0
Trousdale	3.0	...	...	...	3.0	.8	...	2.2
Unicoi	168.7	60.9	12.6	48.3	107.8	57.5	.8	49.5
Union	114.1	16.6	15.0	1.6	97.5	60.7	3.2	33.6
Van Buren	120.4	24.5	10.4	14.1	95.9	40.2	4.5	51.2
Warren	126.4	3.9	3.1	.8	122.5	47.0	4.8	70.7
Washington	119.4	38.1	5.7	32.4	81.3	61.0	2.2	18.1
Wayne	328.3	31.0	31.0	...	297.3	208.8	4.4	84.1
Weakley	267.4	18.3	5.4	12.9	249.1	143.8	65.6	39.7
White	226.1	.6	.3	.3	225.5	83.3	7.3	134.9
Williamson	145.9	2.6	..	2.6	143.3	47.4	7.8	88.1
Wilson	37.2	1.0	...	1.0	36.2	12.5	...	23.7
All counties	17,077.8	2,895.7	2,216.2	679.5	14,182.1	7,529.6	787.9	5,864.6

Table 15. *Sawtimber volume in Doyle rule on commercial forest land by species group and diameter class, 1971*

County	All species	Softwood			Hardwood		
		Total	9.0-14.9 inches	15.0 inches and up	Total	11.0-14.9 inches	15.0 inches and up
				Million board feet			
Anderson	170.4	42.5	38.0	4.5	127.9	46.8	81.1
Bedford	37.8	...	...	...	37.8	25.0	12.8
Benton	128.3	8.1	8.1	...	120.2	76.4	43.8
Bledsoe	68.7	18.5	17.8	.7	50.2	33.4	16.8
Blount	269.1	113.7	100.8	12.9	155.4	71.4	84.0
Bradley	74.9	37.8	37.8	...	37.1	15.6	21.5
Campbell	488.7	105.8	86.0	19.8	382.9	153.6	229.3
Cannon	15.1	...	...	...	15.1	9.4	5.7
Carroll	195.7	17.9	16.4	1.5	177.8	86.0	91.8
Carter	287.8	96.1	25.3	70.8	191.7	84.0	107.7
Cheatham	162.1	...	...	...	162.1	50.9	111.2
Chester	109.5	35.1	33.6	1.5	74.4	44.4	30.0
Claiborne	161.9	23.0	22.1	.9	138.9	83.0	55.9
Clay	128.9	5.0	5.0	...	123.9	75.4	48.5
Cocke	294.7	89.5	40.4	49.1	205.2	73.8	131.4
Coffee	173.4	...	...	...	173.4	64.5	108.9
Crockett	45.6	4.2	...	4.2	41.4	5.7	35.7
Cumberland	361.6	119.0	88.4	30.6	242.6	114.4	128.2
Davidson	122.4	...	...	...	122.4	51.3	71.1
Decatur	181.1	7.6	6.8	.8	173.5	101.9	71.6
De Kalb	85.7	2.3	2.3	...	83.4	28.0	55.4
Dickson	267.3	...	...	...	267.3	134.2	133.1
Dyer	230.4	...	...	...	230.4	50.0	180.4
Fayette	117.0	3.3	3.3	...	113.7	25.7	88.0
Fentress	358.4	143.2	106.7	36.5	215.2	106.6	108.6
Franklin	335.0	1.1	1.1	...	333.9	151.9	182.0
Gibson	80.9	...	...	...	80.9	33.0	47.9
Giles	92.1	...	...	...	92.1	41.3	50.8
Grainger	156.9	18.1	15.2	2.9	138.8	50.2	88.6
Greene	210.8	34.6	19.3	15.3	176.2	52.8	123.4
Grundy	219.7	20.5	18.1	2.4	199.2	79.7	119.5
Hamblen	49.9	3.7	3.7	...	46.2	22.8	23.4
Hamilton	289.6	135.4	96.1	39.3	154.2	62.2	92.0
Hancock	113.4	5.5	3.2	2.3	107.9	46.0	61.9
Hardeman	273.1	43.7	36.4	7.3	229.4	125.4	104.0
Hardin	273.8	49.1	43.3	5.8	224.7	110.7	114.0
Hawkins	251.6	28.2	27.0	1.2	223.4	68.6	154.8
Haywood	199.7	...	...	...	199.7	39.8	159.9
Henderson	244.8	37.6	37.6	...	207.2	118.3	88.9
Henry	156.2	...	...	...	156.2	74.0	82.2
Hickman	253.5	3.9	2.5	1.4	249.6	150.9	98.7
Houston	112.9	1.1	...	1.1	111.8	56.6	55.2
Humphreys	170.9	2.0	1.3	.7	168.9	107.5	61.4
Jackson	131.7	1.4	1.4	...	130.3	57.9	82.4
Jefferson	85.6	7.0	7.0	...	78.6	32.0	46.6
Johnson	193.8	47.8	15.2	32.6	146.0	63.8	82.2
Knox	198.9	38.5	31.2	7.3	160.4	29.5	130.9
Lake	93.7	...	...	...	93.7	6.5	87.2

26

County	All species	Softwood			Hardwood		
		Total	9.0-14.9 inches	15.0 inches and up	Total	11.0-14.9 inches	15.0 inches and up
				Million board feet			
Lauderdale	470.0	...	...	...	470.0	71.8	398.2
Lawrence	175.6	...	...	...	175.6	89.3	86.3
Lewis	116.8	6.8	6.8	...	110.0	80.9	29.1
Lincoln	36.0	...	...	...	36.0	21.7	14.3
Loudon	73.7	14.0	12.7	1.3	59.7	17.4	42.3
McMinn	178.8	68.2	46.9	21.3	110.6	49.4	61.2
McNairy	151.2	56.6	40.5	16.1	94.6	62.1	32.5
Macon	56.7	...	...	...	56.7	32.2	24.5
Madison	246.4	1.5	1.5	...	244.9	67.2	177.7
Marion	357.4	52.8	34.0	18.8	304.6	149.9	154.7
Marshall	59.8	1.6	1.6	...	58.2	20.6	37.6
Maury	117.1	...	...	...	117.1	63.6	63.5
Meigs	86.7	31.7	30.6	1.1	55.0	27.1	27.9
Monroe	582.8	274.9	189.7	85.2	307.9	122.0	185.9
Montgomery	96.8	...	...	...	96.8	34.1	62.7
Moore	55.0	3.6	3.6	...	51.4	18.3	33.1
Morgan	353.5	70.4	57.4	13.0	283.1	133.6	149.5
Obion	158.3	57.8	5.9	51.9	100.5	29.7	70.8
Overton	271.8	52.2	39.5	12.7	219.6	132.1	87.5
Perry	183.4	1.2	1.2	...	182.2	136.8	45.4
Pickett	87.1	2.5	2.5	...	84.6	31.5	53.1
Polk	483.2	284.0	232.8	51.2	199.2	92.6	106.6
Putnam	199.4	15.7	11.8	3.9	183.7	79.5	104.2
Rhea	144.9	28.7	20.5	8.2	116.2	52.2	64.0
Roane	116.2	19.8	17.7	2.1	96.4	41.6	54.8
Robertson	123.0	...	...	...	123.0	23.6	99.4
Rutherford	11.0	...	...	...	11.0	9.2	1.8
Scott	561.9	137.5	122.5	15.0	424.4	228.6	195.8
Sequatchie	153.5	56.0	46.7	9.3	97.5	45.9	51.6
Sevier	198.9	65.1	54.2	10.9	133.8	47.3	86.5
Shelby	120.3	2.0	2.0	...	118.3	24.9	93.4
Smith	43.9	.9	.9	...	43.0	8.7	34.3
Stewart	345.3	10.2	10.2	...	335.1	144.1	191.0
Sullivan	98.3	29.6	16.3	13.3	68.7	34.3	34.4
Sumner	121.4	1.1	...	1.1	120.3	27.5	92.8
Tipton	59.8	...	...	...	59.8	27.0	32.8
Trousdale	3.0	...	...	...	3.0	3.0	...
Unicoi	168.7	60.9	35.6	25.3	107.8	35.7	72.1
Union	114.1	16.6	14.0	2.6	97.5	27.2	70.3
Van Buren	120.4	24.5	20.1	4.4	95.9	51.1	44.8
Warren	126.4	3.9	3.9	...	122.5	51.0	71.5
Washington	119.4	38.1	20.1	18.0	81.3	22.8	58.5
Wayne	328.3	31.0	31.0	...	297.3	207.1	90.2
Weakley	267.4	18.3	13.7	4.6	249.1	56.7	192.4
White	226.1	.6	.3	.3	225.5	85.4	140.1
Williamson	145.9	2.6	1.0	1.6	143.3	59.3	84.0
Wilson	37.2	1.0	1.0	...	36.2	16.5	19.7
All counties	17,077.8	2,895.7	2,149.1	746.6	14,182.1	6,066.9	8,115.2

Table 16. *Growing-stock volume of softwoods on commercial forest land by forest type, 1971*

County	Total	White pine	Loblolly-shortleaf pine	Oak-pine	Cedar	Oak-hickory	Oak-gum-cypress	Elm-ash-cottonwood	Maple-beech-birch
					Million cubic feet				
Anderson	23.3	...	5.9	10.9	1.7	4.8	..	...	...
Bedford	.8	...	...	...	.8	...	...	...	...
Benton	5.8	...	3.7	2.1	..	...	...	...	...
Bledsoe	15.6	...	10.7	1.7		3.2	...	...	...
Blount	65.4	9.6	13.2	28.4	...	14.2	...	...	...
Bradley	64.9	...	58.1	.	...	6.8	...	...	...
Campbell	62.2	...	50.8	8.2	...	3.2	...	...	...
Cannon	1.3	...	...	.8	...	.5	...	...	...
Carroll	14.1	...	6.2	5.5	.4	2.0	...	...	...
Carter	37.2	11.4	7.6	7.9	...	9.7	...	...	0.6
Cheatham	1.5	...	...	.	1.5	...	...	...	...
Chester	19.9	...	8.1	10.9	...	.9	...	...	...
Claiborne	17.8	...	5.6	3.9	.2	8.1	...	...	...
Clay	1.8	...	...	.	...	1.8	...	...	...
Cocke	39.1	...	3.1	23.9	...	12.1	...	...	...
Coffee	...	...	...	...	..	...	..	...	...
Crockett	1.1	...	.	...	...	...	1.1	...	...
Cumberland	66.3	...	18.2	37.5	...	10.6	...	...	...
Davidson	...	...	...	...	...	...	...	...	...
Decatur	10.4	...	7.5	1.2	.5	1.2	...	...	...
De Kalb	5.4	...	..	.	5.3	.1	...	...	...
Dickson	.2	...	..	.	...	.2	...	...	...
Dyer	...	...	...	...	...	...	...	...	..
Fayette	3.0	...	.2	...	.	2.8	..	...	..
Fentress	75.9	...	34.5	26.8	..	12.5	..	...	2.1
Franklin	4.4	...	...	...	1.5	2.5	...	...	.4
Gibson	..	...	...	...	...	...	...	...	...
Giles	1.2	...	...	...	...	1.2	...	...	...
Grainger	12.0	...	...	...	3.3	8.7	...	...	...
Greene	18.2	...	1.5	7.1	1.4	8.2	...	...	...
Grundy	14.8	...	2.5	9.2	...	3.1	...	...	...
Hamblen	6.6	...	4.5	...	.6	1.5	...	...	...
Hamilton	66.1	...	38.9	19.9	...	7.3	...	...	...
Hancock	2.4	...	...	...	...	2.4	...	...	...
Hardeman	27.3	..	21.6	...	...	3.1	2.6	...	...
Hardin	38.4	...	19.1	12.8	..	6.0	.5	...	...
Hawkins	26.8	...	12.9	7.2	1.8	4.9	...	...	...
Haywood	...	...	...	...	...	...	...	...	...
Henderson	26.6	...	22.7	1.4	1.5	1.0	...	...	...
Henry	...	...	...	..	...	...	..	...	...
Hickman	3.0	...	2.8	...	...	.2	..	...	...
Houston	.6	...	...	..	.6	...	...	...	...
Humphreys	1.6	...	...	...	.9	.7	..	...	..
Jackson	5.8	...	...	.	5.1	.7	...	...	...
Jefferson	5.8	...	3.6	.6	1.4	.2	...	...	...
Johnson	19.1	...	...	8.8	...	10.3	...	...	..
Knox	29.4	...	13.5	8.5	2.6	4.8	...	...	...
Lake	...	...	..	...	...	...	...	...	...

28

Table 16. *Growing-stock volume of softwoods on commercial forest land by forest type, 1971*
(Continued)

County	Total	White pine	Loblolly-shortleaf pine	Oak-pine	Cedar	Oak-hickory	Oak-gum-cypress	Elm-ash-cottonwood	Maple-beech-birch
					Million cubic feet				
Lauderdale	...	...	...	...	...	...	...	...	...
Lawrence	...	...	...	...	...	...	...	...	...
Lewis	3.5	...	...	3.0	...	.5	...	...	...
Lincoln	4.3	...	...	...	3.6	.7	...	...	...
Loudon	15.9	...	11.4	2.9	.7	.9	...	...	...
McMinn	53.7	...	30.2	15.2	1.6	6.7	...	...	...
McNairy	31.7	...	22.3	7.1	...	1.3	1.0	...	...
Macon	...	...	...	...	...	...	...	...	...
Madison	1.2	...	...	...	1.2	...	...	...	...
Marion	24.9	...	...	18.8	...	6.1	...	...	...
Marshall	2.3	...	...	...	1.8	.5	...	...	...
Maury	...	...	...	...	...	...	...	...	...
Meigs	30.3	...	12.5	12.2	...	5.6	...	...	...
Monroe	153.6	2.6	99.2	28.4	.2	23.2	...	...	...
Montgomery	1.7	...	...	...	.2	1.5	...	...	...
Moore	1.9	...	...	...	...	1.9	...	...	...
Morgan	37.7	...	.3	17.0	...	20.4	...	...	...
Obion	17.3	...	...	...	...	...	17.3	...	...
Overton	20.7	...	12.7	5.8	...	2.2	...	...	...
Perry	1.7	...	...	...	1.1	.6	...	...	...
Pickett	4.6	...	.3	3.2	...	1.1	...	...	...
Polk	160.8	...	110.2	44.6	...	6.0	...	...	...
Putnam	8.5	...	...	2.4	.8	5.3	...	...	...
Rhea	16.4	...	4.7	7.2	...	4.5	...	...	...
Raone	23.4	...	11.9	3.9	1.3	6.3	...	...	...
Robertson	...	...	...	...	...	...	...	...	...
Rutherford	5.6	...	...	...	5.6	...	...	...	...
Scott	78.6	4.0	38.6	11.8	.	23.7	...	...	.5
Sequatchie	28.8	...	7.5	16.2	...	5.1	...	...	...
Sevier	48.3	...	17.7	22.4	...	8.2	...	...	...
Shelby	1.0	...	...	...	...	...	1.0	...	...
Smith	2.3	...	...	...	1.9	.4	...	...	...
Stewart	4.0	...	...	...	4.0	...	...	...	...
Sullivan	17.2	8.0	2.3	.4	...	5.3	...	...	1.2
Sumner	1.2	...	...	...	.6	.6	...	...	...
Tipton	...	...	...	...	...	...	...	...	...
Trousdale	.4	...	...	...	...	.4	...	...	...
Unicoi	26.1	6.4	...	17.0	...	2.7	...	...	...
Union	22.4	...	10.4	8.5	1.8	1.7	...	...	...
Van Buren	16.6	...	2.8	9.0	...	4.8	...	...	...
Warren	6.0	...	3.6	...	.9	1.5	...	...	...
Washington	20.6	...	...	15.5	...	5.1	...	...	...
Wayne	39.0	...	16.3	14.7	1.2	6 ?	...	...	...
Weakley	12.3	...	6.2	...	...	...	6.1	...	...
White	1.9	...	.1	...	.6	1.2	...	...	...
Williamson	4.8	...	...	...	4.1	.7	...	...	...
Wilson	3.5	...	...	...	1.1	2.4	...	...	...
All counties	1,799.8	42.0	798.2	532.4	65.4	327.4	29.6	...	4.8

Table 17. *Growing-stock volume of hardwoods on commercial forest land by forest type, 1971*

County	Total	White pine	Loblolly-shortleaf pine	Oak-pine	Cedar	Oak-hickory	Oak-gum-cypress	Elm-ash-cottonwood	Maple-beech-birch
					Million cubic feet				
Anderson	80.1	...	...	7.1	0.5	72.5	...	...	...
Bedford	31.4	..	...	...	2.6	21.6	7.2	...	...
Benton	115.7	...	...	1.9	.9	106.5	6.4	...	...
Bledsoe	54.3	...	.6	3.4	...	50.3	...	...	...
Blount	77.6	4.7	...	20.6	...	52.3	...	..	...
Bradley	35.3	...	6.3	..	...	29.0	...	..	...
Campbell	184.2	...	8.5	4.2	...	171.5	...	...	...
Cannon	27.0	...	...	3.1	.6	23.3	...	...	...
Carroll	117.0	..	.1	1.6	1.3	75.0	34.1	4.9	...
Carter	130.9	4.0	3.5	8.5	...	104.0	...	...	10.9
Cheatham	82.6	...	...	...	5.1	77.5	...	...	...
Chester	55.9	...	.8	6.7	...	33.9	14.5	...	...
Claiborne	94.3	..	.2	..	2.1	82.8	...	...	9.2
Clay	67.5	...	..	...	.9	66.6	...	...	...
Cocke	130.1	...	.8	12.1	...	113.0	...	...	4.2
Coffee	98.0	...	...	...	...	90.3	7.7	...	...
Crockett	15.4	...	...	...	...	...	15.4	...	...
Cumberland	181.0	...	3.5	36.3	...	141.2	...	...	...
Davidson	66.5	...	...	...	.8	65.7	...	...	...
Decatur	116.4	...	.2	1.9	1.0	113.3	...	...	...
De Kalb	47.9	...	...	...	2.4	32.7	12.8	...	...
Dickson	168.4	...	...	...	...	168.4	...	...	...
Dyer	86.4	...	...	...	...	24.9	46.2	15.3	...
Fayette	55.9	...	...	...	...	32.6	23.3	...	...
Fentress	123.4	...	6.8	14.7	...	99.8	...	...	2.1
Franklin	168.3	...	...	...	1.6	160.8	...	...	5.9
Gibson	49.4	...	...	...	...	31.0	18.4	...	...
Giles	68.6	...	...	.3	...	66.0	2.3	...	...
Grainger	72.5	...	...	...	7.3	65.2	...	...	...
Greene	81.9	...	.3	2.8	..	78.8	...	...	...
Grundy	112.7	...	2.2	4.3	...	106.2	...	...	...
Hamblen	25.0	...	.3	...	3.5	21.2	...	...	...
Hamilton	84.0	...	4.8	13.0	...	66.2	...	...	...
Hancock	59.5	...	...	...	...	59.5	...	...	...
Hardeman	154.5	...	4.7	...	...	108.6	37.1	4.1	...
Hardin	146.2	...	4.5	14.9	...	79.5	47.3	...	...
Hawkins	117.6	...	2.0	3.7	2.8	109.1	...	...	...
Haywood	88.9	...	...	...	...	16.8	65.0	7.1	...
Henderson	124.5	...	.9	.9	3.9	108.7	10.1	...	...
Henry	110.7	...	...	...	...	47.8	62.9	...	...
Hickman	201.1	...	...	...	...	201.1	...	...	...
Houston	79.8	...	...	...	...	79.8	...	...	...
Humphreys	166.6	...	...	...	5.1	161.5	...	...	...
Jackson	65.7	...	...	...	6.3	59.4	...	...	...
Jefferson	34.2	...	1.9	...	1.9	30.4	...	...	...
Johnson	104.3	...	...	6.0	...	91.6	...	...	6.7
Knox	62.5	...	5.0	9.8	.8	46.9	...	...	...
Lake	31.0	...	...	...	...	...	6.0	25.0	...

Table 17. *Growing-stock volume of hardwoods on commercial forest land by forest type, 1971*
(Continued)

County	Total	White pine	Loblolly-shortleaf pine	Oak-pine	Cedar	Oak-hickory	Oak-gum-cypress	Elm-ash-cottonwood	Maple-beech-birch
						— Million cubic feet —			
Lauderdale	173.0	...	...	...	...	11.6	111.7	49.7	...
Lawrence	123.9	...	...	...	...	117.6	...	6.3	...
Lewis	110.7	...	...	2.2	...	108.5	.	...	...
Lincoln	41.1	...	...	...	18.7	22.2	.2	..	...
Loudon	27.1	...	.8	2.1	.1	24.1	.	...	...
McMinn	66.3	...	6.2	10.1	...	50.0	...	...	...
McNairy	86.9	...	3.7	6.8	...	59.8	16.6	...	...
Macon	57.1	...	...	...	...	57.1	...	...	...
Madison	104.5	...	...	...	.4	76.2	17.5	10.4	...
Marion	162.4	...	...	20.1	..	135.0	...	1.6	5.7
Marshall	30.8	...	...	...	7.0	23.8	.	...	...
Maury	67.5	...	...	...	.2	57.2	10.1	...	..
Meigs	33.7	...	...	9.8	..	23.9	...	...	...
Monroe	167.0	.3	16.4	19.2	1.2	96.5	...	...	33.4
Montgomery	67.6	...	...	...	3.1	50.9	13.6	...	...
Moore	29.8	...	...	...	..	29.8	..	...	...
Morgan	170.0	...	...	20.8	...	149.2	...	...	...
Obion	49.3	...	...	...	...	22.0	21.4	5.9	...
Overton	155.3	...	1.5	7.4	...	146.4	...	...	...
Perry	172.7	...	...	...	3.7	164.8	4.2	...	...
Pickett	48.0	...	1.8	2.0	...	44.2	...	...	...
Polk	113.2	...	28.7	48.8	...	35.7	...	...	...
Putnam	125.8	...	...	1.8	1.8	110.8	...	...	11.4
Rhea	76.9	...	.4	12.5	..	64.0	...	...	...
Roane	66.5	...	1.0	3.6	2.5	59.4	...	...	...
Robertson	55.0	...	...	...	..	55.0	...	...	...
Rutherford	25.6	...	...	...	8.0	17.6	...	...	...
Scott	242.5	3.8	6.3	11.5	...	207.7	...	...	13.2
Sequatchie	62.3	...	1.1	9.4	...	51.8	...	...	...
Sevier	79.2	...	8.6	18.4	.	52.2	...	...	...
Shelby	58.6	...	...	..	...	23.9	20.5	14.2	...
Smith	37.3	...	...	...	6.6	30.7	...	...	...
Stewart	201.2	...	...	..	2.6	198.6	...	...	...
Sullivan	55.0	1.6	.4	1.4	.1	48.7	...	...	2.8
Sumner	51.5	...	...	..	...	51.5	...	...	...
Tipton	36.0	...	...	...	...	36.0	...	..	...
Trousdale	5.5	...	...	..	...	5.5	...	...	...
Unicoi	65.1	.6	...	10.4	..	48.1	...	...	6.0
Union	54.7	...	2.0	10.4	.9	41.4	...	...	...
Van Buren	56.4	...	.8	6.3	...	49.3	...	...	...
Warren	87.5	...	...	...	2.0	85.5	...	...	...
Washington	48.6	...	...	13.0	...	35.6	...	...	...
Wayne	276.1	...	.7	9.7	3.8	256.8	...	5.1	...
Weakley	86.4	...	1.9	.	..	10.5	74.0	...	...
White	122.0	...	.4	.	.5	121.0	...	.1	...
Williamson	80.7	...	...	2.9	4.1	67.1	...	6.6	...
Wilson	29.0	...	...	...	1.3	27.7	...	...	...
All counties	8,596.0	15.0	140.6	438.4	120.0	6,907.7	706.5	156.3	111.5

Table 18. *Sawtimber volume of softwoods on commercial forest land by forest type, 1971*

County	Total	White pine	Loblolly-shortleaf pine	Oak-pine	Cedar	Oak-hickory	Oak-gum-cypress	Elm-ash-cottonwood	Maple-beech-birch
					Million board feet				
Anderson	73.5	...	19.7	37.2	1.2	15.4	...	...	...
Bedford	...	...	...	.	...	...	...	...	...
Benton	13.8	...	13.8	...	..	...	...	...	...
Bledsoe	34.6	...	22.7	3.3	..	8.6	...	...	...
Blount	187.0	30.6	14.7	88.7	...	53.0	...	...	...
Bradley	63.3	...	49.3	...	...	14.0	...	...	...
Campbell	169.4	...	122.6	34.2	...	12.6	...	...	...
Cannon	...	...	...	.	...	...	...	...	...
Carroll	29.7	...	3.1	26.6	..	...	...	..	...
Carter	143.0	58.3	11.7	32.5	...	37.7	...	...	2.8
Cheatham	...	...	...	...	...	...	...	...	...
Chester	58.8	...	19.5	39.3	...	...	...	...	...
Claiborne	38.0	...	3.0	6.9	.7	27.4	...	...	...
Clay	7.0	...	...	...	...	7.0	...	...	...
Cocke	141.3	...	9.0	87.9	...	44.4	...	...	...
Coffee	...	...	...	.	...	...	...	...	...
Crockett	5.6	...	...	.	...	...	5.6	...	...
Cumberland	203.4	...	51.5	113.5	...	38.4	...	...	...
Davidson	...	...	...	...	...	...	...	...	...
Decatur	11.4	...	3.3	5.4	.9	1.8	...	...	...
De Kalb	1.5	...	...	...	1.5	...	...	...	...
Dickson	...	...	...	...	...	...	...	...	...
Dyer	...	...	...	...	...	...	...	...	...
Fayette	4.6	...	...	.	...	4.6	...	...	...
Fentress	225.8	...	114.6	66.1	...	34.6	..	...	10.5
Franklin	1.4	...	...	...	...	1.4	...	...	...
Gibson	...	...	...	.	...	...	...	...	...
Giles	...	...	...	...	...	...	...	...	...
Grainger	30.1	...	...	...	5.0	25.1	...	...	...
Greene	52.6	...	...	13.6	.5	38.5	...	...	...
Grundy	33.3	...	1.3	20.4	...	11.6	...	...	...
Hamblen	5.3	...	2.4	...	.4	2.5	...	...	...
Hamilton	217.7	...	155.4	37.5	...	24.8	...	...	...
Hancock	8.9	...	...	...	...	8.9	...	...	...
Hardeman	73.2	...	57.4	...	...	5.1	10.7	...	...
Hardin	81.8	...	48.8	21.5	...	11.5	...	...	...
Hawkins	43.0	...	9.5	17.7	2.5	13.3	...	...	...
Haywood	...	...	...	.	.	...	...	...	...
Henderson	66.2	...	63.3	1.2	1.7	...	...	...	...
Henry	...	...	...	...	...	...	...	...	...
Hickman	6.7	...	6.7	...	...	...	...	...	...
Houston	1.8	...	...	...	1.8	...	...	...	...
Humphreys	3.1	...	...	...	2.0	1.1	...	...	...
Jackson	1.1	...	...	.	1.1	...	...	...	...
Jefferson	10.4	...	7.9	.6	1.9	...	...	...	...
Johnson	73.4	...	...	37.6	...	35.8	...	...	...
Knox	59.2	...	19.1	29.5	5.0	5.6	...	...	...
Lake	...	...	...	...	...	...	...	...	...

Table 18. *Sawtimber volume of softwoods on commercial forest land by forest type, 1971* (Continued)

County	Total	White pine	Loblolly-shortleaf pine	Oak-pine	Cedar	Oak-hickory	Oak-gum-cypress	Elm-ash-cottonwood	Maple-beech-birch
				— Million board feet —					
Lauderdale	...	...	...	...	...	...	...	...	...
Lawrence	...	...	...	...	...	...	...	...	...
Lewis	11.5	...	...	9.2	...	2.3	...	...	...
Lincoln	...	...	...	...	...	...	...	...	...
Loudon	23.2	...	11.9	9.0	1.6	.7	...	...	...
McMinn	110.2	...	40.9	44.5	1.2	23.6	...	...	...
McNairy	94.1	...	72.7	13.9	...	2.3	5.2	...	...
Macon	...	...	...	...	...	...	...	...	...
Madison	2.0	...	...	...	2.0	...	...	...	...
Marion	83.8	...	...	65.9	...	17.9	...	...	...
Marshall	2.7	...	...	...	2.7	...	...	...	...
Maury	...	...	...	...	...	...	...	...	...
Meigs	53.5	...	3.3	27.5	...	22.7	...	...	...
Monroe	429.2	3.0	264.8	82.1	...	79.3	...	...	...
Montgomery	...	...	...	...	...	...	...	...	...
Moore	6.4	...	...	...	...	6.4	...	...	...
Morgan	122.0	..	.8	59.3	...	61.9	..	...	...
Obion	87.0	...	...	...	...	...	87.0	...	...
Overton	88.8	...	56.8	29.0	...	3.0	..	...	...
Perry	2.0	...	...	...	2.0	...	...	...	...
Pickett	3.1	...	2.6	...	...	.5	...	...	...
Polk	471.0	...	295.7	147.8	..	27.5	...	...	..
Putnam	25.1	...	...	8.1	...	17.0	...	..	...
Rhea	44.8	...	2.2	25.5	...	17.1	...	..	...
Roane	35.0	...	15.0	4.9	.8	14.3	...	...	..
Robertson	...	...	...	...	...	...	...	...	...
Rutherford	...	...	...	...	...	...	...	...	...
Scott	230.7	10.0	127.4	19.8	...	70.1	...	...	3.4
Sequatchie	92.8	...	24.9	52.3	...	15.6	...	...	...
Sevier	106.9	..	33.3	51.1	..	22.5	...	...	...
Shelby	4.0	...	...	...	...	...	4.0	...	...
Smith	.5	...	...	...	.5	...	...	...	...
Stewart	17.0	...	.	...	17.0	...	...	...	..
Sullivan	46.1	27.2	4.8	.5	...	11.9	...	...	1.7
Sumner	2.6	...	...	...	...	2.6	...	...	...
Tipton	...	...	...	...	..	...	..	...	...
Trousdale	...	...	...	...	...	...	...	...	...
Unicoi	98.6	24.7	...	65.7	...	8.2	...	...	...
Union	27.3	...	13.0	7.9	2.4	4.0	...	...	...
Van Buren	41.3	...	11.0	27.4	...	2.9	...	...	...
Warren	7.1	...	5.3	...	...	1.8	...	...	...
Washington	64.4	...	...	48.5	...	15.9	...	...	...
Wayne	52.4	...	18.7	19.8	...	13.9	...	...	...
Weakley	24.9	..	3.3	...	...	...	21.6	...	...
White	.8	...	..	...	.5	.3	...	..	...
Williamson	4.8	...	...	...	1.7	3.1	..	...	...
Wilson	.6	...	..	...	.6	...	...	...	...
All counties	4,699.1	153.8	1,836.1	1,543.5	59.2	954.0	134.1	...	18.4

33

Table 19. *Sawtimber volume of hardwoods on commercial forest land by forest type, 1971*

County	Total	White pine	Loblolly-shortleaf pine	Oak-pine	Cedar	Oak-hickory	Oak-gum-cypress	Elm-ash-cottonwood	Maple-beech-birch
						Million board feet			
Anderson	200.3	...	...	24.4	...	175.9	...	...	...
Bedford	64.3	...	...	...	3.7	32.1	28.5	...	...
Benton	205.6	...	...	.6	...	197.3	7.7	...	...
Bledsoe	91.3	...	1.1	.9	...	89.3	...	...	...
Blount	228.1	12.6	...	74.4	...	141.1	...	...	...
Bradley	63.2	...	2.7	...	...	60.5	...	...	...
Campbell	547.5	...	17.9	11.5	...	518.1	...	...	...
Cannon	31.3	...	...	2.1	...	29.2	...	...	...
Carroll	280.7	...	...	3.4	1.8	187.8	78.1	9.6	...
Carter	296.0	11.7	...	18.3	...	252.4	...	...	13.6
Cheatham	243.6	...	...	...	17.6	226.0	...	...	...
Chester	119.6	...	2.0	10.5	...	78.2	28.9	...	...
Claiborne	226.6	...	...	...	5.1	194.0	...	...	27.5
Clay	183.3	...	...	...	4.7	178.6	...	...	...
Cocke	306.4	...	3.4	24.8	...	269.5	...	...	8.7
Coffee	263.0	...	...	...	...	235.7	27.3	...	...
Crockett	54.4	...	...	...	...	...	54.4	...	...
Cumberland	392.5	...	3.9	80.2	...	308.4	...	...	...
Davidson	184.3	...	...	...	...	184.3	...	...	...
Decatur	285.4	...	...	3.1	1.5	280.8	...	...	...
De Kalb	127.7	...	...	...	...	85.3	42.4	...	...
Dickson	415.2	...	...	...	...	415.2	...	...	...
Dyer	343.7	...	...	...	...	61.8	211.9	70.0	...
Fayette	159.1	...	...	...	...	85.9	73.2	...	...
Fentress	314.4	...	16.1	26.3	...	265.3	...	...	6.7
Franklin	508.3	...	...	...	2.5	484.8	...	...	21.0
Gibson	129.4	...	...	...	...	71.7	57.7	...	...
Giles	142.4	...	...	...	...	137.3	5.1	...	...
Grainger	203.1	...	...	...	14.4	188.7	...	...	...
Greene	255.2	...	1.3	5.7	...	248.2	...	...	...
Grundy	300.3	...	1.3	13.0	...	286.0	...	...	...
Hamblen	66.9	...	...	...	15.1	51.8	...	...	...
Hamilton	233.1	...	7.5	30.1	...	195.5	...	...	...
Hancock	167.0	...	...	...	...	167.0	...	...	...
Hardeman	352.7	...	9.9	...	...	216.8	113.2	12.8	...
Hardin	347.5	...	6.1	27.9	...	186.9	126.6	...	...
Hawkins	314.0	...	.9	1.5	6.3	305.3	...	...	...
Haywood	286.7	...	...	...	...	38.8	229.3	18.6	...
Henderson	331.0	...	2.6	...	14.0	298.2	16.2	...	...
Henry	259.1	...	...	...	...	108.1	151.0	...	...
Hickman	392.7	...	...	...	...	392.7	...	...	...
Houston	174.6	...	...	...	...	174.6	...	...	...
Humphreys	283.5	...	...	...	2.7	280.8	...	...	...
Jackson	200.0	...	...	...	10.0	190.0	...	...	...
Jefferson	114.6	...	3.5	...	2.4	108.7	...	...	...
Johnson	222.1	...	...	17.0	...	181.8	...	...	23.3
Knox	227.8	...	12.2	40.1	2.1	173.4	...	...	...
Lake	132.0	...	...	...	...	...	18.1	113.9	...

Table 19. *Sawtimber volume of hardwoods on commercial forest land by forest type, 1971* (Continued)

County	Total	White pine	Loblolly-shortleaf pine	Oak-pine	Cedar	Oak-hickory	Oak-gum-cypress	Elm-ash-cottonwood	Maple-beech-birch
				— — — Million board feet — — —					
Lauderdale	700.0	...	...	..	...	27.6	425.0	247.4	..
Lawrence	274.3	...	...	...	...	265.3	...	9.0	..
Lewis	185.8	...	...	1.3	...	184.5	..	..	..
Lincoln	72.2	...	...	.	33.6	38.6	..	..	..
Loudon	87.7	...	1.2	3.3	..	83.2	..	..	..
McMinn	164.9	...	13.0	22.8	...	129.1	...	..	...
McNairy	161.2	...	2.1	13.2	...	115.9	30.0	...	...
Macon	99.5	...	...	.	...	99.5	...	...	...
Madison	346.0	...	...	...	...	275.4	67.3	3.3	...
Marion	470.0	...	...	64.6	...	379.7	...	4.4	21.3
Marshall	91.9	...	...	...	22.1	69.8	...	..	..
Maury	173.1	...	...	...	...	134.2	38.9	...	...
Meigs	82.7	...	...	8.4	...	74.3	..	...	...
Monroe	456.3	.8	37.3	39.1	...	236.5	...	...	142.6
Montgomery	149.6	...	...	...	5.3	111.8	32.5	...	..
Moore	76.4	...	...	.	...	76.4	...	...	..
Morgan	430.8	...	...	40.3	...	390.5	...	...	..
Obion	147.3	...	...	...	...	82.0	50.3	15.0	...
Overton	352.9	...	3.1	6.5	...	343.3	...	...	...
Perry	302.7	...	...	...	.7	290.9	11.1	...	...
Pickett	126.3	...	7.6	5.3	...	113.4	..	...	...
Polk	293.5	...	74.0	124.5	...	95.0	..	...	...
Putnam	288.1	...	...	4.8	...	243.4	...	...	39.9
Rhea	179.9	...	1.5	27.6	...	150.8	...	...	...
Roane	148.1	...	3.4	10.0	6.2	128.5	...	...	...
Robertson	176.7	...	...	...	...	176.7	...	...	...
Rutherford	17.9	...	...	...	8.9	9.0	...	...	...
Scott	624.2	11.2	16.9	23.6	...	546.6	...	...	25.9
Sequatchie	154.7	...	2.8	16.2	...	135.7	..	...	..
Sevier	196.5	...	22.5	27.1	...	146.9	...	...	...
Shelby	169.7	...	...	...	...	62.1	71.7	35.9	...
Smith	59.9	...	...	...	5.8	54.1	...	...	...
Stewart	509.3	...	...	...	10.8	498.5	...	...	...
Sullivan	110.2	4.1	...	3.1	...	99.9	...	...	3.1
Sumner	174.7	...	...	...	...	74.7	...	...	...
Tipton	105.7	...	...	...	...	105.7	...	...	...
Trousdale	7.4	...	...	...	...	7.4	...	...	...
Unicoi	161.2	...	...	29.3	...	128.3	...	...	3.6
Union	151.3	...	4.9	19.6	1.9	124.9	...	...	...
Van Buren	153.9	...	2.3	15.5	...	136.1	...	...	...
Warren	198.6	...	...	...	3.3	195.3	...	...	...
Washington	117.2	...	...	38.3	...	78.9	...	...	...
Wayne	472.9	...	...	18.1	10.2	431.8	..	12.8	...
Weakley	337.0	...	...	...	..	38.6	298.4	...	...
White	339.7	...	...	...	...	339.7	...	...	...
Williamson	212.6	...	...	6.2	6.2	175.9	...	24.3	...
Wilson	57.1	...	...	...	...	57.1	...	...	...
All counties	21,641.1	40.4	285.0	984.5	218.9	16,903.3	2,294.8	577.0	337.2

Table 20. *Growing-stock volume of softwoods on commercial forest land by stand-size class, 1971*

County	Total	Saw-timber	Pole-timber	Sapling and seedling	Non-stocked areas	County	Total	Saw-timber	Pole-timber	Sapling and seedling	Non-stocked areas
	– – – – – Million cubic feet – – – – –						– – – – – Million cubic feet – – – – –				
Anderson	23.3	10.7	2.5	10.1	...	Lauderdale	...	...	...	...	...
						Lawrence	...	...	...	...	...
Bedford	.8	...	...	.8	...	Lewis	3.5	...	3.5	...	...
Benton	5.8	...	2.1	3.7	...	Lincoln	4.3	...	2.4	1.9	...
Bledsoe	15.6	1.6	9.1	4.9	...	Loudon	15.9	3.3	10.6	2.0	...
Blount	65.4	29.9	23.0	12.5	...						
Bradley	64.9	...	56.5	8.4	...	McMinn	53.7	15.4	22.6	15.7	...
						McNairy	31.7	11.4	16.0	4.3	...
Campbell	62.2	26.0	36.2	...	...	Macon	...	...	...	...	...
Cannon	1.3	...	1.0	.3	...	Madison	1.2	...	...	1.2	...
Carroll	14.1	5.9	8.2	...	...	Marion	24.9	16.0	4.8	4.1	...
Carter	37.2	28.5	8.1	.6	...	Marshall	2.3	...	.5	1.8	...
Cheatham	1.5	...	...	1.5	...	Maury	...	...	...	...	...
Chester	19.9	11.4	7.9	.6	...	Meigs	30.3	1.4	24.1	4.8	...
Claiborne	17.8	6.1	7.4	4.3	...	Monroe	153.6	66.7	58.7	28.2	...
Clay	1.8	1.3	.5	...	...	Montgomery	1.7	1.5	...	.2	...
Cocke	39.1	18.8	13.3	7.0	...	Moore	1.9	1.9	...	...	...
Coffee	...	...	...	...	...	Morgan	37.7	19.9	12.8	5.0	...
Crockett	1.1	1.1	...	...	...						
Cumberland	66.3	31.2	26.8	8.3	...	Obion	17.3	17.3	...	...	...
						Overton	20.7	12.9	7.8	...	...
Davidson	...	...	...	...	...						
Decatur	10.4	.7	8.0	1.7	...	Perry	1.7	...	1.3	.4	...
De Kalb	5.4	...	2.5	2.9	...	Pickett	4.6	.2	4.1	.3	...
Dickson	.2	...	...	.2	...	Polk	160.8	97.8	57.5	5.5	...
Dyer	...	...	...	...	...	Putnam	8.5	5.4	3.0	.1	...
Fayette	3.0	...	1.9	1.1	...	Rhea	16.4	2.9	5.5	8.0	...
Fentress	75.9	33.1	25.8	17.0	...	Roane	23.4	5.0	11.4	7.0	...
Franklin	4.4	1.3	2.5	.6	...	Robertson	...	...	...	...	...
						Rutherford	5.6	...	3.0	2.6	...
Gibson	...	...	...	...	...						
Giles	1.2	...	1.2	...	...	Scott	78.6	38.3	25.6	14.7	...
Grainger	12.0	3.6	4.6	3.8	...	Sequatchie	28.8	10.1	9.3	9.4	...
Greene	18.2	6.6	4.0	7.6	...	Sevier	48.3	18.6	18.9	10.8	...
Grundy	14.8	4.9	3.8	6.1	...	Shelby	1.0	1.0	...	...	...
						Smith	2.3	...	1.9	.4	...
Hamblen	6.6	...	6.0	.6	...	Stewart	4.0	4.0	...	...	...
Hamilton	66.1	34.5	12.4	19.2	...	Sullivan	17.2	10.5	4.0	2.7	...
Hancock	2.4	2.0	...	.4	...	Sumner	1.2	...	...	1.2	...
Hardeman	27.3	13.9	11.8	1.6	...						
Hardin	38.4	10.6	20.7	7.1	...	Tipton	...	...	...	...	...
Hawkins	26.8	.8	18.7	7.3	...	Trousdale	.4	...	...	.4	...
Haywood	...	...	...	...	...						
Henderson	26.6	17.6	7.6	1.4	...	Unicoi	26.1	22.2	.9	3.0	...
Henry	...	...	...	...	...	Union	22.4	2.0	18.6	1.8	...
Hickman	3.0	...	2.8	.2	...	Van Buren	16.6	5.1	3.6	7.9	...
Houston	.6	...	...	.6	...						
Humphreys	1.6	.7	.9	...	...	Warren	6.0	.4	1.1	4.5	...
						Washington	20.6	14.8	5.3	.5	...
Jackson	5.8	...	5.1	.7	...	Wayne	39.0	6.7	27.9	4.4	...
Jefferson	5.8	...	.2	5.6	...	Weakley	12.3	1.5	10.8	...	...
Johnson	19.1	11.6	5.9	1.6	...	White	1.9	.5	.4	1.0	...
						Williamson	4.8	.7	2.7	1.4	...
Knox	29.4	10.7	7.6	11.1	...	Wilson	3.5	...	2.4	1.1	...
Lake	...	...	...	...	...	All counties	1,799.8	740.5	739.6	319.7	...

36

Table 21. *Growing-stock volume of hardwoods on commercial forest land by stand-size class, 1971*

County	Total	Saw-timber	Pole-timber	Sapling and seedling	Non-stocked areas	County	Total	Saw-timber	Pole-timber	Sapling and seedling	Non-stocked areas
	— — — — Million cubic feet — — — —						⇁ — — — — Million cubic feet — — — —				
Anderson	80.1	32.5	36.2	11.4	...	Lauderdale	173.0	161.4	11.6	...	...
						Lawrence	123.9	35.0	58.8	30.1	...
Bedford	31.4	11.9	10.8	8.7	...	Lewis	110.7	30.5	65.5	14.7	...
Benton	115.7	34.7	76.1	4.9	...	Lincoln	41.1	9.1	24.3	7.7	...
Bledsoe	54.3	4.9	26.2	23.2	...	Loudon	27.1	18.5	7.6	1.0	...
Blount	77.6	42.5	28.5	6.6	...						
Bradley	35.3	15.8	17.7	1.8	...	McMinn	66.3	40.7	9.0	16.6	...
						McNairy	86.9	12.4	51.4	23.1	...
Campbell	184.2	99.7	75.9	8.6	...	Macon	57.1	11.3	39.0	6.8	...
Cannon	27.0	3.5	19.0	4.5	...	Madison	104.5	59.3	37.0	8.2	...
Carroll	117.0	44.2	62.0	10.8	...	Marion	162.4	80.8	56.3	25.3	...
Carter	130.9	74.9	50.4	5.6	...	Marshall	30.8	11.7	10.6	8.5	...
Cheatham	82.6	50.8	26.7	5.1	...	Maury	67.5	31.6	26.3	9.6	...
Chester	55.9	25.2	22.3	8.4	...	Meigs	33.7	10.3	16.5	6.9	...
Claiborne	94.3	37.3	41.8	15.0	0.2	Monroe	167.0	75.4	57.1	34.5	...
Clay	67.5	40.8	25.8	.9	...	Montgomery	67.6	30.5	22.2	14.9	...
Cocke	130.1	60.3	64.7	5.1	...	Moore	29.8	4.8	25.0	...	...
Coffee	98.0	49.9	48.1	...	...	Morgan	170.0	94.1	49.8	26.1	...
Crockett	15.4	15.4	...	...							
Cumberland	181.0	72.1	84.3	24.6	...	Obion	49.3	32.7	9.2	7.4	...
						Overton	155.3	49.0	90.0	16.3	...
Davidson	66.5	35.8	17.4	13.3	...						
Decatur	116.4	54.5	50.7	11.2	...	Perry	172.7	33.4	121.3	18.0	...
De Kalb	47.9	25.3	7.7	14.9	...	Pickett	48.0	10.3	31.3	6.4	...
Dickson	168.4	106.3	55.9	6.2	...	Polk	113.2	74.6	28.1	10.5	...
Dyer	86.4	86.4	...	...	...	Putnam	125.8	67.1	48.0	10.7	...
Fayette	55.9	12.5	31.9	11.5	...	Rhea	76.9	14.8	35.4	26.7	...
Fentress	123.4	68.6	36.6	18.2	...	Roane	66.5	17.3	25.2	24.0	...
Franklin	168.3	96.1	57.7	14.5	...	Robertson	55.0	33.7	15.4	5.9	...
						Rutherford	25.6	...	20.6	5.0	...
Gibson	49.4	25.4	23.8	.2	...						
Giles	68.6	21.0	31.9	14.9	.8	Scott	242.5	92.2	105.3	45.0	...
Grainger	72.5	43.2	23.4	5.9	...	Sequatchie	62.3	19.4	29.3	13.6	...
Greene	81.9	36.7	14.3	30.9	...	Sevier	79.2	34.4	32.9	11.9	...
Grundy	112.7	53.3	38.2	21.2	...	Shelby	58.6	23.4	27.8	7.4	...
						Smith	37.3	...	29.4	7.9	...
Hamblen	25.0	16.2	5.3	3.5	...	Stewart	201.2	98.2	85.2	17.8	...
Hamilton	84.0	51.3	14.0	18.7	...	Sullivan	55.0	23.1	24.7	7.2	...
Hancock	59.5	29.3	24.3	5.9	...	Sumner	51.5	43.5	...	8.0	...
Hardeman	154.5	58.6	77.0	18.9	...						
Hardin	146.2	70.5	57.5	18.2	...	Tipton	36.0	28.9	...	7.1	...
Hawkins	117.6	48.5	52.5	16.6	...	Trousdale	5.5	...	4.4	1.1	...
Haywood	88.9	73.8	15.1	...	...						
Henderson	124.5	37.2	75.1	12.2	...	Unicoi	65.1	44.0	14.2	6.9	...
Henry	110.7	45.5	64.3	.9	...	Union	54.7	35.4	15.7	3.6	...
Hickman	201.1	46.5	118.2	36.4	...						
Houston	79.8	48.6	24.8	6.4	...	Van Buren	56.4	19.0	27.0	10.4	...
Humphreys	166.6	35.9	101.8	28.9	...						
						Warren	87.5	26.0	47.0	14.5	...
Jackson	65.7	28.0	32.7	5.0	...	Washington	48.6	31.7	10.7	6.2	...
Jefferson	34.2	18.4	8.9	6.9	...	Wayne	276.1	40.6	219.1	16.4	...
Johnson	104.3	31.0	69.1	4.2	.	Weakley	86.4	53.0	22.9	10.5	...
Knox	62.5	39.1	6.6	16.8	...	White	122.0	71.0	44.1	6.9	...
						Williamson	80.7	33.0	18.7	29.0	...
Lake	31.0	31.0	...	...	...	Wilson	29.0	...	23.5	5.5	...
						All counties	8,596.0	3,858.0	3,627.6	1,109.4	1.0

37

Table 22. *Sawtimber volume of softwoods on commercial forest land by stand-size class, 1971*

County	Total	Saw-timber	Pole-timber	Sapling and seedling	Non-stocked areas	County	Total	Saw-timber	Pole-timber	Sapling and seedling	Non-stocked areas
Anderson	73.5	38.6	7.3	27.6	...	Lauderdale	...	...	...	...	...
						Lawrence	...	...	...	...	...
Bedford	...	...	...	...	...	Lewis	11.5	...	11.5	...	...
Benton	13.8	...	...	13.8	...	Lincoln	...	...	...	...	...
Bledsoe	34.6	6.8	15.1	12.7	...	Loudon	23.2	9.7	11.1	2.4	...
Blount	187.0	110.0	39.8	37.2	...						
Bradley	63.3	...	54.3	9.0	...	McMinn	110.2	65.5	25.8	18.9	...
						McNairy	94.1	49.1	35.7	9.3	...
Campbell	169.4	118.0	51.4	...	...	Macon	...	...	...	...	...
Cannon	...	...	...	...	...	Madison	2.0	...	...	2.0	...
Carroll	29.7	26.6	3.1	...	...	Marion	83.8	60.0	13.3	10.5	...
Carter	143.0	127.4	15.1	.5	...	Marshall	2.7	...	...	2.7	...
Cheatham	...	...	...	...	...	Maury	.	...	...	...	...
Chester	58.8	38.8	20.0	...	...	Meigs	53.5	7.3	33.5	12.7	...
Claiborne	38.0	24.6	5.4	8.0	...	Monroe	429.2	239.4	125.2	64.6	...
Clay	7.0	7.0	...	...	...	Montgomery	...	...	...	...	...
Cocke	141.3	86.7	33.1	21.5	...	Moore	6.4	6.4	...	...	...
Coffee	...	...	...	...	...	Morgan	122.0	87.5	28.4	6.1	...
Crockett	5.6	5.6	...	...	...						
Cumberland	203.4	114.9	66.3	22.2	...	Obion	87.0	87.0	...	...	...
						Overton	88.8	56.8	32.0	...	...
Davidson	...	...	...	...	...						
Decatur	11.4	...	5.1	6.3	...	Perry	2.0	...	2.0	...	...
De Kalb	1.5	...	1.2	.3	...	Pickett	3.1	.5	2.6	...	...
Dickson	...	...	...	...	...	Polk	471.0	350.7	109.5	10.8	...
Dyer	...	...	...	...	...	Putnam	25.1	20.6	4.5	...	...
Fayette	4.6	...	4.6	...	...	Rhea	44.8	10.8	11.1	22.9	...
Fentress	225.8	136.5	52.7	36.6	...	Roane	35.0	16.6	8.0	10.4	...
Franklin	1.4	...	1.4	...	...	Robertson	...	...	...	...	...
						Rutherford	...	...	...	...	...
Gibson	...	...	...	...	...						
Giles	...	...	...	...	...	Scott	230.7	143.1	56.7	30.9	...
Grainger	30.1	17.4	8.6	4.1	...	Sequatchie	92.8	34.9	32.3	25.6	...
Greene	52.6	35.7	4.2	12.7	...	Sevier	106.9	56.9	28.9	21.1	...
Grundy	33.3	15.7	4.8	12.8	...	Shelby	4.0	4.0	...	...	...
						Smith	.5	...	.5	...	...
Hamblen	5.3	...	4.9	.4	...	Stewart	17.0	17.0	...	...	...
Hamilton	217.7	150.1	23.0	44.6	...	Sullivan	46.1	34.1	6.7	5.3	...
Hancock	8.9	8.9	...	...	...	Sumner	2.6	...	...	2.6	...
Hardeman	73.2	48.0	24.4	.8	...						
Hardin	81.8	38.5	21.8	21.5	...	Tipton	...	...	...	...	...
Hawkins	43.0	3.1	28.0	11.9	...	Trousdale	...	...	...	...	...
Haywood	...	...	...	...	...						
Henderson	66.2	60.1	4.4	1.7	...	Unicoi	98.6	84.4	1.5	12.7	...
Henry	...	...	...	...	...	Union	27.3	4.6	20.3	2.4	...
Hickman	6.7	...	6.7	...	...	Van Buren	41.3	23.1	1.8	16.4	...
Houston	1.8	...	...	1.8	...						
Humphreys	3.1	1.1	2.0	...	...	Warren	7.1	1.8	...	5.3	...
						Washington	64.4	53.5	10.1	.8	...
Jackson	1.1	...	1.1	...	...	Wayne	52.4	19.9	21.5	11.0	...
Jefferson	10.4	...	...	10.4	...	Weakley	24.9	7.6	17.3	...	...
Johnson	73.4	48.0	21.2	4.2	...	White	.8	.3	...	.5	...
						Williamson	4.8	3.1	1.2	.5	...
Knox	59.2	20.1	6.0	33.1	...	Wilson	.6	...	...	.6	...
Lake	...	...	...	...	...	All counties	4,699.1	2,844.4	1,190.0	664.7	...

38

Table 23. *Sawtimber volume of hardwoods on commercial forest land by stand-size class, 1971*

County	Total	Saw-timber	Pole-timber	Sapling and seedling	Non-stocked areas	County	Total	Saw-timber	Pole-timber	Sapling and seedling	Non-stocked areas

– – – – – Million board feet – – – – –   *– – – – – Million board feet – – – – –*

County	Total	Saw-timber	Pole-timber	Sapling and seedling	Non-stocked areas	County	Total	Saw-timber	Pole-timber	Sapling and seedling	Non-stocked areas
Anderson	200.3	109.4	63.1	27.8	...	Lauderdale	700.0	672.4	27.6	...	...
						Lawrence	274.3	120.8	97.7	55.8	...
Bedford	64.3	48.6	12.1	3.6	...	Lewis	185.8	77.1	96.6	12.1	...
Benton	205.6	93.9	104.8	6.9	...	Lincoln	72.2	24.0	40.6	7.6	...
Bledsoe	91.3	15.1	41.2	35.0	...	Loudon	87.7	66.1	19.8	1.8	...
Blount	228.1	157.1	65.7	5.3	...						
Bradley	63.2	39.0	24.2	...	...	McMinn	164.9	123.6	11.5	29.8	
						McNairy	161.2	42.8	55.4	63.0	...
Campbell	547.5	378.9	152.1	16.5	...	Macon	99.5	29.9	48.5	21.1	...
Cannon	31.3	15.7	11.3	4.3	...	Madison	346.0	247.7	67.5	30.8	...
Carroll	280.7	166.4	99.9	14.4	...	Marion	470.0	292.4	105.5	72.1	...
Carter	296.0	217.2	65.6	13.2	...	Marshall	91.9	32.4	22.7	36.8	...
Cheatham	243.6	170.1	55.9	17.6	...	Maury	173.1	129.4	33.9	9.8	...
Chester	119.6	82.4	22.6	14.6	...	Meigs	82.7	42.5	21.4	18.8	...
Claiborne	226.6	112.4	89.1	24.2	0.9	Monroe	456.3	271.0	104.7	80.6	...
Clay	183.3	146.7	31.9	4.7	...	Montgomery	149.6	121.4	12.8	15.4	...
Cocke	306.4	194.8	102.7	8.9	...	Moore	76.4	69.7	6.7	...	...
Coffee	263.0	201.8	58.1	3.1	...	Morgan	430.8	291.7	91.3	47.8	...
Crockett	54.4	54.4	...	...	...						
Cumberland	392.5	201.3	132.6	58.6	...	Obion	147.3	113.3	13.3	20.7	...
						Overton	352.9	156.9	171.7	24.3	...
Davidson	184.3	109.5	30.0	44.8	...						
Decatur	285.4	175.2	89.3	20.9	...	Perry	302.7	91.6	181.9	29.2	...
De Kalb	127.7	101.1	13.8	12.8	...	Pickett	126.3	27.8	75.2	23.3	...
Dickson	415.2	291.1	112.4	11.7	...	Polk	293.5	230.1	45.0	18.4	...
Dyer	343.7	343.7	...	...	...	Putnam	288.1	203.0	65.1	20.0	...
Fayette	159.1	54.8	86.5	17.8	...	Rhea	179.9	53.9	65.4	60.6	...
Fentress	314.4	232.9	53.6	27.9	...	Roane	148.1	51.8	38.7	57.6	...
Franklin	508.3	329.1	143.3	35.9	...	Robertson	176.7	129.4	31.9	15.4	...
						Rutherford	17.9	...	13.1	4.8	...
Gibson	129.4	82.8	46.6	...	...						
Giles	142.4	73.9	54.4	14.1	...	Scott	624.2	312.4	204.4	107.4	...
Grainger	203.1	127.4	58.4	17.3	...	Sequatchie	154.7	73.9	55.9	24.9	...
Greene	255.2	136.7	31.0	87.5	...	Sevier	196.5	120.2	47.6	28.7	...
Grundy	300.3	182.9	75.6	41.8	...	Shelby	169.7	85.5	68.7	15.5	...
						Smith	59.9	44.3	12.1	3.5	...
Hamblen	66.9	42.8	9.0	15.1	...	Stewart	509.3	300.5	168.6	40.2	...
Hamilton	233.1	171.7	19.4	42.0	...	Sullivan	110.2	60.1	37.5	12.6	...
Hancock	167.0	92.8	63.9	10.3	...	Sumner	174.7	145.1	...	29.6	...
Hardeman	352.7	196.2	119.7	36.8	...						
Hardin	347.5	221.2	93.4	32.9	...	Tipton	105.7	74.5	...	31.2	...
Hawkins	314.0	185.7	90.0	38.3	...	Trousdale	7.4	...	5.4	2.0	...
Haywood	286.7	256.1	30.6	...	...						
Henderson	331.0	145.5	156.4	29.1	...	Unicoi	161.2	128.2	8.0	25.0	...
Henry	259.1	135.1	124.0	...	...	Union	151.3	125.0	20.8	5.5	...
Hickman	392.7	148.4	189.5	54.8	...						
Houston	174.6	147.8	20.1	6.7	...	Van Buren	153.9	73.6	59.1	21.2	...
Humphreys	283.5	107.9	132.1	43.5	...						
						Warren	198.6	89.7	79.9	29.0	...
Jackson	200.0	146.4	51.5	2.1	...	Washington	117.2	96.8	17.5	2.9	...
Jefferson	114.6	69.1	28.2	17.3	...	Wayne	472.9	128.3	331.1	13.5	...
Johnson	222.1	107.7	113.5	.9	...	Weakley	337.0	257.4	41.0	38.6	...
						White	339.7	257.1	70.0	12.6	...
Knox	227.8	169.2	10.0	48.6	...	Williamson	212.6	133.5	31.4	47.7	...
						Wilson	57.1	...	48.9	8.2	...
Lake	132.0	132.0	...	...	...	All counties	21,641.1	13,340.7	6,052.5	2,247.0	.9

39

Table 24. *Net annual growth of growing stock on commercial forest land by species group and county, 1970*

County	All species	Soft-wood	Hardwood Total	Oak	Other	County	All species	Soft-wood	Hardwood Total	Oak	Other
			Million cubic feet						Million cubic feet		
Anderson	5.1	1.3	3.8	2.0	1.8	Lauderdale	6.7	...	6.7	1.0	5.7
						Lawrence	6.1	...	6.1	3.1	3.0
Bedford	2.2	.2	2.0	.2	1.8	Lewis	6.7	.4	6.3	5.4	.9
Benton	6.3	.3	6.0	4.2	1.8	Lincoln	2.7	.5	2.2	1.0	1.2
Bledsoe	4.5	1.0	3.5	3.1	.4	Loudon	2.0	1.1	.9	.6	.3
Blount	7.3	3.3	4.0	2.4	1.6	McMinn	7.1	4.0	3.1	1.5	1.6
Bradley	6.1	3.8	2.3	1.3	1.0	McNairy	7.4	2.1	5.3	3.1	2.2
Campbell	11.0	2.9	8.1	4.4	3.7	Macon	2.7	...	2.7	.4	2.3
Cannon	2.4	.3	2.1	.3	1.8	Madison	4.5	.1	4.4	2.5	1.9
Carroll	7.6	.8	6.8	2.5	4.3	Marion	7.3	1.2	6.1	3.7	2.4
Carter	7.2	1.0	6.2	3.0	3.2	Marshall	1.6	.3	1.3	.4	.9
Cheatham	3.7	.8	2.9	1.7	1.2	Maury	3.5	...	3.5	1.0	2.5
Chester	3.8	.9	2.9	1.5	1.4	Meigs	3.2	1.6	1.6	.9	.7
Claiborne	5.4	1.4	4.0	1.9	2.1	Monroe	16.0	8.2	7.8	5.1	2.7
Clay	2.9	.1	2.8	1.4	1.4	Montgomery	4.4	.1	4.3	1.3	3.0
Cocke	7.8	1.2	6.6	3.7	2.9	Moore	1.4	.1	1.3	.4	.9
Coffee	4.7	...	4.7	3.3	1.4	Morgan	8.7	2.1	6.6	4.1	2.5
Crockett	.6	(¹)	.6	.3	.3	Obion	3.0	.4	2.6	.4	2.2
Cumberland	10.8	3.4	7.4	5.3	2.1	Overton	7.4	.7	6.7	2.3	4.4
Davidson	2.4	...	2.4	1.3	1.1	Perry	8.3	.3	8.0	5.5	2.5
Decatur	5.4	.9	4.5	2.9	1.6	Pickett	2.9	.3	2.6	.6	2.0
De Kalb	2.7	.2	2.5	.6	1.9	Polk	12.1	7.2	4.9	3.2	1.7
Dickson	9.0	(¹)	9.0	4.7	4.3	Putnam	5.7	.5	5.2	2.1	3.1
Dyer	3.2	...	3.2	1.7	1.5	Rhea	5.0	1.4	3.6	2.4	1.2
Fayette	3.4	.1	3.3	2.6	.7	Roane	5.3	1.7	3.6	2.7	.9
Fentress	10.1	5.3	4.8	3.3	1.5	Robertson	1.8	...	1.8	.9	.9
Franklin	6.9	.5	6.4	4.7	1.7	Rutherford	2.0	.3	1.7	.3	1.4
Gibson	3.2	...	3.2	1.5	1.7	Scott	15.3	4.3	11.0	5.8	5.2
Giles	4.3	(¹)	4.3	1.4	2.9	Sequatchie	4.1	1.5	2.6	1.8	.8
Grainger	4.1	.5	3.6	1.5	2.1	Sevier	7.0	2.8	4.2	2.6	1.6
Greene	5.1	1.3	3.8	1.6	2.2	Shelby	3.1	(¹)	3.1	.4	2.7
Grundy	6.4	.8	5.6	3.1	2.5	Smith	2.6	.1	2.5	.6	1.9
Hamblen	1.9	.7	1.2	.7	.5	Stewart	9.1	.2	8.9	5.5	3.4
Hamilton	7.2	3.6	3.6	2.2	1.4	Sullivan	3.9	.9	3.0	1.4	1.6
Hancock	2.2	.1	2.1	.8	1.3	Sumner	2.2	.6	1.6	.7	.9
Hardeman	9.5	1.9	7.6	4.9	2.7	Tipton	1.5	...	1.5	.1	1.4
Hardin	10.9	3.4	7.5	3.5	4.0	Trousdale	.3	(¹)	.3	(¹)	.3
Hawkins	7.6	1.6	6.0	2.8	3.2	Unicoi	4.1	.9	3.2	1.2	2.0
Haywood	4.4	...	4.4	2.6	1.8	Union	4.3	1.7	2.6	1.0	1.6
Henderson	7.7	2.0	5.7	2.1	3.6	Van Buren	4.0	1.2	2.8	1.1	1.7
Henry	5.2	...	5.2	1.2	4.0	Warren	4.1	.4	3.7	1.5	2.2
Hickman	12.0	.2	11.8	7.8	4.0	Washington	3.0	.7	2.3	1.4	.9
Houston	3.9	(¹)	3.9	2.4	1.5	Wayne	15.9	2.5	13.4	9.0	4.4
Humphreys	8.8	.1	8.7	5.9	2.8	Weakley	3.8	.6	3.2	1.2	2.0
Jackson	3.7	.5	3.2	.7	2.5	White	5.3	.1	5.2	1.9	3.3
Jefferson	1.8	.3	1.5	.7	.8	Williamson	3.8	.1	3.7	1.2	2.5
Johnson	6.0	.8	5.2	3.0	2.2	Wilson	2.2	.1	2.1	.7	1.4
Knox	4.4	2.1	2.3	.9	1.4	All counties	509.1	102.9	406.2	210.6	195.6
Lake	1.2	...	1.2	...	1.2						

¹ Negligible.

40

Table 25. *Net annual growth of sawtimber on commercial forest land by species group and county, 1970*

County	All species	Soft-wood	Hardwood Total	Hardwood Oak	Hardwood Other	County	All species	Soft-wood	Hardwood Total	Hardwood Oak	Hardwood Other
			– – – – Million board feet – – – –						– – – – Million board feet – – – –		
Anderson	15.0	3.5	11.5	7.4	4.1	Lauderdale	34.8	...	34.8	1.7	33.1
						Lawrence	11.8	...	11.8	8.3	3.5
Bedford	4.7	...	4.7	1.2	3.5	Lewis	12.1	.7	11.4	10.1	1.3
Benton	19.2	2.2	17.0	11.3	5.7	Lincoln	4.1	...	4.1	.9	3.2
Bledsoe	5.1	1.6	3.5	2.9	.6	Loudon	4.6	1.7	2.9	2.4	.5
Blount	23.7	12.3	11.4	5.3	6.1						
Bradley	10.9	3.3	7.6	3.1	4.5	McMinn	13.7	7.2	6.5	3.0	3.5
						McNairy	13.0	3.2	9.8	6.3	3.5
Campbell	40.4	13.8	26.6	18.0	8.6	Macon	5.7	...	5.7	1.1	4.6
Cannon	1.3	...	1.3	.6	.7	Madison	18.8	.1	18.7	10.0	8.7
Carroll	22.5	3.1	19.4	10.0	9.4	Marion	39.3	6.0	33.3	20.8	12.5
Carter	19.0	5.8	13.2	7.1	6.1	Marshall	5.1	.1	5.0	1.2	3.8
Cheatham	7.1	...	7.1	3.7	3.4	Maury	14.5	...	14.5	2.1	12.4
Chester	11.8	3.2	8.6	3.4	5.2	Meigs	7.3	2.4	4.9	3.8	1.1
Claiborne	11.9	1.6	10.3	5.1	5.2	Monroe	48.0	28.1	19.9	9.6	10.3
Clay	7.0	.4	6.6	4.3	2.3	Montgomery	10.7	...	10.7	3.3	7.4
Cocke	21.0	4.3	16.7	9.1	7.6	Moore	5.2	.2	5.0	4.0	1.0
Coffee	10.1	...	10.1	7.4	2.7	Morgan	25.9	9.0	16.9	7.2	9.7
Crockett	1.9	.1	1.8	1.1	.7						
Cumberland	35.4	12.5	22.9	18.4	4.5	Obion	11.3	1.9	9.4	1.1	8.3
						Overton	22.5	4.1	18.4	6.1	12.3
Davidson	6.6	...	6.6	4.3	2.3						
Decatur	17.4	1.7	15.7	12.2	3.5	Perry	19.3	.1	19.2	12.0	7.2
De Kalb	5.6	.1	5.5	2.5	3.0	Pickett	8.1	.9	7.2	1.8	5.4
Dickson	22.0	...	22.0	13.5	8.5	Polk	43.6	25.2	18.4	11.4	7.0
Dyer	15.2	...	15.2	8.4	6.8	Putnam	14.3	1.0	13.3	4.5	8.8
Fayette	6.1	.1	6.0	4.5	1.5	Rhea	16.4	5.4	11.0	4.7	6.3
Fentress	29.6	20.6	9.0	5.5	3.5	Roane	12.8	4.9	7.9	6.3	1.6
Franklin	20.4	.1	20.3	17.0	3.3	Robertson	5.7	...	5.7	3.8	1.9
						Rutherford	3.5	...	3.5	.3	3.2
Gibson	5.0	...	5.0	2.3	2.7						
Giles	9.5	...	9.5	2.8	6.7	Scott	47.2	22.7	24.5	11.4	13.1
Grainger	11.3	1.4	9.9	5.3	4.6	Sequatchie	9.7	5.8	3.9	2.7	1.2
Greene	15.3	3.7	11.6	3.7	7.9	Sevier	12.8	5.9	6.9	5.3	1.6
Grundy	17.2	4.3	12.9	6.2	6.7	Shelby	9.3	.2	9.1	.6	8.5
						Smith	4.6	(¹)	4.6	1.7	2.9
Hamblen	5.1	.8	4.3	1.7	2.6	Stewart	23.9	1.2	22.7	14.6	8.1
Hamilton	28.8	18.1	10.7	8.3	2.4	Sullivan	8.0	3.4	4.6	3.4	1.2
Hancock	16.1	.3	15.8	7.1	8.7	Sumner	5.5	(¹)	5.5	3.1	2.4
Hardeman	26.2	5.3	20.9	13.5	7.4						
Hardin	30.8	8.2	22.6	12.0	10.6	Tipton	7.2	...	7.2	.2	7.0
Hawkins	16.4	4.6	11.8	9.2	2.6	Trousdale	2.2	...	2.2	.1	2.1
Haywood	19.9	...	19.9	8.1	11.8						
Henderson	19.8	5.9	13.9	7.2	6.7	Unicoi	9.7	4.7	5.0	2.6	2.4
Henry	14.4	...	14.4	5.4	9.0	Union	6.6	2.1	4.5	2.9	1.6
Hickman	27.6	.6	27.0	18.1	8.9						
Houston	18.6	(¹)	18.6	8.2	10.4	Van Buren	9.2	2.5	6.7	4.1	2.6
Humphreys	19.8	.1	19.7	11.2	8.5	Warren	10.3	.4	9.9	5.6	4.3
						Washington	7.1	2.1	5.0	2.2	2.8
Jackson	13.3	.1	13.2	2.4	10.8	Wayne	32.6	3.7	28.9	22.5	6.4
Jefferson	5.1	.5	4.6	3.2	1.4	Weakley	20.0	1.5	18.5	5.1	13.4
Johnson	13.2	1.9	11.3	5.6	5.7	White	14.5	(¹)	14.5	4.7	9.8
						Williamson	10.9	.1	10.8	3.8	7.0
Knox	10.8	4.4	6.4	3.7	2.7	Wilson	2.0	(¹)	2.0	.8	1.2
Lake	7.7	...	7.7	...	7.7	All counties	1,428.2	309.0	1,119.2	577.7	541.5

¹ Negligible.

41

Table 26. *Timber removals from growing stock on commercial forest land by species group and county, 1970*

County	All species	Soft-wood	Hardwood Total	Oak	Other
			Million cubic feet		
Anderson	3.1	0.2	2.9	...	2.9
Bedford	1.3	.1	1.2	0.3	.9
Benton	2.0	(¹)	2.0	.6	1.4
Bledsoe	3.1	.7	2.4	1.6	.8
Blount	2.4	.9	1.5	.6	.9
Bradley	3.6	2.5	1.1	1.1	...
Campbell	3.1	.5	2.6	1.7	.9
Cannon	1.2	.3	.9	.6	.3
Carroll	3.6	.3	3.3	2.0	1.3
Carter	1.1	.4	.7	...	.7
Cheatham	1.3	(¹)	1.3	...	1.3
Chester	3.4	.4	3.0	1.8	1.2
Claiborne	2.2	.2	2.0	.2	1.8
Clay	1.2	(¹)	1.2	.8	.4
Cocke	1.7	.8	.9	.9	...
Coffee	3.7	...	3.7	1.7	2.0
Crockett	.6	.1	.5	...	.5
Cumberland	3.2	.6	2.6	2.6	...
Davidson	.9	...	.9	...	.9
Decatur	2.5	.1	2.4	1.1	1.3
De Kalb	1.2	.1	1.1	.8	.3
Dickson	2.3	(¹)	2.3	1.5	.8
Dyer	3.5	...	3.5	.9	2.6
Fayette	2.4	(¹)	2.4	1.1	1.3
Fentress	3.6	.7	2.9	1.1	1.8
Franklin	3.5	.1	3.4	2.7	.7
Gibson	1.1	...	1.1	.5	.6
Giles	1.8	.2	1.6	.4	1.2
Grainger	2.2	.1	2.1	...	2.1
Greene	1.4	.2	1.2	1.2	...
Grundy	2.7	.5	2.2	1.3	.9
Hamblen	2.6	.1	2.5	...	2.5
Hamilton	2.3	1.0	1.3	1.3	...
Hancock	.5	(¹)	.5	.3	.2
Hardeman	4.3	1.0	3.3	1.6	1.7
Hardin	5.4	.9	4.5	2.9	1.6
Hawkins	1.3	.1	1.2	1.2	...
Haywood	2.3	...	2.3	1.8	.5
Henderson	3.0	.2	2.8	1.2	1.6
Henry	2.5	...	2.5	...	2.5
Hickman	3.1	(¹)	3.1	2.1	1.0
Houston	1.2	...	1.2	.3	.9
Humphreys	3.0	(¹)	3.0	2.3	.7
Jackson	.9	(¹)	.9	.1	.8
Jefferson	2.0	(¹)	2.0	...	2.0
Johnson	1.5	.5	1.0	.5	.5
Knox	1.6	.4	1.2	.8	.4
Lake	.8	...	.8	...	.8
Lauderdale	4.7	...	4.7	.3	4.4
Lawrence	4.2	...	4.2	2.3	1.9
Lewis	2.0	.1	1.9	1.5	.4
Lincoln	1.6	.2	1.4	.6	.8
Loudon	1.2	.2	1.0	.5	.5
McMinn	2.9	2.0	.9	.5	.4
McNairy	4.8	.7	4.1	1.5	2.6
Macon	1.8	...	1.8	.2	1.6
Madison	3.5	.3	3.2	1.0	2.2
Marion	2.1	.3	1.8	1.3	.5
Marshall	1.1	.3	.8	.5	.3
Maury	1.4	...	1.4	.1	1.3
Meigs	1.4	.7	.7	.3	.4
Monroe	4.9	3.1	1.8	1.6	.2
Montgomery	2.4	(¹)	2.4	1.1	1.3
Moore	.8	.1	.7	.1	.6
Morgan	2.7	.7	2.0	1.4	.6
Obion	6.0	.7	5.3	...	5.3
Overton	1.9	(¹)	1.9	1.9	...
Perry	2.7	(¹)	2.7	1.4	1.3
Pickett	1.1	...	1.1	...	1.1
Polk	3.7	2.5	1.2	1.2	...
Putnam	3.1	.4	2.7	...	2.7
Rhea	3.2	1.4	1.8	1.4	.4
Roane	1.8	.9	.9	.4	.5
Robertson	1.8	...	1.8	...	1.8
Rutherford	1.6	.7	.9	.9	...
Scott	5.2	.5	4.7	2.0	2.7
Sequatchie	1.8	.2	1.6	.9	.7
Sevier	.8	.4	.4	...	.4
Shelby	3.2	.3	2.9	1.4	1.5
Smith	1.0	.1	.9	.3	.6
Stewart	1.7	(¹)	1.7	1.2	.5
Sullivan	1.9	(¹)	1.9	1.3	.6
Sumner	1.2	.1	1.1	.2	.9
Tipton	1.3	...	1.3	...	1.3
Trousdale	.1	(¹)	.1	...	.1
Unicoi	1.5	.3	1.2	1.2	...
Union	.9	.2	.7	.7	...
Van Buren	1.1	.1	1.0	.6	.4
Warren	2.2	.3	1.9	.9	1.0
Washington	1.1	.1	1.0	...	1.0
Wayne	3.8	.5	3.3	2.0	1.3
Weakley	2.9	.3	2.6	.8	1.8
White	2.9	(¹)	2.9	2.0	.9
Williamson	1.2	.2	1.0	.9	.1
Wilson	1.0	.1	.9	.2	.7
All counties	216.4	33.2	183.2	84.1	99.1

¹ Negligible.

42

Table 27. *Timber removals from sawtimber on commercial forest land by species group and county, 1970*

County	All species	Soft-wood	Hardwood Total	Oak	Other	County	All species	Soft-wood	Hardwood Total	Oak	Other
			– – – – Million board feet – – – –						– – – – Million board feet – – – –		
Anderson	13.1	0.7	12.4	...	12.4	Lauderdale	21.8	...	21.8	1.3	20.5
						Lawrence	15.0	...	15.0	5.8	9.2
Bedford	4.6	...	4.6	2.2	2.4	Lewis	7.4	.3	7.1	5.5	1.6
Benton	8.2	.1	8.1	2.0	6.1	Lincoln	5.9	...	5.9	2.8	3.1
Bledsoe	9.2	2.5	6.7	5.1	1.6	Loudon	3.5	.6	2.9	1.8	1.1
Blount	7.3	2.9	4.4	1.4	3.4						
Bradley	9.0	6.8	2.2	...	2.2	McMinn	9.3	6.2	3.1	1.5	1.6
						McNairy	19.7	1.1	18.6	6.8	11.8
Campbell	11.1	1.9	9.2	5.8	3.0	Macon	7.9	...	7.9	.9	7.0
Cannon	3.9	...	3.9	3.1	.8	Madison	13.4	1.4	12.0	5.0	7.0
Carroll	13.7	.2	13.5	8.8	4.7	Marion	8.0	1.5	6.5	4.4	2.1
Carter	4.0	1.9	2.1	...	2.1	Marshall	4.7	2.3	2.4	2.0	.4
Cheatham	5.9	...	5.9	3.5	2.4	Maury	5.6	...	5.6	...	5.6
Chester	7.6	1.5	6.1	4.7	1.4	Meigs	4.6	2.6	2.0	1.4	.6
Claiborne	9.0	.9	8.1	2.0	6.1	Monroe	20.5	14.1	6.4	6.0	.4
Clay	5.0	(¹)	5.0	2.6	2.4	Montgomery	8.7	...	8.7	3.6	5.1
Cocke	6.9	3.5	3.4	3.4	...	Moore	4.9	2.0	2.9	...	2.9
Coffee	12.8	...	12.8	4.8	8.0	Morgan	9.2	2.8	6.4	4.5	1.9
Crockett	2.5	.3	2.2	...	2.2						
Cumberland	10.5	1.9	8.6	8.6	...	Obion	19.6	3.9	15.7	...	15.7
						Overton	8.3	.1	8.2	...	8.2
Davidson	2.9	...	2.9	1.0	1.9						
Decatur	11.6	.4	11.2	9.4	1.8	Perry	11.7	.(¹)	11.7	5.8	5.9
De Kalb	5.6	.8	4.8	2.0	2.8	Pickett	4.6	(¹)	4.6	...	4.6
Dickson	10.3	...	10.3	6.7	3.6	Polk	17.6	12.9	4.7	4.7	...
Dyer	14.3	...	14.3	4.0	10.3	Putnam	11.9	1.1	10.8	...	10.8
Fayette	8.7	.1	8.6	3.7	4.9	Rhea	9.3	5.3	4.0	4.0	...
Fentress	12.9	3.0	9.9	3.5	6.4	Roane	5.4	2.8	2.6	...	2.6
Franklin	14.7	.3	14.4	12.4	2.0	Robertson	7.4	...	7.4	3.8	3.6
						Rutherford	3.3	...	3.3	3.3	...
Gibson	4.4	...	4.4	2.0	2.4						
Giles	6.1	...	6.1	1.9	4.2	Scott	22.0	2.0	20.0	7.8	12.2
Grainger	7.2	.3	6.9	...	6.9	Sequatchie	5.0	.5	4.5	3.2	1.3
Greene	5.3	.7	4.6	...	4.6	Sevier	2.0	.9	1.1	...	1.1
Grundy	11.3	1.9	9.4	...	9.4	Shelby	11.4	1.5	9.9	3.6	6.3
						Smith	3.9	.4	3.5	1.3	2.2
Hamblen	8.5	.3	8.2	...	8.2	Stewart	7.8	(¹)	7.8	5.7	2.1
Hamilton	7.4	3.8	3.6	...	3.6	Sullivan	5.7	.1	5.6	4.7	.9
Hancock	2.1	.1	2.0	1.3	.7	Sumner	4.5	.3	4.2	1.0	3.2
Hardeman	18.0	2.9	15.1	6.9	8.2						
Hardin	20.6	2.8	17.8	7.4	10.4	Tipton	5.5	...	5.5	...	5.5
Hawkins	4.7	.4	4.3	4.3	...	Trousdale	.3	...	.3	.1	.2
Haywood	10.6	...	10.6	8.1	2.5						
Henderson	12.3	.4	11.9	2.3	9.6	Unicoi	6.1	1.8	4.3	4.3	...
Henry	9.7	...	9.7	...	9.7	Union	3.8	.9	2.9	2.9	...
Hickman	12.0	.2	11.8	7.4	4.4						
Houston	5.4	(¹)	5.4	1.6	3.8	Van Buren	5.4	.6	4.8	2.8	2.0
Humphreys	10.3	(¹)	10.3	8.7	1.6						
						Warren	8.6	.7	7.9	4.7	3.2
Jackson	4.0	(¹)	4.0	.5	3.5	Washington	3.6	.2	3.4	...	3.4
Jefferson	6.4	.2	6.2	...	6.2	Wayne	14.8	1.9	12.9	7.9	5.0
Johnson	6.6	2.6	4.0	2.3	1.7	Weakley	12.5	.7	11.8	3.6	8.2
						White	11.8	.2	11.6	8.1	3.5
Knox	4.7	1.3	3.4	2.4	1.0	Williamson	6.4	2.3	4.1	4.1	...
						Wilson	2.7	.4	2.3	1.6	.7
Lake	3.7	...	3.7	...	3.7	All counties	819.6	124.0	695.6	300.1	395.5

¹ Negligible.

43

Table 28. *Mortality of growing stock and sawtimber on commercial forest land by species group, 1970*

County	Growing stock			Sawtimber		
	All species	Softwood	Hardwood	All species	Softwood	Hardwood
	— Million cubic feet —			*— Million board feet —*		
Anderson	0.4	...	0.4	0.9	...	0.9
Bedford	.7	0.1	.6	1.3	...	1.3
Benton	.5	.1	.4	.5	...	.5
Bledsoe	.4	...	.4	1.6	...	1.6
Blount	1.9	.9	1.0	6.8	3.2	3.6
Bradley	.2	...	.2	.9	...	.9
Campbell	1.6	.8	.8	3.4	.9	2.5
Cannon	.3	...	.3	...	...	...
Carroll	.2	.	.2	...		
Carter	.1	...	.1	...	...	..
Cheatham	.7	.1	.6	1.6	...	1.6
Chester	...	...	...	...		...
Claiborne	.2		.2	.8		.8
Clay	.1	...	.1	...	...	...
Cocke	.6	.2	.4	2.5	.8	1.7
Coffee	.8	...	.8	1.9	...	1.9
Crockett	...		...	...		...
Cumberland	.8		.8	1.6	...	1.6
Davidson	.3		.3	1.3	...	1.3
Decatur	1.1	...	1.1	1.3	...	1.3
De Kalb	.5	...	.5	1.8	...	1.8
Dickson	.4		.4	.5	...	.5
Dyer	.5		.5	.8		.8
Fayette	.3	...	.3	.5	...	.5
Fentress	1.0	.5	.5	2.0	1.0	1.0
Franklin	.8	...	.8	2.8	...	2.8
Gibson	.2		.2	.7		.7
Giles	...	...	...	...	...	...
Grainger	.2	.1	.1	1.2	.8	.4
Greene	.6	.3	.3	...	...	...
Grundy	.4	...	.4	1.2	...	1.2
Hamblen	...	...		...	...	
Hamilton	.1	.1		.5	.5	
Hancock	...		...	...	...	
Hardeman	.4	...	.4	...	...	...
Hardin	.3	...	.3	...	...	...
Hawkins	.6	.1	.5	1.7	.5	1.2
Haywood	.1	...	.1	...	...	...
Henderson	1.1	.2	.9	1.3	.7	.6
Henry	1.8	...	1.8	1.2	...	1.2
Hickman	.5		.5	.3		.3
Houston	.2		.2	.4		.4
Humphreys	1.5	...	1.5	1.9	...	1.9
Jackson	.2		.2	.5		.5
Jefferson	.3		.3	.4		.4
Johnson	...		...	...		...
Knox	.3		.3	.9		.9
Lake	.1	...	.1	...	...	...

Table 28. *Mortality of growing stock and sawtimber on commercial forest land by species group, 1970* (Continued)

County	Growing stock			Sawtimber		
	All species	Softwood	Hardwood	All species	Softwood	Hardwood
	— Million cubic feet —			*— Million board feet —*		
Lauderdale	1.0	...	1.0	4.9	...	4.9
Lawrence	.1		.1	...		...
Lewis	.1		.1	...	...	...
Lincoln	.2		.2	.6		.6
Loudon	.1	...	.1	...	...	...
McMinn	.8	.4	.4	2.5	.7	1.8
McNairy	1.2	.2	1.0	3.8	.6	3.2
Macon	.1	...	.1	.5	...	.5
Madison	.6	...	.6	.4	...	.4
Marion	.7	.2	.5	1.8	.5	1.3
Marshall	.4	...	.4	.8	...	.8
Maury	.1	...	.1	...	...	...
Meigs	.1	.1	...	...		...
Monroe	.8	.6	.2	3.1	3.1	
Montgomery	.2	...	.2	...	...	...
Moore	...	...	...	...	...	...
Morgan	.6	.2	.4	1.6	1.2	.4
Obion	.5	.1	.4	2.5	.9	1.6
Overton	.6	.2	.4	...	...	...
Perry	.7		.7	...		...
Pickett	...	...	...	...		...
Polk	1.8	.6	1.2	4.4	.7	3.7
Putnam	...	...	...	...	...	...
Rhea	.7	.3	.4	1.5	.8	.7
Roane	(¹)	...	(¹)	...	...	...
Robertson	.1		.1	...	...	...
Rutherford	.3	...	.3	.5	...	.5
Scott	1.2	.2	1.0	3.5	.5	3.0
Sequatchie	.2	...	.2	...	...	...
Sevier	.3	.2	.1	1.5	.8	.7
Shelby	.4	...	.4	1.0	...	1.0
Smith	.2	(¹)	.2	.7		.7
Stewart	.7	...	.7	.9		.9
Sullivan	.2	.1	.1	...		...
Sumner	.3	...	.3	1.1	...	1.1
Tipton						
Trousdale	...		...	...	...	...
Unicoi	.5	.1	.4	2.0	.7	1.3
Union	.3	.2	.1	...	...	...
Van Buren	.4	.1	.3	...		...
Warren	.8	.3	.5	1.2	...	1.2
Washington	.2	...	.2	.8	...	.8
Wayne	.7	.1	.6	.7	.3	.4
Weakley	.7	...	.7	2.5	...	2.5
White	.5	...	.5	1.4	...	1.4
Williamson	.3	...	.3	...	...	...
Wilson	.3	...	.3	1.6	...	1.6
All counties	43.3	7.7	35.6	94.8	19.2	75.6

¹ Negligible.

45

Table 29. *Net annual change in growing stock and sawtimber on commercial forest land by species group and county, 1970*

County	Growing stock			Sawtimber		
	All species	Softwood	Hardwood	All species	Softwood	Hardwood
	– – Million cubic feet – –			– – Million board feet – –		
Anderson	+ 2.0	+ 1.1	+ 0.9	+ 1.9	+ 2.8	− 0.9
Bedford	+ .9	+ .1	+ .8	+ .1	(¹)	+ .1
Benton	+ 4.3	+ .3	+ 4.0	+ 11.0	+ 2.1	+ 8.9
Bledsoe	+ 1.4	+ .3	+ 1.1	− 4.1	− .9	− 3.2
Blount	+ 4.9	+ 2.4	+ 2.5	+ 16.4	+ 9.4	+ 7.0
Bradley	+ 2.5	+ 1.3	+ 1.2	+ 1.9	− 3.5	+ 5.4
Campbell	+ 7.9	+ 2.4	+ 5.5	+ 29.3	+ 11.9	+ 17.4
Cannon	+ 1.2	(¹)	+ 1.2	− 2.6	(¹)	− 2.6
Carroll	+ 4.0	+ .5	+ 3.5	+ 8.8	+ 2.9	+ 5.9
Carter	+ 6.1	+ .6	+ 5.5	+ 15.0	+ 3.9	+ 11.1
Cheatham	+ 2.4	+ .8	+ 1.6	+ 1.2	(¹)	+ 1.2
Chester	+ .4	+ .5	− .1	+ 4.2	+ 1.7	+ 2.5
Claiborne	+ 3.2	+ 1.2	+ 2.0	+ 2.9	+ .7	+ 2.2
Clay	+ 1.7	+ .1	+ 1.6	+ 2.0	+ .4	+ 1.6
Cocke	+ 6.1	+ .4	+ 5.7	+ 14.1	+ .8	+ 13.3
Coffee	+ 1.0	(¹)	+ 1.0	− 2.7	(¹)	− 2.7
Crockett	(¹)	− .1	+ .1	− .6	− .2	− .4
Cumberland	+ 7.6	+ 2.8	+ 4.8	+ 24.9	+ 10.6	+ 14.3
Davidson	+ 1.5	(¹)	+ 1.5	+ 3.7	(¹)	+ 3.7
Decatur	+ 2.9	+ .8	+ 2.1	+ 5.8	+ 1.3	+ 4.5
De Kalb	+ 1.5	+ .1	+ 1.4	(¹)	− .7	+ .7
Dickson	+ 6.7	(¹)	+ 6.7	+ 11.7	(¹)	+ 11.7
Dyer	− .3	(¹)	− .3	+ .9	(¹)	+ .9
Fayette	+ 1.0	+ .1	+ .9	− 2.6	(¹)	− 2.6
Fentress	+ 6.5	+ 4.6	+ 1.9	+ 16.7	+ 17.6	− .9
Franklin	+ 3.4	+ .4	+ 3.0	+ 5.7	− .2	+ 5.9
Gibson	+ 2.1	(¹)	+ 2.1	+ .6	(¹)	+ .6
Giles	+ 2.5	− .2	+ 2.7	+ 3.4	(¹)	+ 3.4
Grainger	+ 1.9	+ .4	+ 1.5	+ 4.1	+ 1.1	+ 3.0
Greene	+ 3.7	+ 1.1	+ 2.6	+ 10.0	+ 3.0	+ 7.0
Grundy	+ 3.7	+ .3	+ 3.4	+ 5.9	+ 2.4	+ 3.5
Hamblen	− .7	+ .6	− 1.3	− 3.4	+ .5	− 3.9
Hamilton	+ 4.9	+ 2.6	+ 2.3	+ 21.4	+ 14.3	+ 7.1
Hancock	+ 1.7	+ .1	+ 1.6	+ 14.0	+ .2	+ 13.8
Hardeman	+ 5.2	+ .9	+ 4.3	+ 8.2	+ 2.4	+ 5.8
Hardin	+ 5.5	+ 2.5	+ 3.0	+ 10.2	+ 5.4	+ 4.8
Hawkins	+ 6.3	+ 1.5	+ 4.8	+ 11.7	+ 4.2	+ 7.5
Haywood	+ 2.1	(¹)	+ 2.1	+ 9.3	(¹)	+ 9.3
Henderson	+ 4.7	+ 1.8	+ 2.9	+ 7.5	+ 5.5	+ 2.0
Henry	+ 2.7	(¹)	+ 2.7	+ 4.7	(¹)	+ 4.7
Hickman	+ 8.9	+ .2	+ 8.7	+ 15.6	+ .4	+ 15.2
Houston	+ 2.7	(¹)	+ 2.7	+ 13.2	(¹)	+ 13.2
Humphreys	+ 5.8	+ .1	+ 5.7	+ 9.5	+ .1	+ 9.4
Jackson	+ 2.8	+ .5	+ 2.3	+ 9.3	+ .1	+ 9.2
Jefferson	− .2	+ .3	− .5	− 1.3	+ .3	− 1.6
Johnson	+ 4.5	+ .3	+ 4.2	+ 6.6	− .7	+ 7.3
Knox	+ 2.8	+ 1.7	+ 1.1	+ 6.1	+ 3.1	+ 3.0
Lake	+ .4	(¹)	+ .4	+ 4.0	(¹)	+ 4.0

Table 29. *Net annual change in growing stock and sawtimber on commercial forest land by species group and county, 1970* (Continued)

County	Growing stock			Sawtimber		
	All species	Softwood	Hardwood	All species	Softwood	Hardwood
	— — Million cubic feet — —			— — Million board feet — —		
Lauderdale	+ 2.0	(¹)	+ 2.0	+ 13.0	(¹)	+ 13.0
Lawrence	+ 1.9	(¹)	+ 1.9	− 3.2	(¹)	− 3.2
Lewis	+ 4.7	+ .3	+ 4.4	+ 4.7	+ .4	+ 4.3
Lincoln	+ 1.1	+ .3	+ .8	− 1.8	(¹)	− 1.8
Loudon	+ .8	+ .9	− .1	+ 1.1	+ 1.1	(¹)
McMinn	+ 4.2	+ 2.0	+ 2.2	+ 4.4	+ 1.0	+ 3.4
McNairy	+ 2.6	+ 1.4	+ 1.2	− 6.7	+ 2.1	− 8.8
Macon	+ .9	(¹)	+ .9	− 2.2	(¹)	− 2.2
Madison	+ 1.0	− .2	+ 1.2	+ 5.4	− 1.3	+ 6.7
Marion	+ 5.2	+ .9	+ 4.3	+ 31.3	+ 4.5	+ 26.8
Marshall	+ .5	(¹)	+ .5	+ .4	− 2.2	+ 2.6
Maury	+ 2.1	(¹)	+ 2.1	+ 8.9	(¹)	+ 8.9
Meigs	+ 1.8	+ .9	+ .9	+ 2.7	− .2	+ 2.9
Monroe	+ 11.1	+ 5.1	+ 6.0	+ 27.5	+ 14.0	+ 13.5
Montgomery	+ 2.0	+ .1	+ 1.9	+ 2.0	(¹)	+ 2.0
Moore	+ .6	(¹)	+ .6	+ .3	− 1.8	+ 2.1
Morgan	+ 6.0	+ 1.4	+ 4.6	+ 16.7	+ 6.2	+ 10.5
Obion	− 3.0	− .3	− 2.7	− 8.3	− 2.0	− 6.3
Overton	+ 5.5	+ .7	+ 4.8	+ 14.2	+ 4.0	+ 10.2
Perry	+ 5.6	+ .3	+ 5.3	+ 7.6	+ .1	+ 7.5
Pickett	+ 1.8	+ .3	+ 1.5	+ 3.5	+ .9	+ 2.6
Polk	+ 8.4	+ 4.7	+ 3.7	+ 26.0	+ 12.3	+ 13.7
Putnam	+ 2.6	+ .1	+ 2.5	+ 2.4	− .1	+ 2.5
Rhea	+ 1.8	(¹)	+ 1.8	+ 7.1	+ .1	+ 7.0
Roane	+ 3.5	+ .8	+ 2.7	+ 7.4	+ 2.1	+ 5.3
Robertson	(¹)	(¹)	(¹)	− 1.7	(¹)	− 1.7
Rutherford	+ .4	− .4	+ .8	+ .2	(¹)	+ .2
Scott	+ 10.1	+ 3.8	+ 6.3	+ 25.2	+ 20.7	+ 4.5
Sequatchie	+ 2.3	+ 1.3	+ 1.0	+ 4.7	+ 5.3	− .6
Sevier	+ 6.2	+ 2.4	+ 3.8	+ 10.8	+ 5.0	+ 5.8
Shelby	− .1	− .3	+ .2	− 2.1	− 1.3	− .8
Smith	+ 1.6	(¹)	+ 1.6	+ .7	− .4	+ 1.1
Stewart	+ 7.4	+ .2	+ 7.2	+ 16.1	+ 1.2	+ 14.9
Sullivan	+ 2.0	+ .9	+ 1.1	+ 2.3	+ 3.3	− 1.0
Sumner	+ 1.0	+ .5	+ .5	+ 1.0	− .3	+ 1.3
Tipton	+ .2	(¹)	+ .2	+ 1.7	(¹)	+ 1.7
Trousdale	+ .2	(¹)	+ .2	+ 1.9	(¹)	+ 1.9
Unicoi	+ 2.6	+ .6	+ 2.0	+ 3.6	+ 2.9	+ .7
Union	+ 3.4	+ 1.5	+ 1.9	+ 2.8	+ 1.2	+ 1.6
Van Buren	+ 2.9	+ 1.1	+ 1.8	+ 3.8	+ 1.9	+ 1.9
Warren	+ 1.9	+ .1	+ 1.8	+ 1.7	− .3	+ 2.0
Washington	+ 1.9	+ .6	+ 1.3	+ 3.5	+ 1.9	+ 1.6
Wayne	+ 12.1	+ 2.0	+ 10.1	+ 17.8	+ 1.8	+ 16.0
Weakley	+ .9	+ .3	+ .6	+ 7.5	+ .8	+ 6.7
White	+ 2.4	+ .1	+ 2.3	+ 2.7	− .2	+ 2.9
Williamson	+ 2.6	− .1	+ 2.7	+ 4.5	− 2.2	+ 6.7
Wilson	+ 1.2	(¹)	+ 1.2	− .7	− .4	− .3
All counties	+292.7	+ 69.7	+223.0	+608.6	+185.0	+423.6

¹ Negligible.

Table 30. *Average volume per acre of growing stock and sawtimber on commercial forest land by species group and ownership class, 1971*

Ownership class	Growing stock			Sawtimber		
	All species	Softwood	Hardwood	All species	Softwood	Hardwood
	– – – Cubic feet – – –			– – – Board feet – – –		
STATE OF TENNESSEE						
National forest	1,228	435	793	3,496	1,440	2,056
Other public	1,055	288	767	3,156	905	2,251
Forest industry	806	152	654	2,146	398	1,748
Farmer	793	109	684	1,967	276	1,691
Misc. private	751	116	635	1,815	256	1,559
All ownerships	811	140	671	2,055	367	1,688
WEST						
National forest	. . .	. . .	. . .	. . .	. . .	. . .
Other public	1,679	415	1,264	6,799	1,691	5,108
Forest industry	1,575	8	1,567	6,460	46	6,414
Farmer	891	51	840	2,524	132	2,392
Misc. private	732	85	647	1,713	173	1,540
All ownerships	927	88	839	2,752	255	2,497
WEST CENTRAL						
National forest	. . .	. . .	. . .	. . .	. . .	. . .
Other public	925	57	868	2,207	144	2,063
Forest industry	807	56	751	1,577	112	1,465
Farmer	821	27	794	1,617	54	1,563
Misc. private	739	63	676	1,465	104	1,361
All ownerships	794	47	747	1,587	88	1,499
CENTRAL						
National forest	. . .	. . .	. . .	. . .	. . .	. . .
Other public	701	42	659	1,730	20	1,710
Forest industry	678	. . .	678	1,897	. . .	1,897
Farmer	559	18	541	1,317	12	1,305
Misc. private	617	21	596	1,512	11	1,501
All ownerships	592	20	572	1,428	12	1,416
PLATEAU						
National forest	. . .	. . .	. . .	. . .	. . .	. . .
Other public	1,015	342	673	2,711	1,025	1,686
Forest industry	661	179	482	1,848	552	1,296
Farmer	920	189	731	2,290	624	1,666
Misc. private	798	108	690	2,129	273	1,856
All ownerships	820	152	668	2,163	443	1,720
EAST						
National forest	1,228	435	793	3,496	1,440	2,056
Other public	951	584	367	2,456	1,645	811
Forest industry	796	454	342	1,720	1,010	710
Farmer	838	225	613	2,208	531	1,677
Misc. private	812	277	535	1,913	630	1,283
All ownerships	900	300	600	2,328	780	1,548

Table 31. *Growing-stock volume on commercial forest land by Resource region and species, 1971*

Species	State	West	West central	Central	Plateau	East
	------ Million cubic feet -------					
Softwood:						
Shortleaf pine	634.7	69.8	51.6	...	202.0	311.3
Loblolly pine	184.5	46.9	39.5	1.4	10.6	86.1
Virginia pine	560.8	...	2.8	1.3	191.9	364.8
Pitch pine	71.2	...	...	...	.9	70.3
White pine	151.1	...	...	...	23.5	127.6
Hemlock	55.2	...	...	...	27.5	27.7
Redcedar	103.6	10.5	13.8	43.3	11.1	24.9
Other softwoods	38.7	28.3	.3	...	...	10.1
All softwoods	1,799.8	155.5	108.0	46.0	467.5	1,022.8
Hardwood:						
Select white oaks [1]	1,305.4	140.2	485.9	184.8	323.3	171.2
Select red oaks [2]	554.7	112.1	96.0	75.1	114.7	156.8
Other white oaks	1,016.6	71.7	192.7	80.8	264.7	406.7
Other red oaks	1,486.4	248.9	314.4	206.6	335.1	381.4
Pecan	5.7	5.7	...	...	...	...
Other hickories	1,191.5	123.0	268.1	220.0	340.7	239.7
Sweetgum	337.4	203.8	62.9	28.4	15.8	26.5
Tupelo and blackgum	196.4	52.8	28.3	18.6	56.0	40.7
Hard maple	200.0	15.6	20.2	51.8	86.2	26.2
Soft maple	264.1	51.7	13.5	26.8	71.0	101.1
Beech	138.5	19.7	22.1	27.1	38.5	31.1
Ash	259.0	90.6	28.5	63.3	44.8	31.8
Basswood	52.7	...	...	9.9	22.7	20.1
Yellow-poplar	724.0	68.1	86.1	82.1	241.8	245.9
Black walnut	73.0	1.1	12.2	31.8	7.0	20.9
Black cherry	54.5	9.9	7.3	17.2	10.0	10.1
Magnolia (*Magnolia* spp.)	26.5	2.4	...	...	14.0	10.1
American elm	105.5	50.1	12.0	32.7	3.1	7.6
Other elms	83.7	24.3	20.7	23.2	7.4	8.1
Hackberry	68.2	19.2	4.3	42.9	.2	1.6
Sycamore	73.0	29.1	15.2	14.5	3.0	11.2
Other hardwoods	379.2	144.3	20.0	64.5	56.1	94.3
All hardwoods	8,596.0	1,484.3	1,710.4	1,302.1	2,056.1	2,043.1
All species	10,395.8	1,639.8	1,818.4	1,348.1	2,523.6	3,065.9

[1] Includes white, swamp chestnut, swamp white, chinkapin, and bur oaks.
[2] Includes northern red, Shumard, and cherrybark oaks.

49

Table 32. *Sawtimber volume on commercial forest land by Resource region and species, 1971*

Species	State	West	West central	Central	Plateau	East
	— — — — — — Million board feet — — — — — —					
Softwood:						
Shortleaf pine	1.691.5	208.1	139.6	...	539.9	803.9
Loblolly pine	280.6	100.6	26.5	...	45.8	107.7
Virginia pine	1,428.6	...	5.3	7.0	556.0	860.3
Pitch pine	217.1	...	...	...	1.9	215.2
White pine	622.3	...	...	...	93.6	528.7
Hemlock	·211.9	...	...	...	117.6	94.3
Redcedar	95.0	11.4	30.1	20.2	8.6	24.7
Other softwoods	152.1	130.0	...	...		22.1
All softwoods	4,699.1	450.1	201.5	27.2	1,363.4	2,656.9
Hardwood:						
Select white oaks [1]	3,133.0	412.3	1,003.8	493.6	723.8	499.5
Select red oaks [2]	1,781.0	402.0	236.5	259.2	404.9	478.4
Other white oaks	2,494.0	158.5	325.0	210.4	663.1	1,137.0
Other red oaks	3,966.6	657.1	733.8	641.4	929.9	1,004.4
Pecan	20.8	20.8	...	...	...	...
Other hickories	2,796.4	376.9	442.0	449.9	911.8	615.8
Sweetgum	839.8	607.2	71.8	85.8	28.2	46.8
Tupelo and blackgum	410.9	112.7	41.6	28.6	149.0	79.0
Hard maple	460.4	23.9	33.0	114.5	211.7	77.3
Soft maple	446.5	120.6	23.3	58.4	118.5	125.7
Beech	440.9	66.2	65.2	91.5	143.8	74.2
Ash	624.6	268.6	56.9	122.3	115.5	61.3
Basswood	164.5	...	...	33.6	70.3	60.6
Yellow-poplar	2,112.1	215.8	275.6	273.0	616.9	730.8
Black walnut	147.4	...	19.3	61.8	17.0	49.3
Black cherry	74.6	7.6	7.2	27.0	22.0	10.8
Magnolia (*Magnolia* spp.)	71.3	7.0	...	...	30.2	14.1
American elm	240.7	143.0	17.4	60.5	3.2	16.6
Other elms	162.6	57.5	31.0	40.1	18.2	15.8
Hackberry	151.2	83.8	8.2	75.3	...	3.9
Sycamore	232.4	107.3	31.5	54.0	5.9	33.7
Other hardwoods	869.4	586.5	11.2	43.2	39.6	138.9
All hardwoods	21,641.1	4,415.3	3,434.3	3,224.1	5,293.5	5,273.9
All species	26,340.2	4,865.4	3,635.8	3,251.3	6,656.9	7,930.8

[1] Includes white, swamp chestnut, swamp white, chinkapin, and bur oaks.
[2] Includes northern red, Shumard, and cherrybark oaks.

50

Table 33. *Sampling errors for commercial forest land, growing-stock, and saw-timber volume by species group, 1971*

County	Commercial forest land	Growing stock			Sawtimber		
		All species	Soft-wood	Hard-wood	All species	Soft-wood	Hard-wood
				– – – Percent – – –			
Anderson	2	13	37	16	19	40	22
Bedford	2	33	(¹)	35	46	. . .	46
Benton	4	14	(¹)	15	20	(¹)	22
Bledsoe	4	14	36	19	21	(¹)	36
Blount	3	15	22	19	21	27	24
Bradley	7	8	26	42	28	32	(¹)
Campbell	3	9	18	10	13	26	15
Cannon	2	16	(¹)	16	34	. . .	41
Carroll	2	12	(¹)	14	24	(¹)	26
Carter	2	11	38	11	17	44	15
Cheatham	2	24	(¹)	24	32	. . .	31
Chester	5	16	48	20	25	(¹)	33
Claiborne	3	14	38	17	22	40	23
Clay	2	33	(¹)	34	50	. . .	(¹)
Cocke	2	12	25	16	17	31	24
Coffee	4	18	. . .	18	26	. . .	26
Crockett	4	. . .	. . .	. . .	. . .	. . .	. . .
Cumberland	2	9	17	10	12	24	17
Davidson	1	37	. . .	37	38	. . .	41
Decatur	3	10	(¹)	12	16	(¹)	18
De Kalb	3	27	(¹)	32	47	(¹)	42
Dickson	1	13	(¹)	13	21	. . .	17
Dyer	3	25	. . .	25	31	. . .	31
Fayette	2	37	(¹)	39	48	(¹)	50
Fentress	2	11	16	13	18	23	19
Franklin	3	11	(¹)	11	16	(¹)	15
Gibson	3	32	. . .	31	36	. . .	36
Giles	2	15	(¹)	15	27	. . .	24
Grainger	3	18	26	21	21	38	23
Greene	2	15	33	18	22	45	24
Grundy	1	12	37	13	19	(¹)	20
Hamblen	4	36	(¹)	(¹)	48	49	(¹)
Hamilton	3	15	32	16	24	46	24
Hancock	2	30	(¹)	31	35	(¹)	35
Hardeman	1	11	44	13	19	(¹)	21
Hardin	2	9	25	12	15	38	18
Hawkins	3	13	31	18	24	33	28
Haywood	1	19	. . .	19	23	. . .	23
Henderson	4	16	(¹)	17	22	(¹)	22
Henry	3	21	. . .	21	30	. . .	30
Hickman	2	7	(¹)	8	13	(¹)	13
Houston	2	19	(¹)	19	34	(¹)	34
Humphreys	2	10	(¹)	10	17	(¹)	17
Jackson	4	29	45	33	(¹)	(¹)	33
Jefferson	5	21	32	27	29	(¹)	33
Johnson	4	15	32	17	23	37	27
Knox	2	18	33	25	24	45	31
Lake	2	(¹)	. . .	(¹)	(¹)	. . .	(¹)

Table 33. *Sampling errors for commercial forest land, growing-stock, and saw-timber volume by species group, 1971* (Continued)

County	Commercial forest land	Growing stock			Sawtimber		
		All species	Soft-wood	Hard-wood	All species	Soft-wood	Hard-wood
				- - Percent - -			
Lauderdale	3	27	. . .	27	34	. . .	34
Lawrence	1	14	. . .	14	23	. . .	23
Lewis	5	13	(¹)	14	19	(¹)	21
Lincoln	2	24	36	26	36	. . .	(¹)
Loudon	9	23	43	36	32	(¹)	42
McMinn	3	13	18	22	25	35	28
McNairy	1	13	37	15	21	49	22
Macon	4	15	. . .	15	23	. . .	23
Madison	3	19	(¹)	19	33	(¹)	33
Marion	2	11	28	11	14	38	16
Marshall	3	32	45	36	41	(¹)	46
Maury	2	21	. . .	21	32	. . .	34
Meigs	4	23	37	32	37	35	(¹)
Monroe	1	9	15	17	14	18	24
Montgomery	3	22	(¹)	22	37	. . .	36
Moore	3	27	(¹)	31	40	(¹)	35
Morgan	2	10	23	11	14	31	16
Obion	2	39	(¹)	25	48	(¹)	30
Overton	3	12	31	11	18	36	18
Perry	1	7	(¹)	8	13	(¹)	13
Pickett	2	21	(¹)	20	20	(¹)	30
Polk	2	10	13	13	13	16	17
Putnam	3	12	48	13	19	(¹)	20
Rhea	3	10	24	13	18	36	20
Roane	4	10	25	15	17	34	21
Robertson	1	33	. . .	33	37	. . .	40
Rutherford	2	30	49	36	44	. . .	(¹)
Scott	3	6	16	9	10	23	14
Sequatchie	5	16	26	18	24	36	27
Sevier	3	12	19	17	19	24	27
Shelby	2	20	(¹)	20	28	(¹)	28
Smith	5	35	(¹)	36	(¹)	(¹)	(¹)
Stewart	3	10	(¹)	10	13	(¹)	14
Sullivan	1	17	47	17	23	(¹)	22
Sumner	3	44	(¹)	46	45	(¹)	43
Tipton	4	(¹)	. . .	(¹)	(¹)	. . .	(¹)
Trousdale	3	50	(¹)	(¹)	46	. . .	50
Unicoi	5	15	37	20	20	37	29
Union	5	13	34	20	25	33	30
Van Buren	4	16	34	19	22	(¹)	28
Warren	2	10	(¹)	15	17	(¹)	24
Washington	1	18	39	16	29	47	27
Wayne	2	6	35	7	12	43	13
Weakley	2	49	(¹)	(¹)	(¹)	(¹)	(¹)
White	4	16	(¹)	13	23	(¹)	19
Williamson	3	13	45	15	20	. . .	23
Wilson	4	39	49	41	(¹)	(¹)	45
All counties	0.3	1.7	4.1	1.9	2.7	6.4	3.0

¹ Exceeds 50 percent.

Table 34. *Sampling errors for growth on growing stock and sawtimber on commercial forest land by species group and county, 1970*

County	Growing stock			Sawtimber		
	All species	Softwood	Hardwood	All species	Softwood	Hardwood
	- - - - - - - - - - - *Percent* - - - - - - - - - - -					
Anderson	24	41	27	33	44	38
Bedford	(¹)	(¹)	(¹)	(¹)	. . .	(¹)
Benton	23	(¹)	24	30	(¹)	32
Bledsoe	24	46	27	29	46	32
Blount	27	38	31	31	38	39
Bradley	37	43	(¹)	(¹)	48	(¹)
Campbell	18	37	19	27	(¹)	26
Cannon	47	(¹)	46	48	. . .	48
Carroll	22	(¹)	23	28	(¹)	29
Carter	23	36	23	27	44	30
Cheatham	41	(¹)	41	45	. . .	45
Chester	31	(¹)	33	46	(¹)	(¹)
Claiborne	25	(¹)	25	28	42	29
Clay	48	(¹)	49	(¹)	(¹)	(¹)
Cocke	22	29	23	26	34	30
Coffee	33	. . .	33	37	. . .	37
Crockett	(¹)	(¹)	(¹)	(¹)	(¹)	(¹)
Cumberland	15	25	16	23	34	23
Davidson	48	. . .	48	(¹)	. . .	(¹)
Decatur	24	(¹)	22	28	(¹)	30
De Kalb	37	(¹)	39	(¹)	(¹)	(¹)
Dickson	27	(¹)	27	28	. . .	28
Dyer	49	. . .	49	(¹)	. . .	(¹)
Fayette	(¹)	(¹)	(¹)	(¹)	(¹)	(¹)
Fentress	18	25	18	26	35	25
Franklin	20	(¹)	20	25	(¹)	25
Gibson	(¹)	. . .	(¹)	(¹)	. . .	(¹)
Giles	20	(¹)	20	39	. . .	39
Grainger	28	34	29	40	47	44
Greene	22	40	25	38	(¹)	45
Grundy	22	42	24	31	(¹)	33
Hamblen	(¹)	(¹)	(¹)	(¹)	(¹)	(¹)
Hamilton	21	30	26	30	42	38
Hancock	37	(¹)	38	(¹)	(¹)	(¹)
Hardeman	19	40	20	26	(¹)	26
Hardin	17	33	18	21	41	24
Hawkins	21	36	23	29	40	37
Haywood	39	. . .	39	40	. . .	40
Henderson	22	. . .	24	35	(¹)	29
Henry	36	. . .	36	48	. . .	48
Hickman	15	(¹)	16	22	(¹)	22
Houston	31	(¹)	31	38	(¹)	38
Humphreys	18	(¹)	18	27	(¹)	27
Jackson	33	(¹)	35	(¹)	(¹)	(¹)
Jefferson	33	42	37	48	(¹)	(¹)
Johnson	24	34	26	31	38	33
Knox	31	41	36	34	(¹)	38
Lake	(¹)	. . .	(¹)	(¹)	. . .	(¹)

53

Table 34. *Sampling errors for growth on growing stock and sawtimber on com-*
mercial forest land by species group and county, 1970 (Continued)

County	Growing stock			Sawtimber		
	All species	Softwood	Hardwood	All species	Softwood	Hardwood
– – – – – – – – – – Percent – – – – – – – – – – –						
Lauderdale	49		49	(¹)	. . .	(¹)
Lawrence	22	. . .	22	33	. . .	33
Lewis	24	(¹)	24	39	(¹)	41
Lincoln	42	(¹)	43	(¹)	. . .	(¹)
Loudon	39	(¹)	41	40	(¹)	(¹)
McMinn	23	29	27	33	40	40
McNairy	25	35	30	25	44	29
Macon	36	. . .	36	49	. . .	49
Madison	34	. . .	34	38	(¹)	38
Marion	18	39	20	28	48	31
Marshall	43	(¹)	42	(¹)	(¹)	(¹)
Maury	30	. . .	30	(¹)	. . .	(¹)
Meigs	36	(¹)	41	42	45	(¹)
Monroe	16	20	20	19	22	27
Montgomery	33	(¹)	33	42	. . .	42
Moore	(¹)	(¹)	(¹)	(¹)	(¹)	(¹)
Morgan	16	22	17	22	38	25
Obion	48	(¹)	46	(¹)	(¹)	(¹)
Overton	24	(¹)	23	29	(¹)	30
Perry	17	(¹)	17	22	(¹)	27
Pickett	39	(¹)	42	43	(¹)	46
Polk	18	20	20	24	28	34
Putnam	22	46	23	34	(¹)	36
Rhea	23	44	25	39	(¹)	39
Roane	21	34	24	31	(¹)	29
Robertson	(¹)	. . .	(¹)	(¹)	. . .	(¹)
Rutherford	39	(¹)	43	(¹)	. . .	(¹)
Scott	16	26	18	23	38	25
Sequatchie	24	30	28	30	39	40
Sevier	22	31	24	26	32	32
Shelby	34	(¹)	35	47	(¹)	48
Smith	44	(¹)	44	(¹)	(¹)	(¹)
Stewart	20	(¹)	21	23	(¹)	24
Sullivan	25	(¹)	25	32	(¹)	37
Sumner	47	(¹)	(¹)	(¹)	. . .	(¹)
Tipton	(¹)	. . .	(¹)	(¹)	. . .	(¹)
Trousdale	(¹)	(¹)	(¹)	(¹)	. . .	(¹)
Unicoi	31	46	34	31	44	38
Union	26	39	30	30	(¹)	33
Van Buren	31	46	34	34	(¹)	41
Warren	25	(¹)	26	34	(¹)	35
Washington	32	46	33	46	(¹)	(¹)
Wayne	14	37	15	23	44	26
Weakley	(¹)	(¹)	(¹)	(¹)	(¹)	(¹)
White	24	44	24	31	(¹)	31
Williamson	22	(¹)	23	28	(¹)	29
Wilson	48	(¹)	48	(¹)	(¹)	(¹)
All counties	2.4	5.3	2.7	3.8	7.7	4.3

¹ Exceeds 50 percent.

Table 35. *Sampling errors for timber removals from growing stock and sawtimber on commercial forest land by species group and county, 1970*

County	Growing stock			Sawtimber		
	All species	Softwood	Hardwood	All species	Softwood	Hardwood
	‒ ‒ ‒ ‒ ‒ ‒ ‒ ‒ ‒ ‒ Percent ‒ ‒ ‒ ‒ ‒ ‒ ‒ ‒ ‒ ‒					
Anderson	29	22	31	26	(¹)	27
Bedford	45	(¹)	48	43	(¹)	43
Benton	34	(¹)	35	32	(¹)	32
Bledsoe	26	12	34	28	36	36
Blount	27	11	43	30	30	46
Bradley	16	7	50	25	20	(¹)
Campbell	28	15	33	27	42	31
Cannon	44	(¹)	(¹)	47	(¹)	47
Carroll	25	21	27	25	(¹)	25
Carter	42	18	(¹)	39	37	(¹)
Cheatham	47	(¹)	47	38	(¹)	38
Chester	25	19	28	30	43	36
Claiborne	35	26	38	31	(¹)	34
Clay	47	(¹)	49	42	(¹)	42
Cocke	29	11	(¹)	29	27	(¹)
Coffee	28	(¹)	28	26	(¹)	26
Crockett	(¹)	48	(¹)	(¹)	(¹)	(¹)
Cumberland	27	13	33	27	41	32
Davidson	(¹)	(¹)	(¹)	(¹)	(¹)	(¹)
Decatur	31	33	32	26	(¹)	27
De Kalb	48	(¹)	(¹)	37	49	42
Dickson	34	(¹)	35	29	(¹)	29
Dyer	26	(¹)	26	23	(¹)	23
Fayette	32	(¹)	32	30	(¹)	30
Fentress	25	12	31	24	33	30
Franklin	29	43	29	25	(¹)	25
Gibson	48	(¹)	48	42	(¹)	42
Giles	39	(¹)	43	38	(¹)	38
Grainger	35	42	36	36	(¹)	37
Greene	42	25	48	40	(¹)	45
Grundy	30	15	36	26	41	30
Hamblen	33	47	34	33	(¹)	34
Hamilton	27	11	46	28	26	(¹)
Hancock	(¹)	(¹)	(¹)	(¹)	(¹)	(¹)
Hardeman	21	13	27	20	30	23
Hardin	19	12	23	19	38	21
Hawkins	46	38	49	44	(¹)	47
Haywood	33	(¹)	33	27	(¹)	27
Henderson	27	26	29	24	(¹)	25
Henry	31	(¹)	31	28	(¹)	28
Hickman	27	49	27	26	(¹)	26
Houston	46	(¹)	46	39	(¹)	39
Humphreys	28	(¹)	28	26	(¹)	28
Jackson	(¹)	(¹)	(¹)	46	(¹)	46
Jefferson	36	50	37	38	(¹)	39
Johnson	37	15	(¹)	32	32	49
Knox	38	17	50	40	45	(¹)
Lake	(¹)	(¹)	(¹)	46	(¹)	46

Table 35. *Sampling errors for timber removals from growing stock and sawtimber on commercial forest land by species group and county, 1970* (Continued)

County	Growing stock			Sawtimber		
	All species	Softwood	Hardwood	All species	Softwood	Hardwood
	----------- Percent ------------					
Lauderdale	23	(¹)	23	19	(¹)	19
Lawrence	24	(¹)	24	23	(¹)	23
Lewis	35	44	36	33	(¹)	34
Lincoln	43	(¹)	46	38	(¹)	38
Loudon	44	24	(¹)	48	(¹)	(¹)
McMinn	18	7	(¹)	23	21	(¹)
McNairy	21	14	24	19	49	20
Macon	39	(¹)	39	33	(¹)	33
Madison	26	22	28	23	44	25
Marion	35	20	40	31	46	37
Marshall	46	(¹)	(¹)	33	28	(¹)
Maury	46	(¹)	46	39	(¹)	39
Meigs	31	12	(¹)	35	32	(¹)
Monroe	15	6	40	15	14	38
Mongomery	34	(¹)	34	31	(¹)	31
Moore	(¹)	(¹)	(¹)	34	30	(¹)
Morgan	28	12	38	39	34	37
Obion	19	14	21	18	27	22
Overton	38	(¹)	39	33	(¹)	33
Perry	30	(¹)	30	26	(¹)	26
Pickett	(¹)	(¹)	(¹)	44	(¹)	44
Polk	16	7	49	16	14	45
Putnam	28	16	32	26	(¹)	28
Rhea	23	9	39	25	22	49
Roane	29	11	(¹)	33	30	(¹)
Robertson	40	(¹)	40	34	(¹)	34
Rutherford	36	36	(¹)	(¹)	(¹)	(¹)
Scott	22	14	25	19	41	21
Sequatchie	38	26	42	40	(¹)	44
Sevier	41	16	(¹)	(¹)	(¹)	(¹)
Shelby	26	23	29	25	42	28
Smith	(¹)	(¹)	(¹)	44	(¹)	49
Stewart	38	(¹)	38	33	(¹)	33
Sullivan	37	(¹)	38	40	(¹)	41
Sumner	49	(¹)	(¹)	42	(¹)	45
Tipton	43	(¹)	43	37	(¹)	37
Trousdale	(¹)	(¹)	(¹)	(¹)	(¹)	(¹)
Unicoi	38	18	48	35	38	47
Union	49	23	(¹)	45	(¹)	(¹)
Van Buren	47	31	(¹)	39	(¹)	43
Warren	34	20	39	31	(¹)	33
Washington	(¹)	46	(¹)	50	(¹)	(¹)
Wayne	24	16	27	25	46	28
Weakley	27	21	30	25	(¹)	26
White	31	(¹)	31	27	(¹)	27
Williamson	(¹)	(¹)	(¹)	32	29	46
Wilson	(¹)	(¹)	(¹)	(¹)	(¹)	(¹)
All counties	3.2	2.3	3.8	3.0	4.7	3.5

¹ Exceeds 50 percent.

Table 36. *Sampling errors for growing-stock volume on commercial forest land by Resource region and species, 1971*

Species	State	West	West central	Central	Plateau	East
			— — — — — — Percent — — — — — — —			
Softwood:						
Shortleaf pine	8	28	23	. . .	15	11
Loblolly pine	19	43	39	(¹)	41	26
Virginia pine	8	. . .	(¹)	(¹)	14	9
Pitch pine	23	. . .	. . .	. . .	(¹)	22
White pine	16	. . .	. . .	. . .	26	18
Hemlock	26	. . .	. . .	. . .	30	28
Redcedar	10	27	33	16	24	17
Other softwoods	28	(¹)	(¹)	. . .	. . .	(¹)
All softwoods	4.1	21.2	18.2	15.2	6.5	5.6
Hardwood:						
Select white oaks	4	13	6	12	7	8
Select red oaks	7	26	10	18	10	10
Other white oaks	4	14	9	18	9	7
Other red oaks	4	12	6	13	6	7
Pecan	49	46	. . .	. . .	. . .	. . .
Other hickories	4	15	7	12	7	8
Sweetgum	12	18	16	34	24	22
Tupelo and blackgum	7	17	13	22	11	12
Hard maple	10	41	21	18	17	29
Soft maple	7	20	30	24	12	10
Beech	11	32	21	25	21	20
Ash	18	(¹)	25	19	19	19
Basswood	20	. . .	. . .	34	29	38
Yellow-poplar	6	24	12	18	11	11
Black walnut	11	(¹)	24	15	34	22
Black cherry	13	36	28	25	27	27
Magnolia (*Magnolia* spp.)	20	(¹)	. . .	. . .	30	27
American elm	12	20	27	18	(¹)	25
Other elms	11	21	22	18	29	28
Hackberry	22	(¹)	(¹)	20	(¹)	. . .
Sycamore	18	35	33	30	42	40
Other hardwoods	9	21	30	26	19	18
All hardwoods	1.9	6.6	3.2	5.7	3.1	3.8
All species	1.7	6.2	2.9	5.5	2.8	2.8

¹ Exceeds 50 percent.

Table 37. *Sampling errors for sawtimber volume on commercial forest land by Resource region and species, 1971*

Species	State	West	West central	Central	Plateau	East
	– – – – – – – *Percent* – – – – – – –					
Softwood:						
Shortleaf pine	11	32	28	. . .	20	15
Loblolly pine	30	(¹)	(¹)	. . .	(¹)	35
Virginia pine	10	. . .	(¹)	(¹)	19	11
Pitch pine	26	. . .	. . .	. . .	(¹)	26
White pine	16	. . .	. . .	. . .	27	19
Hemlock	28	. . .	. . .	. . .	32	35
Redcedar	22	49	(¹)	40	37	25
Other softwoods	36	(¹)	. . .	. . .	. . .	(¹)
All softwoods	6.4	28.7	23.0	35.0	9.3	7.6
Hardwood:						
Select white oaks	5	15	9	16	10	10
Select red oaks	10	35	12	21	12	12
Other white oaks	6	18	13	24	11	9
Other red oaks	5	16	9	15	8	9
Pecan	(¹)	(¹)	. . .	. . .	. . .	. . .
Other hickories	6	23	9	20	9	10
Sweetgum	17	22	25	38	34	29
Tupelo and blackgum	9	24	21	42	14	19
Hard maple	15	(¹)	40	21	24	48
Soft maple	12	27	36	35	16	17
Beech	13	45	23	34	22	24
Ash	14	(¹)	33	27	24	22
Basswood	22	. . .	. . .	41	37	36
Yellow-poplar	8	27	14	25	15	13
Black walnut	14	. . .	39	23	42	24
Black cherry	21	(¹)	(¹)	34	36	(¹)
Magnolia (*Magnolia* spp.)	27	(¹)	. . .	. . .	35	41
American elm	18	26	(¹)	30	(¹)	35
Other elms	17	36	31	29	(¹)	37
Hackberry	32	(¹)	(¹)	36	. . .	(¹)
Sycamore	20	(¹)	38	33	(¹)	43
Other hardwoods	15	27	(¹)	(¹)	36	33
All hardwoods	3.0	10.0	5.2	8.1	4.7	5.3
All species	2.7	9.5	5.0	8.5	4.2	4.3

¹ Exceeds 50 percent.

U. S. Department of Agriculture
Forest Service Resource Bulletin SO-33

Forest Statistics
for
Southwest Alabama Counties

Arnold Hedlund

and

J. M. Earles

Southern Forest Experiment Station
New Orleans, Louisiana
Forest Service, U. S. Department of Agriculture

1972

Forest Statistics
for
Southwest Alabama Counties

Arnold Hedlund and J. M. Earles

This report tabulates information from a new forest inventory of counties in southwestern Alabama. The tables are intended for use as source data in compiling estimates for groups of counties. Because the sampling procedure is designed primarily to furnish inventory data for the State as a whole, estimates for individual counties have limited and variable accuracy.

The data on forest acreage and timber volume were secured by a systematic sampling method involving a forest-nonforest classification on aerial photographs and on-the-ground measurements of trees at sample locations. The sample locations were at the intersections of a grid of lines spaced 3 miles apart. At each forested location, 10 small plots were uniformly distributed on an area of about 1 acre.

The sampling errors to which the county area and volume totals are liable (on a probability of two chances out of three) are shown in table 1.

An approximation of sampling errors for groups of counties may be obtained by using the formula:

$$e = \frac{(SE) \sqrt{\text{specified volume or area}}}{\sqrt{\text{volume or area total in question}}}$$

Where: e = Estimated sampling error of the volume or area total in question

SE = Specified sampling error for the State.

The error decreases when data for two or more counties are grouped. Conversely, as data for individual counties are broken down by various subdivisions, the possibility of error increases and is greatest for the smallest items. Sampling errors associated with the estimates of the principal timber species in this report are shown in table 2.

Because of differences in standards of tree measurement, direct comparisons cannot be made between the estimates in this report and those from the survey of 1963. In table 3, changes between the two surveys are summarized in terms of current measurement standards.

It is anticipated that data for other counties of Alabama will be published as field work progresses. A Statewide interpretive report will be issued when all counties have been inventoried; it will include an evaluation of timber trends since 1963.

Table 1. *Sampling errors [1] for forest land and timber volume, 1972*

County	Commercial forest land	Growing stock	Saw-timber
	– – – Percent – – –		
Baldwin	2	9	10
Choctaw	1	8	11
Clarke	1	6	8
Conecuh	1	10	13
Covington	1	10	14
Escambia	1	10	12
Marengo	2	8	12
Mobile	1	12	15
Monroe	1	7	10
Sumter	2	10	14
Washington	1	8	10
Wilcox	2	8	10
All counties	0.4	2.5	3.3

[1] By random-sampling formula.

Table 2. *Sampling errors for timber volume by species, 1972*

Species	Growing stock	Sawtimber
	- - Percent - -	
Softwood:		
Longleaf pine	8	10
Slash pine	10	11
Shortleaf pine	8	9
Loblolly pine	5	6
Spruce pine	17	19
Redcedar	43	(¹)
Cypress	30	32
All softwoods	3.4	4.1
Hardwood:		
Select white oaks	11	13
Select red oaks	15	17
Other white oaks	12	16
Other red oaks	6	8
Pecan	43	49
Other hickories	10	12
Persimmon	27	(¹)
Maple	29	(¹)
Beech	20	23
Sweetgum	8	11
Blackgum	12	13
Other gums	23	24
White ash	35	44
Other ashes	21	22
Sycamore	28	36
Basswood	29	36
Yellow-poplar	11	13
Magnolia	22	42
Sweetbay	14	19
Willow	40	(¹)
Black cherry	34	(¹)
American elm	20	27
Other elms	18	29
Hackberry	23	30
Dogwood	15	. . .
Holly	28	(¹)
Other hardwoods	45	(¹)
All hardwoods	4.3	5.5
All species	2.5	3.3

¹ Exceeds 50 percent.

Table 3. *Change¹ in forest resource since 1963*

Item	Change
	Percent
Commercial forest land	+ 0.2
Growing-stock volume:	
Softwood	+ 11
Hardwood	+ 2
All species	+ 7
Sawtimber volume:	
Softwood	+ 14
Hardwood	− 1
All species	+ 10

¹ Based on 1972 measurement standards.

DEFINITIONS OF TERMS

Acceptable trees.—Growing-stock trees of commercial species that meet specified standards of size and quality but do not qualify as desirable trees.

Commercial forest land.—Forest land producing or capable of producing crops of industrial wood and not withdrawn from timber utilization.

Desirable trees.—Growing-stock trees that are of commercial species, have no defects in quality for timber products, are of relatively high vigor, and contain no pathogens that may result in death or serious deterioration before rotation age.

Forest type.—A classification of forest land based upon the species forming a plurality of live-tree stocking.

Growing-stock trees.—Live trees that are of commercial species and qualify as desirable or acceptable trees.

Growing-stock volume.—Net volume in cubic feet of growing-stock trees at least 5.0 inches in diameter at breast height, from a 1-foot stump to a minimum 4.0-inch top diameter outside bark of the central stem, or to the point where the central stem breaks into limbs.

Poletimber trees.—Growing-stock trees of commercial species at least 5.0 inches in diameter at breast height, but smaller than sawtimber size.

Sawtimber trees.—Live trees that are of commercial species, contain at least a 12-foot saw log, and meet regional specifications for freedom from defect. Softwoods must be at least 9.0 inches in diameter at breast height and hardwoods at least 11.0 inches.

Sawtimber volume.—Net volume of the saw-log portion of live sawtimber in board feet, International ¼-inch rule.

Site class.—A classification of forest land in terms of inherent capacity to grow crops of industrial wood.

Stand-size class.—A classification of forest land based on the size class of growing-stock trees on the area; that is, sawtimber, poletimber, or seedling and saplings.

Table 4 . *Commercial forest land by ownership class, 1972*

County	All ownerships	National forest	Other public	Forest industry	Farmer	Misc. private
			- - - - - - - - - - *Thousand acres* - - - - - - - - - -			
Baldwin	702.1	...	5.7	286.0	114.5	295.9
Choctaw	504.0	...	3.9	150.0	102.0	248.1
Clarke	722.4	...	8.2	291.2	112.0	311.0
Conecuh	428.4	...	(1/)	170.1	132.3	126.0
Covington	450.0	54.2	2.1	156.0	158.5	79.2
Escambia	490.2	32.0	4.0	216.6	61.3	176.3
Marengo	402.6	...	1.0	79.2	165.0	157.4
Mobile	522.9	...	24.4	50.4	92.5	355.6
Monroe	508.8	...	3.3	164.3	196.0	145.2
Sumter	390.6	...	1.4	124.0	155.0	110.2
Washington	622.2	...	1.4	79.3	107.4	434.1
Wilcox	421.8	...	4.3	57.0	153.9	206.6
All counties	6,166.0	86.2	59.7	1,824.1	1,550.4	2,645.6

1/ Negligible.

Table 5. *Commercial forest land by forest type, 1972*

County	All types	Longleaf-slash pine	Loblolly-shortleaf pine	Oak-pine	Oak-hickory	Oak-gum-cypress	Elm-ash-cottonwood
			- - - - - - - - - - - - - *Thousand acres* - - - - - - - - - - - - -				
Baldwin	702.1	283.9	58.5	156.0	47.7	156.0	...
Choctaw	504.0	...	186.0	132.0	108.0	72.0	6.0
Clarke	722.4	...	308.0	151.2	117.6	134.4	11.2
Concuh	428.4	12.6	119.7	94.5	163.8	37.8	...
Covington	450.0	144.0	72.0	84.0	102.0	48.0	...
Escambia	490.2	245.1	22.8	119.7	39.9	62.7	...
Marengo	402.6	...	151.8	99.0	59.4	92.4	...
Mobile	522.9	201.6	31.5	126.0	81.9	81.9	...
Monroe	508.8	21.2	111.3	137.8	148.4	84.8	5.3
Sumter	390.6	...	117.8	55.8	124.0	86.8	6.2
Washington	622.2	158.6	103.7	176.9	85.4	97.6	...
Wilcox	421.8	11.4	131.1	125.4	91.2	62.7	...
All counties	6,166.0	1,078.4	1,414.2	1,458.3	1,169.3	1,017.1	28.7

3

Table 6. *Commercial forest land by stand-size class, 1972*

County	All classes	Sawtimber	Poletimber	Sapling and seedling	Nonstocked areas
		- - - - - - - - *Thousand acres* - - - - - - -			
Baldwin	702.1	268.7	112.7	312.0	8.7
Choctaw	504.0	180.0	174.0	150.0	...
Clarke	722.4	386.4	168.0	168.0	...
Conecuh	428.4	182.7	107.1	132.3	6.3
Covington	450.0	168.0	114.0	162.0	6.0
Escambia	490.2	216.6	96.9	176.7	...
Marengo	402.6	158.4	118.8	125.4	...
Mobile	522.9	126.0	126.0	252.0	18.9
Monroe	508.8	201.4	143.1	164.3	...
Sumter	390.6	192.2	68.2	130.2	...
Washington	622.2	250.1	164.7	207.4	...
Wilcox	421.8	216.6	108.3	96.9	...
All counties	6,166.0	2,547.1	1,501.8	2,077.2	39.9

Table 7. *Commercial forest land by site class, 1972*

County	All classes	165 cu. ft. or more	120-165 cu. ft.	85-120 cu.ft.	50-85 cu.ft.	Less than 50 cu. ft.
		- - - - - - - - - - *Thousand acres* - - - - - - - - - -				
Baldwin	702.1	...	19.5	188.5	444.2	49.9
Choctaw	504.0	30.0	84.0	276.0	114.0	...
Clarke	722.4	39.2	190.4	291.2	184.8	16.8
Conecuh	428.4	50.4	207.9	157.5	12.6	...
Covington	450.0	30.0	102.0	162.0	150.0	6.0
Escambia	490.2	...	45.6	176.7	245.1	22.8
Marengo	402.6	6.6	118.8	204.6	72.6	...
Mobile	522.9	...	12.6	107.1	296.1	107.1
Monroe	508.8	10.6	90.1	164.3	164.3	79.5
Sumter	390.6	18.6	80.6	173.6	99.2	18.6
Washington	622.2	6.1	48.8	250.1	298.9	18.3
Wilcox	421.8	11.4	51.3	188.1	165.3	5.7
All counties	6,166.0	202.9	1,051.6	2,339.7	2,247.1	324.7

4

Table 8. *Cordage of growing stock on commercial forest land by species group, 1972*

County	All species	Softwood			Hardwood			
		Total	Pine	Other	Total	Oak	Gum	Other
			- - - - - - - - - - Thousand cords - - - - - - - - -					
Baldwin	10,382	6,127	5,472	655	4,255	775	2,149	1,331
Choctaw	7,897	5,067	4,914	153	2,830	1,188	884	758
Clarke	12,910	7,740	7,560	180	5,170	1,763	1,703	1,704
Conecuh	6,632	3,256	3,245	11	3,376	1,221	1,136	1,019
Covington	5,856	4,087	4,068	19	1,769	506	703	560
Escambia	6,562	4,823	4,815	8	1,739	515	436	788
Marengo	5,866	3,247	3,163	84	2,619	1,066	534	1,019
Mobile	5,169	3,121	2,884	237	2,048	349	1,051	648
Monroe	7,683	3,659	3,580	79	4,024	1,434	1,212	1,378
Sumter	6,348	3,208	3,152	56	3,140	1,270	816	1,054
Washington	8,395	4,829	4,689	140	3,566	1,180	1,001	1,385
Wilcox	7,410	3,701	3,678	23	3,709	1,550	987	1,172
All counties	91,110	52,865	51,220	1,645	38,245	12,817	12,612	12,816

Table 9. *Growing-stock volume on commercial forest land by species group, 1972*

County	All species	Softwood			Hardwood			
		Total	Pine	Other	Total	Oak	Gum	Other
			- - - - - - - - - - - Million cubic feet - - - - - - - - - - - -					
Baldwin	744.6	459.5	410.4	49.1	285.1	51.9	144.0	89.2
Choctaw	569.6	380.0	368.5	11.5	189.6	79.6	59.2	50.8
Clarke	926.9	580.5	567.0	13.5	346.4	118.1	114.1	114.2
Conecuh	470.4	244.2	243.4	.8	226.2	81.8	76.1	68.3
Covington	425.0	306.5	305.1	1.4	118.5	33.9	47.1	37.5
Escambia	478.2	361.7	361.1	.6	116.5	34.5	29.2	52.8
Marengo	419.0	243.5	237.2	6.3	175.5	71.4	35.8	68.3
Mobile	371.3	234.1	216.3	17.8	137.2	23.4	70.4	43.4
Monroe	544.0	274.4	268.5	5.9	269.6	96.1	81.2	92.3
Sumter	451.0	240.6	236.4	4.2	210.4	85.1	54.7	70.6
Washington	601.1	362.2	351.7	10.5	238.9	79.0	67.1	92.8
Wilcox	526.1	277.6	275.9	1.7	248.5	103.9	66.1	78.5
All counties	6,527.2	3,964.8	3,841.5	123.3	2,562.4	858.7	845.0	858.7

5

Table 10. *Sawtimber volume on commercial forest land by species group, 1972*

County	All species	Softwood			Hardwood			
		Total	Pine	Other	Total	Oak	Gum	Other
- - - - - - - - - - - - - *Million board feet* - - - - - - - - - - - - -								
Baldwin	2,911.1	2,078.6	1,857.4	221.2	832.5	173.1	417.5	241.9
Choctaw	2,105.6	1,683.6	1,616.4	67.2	422.0	238.8	84.2	99.0
Clarke	3,639.4	2,732.2	2,670.4	61.8	907.2	376.8	262.0	268.4
Conecuh	1,734.0	1,127.2	1,123.3	3.9	606.8	274.3	194.5	138.0
Covington	1,475.3	1,279.3	1,272.1	7.2	196.0	66.2	64.5	65.3
Escambia	1,850.6	1,545.8	1,545.8	...	304.8	124.9	67.4	112.5
Marengo	1,475.5	939.8	910.8	29.0	535.7	243.3	101.9	190.5
Mobile	1,192.5	890.3	818.2	72.1	302.2	79.4	170.2	52.6
Monroe	1,865.0	1,087.6	1,057.9	29.7	777.4	368.4	164.2	244.8
Sumter	1,837.5	1,224.4	1,216.9	7.5	613.1	319.9	120.3	172.9
Washington	2,043.6	1,433.7	1,386.7	47.0	609.9	225.2	182.5	202.2
Wilcox	1,771.1	1,053.4	1,053.4	...	717.7	343.4	167.2	207.1
All counties	23,901.2	17,075.9	16,529.3	546.6	6,825.3	2,833.7	1,996.4	1,995.2

Table 11. *Sawtimber volume on commercial forest land by species group and diameter class, 1972*

County	All species	Softwood			Hardwood		
		Total	9.0-14.9 inches	15.0 inches and up	Total	11.0-14.9 inches	15.0 inches and up
- - - - - - - - - - - *Million board feet* - - - - - - - - - - - -							
Baldwin	2,911.1	2,078.6	1,492.3	586.3	832.5	272.3	560.2
Choctaw	2,105.6	1,683.6	1,047.5	636.1	422.0	211.5	210.5
Clarke	3,639.4	2,732.2	1,570.2	1,162.0	907.2	374.3	532.9
Conecuh	1,734.0	1,127.2	615.0	512.2	606.8	349.9	256.9
Covington	1,475.3	1,279.3	884.8	394.5	196.0	134.4	61.6
Escambia	1,850.6	1,545.8	1,103.2	442.6	304.8	112.1	192.7
Marengo	1,475.5	939.8	603.4	336.4	535.7	189.6	346.1
Mobile	1,192.5	890.3	651.3	239.0	302.2	118.8	183.4
Monroe	1,865.0	1,087.6	739.6	348.0	777.4	324.8	452.6
Sumter	1,837.5	1,224.4	666.7	557.7	613.1	249.1	364.0
Washington	2,043.6	1,433.7	890.8	542.9	609.9	220.7	389.2
Wilcox	1,771.1	1,053.4	690.9	362.5	717.7	307.9	409.8
All counties	23,901.2	17,075.9	10,955.7	6,120.2	6,825.3	2,865.4	3,959.9

6

Table 12. *Growing-stock volume of softwoods on commercial forest land by forest type, 1972*

County	All types	Longleaf-slash pine	Loblolly-shortleaf pine	Oak-pine	Oak-hickory	Oak-gum-cypress	Elm-ash-cottonwood
			- - - - - - Million cubic feet - - - - - -				
Baldwin	459.5	272.2	34.3	77.0	11.7	64.3	...
Choctaw	380.0	...	235.9	101.7	23.5	18.9	...
Clarke	580.5	...	390.0	141.2	26.3	17.3	5.7
Conecuh	244.2	13.0	113.8	88.4	24.9	4.1	...
Covington	306.5	145.8	87.6	52.2	12.0	8.9	...
Escambia	361.7	252.9	12.8	69.7	4.3	22.0	...
Marengo	243.5	...	164.5	62.3	8.4	8.3	...
Mobile	234.1	124.2	26.0	49.3	7.0	27.6	...
Monroe	274.4	13.4	101.8	103.8	38.8	16.6	...
Sumter	240.6	...	181.8	31.6	22.0	5.2	...
Washington	362.2	134.6	87.4	105.0	12.5	22.7	...
Wilcox	277.6	4.5	155.5	87.1	23.9	6.6	...
All counties	3,964.8	960.6	1,591.4	969.3	215.3	222.5	5.7

Table 13. *Growing-stock volume of hardwoods on commercial forest land by forest type, 1972*

County	All types	Longleaf-slash pine	Loblolly-shortleaf pine	Oak-pine	Oak-hickory	Oak-gum-cypress	Elm-ash-cottonwood
			- - - - - - Million cubic feet - - - - - -				
Baldwin	285.1	12.5	2.9	22.5	13.1	234.1	...
Choctaw	189.6	...	30.7	43.0	50.0	65.4	0.5
Clarke	346.4	...	60.3	77.4	51.6	149.8	7.3
Conecuh	226.2	1.2	24.3	61.6	80.5	58.6	...
Covington	118.5	9.1	10.5	14.6	28.6	55.7	...
Escambia	116.5	10.1	2.0	22.4	10.5	71.5	...
Marengo	175.5	...	23.6	40.9	36.8	74.2	...
Mobile	137.2	7.5	10.4	30.3	5.4	83.6	...
Monroe	269.6	1.1	13.0	61.5	106.3	85.3	2.4
Sumter	210.4		32.0	22.9	63.6	87.5	4.4
Washington	238.9	6.1	15.3	58.7	39.6	119.2	...
Wilcox	248.5	.1	22.1	63.6	63.4	99.3	...
All counties	2,562.4	47.7	247.1	519.4	549.4	1,184.2	14.6

Table 14. *Sawtimber volume of softwoods on commercial forest land by forest type, 1972*

County	All types	Longleaf-slash pine	Loblolly-shortleaf pine	Oak-pine	Oak-hickory	Oak-gum-cypress	Elm-ash-cottonwood
		- - - - - - - - - - - - *Million board feet* - - - - - - - - - - - -					
Baldwin	2,078.6	1,224.0	146.2	352.5	52.1	303.8	...
Choctaw	1,683.6	...	1,007.1	463.7	106.9	105.9	...
Clarke	2,732.2	...	1,807.1	704.8	112.5	83.3	24.5
Conecuh	1,127.2	46.0	440.2	494.2	125.1	21.7	...
Covington	1,279.3	575.5	401.3	205.6	51.1	45.8	...
Escambia	1,545.8	994.4	50.5	362.7	22.7	115.5	...
Marengo	939.8	...	591.8	273.0	34.3	40.7	...
Mobile	890.3	444.8	91.8	212.5	15.1	126.1	...
Monroe	1,087.6	60.5	296.1	470.8	173.5	86.7	...
Sumter	1,224.4	...	934.4	155.4	103.9	30.7	...
Washington	1,433.7	472.1	333.6	462.1	53.0	112.9	...
Wilcox	1,053.4	8.5	569.6	354.4	98.6	22.3	...
All counties	17,075.9	3,825.8	6,669.7	4,511.7	948.8	1,095.4	24.5

Table 15. *Sawtimber volume of hardwoods on commercial forest land by forest type, 1972*

County	All types	Longleaf-slash pine	Loblolly-shortleaf pine	Oak-pine	Oak-hickory	Oak-gum-cypress	Elm-ash-cottonwood
		- - - - - - - - - - - *Million board feet* - - - - - - - - - - -					
Baldwin	832.5	35.5	1.7	53.6	31.5	710.2	...
Choctaw	422.0	...	53.1	103.7	97.7	167.5	...
Clarke	907.2	...	99.6	205.7	124.5	453.0	24.4
Conecuh	606.8	2.0	73.0	183.8	202.2	145.8	...
Covington	196.0	22.5	18.2	29.0	33.1	93.2	...
Escambia	304.8	34.3	5.8	45.4	24.2	195.1	...
Marengo	535.7	...	54.5	85.7	146.3	249.2	...
Mobile	302.2	13.8	32.2	61.1	8.9	186.2	...
Monroe	777.4	2.0	20.0	141.3	321.4	283.8	8.9
Sumter	613.1	...	69.5	83.6	186.9	257.8	15.3
Washington	609.9	9.8	32.3	111.2	99.7	356.9	...
Wilcox	717.7	...	36.6	158.1	172.8	350.2	...
All counties	6,825.3	119.9	496.5	1,262.2	1,449.2	3,448.9	48.6

Table 16. *Growing-stock volume of softwoods on commercial forest land by stand-size class, 1972*

County	All classes	Sawtimber	Poletimber	Sapling and seedling	Nonstocked areas
		- - - - - - - - *Million cubic feet* - - - - - - - -			
Baldwin	459.5	326.7	61.6	70.8	0.4
Choctaw	380.0	240.9	91.7	47.4	
Clarke	580.5	465.3	80.9	34.3	
Conecuh	244.2	163.7	61.0	19.5	
Covington	306.5	231.4	48.1	27.0	
Escambia	361.7	258.4	75.7	27.6	
Marengo	243.5	137.4	80.9	25.2	...
Mobile	234.1	126.2	57.7	49.4	.8
Monroe	274.4	136.1	97.0	41.3	...
Sumter	240.6	206.9	18.4	15.3	
Washington	362.2	208.9	117.5	35.8	...
Wilcox	277.6	201.3	63.4	12.9	...
All counties	3,964.8	2,703.2	853.9	406.5	1.2

Table 17. *Growing-stock volume of hardwoods on commercial forest land by stand-size class, 1972*

County	All classes	Sawtimber	Poletimber	Sapling and seedling	Nonstocked areas
		- - - - - - - - *Million cubic feet* - - - - - - - -			
Baldwin	285.1	201.6	58.6	24.9	
Choctaw	189.6	90.7	83.3	15.6	
Clarke	346.4	242.6	86.2	17.6	
Conecuh	226.2	136.8	70.5	18.9	
Covington	118.5	45.0	61.0	12.5	
Escambia	116.5	76.5	34.8	5.2	
Marengo	175.5	108.4	50.5	16.6	
Mobile	137.2	81.9	45.2	10.1	
Monroe	269.6	186.1	63.8	19.7	
Sumter	210.4	140.7	43.3	26.4	
Washington	238.9	154.9	62.0	22.0	...
Wilcox	248.5	190.3	37.2	21.0	...
All counties	2,562.4	1,655.5	696.4	210.5	...

Table 18. *Sawtimber volume of softwoods on commercial forest land by stand-size class, 1972*

County	All classes	Sawtimber	Poletimber	Sapling and seedling	Nonstocked areas
	- - - - - - - Million board feet - - - - - - -				
Baldwin	2,078.6	1,666.0	137.9	274.7	...
Choctaw	1,683.6	1,208.7	285.8	189.1	...
Clarke	2,732.2	2,373.0	237.5	121.7	...
Conecuh	1,127.2	879.4	169.5	78.3	...
Covington	1,279.3	1,074.7	117.0	87.6	...
Escambia	1,545.8	1,251.9	214.0	79.9	...
Marengo	939.8	625.5	230.6	83.7	...
Mobile	890.3	602.0	142.7	142.7	2.9
Monroe	1,087.6	679.5	288.3	119.8	...
Sumter	1,224.4	1,095.9	61.4	67.1	...
Washington	1,433.7	993.7	344.5	95.5	...
Wilcox	1,053.4	864.8	146.0	42.6	...
All counties	17,075.9	13,315.1	2,375.2	1,382.7	2.9

Table 19. *Sawtimber volume of hardwoods on commercial forest land by stand-size class, 1972*

County	All classes	Sawtimber	Poletimber	Sapling and seedling	Nonstocked areas
	- - - - - - - Million board feet - - - - - - -				
Baldwin	832.5	655.4	108.9	68.2	
Choctaw	422.0	274.6	127.3	20.1	
Clarke	907.2	752.1	128.3	26.8	
Conecuh	606.8	427.7	150.4	28.7	
Covington	196.0	115.0	66.6	14.4	
Escambia	304.8	251.8	40.2	12.8	
Marengo	535.7	415.1	92.7	27.9	
Mobile	302.2	235.8	48.7	17.7	
Monroe	777.4	622.6	116.3	38.5	
Sumter	613.1	480.3	64.2	68.6	
Washington	609.9	471.4	102.7	35.8	...
Wilcox	717.7	623.6	52.9	41.2	...
All counties	6,825.3	5,325.4	1,099.2	400.7	...

Table 20. *Growing-stock volume on commercial forest land by species and diameter class, 1972*

Species	All classes	Diameter class (inches at breast height) — Million cubic feet									
		5.0–6.9	7.0–8.9	9.0–10.9	11.0–12.9	13.0–14.9	15.0–16.9	17.0–18.9	19.0–20.9	21.0–28.9	29.0 and larger
Softwood:											
Longleaf pine	825.7	62.3	136.1	177.1	203.8	154.1	71.0	17.3	4.0	...	...
Slash pine	571.2	71.4	106.6.	112.4	102.4	72.3	55.0	29.7	13.5	7.9	...
Shortleaf pine	644.9	62.2	91.9	119.4	151.1	103.1	72.1	30.5	10.3	4.3	...
Loblolly pine	1,668.9	144.2	198.6	235.1	268.5	276.7	212.3	165.4	83.5	79.1	5.5
Spruce pine	130.8	8.7	11.3	8.7	13.9	26.1	18.6	19.9	12.2	9.8	1.6
Redcedar	21.7	4.9	8.0	2.9	3.4	.9	...	...	...	...	...
Cypress	101.6	2.4	7.8	8.2	9.0	10.4	13.0	9.4	8.6	32.2	.6
Total	3,964.8	356.1	560.3	663.8	752.1	643.6	442.7	272.2	132.1	134.2	7.7
Hardwood:											
Select white oaks	141.4	11.7	16.3	18.7	20.4	25.8	16.6	16.0	7.8	6.9	1.2
Select red oaks	75.1	2.5	5.0	8.4	8.9	6.5	7.6	8.6	4.7	21.8	1.1
Other white oaks	99.5	10.0	18.4	12.5	13.0	8.8	9.2	8.3	4.2	13.3	1.8
Other red oaks	542.7	59.1	67.9	79.6	76.8	80.2	54.7	41.0	20.8	49.2	13.4
Pecan	25.8	.6	2.0	3.1	3.1	5.9	1.7	1.7	2.2	4.5	1.0
Other hickories	131.3	11.0	13.1	19.5	22.3	22.7	17.1	9.6	2.4	12.4	1.2
Persimmon	6.5	1.2	2.8	2.0	.5	...	...	...	...	...	...
Maple	56.3	1.2	14.1	12.8	5.3	3.6	4.6	1.9	1.6	.5	...
Beech	34.4	1.5	2.3	2.8	4.4	4.4	6.6	4.7	4.2	3.5	...
Sweetgum	420.8	66.6	72.2	74.3	63.2	50.9	29.8	27.5	15.6	20.4	.3
Blackgum	224.9	30.8	44.3	54.3	32.9	25.6	18.8	8.8	5.0	4.4	...
Other gums	199.3	9.7	27.2	34.3	18.3	31.6	33.4	17.8	11.6	14.7	.7
White ash	27.2	1.2	1.8	2.2	2.3	4.1	6.4	2.1	1.1	6.0	...
Other ashes	70.3	7.2	12.9	9.7	8.5	12.6	7.7	2.9	5.9	2.9	...
Sycamore	18.5	1.9	2.0	1.3	.7	2.0	1.2	3.5	2.2	2.2	...
Basswood	10.6	1.1	.7	1.3	1.7	1.9	2.0	1.2	...	...	...
Yellow-poplar	136.7	8.7	13.0	18.4	14.8	20.7	15.0	24.3	11.1	9.7	.5
Magnolia (*Magnolia* spp.)	12.0	2.5	2.8	1.3	1.3	.5	.9	2.2	...	...	1.0
Sweetbay	152.0	26.3	28.3	33.5	29.4	15.7	8.8	4.5	2.6	2.9	...
Willow	6.3	1.1	1.1	2.2	1.9	...	...	...	...	...	...
Black cherry	3.5	.6	1.3	.7	...	.9	...	...	...	...	...
American elm	31.3	2.4	3.2	6.3	4.5	7.8	3.0	2.2	1.0	.4	...
Other elms	27.5	4.3	6.9	3.9	4.0	2.0	2.9	.5	1.1	1.9	.5
Hackberry	64.3	5.8	8.6	11.8	8.5	5.8	9.9	5.6	3.8	4.5	...
Dogwood	14.2	12.5	1.7	...	...	...	...	...	...	...	...
Holly	6.8	2.6	2.3	1.0	.4	.5	...	...	...	...	...
Other hardwoods	23.2	5.7	1.1	2.3	1.9	1.9	3.0	2.0	1.6	3.7	...
Total	2,562.4	301.0	374.2	418.3	349.0	342.4	261.1	196.9	110.5	186.3	22.7
All species	6,527.2	657.1	934.5	1,082.1	1,101.1	986.0	703.8	469.1	242.6	320.5	30.4

1/ Detailed county statistics by species and diameter class are available upon request.

11

Table 21. *Sawtimber volume on commercial forest land by species and diameter class, 1972*

Species	All classes	Diameter class (inches at breast height)							
		9.0–10.9	11.0–12.9	13.0–14.9	15.0–16.9	17.0–18.9	19.0–20.9	21.0–28.9	29.0 and larger
		– – – – – – – – – – – – – – – – Million board feet – – – – – – – – – – – – – – – –							
Softwood:									
Longleaf pine	3,522.0	810.5	1,175.0	945.5	453.7	112.1	25.2	...	...
Slash pine	2,279.3	518.8	611.9	450.2	360.0	195.5	89.8	53.1	...
Shortleaf pine	2,552.1	576.6	791.1	550.8	390.0	164.6	54.1	24.9	...
Loblolly pine	7,595.5	999.4	1,456.2	1,641.9	1,323.9	1,059.9	553.0	525.7	35.5
Spruce pine	580.4	42.7	69.8	139.8	98.5	108.1	64.4	48.9	8.2
Redcedar	46.9	14.9	17.5	5.2	4.3	...	...	5.0	...
Cypress	499.7	36.6	46.1	55.2	71.9	52.5	50.8	184.1	2.5
Total	17,075.9	2,999.5	4,167.6	3,788.6	2,702.3	1,692.7	837.3	841.7	46.2
Hardwood:									
Select white oaks	506.2	...	96.5	131.5	92.7	89.4	46.3	41.8	8.0
Select red oaks	319.1	...	35.7	33.3	38.5	48.1	26.6	130.9	6.0
Other white oaks	306.8	...	57.5	45.9	48.5	47.1	23.0	71.9	12.9
Other red oaks	1,701.6	...	309.0	399.9	290.0	224.1	117.9	285.0	75.4
Pecan	84.8	...	10.3	24.4	8.6	6.6	9.9	20.6	4.4
Other hickories	367.3	...	79.1	95.2	75.6	42.6	11.1	57.3	6.4
Persimmon	1.6	...	1.6	...	...	...	...	...	...
Maple	63.8	...	17.6	12.7	16.0	7.7	7.7	2.1	...
Beech	108.0	...	14.3	16.6	25.5	16.7	18.7	16.2	...
Sweetgum	1,005.2	...	254.3	248.1	153.4	147.4	86.2	115.0	.8
Blackgum	445.4	...	125.1	120.8	100.0	47.3	27.8	24.4	...
Other gums	545.8	...	52.4	123.9	149.6	86.0	57.7	73.3	2.9
White ash	97.8	...	7.2	17.2	29.3	8.8	6.0	29.3	...
Other ashes	162.6	...	25.2	52.0	32.3	13.4	28.3	11.4	...
Sycamore	49.6	...	2.2	6.1	4.5	17.0	10.5	9.3	...
Basswood	34.3	...	6.0	9.4	9.8	5.5	...	...	3.6
Yellow-poplar	419.4	...	45.4	88.1	67.0	113.3	55.8	45.3	4.5
Magnolia (*Magnolia* spp.)	20.9	...	4.3	1.2	3.6	9.7	...	2.1	...
Sweetbay	230.2	...	91.1	59.8	35.1	19.2	10.6	14.4	...
Willow	5.5	...	5.5	...	...	...	...	...	...
Black cherry	2.7	...	...	2.7	...	...	...	...	...
American elm	80.0	...	14.5	32.3	13.6	10.8	4.5	1.2	3.1
Other elms	52.7	...	16.0	8.0	12.8	1.5	5.4	9.0	...
Hackberry	152.4	...	27.4	22.5	41.4	23.1	18.1	19.9	...
Holly	2.2	...	.4	1.8	...	...	...	...	...
Other hardwoods	59.4	...	6.7	6.7	12.9	8.2	7.6	17.3	...
Total	6,825.3	...	1,305.3	1,560.1	1,260.7	993.8	579.7	997.7	128.0

Table 22. *Average volume per acre of growing stock and sawtimber on commercial forest land by species group and ownership class, 1972*

Ownership	Growing stock			Sawtimber		
	All species	Softwood	Hardwood	All species	Softwood	Hardwood
	- - - - Cubic feet - - - -			- - - - Board feet - - - -		
National forest	1,134	994	140	4,606	4,340	266
Other public	1,111	709	402	4,757	3,203	1,554
Forest industry	1,224	820	404	4,895	3,811	1,084
Farmer	993	532	461	3,420	2,217	1,203
Misc. private	979	573	406	3,398	2,314	1,084
All ownerships	1,059	643	416	3,876	2,769	1,107

13

Forest Statistics
for
North Alabama Counties

Arnold Hedlund

and

J. M. Earles

Southern Forest Experiment Station
New Orleans, Louisiana
Forest Service, U. S. Department of Agriculture

1972

Forest Statistics
for
North Alabama Counties

Arnold Hedlund and J. M. Earles

This report tabulates information from a new forest inventory of counties in northern Alabama. The tables are intended for use as source data in compiling estimates for groups of counties. Because the sampling procedure is designed primarily to furnish inventory data for the State as a whole, estimates for individual counties have limited and variable accuracy.

The data on forest acreage and timber volume were secured by a systematic sampling method involving a forest-nonforest classification on aerial photographs and on-the-ground measurements of trees at sample locations. The sample locations were at the intersections of a grid of lines spaced 3 miles apart. At each forested location, 10 small plots were uniformly distributed on an area of about 1 acre.

The sampling errors to which the county area and volume totals are liable (on a probability of two chances out of three) are shown in table 1.

An approximation of sampling errors for groups of counties may be obtained by using the formula:

$$e = \frac{(SE)\sqrt{\text{specified volume or area}}}{\sqrt{\text{volume or area total in question}}}$$

Where: e = Estimated sampling error of the volume or area total in question
SE = Specified sampling error for the State.

The error decreases when data for two or more counties are grouped. Conversely, as data for

Table 1. *Sampling errors* [1] *for forest land and timber volume, 1972*

County	Commercial forest land	Growing stock	Saw-timber
	– – – – *Percent* – – – –		
Colbert	1	11	16
De Kalb	2	11	17
Franklin	2	8	12
Jackson	1	6	9
Lauderdale	2	11	20
Lawrence	1	12	20
Limestone	1	11	19
Madison	1	11	21
Marshall	2	15	24
Morgan	2	11	17
All counties	0.5	3.4	5.6

[1] By random-sampling formula.

individual counties are broken down by various subdivisions, the possibility of error increases and is greatest for the smallest items. Sampling errors associated with the estimates of the principal timber species in this report are shown in table 2.

Because of differences in standards of tree measurement, direct comparisons cannot be made between the estimates in this report and those from the survey of 1963. In table 3, changes between the two surveys are summarized in terms of current measurement standards.

Table 2. *Sampling errors for timber volume by species, 1972*

Species	Growing stock	Sawtimber
	– – Percent – –	
Softwood:		
Shortleaf pine	12	17
Loblolly pine	13	17
Virginia pine	19	24
Other softwoods	38	(¹)
Total	8.7	13.0
Hardwood:		
Select white oaks	9	12
Select red oaks	14	16
Other white oaks	11	16
Other red oaks	8	10
Hickory	8	11
Persimmon	31	(¹)
Hard maple	36	(¹)
Soft maple	30	46
Beech	39	43
Sweetgum	15	26
Blackgum	14	21
White ash	16	21
Sycamore	41	45
Basswood	40	(¹)
Yellow-poplar	13	17
Black walnut	31	43
Black cherry	35	(¹)
American elm	24	33
Other elms	17	31
Hackberry	34	49
Black locust	48	(¹)
Dogwood	41	. . .
Other hardwoods	24	44
Total	4.0	6.1
All species	3.4	5.6

¹ Exceeds 50 percent.

Table 3. *Change ¹ in forest resource since 1963*

Item	Change
	Percent
Commercial forest land	– 3.4
Growing-stock volume:	
Softwood	+ 71
Hardwood	+ 12
All species	+ 24
Sawtimber volume:	
Softwood	+ 85
Hardwood	+ 10
All species	+ 26

¹ Based on 1972 measurement standards.

It is anticipated that data for other counties of Alabama will be published as field work progresses. A Statewide interpretive report will be issued when all counties have been inventoried; it will include an evaluation of timber trends since 1963.

DEFINITIONS OF TERMS

Acceptable trees.—Growing-stock trees of commercial species that meet specified standards of size and quality but do not qualify as desirable trees.

Commercial forest land.—Forest land producing or capable of producing crops of industrial wood and not withdrawn from timber utilization.

Desirable trees.—Growing-stock trees that are of commercial species, have no defects in quality for timber products, are of relatively high vigor, and contain no pathogens that may result in death or serious deterioration before rotation age.

Forest type.—A classification of forest land based upon the species forming a plurality of live-tree stocking.

Growing-stock trees.—Live trees that are of commercial species and qualify as desirable or acceptable trees.

Growing-stock volume.—Net volume in cubic feet of growing-stock trees at least 5.0 inches in diameter at breast height, from a 1-foot stump to a minimum 4.0-inch top diameter outside bark of the central stem, or to the point where the central stem breaks into limbs.

Poletimber trees.—Growing-stock trees of commercial species at least 5.0 inches in diameter at breast height but smaller than sawtimber size.

Sawtimber trees.—Live trees that are of commercial species, contain at least a 12-foot saw log, and meet regional specifications for freedom from defect. Softwoods must be at least 9.0 inches in diameter at breast height and hardwoods at least 11.0 inches.

Sawtimber volume.—Net volume of the saw-log portion of live sawtimber in board feet, International ¼-inch rule.

Site class.—A classification of forest land in terms of inherent capacity to grow crops of industrial wood.

Stand-size class.—A classification of forest land based on the size class of growing-stock trees on the area; that is, sawtimber, poletimber, or seedling and saplings.

2

Table 4. *Commercial forest land by ownership class, 1972*

County	All ownerships	National forest	Other public	Forest industry	Farmer	Misc. private
			- - - - - - - - - Thousand acres - - - - - - - - - -			
Colbert	222.3	...	11.3	11.4	91.9	107.7
De Kalb	246.4	...	5.8	22.4	135.4	82.8
Franklin	265.0	1.6	1.4	60.0	125.9	76.1
Jackson	436.8	...	14.9	44.8	259.5	117.6
Lauderdale	154.0	...	4.0	11.0	110.8	28.2
Lawrence	203.5	88.7	1.8	...	88.6	24.4
Limestone	77.9	...	5.6	...	53.7	18.6
Madison	180.0	...	17.9	6.0	84.6	71.5
Marshall	173.6	...	12.6	22.4	73.3	65.3
Morgan	157.5	...	7.8	...	122.4	27.3
All counties	2,117.0	90.3	83.1	178.0	1,146.1	619.5

Table 5. *Commercial forest land by forest type, 1972*

County	All types	Loblolly-shortleaf pine	Oak-pine	Oak-hickory	Oak-gum-cypress	Elm-ash-cottonwood
			- - - - - - - - Thousand acres - - - - - - - -			
Colbert	222.3	17.1	57.0	136.8	5.7	5.7
De Kalb	246.4	84.0	50.4	112.0	...	
Franklin	265.0	55.0	65.0	145.0	...	
Jackson	436.8	16.8	28.0	369.6	22.4	
Lauderdale	154.0	5.5	22.0	115.5	11.0	
Lawrence	203.5	38.5	16.5	132.0	16.5	
Limestone	77.9	4.1	4.1	45.1	24.6	
Madison	180.0	18.0	12.0	102.0	48.0	
Marshall	173.6	50.4	39.2	84.0	...	...
Morgan	157.5	36.0	31.5	58.5	31.5	...
All counties	2,117.0	325.4	325.7	1,300.5	159.7	5.7

Table 6. *Commercial forest land by stand-size class, 1972*

County	All classes	Sawtimber	Poletimber	Sapling and seedling	Nonstocked areas
			Thousand acres		
Colbert	222.3	22.8	96.9	102.6	
De Kalb	246.4	56.0	100.8	89.6	
Franklin	265.0	15.0	155.0	95.0	
Jackson	436.8	156.8	173.6	106.4	
Lauderdale	154.0	44.0	55.0	55.0	
Lawrence	203.5	38.5	88.0	77.0	
Limestone	77.9	32.8	32.8	12.3	
Madison	180.0	48.0	90.0	42.0	
Marshall	173.6	67.2	67.2	39.2	...
Morgan	157.5	45.0	58.5	54.0	...
All counties	2,117.0	526.1	917.8	673.1	...

Table 7. *Commercial forest land by site class, 1972*

County	All classes	165 cu. ft. or more	120-165 cu.ft.	85-120 cu.ft.	50-85 cu.ft.	Less than 50 cu. ft.
			Thousand acres			
Colbert	222.3	...	11.4	51.3	153.9	5.7
De Kalb	246.4	...	...	16.8	168.0	61.6
Franklin	265.0	5.0	15.0	105.0	115.0	25.0
Jackson	436.8	5.6	...	61.6	252.0	117.6
Lauderdale	154.0	...	...	66.0	71.5	16.5
Lawrence	203.5	...	...	33.0	137.5	33.0
Limestone	77.9	...	12.3	36.9	28.7	...
Madison	180.0	6.0	24.0	30.0	78.0	42.0
Marshall	173.6	...	11.2	61.6	84.0	16.8
Morgan	157.5	...	4.5	90.0	49.5	13.5
All counties	2,117.0	16.6	78.4	552.2	1,138.1	331.7

4

Table 8. *Cordage of growing stock on commercial forest land by species group, 1972*

County	All species	Softwood			Hardwood			
		Total	Pine	Other	Total	Oak	Gum	Other
				- - - - - - - - - Thousand cords - - - - - - - -				
Colbert	2,247	340	337	3	1,907	1,030	176	701
De Kalb	2,560	1,260	1,260	...	1,300	825	145	330
Franklin	3,131	1,127	1,118	9	2,004	1,010	169	825
Jackson	6,140	533	390	143	5,607	2,830	431	2,346
Lauderdale	1,772	165	165	...	1,607	1,005	96	506
Lawrence	2,180	679	603	76	1,501	964	154	383
Limestone	1,204	189	185	4	1,015	545	149	321
Madison	2,259	428	360	68	1,831	706	170	955
Marshall	2,816	1,429	1,393	36	1,387	657	194	536
Morgan	2,096	717	702	15	1,379	585	315	479
All counties	26,405	6,867	6,513	354	19,538	10,157	1,999	7,382

Table 9. *Growing-stock volume on commercial forest land by species group, 1972*

County	All species	Softwood			Hardwood			
		Total	Pine	Other	Total	Oak	Gum	Other
				- - - - - - - - - Million cubic feet - - - - - - - -				
Colbert	153.3	25.5	25.3	0.2	127.8	69.0	11.8	47.0
De Kalb	181.6	94.5	94.5	...	87.1	55.3	9.7	22.1
Franklin	218.8	84.5	83.8	.7	134.3	67.7	11.3	55.3
Jackson	415.7	40.0	29.3	10.7	375.7	189.6	28.9	157.2
Lauderdale	120.1	12.4	12.4	...	107.7	67.4	6.4	33.9
Lawrence	151.5	50.9	45.2	5.7	100.6	64.6	10.3	25.7
Limestone	82.2	14.2	13.9	.3	68.0	36.5	10.0	21.5
Madison	154.8	32.1	27.0	5.1	122.7	47.3	11.4	64.0
Marshall	200.1	107.2	104.5	2.7	92.9	44.0	13.0	35.9
Morgan	146.2	53.8	52.7	1.1	92.4	39.2	21.1	32.1
All counties	1,824.3	515.1	488.6	26.5	1,309.2	680.6	133.9	494.7

Table 10. *Sawtimber volume on commercial forest land by species group, 1972*

County	All species	Softwood			Hardwood			
		Total	Pine	Other	Total	Oak	Gum	Other
- - - - - - - - - - Million board feet - - - - - - - - - - -								
Colbert	310.3	46.9	46.9	...	263.4	182.1	6.2	75.1
De Kalb	418.6	223.9	223.9	...	194.7	132.6	21.2	40.9
Franklin	372.6	131.4	131.4	...	241.2	147.1	8.1	86.0
Jackson	1,164.9	123.9	108.9	15.0	1,041.0	634.6	53.7	352.7
Lauderdale	268.2	25.1	25.1	...	243.1	166.9	7.6	68.6
Lawrence	387.4	170.2	156.0	14.2	217.2	156.4	18.5	42.3
Limestone	270.8	73.0	73.0	...	197.8	131.4	16.8	49.6
Madison	345.1	94.9	90.2	4.7	250.2	124.2	21.5	104.5
Marshall	633.8	414.9	414.9	...	218.9	125.1	27.8	66.0
Morgan	375.7	149.8	144.4	5.4	225.9	94.6	54.1	77.2
All counties	4,547.4	1,454.0	1,414.7	39.3	3,093.4	1,895.0	235.5	962.9

Table 11. *Sawtimber volume on commercial forest land by species group and diameter class, 1972*

County	All species	Softwood			Hardwood		
		Total	9.0-14.9 inches	15.0 inches and up	Total	11.0-14.9 inches	15.0 inches and up
- - - - - - - Million board feet - - - - - - -							
Colbert	310.3	46.9	39.7	7.2	263.4	181.0	82.4
De Kalb	418.6	223.9	163.8	60.1	194.7	98.6	96.1
Franklin	372.6	131.4	116.9	14.5	241.2	158.9	82.3
Jackson	1,164.9	123.9	99.8	24.1	1,041.0	557.5	483.5
Lauderdale	268.2	25.1	25.1	...	243.1	122.8	120.3
Lawrence	387.4	170.2	76.3	93.9	217.2	70.6	146.6
Limestone	270.8	73.0	21.2	51.8	197.8	60.2	137.6
Madison	345.1	94.9	70.4	24.5	250.2	123.1	127.1
Marshall	633.8	414.9	171.1	243.8	218.9	113.3	105.6
Morgan	375.7	149.8	115.6	34.2	225.9	84.3	141.6
All counties	4,547.4	1,454.0	899.9	554.1	3,093.4	1,570.3	1,523.1

Table 12. *Growing-stock volume of softwoods on commercial*
forest land by forest type, 1972

County	All types	Loblolly-shortleaf pine	Oak-pine	Oak-hickory	Oak-gum-cypress
			- - - - Million cubic feet - - - -		
Colbert	25.5	3.2	14.5	7.8	...
De Kalb	94.5	57.1	23.7	13.7	...
Franklin	84.5	51.9	24.9	7.7	...
Jackson	40.0	11.4	12.2	16.4	...
Lauderdale	12.4	1.1	7.0	4.3	...
Lawrence	50.9	26.0	3.5	21.0	0.4
Limestone	14.2	4.2	6.0	.7	3.3
Madison	32.1	12.3	6.3	2.0	11.5
Marshall	107.2	73.8	27.1	6.3	...
Morgan	53.8	36.1	12.0	5.7	...
All counties	515.1	277.1	137.2	85.6	15.2

Table 13. *Growing-stock volume of hardwoods on commercial forest land by*
forest type, 1972

County	All types	Loblolly-shortleaf pine	Oak-pine	Oak-hickory	Oak-gum-cypress	Elm-ash-cottonwood
			- - - - - - Million cubic feet - - - - - -			
Colbert	127.8	1.1	16.0	97.8	8.4	4.5
De Kalb	87.1	8.8	17.7	60.6	...	...
Franklin	134.3	15.6	22.5	96.2	...	...
Jackson	375.7	1.7	8.7	332.6	32.7	...
Lauderdale	107.7	.3	3.9	92.7	10.8	...
Lawrence	100.6	4.1	3.5	84.8	8.2	...
Limestone	68.0	1.7	2.1	39.5	24.7	...
Madison	122.7	1.5	1.3	79.9	40.0	...
Marshall	92.9	6.9	26.0	60.0	...	...
Morgan	92.4	8.4	10.5	40.0	33.5	...
All counties	1,309.2	50.1	112.2	984.1	158.3	4.5

7

Table 14. *Sawtimber volume of softwoods on commercial forest land by forest type, 1972*

County	All types	Loblolly-shortleaf pine	Oak-pine	Oak-hickory	Oak-gum-cypress
		- - - - *Million board feet* - - - -			
Colbert	46.9	1.9	33.6	11.4	...
De Kalb	223.9	111.6	68.4	43.9	...
Franklin	131.4	73.5	44.2	13.7	...
Jackson	123.9	39.2	52.0	32.7	...
Lauderdale	25.1	2.8	20.3	2.0	...
Lawrence	170.2	80.0	5.9	83.1	1.2
Limestone	73.0	18.3	32.2	3.9	18.6
Madison	94.9	29.0	20.5	1.5	43.9
Marshall	414.9	297.0	106.5	11.4	...
Morgan	149.8	96.7	37.1	16.0	...
All counties	1,454.0	750.0	420.7	219.6	63.7

Table 15. *Sawtimber volume of hardwoods on commercial forest land by forest type, 1972*

County	All types	Loblolly-shortleaf pine	Oak-pine	Oak-hickory	Oak-gum-cypress	Elm-ash-cottonwood
		- - - - - - - *Million board feet* - - - - - - -				
Colbert	263.4	2.2	20.4	222.6	10.7	7.5
De Kalb	194.7	8.6	41.1	145.0	...	...
Franklin	241.2	28.5	35.8	176.9	...	...
Jackson	1,041.0	2.7	13.1	941.7	83.5	...
Lauderdale	243.1	...	4.9	219.2	19.0	...
Lawrence	217.2	9.5	1.8	193.6	12.3	...
Limestone	197.8	2.6	6.7	119.3	69.2	...
Madison	250.2	4.4	2.2	155.7	87.9	...
Marshall	218.9	11.8	74.3	132.8	...	...
Morgan	225.9	7.1	14.1	96.6	108.1	...
All counties	3,093.4	77.4	214.4	2,403.4	390.7	7.5

8

Table 16. *Growing-stock volume of softwoods on commercial forest*
land by stand-size class, 1972

County	All classes	Sawtimber	Poletimber	Sapling and seedling	Nonstocked areas
	- - - - - Million cubic feet - - - - -				
Colbert	25.5	0.5	10.5	14.5	
De Kalb	94.5	24.7	58.1	11.7	
Franklin	84.5	8.0	64.0	12.5	
Jackson	40.0	2.2	29.4	8.4	
Lauderdale	12.4	...	5.3	7.1	
Lawrence	50.9	29.8	15.2	5.9	
Limestone	14.2	13.9	.3	...	
Madison	32.1	17.1	11.0	4.0	
Marshall	107.2	83.1	17.5	6.6	...
Morgan	53.8	24.4	18.9	10.5	...
All counties	515.1	203.7	230.2	81.2	...

Table 17. *Growing-stock volume of hardwoods on commercial forest land*
by stand-size class, 1972

County	All classes	Sawtimber	Poletimber	Sapling and seedling	Nonstocked areas
	- - - - - Million cubic feet - - - - -				
Colbert	127.8	24.2	85.2	18.4	...
De Kalb	87.1	44.5	27.9	14.7	...
Franklin	134.3	15.4	90.0	28.9	...
Jackson	375.7	213.1	124.0	38.6	...
Lauderdale	107.7	48.5	42.0	17.2	...
Lawrence	100.6	25.8	62.2	12.6	
Limestone	68.0	36.6	28.7	2.7	
Madison	122.7	47.8	66.5	8.4	...
Marshall	92.9	40.1	47.2	5.6	...
Morgan	92.4	44.7	36.9	10.8	...
All counties	1,309.2	540.7	610.6	157.9	...

Table 18. *Sawtimber volume of softwoods on commercial forest land by stand-size class, 1972*

County	All classes	Sawtimber	Poletimber	Sapling and seedling	Nonstocked areas
	- - - - - - *Million board feet* - - - - - -				
Colbert	46.9	2.5	17.5	26.9	...
De Kalb	223.9	108.1	94.8	21.0	...
Franklin	131.4	22.6	80.3	28.5	...
Jackson	123.9	11.4	90.7	21.8	...
Lauderdale	25.1	...	2.8	22.3	...
Lawrence	170.2	130.7	32.3	7.2	...
Limestone	73.0	73.0	...	...	
Madison	94.9	73.7	9.8	11.4	...
Marshall	414.9	384.9	22.7	7.3	...
Morgan	149.8	73.7	43.2	32.9	...
All counties	1,454.0	880.6	394.1	179.3	...

Table 19. *Sawtimber volume of hardwoods on commercial forest land by stand-size class, 1972*

County	All classes	Sawtimber	Poletimber	Sapling and seedling	Nonstocked areas
	- - - - - - *Million board feet* - - - - - -				
Colbert	263.4	93.1	143.2	27.1	...
De Kalb	194.7	128.4	30.3	36.0	...
Franklin	241.2	43.3	161.6	36.3	...
Jackson	1,041.0	759.0	213.3	68.7	
Lauderdale	243.1	175.9	48.8	18.4	...
Lawrence	217.2	81.5	122.4	13.3	...
Limestone	197.8	138.8	56.6	2.4	...
Madison	250.2	142.4	96.4	11.4	...
Marshall	218.9	107.2	102.6	9.1	...
Morgan	225.9	161.6	51.0	13.3	...
All counties	3,093.4	1,831.2	1,026.2	236.0	...

11

Species	All classes	Diameter class (inches at breast height) – Million cubic feet									
		5.0-6.9	7.0-8.9	9.0-10.9	11.0-12.9	13.0-14.9	15.0-16.9	17.0-18.9	19.0-20.9	21.0-28.9	29.0 and larger
Softwood:											
Shortleaf pine	149.6	37.2	41.0	37.2	20.7	7.7	3.7	0.7	1.4	...	...
Loblolly pine	250.1	39.3	36.0	23.7	30.5	27.4	31.5	20.5	13.0	28.2	...
Virginia pine	88.9	24.5	32.7	13.5	11.9	5.7	.6	...	...	...	...
Other softwoods	26.5	9.8	9.2	3.7	1.1	1.5	.5	.4	.3	...	...
Total	515.1	110.8	118.9	78.1	64.2	42.3	36.3	21.6	14.7	28.2	...
Hardwood:											
Select white oaks	224.8	21.8	31.3	40.4	43.0	32.9	19.7	11.2	8.8	10.3	5.4
Select red oaks	74.4	6.4	5.2	9.3	12.4	11.8	11.9	9.1	2.6	5.2	.5
Other white oaks	153.0	24.7	29.0	25.9	21.8	23.5	11.7	8.5	4.2	3.7	...
Other red oaks	228.4	27.6	30.6	42.3	32.3	34.4	29.9	9.9	9.6	7.2	4.6
Hickory	266.4	28.4	46.8	59.6	45.5	32.9	25.6	8.4	9.6	9.6	...
Persimmon	4.4	1.9	.9	.5	...	...	1.1	...	...	...	...
Hard maple	11.9	2.6	1.6	1.9	2.6	2.5	.3	...	...	.4	...
Soft maple	22.5	3.4	2.4	3.9	.7	2.9	4.4	1.7	1.8	1.3	...
Beech	4.1	.4	.3	.7	...	.5	1.0	...	.5	.5	.2
Sweetgum	93.9	17.7	21.5	23.9	12.4	6.9	4.6	4.8	.9	1.2	...
Blackgum	40.0	6.2	8.7	6.4	4.4	4.5	4.8	3.6	1.4	...	...
White ash	27.0	4.1	3.5	3.4	3.4	4.4	3.9	2.0	1.2	1.1	1.4
Sycamore	5.2	...	...	.6	.2	1.3	...	1.1	...	.6	...
Basswood	4.9	...	2.5	1.0	.5	.5	...	...	...	.4	...
Yellow-poplar	54.0	5.9	10.7	6.4	6.9	6.2	7.8	3.5	2.1	3.6	.9
Black walnut	7.0	1.0	1.2	.9	1.7	1.2	.5	.5	...	...	...
Black cherry	4.8	1.0	1.2	.8	1.3	...	...	...	...	.5	...
American elm	11.4	1.2	1.7	2.7	1.3	1.3	.4	1.9	.3	.6	...
Other elms	17.4	3.2	4.6	4.6	2.9	.1	.7	.9	.4	...	...
Hackberry	9.5	.7	2.4	3.5	1.6	.3	.3	.2	...	...	...
Black locust	4.1	.9	.5	1.1	.4	1.2	...	...	...	.5	...
Dogwood	2.6	2.1	.5	...	...	...	...	...	...	...	...
Other hardwoods	37.5	5.3	9.9	7.9	3.0	3.6	2.3	1.8	2.5	1.2	...
Total	1,309.2	166.5	217.0	247.7	198.3	172.9	130.9	69.1	45.9	47.9	13.0
All species	1,824.3	277.3	335.9	325.8	262.5	215.2	167.2	90.7	60.6	76.1	13.0

1/ Detailed county statistics by species and diameter class available upon request.

Table 21. *Sawtimber volume on commercial forest land by species and diameter class, 1972* [1]

| Species | All classes | Diameter class (inches at breast height) — — — — Million board feet — — — — | | | | | | | |
		9.0-10.9	11.0-12.9	13.0-14.9	15.0-16.9	17.0-18.9	19.0-20.9	21.0-28.9	29.0 and larger
Softwood:									
Shortleaf pine	353.8	184.3	101.3	40.6	19.7	1.5	6.4	...	...
Loblolly pine	902.7	92.8	151.4	140.7	174.6	111.4	72.3	159.5	...
Virginia pine	158.2	65.4	60.6	28.8	3.4	...	...	...	...
Other softwoods	39.3	19.7	5.9	8.4	2.1	2.2	1.0	...	...
Total	1,454.0	362.2	319.2	218.5	199.8	115.1	79.7	159.5	...
Hardwood:									
Select white oaks	651.6	...	184.1	164.5	106.9	56.4	50.2	60.8	28.7
Select red oaks	266.3	...	50.6	60.2	63.0	46.8	13.4	29.3	3.0
Other white oaks	358.8	...	88.9	116.4	63.4	45.6	24.4	20.1	...
Other red oaks	618.3	...	132.0	170.6	150.4	52.1	50.8	38.1	24.3
Hickory	525.1	...	165.9	130.0	105.0	38.3	41.8	44.1	...
Persimmon	5.0	...	...	...	5.0	...	...	...	...
Hard maple	19.4	...	7.3	9.2	.9	...	8.0	2.0	...
Soft maple	47.7	...	2.0	10.2	15.1	7.0	2.2	5.4	...
Beech	10.5	...	...	1.2	3.9	...	4.2	2.0	1.2
Sweetgum	143.5	...	48.3	33.3	22.9	27.1	8.4	7.7	...
Blackgum	92.0	...	16.6	20.3	25.8	20.9	8.4	...	...
White ash	66.1	...	12.5	18.3	16.3	8.8	5.1	5.1	...
Sycamore	19.6	...	.5	4.5	...	3.5	...	4.7	6.4
Basswood	5.6	...	1.7	2.1	...	...	...	1.8	...
Yellow-poplar	125.2	...	22.8	24.3	34.6	15.3	8.8	15.0	4.4
Black walnut	15.1	...	6.0	4.5	2.0	2.6	...	...	...
Black cherry	5.9	...	3.9	...	...	...	...	2.0	...
American elm	24.2	...	3.5	6.4	1.6	8.0	1.5	3.2	...
Other elms	19.6	...	10.3	.6	2.5	4.1	2.1	...	...
Hackberry	8.3	...	4.4	.5	1.1	.9	...	1.4	...
Black locust	7.2	...	1.7	5.5	...	...	...	...	...
Other hardwoods	58.4	...	9.1	15.6	10.0	8.1	9.8	5.8	...
Total	3,093.4	...	772.1	798.2	630.4	345.5	230.7	248.5	68.0
All species	4,547.4	362.2	1,091.3	1,016.7	830.2	460.6	310.4	408.0	68.0

[1] Detailed county statistics by species and diameter class available upon request.

Table 22. *Average volume per acre of growing stock and sawtimber on commercial forest land by species group and ownership class, 1972*

Ownership	Growing stock			Sawtimber		
	All species	Softwood	Hardwood	All species	Softwood	Hardwood
	- - - Cubic feet - - -			- - - Board feet - - -		
National forest	949	320	629	2,812	1,319	1,493
Other public	827	294	533	2,092	898	1,194
Forest industry	933	323	610	2,704	1,161	1,543
Farmer	872	222	650	2,125	598	1,527
Misc. private	813	241	572	1,941	594	1,347
All ownerships	861	243	618	2,148	687	1,461

FOREST RESOURCES
OF
TENNESSEE

Paul A. Murphy

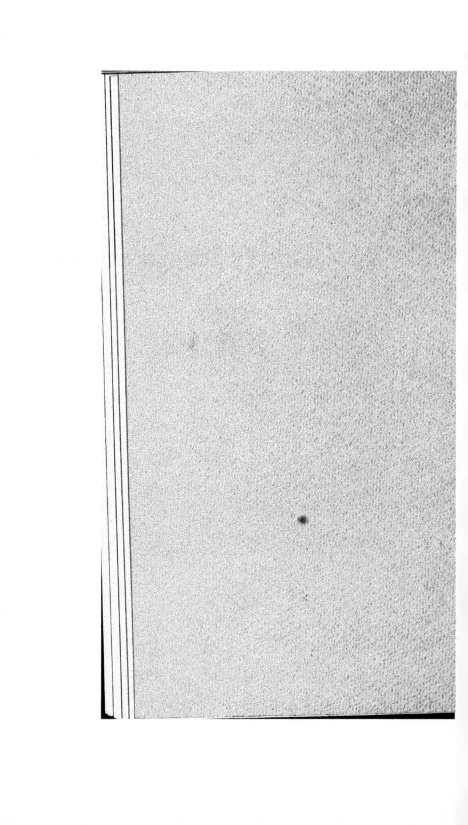

FOREST RESOURCES
OF
TENNESSEE

Paul A. Murphy

U. S. DEPARTMENT OF AGRICULTURE
FOREST SERVICE

SOUTHERN FOREST EXPERIMENT STATION
New Orleans, Louisiana

1972

Contents

Highlights

This report states the principal findings of a new forest survey of Tennessee. Data for growth and cut are given for 1970, and the inventory is reported for January 1, 1971. A canvass of forest products output in 1970 also contributed information.

Because forests were cleared for agriculture, the amount of land available for timber production is now 12.8 million acres, a decline of 5 percent from 1961. About three-fourths of the diversion was to pasture, mostly in central Tennessee. The rest occurred in the western part of the State for row crops such as cotton, corn, and soybeans.

The only substantial change in ownership patterns was a 14-percent decline in farmer-owned forest—a consequence of land clearing. Although public ownership in the federal category increased moderately, private owners still hold the bulk of the commercial forest area: about 90 percent.

Despite the loss in forest area, the timber supply picture has brightened considerably. Softwood growing stock rose 26 percent, while hardwood increased 11 percent.

Softwood growing stock now totals 1.8 billion cubic feet. Most of it is shortleaf pine and Virginia pine, both of which are most abundant in eastern Tennessee. About 58 percent is large enough to be considered sawtimber; the remaining is poletimber. Most of the volume increase was in trees 6 to 12 inches in diameter.

About 8.6 billion cubic feet are in hardwood growing stock trees, chiefly oaks, hickories, and yellow-poplar. Sawtimber now comprises 57 percent of the growing stock volume—equivalent to 22 billion board feet. Most of the volume increase was in trees 10 to 16 inches in diameter.

Stocking has improved and has stimulated growth considerably. In 1970, growth was 40 cubic feet per acre, an increase over the 1960 growth of 30 cubic feet. A promise of still further increase lies in the present excess of growth over cut for both hardwoods and softwoods.

The number of sawmills in Tennessee has declined since 1960. The attrition was in small mills, which cut most of the softwoods. The subsequent drop in softwood saw log production has had a salutary effect on the pine resource. The larger mills process mainly hardwood, and, though they more than doubled in number, hardwood saw log output for 1970 was slightly below its 1960 level.

Because of expansion in the State's pulping capacity in the last decade, pulpwood production reached a record level in 1970. Nevertheless, Tennessee mills import over one-half of their requirements from other States. Use of wood residues for pulp has been increasing steadily for the last 10 years.

Veneer and cooperage plants decreased both in number and in output. As a consequence of the decline of these industries and the closing of many small sawmills, the total volume of timber products cut was less in 1970 than in 1960.

Despite the recent resource improvement, hardwood forest types occupy almost 5 million acres that are better suited to growing pines, and cull trees preempt much growing space that could be occupied by growing stock. By remedying these conditions, Tennessee can help supply the increased requirements of its pulpmills and maintain its hardwood sawmill industry.

Resource Trends

FOREST AREA

Forests occupy 13.1 million acres or 50 percent of the land area in Tennessee (fig. 1). About 12.8 million acres are classified as commercial—that is, they are capable of growing trees for timber products, and cutting is permitted. Some 300,000 acres are reserved from cutting. Total commercial acreage is 5 percent less than at the time of the last previous forest survey in 1961 (table I). This decline reverses a trend of increasing acreage that had been documented in 1961.[1] Nevertheless, there is still more forest now than 20 years ago.

[1] Sternitzke, H. S. Tennessee forests. USDA Forest Serv. South. Forest Exp. Stn. Forest Surv. Release 86, 29 p. 1962.

Table I. *Commercial forest land in 1971 and change since 1961*

Region	Commercial forest	Change since last survey	Proportion of region forested [1]
	Thousand acres	*Percent*	*Percent*
West	1,768.5	− 7	29
West Central	2,290.9	− 1	67
Central	2,276.3	−12	36
Plateau	3,077.0	− 3	70
East	3,407.1	− 2	54
All regions	12,819.8	− 5	49

[1] Total forest, including noncommercial, as a proportion of total area in the region.

Loss in Forest Area

Much of the loss was a consequence of farm owners increasing their pasture and arable acreage by clearing forest land (table II). The declines have been greatest in the Central, Plateau, and West regions.

Statewide, 1.2 million of the acres designated by the 1961 survey as commercial forest land have been converted to agricultural use. About 75 percent went into pasture, and most of the remainder into row crops—soybeans, cotton, and corn. The change to pasture occurred mostly in the Central and Plateau regions, the shift to row crops in the West region.

Other uses, chiefly urban and highway expansion, claimed an additional 309,000 acres.

While large acreages were being cleared, nearly a million acres of crop and pasture land were allowed to revert to forest. The reversions were insufficient to offset the withdrawals, and the net loss diminished the growing stock inventory. Moreover, the effect was greater than is indicated by acreage changes alone. Land diverted from commercial forest usually contains some growing stock; land reverting to forest usually has no timber at all.

Additions to forests will continue to come from former farm lands, but a substantial di-

Table II. *Changes in commercial forest land, 1961-1971*

Region	Net change	Additions from:			Diversions to:		
		Total	Nonforest	Noncommercial forest	Total	Agriculture	Other
	‒ ‒ ‒ ‒ ‒ ‒ ‒ ‒ ‒ ‒ ‒ ‒ ‒ ‒ *Thousand acres* ‒ ‒ ‒ ‒ ‒ ‒ ‒ ‒ ‒ ‒ ‒ ‒ ‒						
West	−130.8	126.3	126.3	...	257.1	221.8	35.3
West Central	− 11.8	67.5	67.5	..	79.3	70.2	9.1
Central	−304.2	307.0	307.0	...	611.2	557.9	53.3
Plateau	−101.0	264.4	264.4	...	365.4	208.5	156.9
East	− 64.8	95.8	85.8	10.0	160.6	105.6	55.0
All regions	−612.6	861.0	851.0	10.0	1,473.6	1,164.0	[1] 309.6

[1] Includes 34,300 acres diverted to water impoundments and 63,000 acres transferred to noncommercial forest.

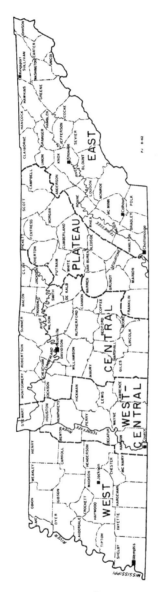

Figure 1. Forest resource regions in Tennessee.

3

version to agriculture will also persist, and urbanization and other uses will continue to expand. Therefore, the prospect is that the current decline will continue.

Change in Ownership

Ninety percent of the forest land is privately owned.[2] Farmers hold a substantial amount—about 5 million acres. Chiefly because of the clearing for pasture and crops, acreage in this class diminished 14 percent since 1961.

Miscellaneous private owners hold about 5.3 million acres. Within this group, individuals own the bulk—some 4.6 million acres; the rest is in corporate ownership. There was little acreage change for either category since 1961.

Forest industry holdings increased 175,500 acres to a total of 1.1 million. These firms have better resources for forest management than do most other private owners.

Public ownership increased moderately. The biggest single change was the acquisition by TVA of 64,000 acres in the Land-Between-The-Lakes area.

Forest Type

The forest type covering any area is partly the result of past uses and disturbances. Fire, logging, and reversion of agricultural land to forest all affect the species composition. Forest lands in Tennessee may be divided into three basic site classes—pine, upland hardwood, and bottom-land hardwood—according to their suit-

[2] Table 2 in the appendix shows the acres of commercial forest land by ownership classes.

ability for growing certain timber types. These classes do not necessarily describe what types are actually present; rather, they indicate what commercial types the sites are best able to support.

About 5.9 million acres, 46 percent of the commercial forest area, are suitable for Virginia pine, shortleaf pine, and, in some places, loblolly pine. Most pine sites occur in the East and Plateau regions (fig. 2). The primary forest types now on these sites are loblolly-shortleaf pine, oak-pine, and oak-hickory (table III). Thus a great proportion of the pine sites are presently supporting hardwood. The oak-hickory type alone occupies 3.5 million acres that could grow pine.

Sites best suited for upland hardwoods comprise 48 percent of the total. They are most numerous in the Central and West Central regions, but all regions have substantial acreages. This class lost more land to agriculture

Table III. *Commercial forest land by forest types and sites*

Forest type	Site		
	Southern pine	Upland hardwood	Bottom-land hardwood
	– – – – *Thousand acres* – – – –		
White pine	28.9	10.0	...
Cedar	188.3	483.7	21.8
Loblolly-shortleaf pine	998.8	...	...
Oak-pine [1]	1,164.7	33.3	..
Oak-hickory	3,532.3	5,575.7	...
Oak-gum-cypress	...	..	547.2
Elm-ash-cottonwood	..	...	150.7
Maple-beech-birch	...	84.4	...
All types	5,913.0	6,187.1	719.7

[1] Includes white pine-hardwood type.

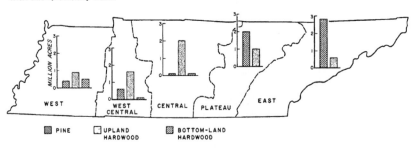

WEST WEST CENTRAL CENTRAL PLATEAU EAST

▨ PINE ☐ UPLAND HARDWOOD ▨ BOTTOM-LAND HARDWOOD

Figure 2. *Commercial forest land by region and site.*

4

than any other. The primary forest types are oak-hickory, cedar, and maple-beech-birch. The oak-hickory is overwhelmingly the largest while the maple-beech-birch occurs only in the Plateau and East regions. Some redcedar is also present, mainly in the Central region. Most of the existing upland types—including the cedar—are suitable.

Only 6 percent of the commercial forest land is in the bottom-land hardwood site class, and the only substantial occurrence is in the West region. Elm-ash-cottonwood and oak-gum-cypress stands occupy these sites and are considered desirable.

TIMBER VOLUME

The commercial forests of Tennessee contained over 12 billion cubic feet of wood in 1971. This total includes the volumes of rough and rotten trees that are unsuitable for timber products. Growing stock trees, which are neither rough nor rotten, made up 10.4 billion cubic feet of the total volume.

Specifications for growing stock trees and methods of computing tree volumes have changed since the last survey. Therefore, the 1961 volume data were adjusted to permit direct comparisons with 1971.

Softwood Volume Increased Moderately

Softwood volume increased 26 percent, from 1.4 billion to 1.8 billion cubic feet, between surveys (table IV). Most is shortleaf pine and Virginia pine (fig. 3). The East and Plateau regions have 81 percent of the shortleaf pine and 99 percent of the Virginia pine. The gains

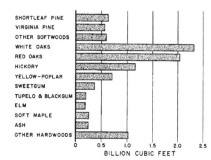

Figure 3. *Growing stock by species.*

were not uniform throughout the range of tree diameters (fig. 4). Most of the increase was in the 6- to 12-inch classes.

Because pines as a group have good form and low incidence of decay, virtually all can be considered as growing stock (fig. 5). About 42 percent of the growing stock volume is in poletimber. Sawtimber comprises 58 percent, or almost 4.7 billion board feet.

Table IV. *Growing stock volume in 1971 and change since 1961*

Region	Softwood		Hardwood	
	Volume	Change	Volume	Change
	Million cu. ft.	Percent	Million cu. ft.	Percent
West	155.5	+58	1,484.3	+ 3
West Central	108.0	+62	1,710.4	+18
Central	46.0	+65	1,302.1	+ 8
Plateau	467.5	+ 7	2,056.1	+ 7
East	1,022.8	+28	2,043.1	+20
All regions	1,799.8	+26	8,596.0	+11

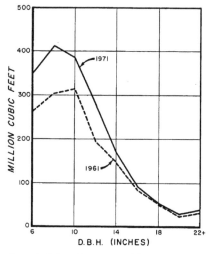

Figure 4. *Softwood growing stock by tree diameter, 1961 and 1971.*

5

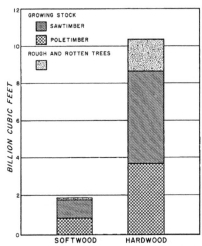

Figure 5. *Volume of softwoods and hardwoods by class of timber.*

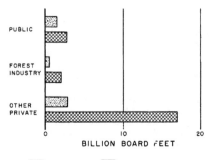

Figure 6. *Sawtimber volume by class of ownership.*

Softwood sawtimber volume increased 22 percent (table V). The small sawmills in Tennessee cut chiefly softwood, and a recent decline in the number of these mills[a] has diminished the pressure on the resource.

Table V. *Sawtimber volume in 1971 and change since 1961*

Region	Softwood		Hardwood	
	Volume	Change	Volume	Change
	Million bd. ft.	*Percent*	*Million bd. ft.*	*Percent*
West	450.1	+40	4,415.3	+ 5
West Central	201.5	+80	3,434.3	+27
Central	27.2	+28	3,224.1	+ 9
Plateau	1,363.3	+24	5,293.5	+12
East	2,656.9	+15	5,273.9	+18
All regions	4,699.0	+22	21,641.1	+14

Most of the sawtimber volume is in nonindustrial private ownership (fig. 6), but some is on industrial or public land. The regional distribution follows that of growing stock most of it is in the East and Plateau regions.

[a] Bertelson, D. F. Tennessee forest industries. USDA Forest Serv. Resour. Bull. SO-30, 27 p. South. Forest Exp. Stn., New Orleans, La. 1971.

Hardwood Volume Increased Slightly

Despite the loss of 600,000 acres of commercial forest land between surveys, hardwood growing stock volume increased from 7.7 billion to 8.6 billion cubic feet, or 11 percent (table IV).

White oaks, red oaks, hickories, and yellow-poplar comprise most of the growing stock volume (fig. 3). The oaks are most abundant in the East, Plateau, and West Central regions, while over two-thirds of the yellow-poplar volume is in the East and Plateau regions.

Tennessee's forests contain almost 10.3 billion cubic feet of hardwood. About 16 percent is in rough and rotten trees; the hardwoods do not have the pines' inherently better form and low incidence of decay. Some 8.6 billion cubic feet of the total is growing stock; poletimber trees comprise 43 percent of the growing stock volume, and the remainder is in sawtimber.

Hardwood sawtimber volume is 22 billion board feet, 14 percent more than in the previous survey (table V). The overwhelming part is privately owned (fig. 6). Saw log quality improved slightly; about 36 percent of the hardwood sawtimber volume is now in grade-2 logs or better.

Most of the volume increase was in trees 10 to 16 inches in diameter (fig. 7).

6

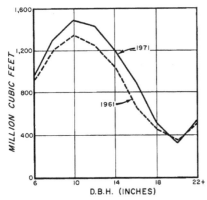

Figure 7. *Hardwood growing stock by tree diameter, 1961 and 1971.*

GROWTH AND REMOVALS

In 1970, the inventory of growing stock in Tennessee increased by almost 293 million cubic feet (table VI). This increase is net growth minus removals. Growth exceeded removals by a wide margin for both hardwoods and softwoods.

Table VI. *Summary of volume-change statistics, 1970*

Item	Growing stock			Sawtimber	
	Soft-wood	Hard-wood	All species	Soft-wood	Hard-wood
	Million cubic feet			*Million board feet*	
Net growth, 1970	102.9	406.2	509.1	309.0	1,119.2
Timber removals, 1970	33.2	183.2	216.4	124.0	695.6
Net change, 1970	+69.7	+223.0	+292.7	+185.0	+423.6

Removals totaled more than 216 million cubic feet in 1970, and the hardwood cut greatly exceeded that of softwoods. A favorable growth-cut ratio existed for most species. In cypress, tupelo, and blackgum, however, the ratios indicate that the sawtimber inventory is being reduced.

Gross growth for 1970 was about 552 million cubic feet. This growth can be divided into five components: (1) survivor growth—the increment in net volume of trees in the growing stock at the beginning of the year and surviving to its end; (2) ingrowth—the net volume of trees at the time they grew into growing stock during 1970; (3) growth on ingrowth—the increment in net volume of trees after they grew into growing stock; (4) growth on removals—the increment in net volume of growing stock trees that were cut during the year; (5) mortality—the net volume in growing stock trees that died during the year.

Survivor growth made up 74 percent of the gross growth during 1970, ingrowth and growth on ingrowth contributed 17 percent, and growth on trees removed added another 1 percent (table VII). The volume of trees dying was 8 percent of gross growth.

Survivor growth was the biggest growth component for the hardwood species group. It also accounted for the greatest part of gross growth in softwoods, except that in the Central region ingrowth was the biggest component. Substantial softwood ingrowth also occurred in the West Central region.

The net growth was about 509 million cubic feet, of which 52 percent occurred in the Plateau and East regions. These regions also contained most of the growing stock volume. The West Central region contributed 18 percent to net growth, the West 16, and the Central region 14.

Net volume growth can be compared with its potential to determine how fully the sites are being utilized. The growth potential of each survey plot was determined, and the results indicate that the commercial forest land in Tennessee has an average potential productivity of 71 cubic feet per acre annually. In 1970, net annual growth was 40 cubic feet per acre, or only 56 percent of potential. Why is growth not at its capacity? Stocking and stand structure provide an answer.

Stocking is a measure of the extent to which the growth potential of a site is utilized by trees, and it is determined by comparing the stand density (in terms of number of trees or basal area) with a specified standard. Full or 100 percent stocking is the level at which there is no increase in growth with an increase in stocking.

About 80 percent of the commercial forest land in Tennessee is less than fully stocked with growing stock trees. In some stands, space is preempted by rough and rotten trees; conse-

7

quently, little natural improvement will occur until this space is made available to growing stock. In other stands part of the space is unoccupied by any trees, good or bad.

Stand structure also affects per-acre volume growth. About 4.6 million acres of commercial forest land are either nonstocked or in sapling or seedling stands. Another 4.9 million acres are in poletimber, and sawtimber occupies 3.3 million acres. Thus over one-third are in seedling and sapling stands, which contribute little volume growth.

Table VII. *Growth components of growing stock on commercial forest land by species group and resource region, Tennessee, 1970*

Region and species group	Growth components					Total	
	Survivor growth	Ingrowth	Growth on ingrowth	Growth on removals	Mortality	Gross growth	Net growth
	– – – – – – – – – – – – – Million cubic feet – – – – – – – – – – – – –						
West							
Softwood	7.1	1.6	(¹)	0.2	0.5	9.4	8.9
Hardwood	61.4	7.8	0.2	1.5	8.6	79.5	70.9
Total	68.5	9.4	.2	1.7	9.1	88.9	79.8
West Central							
Softwood	5.2	3.0	(¹)	.1	.2	8.5	8.3
Hardwood	69.4	15.0	.2	.5	6.2	91.3	85.1
Total	74.6	18.0	.2	.6	6.4	99.8	93.4
Central							
Softwood	1.9	2.3	(¹)	.1	.2	4.5	4.3
Hardwood	50.9	13.1	.2	.7	6.3	71.2	64.9
Total	52.8	15.4	.2	.8	6.5	75.7	69.2
Plateau							
Softwood	21.5	4.5	.1	.1	2.5	28.7	26.2
Hardwood	71.2	16.1	.2	.8	7.5	95.8	88.3
Total	92.7	20.6	.3	.9	10.0	124.5	114.5
East							
Softwood	42.3	12.2	.2	.5	4.3	59.5	55.2
Hardwood	77.1	18.9	.2	.8	7.0	104.0	97.0
Total	119.4	31.1	.4	1.3	11.3	163.5	152.2
All regions							
Softwood	78.0	23.6	.3	1.0	7.7	110.6	102.9
Hardwood	330.0	70.9	1.0	4.3	35.6	441.8	406.2
Total	408.0	94.5	1.3	5.3	43.3	552.4	509.1

¹ Negligible.

Timber Products Output

Tennessee's output of industrial roundwood in 1970 was 137 million cubic feet,[1] a decline of 6 percent from 1960. An additional 24 million cubic feet were cut for domestic use, chiefly firewood.

LARGE SAWMILLS INCREASE

In 1970, the total saw log production was 534 million board feet or 89 million cubic feet (fig. 8). Most of the saw logs harvested in Tennessee also received primary processing there. Imports and exports were a small fraction of the total.

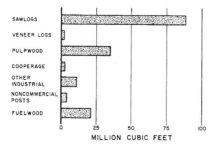

Figure 8. *Output of Tennessee roundwood by product, 1970.*

Softwood saw logs comprised 69 million board feet. Two-thirds of this volume was southern pine, and the remainder was cypress, white pine, redcedar, and hemlock.

Softwood lumber is sawn mainly by small mills. That two-thirds of the softwood saw logs were converted into lumber without having crossed a county line attests both the modest requirements of individual mills and their aggregate importance in the State's softwood lumber industry.

Softwood saw log production was 56 percent less than in 1960. Considerable attrition of

Tennessee sawmills has occurred in the last 25 years. In 1946, there were 2,789 sawmills: that number had decreased to 1,135 in 1960 and 546 in 1970. Competition from larger mills, equipment obsolescence, and rising labor costs all contributed to the decline.

The output of hardwood saw logs in 1970 was 465 million board feet, slightly less than the 1960 total of 477 million. Oaks comprised 59 percent of the total.

The large mills process mainly hardwood saw logs. Mills cutting at least 3 million board feet annually more than doubled in number during the last decade. As an indication of the roundwood requirements of these plants, almost half of the hardwood saw log volume cut in Tennessee was transported across county boundaries for primary processing.

Locations of sawmills and other primary wood-using plants are mapped in figure 9.

PULPWOOD PRODUCTION A RECORD

With construction of two mills and expansion of existing facilities, Tennessee's 24-hour pulping capacity rose from 2,357 tons in 1960 to 3,670 tons in 1970. Daily capacity of the average mill increased from 471 to 524 tons.

The 1970 pulpwood harvest reflects the industry expansion. A total of 437,000 cords were removed from Tennessee's forests[1]—a 24 percent increase over 1960 and a record for the State. Concurrently with the pulping capacity, the rate of pulpwood production has been increasing since 1966.

Over half of the cordage is hardwood. Ten years ago the proportion of pine was greater than that of hardwood, but since 1964 hardwood has exceeded pine.

Despite the increase in pulpwood harvest, more than half the wood used by Tennessee

[1] Beltz, R. C. **Southern pulpwood production, 1970.** USDA Forest Serv. Resour. Bull. SO-28, 22 p. South. Forest Exp. Stn., New Orleans, La. 1971.

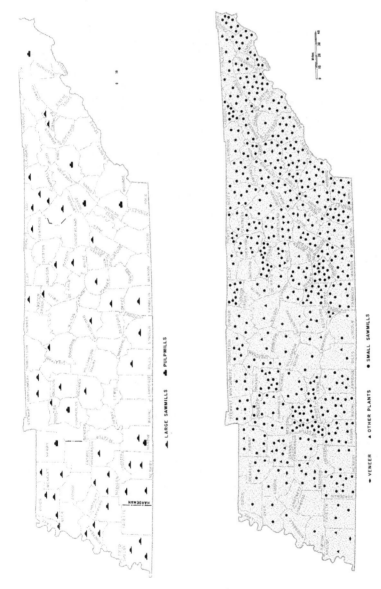

LARGE SAWMILLS   ● PULPMILLS

● VENEER   ▲ OTHER PLANTS   ● SMALL SAWMILLS

Figure 9. Primary wood-using industries in Tennessee, 1970.

10

pulpmills is imported. These imports, chiefly southern pine, totaled 505,000 cords in 1970; only 40,000 cords were exported.

OTHER PRODUCTS

Veneer log production in 1970 was 7 million board feet, a decline of 37 percent from 1960 and a very small fraction of the total roundwood output. Hardwoods, mostly yellow-poplar and sweetgum, comprised 99 percent of the total. The number of veneer mills dropped from nine to six during the decade.

Cooperage is also a declining industry; the number of mills decreased by two-thirds during the decade. Output of cooperage bolts dropped accordingly to 11 million board feet —a decline of 58 percent from 1960. Most of the bolts were white oak for tight cooperage.

Other products comprised less than 8 percent of the total. Among these are handlestock, charcoal, commercial posts, excelsior, furniture stock, mine timbers, miscellaneous dimension, piling, poles, and shuttleblocks.

Domestic use, largely for fuel, was 50 percent of the total roundwood production in 1949, 20 percent in 1960, and 15 percent in 1970. Movement of rural populations to the cities and a switch to more modern fuels among those remaining in the country explain the steady decrease in fuelwood.

PLANT RESIDUES AND BYPRODUCTS

In 1970, Tennessee forest industries produced 51 million cubic feet of residues in converting roundwood into primary products. This total was equally divided between coarse and fine residues. Coarse residue is material, such as slabs and edgings, that can be made into pulp chips. Fine residue consists mainly of sawdust and shavings, which cannot be converted into pulp chips.

More than half of the residue was utilized. Ten million cubic feet went into pulp and particleboard; the use of residues in pulp has been expanding consistently since 1960. About 12 million cubic feet were burned for fuel, and more than 5 million cubic feet were used for other products such as animal bedding, charcoal, and soil mulch.

The nonutilized portion of the residues totaled 23 million cubic feet in 1970—equivalent to the growing stock volume on 29,000 acres of Tennessee's commercial forest land. Two-thirds of the unused residues are fines.

Timber Supply Outlook

Demand for timber will probably increase. But what about the supply? Projections can aid in evaluating Tennessee's prospects of satisfying future demand. Projections are not predictions, since no attempt is made to estimate what conditions will be in the future. They show only what will occur if certain assumptions hold true.

Two projections, prospective cut and potential cut, were made for Tennessee. In the propective cut, the assumption is that the cut will be brought into balance with growth. In the potential cut, it is assumed that forest management will be intensified so that there will be a better balance of tree sizes in 30 years, the end of the projection period.

PROSPECTIVE CUT

In this projection the cut is adjusted each year until the last year of the projection period, when it is assumed to equal the growth on growing stock (figs. 10 and 11). The other assumptions are that the commercial forest area, growth rates, and mortality rates will not change.

The growth-cut ratios were favorable for softwoods in 1970: 3.1 for growing stock and 2.5 for sawtimber. These ratios mean that the annual cut can be increased without diminishing the softwood inventory. In the year 2,000 the growth and cut are 135 million cubic feet (fig. 10).

Most of the inventory increase will be in the lower diameter classes (fig. 12). About 75 percent of the softwood sawtimber volume is in the 14-inch class and less.

The proportions of growth to cut for hardwood in 1970 were 2.2 for growing stock and 1.6 for sawtimber. As in softwood, the cut of growing stock trees can be increased greatly during the projection period (fig. 11). In the

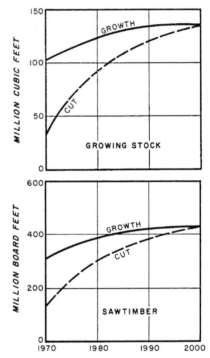

Figure 10. *Prospective growth and cut of softwood, 1970-2000.*

year 2000, growth and cut are 556 million cubic feet.

Growth and cut are initially favorable for hardwood sawtimber. As the projection period proceeds, however, the ratio diminishes. By 1977, and for every year thereafter, the cut is larger than the growth. The result is a diminution of the sawtimber inventory (fig. 13).

12

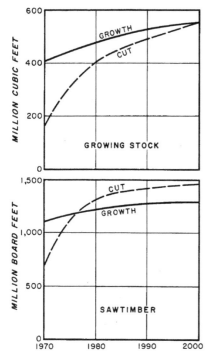

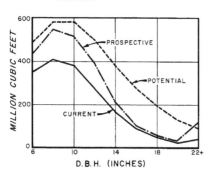

Figure 11. *Prospective growth and cut of hardwood, 1970-2000.*

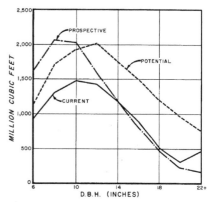

Figure 12. *Comparison of 1971 softwood growing stock with prospective and potential inventories of 2001.*

Figure 13. *Comparison of 1971 hardwood growing stock with prospective and potential inventories of 2001.*

The management goal in the prospective cut is a modest one. The deficit of trees in the upper diameter classes was not considered; consequently, a reduction of the hardwood sawtimber inventory occurred. More ambitious management goals are possible, and they are considered in the potential cut.

POTENTIAL CUT

In calculating the potential cut, it is assumed that the commercial forest area will remain the same as now but that the oak-pine forest type will be converted to pure pine by the end of the projection period. With the conversion there will be 2.9 million acres in the softwood type and 9.9 million acres in the hardwood type. Growth and mortality rates remain unchanged.

To correct the deficit of trees in the larger diameter classes, a goal for both types is to improve the distribution of tree sizes by adjusting the annual cut. With the 1971 inventory and the desired inventory of 2001 as the bases, stand tables for each year of the projection period were found by interpolation. The cut each year was adjusted so that the interpolated stand was attained. In the early years of the projection period the cut is reduced, but as growth rebuilds the inventory the removals

13

are increased. The cut is concentrated in the lower tree sizes so that the deficit in large trees is gradually ameliorated.

The specific goals for the softwood type are a basal area of 80 square feet per acre and a growing stock proportion of 97 percent of the total stand. The goals for the hardwood type are a density of 90 square feet per acre and a growing stock proportion of 90 percent of the total stand.

If these goals are achieved, Tennessee's forests will have an annual growth of 704 million cubic feet or 55 cubic feet per acre in 2000. The growing stock needed for this growth is seen in figures 12 and 13. Softwood comprises 20 percent of the inventory.

Although the cubic-foot growth does not increase much, the sawtimber growth is increased markedly—to 187 board feet per acre in the year 2000, as opposed to 135 board feet for the prospective cut in 2000 and 111 board feet at present.

The potential inventory for both species groups has much more volume in the higher diameter classes than does the 1971 inventory. Thus, the potential cut indicates that Tennessee's forests could furnish much more timber than they now do.

Management Opportunities

PINE SITES

Tennessee is considered primarily a hardwood State. However, 46 percent or 5.9 million acres of the commercial forest area belong in the pine site class. Since only about 1 million acres are currently in pine, almost 5 million acres are candidates for conversion. The time for conversion depends upon the management potential of the present stands.

Pine sites that are poorly stocked with growing stock trees total 594,000 acres. These stands have little management potential and are candidates for immediate conversion. Only 59,000 acres have an adequate pine seed source; the remaining would have to be planted or seeded.

The other pine sites contain stands that are at least 60 percent stocked with growing stock trees. The stands can be managed and regenerated to pure pine subsequently. These areas total 5.3 million acres, and only 1.6 million acres have an adequate pine seed source.

HARDWOOD SITES

One problem with the hardwood resource is an unfavorable distribution of tree sizes. As indicated by the projection of potential cut, a better distribution may be obtained by concentrating annual removals on trees too small for saw logs. The hardwood pulpwood market offers an outlet for this material.

Another problem is inadequate stocking with desirable trees. Desirable trees are growing stock which have high vigor, possess no serious defects to limit prospective or present use, and contain no pathogens likely to cause death or serious deterioration before rotation age. Acceptable trees are growing stock that do not qualify as desirable. Sample plots of the survey were classified according to their condition class—that is, as having poor, medium, or good stocking of desirable trees—and these data

were used to estimate the amount of commercial forest land in each condition class.

Poorly Stocked Stands

Some 1.4 million acres of hardwood sites are poorly stocked with growing stock trees. All regions have some acreage in this condition class, but a large proportion occurs in the Central region. Some areas are suitable for the planting of yellow-poplar; on others, cull tree removal may facilitate natural restocking.

Another 5.4 million acres are poorly stocked with desirable trees but have medium or better stocking of growing stock trees. More hardwood sites occur in this condition class than any other. Stands can be improved by removing cull trees and favoring desirable trees in intermediate cuts or thinnings.

Medium Stocked Stands

On 16,000 acres desirable trees supply medium stocking, and less than 30 percent of the area is occupied by other trees or conditions that prevent occupancy by desirable trees. These areas occur in the Central and Plateau regions. No stand treatments are necessary.

On 81,000 acres of hardwood sites desirable trees provide medium stocking, but 30 percent or more of the area is occupied by other trees. This condition class occurs in the Central, Plateau, and West regions. Thinning of acceptable trees and removal of culls can improve stocking of desirable trees.

Well Stocked Stands

About 6,000 acres are well stocked with desirable trees, but not overstocked. All are in the West Central region. Since these stands have maximum growth in desirable trees, no special treatments are necessary.

RESOURCE IMPROVEMENT

Despite the net loss of about 600,000 acres of commercial forest since 1961, the timber resource of Tennessee has improved. Among the improvements are increases in stocking, volume of desirable species, and growth. However, problems still remain. Only 20 percent of the commercial forest area is well stocked, large trees are scarce, and hardwoods occupy many acres that could support pine.

Two ways of improving the resource have been mentioned. One is the conversion of suitable areas to pine. The other is stand treatment in the hardwood type.

The identification of stand conditions and pine sites does not necessarily mean that improvements should be undertaken. In some situations, the cost of improvement may be greater than the financial returns, and the gains from some treatments, such as cull tree removal, are sometimes difficult to assess. Nevertheless, some priorities can be outlined on the basis of cost and technical feasibility.

Priorities on pine sites can be assigned on the basis of conversion cost. If stands that can be profitably managed are excluded, the first priority would be sites that can be regenerated naturally to pine. Some stands already have pine reproduction, which can be released by harvesting or deadening any competing overstory. Others have a pine seed source but no reproduction. On these areas a pine understory can be established naturally before the overstory is eliminated.

Conversions which necessitate artificial regeneration of pine are second in priority. Conversion costs will vary widely according to stand conditions. Some areas have a few large trees which can be deadened economically. Most stands, however, are composed of many stems of varying sizes, and heavy machinery is needed to clear and prepare for planting. Machine clearing is expensive, but there is no other way of restoring these sites.

On hardwood sites management should be aimed at increasing the stocking of desirable trees. Ranking first in priority is the harvesting of merchantable but less desirable trees, next is deadening of large culls, and finally is deadening of small culls. The harvesting of less desirable trees can provide an immediate economic return while freeing growing space. Large culls can be treated singly, while blanket treatment may be needed for small culls. In some cases, areas can be cleared of their present stand and profitably planted to yellow-poplar.

Though the stand treatments outlined here require the careful judgement of foresters and often will entail a large financial outlay, they are feasible in many situations. The extent to which land managers adopt them will determine the future productivity of Tennessee's forests.

Appendix

SURVEY METHODS

The data on forest acreage and timber volume in this report were secured by a sampling method involving a forest-nonforest classification on aerial photographs and on-the-ground measurements of trees at sample locations. The sample locations were at the intersections of a grid of lines spaced 3 miles apart. In Tennessee, 121,290 photographic classifications were made and 4,665 ground sample locations were visited.

The initial estimates of forest area that were obtained with the aerial photographs were adjusted on the basis of the ground check.

A cluster of 10 variable-radius plots was installed at each ground sample location. Each sample tree on the variable-radius plots represented 3.75 square feet of basal area per acre. Trees less than 5.0 inches in diameter were tallied on fixed-radius plots around the plot centers. Together, these samples provided most of the information for the new inventory. A subsample of trees on the plots was measured in detail to obtain data for calculating timber volumes.

The plots established by the prior survey were remeasured to determine the elements of change and were the basis for estimating growth, mortality, removals, and changes in land use.

With the assistance of the Tennessee Valley Authority and the Tennessee Department of Conservation, a special study was made to determine product output. It consisted of a canvass of all primary wood-using plants active in Tennessee during 1970. Out-of-State firms known to use Tennessee roundwood were also contacted. Additionally, fuelwood and other domestic uses were determined from an area sample.

RELIABILITY OF THE DATA

Reliability of the estimates may be affected by two types of errors. The first stems from the use of a sample to estimate the whole and from variability of the items being sampled. This type is termed sampling error; it is susceptible to a mathematical evaluation of the probability of error. The second type—often referred to as reporting or estimating error—derives from mistakes in measurement, judgment, or recording, and from limitations of method or equipment. Its effects cannot be appraised mathematically, but the Forest Service constantly attempts to hold it to a minimum by proper training and good supervision, and by emphasis on careful work.

Statistical analysis of the data indicates a sampling error of plus or minus 0.3 percent for the estimate of total commercial forest area, 1.7 percent for total cubic volume, and 2.7 percent for total board-foot volume. As these totals are broken down by forest type, species, tree diameter, and other subdivisions, the possibility of error increases and is greatest for the smallest items. The order of this increase is suggested in the following tabulation, which shows the sampling error to which the timber volume and area estimates are liable, two chances out of three:

Commercial forest area	Sampling error [1]	Cubic volume [2]	Sampling error [1]	Board-foot volume [3]	Sampling error [1]
Thousand acres	Percent	Million cubic feet	Percent	Million board feet	Percent
12,819.8	0.3				
1,153.8	1.0	10,395.8	1.7	.	...
288.4	2.0	7,454.5	2.0	26,340.2	2.7
128.2	3.0	3,313.1	3.0	21,335.6	3.0
72.1	4.0	1,863.6	4.0	12,001.3	4.0
46.2	5.0	1,192.7	5.0	7,680.8	5.0
11.5	10.0	298.2	10.0	1,920.2	10.0
5.1	15.0	132.5	15.0	853.4	15.0
2.9	20.0	74.5	20.0	480.1	20.0
1.8	25.0	47.7	25.0	307.2	25.0

[1] By random-sampling formula.
[2] Growing-stock volume on commercial forest land.
[3] Sawtimber volume on commercial forest land.

The sampling error to which the estimates of growth, mortality, and removals are liable, on a probability of two chances out of three, are:

Net annual growth				Annual removals			
Cubic volume	Sampling error [1]	Board foot volume	Sampling error [1]	Cubic volume	Sampling error [1]	Board foot volume	Sampling error [1]
Million cubic feet	Percent	Million board feet	Percent	Million cubic feet	Percent	Million board feet	Percent
509.1	2.4						
325.8	3.0	1,428.2	3.8	216.4	3.2	819.6	3.0
183.3	4.0	1,289.0	4.0	138.5	4.0	461.0	4.0
117.3	5.0	824.9	5.0	88.6	5.0	295.1	5.0
29.3	10.0	206.2	10.0	22.2	10.0	73.8	10.0
13.0	15.0	91.7	15.0	9.8	15.0	32.8	15.0
7.3	20.0	51.6	20.0	5.5	20.0	18.4	20.0
4.7	25.0	33.0	25.0	3.5	25.0	11.8	25.0

[1] By random-sampling formula.

DEFINITIONS OF TERMS

Forest Land Class

Forest land.—Land at least 16.7 percent stocked by forest trees of any size, or formerly having such tree cover and not currently developed for non-forest use.

Commercial forest land.—Forest land that is producing or is capable of producing crops of industrial wood and not withdrawn from timber utilization.

Nonstocked land.—Commercial forest land less than 16.7 percent stocked with growing-stock trees.

Productive-reserved forest land.—Productive public forest land withdrawn from timber utilization through statute or administrative regulation.

Unproductive forest land.—Forest land incapable of yielding crops of industrial wood because of adverse site conditions.

Tree Species

Commercial species.—Tree species presently or prospectively suitable for industrial wood products; excludes so-called weed species such as blackjack oak and blue beech.

Hardwoods.—Dicotyledonous trees, usually broad-leaved and deciduous.

Softwoods.—Coniferous trees, usually evergreen, having needle or scale-like leaves.

Forest Type

White pine.—Forests in which eastern white pine comprises a plurality of the stocking. Common associates include hemlock, birch, and maple.

Spruce-fir.—Forests in which spruce or true firs, singly or in combination, comprise a plurality of the stocking. Common associates include maple, birch, and hemlock.

Loblolly-shortleaf pine.—Forests in which southern pines comprise a plurality of the stocking. Common associates include oak, hickory, and gum.

Oak-pine.—Forests in which hardwoods (usually upland oaks) comprise a plurality of the stocking but in which softwoods, except cypress and eastern redcedar, comprise 25-50 percent of the stocking. Common associates include gum, hickory, and yellow-poplar.

Cedar.—Forests in which eastern redcedar comprises 25 percent or more of the stocking. Common associates include southern pines, oak, and hickory.

Oak-hickory.—Forests in which upland oaks or hickory, singly or in combination, comprise a plurality of the stocking except where pines comprise 25-50 percent, in which case the stand is classified oak-pine. Common associates include yellow-poplar, elm, maple, and black walnut.

Oak-gum-cypress.—Bottom-land forests in which tupelo, blackgum, sweetgum, oaks, or southern cypress, singly or in combination, comprise a plurality of stocking except where pines comprise 25-50 percent, in which case the stand is classified oak-pine. Common associates include cottonwood, willow, ash, elm, hackberry, and maple.

Elm-ash-cottonwood.—Forests in which elm, ash, or cottonwood, singly or in combination, comprise a plurality of the stocking. Common associates include willow, sycamore, beech, and maple.

Maple-beech-birch.—Forests in which sugar maple, beech, or yellow birch, singly or in combination, comprise a plurality of the stocking. Common associates include hemlock, elm, basswood, and white pine.

Class of Timber

Growing stock trees.—Sawtimber trees, poletimber trees, saplings, and seedlings; that is, all live trees except rough and rotten trees.

18

Desirable trees.—Growing-stock trees that have no serious defects to limit present or prospective use, are of relatively high vigor, and contain no pathogens that may result in death or serious deterioration before rotation age. They comprise the type of trees that forest managers aim to grow; that is, the trees favored in silvicultural operations.

Acceptable trees.—Trees meeting the specifications for growing stock but not qualifying as desirable trees.

Sawtimber trees.—Live trees of commercial species, 9.0 inches and larger in diameter at breast height for softwoods and 11.0 inches and larger for hardwoods, and containing at least one 12-foot saw log.

Poletimber trees.—Live trees of commercial species 5.0 to 9.0 inches in d.b.h. for softwoods and 5.0 to 11.0 inches for hardwoods, and of good form and vigor.

Saplings.—Live trees of commercial species, 1.0 inch to 5.0 inches in d.b.h. and of good form and vigor.

Rough and rotten trees.—Live trees that are unmerchantable for saw logs now or prospectively because of defect, rot, or species.

Salvable dead trees.—Standing or down dead trees that are considered currently or potentially merchantable.

Stand-Size Class

Sawtimber stands.—Stands at least 16.7 percent stocked with growing-stock trees, with half or more of this stocking in sawtimber or poletimber trees, and with sawtimber stocking at least equal to poletimber stocking.

Poletimber stands.—Stands at least 16.7 percent stocked with growing-stock trees, with half or more of this stocking in sawtimber or poletimber trees, and with poletimber stocking exceeding that of sawtimber stocking.

Sapling-seedling stands.—Stands at least 16.7 percent stocked with growing-stock trees, with more than half of this stocking in saplings or seedlings.

Nonstocked areas.—Commercial forest lands less than 16.7 percent stocked with growing-stock trees.

Stocking

Stocking is a measure of the extent to which the growth potential of the site is utilized by trees or preempted by vegetative cover. Stocking is determined by comparing the stand density in terms of number of trees or basal area with a specified standard. Full stocking is assumed to range from 100 to 133 percent of the stocking standard.

The tabulation below shows the density standard in terms of trees per acre, by size class, required for full stocking:

D.b.h. (inches)	Number of trees	D.b.h. (inches)	Number of trees
Seedlings	600	16	72
2	560	18	60
4	460	20	51
6	340	22	42
8	240	24	36
10	155	26	31
12	115	28	27
14	90	30	24

Volume

Volume of sawtimber.—Net volume of the sawlog portion of live sawtimber trees in board feet of the International rule, ¼-inch kerf.

Volume of growing stock.—Volume of sound wood in the bole of sawtimber and poletimber trees from stump to a minimum 4.0-inch top outside bark or to the point where the central stem breaks into limbs.

Volume of timber.—The volume of sound wood in the bole of growing stock, rough, rotten, and salvable dead trees 5.0 inches and larger in d.b.h. from stump to a minimum 4.0-inch top outside bark or to the point where the central stem breaks into limbs.

Area Condition Class

A classification of commercial forest land based upon stocking by desirable trees and other conditions affecting current and prospective timber growth.

Class 10.—Areas 100 percent or more stocked with desirable trees and not overstocked.

Class 20.—Areas 100 percent or more stocked with desirable trees and overstocked with all live trees.

Class 30.—Areas 60 to 100 percent stocked with desirable trees and with less than 30 percent of the area controlled by other trees, inhibiting vegetation, slash, or nonstockable conditions.

Class 40.—Areas 60 to 100 percent stocked with desirable trees and with 30 percent or more of the area controlled by other trees, or conditions that ordinarily prevent occupancy by desirable trees.

Class 50.—Areas less than 60 percent stocked with desirable trees, but with 100 percent or more stocking of growing-stock trees.

Class 60.—Areas less than 60 percent stocked with desirable trees, but with 60 to 100 percent stocking of growing-stock trees.

Class 70.—Areas less than 60 percent stocked with desirable trees and with less than 60 percent stocking of growing-stock trees.

19

Miscellaneous Definitions

Basal area.—The area in square feet of the cross section at breast height of a single tree or of all the trees in a stand, usually expressed as square feet per acre.

D.b.h. (Diameter breast high).—Tree diameter in inches, outside bark, measured at 4½ feet above ground.

Diameter classes.—The 2-inch diameter classes extend from 1.0 inch below to 0.9 inch above the stated midpoint. Thus, the 12-inch class includes trees 11.0 inches through 12.9 inches d.b.h.

Site classes.—A classification of forest land in terms of inherent capacity to grow crops of industrial wood.

Log grades.—A classification of logs based on external characteristics as indicators of quality or value.

Gross growth.—Annual increase in net volume of trees in the absence of cutting and mortality.

Net annual growth.—The increase in volume of a specified size class for a specific year. Components of net annual growth include the increment in net volume of trees at the beginning of the specific year surviving to its end plus volume of trees reaching the size class during the year minus the volume of trees that died during the year minus the net volume of trees that become rough or rotten during the year.

Mortality.—Number or sound-wood volume of live trees dying from natural causes during a specified period.

Timber removals.—The net volume of growing-stock trees removed from the inventory by harvesting, cultural operations such as timber-stand improvement, land clearing, or changes in land use.

Timber products.—Roundwood products and plant byproducts. Timber products output includes roundwood products cut from growing stock on commercial forest land; from other sources, such as cull trees, salvable dead trees, limbs, and saplings; from trees on noncommercial and nonforest lands; and from plant byproducts.

Roundwood products.—Logs, bolts, or other round sections cut from trees for industrial or consumer uses. Included are saw logs, veneer logs and bolts, cooperage logs and bolts, pulpwood, fuelwood, piling, poles and posts, hewn ties, mine timbers, and various other round, split, or hewn products.

Logging residues.—The unused portions of trees cut or killed by logging.

Plant byproducts.—Wood products, such as pulp chips, obtained incidental to manufacture of other products.

Plant residues.—Wood materials from manufacturing plants not utilized for some product. Included are slabs, edgings, trimmings, miscuts, sawdust, shavings, veneer cores and clippings, and pulp screening.

STANDARD TABLES

NOTE: Regional tables, identical in format to standard State tables 1-22, are available for each of the five forest resource regions in Tennessee. They are free on request to the Southern Forest Experiment Station.

Table 1. *Area by land classes, Tennessee, 1971*

Land class	Area
	Thousand acres
Forest:	
Commercial	12,819.8
Productive-reserved	316.5
Unproductive	...
Total forest	13,136.3
Nonforest:	
Cropland [1]	7,855.2
Pasture and range [1]	1,808.2
Other [2]	3,675.2
Total nonforest	13,338.6
All land [3]	26,474.9

[1] Source: Census of Agriculture.
[2] Includes swampland, industrial and urban areas, other nonforest land, and 36,500 acres classed as water by Forest Survey standards but defined by the Bureau of the Census as land.
[3] Source: United States Bureau of the Census, Land and Water Area of the United States.

Table 2. *Area of commercial forest land by ownership classes, Tennessee, 1971*

Ownership class	Area
	Thousand acres
Public:	
National forest	599.7
Other federal	340.3
State	324.0
County and municipal	22.2
Total public	1,286.2
Private:	
Forest industry [1]	1,121.4
Farmer	5,079.1
Miscellaneous private:	
Individual	4,577.2
Corporate	755.9
Total private	11,533.6
All ownerships	12,819.8

[1] Not including 53,700 acres of farmer-owned and miscellaneous private lands leased to forest industry.

Table 3. *Area of commercial forest land by stand-size and ownership classes, Tennessee, 1971*

Stand-size class	All ownerships	National forest	Other public	Forest industry	Farmer and misc. private
	- - - - - - - - - - Thousand acres - - - - - - - - - -				
Sawtimber	3,297.8	257.0	297.8	233.2	2,509.8
Poletimber	4,893.6	230.6	271.5	432.2	3,959.3
Sapling and seedling	4,595.9	112.1	117.2	456.0	3,910.6
Nonstocked areas	32.5	...	...	...	32.5
All classes	12,819.8	599.7	686.5	1,121.4	10,412.2

Table 4. *Area of commercial forest land by stand-volume and ownership classes, Tennessee, 1971*

Stand-volume per acre [1]	All ownerships	National forest	Other public	Forest industry	Farmer and misc. private
	- - - - - - - - - Thousand acres - - - - - - - - -				
Less than 1,500 board feet	6,953.0	153.2	272.7	617.0	5,910.1
1,500 to 5,000 board feet	4,555.9	285.5	265.2	380.8	3,624.4
More than 5,000 board feet	1,310.9	161.0	148.6	123.6	877.7
All classes	12,819.8	599.7	686.5	1,121.4	10,412.2

[1] International ¼-inch rule.

22

Table 5. *Area of commercial forest land by stocking classes based on selected stand components, Tennessee, 1971*

Stocking percentage	All trees	Growing-stock trees			Rough and rotten trees	Inhibiting vegetation
		Total	Desirable	Acceptable		
		– – – – – – – – – – – Thousand acres – – – – – – – – – – –				
160 or more	11.6	11.6	...	...		
150 to 160	28.0	11.7	.	...		
140 to 150	275.0	50.7	...	5.3		
130 to 140	629.2	147.8	11.1	15.2		
120 to 130	1,420.9	318.5	5.7	27.9	...	...
110 to 120	2,706.6	773.4	35.1	124.0	...	
100 to 110	3,254.3	1,286.7	22.3	298.5	6.4	
90 to 100	2,431.9	1,917.3	62.4	782.7	...	
80 to 90	1,194.4	2,514.5	67.0	1,498.3	23.5	...
70 to 80	477.9	2,193.5	164.5	2,201.8	71.3	
60 to 70	236.5	1,619.2	243.2	2,262.2	171.8	
50 to 60	97.7	1,170.6	370.8	2,121.9	415.4	...
40 to 50	44.9	525.0	669.8	1,669.1	932.0	...
30 to 40	10.9	190.6	1,150.4	989.2	1,902.2	5.4
20 to 30	...	50.9	1,962.2	529.0	3,203.2	14.2
10 to 20	...	26.4	3,134.4	169.4	3,598.0	75.6
Less than 10	...	11.4	4,920.9	125.3	2,496.0	12,724.6
All areas	12,819.8	12,819.8	12,819.8	12,819.8	12,819.8	12,819.8

Table 6. *Area of commercial forest land by area-condition and ownership classes, Tennessee, 1971*

Area-condition class	All ownerships	National forest	Other public	Forest industry	Farmer and misc. private
	– – – – – – – – Thousand acres – – – – – – – –				
10	50.8	...	8.0	10.6	32.2
20	23.4	...	5.3	14.8	3.3
30	79.4	...	5.3	11.1	63.0
40	457.7	11.7	10.1	45.8	390.1
50	2,129.7	148.6	96.4	251.0	1,633.7
60	8,103.9	330.7	458.4	630.2	6,684.6
70	1,974.9	108.7	103.0	157.9	1,605.3
All classes	12,819.8	599.7	686.5	1,121.4	10,412.2

Table 7. *Area of commercial forest land by site and ownership classes, Tennessee, 1971*

Site class	All owner-ships	National forest	Other public	Forest industry	Farmer and misc. private
	– – – – – – – – Thousand acres – – – – – – – –				
165 cu. ft. or more	165.2	...	16.8	40.6	107.8
120 to 165 cu. ft.	379.7	5.5	50.6	11.3	312.3
85 to 120 cu. ft.	2,465.7	104.9	160.0	151.4	2,049.4
50 to 85 cu. ft.	6,497.2	334.1	335.5	626.2	5,201.4
Less than 50 cu. ft.	3,312.0	155.2	123.6	291.9	2,741.3
All classes	12,819.8	599.7	686.5	1,121.4	10,412.2

Table 8. *Area of commercial forest land by forest types and ownership classes, Tennessee, 1971*

Type	All ownerships	Public	Private
	– – Thousand acres – –		
White pine	38.9	21.9	17.0
Loblolly-shortleaf pine	998.8	151.0	847.8
Oak-pine	1,198.0	199.3	998.7
Cedar	693.8	39.9	653.9
Oak-hickory	9,108.0	759.6	8,348.4
Oak-gum-cypress	547.2	80.6	466.6
Elm-ash-cottonwood	150.7	10.3	140.4
Maple-beech-birch	84.4	23.6	60.8
All types	12,819.8	1,286.2	11,533.6

Table 9. *Area of noncommercial forest land by forest types, Tennessee, 1971*

Type	All areas	Productive-reserved areas	Un-productive areas
	– – Thousand acres – –		
Spruce-fir	15.6	15.6	...
White pine	55.8	55.8	...
Loblolly-shortleaf pine	11.6	11.6	...
Oak-pine	44.8	44.8	...
Oak-hickory	155.4	155.4	...
Maple-beech-birch	33.3	33.3	...
All types	316.5	316.5	...

Table 10. *Number of growing-stock trees on commercial forest land by species and diameter classes, Tennessee, 1971*

Species	Diameter class (inches at breast height)										
	All classes	5.0-6.9	7.0-8.9	9.0-10.9	11.0-12.9	13.0-14.9	15.0-16.9	17.0-18.9	19.0-20.9	21.0-28.9	29.0 and larger
	– – – – – – – – – – – – – – Thousand trees – – – – – – – – – – – – – –										
Softwood:											
Shortleaf pine	87,357	38,984	25,285	14,274	5,672	2,035	773	276	46	12	...
Loblolly	41,421	25,349	11,335	3,068	1,132	323	157	39	9	9	...
Virginia pine	90,244	44,833	22,900	12,916	6,396	2,507	471	166	38	17	...
Pitch pine	10,300	5,353	2,070	1,487	553	466	157	124	82	8	...
Table-Mountain pine	1,694	653	579	199	134	78	51	...	...	...	...
White pine	10,346	2,299	2,474	2,021	1,219	892	608	410	182	216	25
Hemlock	4,646	1,141	1,391	705	516	383	295	71	77	58	9
Redcedar	39,590	26,602	9,703	2,313	638	171	113	42	8	...	...
Cypress	1,201	254	233	118	194	· 123	90	42	64	52	31
Total	286,799	145,468	75,970	37,101	16,454	6,978	2,715	1,170	506	372	65
Hardwood:											
Select white oaks [1]	152,596	59,511	37,136	25,248	14,328	8,469	4,269	2,261	626	715	33
Select red oaks [2]	43,665	13,159	8,712	8,253	5,018	3,700	2,210	1,070	559	901	83
Other white oaks	123,406	47,902	30,341	19,141	11,925	7,216	3,721	1,642	788	672	58
Other red oaks	159,268	59,216	35,887	26,934	15,777	10,894	5,827	2,422	1,063	1,066	182
Pecan	328	139	...	105	...	...	...	39	36	9	...
Other hickories	152,454	64,133	39,867	23,605	13,065	6,367	3,096	1,257	510	533	21
Sweetgum	36,090	13,696	9,646	5,940	3,600	1,460	996	432	129	175	16
Tupelo and blackgum	29,164	12,619	8,064	3,942	2,284	1,245	472	290	172	76	...
Hard maple	25,806	10,668	6,706	4,060	1,776	1,380	596	229	215	168	8
Soft maple	42,044	21,189	10,087	5,792	2,787	791	811	338	132	109	8
Beech	12,496	3,592	3,639	1,941	885	797	672	324	276	354	16
Ash	33,236	16,666	7,236	4,291	1,721	1,323	850	381	421	342	5
Cottonwood	865	171	...	...	...	80	193	77	68	245	31
Basswood	4,375	1,435	1,232	636	402	300	123	120	62	65	...
Yellow-poplar	61,389	22,608	13,792	9,417	6,905	3,946	2,732	955	666	342	26
Black walnut	9,788	3,385	2,866	1,766	1,064	465	189	31	22	...	...
Black cherry	9,065	3,995	3,170	1,001	563	223	69	44	...	...	...
Willow	1,730	732	380	38	153	...	89	232	81	25	...
Magnolia (*Magnolia* spp.)	2,400	734	723	349	330	154	47	26	10	27	...
American elm	16,248	7,912	3,639	2,531	1,024	515	232	171	98	97	29
Other elms	15,206	8,569	2,787	2,194	961	415	107	43	104	26	...
Hackberry	10,597	4,760	2,740	1,374	805	433	330	80	63	12	...
Sycamore	5,106	1,417	996	949	661	397	299	102	95	187	3
Other hardwoods	66,964	45,409	13,221	4,257	1,734	1,210	587	248	121	161	16
Total	1,014,286	423,617	242,867	153,764	87,768	51,780	28,517	12,814	6,317	6,307	535
All species	1,301,085	569,085	318,837	190,865	104,222	58,758	31,232	13,984	6,823	6,679	600

[1] Includes white, swamp chestnut, swamp white, chinkapin and bur oaks.
[2] Includes northern red, Shumard, and cherrybark oaks.

24

Table 11. *Volume of timber on commercial forest land by class of timber and by softwoods and hardwoods, Tennessee, 1971*

Class of timber	All species	Soft-wood	Hard-wood
	-- Million cubic feet --		
Sawtimber trees:			
Saw-log portion	4,615.9	893.8	3,722.1
Upper-stem portion	1,288.9	144.9	1,144.0
Total	5,904.8	1,038.7	4,866.1
Poletimber	4,491.0	761.1	3,729.9
All growing stock	10,395.8	1,799.8	8,596.0
Rough trees	1,111.6	37.1	1,074.5
Rotten trees	605.0	20.7	584.3
Salvable dead trees	26.8	12.8	14.0
All timber	12,139.2	1,870.4	10,268.8

Table 12. *Volume of growing stock and sawtimber on commercial forest land by ownership classes and by softwoods and hardwoods, Tennessee, 1971*

Ownership class	Growing stock			Sawtimber		
	All species	Soft-wood	Hard-wood	All species	Soft-wood	Hard-wood
	-- Million cubic feet --			-- Million board feet --		
National forest	736.5	261.0	475.5	2,096.5	863.6	1,232.9
Other public	724.6	197.8	526.8	2,166.7	621.6	1,545.1
Forest industry	904.3	170.8	733.5	2,406.6	446.3	1,960.3
Farmer and misc. private	8,030.4	1,170.2	6,860.2	19,670.4	2,767.6	16,902.8
All ownerships	10,395.8	1,799.8	8,596.0	26,340.2	4,699.1	21,641.1

Table 13. *Volume of growing stock on commercial forest land by species and diameter classes, Tennessee, 1971*

Species	Diameter class (inches at breast height)										
	All classes	5.0-6.9	7.0-8.9	9.0-10.9	11.0-12.9	13.0-14.9	15.0-16.9	17.0-18.9	19.0-20.9	21.0-28.9	29.0 and larger
	-- Million cubic feet --										
Softwood:											
Shortleaf pine	634.7	111.5	157.2	163.2	103.6	52.7	30.0	13.2	2.6	0.7	...
Loblolly pine	184.5	61.3	58.3	29.3	19.2	8.0	4.9	2.0	.8	.7	...
Virginia pine	560.8	109.9	127.2	135.4	106.7	57.3	14.7	6.5	2.1	1.0	...
Pitch pine	71.2	12.6	11.0	12.0	7.8	11.6	5.7	6.0	4.1	.4	...
Table-Mountain pine	10.1	1.4	2.9	1.6	1.8	1.4	1.0	...	...	...	..
White pine	151.1	5.4	13.2	20.0	19.7	22.2	19.6	18.2	9.9	19.0	3.9
Hemlock	55.2	2.4	7.5	7.4	7.2	8.9	9.3	2.9	4.4	4.3	.9
Redcedar	103.6	43.5	32.9	15.0	6.2	2.6	2.4	.9	.1	...	...
Cypress	28.6	1.0	1.9	.8	3.1	3.6	2.9	2.7	3.6	4.3	4.7
Total	1,799.8	349.0	412.1	384.7	275.3	168.3	90.5	52.4	27.6	30.4	9.5
Hardwood:											
Select white oaks	1,305.4	136.4	196.6	248.2	229.2	194.1	130.6	87.5	30.8	49.3	2.7
Select red oaks	554.7	33.6	51.3	84.3	82.4	84.2	70.4	40.4	28.8	69.8	9.5
Other white oaks	1,016.6	107.4	158.6	172.7	179.2	154.2	103.8	60.2	35.7	39.7	5.1
Other red oaks	1,486.4	135.7	192.3	255.0	245.0	237.8	173.6	95.8	52.7	74.0	24.5
Pecan	5.7	.2	...	1.0	...	...	...	1.8	2.3	.4	...
Other hickories	1,191.5	135.8	217.7	235.7	219.0	153.5	101.8	52.8	28.9	43.6	2.7
Sweetgum	337.4	30.0	55.4	64.5	68.5	39.9	34.6	18.6	8.2	15.2	2.5
Tupelo and blackgum	196.4	23.9	38.8	35.6	33.8	26.6	13.9	11.1	7.5	5.2	...
Hard maple	200.0	24.6	35.5	35.9	27.5	29.2	17.0	9.0	10.1	11.2	1.0
Soft maple	264.1	50.5	54.4	51.9	43.1	17.6	23.4	10.3	5.9	6.2	.8
Beech	138.5	7.9	17.6	16.2	12.3	15.9	17.3	11.1	12.7	26.3	1.2
Ash	259.0	36.9	41.8	41.5	27.9	29.0	26.0	13.7	19.1	22.7	.4
Cottonwood	54.8	.3	...	...	...	3.2	8.1	3.9	6.0	27.9	5.4
Basswood	52.7	3.4	6.5	7.3	7.7	8.8	4.6	5.7	3.3	5.4	...
Yellow-poplar	724.0	58.3	85.6	107.4	138.8	111.0	102.3	46.8	40.7	29.3	3.8
Black walnut	73.0	8.8	14.8	15.2	16.5	10.2	5.5	1.1	.9	...	...
Black cherry	54.5	9.4	15.9	10.6	9.2	4.7	2.8	1.9	...	...	...
Willow	30.0	1.5	2.3	.4	2.3	...	4.5	12.3	4.3	2.4	...
Magnolia (*Magnolia* spp.)	26.5	1.9	4.0	4.8	5.9	4.5	1.9	1.1	.5	1.9	...
American elm	105.5	16.3	16.1	21.2	15.8	10.9	5.4	5.8	4.3	5.5	4.2
Other elms	83.7	16.4	13.7	17.9	15.0	9.6	2.9	1.2	4.9	2.1	...
Hackberry	68.2	8.1	13.0	10.8	10.4	9.6	9.4	3.8	2.3	.8	...
Sycamore	73.0	2.9	5.8	11.1	11.2	10.2	8.9	3.5	4.3	14.7	.4
Other hardwoods	294.4	89.4	65.3	39.1	28.8	25.7	15.9	10.4	5.9	12.1	1.8
Total	8,596.0	939.6	1,302.0	1,488.3	1,429.5	1,190.4	884.6	509.8	320.1	465.7	66.0
All species	10,395.8	1,288.6	1,714.1	1,873.0	1,704.8	1,358.7	975.1	562.2	347.7	496.1	75.5

25

Table 14. *Volume of sawtimber on commercial forest land by species and diameter classes, Tennessee, 1971*

Species	Diameter class (inches at breast height)								
	All classes	9.0-10.9	11.0-12.9	13.0-14.9	15.0-16.9	17.0-18.9	19.0-20.9	21.0-28.9	29.0 and larger
	-- -- -- -- -- -- -- -- -- Million board feet -- -- -- -- -- -- -- -- --								
Softwood:									
Shortleaf pine	1,691.5	665.2	501.8	270.4	163.1	72.4	14.6	4.0	..
Loblolly pine	280.6	104.2	91.5	41.7	25.0	10.6	3.9	3.7	...
Virginia pine	1,428.6	510.6	498.4	291.3	75.0	36.1	11.6	5.6	...
Pitch pine	217.1	36.7	35.5	59.8	30.0	31.0	22.3	1.8	...
Table-Mountain pine	22.1	4.6	5.6	7.1	4.8	...	...	...	...
White pine	622.3	71.7	89.3	106.7	98.0	89.3	50.0	98.2	19.1
Hemlock	211.9	27.7	30.3	43.3	44.1	14.2	25.6	22.2	4.5
Cypress	130.0	1.4	12.7	18.9	14.4	16.4	18.6	22.2	25.4
Redcedar	95.0	43.0	24.1	12.2	10.7	4.5	.5	...	..
Total	4,699.1	1,465.1	1,289.2	851.4	465.1	274.5	147.1	157.7	49.0
Hardwood:									
Select white oaks	3,133.0	...	847.3	845.5	608.1	421.4	147.3	251.0	12.4
Select red oaks	1,781.0	...	315.7	382.7	331.5	200.5	140.1	363.6	46.9
Other white oaks	2,494.0	...	659.9	664.7	477.5	287.3	178.5	198.9	27.2
Other red oaks	3,966.6	...	901.1	1,028.0	796.5	473.2	261.9	390.0	115.9
Pecan	20.8	...	...	...	...	8.7	9.4	2.7	...
Other hickories	2,796.4	...	881.9	714.0	516.8	268.4	156.8	244.0	14.5
Sweetgum	839.8	...	255.7	186.6	165.9	93.7	41.5	82.5	13.9
Tupelo and blackgum	410.9	...	119.5	106.8	69.8	54.9	34.7	25.2	...
Hard maple	460.4	...	99.5	122.5	78.7	45.1	51.1	57.9	5.6
Soft maple	446.5	...	158.1	73.6	102.2	46.5	28.8	31.9	5.4
Beech	440.9	...	43.7	65.8	81.6	58.5	65.5	118.8	7.0
Ash	624.6	...	103.1	133.6	121.7	68.2	90.1	105.8	2.1
Cottonwood	278.6	...	...	13.5	38.4	20.6	31.7	143.9	30.5
Basswood	164.5	...	29.2	43.0	21.7	27.3	15.7	27.6	..
Yellow-poplar	2,112.1	...	528.1	494.9	485.1	228.7	204.4	150.9	20.0
Black walnut	147.4	..	65.0	47.3	24.9	6.1	4.1	...	...
Black cherry	74.6	..	31.6	20.6	13.2	9.2	...	...	...
Willow '	145.3	...	8.3	...	28.0	67.6	28.7	12.7	..
Magnolia (*Magnolia* spp.)	71.3	...	25.6	19.4	8.6	5.6	2.9	9.2	..
American elm	240.7	...	60.5	46.6	26.4	31.7	21.7	30.6	23.2
Other elms	162.6	...	60.6	41.4	13.4	6.2	25.7	15.3	...
Hackberry	151.2	...	37.1	39.7	42.2	17.9	11.4	2.9	...
Sycamore	232.4	...	31.7	44.7	40.4	14.3	23.3	75.3	2.7
Other hardwoods	445.5	...	108.9	111.4	75.6	50.9	27.8	61.2	9.7
Total	21,641.1	...	5,372.1	5,246.3	4,168.2	2,512.5	1,603.1	2,401.9	337.0
All species	26,340.2	1,465.1	6,661.3	6.097.7	4,633.3	2,787.0	1,750.2	2,559.6	386.0

26

Table 15. *Volume of sawtimber on commercial forest land by species and log grade, Tennessee, 1971*

Species	All grades	Grade 1	Grade 2	Grade 3	Grade 4
	– – – – – – Million board feet – – – – – –				
Softwood:					
Yellow pines [1]	3,639.9	371.7	429.3	2,838.9	([2])
Cypress [1]	130.0	37.8	20.5	71.7	([2])
Redcedar [3]	95.0	95.0	([2])	([2])	([2])
Other softwoods [4]	834.2	27.4	113.5	397.5	295.8
Total	4,699.1	531.9	563.3	3,308.1	295.8
Hardwood:[5]					
Select white and red oaks	4,914.0	848.9	1,069.8	2,386.8	608.5
Other white and red oaks	6,460.6	1,044.2	1,251.4	3,289.1	875.9
Hickory	2,817.2	375.0	493.6	1,545.9	402.7
Hard maple	460.4	65.8	75.2	241.8	77.6
Sweetgum	839.8	119.8	164.2	417.6	138.2
Ash, walnut, and black cherry	846.6	182.9	197.6	390.7	75.4
Yellow-poplar	2,112.1	362.6	351.6	965.6	423.3
Other hardwoods	3,190.4	553.1	633.2	1,466.4	537.7
Total	21,641.1	3,552.3	4,236.6	10,703.9	3,148.3
All species	26,340.2	4,084.2	4,799.9	14,012.0	3,444.1

[1] Based on **Southern Pine Log Grades for Yard and Structural Lumber,** Research Paper SE-39, published by the Southeastern Forest Experiment Station in 1968.
[2] Not applicable.
[3] All redcedar saw logs are graded as No. 1.
[4] Based on **Trial Log Grades for Eastern White Pine,** prepared by the Northeastern Forest Experiment Station in 1960.
[5] Grades 1-3 are based on **Hardwood Log Grades for Standard Lumber,** issued by the U. S. Forest Products Laboratory under the designation D1737A in 1961. Grade-4 tie and timber log specifications are based chiefly on knot size and log soundness.

Table 16. *Annual growth and removals of growing stock on commercial forest land by species, Tennessee, 1970*

Species	Net annual growth	Annual removals
	Million cubic feet	
Softwood:		
Yellow pines	85.1	20.9
White pine	5.3	2.8
Cypress	.7	1.7
Other softwoods	11.8	7.8
Total	102.9	33.2
Hardwood:		
Select white and red oaks	85.7	36.2
Other white and red oaks	124.9	47.9
Hickory	51.1	21.0
Hard maple	9.3	3.3
Sweetgum	13.7	8.5
Tupelo and blackgum	8.3	4.2
Ash, walnut, and black cherry	19.4	10.1
Yellow-poplar	27.8	10.0
Other hardwoods	66.0	42.0
Total	406.2	183.2
All species	509.1	216.4

Table 17. *Annual growth and removals of growing stock on commercial forest land by ownership classes and by softwoods and hardwoods, Tennessee, 1970*

Ownership class	Net annual growth			Annual removals		
	All species	Soft-wood	Hard-wood	All species	Soft-wood	Hard-wood
	— — — — — — — — — Million cubic feet — — — — — — — — —					
National forest	36.7	14.1	22.6	9.5	3.4	6.1
Other public	36.2	11.4	24.8	12.5	1.4	11.1
Forest industry	44.5	9.9	34.6	14.1	1.1	13.0
Farmer and misc. private	391.7	67.5	324.2	180.3	27.3	153.0
All ownerships	509.1	102.9	406.2	216.4	33.2	183.2

Table 18. *Annual growth and removals of sawtimber on commercial forest land by species, Tennessee, 1970*

Species	Net annual growth	Annual removals
	Million board feet	
Softwood:		
Yellow pines	267.5	67.4
White pine	24.2	13.5
Cypress	3.1	9.0
Other softwoods	14.2	34.1
Total	309.0	124.0
Hardwood:		
Select white and red oaks	235.6	137.2
Other white and red oaks	342.1	162.9
Hickory	151.6	81.6
Hard maple	23.6	14.5
Sweetgum	38.3	33.0
Tupelo and blackgum	14.7	15.1
Ash, walnut, and black cherry	57.7	37.5
Yellow-poplar	102.7	51.8
Other hardwoods	152.9	162.0
Total	1,119.2	695.6
All species	1,428.2	819.6

Table 19. *Annual growth and removals of sawtimber on commercial forest land by ownership classes and by softwoods and hardwoods, Tennessee, 1970*

Ownership class	Net annual growth			Annual removals		
	All species	Soft-wood	Hard-wood	All species	Soft-Hard-	Hard-wood
	— — — — — — — Million board feet — — — — — — —					
National forest	111.4	51.9	59.5	47.0	18.6	28.4
Other public	122.5	40.2	82.3	45.7	2.4	43.3
Forest industry	138.1	32.4	105.7	48.8	4.5	44.3
Farmer and misc. private	1,056.2	184.5	871.7	678.1	98.5	579.6
All ownerships	1,428.2	309.0	1,119.2	819.6	124.0	695.6

28

Table 20. *Mortality of growing stock and sawtimber on commercial forest land by species, Tennessee, 1970*

Species	Growing stock	Sawtimber
	Million cubic feet	*Million board feet*
Softwood:		
Yellow pines	6.5	14.6
White pine	.4	1.5
Cypress	.3	1.5
Other softwoods	.5	1.6
Total	7.7	19.2
Hardwood:		
Select white and red oaks	3.8	9.1
Other white and red oaks	9.2	23.6
Hickory	4.4	7.5
Hard maple	1.8	.9
Sweetgum	2.1	3.8
Tupelo and blackgum	2.2	5.9
Ash, walnut, and black cherry	2.6	3.8
Yellow-poplar	1.4	3.3
Other hardwoods	8.1	17.7
Total	35.6	75.6
All species	43.3	94.8

Table 21. *Mortality of growing stock and sawtimber on commercial forest land by ownership classes and by softwoods and hardwoods, Tennessee, 1970*

Ownership class	Growing stock			Sawtimber		
	All species	Soft-wood	Hard-wood	All species	Soft-wood	Hard-wood
	– Million cubic feet –			*– Million board feet -*		
National forest	2.7	1.1	1.6	8.7	4.1	4.6
Other public	3.2	.9	2.3	7.9	2.6	5.3
Forest industry	3.8	.7	3.1	7.6	1.5	6.1
Farmer and misc. private	33.6	5.0	28.6	70.6	11.0	59.6
All ownerships	43.3	7.7	35.6	94.8	19.2	75.6

Table 22. *Mortality of growing stock and sawtimber on commercial forest land by causes and by softwoods and hardwoods, Tennessee, 1970*

Cause of death	Growing stock			Sawtimber		
	All species	Soft-wood	Hard-wood	All species	Soft-wood	Hard-wood
	– Million cubic feet –			*– Million board feet –*		
Fire	2.1	0.3	1.8	4.7	1.0	3.7
Insects	.4	.4	. . .	1.7	1.7	. .
Disease	.6	.1	.5	.5	. . .	.5
Other	5.2	1.4	3.8	17.7	4.8	12.9
Unknown	35.0	5.5	29.5	70.2	11.7	58.5
All causes	43.3	7.7	35.6	94.8	19.2	75.6

Table 23. *Total output of timber products by product, by type of material used, and by softwoods and hardwoods, Tennessee, 1970*

Product and species group	Standard units	Total output		Roundwood products		Plant byproducts	
		Number	M cu. ft.	Number	M cu. ft.	Number	M cu. ft.
Saw logs:							
Softwood	M bd. ft. [1]	69,218	11,386	69,218	11,386		
Hardwood	M bd. ft. [1]	464,823	77,486	464,823	77,486	...	...
Total	M bd. ft. [1]	534,041	88,872	534,041	88,872	...	...
Veneer logs and bolts:							
Softwood	M bd. ft.	70	12	70	12		
Hardwood	M bd. ft.	6,941	1,165	6,941	1,165	...	...
Total	M bd. ft	7,011	1,177	7,011	1,177	...	...
Pulpwood:							
Softwood	Std. cords [2]	202,245	16,378	190,105	15,398	12,140	980
Hardwood	Std. cords [2]	365,099	29,211	246,836	19,747	118,263	9,464
Total	Std. cords [2]	567,344	45,589	436,941	35,145	130,403	10,444
Cooperage:							
Softwood	M bd. ft.	112	18	112	18		
Hardwood	M bd. ft.	10,773	1,551	10,773	1,551		...
Total	M bd. ft.	10,885	1,569	10,885	1,569	...	...
Piling:							
Softwood	M linear ft.	6	4	6	4	...	
Hardwood	M linear ft.	...	...	...	...	...	...
Total	M linear ft.	6	4	6	4	...	...
Poles:							
Softwood	M pieces	71	317	71	317		...
Hardwood	M pieces	...	...	...	...		
Total	M pieces	71	317	71	317	...	...
Mine timbers (round):							
Softwood	M cu. ft.	...	...	...	...		...
Hardwood	M cu. ft.	94	94	94	94		
Total	M cu. ft.	94	94	94	94		...
Commercial posts (round and split):							
Softwood	M pieces	762	502	762	502		
Hardwood	M pieces	2	1	2	1	...	...
Total	M pieces	764	503	764	503	...	...
Other:[3]							
Softwood	M cu. ft.	690	690	267	267	423	423
Hardwood	M cu. ft.	14,541	14,541	9,530	9,530	5,011	5,011
Total	M cu. ft.	15,231	15,231	9,797	9,797	5,434	5,434
Total industrial products:							
Softwood	...	...	...	...	27,904		1,403
Hardwood	...	...	...	...	109,574	...	14,475
Total	...	...	...	...	137,478	...	15,878
Noncommercial posts (round and split):							
Softwood	M pieces	987	651	987	651		
Hardwood	M pieces	3,671	2,416	3,671	2,416	...	...
Total	M pieces	4,658	3,067	4,658	3,067	...	...
Fuelwood:							
Softwood	Std. cords	44,832	3,379	2,538	190	[4] 42,294	[4] 3,189
Hardwood	Std. cords	384,370	28,828	274,770	20,608	[4] 109,600	[4] 8,220
Total	Std. cords	429,202	32,207	277,308	20,798	[4] 151,894	[4] 11,409
All products:							
Softwood	...	...	...	...	28,745		4,592
Hardwood	...	...	...	...	132,598	...	22,695
Total	...	...	...	...	161,343	...	27,287

[1] International ¼-inch rule.
[2] Rough wood basis (for example, chips converted to equivalent standard cords).
[3] Includes chemical wood, handle stock, miscellaneous dimension, miscellaneous domestic use, and other minor industrial products. Additionally, byproducts include material used for livestock bedding, mulch, etc.
[4] Includes plant byproducts used for industrial and domestic fuel.

30

Table 24. *Output of roundwood products by source and by softwoods and hardwoods, Tennessee, 1970*

Product and species group	All sources	Growing-stock trees [1]			Rough and rotten trees	Salvable dead trees [2]	Other sources [2]
		Total	Saw-timber	Pole-timber			
	– – – – – – – – – Thousand cubic feet – – – – – – – – –						
Industrial products:							
Saw logs:							
Softwood	11,386	11,310	11,268	42	14	. . .	62
Hardwood	77,486	74,604	74,511	93	1,023	1,812	47
Total	88,872	85,914	85,779	135	1,037	1,812	109
Veneer logs and bolts:							
Softwood	12	12	12	. .	. . .	.	. . .
Hardwood	1,165	1,145	1,145	. .	15	.	5
Total	1,177	1,157	1,157	. .	15	.	5
Pulpwood:							
Softwood	15,398	14,663	10,109	4,554	102	. . .	633
Hardwood	19,747	15,863	8,909	6,954	2,995	51	838
Total	35,145	30,526	19,018	11,508	3,097	51	1,471
Misc. industrial products:							
Cooperage:							
Softwood	18	18	17	1	. . .	. .	. . .
Hardwood	1,551	1,530	1,530	. . .	11	.	10
Total	1,569	1,548	1,547	1	11	.	10
Piling:							
Softwood	4	4	4	. .	. . .	. .	. . .
Hardwood	. . .	. . .	. . .	. . .	. . .	. . .	. . .
Total	4	4	4	. .	. .	.	.
Poles:							
Softwood	317	315	279	36	. . .	. . .	2
Hardwood	. . .	. . .	. . .	. . .	. . .	. . .	. . .
Total	317	315	279	36	. .	.	2
Mine timbers (round):							
Softwood	. . .	. . .	. . .	. . .	. . .	. . .	. . .
Hardwood	94	94	. .	94	. . .	. . .	. .
Total	94	94	. . .	94	. .	.	. .
Commercial posts (round and split):							
Softwood	502	457	. .	457	.	. .	45
Hardwood	1	1	.	1	. . .	. . .	. . .
Total	503	458	.	458	.	. . .	45
Other:							
Softwood	267	246	94	152	. . .	. . .	21
Hardwood	9,530	9,008	6,057	2,951	177	79	266
Total	9,797	9,254	6,151	3,103	177	79	287
All misc. industrial products:							
Softwood	1,108	1,040	394	646	. . .	. . .	68
Hardwood	11,176	10,633	7,587	3,046	188	79	276
Total	12,284	11,673	7,981	3,692	188	79	344
All industrial products:							
Softwood	27,904	27,025	21,783	5,242	116	. . .	763
Hardwood	109,574	102,245	92,152	10,093	4,221	1,942	1,166
Total	137,478	129,270	113,935	15,335	4,337	1,942	1,929
Noncommercial posts (round and split):							
Softwood	651	588	320	268	28	.	35
Hardwood	2,416	2,180	635	1,545	105	. .	131
Total	3,067	2,768	955	1,813	133	. .	166
Fuelwood:							
Softwood	190	131	70	61	6	13	40
Hardwood	20,608	14,220	6,467	7,753	596	1,388	4,404
Total	20,798	14,351	6,537	7,814	602	1,401	4,444
All products:							
Softwood	28,745	27,744	22,173	5,571	150	13	838
Hardwood	132,598	118,645	99,254	19,391	4,922	3,330	5,701
Total	161,343	146,389	121,427	24,962	5,072	3,343	6,539

[1] On commercial forest land.
[2] Includes noncommercial forest land, nonforest land such as fence rows, trees less than 5.0 inches in diameter, and treetops and limbs.

31

Table 25. *Timber removals from growing stock on commercial forest land by items and by softwoods and hardwoods, Tennessee, 1970*

Item	All species	Soft-wood	Hard-wood
	– Thousand cubic feet –		
Roundwood products:			
Saw logs	85,914	11,310	74,604
Veneer logs and bolts	1,157	12	1,145
Pulpwood	30,526	14,663	15,863
Cooperage logs and bolts	1,548	18	1,530
Piling	4	4	...
Poles	315	315	...
Mine timbers	94	...	94
Posts	3,226	1,045	2,181
Other	9,254	246	9,008
Fuelwood	14,351	131	14,220
All products	146,389	27,744	118,645
Logging residues	37,923	1,958	35,965
Other removals	31,997	3,450	28,547
Total removals	216,309	33,152	183,157

Table 26. *Timber removals from live sawtimber on commercial forest land by items and by softwoods and hardwoods, Tennessee, 1970*

Item	All species	Soft-wood	Hard-wood
	– Thousand board feet –		
Roundwood products:			
Saw logs	504,988	68,380	436,608
Veneer logs and bolts	6,803	69	6,734
Pulpwood	74,710	40,191	34,519
Cooperage logs and bolts	10,393	98	10,295
Piling	26	26	...
Poles	1,609	1,609	...
Mine timbers	...	...	...
Posts	3,730	1,269	2,461
Other	34,327	423	33,904
Fuelwood	31,919	348	31,571
All products	668,505	112,413	556,092
Logging residues	81,096	3,293	77,803
Other removals	69,997	8,306	61,691
Total removals	819,598	124,012	695,586

Table 27. *Volume of plant residues by industrial source and type of residue and by softwoods and hardwoods, Tennessee, 1970*

Species group and type	All industries	Lumber	Veneer and plywood	Other
	– – – – Thousand cubic feet – – – – –			
Softwood:				
Coarse [1]	1,463	1,454	5	4
Fine [2]	1,559	1,502	...	57
Total	3,022	2,956	5	61
Hardwood:				
Coarse	6,097	5,647	115	335
Fine	14,166	13,093	11	1,062
Total	20,263	18,740	126	1,397
All species:				
Coarse	7,560	7,101	120	339
Fine	15,725	14,595	11	1,119
All types	23,285	21,696	131	1,458

[1] Unused material suitable for chipping, such as slabs, edgings, and veneer cores.
[2] Unused material not suitable for chipping, such as sawdust and shavings.

Table 28. *Projections of net annual growth, available cut, and inventory of growing stock and sawtimber on commercial forest land, Tennessee, 1970-2000* [1]

Species group	Growing stock				Sawtimber			
	1970	1980	1990	2000	1970	1980	1990	2000
	– – – – Thousand cubic feet – – – –				– – – – Thousand board feet – – – –			
Softwood:								
Cut	33,200	94,900	120,400	135,300	124,000	301,000	380,000	430,000
Growth	102,900	124,100	134,100	135,300	309,000	384,000	421,000	430,000
Inventory [2]	1,799,800	2,161,200	2,367,500	2,420,000	4,699,100	5,739,000	6,332,000	6,518,000
Hardwood:								
Cut	183,200	404,900	493,300	555,800	695,600	1,270,000	1,420,000	1,456,000
Growth	406,200	478,000	531,800	555,800	1,119,200	1,237,000	1,282,000	1,300,000
Inventory [2]	8,596,000	9,425,600	9,966,100	10,159,800	21,641,100	22,304,000	21,303,000	19,777,000
Total:								
Cut	216,400	499,800	613,700	691,100	819,600	1,571,000	1,800,000	1,886,000
Growth	509,100	602,100	665,900	691,100	1,428,200	1,621,000	1,703,000	1,730,000
Inventory [2]	10,395,800	11,586,800	12,333,600	12,579,800	26,340,200	28,043,000	27,635,000	26,295,000

[1] Based on the assumption that the cut of the growing stock will be in balance with growth by the year 2000, and that forestry progress will continue at the rate indicated by recent trends.
[2] Inventory as of January 1 of the following year.

ALABAMA
FOREST INDUSTRIES

Daniel F. Bertelson

Southern Forest Experiment Station
Forest Service
U. S. Department of Agriculture

ALABAMA FOREST INDUSTRIES

Daniel F. Bertelson

Alabama forests supplied 718 million cubic feet of roundwood to forest industries during 1971. Softwoods, mainly pine, made up over seven-tenths of the total. In terms of volume harvested, pulpwood was the leading product, with saw logs second. The two combined accounted for 91 percent of the roundwood produced. These are some of the major findings of a 1971 canvass of all primary forest industries using wood from Alabama.

Although the number of primary wood-using mills in the State decreased, the total timber harvest increased 70 percent since 1962 (fig. 1). The increase in roundwood output was due to expansion of the pulping industry, introduction of southern pine plywood manufacturing, and an increase in the average size of sawmills.

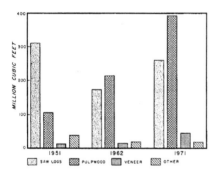

Figure 1. – Output of industrial roundwood in Alabama, by products, 1951–1971.

SAW LOGS

Alabama harvested almost 1.5 billion board feet of saw logs in 1971, an increase of about 0.4 billion board feet over 1962. Softwoods, mostly pine, accounted for about three-fourths of the production. Some cypress and redcedar were also harvested. Oaks supplied over half the hardwood saw logs, with yellow-poplar, sweetgum, tupelo, and blackgum making up most of the remainder.

Trends in size and number of sawmills that began in the late 1940's are continuing. Alabama's 323 sawmills in 1971 is about one-tenth the number in 1946 and a little over half those active in 1962. Large sawmills, those cutting in excess of 3 million board feet annually, increased from 74 mills 9 years ago to the present 135. The portable sawmill, a common sight 25 years ago, is a thing of the past. The trend to larger more efficient mills will, in the next 10 years, continue to take its toll of small sawmills. Rising wages will limit the ability of small mills to compete. A bill in the U. S. Senate at the time of this writing may speed the process. It would extend minimum wage protection to sawmill and logging workers in companies with fewer than eight employees. This bill would affect about 7,000 workers, mostly in the South. Large mills with modern equipment can offset wage increases through automation, which raises output per man-hour, and through sale of plant byproducts.

The application of new technology is apparent in the 11 Alabama sawmills with chipping headrigs, which produce more chips and less sawdust than conventional band and circular saws. All 11 are large, and together they accounted for 28 percent of all softwood logs sawn in the State. Chipping headrigs are used almost exclusively on softwood logs.

In 1951 the average sawmill produced less than 1 million board feet annually. This average rose to almost 2 million in 1962 and to over 4.5 million in 1971. Individual mill production ranged from less than 5,000 to over 90 million board feet. Forty-three mills produced over 10 million board feet in 1971. Large sawmills processed 90 percent of the sawn wood in Alabama; over three-fourths of their production was softwood. Small sawmills processed equal amounts of softwood and hardwood.

Almost half of the saw logs harvested crossed county lines before being cut into lumber. This pattern indicates the dominance of the large sawmills. Small mills will generally cut logs from their home county. Larger mills reach into surrounding counties to obtain enough logs to maintain plant production. Interstate movement was minor, with only 3 percent of the total saw-log harvest shipped to mills in surrounding States. Alabama sawmills imported 84 million board feet of saw logs.

PULPWOOD

Alabama is the leading supplier of pulpwood in the Gulf States. Round pulpwood production in 1971 was in excess of 4.8 million cords, accounting for 55 percent of the State's timber harvest. Although pulpwood harvest was 6 percent lower than the record high of 1970, it has increased by some 2 million cords since 1962. Until 1971, Alabama's pulpwood output had increased or remained constant for two decades (fig. 2).

Softwoods (exclusively pine) are still the main pulp species, but the proportion of hardwoods has greatly increased in the last 15 years. Before 1957 hardwoods accounted for less than 5 percent of the pulpwood output. This percent increased to 24 in 1962 and has leveled off around 30 percent for the last 4 years. Oaks and gums were the dominant hardwoods cut, contributing three-fourths of the hardwood output.

Alabama exported some 1.4 million cords of pulpwood to six neighboring States while importing almost 0.8 million cords from four adjacent States. Over 71 percent of the pulpwood harvested in Alabama was processed at pulpmills within the State.

Construction of six new plants as well as expansion of existing facilities has more than doubled Alabama's pulping capability from 5,093 tons per day in 1962 to 11,443 tons in 1971. The 15 pulpmills have an average pulping capacity of 764 tons per day, compared to 566 tons in 1962. Individual mill capacity ranges from 48 to 1,590 tons daily.

Alabama pulpmills processed 4.2 million cords of roundwood in 1971, of which 82 percent came from Alabama forests. The ratio of softwoods to hardwoods was 7 to 3, the same as the ratio for pulpwood harvested in the State.

The South now supplies two-thirds of the Nation's pulpwood bolts. Needs for pulp products are expected to at least double by the year 2000. As more lands in the North and West are set aside for recreation, the South will be depended upon increasingly to expand its output. Alabama, second only to Georgia in pulpwood production in the South, will have to expand its harvest to meet future demands for paper.

In addition to the roundwood volume, the equivalent of 1.4 million cords of Alabama plant byproducts were used by pulpmills. This volume represents almost one-fourth of the total pulpwood production. The use

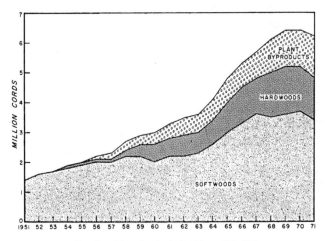

Figure 2. – Pulpwood production in Alabama, 1951–1971.

of plant byproducts has more than doubled since 1962 and has increased 17 percent in the last year. Further impressive increases are unlikely, because more than 93 percent of the State's coarse residues are already being sold as byproducts to the pulp industry. Use of chipped byproducts will increase with the expansion of other forest industries. Also, installation of chipping headrigs, which produce more chips and less sawdust, will increase the volume of plant byproducts available for pulpmills.

VENEER

Alabama forests produced 278 million board feet of veneer logs in 1971, almost three times the 1962 harvest (fig. 3). The great increase is due completely to the emergence of the southern pine plywood industry. Alabama had 32 veneer plants in operation in 1971, six of which produced plywood. These six plants accounted for almost 99 percent of the softwood veneer logs processed in the State.

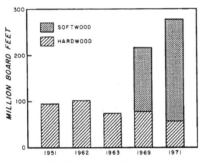

Figure 3. – Softwood and hardwood veneer – log production, 1951–1971.

The southern pine plywood industry began in late 1963 in Arkansas. Since then it has become a major industry, with 53 plants across the South producing over 20 percent of the Nation's softwood plywood. Alabama's six plywood plants have a capacity to produce 587 million square feet of plywood annually (3/8-inch basis). In 1971 these plants processed 216 million board feet of veneer logs, representing 77 percent of the total volume processed by the State's 32 plants. The southern pine plywood industry, less than 9 years old, is expanding and will continue to do so. One limiting factor to the rate of expansion may be the particleboard industry. This industry, which uses wood residues, is expanding, and its product can be substituted for plywood in some phases of construction.

Alabama's hardwood veneer mills, like those in other Midsouth States, have been declining both in number and total output for a number of years. In 1951, 42 veneer mills consumed 96 million board feet of veneer logs. The 26 active mills in 1971 processed on the average more per plant, but total consumption dropped by 31 million board feet. Two factors have contributed to the decline of this industry—product substitution and scarcity of veneer logs. New products such as paperboard, overlays, and painted grain are being substituted for hardwood veneer. Timber suited to hardwood veneer production occurs in trees 18 inches and larger in diameter. Much of the existing volume in these sizes occurs either in small groups that cannot be harvested economically or in species that are in little demand for veneer.

OTHER PRODUCTS

Alabama is one of the top producers of southern pine poles. Over 1 million trees, mostly from the southwestern part of the State, were cut for poles in 1971. The pole volume accounted for 2 percent of the total timber harvest. All other products consumed less than 1 percent of the total roundwood output in Alabama. These products include commercial posts, piling, furniture stock, cooperage, handlestock, miscellaneous dimension, excelsior, and shuttleblocks.

PLANT RESIDUES

In the conversion of roundwood into primary products, more than 163 million cubic feet of various wood residues were generated. Seven-tenths of this volume was in coarse items such as slabs, edgings, cull pieces, and other material suitable for conversion into pulp chips. The rest was comprised of finer particles such as sawdust and shavings.

Over 70 percent, or 115 million cubic feet, went into the production of pulp and particleboard. Almost 13 million cubic feet of material, both coarse and fine, were burned for domestic and industrial fuel. Another 2.8 million cubic feet were used for miscellaneous purposes such as charcoal, animal bedding, and soil mulch.

Alabama forest industries converted 85 percent of their wood residues into plant byproducts in 1971. The remaining 24 million cubic feet of residues were mostly fine particles with no available market. Pulp chips are by far the most profitable byproduct, and Alabama industries used over 93 percent of the coarse residues for this purpose. The ratio of coarse material to fine particles was larger than expected due to the use of chipping headrigs and tree-length logging. Installation of chipping headrigs has increased the volume of chipped byproducts and reduced the amount of fine particles. Tree-length logging has also boosted chip production. Tops and cull sections otherwise left in the woods are brought to the plant and processed into chips.

Over 2 million tons of bark were produced by Alabama forest industries in 1971, and less than two-thirds of this material was used. Industrial fuel ac-counted for 96 percent of this use. Small amounts went into charcoal, domestic fuel, animal bedding, and soil mulch. Almost 1 million tons of bark were wasted. Considerable research is being done to find profitable uses for it. The tremendous amount of bark produced in Alabama each year represents a great potential for added income to the State's forest industries.

The locations of all primary wood-using plants in Alabama are shown in figure 4.

Figure 4. – *Primary wood-using plants in Alabama, 1971.*

Table 1. – *Volume of industrial roundwood, 1971*

Product	Standard units	Volume in standard units			Roundwood volume		
		All species	Softwood	Hardwood	All species	Softwood	Hardwood
					– – – – – – *M cu. ft.* – – – – – –		
Saw logs	M bd. ft. [1]	1,481,515	1,095,586	385,929	261,761	195,343	66,418
Veneer logs	M bd. ft. [1]	278,050	221,031	57,019	45,287	35,719	9,568
Pulpwood	Std. cords	4,858,671	3,429,940	1,428,731	392,126	277,825	114,301
Piling	M linear ft.	805	805	...	645	645	...
Poles	M pieces	1,002	1,002	...	14,231	14,231	...
Posts	M pieces	1,975	1,974	1	1,147	1,146	1
Misc. products [2]	M cu. ft.	2,938	704	2,234	2,938	704	2,234
Total					718,135	525,613	192,522

[1] International ¼-inch rule.
[2] Includes furniture stock, cooperage, miscellaneous dimension, handlestock, excelsior, and shuttleblocks.

Table 2. – *Industrial roundwood, by species, 1971*

Species group	Saw logs	Veneer logs	Pulpwood	Piling	Poles	Posts	Miscellaneous products
	– – – – *M bd. ft.* [1] – – – –		*Std. cords*	*M linear ft.*	– – *M pieces* – –		*M cu. ft.*
Softwood:							
Pines	1,090,005	219,521	3,429,940	805	1,002	1,974	674
Cypress	4,169	1,510	...	...	...	...	...
Other softwoods	1,412	...	...	...	...	...	30
Total	1,095,586	221,031	3,429,940	805	1,002	1,974	704
Hardwood:							
Black and tupelo gums	52,888	16,710	[2] 472,422	...	...	1	179
Sweetgum	24,599	6,810	...	...	...	...	48
Red oaks	147,697	6,973	[3] 602,726	...	...	...	702
White oaks	55,867	2,719	...	...	...	...	516
Other hardwoods	104,878	23,807	353,583	...	...	...	789
Total	385,929	57,019	1,428,731	...	...	1	2,234
All species	1,481,515	278,050	4,858,671	805	1,002	1,975	2,938

[1] International ¼-inch rule.
[2] Black and tupelo combined with sweetgum.
[3] Red and white oaks combined.

Table 3. – *Residues produced by primary wood-using plants, 1971*

Type of industry [1]	All species			Softwood			Hardwood		
	Total	Fine [2]	Coarse [3]	Total	Fine [2]	Coarse [3]	Total	Fine [2]	Coarse [3]
	– – – – – – – – – – – – – – *M cu. ft.* – – – – – – – – – – – – – –								
Lumber	140,450	47,374	93,076	106,492	32,982	73,510	33,958	14,392	19,566
Veneer	21,523	875	20,648	16,706	680	16,026	4,817	195	4,622
Piling, poles, and posts	124	124	...	124	124	...	...	...	...
Miscellaneous products	1,144	608	536	349	164	185	795	444	351
All products	163,241	48,981	114,260	123,671	33,950	89,721	39,570	15,031	24,539

[1] Excludes woodpulp industry.
[2] Fine residues include sawdust, screenings, and other material generally too small for chipping.
[3] Coarse residues include slabs, edgings, trimmings, and other material generally suitable for chipping.

Table 4. – *Volume of primary plant byproducts, 1971*

Source industry [1]	Type of use	All species	Softwood	Hardwood
		— — — — — — — *M cu. ft.* — — — — — —		
Lumber	Fuel [2]	12,076	9,311	2,765
	Fiber [3]	95,397	78,256	17,141
	Other [4]	10,229	6,867	3,362
	Total	117,702	94,434	23,268
Veneer	Fuel	305	254	51
	Fiber	19,663	15,463	4,200
	Other	890	890	...
	Total	20,858	16,607	4,251
Piling, poles, and	Fuel	32	32	...
posts	Fiber	22	22	...
	Other	...	...	...
	Total	54	54	...
Miscellaneous	Fuel	424	197	227
industries	Fiber	33	...	33
	Other	328	11	317
	Total	785	208	577
All industries	Fuel	12,837	9,794	3,043
	Fiber	115,115	93,741	21,374
	Other	11,447	7,768	3,679
	Total	139,399	111,303	28,096

[1] Excludes woodpulp industry.
[2] Includes all residues used as fuel by industrial plants and domestic fuel either sold or given away.
[3] Includes all residues used in manufacture of fiber products, such as pulp or hardboard.
[4] Includes residues used as livestock bedding, mulch, floor sweepings, and specialty items.

Table 5. – *Movement of industrial roundwood, by product, 1971*

Product	Unit	Out of State receipts	Logged and remained in State	Logged and shipped out of State	Total receipts	Total production
		— — — — — — — — — — — — — *Standard units* — — — — — — — — — — — — —				
Saw logs	M bd. ft. [1]	83,501	1,433,156	48,359	1,516,657	1,481,515
Veneer	M bd. ft. [1]	17,884	263,697	14,353	281,581	278,050
Pulpwood	Std. cords	763,843	3,469,153	1,389,518	4,232,996	4,858,671
Piling	M linear ft.	56	805	...	861	805
Poles	M pieces	59	987	15	1,046	1,002
Posts	M pieces	73	1,975	...	2,048	1,975
Misc. products	M cu. ft.	894	2,148	790	3,042	2,938

[1] International ¼-inch rule.

Table 6. – *Saw-log production by county, 1971*

County	All species	Softwood	Hardwood	County	All species	Softwood	Hardwood
	– – – – – *M board feet* [1] – – – – –				– – – – – *M board feet* [1] – – – – –		
Autauga	11,565	7,848	3,717	Jackson	15,732	9,383	6,349
				Jefferson	39,852	31,835	8,017
Baldwin	42,110	30,235	11,875				
Barbour	35,093	27,167	7,926	Lamar	16,294	9,717	6,577
Bibb	34,787	26,596	8,191	Lauderdale	5,547	503	5,044
Blount	8,732	7,088	1,644	Lawrence	7,248	3,381	3,867
Bullock	15,291	11,402	3,889	Lee	15,216	12,367	2,849
Butler	27,858	21,433	6,425	Limestone	3,411	530	2,881
				Lowndes	20,658	15,781	4,877
Calhoun	11,174	9,564	1,610				
Chambers	14,386	10,892	3,494	Macon	12,005	8,363	3,642
Cherokee	8,631	5,181	3,450	Madison	2,384	580	1,804
Chilton	19,987	13,927	6,060	Marengo	30,057	19,795	10,262
Choctaw	68,862	60,707	8,155	Marion	14,502	7,094	7,408
Clarke	109,047	87,654	21,393	Marshall	5,175	2,505	2,670
Clay	17,222	12,008	5,214	Mobile	19,609	13,749	5,860
Cleburne	7,966	5,789	2,177	Monroe	46,518	38,139	8,379
Coffee	5,507	2,837	2,670	Montgomery	7,802	5,548	2,254
Colbert	8,528	3,254	5,274	Morgan	6,796	4,151	2,645
Conecuh	38,742	32,652	6,090				
Coosa	10,379	8,782	1,597	Perry	26,651	19,259	7,392
Covington	25,396	24,552	844	Pickens	37,922	27,473	10,449
Crenshaw	23,279	16,444	6,835	Pike	42,891	19,645	23,246
Cullman	14,995	10,873	4,122				
				Randolph	11,263	7,679	3,584
Dale	14,950	12,929	2,021	Russell	19,690	16,534	3,156
Dallas	21,613	15,617	5,996				
De Kalb	5,272	1,781	3,491	St. Clair	9,887	5,477	4,410
				Shelby	20,802	19,752	1,050
Elmore	8,043	7,930	113	Sumter	59,397	50,788	8,609
Escambia	17,246	17,071	175				
Etowah	4,945	3,264	1,681	Talladega	14,860	11,318	3,542
				Tallapoosa	21,692	13,303	8,389
Fayette	12,969	7,970	4,999	Tuscaloosa	47,756	30,787	16,969
Franklin	10,408	2,985	7,423				
				Walker	42,092	30,532	11,560
Geneva	9,330	7,547	1,783	Washington	54,539	46,091	8,448
Greene	20,038	13,579	6,459	Wilcox	55,043	42,630	12,413
				Winston	28,175	17,135	11,040
Hale	26,931	19,330	7,601				
Henry	7,274	5,667	1,607	All counties	1,481,515	1,095,586	385,929
Houston	1,493	1,207	286				

[1] International ¼-inch rule.

8

Table 7. — *Saw-log movement, 1971*

County [1]	Logged and remained in county	Outgoing shipments	Incoming shipments	Total log receipts	County [1]	Logged and remained in county	Outgoing shipments	Incoming shipments	Total log receipts
	– – – – – – *M bd. ft.* [2] – – – – – –					– – – – – – *M bd. ft.* [2] – – – – – –			
Baldwin	10,152	31,958	498	10,650	Lamar	4,514	11,780	374	4,888
Barbour	27,860	7,233	15,666	43,526	Lauderdale	4,099	1,448	5,050	9,149
Bibb	23,144	11,643	32,400	55,544					
Blount	1,987	6,745	2,353	4,340	Macon	6,679	5,326	3,292	9,971
					Marengo	18,954	11,103	18,883	37,837
Calhoun	8,565	2,609	2,974	11,539	Marion	8,383	6,119	6,014	14,397
Cherokee	4,392	4,239	15	4,407	Mobile	18,435	1,174	69,232	87,667
Chilton	5,971	14,016	2,085	8,056	Morgan	4,572	2,224	1,854	6,426
Choctaw	25,329	43,533	16,555	41,884					
Clarke	84,437	24,610	37,333	121,770	Pickens	31,019	6,903	15,286	46,305
Clay	9,526	7,696	10,689	20,215	Pike	17,005	25,886	8,387	25,392
Cleburne	3,942	4,024	862	4,804					
Coffee	1,558	3,949	209	1,767	Randolph	5,991	5,272	672	6,663
Colbert	6,747	1,781	1,577	8,324	Russell	14,356	5,334	5,789	20,145
Coosa	4,088	6,291	5,311	9,399					
Crenshaw	16,547	6,732	11,536	28,083	St. Clair	5,253	4,634	5,574	10,827
Cullman	12,379	2,616	12,235	24,614	Shelby	13,155	7,647	15,961	29,116
					Sumter	52,699	6,698	32,555	85,254
Dale	10,052	4,898	4,825	14,877					
Dallas	5,951	15,662	49,191	55,142	Talladega	10,174	4,686	6,982	17,156
De Kalb	4,134	1,138	1,380	5,514	Tallapoosa	7,277	14,415	4,941	12,218
					Tuscaloosa	32,732	15,024	24,634	57,366
Elmore	7,912	131	4,270	12,182					
Escambia	11,804	5,442	21,537	33,341	Walker	22,748	19,344	24,279	47,027
Etowah	3,168	1,777	2,093	5,261	Washington	27,435	27,104	2,142	29,577
					Winston	18,895	9,280	16,940	35,835
Fayette	10,684	2,285	7,473	18,157					
Franklin	9,376	1,032	9,627	19,003	All other counties	153,438	234,972	173,912	327,350
Jackson	6,245	9,487	6,055	12,300					
Jefferson	11,131	28,721	10,261	21,392	Total	804,894	676,621	711,763	1,516,657

[1] Counties with less than three plants are omitted.
[2] International ¼-inch rule.

Table 8. – *Veneer-log production, by county, 1971*

County [1]	All species	Softwood	Hardwood	County [1]	All species	Softwood	Hardwood
	– – – – – *M bd. ft.* [2] – – – – –				– – – – – *M bd. ft.* [2] – – – – –		
Autauga	3,459	2,304	1,155	Lamar	20	7	13
				Lauderdale	82	...	82
Baldwin	1,591	592	999	Lawrence	137	...	137
Barbour	4,347	1,194	3,153	Lee	4,820	4,217	603
Bibb	1,400	718	682	Limestone	866	...	866
Blount	262	132	130	Lowndes	10,883	9,140	1,743
Bullock	50	50	...				
Butler	37,123	35,525	1,598	Macon	1,411	386	1,025
				Madison	160	...	160
Chambers	655	98	557	Marengo	4,961	4,011	950
Chilton	452	175	277	Marion	1,439	1,395	44
Choctaw	10,527	10,018	509	Mobile	437	198	239
Clarke	23,627	21,722	1,905	Monroe	9,851	7,466	2,385
Clay	280	252	28	Montgomery	3,361	1,612	1,749
Coffee	65	65	...	Morgan	1,117	...	1,117
Conecuh	14,493	12,856	1,637				
Coosa	1,006	112	894	Perry	3,977	3,750	227
Covington	17,436	16,681	755	Pickens	7,154	752	6,402
Crenshaw	6,934	5,912	1,022	Pike	1,360	607	753
Cullman	104	16	88				
				Russell	195	82	113
Dale	3,296	1,988	1,308				
Dallas	8,017	7,640	377	St. Clair	282	228	54
				Shelby	268	268	...
Elmore	2,418	542	1,876	Sumter	5,435	5,410	25
Escambia	4,214	534	3,680				
Etowah	59	...	59	Talladega	793	356	437
				Tuscaloosa	2,898	2,007	891
Fayette	266	145	121				
				Walker	4,839	4,838	1
Geneva	2,950	2,282	668	Washington	957	639	318
Greene	8,770	4,043	4,727	Wilcox	23,151	19,831	3,320
				Winston	1,161	994	167
Hale	2,789	1,085	1,704				
Henry	6,799	4,716	2,083	All counties	278,050	221,031	57,019
Houston	1,427	221	1,206				
Jefferson	21,219	21,219	...				

[1] Counties with negligible output are omitted.
[2] International ¼-inch rule.

Table 9. – *Piling production, by county, 1971*

County [1]	All species (softwood)	County [1]	All species (softwood)	County [1]	All species (softwood)
	– *M linear ft.* –		– *M linear ft.* –		– *M linear ft.* –
Choctaw	62	Jefferson	1	Tuscaloosa	?
Clarke	24				
		Marengo	20	Walker	2
		Monroe	6	Washington	24
Escambia	560			Wilcox	6
Greene	14	Perry	14		
				All counties	805
Hale	14	Sumter	56		

[1] Counties with negligible output are omitted.

10

Table 10. – *Pole production, by county, 1971*

County [1]	All species (softwood)	County [1]	All species (softwood)	County [1]	All species (softwood)
	– M pieces –		– M pieces –		– M pieces –
Autauga	10	Dallas	14	Montgomery	2
Baldwin	133	Escambia	75	Perry	69
Bibb	89			Pickens	57
Butler	19	Greene	3	Pike	17
Chilton	30	Hale	31	Shelby	30
Choctaw	12			Sumter	14
Clarke	9	Lowndes	14	Tuscaloosa	55
Coffee	17				
Conecuh	38	Marengo	11	Washington	58
Covington	105	Mobile	58		
Crenshaw	20	Monroe	11	All counties	1,002

[1] Counties with negligible output are omitted.

Table 11. – *Commercial post production, by county, 1971*

County [1]	All species	County [1]	All species	County [1]	All species
	– M pieces –		– M pieces –		– M pieces –
Autauga	22	Dallas	26	Montgomery	3
Baldwin	116	Escambia	20	Perry	122
Barbour	8			Pickens	18
Bibb	136	Hale	40	Pike	14
Butler	7	Henry	13	St. Clair	1
Chilton	69	Jefferson	82	Shelby	69
Clarke	136				
Coffee	14	Lowndes	~	Tuscaloosa	207
Conecuh	14			Walker	107
Coosa	9	Marengo	251	Washington	18
Covington	348	Mobile	34		
Crenshaw	14	Monroe	51	All species	1,975

[1] Counties with negligible output are omitted.

11

Table 12. – *Output of miscellaneous products, by county, 1971*

County 1/	All species	Softwood	Hardwood	County 1/	All species	Softwood	Hardwood
	– – – – – *M cubic feet* – – – – –				– – – – – *M cubic feet* – – – – –		
Baldwin	22	...	22	Lauderdale	40		40
Barbour	9	...	9	Limestone	6		6
Blount	104	104	...				
Butler	9	...	9	Madison	149		141
				Marengo	91		91
Clarke	61	...	61	Marion	24		24
Colbert	6	...	6	Marshall	43	...	43
Cullman	104	104	...	Mobile	2	...	2
				Monroe	41	39	2
Escambia			1	Montgomery	44	...	44
				Morgan	11	5	6
Fayette	35	...	35				
Franklin	6		6	Pickens	87		87
Greene	44	...	44	Sumter	74		74
Hale	513	...	513	Tuscaloosa	341	...	341
Jackson	241	17	224	Wilcox	540	427	113
Jefferson	34	...	34				
				All counties	2,938	704	2,234
Lamar	256	...	256				

1/ Counties with negligible output are omitted.

Table 13. – *Industrial roundwood production, by county, 1971*

County	All species	Softwood	Hardwood	County	All species	Softwood	Hardwood
	– – – – – *M cubic feet* – – – – –				– – – – – *M cubic feet* – – – – –		
Autauga	6,833	4,147	2,686	Cullman	7,016	6,057	959
Baldwin	29,393	23,130	6,263	Dale	10,084	7,028	3,056
Barbour	15,791	12,044	3,747	Dallas	13,607	8,550	5,057
Bibb	13,091	10,246	2,845	De Kalb	2,327	1,635	692
Blount	4,362	3,907	455				
Bullock	5,683	4,360	1,323	Elmore	6,017	4,482	1,535
Butler	22,656	15,848	6,808	Escambia	16,111	13,935	2,176
				Etowah	3,551	3,195	356
Calhoun	5,388	4,657	731				
Chambers	8,111	6,105	2,006	Fayette	4,824	3,710	1,114
Cherokee	4,179	3,384	795	Franklin	3,964	2,487	1,477
Chilton	9,968	7,273	2,695				
Choctaw	31,394	19,550	11,844	Geneva	5,626	4,674	952
Clarke	35,583	25,551	10,032	Greene	9,411	5,411	4,000
Clay	10,598	7,338	3,260				
Cleburne	6,475	5,694	781	Hale	10,258	6,522	3,736
Coffee	4,882	3,438	1,444	Henry	6,975	4,953	2,022
Colbert	1,910	965	945	Houston	3,803	2,988	815
Conecuh	19,578	15,017	4,561				
Coosa	12,464	9,106	3,358	Jackson	3,504	2,049	1,455
Covington	17,421	15,193	2,228	Jefferson	13,425	11,806	1,619
Crenshaw	12,206	8,590	3,616				

Table 13. – *Industrial roundwood production, by county, 1971* (continued)

County	All species	Softwood	Hardwood	County	All species	Softwood	Hardwood
	– – – – – M cubic feet – – – – –				– – – – – M cubic feet – – – – –		
Lamar	7,070	5,258	1,812	Pike	13,643	8,349	5,294
Lauderdale	1,783	695	1,088				
Lawrence	1,586	765	821	Randolph	9,431	6,971	2,460
Lee	9,763	8,686	1,077	Russell	7,755	7,055	700
Limestone	906	116	790				
Lowndes	11,976	8,819	3,157	St. Clair	6,413	5,354	1,059
				Shelby	8,730	7,558	1,172
Macon	6,359	4,929	1,430	Sumter	19,588	13,667	5,921
Madison	625	131	494				
Marengo	19,915	11,592	8,323	Talladega	6,803	5,328	1,475
Marion	6,850	5,319	1,531	Tallapoosa	15,940	11,783	4,157
Marshall	2,149	1,646	503	Tuscaloosa	15,000	11,032	3,968
Mobile	14,215	11,544	2,671				
Monroe	23,271	16,165	7,106	Walker	15,435	12,570	2,865
Montgomery	8,321	5,812	2,509	Washington	22,589	17,250	5,339
Morgan	2,106	1,054	1,052	Wilcox	24,750	16,667	8,083
				Winston	8,361	6,139	2,222
Perry	12,415	8,607	3,808				
Pickens	15,918	9,727	6,191	All counties	718,135	525,613	192,522

Table 14. – *Plant byproducts, by county, 1971*

County 1/	All species		Softwood		Hardwood	
	Fine	Coarse	Fine	Coarse	Fine	Coarse
	– – – – – – – – – – M cubic feet – – – – – – – – – –					
Baldwin	148	661	144	303	4	358
Barbour	. . .	2,793	. . .	2,099	. . .	694
Bibb	976	3,333	910	2,970	66	363
Blount	112	200	68	142	44	58
Butler	1,398	7,113	1,178	6,739	220	374
Calhoun	297	624	261	573	36	51
Cherokee	115	235	46	118	69	117
Chilton	62	468	51	396	11	72
Choctaw	1,144	2,361	1,071	2,220	73	141
Clarke	2,638	8,671	2,348	7,937	290	734
Clay	575	1,241	455	1,074	120	167
Cleburne	56	123	44	104	12	19
Coffee	. . .	76	. . .	23	. . .	53
Colbert	103	395	31	181	72	214
Coosa	. . .	384	. . .	261	. . .	123
Covington	1,107	4,566	1,107	4,566	. . .	. . .
Crenshaw	165	1,579	111	1,121	54	458
Cullman	791	1,324	710	1,272	81	52
Dale	. . .	745	. . .	713	. . .	32
Dallas	282	3,023	196	607	86	2,416
De Kalb	133	196	27	45	106	151
Elmore	59	723	55	718	4	5
Escambia	986	3,230	962	2,775	24	455
Etowah	88	179	15	46	73	133

13

Table 14. – *Plant byproducts, by county, 1971* (continued)

County 1/	All species		Softwood		Hardwood	
	Fine	Coarse	Fine	Coarse	Fine	Coarse
	— — — — — — — — — — — *M cubic feet* — — — — — — — — — — — —					
Fayette	163	981	67	674	96	307
Franklin	389	962	118	364	271	598
Greene	264	721	262	554		167
Hale	149	103		3	149	100
Henry	...	154	...	133	...	21
Jackson	202	615	84	295	118	320
Jefferson	516	1,087	200	378	316	709
Lamar	...	72		39	...	33
Lauderdale	257	600	...	1	257	599
Lawrence	3	4	1	2	2	2
Limestone	22	28	...	1	22	27
Macon	...	546	...	382	...	164
Madison	76	91	10	7	66	84
Marengo	1,071	2,169	418	855	653	1,314
Marion	84	736	30	520	54	216
Mobile	2,117	4,956	1,438	3,039	679	1,917
Monroe	679	1,706	644	1,545	35	161
Montgomery	18	1,798	2	94	16	1,704
Morgan	210	507	118	222	92	285
Perry	67	57	48	42	19	15
Pickens	643	3,385	573	2,090	70	1,295
Pike	...	1,431	...	933	...	498
Randolph	128	330	120	213	8	117
Russell	120	1,220	120	1,151	...	69
St. Clair	330	574	242	468	88	106
Shelby	148	1,761	148	1,485	...	276
Sumter	2,479	4,819	2,261	4,384	218	435
Talladega	454	892	362	770	92	122
Tallapoosa	42	659	26	396	16	263
Tuscaloosa	785	3,123	692	2,292	93	831
Walker	1,022	5,803	768	5,335	254	468
Washington	733	1,806	716	1,785	17	21
Wilcox	2,954	15,487	2,953	14,965	1	522
Winston	750	1,631	487	1,144	263	487
All other counties	830	5,402	739	4,302	91	1,100
Total	28,940	110,459	23,437	87,866	5,503	22,593

1/ Omitted counties have either negligible volume or less than three plants.

14

Table 15. – *Unused plant residues, by county, 1971*

County [1]	All species		Softwood		Hardwood	
	Fine	Coarse	Fine	Coarse	Fine	Coarse
			– – M cubic feet – –			
Baldwin	217	...	18	...	199	...
Barbour	1,345	6	1,020	4	325	2
Bibb	726	88	562	43	164	45
Blount	29	48	1	2	28	46
Butler	65	...	61	...	4	...
Calhoun	57	2	54	1	3	1
Cherokee	32	5	13	3	19	2
Chilton	186	14	137	...	49	14
Choctaw	111	71	21	...	90	71
Clarke	1,111	2	857	1	254	1
Clay	49	58	37	49	12	9
Cleburne	102	91	62	45	40	46
Coffee	62	4	18	3	44	1
Colbert	179	37	75	19	104	18
Coosa	293	291	202	291	91	...
Covington	2	...	2	...	...	...
Crenshaw	726	122	472	81	254	41
Cullman	...	126	...	71	...	55
Dale	448	117	395	80	53	37
Dallas	1,686	1	98	1	1,588	...
De Kalb	60	49	23	25	37	24
Elmore	308	...	308	...	...	...
Escambia	6	...	1	...	5	...
Etowah	94	105	53	71	41	34
Fayette	420	34	264	6	156	28
Franklin	263	19	73	5	190	14
Greene	44	15		9	44	
Hale	3	...	2	...	1	...
Henry	280	773	202	291	78	482
Jackson	256	91	87	32	169	59
Jefferson	224	67	27	36	197	31
Lamar	164	144	89	86	75	58
Lauderdale	114	1	...	...	114	1
Lawrence	25	33	16	22	9	11
Limestone	1	1	...	...	1	1
Macon	320	...	195	...	125	...
Madison	31	2	...	2	31	...
Marengo	295	2	36	...	259	2
Marion	377	70	239	28	138	42
Mobile	743	12	12	10	731	2
Monroe	110	...	90	...	20	...
Montgomery	792	...	22	...	770	...
Morgan	7	5	...	1	7	4
Perry	19	57	14	42	5	15
Pickens	841	182	425	82	416	100
Pike	824	9	459	7	365	2

15

Table 15. – *Unused plant residues, by county, 1971* (continued)

County [1]	All		Softwood		Hardwood	
	Fine	Coarse	Fine	Coarse	Fine	Coarse
				– – – – – – – – – – – – –				*M cubic feet* – – – – – – – – – – – –			
Randolph	89	17	1	8	88	9
Russell	476	. . .	426	. . .	50	. . .
St. Clair	8	53	2	31	6	22
Shelby	772	27	554	8	218	19
Sumter	124	7	. . .	. . .	124	7
Talladega	81	95	12	9	69	86
Tallapoosa	359	. . .	178	. . .	181	. . .
Tuscaloosa	1,047	218	451	29	596	189
Walker	528	125	389	58	139	67
Washington	131	. . .	131	. . .	. . .	. . .
Wilcox	197	98	116	85	81	13
Winston	404	343	170	170	234	173
All counties	1,778	64	1,341	8	437	56
Total	20,041	3,801	10,513	1,855	9,528	1,946

[1] Omitted counties have either negligible volume or less than three plants.

Table 16. – *Bark used, by county, 1971*

County [1]	All species	Softwood	Hardwood	County [1]	All species	Softwood	Hardwood
	– – – – – – *Tons* – – – – – – –				– – – – – – *Tons* – – – – – – –		
Baldwin	751	127	624	Greene	212	. . .	212
Barbour	29	16	13				
Bibb	24,354	23,146	1,208	Hale	44	22	22
Blount	35	5	30				
				Jefferson	4,094	118	3,976
Calhoun	1,978	1,577	401				
Cherokee	399	138	261	Lauderdale	491	6	485
Chilton	15	. . .	15	Lawrence	54,525	38,724	15,801
Choctaw	122,727	52,558	70,169	Limestone	318	2	316
Clarke	25,030	20,565	4,465				
Clay	4,909	3,770	1,139	Madison	803	90	713
Cleburne	55	2	53	Marengo	93,265	51,570	41,695
Coffee	23	15	8	Mobile	364,256	229,022	135,234
Colbert	2,137	591	1,546	Monroe	2,393	1,635	758
Coosa	1,424	7	1,417	Montgomery	2,922	205	2,717
Covington	307	307	. . .	Morgan	2,402	1,441	961
Crenshaw	772	83	689				
Cullman	8,031	7,549	482	Perry	547	358	189
				Pickens	4,036	3,304	732
Dallas	22,921	913	22,008				
De Kalb	810	1	809	Randolph	31	19	12
				Russell	64,354	62,095	2,259
Elmore	710	645	65				
Escambia	130,707	95,770	34,937	Shelby	16	3	13
				Sumter	2,306	667	1,639
Franklin	2,546	536	2,010				

Table 16. – *Bark used, by county, 1971* (continued)

County [1]	All species	Softwood	Hardwood	County [1]	All species	Softwood	Hardwood
	– – – – – – *Tons* – – – – – – – –				– – – – – – *Tons* – – – – – – – –		
Talladega	134,159	107,228	26,931	Wilcox	156,882	147,376	9,506
Tallapoosa	274	47	227				
Tuscaloosa	36	...	36	All other counties	118,247	105,326	12,921
Walker	9,870	8,992	878				
Washington	9,295	9,030	265	Total	1,376,448	975,601	400,847

[1] Omitted counties have either negligible volume or less than three plants.

Table 17. – *Unused bark, by county, 1971*

County [1]	All species	Softwood	Hardwood	County [1]	All species	Softwood	Hardwood
	– – – – – – *Tons* – – – – – – – –				– – – – – – *Tons* – – – – – – – –		
Baldwin	8,895	5,804	3,091	Lauderdale	5,202	3	5,199
Barbour	18,962	12,794	6,168	Lawrence	319	184	135
Bibb	11,684	8,527	3,157	Limestone	1	1	...
Blount	2,032	864	1,168				
Butler	41,324	37,361	3,963	Macon	4,364	2,416	1,948
				Madison	562	23	539
Calhoun	2,474	2,273	201	Marengo	10,545	4,785	5,760
Cherokee	1,715	603	1,112	Marion	6,368	3,371	2,997
Chilton	3,325	2,367	958	Mobile	19,923	9,170	10,753
Choctaw	29,780	14,499	15,281	Monroe	8,769	8,066	703
Clarke	99,246	60,319	38,927	Montgomery	22,963	9,051	13,912
Clay	3,256	2,334	922	Morgan	1,701	11	1,690
Cleburne	2,009	1,231	778				
Coffee	873	198	675	Perry	4,417	4,228	189
Colbert	1,911	711	1,200	Pickens	21,585	9,635	11,950
Coosa	2,538	2,538	...	Pike	11,368	5,705	5,663
Covington	28,729	28,729	...				
Crenshaw	12,020	7,284	4,736	Randolph	2,957	1,469	1,488
Cullman	1,974	1,130	844	Russell	7,680	6,887	793
Dale	5,762	4,929	833	St. Clair	4,531	3,052	1,479
Dallas	107,983	64,828	43,155	Shelby	13,339	9,950	3,389
De Kalb	2,030	583	1,447	Sumter	39,642	35,925	3,717
Elmore	3,784	3,784	...	Talladega	47,220	36,734	10,486
Escambia	22,324	19,656	2,668	Tallapoosa	5,321	2,476	2,845
Etowah	2,581	783	1,798	Tuscaloosa	29,626	18,210	11,416
Fayette	8,086	4,154	3,932	Walker	20,377	15,131	5,246
Franklin	7,039	1,831	5,208	Washington	4,583	4,583	...
				Wilcox	6,375	2,036	4,339
Greene	4,453	3,360	1,093	Winston	15,959	8,198	7,761
Henry	6,613	2,626	3,987	All other counties	37,470	26,082	11,388
Jackson	6,456	2,119	4,337				
Jefferson	6,749	2,759	3,990	Total	811,995	529,402	282,593
Lamar	2,221	1,042	1,179				

[1] Omitted counties have either negligible volume or less than three plants.

17

Table 18. – *Large sawmills* 1/

County	Firm	Plant	
		Location	Address 2/
Baldwin	Crosby Lumber Co., Inc. 3/	Bay Minette	
	J. M. McMillan Sawmill, Inc. 3/	Stockton	Box 79
Barbour	Boutwell Lumber Co. 3/	Louisville	Box 97, Brundidge
	Brabham Lumber Co. 3/	Eufaula	1100 Dale Road
	Clayton Wood Products 3/	Clayton	
	Dixon Lumber Co. 3/	Eufaula	Drawer K
	Garrison Brothers Lumber Co. 3/	Eufaula	Box 329
Bibb	Olon Belcher Lumber Co. 3/	Brent	Box 160
	Steve Bowman Lumber Co. 3/	Centreville	Box 158
	Bill Brown Lumber Co., 3/	Briarfield	
	Centreville Lumber Co. Inc.	Centreville	Hwy. 82
	Fox Lumber Co. 3/	Centreville	Box 37
	Leonard Kornegay Sawmill 3/	Eoline	Rt. 1, Centreville
	Brown Mitchell Lumber Co. 3/	Briarfield	Box 305, Brent
Blount	Mooneyham Lumber Co. 3/	Rainbow	Rt. 1, Blountsville
Bullock	Midway Lumber Co. 3/	Union Springs	Box 97, Louisville
Butler	Union Camp Corp. 3/	Chapman	Box 38
Calhoun	Biddy Lumber Co. 3/	Piedmont	111 N. Harris St.
	Read Lumber Co. 3/	Wellington	Box 171
Chambers	Bailey Brothers Lumber Co. 3/	Abanda	Box 62, Wadley
	East Alabama Lumber Co. 3/	Lafayette	910 9th Ave. S.E.
Cherokee	P. E. M. Mills 3/	Centre	Rt. 1
Chilton	Clanton Lumber Co. 3/	Clanton	Box 309
	Graham Lumber Corp. 3/	Maplesville	Box 67
Choctaw	Clark Lumber Co., Inc. 3/	Silas	Box 117
	Hood Lumber Co., Melvin Division 3/	Melvin	Drawer E, Quitman, Miss.
	Jachin Lumber Co. 3/	Jachin	
	J. W. Lassiter Lumber Co. 3/	Cullomburg	Box 24
	C. F. Littlepage Lumber Co. 3/	Butler	Rt. 1
Clarke	American Can Co., Inc. 3/	Thomasville	Box 145
	Jackson Sawmill Co., Inc. 3/	Jackson	Box 368
	McCorquodale Brothers Co. 2/	Jackson	
	Scotch Lumber Co. 3/	Fulton	
	M. W. Smith Lumber Co. 3/	Jackson	Box 667
Clay	Mellow Valley Wood Processing 3/	Mellow Valley	Box 627, Ashland
	Williamson Lumber Co., Inc. 2/	Ashland	Box 396
Colbert	Cornelius Lumber Co. 3/	Margerum	Rt. 1, Cherokee
	McKinney Lumber Co. 3/	Muscle Shoals	Drawer C
Conecuh	Conecuh Lumber Co. 3/	Evergreen	Drawer 69
	Price Lumber Co., Inc. 3/	Castleberry	Box 309, Evergreen
Coosa	A. J. Broom Lumber Co.	Kellyton	Box 82
	Dunnam Lumber Co., Inc. 3/	Weogufka	Box 1

Table 18. – *Large sawmills* [1]/ (continued)

County	Firm	Plant	
		Location	Address [2]/
Covington	Dixon Lumber Co. [3]/	Andalusia	
	Lockhart Lumber Co., Inc. [3]/	Lockhart	Box 207
Crenshaw	D & D Lumber Co. [3]/	Brantley	Box 45
	Dozier Lumber Co.	Dozier	Box 185
	J. W. Holman Lumber Co., Inc. [3]/	Highland Homes	Box 67
	J. P. Lester Sawmill, Inc. [3]/	Glenwood	Box 155
Cullman	Champion Home Builders [3]/	Cullman	Box 306
Dale	Deloney Lumber Co. [3]/	Ozark	Box 134
Dallas	Fox Lumber Co. [3]/	Plantersville	Box 100
	Miller & Co. Sawmill No. 1 [3]/	Selma	Box 779
	Miller & Co. Sawmill No. 4 [3]/	Selma	Box 779
Elmore	Bass Lumber Co. [3]/	Wetumpka	Rt. 5, Box 29AAA
	Robinson & Son Lumber Co. [3]/	Wetumpka	Box 633
Escambia	T. R. Miller Mill Co., Inc. [3]/	Brewton	Box 708
	Swift Lumber Co. [3]/	Atmore	Drawer M
Etowah	Jones Sawmill, Inc. [3]/	Attalla	Box 1665, Gadsden
Fayette	Carpenter Lumber Co. [3]/	Berry	
	Newman Lumber Co., Inc. [3]/	Belk	Box 22
	B. B. Springer Lumber Co. [3]/	New Hope	Rt. 4, Fayette
	Watkins Brother's Lumber Co. [3]/	Fayette	Box 294
Franklin	D. S. Anderson Lumber Co. [3]/	Haleyville	Rt. 1
	Herman A. Ketton Lumber Co. [3]/	Red Bay	
Geneva	Casey Brothers Lumber Co. [3]/	Slocomb	Box 362
Greene	Colson Lumber Co., Inc. [3]/	Eutaw	Box 68
Henry	Dixie Veneer Co. [3]/	Abbeville	Box 9
Houston	Casey Lumber Co. [3]/	Dothan	Box 1961
Jackson	W. J. Word Lumber Co. [3]/	Scottsboro	Box 907
Jefferson	Buchanan Lumber Co. of Birmingham [3]/	Birmingham	1910 50th St. N.
	W. L. Edge & Son Lumber Co. [3]/	Adger	804 Bessemer Hwy., Birmingham
Lauderdale	T. J. Moss Lumber Co., Inc.	Rogersville	Box 53
Lee	Dudley Lumber Co. [3]/	Salem	Box 7
Lowndes	J. W. Casey Lumber Co. [3]/	Braggs	
Macon	Marble Brothers Lumber Co., Inc. [3]/	Tuskegee	Box 30
	R. P. Self Lumber Co., Inc. [3]/	Notasulga	Box 215
Marengo	Linden Lumber Co., Inc. [3]/	Linden	Box 506
	Miller & Co., Inc. [3]/	Demopolis	Box 2717 W. Jackson St.
	Thomas & Miller Co. [3]/	Linden	

Table 18. – *Large sawmills* [1] (continued)

County	Firm	Plant	
		Location	Address [2]
Marion	Alabama Oak Flooring Co. [3]	Guin	1107 10th Ave. N.
	W. T. Vick Lumber Co. [3]	Hamilton	
Mobile	Buchanan Lumber Mobile, Inc. [3]	Mobile	Box 171
	Gulf Lumber Co. [3]	Mobile	Box 1663
	Mobile River Sawmill-Adams Branch [3]	Mobile	Box 345
	Mobile River Sawmill Division –		
	Scott Paper Co. [3]	Mt. Vernon	
Monroe	F. H. King & Son Lumber Co. [3]	Frisco City	Box 280
	Vredenburgh Div. Longleaf Ind., Inc. [3]	Vredenburgh	
Montgomery	Buchanan Lumber Co. [3]	Montgomery	1203 N. McDonough
Morgan	Somerville Lumber Co. [3]	Somerville	Box 36
Pickens	Abram's Lumber Co.	Benevola	Rt. 5, Gordo
	Carpenter and Shirley Lumber Co. [3]	Gordo	Drawer L
	Floyd Lumber Co. [3]	Gordo	Box F
	Lewis Brothers Lumber Co., Inc. [3]	Aliceville	Box 334
	McShan Lumber Co. [3]	McShan	Box 27
	Pate Lumber Co. [3]	Carrollton	Box 112
	C. E. Reid Lumber Co., Inc. [3]	Reform	Box 428
	Summerville Brothers Lumber Co., Inc. [3]	Aliceville	Box 425
Pike	Ray Gibson Sawmill [3]	Troy	Rt. 1
	Green Wood Products, Inc. [3]	Troy	Box 421
	Helms Lumber Co. [3]	Brundidge	Box 577
	W. J. Sorrell Sawmill [3]	Saco	Rt. 5, Troy
Randolph	S. M. Wylie Co., Inc. [3]	Roanoke	Box 506
Russell	A. B. Carroll Lumber Co., Inc. [3]	Hurtsboro	Box 237
	Phenix Lumber Co. [3]	Phenix City	Box 844
	Walker-Williams Lumber Co., Inc. [3]	Hutchechubee	Box 7
St. Clair	Pell City Wood Products [3]	Pell City	Box 445
	Simmons-Banks Lumber Co. [3]	Springville	Rt. 2, Box 18
Shelby	Mt. Shadows Wood Processing Center [3]	Westover	Box 14
	Seaman Timber Co., Inc. [3]	Montevallo	Box 372
	Shelby County Lumber Co. [3]	Columbiana	Box 758
Sumter	American Can Co., Inc.		
	Allison Lbr. Div. [3]	Bellamy	
	Miller & Co., Inc. [3]	York	Box 549
Talladega	S & R Lumber Co. [3]	Talladega	Box 13
	Jim Wallis Lumber Co., Inc. [3]	Talladega	Box 536
Tallapoosa	Dadeville Chip Co. [3]	Dadeville	Box 328
	Foy Lumber Co., Inc. [3]	Alexander City	Box 303
Tuscaloosa	Newton Brothers Lumber Co., Inc.	Tuscaloosa	Drawer 2627
	Newton Lumber Co. [3]	Tuscaloosa	Box 2181
	Pearson Lumber Co. #1 [3]	Tuscaloosa	Box 1548
	George Roses Lumber Co. [3]	Northport	Box 309
	W. P. Sartain Lumber Co. [3]	Coker	Box 36
	W. G. Sullivan Lumber Co., Inc. [3]	Brownville	Rt. 3, Northport

Table 18. – *Large sawmills* [1] (continued)

County	Firm	Plant	
		Location	Address [2]
Walker	Avery-Guthrie & Sons [3]	Oakman	Box 261
	Birmingham Forest Products, Inc. [3]	Cordova	Drawer H
	Gus Early Lumber Co, [3]	Carbon Hill	302 Railroad Ave.
	Jasper Lumber Co. [3]	Jasper	Box 460
	TMA Forest Products [2]	Jasper	Box 1425
Washington	Carpenter & Dickey Lumber Co., Inc. [3]	Chatom	Box 164
	W. E. Hill Lumber Co., Inc. [3]	Millry	Box 85
	Longleaf Lumber Co. [3]	Chatom	Box 460
Wilcox	MacMillan Bloedel Products, Inc. [3]	Pine Hill	
Winston	Alford Lumber Co.	Double Springs	Hwy. 278 East
	Bankhead Forest Industries, Inc. [3]	Grayson	
	Leburn Burleson [3]	Haleyville	15th Ave.
	TMA Forest Products [2]	Double Springs	

[1] Output of 3 million board feet or more.
[2] Office address specified when different from plant location.
[3] Produced chips for sale to pulpmills.

Table 19. – *Small sawmills* [1]

County	Firm	Plant	
		Location	Address [2]
Autauga	Percy Hill Sawmill	Haynes	Rt. 3, Prattville
Baldwin	O. J. Early Lumber Co., Inc. [3]	Robertsdale	Rt. 1
	Giles Sawmill	Summerdale	Rt. 1
	Russell Lumber Co.	Foley	Rt. 1, Box 262
Barbour	Cowikee Lumber Co. [3]	Eufaula	Box 329
	Elijah Franklin	Lugo	Rt. 1, Comer
	W. D. Linn Sawmill [3]	Abbeyville	
	Louisville Lumber & Builders Supply Co.	Louisville	Rt. 2
Bibb	I. H. Burt & Son Lumber Co. [3]	West Blockton	General Delivery
	Stevensons Lumber Co.	Briarfield	Rt. 1
Blount	D. A. Brothers Sawmill	Oneonta	Rt. 2
	S. B. Parker Sawmill	Blountsville	Box 415
	A. S. Tidwell Lumber Co. [3]	Oneonta	Rt. 1, Box 1
Bullock	Springer Lumber Co. [3]	Union Springs	Box 208
Butler	L. A. Black Timber Co., Inc. [3]	Greenville	Rt. 3
Calhoun	Brooks Lumber Co.	Anniston	Rt. 3
	Rembert Green Sawmill	Jacksonville	
	A. E. Webb Lumber Co. [3]	Anniston	Box 651
	Gerald Willis Lumber Co. [3]	Piedmont	Rt. 3, Box 324B

Table 19. – *Small sawmills* 1/ (continued)

County	Firm	Plant	
		Location	Address 2/
Cherokee	Coley Lumber Co.	Centre	Box 4
	Howard Brothers Sawmill	Collinsville	Rt. 1
	John Myer Sawmill	Collinsville	Rt. 1
Chilton	L. M. Carter Sawmill	Stanton	Rt. 1
Choctaw	Chadwick Lumber Co.	Gilbertown	Rt. 1, Silas
	Davidson Lumber Co. 3/	Gilbertown	Rt. 1
	Etheridge Lumber Co. 3/	Baldon Springs	
	Kelley Sawmill	Lisman	Box 392, Butler
	Robert Tyson Sawmill	Toxey	Rt. 1
Clarke	Max Carnes Tie Co. 3/	Whatley	Rt. 1, Brantley
	Hamilton Tie Mill	Whatley	
	Jones and Arnot Lumber Co. 3/	Jackson	921 Depot Rd.
	E. W. Kelley Lumber Co. 3/	Whatley	Box 38
	Moody Wimberly Sawmill	Carlton	
Clay	Lineville Lumber Co.	Lineville	Box 338
	Wakefield Lumber Co.	Lineville	Box 472
	Wallis and Elliot Lumber Co. 3/	Lineville	Box 265
Cleburne	Baswell Sawmill	Borden Springs	Rt. 1
	Major L. Burns Sawmill 3/	Heflin	Rt. 2, Box 311, Piedmont
	Charles Sons Lumber Co. 3/	Heflin	Rt. 4
	Charles M. Jordan Lumber Co. 3/	Talladega	Rt. 1, Lineville
	F. H. Sanders Lumber Co.	Five Points	Rt. 3, Heflin
Coffee	Elba Wood Products 3/	Elba	Box 276
	LeConte Sawmill	Coffee Springs	Rt. 1
	L. W. Strickland Sawmill	Enterprise	Rt. 2
	Windham Lumber Co. 3/	Elba	Box 424
Colbert	Cherokee Lumber Co., Inc.	Margerum	Rt. 1, Cherokee
	Jack Davis Sawmill	Tuscumbia	Rt. 2
	W. O. Foster Sawmill	Tuscumbia	Rt. 1
	J. R. Holt Sawmill	Tuscumbia	Rt. 2
	Willard E. Howard Sawmill	Tuscumbia	Rt. 1
Coosa	J. R. Bentley Mill	Rockford	Box 133
Crenshaw	Bryan & Son Lumber Co.	Brantley	Rt. 3
	Kimbro Sawmill	Dozier	Rt. 1
Cullman	N. C. Arnold & Sons Lumber Co. 3/	Hanceville	Rt. 1
	Buettner Brothers Lumber Co., Inc. 3/	Cullman	708 7th Ave. W.
	James T. Day	Beech Grove	Rt. 2, Hanceville
	Jones Chapel Sawmill	Jones Chapel	Rt. 13, Cullman
	Myrthe Swann	Beech Grove	
Dale	Charles Lisenby Sawmill	Ozark	415 Dalesville
	M. L. McDaniels Sawmill	Echo	Rt. 1, Ozark
Dallas	Elam Lumber Co.	Selma	Rt. 2, Box 44
De Kalb	R. G. Baty Lumber Co. 3/	Mentone	Rt. 1
	C & H Lumber Co.	Valley Head	
	J. E. Gilbreath Sawmill	Crossville	Rt. 1

Table 19. – *Small sawmills* $\underline{1}/$ (continued)

County	Firm	Plant	
		Location	Address $\underline{2}/$
	Glover Brothers Lumber Co. $\underline{3}/$	Rainsville	Rt. 1
	Fred McDowdy Sawmill	Geraldine	Rt. 2
	Smith Lumber Co.	Rainsville	Rt. 1
	Ralph Spillman Sawmill	Fort Payne	1411 Grand Ave. N.
	Paul Stone Sawmill	Groveoak	Rt. 1
	H. W. Thompson Sawmill	Henagar	Rt. 3
	Wood Products, Inc.	Fort Payne	Box 52
Elmore	Smith Lumber Co.	Eclectic	Box 48
Escambia	D. J. Bondurant Lumber Co. $\underline{3}/$	Flomaton	Hwy. 31 South
	Rebel Craft	Brewton	Rt. 1
	White Pallet Co., Inc. $\underline{3}/$	Flomaton	Rt. 1, Box 42
Etowah	Collins & Lemons Sawmill	Attalla	Rt. 1
	Jones Lumber Co. $\underline{3}/$	Attalla	Walnut Grove Hwy.
	A. G. Kelley Sawmill	Altoona	Rt. 3
	W. T. Lowery Sawmill	Hokes Bluff	Rt. 2, Gadsden
	Pinkston Sawmill	Gadsden	Rt. 1
	Red Shirley Sawmill	Gallant Road	Rt. 2, Box 106, Attalla
	Stanfield Lumber Co.	Attalla	Rt. 2
Fayette	Blakely Lumber Co. $\underline{3}/$	Berry	Box 187
	Clyde Bonner Sawmill	Berry	Rt. 2
	G. Frank Farris Lumber Co.	Glen Allen	Box 74, Eldridge
	E. C. Newman Sawmill	Covin	Rt. 6, Fayette
Franklin	John Amos & Son Lumber Co.	Bethsaida	Rt. 4, Russellville
	T. D. Baker Sawmill	Enterprise	Rt. 1, Phil Campbell
	McKinney Lumber Co.	Russellville	Drawer C, Muscle Shoals
	Paul E. McMahan Sawmill	Russellville	Rt. 6
	Thorn & Thorn Sawmill	Vina	Rt. 2
Geneva	H. C. Register	Luverne	
Greene	Payne Lumber Co.	Boligee	Box 191
Hale	Livingston Sawmill	Akron	Rt. 1, Box 77
	Chess Wilson Sawmill	Havana	Rt. 2, Moundville
Jackson	Lonnie Brown Sawmill	Pisgah	Rt. 1
	Chickamauga Cedar Co.	Stevenson	Drawer B
	Calvin Crabtree Sawmill	Langston	Rt. 1, Mentone
	W. F. Guffey & Son Sawmill	Skyline	Rt. 1, Scottsboro
	B. F. Hawes & Son Lumber Co.	Fabius	Rt. 1, Flat Rock
	Laymon McCarver Sawmill	Stevenson	Rt. 1, Hollywood
	Pete Whisante Sawmill	Fabius	Rt. 1
Jefferson	W. J. Alexander	Quinton	Rt. 2
	James A. Capp's Lumber Co. $\underline{3}/$	Wylam	Box 7010
	H. H. Glenn Lumber Co.	Argo	Rt. 1, Trussville
	Isbell Sawmill	Irondale	1012 Farley Ave., Leeds
	Ketona Lumber Co.	Birmingham	237 Ketona Rd.
	McCorp Lumber Co. $\underline{3}/$	Pinson	Rt. 12, Box 598, Birmingham
	Pinson Valley Lumber Co.	Birmingham	Box 6494

Table 19. – *Small sawmills* 1/ (continued)

County	Firm	Plant Location	Plant Address 2/
Lamar	G. Frank Farris Lumber Co.	Sulligent	Box 74, Eldridge
	Eugene Harrison Sawmill	Crossville	Rt. 2, Vernon
	Knight Brothers Sawmill	Detroit	
	Millport Sawmill Co. 3/	Millport	Box 5
	Redus Newman Sawmill	Belk	Rt. 1, Kennedy
	Richardson Sawmill	Spring Hill Church	Box 32, Millport
	Ruffin & Sanford Sawmill	Millport	Rt. 2, Reform
Lauderdale	Southern Wood Piedmont Co. 3/	Jacksonburg	Box 1206, Florence
	Taylor Lumber Co.	Florence	1308 Sherrod Ave.
	C. F. Williams Sawmill	Anderson	Rt. 1
Lawrence	Littrell Lumber Co.	Moulton	836 Morgan Rd.
	Glen R. Smith Sawmill	Mt. Hope	Rt. 1
Lee	Opelika Lumber Co.	Opelika	Box 749
Limestone	William L. Golden Sawmill	Elkmont	
	R. L. Huber Sawmill	Piney Chapel	Rt. 9, Athens
Lowndes	Ft. Deposit Lumber Co., Inc. 3/	Ft. Deposit	Drawer T
Macon	Sistrunk Brothers Lumber Co. 3/	Society Hill	Rt. 2, Opelika
Madison	George C. Brown & Co.	Gurley	Box 158
	Moss Lumber Industries 3/	Gurley	Box 363
Marengo	Green Coats Sawmill	Old Spring Hill	Box 218, Demopolis
	Dunn Cedar Mill	Linden	
	Rolison Sawmill 3/	Sweetwater	
Marion	Gibbs Lumber Co.	Brilliant	Rt. 1
	Rex Harris 3/	Winfield	Box 471
Marshall	J. R. Centers Sawmill	Poplar Springs	Rt. 1, Albertville
	W. B. Troup Sawmill	Grant	Rt. 2
Mobile	Pratt Turner Sawmill Co. 3/	Citronelle	Box 34B
Montgomery	Travis Senn	Ramer	
Morgan	S. Ball Sawmill	Hartselle	1047 N. Railroad
	Littrell Lumber Mill	Decatur	Box 1827
	Stone Lumber Co. 3/	Decatur	Box 777
	H. C. Turney Sawmill	Somerville	Rt. 3
Perry	V. G. Middlebrooks Sawmill	Marion	Rt. 3
Pickens	House Brothers Sawmill	Millport	Rt. 3
	H. A. Wells Sawmill	Millport	Box 8
Pike	Ray Floyd Sawmill 3/	Troy	Rt. 1, Goshen
	Max Price Sawmill	Troy	1008 N. Three Notch
	Norman Tie & Lumber Co., Inc. 3/	Goshen	
Randolph	Denton Brothers Lumber Co. 3/	Roanoke	
	Herren Brothers	Woodland	Rt. 2
	Bonner Taylor 3/	Forester Chapel	Rt. 1, Wadley

Table 19. – *Small sawmills* [1] (continued)

County	Firm	Plant	
		Location	Address [2]
St. Clair	Orlan M. Busby, Jr. Lumber Co.	Pell City	Rt. 3, Box 306, Leeds
	M. B. Ferguson Sawmill	Cook Springs	Rt. 3, Pell City
	Woodrow Leopard Sawmill	Argo	Rt. 2, Trussville
Shelby	Brackin Sawmill [3]	Calera	Rt. 1
	Marguess & Son Lumber Co.	Calera	Rt. 1, Box 105
	B. L. Owen Lumber Co. [3]	Columbiana	
	Watley Sawmill	New Hope	Rt. 1, Helena
Sumter	Wallace Edmonds Lumber Co.	Emelle	
	Sumter Mfg., Inc.	York	Box 36
	York Tie & Lumber Co. [3]	York	Hwy. 11 W.
Talladega	G. G. & G. Lumber Co.	Pleasant Grove Church	Box 123, Talladega
	Clyde Gunter Sawmill [3]	Munford	Rt. 1, Box 149
	Kelley Sawmill	Sycamore	Rt. 1, Alpine
	Miller Lumber Co.	Sylacauga	Box 134
	Hubert Snider Sawmill	Talladega	302 Heath St.
Tallapoosa	George M. Bunn	Waverly	Rt. 2
	Braxton Cotney [3]	Wadley	Rt. 2
Tuscaloosa	Pete Gamble Sawmill	Caffee Junction	Rt. 1, McCalla
	Hale County Lumber, Inc. [3]	Moundville	Drawer 2627, Tuscaloosa
	North River Lumber Co. [3]	Windham Springs	Box 1548, Tuscaloosa
	Patton Lumber Co. [3]	Tuscaloosa	Box 1547
	Richardson Brothers Lumber Co. [3]	Northport	Box 356
Walker	Addison Lumber Co.	Jasper	Box 662
	Addison & Son Log and Tie Mill	Jasper	Box 250
	Alton Evans	Oakman	
	Leroy Ferrell Sawmill	Jasper	Rt. 7, Box 381
	B. W. Kilgore	Jasper	Holly Grove Road
	Sam Sparks	Carbon Hill	Rt. 1
	Hugh Wells	Oakman	Rt. 1
	Wheeler Whitlow	Sumiton	Rt. 2, Cordova
Washington	T. W. Richardson Sawmill	Frankville	
Wilcox	T. M. Phillips Lumber Co.	Furman	Rt. 1, Greenville
Winston	Commens & Hess	Double Springs	Rt. 2
	James Hogan	Poplar Springs	Rt. 3, Nauvoo
	C. W. Knight & Son Lumber Co. [3]	Haleyville	Box 489
	Jesse Lovette	Natural Bridge	Rt. 3, Haleyville
	Sipsey River Lumber Co. [3]	Double Springs	
	C. S. Walker	Addison	Rt. 2

[1] Output of less than 3 million board feet.
[2] Office address specified when different from plant location.
[3] Produced chips for sale to pulpmills.

Table 20. – *Wood pulpmills*

County	Firm	Location
Autauga	Union Camp Corp.	Montgomery
Choctaw	American Can Co.	Naheola
Clarke	Allied Paper Corp.	Jackson
Dallas	Hammermill Paper Co., Riverdale Div.	Riverdale
Escambia	Container Corp. of America	Brewton
Lawrence	U. S. Plywood-Champion Papers, Inc.	Courtland
Marengo	Gulf States Paper Corp.	Demopolis
Mobile	General Aniline & Film Corp.	Mobile
	International Paper Co.	Mobile
	National Gypsum Co.	Mobile
	Scott Paper Co.	Mobile
Russell	Alabama Kraft Co., Div. Ga. Kraft Co.	Mahrt
Talladega	Kimberly-Clark Corp., Coosa River Newsprint Div.	Coosa Pines
Tuscaloosa	Gulf States Paper Corp.	Tuscaloosa
Wilcox	MacMillan Bloedel United, Inc.	Pine Hill

Table 21. – *Veneer plants*

County	Firm	Location	Address [1]	Type [2]
Baldwin	Bacon-McMillan Manufacturing Co. [3]	Stockton	Box 78	O
Barbour	Alabama Georgia Veneer Co. [3]	Eufaula	Box 21	C
Bibb	Fox Lumber Co.	Centreville	Box 37	O
Blount	Marsh & Standridge Basket Factory	Nector	Rt. 1, Cleveland	C
	Oneonta Basket Factory	Oneonta	206 3rd Ave. W.	C
Butler	Union Camp Corp.* [3]	Chapman	Box 38	O
Chilton	Jemison Basket Co.	Jemison	Box 96	C
Clarke	Scotch Plywood Co.* [3]	Fulton		O
	Winborn Veneer Co. [3]	Allen		C
Covington	Dixon Plywood Co.* [3]	Andalusia		O
Crenshaw	H. E. Browder Veneer Co. [3]	Bradleyton	Box 23, Petrey	C
Cullman	E. Malchow & Sons	Cullman	321 1st Ave. N.	
Dallas	Howell Veneer Co. [3]	Selma	Carren St.	O
Escambia	Harold Brothers Veneer Co., Inc. [3]	East Brewton	Rt. 3	O
	T. R. Miller Mill Co., Inc. [3]	Brewton	Box 708	C

26

Table 21. – *Veneer plants* (continued)

County	Firm	Location	Address [1]	Type [2]
Greene	Knoxville Veneer Co. [3]	Eutaw		C
	Sumter Veneer Co. [3]	Eutaw	Drawer 351	C
Henry	Dixie Veneer Co. [3]	Abbeville	Box 9	O
Houston	Howell Plywood Corp. [3]	Dothan	Box 250	O
Marengo	A. R. Taylor Veneer Co., Inc. [3]	Demopolis	Box 719	C
Monroe	Meridian Plywood, Inc. [3]	Mexia	Box 272, Monroeville	C
Montgomery	Browder Veneer Works, Inc. [3]	Montgomery	1401 N. McDonough St.	C
	Capital Veneer Works, Inc. [3]	Montgomery	1710 Jackson Ferry Rd.	C
Morgan	Decatur Box & Basket Co., Inc. [3]	Decatur	Box 1190	O
Pickens	Aliceville Veneer, Inc. [3]	Aliceville	Box 424	C
St. Clair	Fairmont Basket Works, Inc.	Springville	Box 159	C
Sumter	Sumter Plywood Corp.* [3]	Livingston	Box 1017	O
Tuscaloosa	Thompson & Swaim Veneer, Inc. [3]	Tuscaloosa	Box 2468	O
Walker	Birmingham Forest Products, Inc.* [3]	Cordova	Drawer H	O
Wilcox	Browder Veneer Co., Inc. [3]	Camden	Box 310	C
	MacMillan Bloedel Products, Inc.* [3]	Pine Hill		O
	Millers Bend Lumber Co., Inc. [3]	Pine Hill	Box 309	O

[1] Office address specified when different from plant location.
[2] C=plants producing chiefly container veneer.
   O=plants producing chiefly commercial and other veneers.
[3] Produced chips for sale to pulpmills.
* Produces southern pine plywood.

Table 22. – *Post, pole, and piling plants*

County	Firm	Plant	
		Location	Address
Baldwin	Baldwin Pole & Piling Co., Inc.	Bay Minette	Box 768
Barbour	Loftin Post Co.	Clio	Rt. 2, Box 7
Bibb	Olon Belcher Lumber	Brent	Box 160
	Fox Lumber Co.	Centreville	Box 37
Butler	Union Camp Corp.	Chapman	Box 38
Clarke	Cumberland Gulf Corp.	Walker Springs	Box A
	B. W. Wilson Timber Co.	Thomasville	Box 516, Grove Hill
Covington	W. G. Henson Pole Co.	Lockhart	Box 186
	Lockhart Lumber Co., Inc.	Lockhart	Box 207

Table 22. – *Post, pole, and piling plants* (continued)

County	Firm	Plant	
		Location	Address
Escambia	T. R. Miller Mill Co., Inc.	Brewton	Box 708
	Republic Creosoting Co.	Huxford	Monroeville
Henry	Great Southern Wood Preserving, Inc.	Abbeville	Drawer 415
Jefferson	Birmingham Wood Preserving Co.	Birmingham	5400 10th Ave.
Marengo	Linden Creosote Co.	Linden	Box 402
Mobile	Gulfport Creosoting Co.	Mobile	Box 449
Monroe	Stallworth Timber Co.	Beatrice	Box 38
Montgomery	Koppers Co., Inc.	Montgomery	Box 510
Perry	Cahaba Wood Preserving Co.	Suttle	Box 35
	Southern Timber Co.	Marion	Box 53
Shelby	Seaman Timber Co., Inc.	Montevallo	Box 372
Sumter	C & L Timber Co.	York	Drawer 69
Tuscaloosa	Brown Wood Preserving Co.	Brownville	
Washington	Forest Products Co.	Chatom	Box 232

Table 23. – *Miscellaneous plants*

County	Firm	Plant	
		Location	Address [1]
Cullman	Garden City Heading Co. [2]	Garden City	Box 155
Escambia	Clifford Johnson Dogwood Mill [3]	Brewton	Rt. 1, Box 444
Greene	Eutaw Hardwood Dimension [4]	Eutaw	Box 61
Hale	Chairs, Inc. [5]	Greensboro	Box 477
Jackson	Klepzig Brothers & Wilford [2]	Stevenson	Box 466
Lauderdale	Ramoneda Brothers Stave Mill [2]	Florence	Box 1004
Limestone	Wellford Brothers & Klepin [2]	Athens	Box 508
Madison	Giles & Kendall Co. [5]	Maysville	Box 188, Huntsville
	Textile Hardwood Mfg. Co., Inc. [6]	Huntsville	Box 1227
Marengo	Demopolis Hickory Mill, Inc. [4]	Demopolis	Box 236
Mobile	Lucedale Block Mill	Whistler	Box 12085
Tuscaloosa	Tusco Hardwood Mfg. Co. [6]	Northport	Box 326, Tuscaloosa

Table 23. – *Miscellaneous plants* (continued)

County	Firm	Plant	
		Location	Address 1/
Wilcox	Grief Brothers Corp. – Dallas Cooperage Division Mill 1 2/	Pine Hill	Box 1057, Selma
	Grief Brothers Corp. – Dallas Cooperage Division Mill 2 2/	Pine Apple	Box 1057, Selma
	Wilcox Milling Co., Inc. 6/	Camden	Box 148
	J. A. Winters Co., Inc. 7/	McWilliams	

1/ Office address specified when different from plant location.
2/ Cooperage.
3/ Shuttleblocks.
4/ Handlestock.
5/ Furniture stock.
6/ Miscellaneous dimension mill.
7/ Excelsior.

Forest Statistics
for
Central Alabama Counties

Arnold Hedlund and J. M. Earles

This report tabulates information from a new forest inventory of counties in central Alabama. The tables are intended for use as source data in compiling estimates for groups of counties. Because the sampling procedure is designed primarily to furnish inventory data for the State as a whole, estimates for individual counties have limited and variable accuracy.

The data on forest acreage and timber volume were secured by a systematic sampling method involving a forest-nonforest classification on aerial photographs and on-the-ground measurements of trees at sample locations. The sample locations were at the intersections of a grid of lines spaced 3 miles apart. At each forested location, 10 small plots were uniformly distributed on an area of about 1 acre.

The sampling errors to which the county area and volume totals are liable (on a probability of two chances out of three) are shown in table 1.

An approximation of sampling errors for groups of counties may be obtained by using the formula:

$$e = \frac{(SE) \sqrt{\text{specified volume or area}}}{\sqrt{\text{volume or area total in question}}}$$

Where: e = Estimated sampling error of the volume or area total in question

SE = Specified sampling error for the State.

The error decreases when data for two or more counties are grouped. Conversely, as data for individual counties are broken down by various subdivisions, the possibility of error increases and is greatest for the smallest items. Sampling errors associated with the estimates of the

Table 1. *Sampling errors[1] for forest land and timber volume, 1972*

County	Commercial forest land	Growing stock	Saw-timber
	– – – – Percent – – – –		
Bibb		10	15
Blount		13	18
Calhoun	2	10	13
Cherokee		12	20
Clay		11	16
Cleburne		9	14
Coosa		10	14
Cullman	2	8	14
Etowah		14	20
Fayette		9	16
Greene	2	10	14
Hale	2	11	16
Jefferson	2	10	16
Lamar	3	9	14
Marion	2	8	14
Perry	1	9	13
Pickens	1	8	12
Randolph	3	10	16
St. Clair	2	8	14
Shelby	2	7	13
Talladega	1	11	16
Tuscaloosa	1	7	10
Walker	2	8	13
Winston	2	9	14
All counties	0.4	1.9	3.1

[1] By random-sampling formula.

principal timber species in this report are shown in table 2.

Because of differences in standards of tree measurement, direct comparisons cannot be made between the estimates in this report and those from the survey of 1963. In table 3, changes between the two surveys are summarized in terms of current measurement standards.

3

Table 2. *Sampling errors for timber volume by species, 1972*

Species	West Central		North Central	
	Growing stock	Saw- timber	Growing stock	Saw- timber
	- - - - - Percent - - - - -			
Softwood:				
Longleaf pine	22	25	13	14
Shortleaf pine	8	11	6	8
Loblolly pine	6	8	6	7
Virginia pine	17	26	10	14
Other southern pines	(¹)	(¹)	. . .	. . .
Redcedar	40	(¹)	(¹)	. . .
Cypress	46	50	. . .	. . .
Other softwoods	. . .	. . .	(¹)	. . .
All softwoods	4.6	6.4	3.7	5.3
Hardwood:				
Select white oaks	10	13	9	12
Select red oaks	16	19	16	21
Other white oaks	10	14	8	12
Other red oaks	7	10	6	10
Hickory	16	23	7	11
Persimmon	35	(¹)	(¹)	(¹)
Soft maple	14	19	21	28
Beech	24	28	27	29
Sweetgum	10	18	10	16
Blackgum	20	18	12	18
Other gums	35	48	. . .	. . .
White ash	(¹)	(¹)	28	34
Other ashes	33	49	33	46
Basswood	(¹)	(¹)	35	(¹)
Yellow-poplar	12	16	12	14
Magnolia (*Magnolia* spp.)	33	(¹)	(¹)	. . .
Black cherry	31	. . .	32	(¹)
American elm	23	26	31	50
Other elms	24	32	28	42
River birch	33	36	(¹)	(¹)
Hackberry	35	36	(¹)	. . .
Dogwood	24	. . .	23	. . .
Other hardwoods	(¹)	(¹)	33	(¹)
All hardwoods	5.0	6.9	4.2	6.2
All species	3.0	4.6	2.5	4.1

¹ Exceeds 50 percent.

Table 3. *Change*¹ *in forest resource since 1963*

Item	West Central	North Central
	- - Percent - -	
Commercial forest land	−2.4	−3.5
Growing-stock volume:		
Softwood	+ 37	+ 45
Hardwood	+ 31	+ 19
All species	+ 34	+ 34
Sawtimber volume:		
Softwood	+ 31	+ 44
Hardwood	+ 38	+ 22
All species	+ 34	+ 37

¹ Based on current measurement standards.

DEFINITIONS OF TERMS

Acceptable trees.—Growing-stock trees of commercial species that meet specified standards of size and quality but do not qualify as desirable trees.

Commercial forest land.—Forest land producing or capable of producing crops of industrial wood and not withdrawn from timber utilization.

Desirable trees.—Growing-stock trees that are of commercial species, have no defects in quality for timber products, are of relatively high vigor, and contain no pathogens that may result in death or serious deterioration before rotation age.

Forest type.—A classification of forest land based upon the species forming a plurality of live-tree stocking.

Growing-stock trees.—Live trees that are of commercial species and qualify as desirable or acceptable trees.

Growing-stock volume.—Net volume in cubic feet of growing-stock trees at least 5.0 inches in diameter at breast height, from a 1-foot stump to a minimum 4.0-inch top diameter outside bark of the central stem, or to the point where the central stem breaks into limbs.

Poletimber trees.—Growing-stock trees of commercial species at least 5.0 inches in diameter at breast height but smaller than sawtimber size.

Sawtimber trees.—Live trees that are of commercial species, contain at least a 12-foot saw log, and meet regional specifications for freedom from defect. Softwoods must be at least 9.0 inches in diameter at breast height and hardwoods at least 11.0 inches.

Sawtimber volume.—Net volume of the saw-log portion of live sawtimber in board feet, International ¼-inch rule.

Site class.—A classification of forest land in terms of inherent capacity to grow crops of industrial wood.

Stand-size class.—A classification of forest land based on the size class of growing-stock trees on the area; that is, sawtimber, poletimber, or seedlings and saplings.

Bibb
Fayett
Greene
Hale
Lamar

Marion
Perry
Picken
Tuscal

All co

Table

Table 4. *Commercial forest land by ownership class, West Central region, 1972*

County	All ownerships	National forest	Other public	Forest industry	Farmer	Misc. private
	- - - - - - - - - - *Thousand acres*- - - - - - - - - -					
Bibb	332.8	60.6	3.9	98.8	42.3	127.2
Fayette	307.4	...	7.5	68.9	86.2	144.8
Greene	234.6	...	2.3	35.7	103.7	92.9
Hale	248.0	27.7	2.9	55.8	56.7	104.9
Lamar	285.0	...	.1	39.9	92.7	152.3
Marion	348.1	...	2.5	94.4	95.9	155.3
Perry	286.2	32.9	.4	53.0	102.3	97.6
Pickens	427.5	...	...	136.8	127.4	163.3
Tuscaloosa	696.2	8.5	10.2	153.4	138.0	386.1
All counties	3,165.8	129.7	29.8	736.7	845.2	1,424.4

Table 5. *Commercial forest land by ownership class, North Central region, 1972*

County	All ownerships	National forest	Other public	Forest industry	Farmer	Misc. private
	- - - - - - - - - - *Thousand acres*- - - - - - - - - -					
Blount	245.7	...	6.8	...	87.6	151.3
Calhoun	241.9	15.1	52.2	53.1	76.2	45.3
Cherokee	214.6	...	...	63.8	57.6	93.2
Clay	313.2	65.2	1.6	27.0	91.2	128.2
Cleburne	312.7	79.4	1.9	88.5	52.8	90.1
Coosa	354.0	...	5.0	90.0	59.6	199.4
Cullman	256.5	...	1.2	22.8	141.6	90.9
Etowah	176.9	...	1.4	6.1	97.0	72.4
Jefferson	459.2	...	11.6	...	44.5	403.1
Randolph	270.3		.3	10.2	157.1	102.7
St. Clair	311.1	...	.9	66.3	86.2	157.7
Shelby	400.2	...	12.8	133.4	92.2	161.8
Talladega	291.2	41.6	9.2	22.4	44.5	173.5
Walker	369.2	...	15.5	46.8	67.2	239.7
Winston	319.2	85.8	2.3	62.7	62.3	106.1
All counties	4,535.9	287.1	122.7	693.1	1,217.6	2,215.4

Table 6. *Commercial forest land by forest type, West Central region, 1972*

County	All types	Loblolly-shortleaf pine	Loblolly-pine	Oak-pine	Oak-hickory	Oak-gum-cypress	Elm-ash-cottonwood
			-Thousand acres-				
Bibb	332.8	26.0	130.0	104.0	67.6	5.2	...
Fayette	307.4	...	127.2	53.0	79.5	42.4	5.3
Greene	234.6	...	61.2	40.8	40.8	91.8	...
Hale	248.0	6.2	68.2	86.8	31.0	55.8	...
Lamar	285.0	...	62.7	85.5	57.0	74.1	5.7
Marion	348.1	...	100.3	82.6	159.3	...	5.9
Perry	286.2	15.9	90.1	74.2	63.6	31.8	10.6
Pickens	427.5	...	176.7	102.6	74.1	68.4	5.7
Tuscaloosa	696.2	23.6	247.8	194.7	141.6	88.5	...
All counties	3,165.8	71.7	1,064.2	824.2	714.5	458.0	33.2

Table 7. *Commercial forest land by forest type, North Central region, 1972*

County	All types	Loblolly-shortleaf pine	Loblolly-pine	Oak-pine	Oak-hickory	Oak-gum-cypress	Elm-ash-cottonwood
			-Thousand acres-				
Blount	245.7	...	81.9	81.9	69.3	12.6	...
Calhoun	241.9	...	76.7	82.6	82.6	...	...
Cherokee	214.6	...	98.6	58.0	46.4	11.6	...
Clay	313.2	5.4	102.6	86.4	118.8	...	...
Cleburne	312.7	5.9	129.8	82.6	94.4	...	...
Coosa	354.0	24.0	138.0	102.0	84.0	6.0	...
Cullman	256.5	...	96.9	85.5	74.1	...	...
Etowah	176.9	...	61.0	36.6	73.2	6.1	...
Jefferson	459.2	11.2	207.2	134.4	95.2	5.6	5.6
Randolph	270.3	5.1	117.3	71.4	71.4	5.1	...
St. Clair	311.1	5.1	102.0	76.5	96.9	30.6	...
Shelby	400.2	29.0	116.0	116.0	116.0	17.4	5.8
Talladega	291.2	11.2	89.6	95.2	95.2	...	...
Walker	369.2	...	171.6	93.6	104.0	...	...
Winston	319.2	...	136.8	85.5	96.9	...	...
All counties	4,535.9	96.9	1,726.0	1,288.2	1,318.4	95.0	11.4

Table 8. *Commercial forest land by stand-size class, West Central region, 1972*

County	All classes	Sawtimber	Poletimber	Sapling and seedling	Nonstocked areas
- - - - - - - - Thousand acres- - - - - - - - -					
Bibb	332.8	83.2	130.0	119.6	...
Fayette	307.4	68.9	137.8	95.4	5.3
Greene	234.6	122.4	66.3	45.9	...
Hale	248.0	105.4	68.2	74.4	...
Lamar	285.0	57.0	165.3	62.7	...
Marion	348.1	47.2	153.4	147.5	...
Perry	286.2	127.2	95.4	63.6	...
Pickens	427.5	148.2	131.1	148.2	...
Tuscaloosa	696.2	206.5	236.0	253.7	...
All counties	3,165.8	966.0	1,183.5	1,011.0	5.3

Table 9. *Commercial forest land by stand-size class, North Central region, 1972*

County	All classes	Sawtimber	Poletimber	Sapling and seedling	Nonstocked areas
- - - - - - - - Thousand acres- - - - - - - - -					
Blount	245.7	94.5	69.3	81.9	...
Calhoun	241.9	64.9	94.4	82.6	...
Cherokee	214.6	40.6	63.8	110.2	...
Clay	313.2	59.4	140.4	113.4	...
Cleburne	312.7	88.5	135.7	88.5	...
Coosa	354.0	72.0	144.0	138.0	...
Cullman	256.5	62.7	142.5	51.3	...
Etowah	176.9	36.6	54.9	85.4	...
Jefferson	459.2	100.8	162.4	196.0	...
Randolph	270.3	76.5	61.2	132.6	...
St. Clair	311.1	66.3	122.4	122.4	...
Shelby	400.2	116.0	156.6	121.8	5.8
Talladega	291.2	72.8	128.8	89.6	...
Walker	369.2	114.4	166.4	88.4	...
Winston	319.2	96.9	125.4	96.9	...
All counties	4,535.9	1,162.9	1,768.2	1,599.0	5.8

5

Table 10. *Commercial forest land by site class, West Central region, 1972*

County	All classes	165 cu.ft. or more	120-165 cu.ft.	85-120 cu.ft.	50-85 cu.ft.	Less than 50 cu.ft.
			- - - - - - - - - - *Thousand acres-* - - - - - - - - - -			
Bibb	332.8	...	10.4	124.8	166.4	31.2
Fayette	307.4	...	10.6	111.3	164.3	21.2
Greene	234.6	...	20.4	137.7	61.2	15.3
Hale	248.0	12.4	31.0	136.4	68.2	...
Lamar	285.0	...	17.1	91.2	148.2	28.5
Marion	348.1	5.9	17.7	123.9	182.9	17.7
Perry	286.2	15.9	58.3	100.7	100.7	10.6
Pickens	427.5	5.7	11.4	205.2	176.7	28.5
Tuscaloosa	696.2	...	64.9	224.2	324.5	82.6
All counties	3,165.8	39.9	241.8	1,255.4	1,393.1	235.6

Table 11. *Commercial forest land by site class, North Central region, 1972*

County	All classes	165 cu.ft. or more	120-165 cu.ft.	85-120 cu.ft.	50-85 cu.ft.	Less than 50 cu.ft.
			- - - - - - - - - - *Thousand acres-* - - - - - - - - - -			
Blount	245.7	...	18.9	37.8	163.8	25.2
Calhoun	241.9	...	11.8	82.6	106.2	41.3
Cherokee	214.6	...	5.8	40.6	156.6	11.6
Clay	313.2	...	10.8	86.4	172.8	43.2
Cleburne	312.7	...	5.9	41.3	236.0	29.5
Coosa	354.0	...	18.0	108.0	198.0	30.0
Cullman	256.5	...	...	68.4	171.0	17.1
Etowah	176.9	...	6.1	48.8	97.6	24.4
Jefferson	459.2	5.6	72.8	246.4	128.8	5.6
Randolph	270.3	5.1	5.1	96.9	147.9	15.3
St. Clair	311.1	...	35.7	117.3	142.8	15.3
Shelby	400.2	11.6	40.6	174.0	150.8	23.2
Talladega	291.2	...	...	50.4	190.4	50.4
Walker	369.2	15.6	57.2	145.6	145.6	5.2
Winston	319.2	...	11.4	114.0	188.1	5.7
All counties	4,535.9	37.9	300.1	1,458.5	2,396.4	343.0

Table 12. *Cordage of growing stock on commercial forest land by species group, West Central region, 1972*

County	All species	Softwood			Hardwood			
		Total	Pine	Other	Total	Oak	Gum	Other
				-Thousand cords-				
Bibb	5,004	3,183	3,168	15	1,821	864	515	442
Fayette	3,743	1,730	1,727	3	2,013	860	616	537
Greene	4,197	1,709	1,600	109	2,488	685	864	939
Hale	4,198	2,334	2,331	3	1,864	831	561	472
Lamar	4,015	1,343	1,319	24	2,672	946	1,108	618
Marion	3,414	1,578	1,573	5	1,836	1,097	173	566
Perry	4,285	2,509	2,468	41	1,776	590	501	685
Pickens	5,820	3,335	3,323	12	2,485	1,058	878	549
Tuscaloosa	9,975	4,827	4,800	27	5,148	2,306	1,635	1,207
All counties	44,651	22,548	22,309	239	22,103	9,237	6,851	6,015

Table 13. *Cordage of growing stock on commercial forest land by species group, North Central region, 1972*

County	All species	Softwood			Hardwood			
		Total	Pine	Other	Total	Oak	Gum	Other
				-Thousand cords-				
Blount	3,466	1,575	1,572	3	1,891	990	270	631
Calhoun	2,485	1,473	1,473	...	1,012	579	118	315
Cherokee	1,778	937	937	...	841	612	51	178
Clay	3,250	1,809	1,809	...	1,441	709	235	497
Cleburne	3,895	2,491	2,491	...	1,404	825	155	424
Coosa	3,577	1,979	1,979	...	1,598	737	358	503
Cullman	3,527	1,847	1,844	3	1,680	951	140	589
Etowah	1,585	888	888	...	697	448	76	173
Jefferson	4,992	3,676	3,676	...	1,316	679	215	422
Randolph	2,822	1,668	1,668	...	1,154	543	145	466
St. Clair	3,381	1,917	1,911	6	1,464	785	285	394
Shelby	4,074	2,323	2,323	...	1,751	852	281	618
Talladega	3,222	1,768	1,768	...	1,454	739	240	475
Walker	5,585	3,433	3,433	...	2,152	1,055	294	803
Winston	4,558	2,704	2,700	4	1,854	1,181	112	561
All counties	52,197	30,488	30,472	16	21,709	11,685	2,975	7,049

Table 14. *Growing-stock volume on commercial forest land by species group, West Central region, 1972*

County	All species	Softwood			Hardwood			
		Total	Pine	Other	Total	Oak	Gum	Other
				-Million cubic feet-				
Bibb	360.7	238.7	237.6	1.1	122.0	57.9	34.5	29.6
Fayette	264.6	129.7	129.5	.2	134.9	57.6	41.3	36.0
Greene	294.9	128.2	120.0	8.2	166.7	45.9	57.9	62.9
Hale	299.9	175.0	174.8	.2	124.9	55.7	37.6	31.6
Lamar	279.7	100.7	98.9	1.8	179.0	63.4	74.2	41.4
Marion	241.4	118.4	118.0	.4	123.0	73.5	11.6	37.9
Perry	307.2	188.2	185.1	3.1	119.0	39.5	33.6	45.9
Pickens	416.6	250.1	249.2	.9	166.5	70.9	58.8	36.8
Tuscaloosa	707.0	362.1	360.1	2.0	344.9	154.5	109.5	80.9
All counties	3,172.0	1,691.1	1,673.2	17.9	1,480.9	618.9	459.0	403.0

Table 15. *Growing-stock volume on commercial forest land by species group, North Central region, 1972*

County	All species	Softwood			Hardwood			
		Total	Pine	Other	Total	Oak	Gum	Other
				-Million cubic feet-				
Blount	244.8	118.1	117.9	0.2	126.7	66.3	18.1	42.3
Calhoun	178.3	110.5	110.5	...	67.8	38.8	7.9	21.1
Cherokee	126.6	70.3	70.3	...	56.3	41.0	3.4	11.9
Clay	232.2	135.7	135.7	...	96.5	47.5	15.7	33.3
Cleburne	280.9	186.8	186.8	...	94.1	55.3	10.4	28.4
Coosa	255.5	148.4	148.4	...	107.1	49.4	24.0	33.7
Cullman	251.1	138.5	138.3	.2	112.6	63.7	9.4	39.5
Etowah	113.3	66.6	66.6	...	46.7	30.0	5.1	11.6
Jefferson	363.9	275.7	275.7	...	88.2	45.5	14.4	28.3
Randolph	202.4	125.1	125.1	...	77.3	36.4	9.7	31.2
St. Clair	241.9	143.8	143.3	.5	98.1	52.6	19.1	26.4
Shelby	291.5	174.2	174.2	...	117.3	57.1	18.8	41.4
Talladega	230.0	132.6	132.6	...	97.4	49.5	16.1	31.8
Walker	401.7	257.5	257.5	...	144.2	70.7	19.7	53.8
Winston	327.0	202.8	202.5	.3	124.2	79.1	7.5	37.6
All counties	3,741.1	2,286.6	2,285.4	1.2	1,454.5	782.9	199.3	472.3

Table 16. *Sawtimber volume on commercial forest land by species group, West Central region, 1972*

County	All species	Softwood			Hardwood			
		Total	Pine	Other	Total	Oak	Gum	Other
				-Million board feet-				
Bibb	1,155.2	902.6	901.5	1.1	252.6	146.3	58.2	48.1
Fayette	635.6	380.8	380.8	...	254.8	131.3	56.0	67.5
Greene	1,073.8	552.0	509.0	43.0	521.8	151.0	213.3	157.5
Hale	1,085.5	794.4	794.4	...	291.1	164.7	65.8	60.6
Lamar	599.7	223.9	219.3	4.6	375.8	163.7	132.6	79.5
Marion	480.6	262.0	260.8	1.2	218.6	147.3	13.4	57.9
Perry	1,066.1	796.7	780.6	16.1	269.4	116.5	72.7	80.2
Pickens	1,219.5	821.4	818.2	3.2	398.1	196.6	123.5	78.0
Tuscaloosa	2,030.5	1,194.5	1,189.1	5.4	836.0	453.5	213.6	168.9
All counties	9,346.5	5,928.3	5,853.7	74.6	3,418.2	1,670.9	949.1	798.2

Table 17. *Sawtimber volume on commercial forest land by species group, North Central region, 1972*

County	All species	Softwood			Hardwood			
		Total	Pine	Other	Total	Oak	Gum	Other
				-Million board feet-				
Blount	704.1	352.8	352.8	...	351.3	208.2	53.4	89.7
Calhoun	470.3	318.9	318.9	...	151.4	104.9	13.6	32.9
Cherokee	341.7	210.5	210.5	...	131.2	108.4	5.0	17.8
Clay	603.4	447.4	447.4	...	156.0	97.8	17.8	40.4
Cleburne	724.9	569.5	569.5	...	155.4	103.4	12.3	39.7
Coosa	676.4	455.3	455.3	...	221.1	113.5	35.5	72.1
Cullman	590.3	367.3	367.3	...	223.0	125.4	17.7	79.9
Etowah	270.3	153.3	153.3	...	117.0	93.2	7.1	16.7
Jefferson	1,195.6	999.3	999.3	...	196.3	117.5	13.2	65.6
Randolph	569.2	387.4	387.4	...	181.8	109.5	9.5	62.8
St. Clair	629.4	397.7	397.7	...	231.7	141.3	38.3	52.1
Shelby	743.6	502.3	502.3	...	241.3	136.0	41.6	63.7
Talladega	643.4	445.4	445.4	...	198.0	117.7	21.9	58.4
Walker	1,189.2	905.7	905.7	...	283.5	136.1	29.5	117.9
Winston	957.6	647.5	647.5	...	310.1	232.7	10.1	67.3
All counties	10,309.4	7,160.3	7,160.3	...	3,149.1	1,945.6	326.5	877.0

9

Table 18. *Sawtimber volume on commercial forest land by species group and diameter class, West Central region, 1972*

County	All species	Softwood			Hardwood		
		Total	9.0–14.9 inches	15.0 inches and up	Total	11.0–14.9 inches	15.0 inches and up

- - - - - - - - - - Million board feet - - - - - - - - - - -

County	All species	Total	9.0–14.9 inches	15.0 inches and up	Total	11.0–14.9 inches	15.0 inches and up
Bibb	1,155.2	902.6	562.2	340.4	252.6	139.4	113.2
Fayette	635.6	380.8	279.0	101.8	254.8	163.8	91.0
Greene	1,073.8	552.0	322.1	229.9	521.8	159.0	362.8
Hale	1,085.5	794.4	418.0	376.4	291.1	127.1	164.0
Lamar	599.7	223.9	182.3	41.6	375.8	241.4	134.4
Marion	480.6	262.0	223.5	38.5	218.6	153.7	64.9
Perry	1,066.1	796.7	494.9	301.8	269.4	104.7	164.7
Pickens	1,219.5	821.4	585.3	236.1	398.1	221.6	176.5
Tuscaloosa	2,030.5	1,194.5	775.9	418.6	836.0	408.2	427.8
All counties	9,346.5	5,928.3	3,843.2	2,085.1	3,418.2	1,718.9	1,699.3

Table 19. *Sawtimber volume on commercial forest land by species group and diameter class, North Central region, 1972*

County	All species	Softwood			Hardwood		
		Total	9.0–14.9 inches	15.0 inches and up	Total	11.0–14.9 inches	15.0 inches and up

- - - - - - - - - - Million board feet - - - - - - - - - - -

County	All species	Total	9.0–14.9 inches	15.0 inches and up	Total	11.0–14.9 inches	15.0 inches and up
Blount	704.1	352.8	301.1	51.7	351.3	165.6	185.7
Calhoun	470.3	318.9	242.1	76.8	151.4	84.2	67.2
Cherokee	341.7	210.5	148.4	62.1	131.2	62.6	68.6
Clay	603.4	447.4	329.6	117.8	156.0	98.5	57.5
Cleburne	724.9	569.5	398.0	171.5	155.4	106.7	48.7
Coosa	676.4	455.3	359.2	96.1	221.1	112.7	108.4
Cullman	590.3	367.3	319.5	47.8	223.0	122.4	100.6
Etowah	270.3	153.3	129.3	24.0	117.0	59.2	57.8
Jefferson	1,195.6	999.3	571.4	427.9	196.3	85.9	110.4
Randolph	569.2	387.4	262.5	124.9	181.8	86.2	95.6
St. Clair	629.4	397.7	305.7	92.0	231.7	111.8	119.9
Shelby	743.6	502.3	333.6	168.7	241.3	117.3	124.0
Talladega	643.4	445.4	303.9	141.5	198.0	106.1	91.9
Walker	1,189.2	905.7	703.2	202.5	283.5	173.4	110.1
Winston	957.6	647.5	397.5	250.0	310.1	156.9	153.2
All counties	10,309.4	7,160.3	5,105.0	2,055.3	3,149.1	1,649.5	1,499.6

Table 20. *Growing-stock volume of softwoods on commercial forest land by forest type, West Central region, 1972*

County	All types	Longleaf-slash pine	Loblolly-shortleaf pine	Oak-pine	Oak-hickory	Oak-gum-cypress	Elm-ash-cottonwood
			-Million cubic feet-				
Bibb	238.7	27.1	129.0	74.6	8.0	...	...
Fayette	129.7	...	93.8	24.4	8.7	2.8	...
Greene	128.2	...	67.8	31.3	7.4	21.7	...
Hale	175.0	20.3	69.9	72.5	3.0	9.3	...
Lamar	100.7	...	63.1	24.7	8.0	4.9	...
Marion	118.4	...	79.5	25.1	13.4	...	0.4
Perry	188.2	10.2	90.7	68.2	9.8	7.6	1.7
Pickens	250.1	...	170.2	64.4	7.5	8.0	...
Tuscaloosa	362.1	23.9	200.2	97.9	27.1	13.0	...
All counties	1,691.1	81.5	964.2	483.1	92.9	67.3	2.1

Table 21. *Growing-stock volume of softwoods on commercial forest land by forest type, North Central region, 1972*

County	All types	Longleaf-slash pine	Loblolly-shortleaf pine	Oak-pine	Oak-hickory	Oak-gum-cypress	Elm-ash-cottonwood
			-Million cubic feet-				
Blount	118.1	...	81.4	31.4	4.5	0.8	...
Calhoun	110.5	...	59.4	41.6	9.5	...	...
Cherokee	70.3	...	52.9	12.7	3.2	1.5	...
Clay	135.7	...	75.8	42.3	17.6	...	...
Cleburne	186.8	3.3	137.1	32.7	13.7	...	...
Coosa	148.4	17.2	80.1	41.1	9.4	.6	...
Cullman	138.5	...	95.9	33.9	8.7	...	...
Etowah	66.6	...	45.8	10.3	9.2	1.3	...
Jefferson	275.7	15.0	204.9	45.5	9.9	...	0.4
Randolph	125.1	7.8	62.5	50.6	4.2	...	...
St. Clair	143.8	7.1	90.6	26.6	11.2	8.3	...
Shelby	174.2	18.4	91.6	44.9	19.3	...	...
Talladega	132.6	9.6	62.7	48.0	12.3	...	...
Walker	257.5	...	185.5	55.3	16.7	...	...
Winston	202.8	...	139.5	41.3	22.0	...	...
All counties	2,286.6	78.4	1,465.7	558.2	171.4	12.5	.4

Table 22. *Growing-stock volume of hardwoods on commercial forest land by forest type, West Central region, 1972*

County	All types	Longleaf-slash pine	Loblolly-shortleaf pine	Oak-pine	Oak-hickory	Oak-gum-cypress	Elm-ash-cottonwood
			-Million cubic feet-				
Bibb	122.0	2.9	23.4	54.5	33.7	7.5	...
Fayette	134.9	...	13.0	22.9	54.2	43.0	1.8
Greene	166.7	...	7.1	22.6	27.6	109.4	...
Hale	124.9	1.4	15.2	28.2	6.7	73.4	...
Lamar	179.0	...	3.8	26.4	45.3	101.5	2.0
Marion	123.0	...	8.8	18.4	92.3	...	3.5
Perry	119.0	.8	7.5	34.2	32.9	24.6	19.0
Pickens	166.5	...	19.2	38.3	34.0	71.5	3.5
Tuscaloosa	344.9	3.3	35.5	64.9	111.1	130.1	...
All counties	1,480.9	8.4	133.5	310.4	437.8	561.0	29.8

Table 23. *Growing-stock volume of hardwoods on commercial forest land by forest type, North Central region, 1972*

County	All types	Longleaf-slash pine	Loblolly-shortleaf pine	Oak-pine	Oak-hickory	Oak-gum-cypress	Elm-ash-cottonwood
			-Million cubic feet-				
Blount	126.7		12.3	31.1	67.8	15.5	...
Calhoun	67.8		6.2	17.2	44.4	...	...
Cherokee	56.3		10.8	8.4	24.9	12.2	...
Clay	96.5		9.7	32.5	54.3	...	...
Cleburne	94.1		16.8	24.5	52.8	...	...
Coosa	107.1	1.5	17.4	36.9	44.4	6.9	...
Cullman	112.6	...	15.0	37.2	60.4	...	...
Etowah	46.7	...	4.2	6.5	33.6	2.4	...
Jefferson	88.2	.7	19.4	29.6	34.2	.6	3.7
Randolph	77.3	...	9.0	29.9	36.2	2.2	...
St. Clair	98.1	...	10.5	19.4	50.4	17.8	...
Shelby	117.3	1.2	15.8	30.1	47.7	11.8	10.7
Talladega	97.4	1.1	6.8	33.9	55.6	...	...
Walker	144.2	...	39.6	31.5	73.1	...	...
Winston	124.2	...	19.4	34.2	70.6	...	...
All counties	1,454.5	4.5	212.9	402.9	750.4	69.4	14.4

Table 24. *Sawtimber volume of softwoods on commercial forest land by forest type,*
West Central region, 1972

County	All types	Longleaf-slash pine	Loblolly-shortleaf pine	Oak-pine	Oak-hickory	Oak-gum-cypress	Elm-ash-cottonwood
				-Million board feet-			
Bibb	902.6	95.5	485.5	295.7	25.9	...	...
Fayette	380.8	...	247.0	101.0	25.0	7.8	...
Greene	552.0	...	244.0	147.6	39.6	120.8	...
Hale	794.4	122.2	275.3	324.8	14.7	57.4	...
Lamar	223.9	...	127.5	52.7	28.8	14.9	...
Marion	262.0	...	184.5	50.3	26.0	...	1.2
Perry	796.7	40.9	330.0	327.2	42.8	46.6	9.2
Pickens	821.4	...	465.2	294.8	19.7	41.7	...
Tuscaloosa	1,194.5	103.0	583.5	323.5	102.3	82.2	...
All counties	5,928.3	361.6	2,942.5	1,917.6	324.8	371.4	10.4

Table 25. *Sawtimber volume of softwoods on commercial forest land by forest type,*
North Central region, 1972

County	All types	Longleaf-slash pine	Loblolly-shortleaf pine	Oak-pine	Oak-hickory	Oak-gum-cypress	Elm-ash-cottonwood
				-Million board feet-			
Blount	352.8	...	271.3	68.4	13.1	...	...
Calhoun	318.9	...	154.1	138.1	26.7	...	...
Cherokee	210.5	...	152.9	42.1	10.8	4.7	...
Clay	447.4	...	224.9	153.2	69.3	...	...
Cleburne	569.5	11.3	406.2	102.6	49.4	...	...
Coosa	455.3	70.1	256.1	98.1	26.5	4.5	...
Cullman	367.3	...	269.9	74.5	22.9	...	...
Etowah	153.3	...	91.8	28.6	24.6	8.3	...
Jefferson	999.3	54.6	773.0	141.6	28.3	...	1.8
Randolph	387.4	17.6	151.1	205.8	12.9	...	...
St. Clair	397.7	34.7	198.9	86.8	36.7	40.6	...
Shelby	502.3	47.7	240.3	130.1	84.2	...	...
Talladega	445.4	28.9	188.1	183.0	45.4	...	...
Walker	905.7	...	661.9	195.4	48.4	...	...
Winston	647.5	...	413.2	134.4	99.9	...	...
All counties	7,160.3	264.9	4,453.7	1,782.7	599.1	58.1	1.8

Table 26. *Sawtimber volume of hardwoods on commercial forest land by forest type,*
West Central region, 1972

County	All types	Longleaf-slash pine	Loblolly-shortleaf pine	Oak-pine	Oak-hickory	Oak-gum-cypress	Elm-ash-cottonwood
			- - - - - - - - - - -Million board feet- - - - - - - - - - - -				
Bibb	252.6	5.0	63.5	111.0	51.0	22.1	...
Fayette	254.8	...	24.4	42.5	113.8	71.5	2.6
Greene	521.8		17.5	41.6	74.4	388.3	...
Hale	291.1		40.9	51.7	9.7	188.8	...
Lamar	375.8		7.5	47.8	100.3	220.2	...
Marion	218.6		9.0	22.6	182.7	...	4.3
Perry	269.4	...	13.4	57.5	82.6	65.9	50.0
Pickens	398.1	...	32.1	92.0	70.4	197.5	6.1
Tuscaloosa	836.0	2.3	56.7	130.6	293.0	353.4	...
All counties	3,418.2	7.3	265.0	597.3	977.9	1,507.7	63.0

Table 27. *Sawtimber volume of hardwoods on commercial forest land by forest type,*
North Central region, 1972

County	All types	Longleaf-slash pine	Loblolly-shortleaf pine	Oak-pine	Oak-hickory	Oak-gum-cypress	Elm-ash-cottonwood
			- - - - - - - - - - -Million board feet- - - - - - - - - - -				
Blount	351.3		36.3	82.2	182.9	49.9	...
Calhoun	151.4	...	13.3	38.6	99.5	...	...
Cherokee	131.2		16.7	13.4	64.7	36.4	...
Clay	156.0	...	10.9	38.8	106.3	...	...
Cleburne	155.4		37.9	45.2	72.3	...	...
Coosa	221.1	2.8	29.6	58.4	106.4	23.9	...
Cullman	223.0	...	29.1	68.3	125.6	...	...
Etowah	117.0	...	6.9	11.5	90.8	7.8	...
Jefferson	196.3	2.2	40.0	69.5	66.9	...	17.7
Randolph	181.8	...	10.3	69.3	95.5	6.7	...
St. Clair	231.7	...	19.2	43.4	109.9	59.2	...
Shelby	241.3	1.2	24.0	68.6	112.9	30.8	3.8
Talladega	198.0	1.6	6.1	49.2	141.1	...	...
Walker	283.5	...	82.9	56.8	143.8	...	...
Winston	310.1	...	43.2	87.4	179.5	...	...
All counties	3,149.1	7.8	406.4	800.6	1,698.1	214.7	21.5

Table 28. *Growing-stock volume of softwoods on commercial forest land by stand-size class, West Central region, 1972*

County	All classes	Sawtimber	Poletimber	Sapling and seedling	Nonstocked areas
			- - - - - Million cubic feet- - - - - - -		
Bibb	238.7	133.6	73.3	31.8	...
Fayette	129.7	63.5	50.0	16.2	
Greene	128.2	80.7	34.1	13.4	
Hale	175.0	132.2	23.8	19.0	
Lamar	100.7	35.5	54.9	10.3	
Marion	118.4	27.0	59.2	32.2	
Perry	188.2	128.0	54.1	6.1	
Pickens	250.1	135.6	79.1	35.4	...
Tuscaloosa	362.1	162.8	142.8	56.5	...
All counties	1,691.1	898.9	571.3	220.9	...

Table 29. *Growing-stock volume of softwoods on commercial forest land by stand-size class, North Central region, 1972*

County	All classes	Sawtimber	Poletimber	Sapling and seedling	Nonstocked areas
			- - - - - Million cubic feet- - - - - - -		
Blount	118.1	72.6	26.2	19.3	
Calhoun	110.5	33.0	59.5	18.0	...
Cherokee	70.3	18.6	24.0	27.7	
Clay	135.7	59.5	57.6	18.6	
Cleburne	186.8	97.8	70.3	18.7	
Coosa	148.4	54.0	72.3	22.1	
Cullman	138.5	60.6	68.7	9.2	
Etowah	66.6	14.5	38.9	13.2	
Jefferson	275.7	126.4	108.7	40.6	
Randolph	125.1	64.8	39.3	21.0	
St. Clair	143.8	67.0	50.0	26.8	...
Shelby	174.2	62.8	86.3	24.9	0.2
Talladega	132.6	49.2	70.7	12.7	...
Walker	257.5	131.8	98.2	27.5	...
Winston	202.8	89.8	97.8	15.2	...
All counties	2,286.6	1,002.4	968.5	315.5	.2

15

Table 30. *Growing-stock volume of hardwoods on commercial forest land by stand-size class, West Central region, 1972*

County	All classes	Sawtimber	Poletimber	Sapling and seedling	Nonstocked areas
- - - - - - - - - Million cubic feet- - - - - - - -					
Bibb	122.0	32.9	76.5	12.6	
Fayette	134.9	39.5	81.9	13.5	
Greene	166.7	124.3	36.2	6.2	
Hale	124.9	58.5	57.0	9.4	
Lamar	179.0	57.0	107.4	14.6	
Marion	123.0	28.5	74.5	20.0	
Perry	119.0	70.2	39.7	9.1	
Pickens	166.5	95.7	56.6	14.2	...
Tuscaloosa	344.9	155.8	149.9	39.2	...
All counties	1,480.9	662.4	679.7	138.8	...

Table 31. *Growing-stock volume of hardwoods on commercial forest land by stand-size class, North Central region, 1972*

County	All classes	Sawtimber	Poletimber	Sapling and seedling	Nonstocked areas
- - - - - - - - Million cubic feet- - - - - - -					
Blount	126.7	68.6	47.8	10.3	
Calhoun	67.8	27.0	30.4	10.4	
Cherokee	56.3	31.1	14.1	11.1	
Clay	96.5	20.1	59.9	16.5	
Cleburne	94.1	21.9	57.0	15.2	
Coosa	107.1	25.0	66.3	15.8	
Cullman	112.6	26.7	80.7	5.2	
Etowah	46.7	19.8	13.9	13.0	
Jefferson	88.2	31.5	37.3	19.4	
Randolph	77.3	39.7	16.7	20.9	
St. Clair	98.1	30.5	51.4	16.2	
Shelby	117.3	54.8	51.1	11.4	
Talladega	97.4	53.3	33.4	10.7	
Walker	144.2	56.1	75.8	12.3	...
Winston	124.2	61.3	37.6	25.3	...
All counties	1,454.5	567.4	673.4	213.7	...

16

Table 32. *Sawtimber volume of softwoods on commercial forest land by stand-size class, West Central region, 1972*

County	All classes	Sawtimber	Poletimber	Sapling and seedling	Nonstocked areas
	- - - - - - - - Million board feet- - - - - - - -				
Bibb	902.6	667.5	154.9	80.2	
Fayette	380.8	260.4	96.6	23.8	
Greene	552.0	411.1	95.1	45.8	
Hale	794.4	664.7	65.6	64.1	
Lamar	223.9	115.5	90.4	18.0	
Marion	262.0	110.9	97.1	54.0	
Perry	796.7	638.7	151.5	6.5	
Pickens	821.4	588.3	103.0	130.1	...
Tuscaloosa	1,194.5	759.6	318.1	116.8	...
All counties	5,928.3	4,216.7	1,172.3	539.3	...

Table 33. *Sawtimber volume of softwoods on commercial forest land by stand-size class, North Central region, 1972*

County	All classes	Sawtimber	Poletimber	Sapling and seedling	Nonstocked areas
	- - - - - - - - Million board feet- - - - - - - -				
Blount	352.8	281.5	35.8	35.5	...
Calhoun	318.9	116.8	143.7	58.4	
Cherokee	210.5	82.4	40.1	88.0	
Clay	447.4	267.3	135.7	44.4	
Cleburne	569.5	376.9	170.8	21.8	
Coosa	455.3	242.5	164.0	48.8	
Cullman	367.3	229.6	122.8	14.9	
Etowah	153.3	58.8	64.9	29.6	
Jefferson	999.3	619.2	270.6	109.5	
Randolph	387.4	264.1	70.4	52.9	
St. Clair	397.7	255.8	77.0	64.9	...
Shelby	502.3	282.9	161.6	56.9	0.9
Talladega	445.4	226.0	185.1	34.3	...
Walker	905.7	597.3	227.5	80.9	...
Winston	647.5	427.8	187.8	31.9	...
All counties	7,160.3	4,328.9	2,057.8	772.7	.9

17

Table 34. *Sawtimber volume of hardwoods on commercial forest land by stand-size class, West Central region, 1972*

County	All classes	Sawtimber	Poletimber	Sapling and seedling	Nonstocked areas
		- - - - - - -Million board feet- - - - - - -			
Bibb	252.6	79.6	149.9	23.1	
Fayette	254.8	115.3	119.7	19.8	
Greene	521.8	444.5	64.6	12.7	
Hale	291.1	190.1	88.3	12.7	
Lamar	375.8	191.0	153.6	31.2	
Marion	218.6	73.1	114.6	30.9	
Perry	269.4	200.7	55.9	12.8	
Pickens	398.1	282.6	97.0	18.5	...
Tuscaloosa	836.0	475.7	283.9	76.4	...
All counties	3,418.2	2,052.6	1,127.5	238.1	...

Table 35. *Sawtimber volume of hardwoods on commercial forest land by stand-size class, North Central region, 1972*

County	All classes	Sawtimber	Poletimber	Sapling and seedling	Nonstocked areas
		- - - - - - -Million board feet- - - - - - -			
Blount	351.3	228.2	101.8	21.3	
Calhoun	151.4	92.2	47.8	11.4	
Cherokee	131.2	97.5	10.1	23.6	
Clay	156.0	48.4	80.2	27.4	
Cleburne	155.4	57.0	76.5	21.9	
Coosa	221.1	80.9	121.4	18.8	
Cullman	223.0	78.0	139.9	5.1	
Etowah	117.0	75.0	19.1	22.9	
Jefferson	196.3	97.9	59.6	38.8	
Randolph	181.8	123.3	14.5	44.0	
St. Clair	231.7	112.7	92.5	26.5	
Shelby	241.3	167.4	61.7	12.2	
Talladega	198.0	139.9	46.6	11.5	
Walker	283.5	160.3	108.6	14.6	...
Winston	310.1	198.5	64.6	47.0	...
All counties	3,149.1	1,757.2	1,044.9	347.0	...

Table 36. *Growing-stock volume on commercial forest land by species and diameter class, West Central region, 1972*

Species	All classes	Diameter class (inches at breast height) — Million cubic feet									
		5.0– 6.9	7.0– 8.9	9.0– 10.9	11.0– 12.9	13.0– 14.9	15.0– 16.9	17.0– 18.9	19.0– 20.9	21.0– 28.9	29.0 and larger
Softwood:											
Longleaf pine	103.4	8.5	13.9	18.9	25.1	19.2	10.0	5.8	2.0	...	...
Shortleaf pine	382.6	67.7	94.1	90.0	74.6	33.4	16.2	5.5	.7	0.4	...
Loblolly pine	1,107.9	153.7	197.4	180.7	158.4	125.6	115.0	67.4	49.2	59.4	1.1
Virginia pine	68.7	25.2	18.3	14.6	8.0	1.2	1.1	.3	...	...	...
Other southern pines	10.6	1.4	1.2	.9	.5	2.5	1.5	.7	1.3	.6	...
Redcedar	3.7	1.6	1.5	.4	.2	...	...	...	...	...	...
Cypress	14.2	.6	...	.4	.2	...	2.5	.4	2.8	3.4	3.9
Total	1,691.1	258.7	326.4	305.9	267.0	181.9	146.3	80.1	56.0	63.8	5.0
Hardwood:											
Select white oaks	118.0	11.9	21.2	23.0	16.4	19.1	11.0	7.8	3.5	4.1	...
Select red oaks	40.9	2.3	3.2	8.8	6.1	3.5	4.7	1.9	3.0	3.5	3.9
Other white oaks	111.4	15.1	21.3	18.4	18.4	14.2	12.9	3.6	4.5	2.0	1.0
Other red oaks	348.6	46.1	51.7	63.8	49.3	42.2	34.5	23.6	13.7	18.2	5.5
Hickory	141.3	15.9	21.9	24.5	24.2	28.4	11.8	5.0	4.5	5.1	...
Persimmon	3.4	.7	.8	1.0	.9	...	...	...	...	...	...
Soft maple	34.7	7.4	5.8	5.8	5.2	2.2	3.9	1.9	2.5	...	...
Beech	10.1	.5	.3	1.2	.7	2.0	1.2	.9	1.5	1.3	.5
Sweetgum	307.8	51.8	55.0	60.3	48.8	36.0	28.1	9.0	8.3	10.5	...
Blackgum	93.8	11.0	23.8	20.5	20.5	9.9	4.7	2.1	...	1.4	...
Other gums	57.4	4.8	8.9	15.6	8.4	7.3	4.3	3.7	1.4	2.0	1.0
Ash	19.5	2.8	1.5	3.1	3.2	4.7	1.8	1.1	.6	...	.7
Yellow-poplar	69.0	7.9	12.1	10.0	14.7	6.0	7.5	2.5	2.9	4.8	.6
Magnolia (*Magnolia* spp.)	34.0	4.1	9.6	11.1	5.0	2.7	1.1	.4	...	...	...
Black cherry	2.9	2.1	.4	.4	...	...	...	...	...	...	...
American elm	21.7	1.8	4.8	3.1	3.1	2.6	2.5	1.7	1.4	.3	.4
Other elms	14.3	.6	3.1	4.9	3.2	.6	1.2	.4	...	.3	...
River birch	14.6	1.6	2.0	3.9	2.3	1.1	1.4	1.6	...	.4	.3
Hackberry	20.4	1.8	2.3	4.9	1.8	1.9	2.9	2.4	.8	1.2	.4
Dogwood	3.3	3.1	.2	...	...	...	...	...	...	...	...
Other hardwoods	13.8	3.5	2.4	2.0	1.1	1.0	.5	.7	.6	2.0	...
Total	1,480.9	196.8	252.3	286.3	233.3	185.4	136.0	70.2	49.2	57.1	14.3
All species	3,172.0	455.5	578.7	592.2	500.3	367.3	282.3	150.3	105.2	120.9	19.3

19

Table 37. *Growing-stock volume on commercial forest land by species and diameter class, North Central region, 1972*

Species	All classes	Diameter class (inches at breast height) — Million cubic feet									
		5.0–6.9	7.0–8.9	9.0–10.9	11.0–12.9	13.0–14.9	15.0–16.9	17.0–18.9	19.0–20.9	21.0–28.9	29.0 and larger
Softwood:											
Longleaf pine	170.8	16.2	33.7	38.3	31.1	24.8	12.9	7.4	4.3	2.1	...
Shortleaf pine	599.1	153.0	172.9	125.7	72.7	36.7	28.2	7.7	.6	1.6	...
Loblolly pine	1,268.4	187.5	234.0	228.4	196.2	149.4	104.0	83.5	36.4	46.2	2.8
Virginia pine	247.1	68.8	67.4	50.9	35.0	18.7	4.4	1.9	...	...	...
Other softwoods	1.2	.8	.4	...	..	...	...	...	...	...	...
Total	2,286.6	426.3	508.4	443.3	335.0	229.6	149.5	100.5	41.3	49.9	2.8
Hardwood:											
Select white oaks	183.9	18.0	27.6	27.4	27.0	30.2	22.5	13.7	7.7	9.8	...
Select red oaks	57.5	6.4	6.8	7.2	8.2	6.8	6.9	4.5	3.9	4.9	1.9
Other white oaks	204.9	30.4	45.8	44.3	31.7	27.0	12.0	8.3	3.0	2.0	.4
Other red oaks	336.6	48.7	60.6	63.0	48.6	41.0	31.4	19.7	9.4	12.1	2.1
Hickory	246.5	36.0	51.1	55.5	45.6	27.4	15.7	6.1	4.9	4.2	...
Soft maple	19.3	5.1	2.6	2.6	1.7	2.7	2.0	.2	.6	1.8	...
Beech	12.5	.7	.4	2.7	1.8	1.4	2.2	.9	.3	1.4	.7
Sweetgum	159.2	35.2	37.6	29.8	16.9	16.8	12.9	3.4	3.2	3.4	...
Blackgum	40.1	4.3	8.4	12.1	4.6	5.0	3.4	.9	...	1.4	...
White ash	9.0	.9	1.2	.5	1.1	2.4	.8	...	1.5	.6	...
Other ashes	9.9	1.4	1.7	1.0	.8	2.4	1.0	1.3	.3	...	...
Basswood	4.7	.3	.9	.5	1.1	.9	1.0	...	...	...	...
Yellow-poplar	126.1	8.8	14.5	25.8	21.5	19.3	10.6	12.0	5.8	6.1	1.7
Black cherry	4.0	1.0	1.8	...	.5	.7	...	...	...	...	...
American elm	4.5	.5	1.1	1.0	.9	...	.4	...	...	...	...
Other elms	8.7	2.4	2.4	1.0	2.0	.5	.4	...	...	...	.6
Dogwood	3.7	2.8	.9	...	...	...	...	...	...	...	...
Other hardwoods	23.4	6.4	7.2	3.3	2.8	1.2	1.5	.3	.7	...	...
Total	1,454.5	209.3	272.6	277.7	216.8	185.7	124.7	71.3	41.3	47.7	7.4
All species	3,741.1	635.6	781.0	721.0	551.8	415.3	274.2	171.8	82.6	97.6	10.2

20

Table 38. *Sawtimber volume on commercial forest land by species and diameter class, West Central region, 1972*

Species	All classes	Diameter class (inches at breast height) —Million board feet—							
		9.0–10.9	11.0–12.9	13.0–14.9	15.0–16.9	17.0–18.9	19.0–20.9	21.0–28.9	29.0 and larger
Softwood:									
Longleaf pine	460.4	87.4	142.4	117.3	62.9	37.1	13.3	...	...
Shortleaf pine	1,125.5	445.6	388.5	176.0	80.3	29.8	3.4	1.9	...
Loblolly pine	4,095.1	766.8	844.1	724.1	678.1	420.7	299.6	355.8	5.9
Virginia pine	131.1	75.6	42.6	6.2	5.6	1.1	...	...	...
Other southern pines	41.6	4.1	2.4	14.3	8.5	3.4	6.3	2.6	...
Redcedar	3.3	2.4	.9	...	...	...	...	...	...
Cypress	71.3	1.8	.7	...	13.7	1.2	15.0	18.8	20.1
Total	5,928.3	1,383.7	1,421.6	1,037.9	849.1	493.3	337.6	379.1	26.0
Hardwood:									
Select white oaks	314.2	...	76.1	96.5	56.0	44.1	19.7	21.8	...
Select red oaks	136.3	...	21.9	17.2	25.5	11.4	18.3	20.6	21.4
Other white oaks	282.9	...	81.0	70.2	70.5	17.4	27.1	10.6	6.1
Other red oaks	937.5	...	200.5	206.2	183.0	136.6	72.4	104.2	34.6
Hickory	309.1	...	74.1	113.2	53.0	22.2	22.9	23.7	...
Persimmon	3.0	...	3.0	...	...	...	...	...	...
Soft maple	56.7	...	13.8	8.3	15.8	7.3	11.5	...	...
Beech	33.6	...	2.5	7.3	4.5	3.2	7.4	6.0	2.7
Sweetgum	661.4	...	183.3	172.7	148.2	51.7	47.7	57.8	...
Blackgum	169.2	...	78.4	49.5	23.2	10.5	7.8	7.6	6.1
Other gums	118.5	...	25.2	28.6	22.0	18.3	2.9	10.5	3.2
Ash	48.1	...	10.2	19.3	7.4	5.1	...	...	2.9
Yellow-poplar	150.1	...	44.0	25.7	31.6	11.0	12.4	22.5	...
Magnolia (*Magnolia* spp.)	30.6	...	15.2	9.7	3.9	1.8	...	...	...
American elm	45.7	...	8.5	10.4	8.8	9.0	5.4	1.9	1.7
Other elms	21.4	...	10.7	2.4	4.2	2.5	...	1.6	...
River birch	27.6	...	8.0	4.3	5.5	6.6	...	1.7	1.5
Hackberry	47.5	...	6.4	8.0	10.8	11.5	3.4	5.8	1.6
Other hardwoods	24.8	...	2.9	3.7	1.6	3.3	2.9	10.4	...
Total	3,418.2	...	865.7	853.2	675.5	373.5	261.8	306.7	81.8
All species	9,346.5	1,383.7	2,287.3	1,891.1	1,524.6	866.8	599.4	685.8	107.8

Table 39. *Sawtimber volume on commercial forest land by species and diameter class, North Central region, 1972*

Species	All classes	Diameter class (inches at breast height) ----Million board feet----							
		9.0–10.9	11.0–12.9	13.0–14.9	15.0–16.9	17.0–18.9	19.0–20.9	21.0–28.9	29.0 and larger
Softwood:									
Longleaf pine	660.4	168.5	171.1	149.6	79.7	47.8	29.1	14.6	...
Shortleaf pine	1,383.7	624.1	374.8	191.6	143.2	39.2	3.1	7.7	...
Loblolly pine	4,551.2	984.3	1,044.1	863.1	622.8	515.6	223.5	282.2	15.6
Virginia pine	565.0	252.7	185.8	95.3	21.4	9.8	...	...	...
Total	7,160.3	2,029.6	1,775.8	1,299.6	867.1	612.4	255.7	304.5	15.6
Hardwood:									
Select white oaks	558.3	...	113.0	148.2	117.2	77.4	45.8	56.7	...
Select red oaks	188.4	...	35.3	31.4	36.2	23.3	24.6	28.1	9.5
Other white oaks	400.5	...	136.4	125.4	62.0	46.3	16.5	11.9	2.0
Other red oaks	798.4	...	200.9	190.1	163.4	107.7	53.2	67.4	15.7
Hickory	399.1	...	154.5	108.2	65.7	27.4	22.2	21.1	...
Soft maple	31.8	...	4.3	8.6	8.1	.9	2.3	7.6	...
Beech	33.4	...	5.3	4.9	9.6	3.6	1.5	6.3	2.2
Sweetgum	254.2	...	60.7	76.1	65.5	18.0	15.7	18.2	...
Blackgum	72.3	...	19.9	23.8	15.9	4.1	...	8.6	...
White ash	26.3	...	4.3	9.6	3.7	...	6.8	1.9	...
Other ashes	26.3	...	2.4	9.7	5.7	7.4	1.1	...	...
Yellow-poplar	299.5	...	64.1	76.3	46.7	53.3	23.4	28.4	7.3
American elm	9.0	...	3.9	...	2.3	...	...	...	2.8
Other elms	10.2	...	7.1	1.2	1.9	...	...	...	...
Other hardwoods	41.4	...	14.4	9.5	13.5	1.4	2.6	...	...
Total	3,149.1	...	826.5	823.0	617.4	370.8	215.7	256.2	39.5
All species	10,309.4	2,029.6	2,602.3	2,122.6	1,484.5	983.2	471.4	560.7	55.1

22

Table 40. *Average volume per acre of growing stock and sawtimber on commercial forest land by species group and ownership class, West Central region, 1972*

Ownership class	Growing stock			Sawtimber		
	All species	Softwood	Hardwood	All species	Softwood	Hardwood
	- - -Cubic feet- - -			- - -Board feet- - -		
National forest	1,369	1,138	231	5,942	5,496	446
Other public	913	440	473	2,252	1,292	960
Forest industry	1,019	634	385	2,996	2,057	939
Farmer	933	465	468	2,646	1,620	1,026
Misc. private	1,003	471	532	2,855	1,610	1,245
All ownerships	1,002	534	468	2,953	1,873	1,080

Table 41. *Average volume per acre of growing stock and sawtimber on commercial forest land by species group and ownership class, North Central region, 1972*

Ownership class	Growing stock			Sawtimber		
	All species	Softwood	Hardwood	All species	Softwood	Hardwood
	- - -Cubic feet- - -			- - -Board feet- - -		
National forest	1,085	724	361	3,821	2,948	873
Other public	708	350	358	2,019	1,021	998
Forest industry	776	513	263	1,985	1,465	520
Farmer	861	516	345	2,193	1,466	727
Misc. private	792	474	318	2,220	1,529	691
All ownerships	825	504	321	2,273	1,579	694

23

Arkansas
Forest Industries, 1971

Daniel F. Bertelson

Southern Forest Experiment Station
Forest Service
U. S. Department of Agriculture

1973

Arkansas Forest
Industries, 1971

Daniel F. Bertelson

Southern Forest Experiment Station
New Orleans, La.
Forest Service, U. S. Department of Agriculture

in cooperation with

Arkansas State Forestry Commission

1973

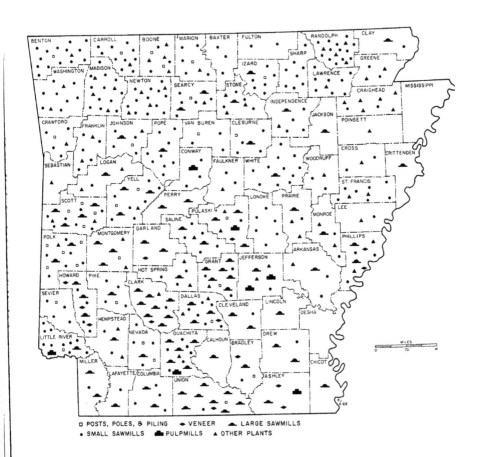

POSTS, POLES, & PILING   VENEER   LARGE SAWMILLS
SMALL SAWMILLS   PULPMILLS   OTHER PLANTS

Primary wood-using plants in Arkansas, 1971

ii

The Report in Brief

Arkansas forests supplied more than 451 million cubic feet of roundwood to forest industries in 1971. Softwoods, mainly pine, made up more than two-thirds of the total. The timber harvest increased 15 percent during the years 1969-1971, while the number of primary wood-using plants decreased. Saw logs and pulpwood comprised 83 percent of the roundwood. Veneer logs made up over 9 percent, with more than half of the remainder going into poles and charcoal wood. Figure 1 shows recent trends in output of these products.

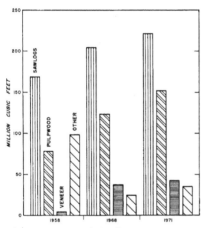

Figure 1.—*Output of industrial roundwood in Arkansas, by product, 1958-1971.*

In converting roundwood into lumber and veneer, Arkansas mills generated 170 million cubic feet of wood residues. Seventy-nine percent of this volume was used for byproducts, mainly pulp chips. The volume of residues and the proportion utilized have both been increasing.

A total of 499 wood-using plants were in operation during 1971. Some small sawmills have been shutting down, and larger mills are increasing their output. Pulpmills have been expanding their capacities, and development of pine veneer plants has more than offset a declining hardwood veneer industry.

These are among the major findings of a canvass of all primary forest industries in Arkansas. In the past, surveys of forest industries have usually been made on a 10-year cycle. Thus, data for Arkansas were gathered in 1948, 1958, and 1968. Because developments in the State have been proceeding rapidly, however, the Arkansas Forestry Commission saw the need for a new survey in 1971. Under supervision of James G. Barnum, Commission personnel visited all primary wood-using plants in the State. Their data were compiled and analyzed by the Forest Resources Research Unit of the Southern Forest Experiment Station.

This report tabulates total State production and shows softwood and hardwood output by county. It also lists names and addresses of all primary forest industries; plant locations are mapped on page ii. For readers who need greater detail, a supplementary report, "Arkansas Product Output and Timber Removals by County," is available without charge from the Southern Forest Experiment Station.

SAW LOGS

Arkansas harvested 1.3 billion board feet of saw logs in 1971, about half of the State's total roundwood production. Softwoods, mostly pine but including some cypress and eastern redcedar, made up two-thirds of the volume. Oaks accounted for 62 percent of the hardwood saw logs with the gums second in volume harvested. Some 67 million board feet of saw logs came from out of the State. This was almost three times the amount exported to surrounding States.

For the last 25 years, the trend in the South has been toward fewer but larger sawmills. Thus, 78 Arkansas sawmills shut down in the last 3 years, but average production per mill increased from 2.8 million board feet in 1968 to 3.7 in 1971. Of the mills that closed, only one was large (cutting at least 3 million board feet annually).

Receipts at the 92 large mills now in operation accounted for almost 90 percent of the State's saw log production.

Arkansas still has 278 small sawmills. They vary widely in size and equipment, but for most the annual production is considerably less than 3 million feet. Many lack dry kilns and planers, and only a few have equipment for converting their residues into pulp chips. Ownership changes rapidly, and continued closures may be expected. In contrast to the situation 10 or 15 years ago, however, the great majority of surviving small mills are at fixed locations. In Arkansas, as elsewhere, the portable mill has become a rarity.

PULPWOOD

Arkansas' harvest of round pulpwood in 1971 totaled 1.9 million cords, an increase of 23 percent since 1968 (fig. 2). Pine bolts accounted for nearly two-thirds of the total. Oaks and gums were the dominant hardwoods.

Although the number of pulpmills in Arkansas remained constant, plant expansion raised the combined total capacity of the seven mills from 4,113 tons per day in 1968 to 4,740 tons in 1971. Capabilities of individual mills range from 140 to 1,700 tons daily.

In addition to roundwood the pulpmills used the equivalent of 1.3 million cords of plant

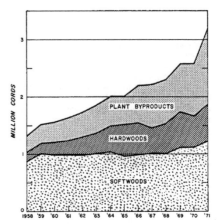

Figure 2.—*Pulpwood production in Arkansas, 1958-1971.*

byproducts in 1971. This volume represents over two fifths of the total pulpwood production in the State. Use of plant byproducts has increased 69 percent since 1968; almost all of this wood comes from the big mills that saw most of the State's pine saw logs or manufacture southern pine plywood.

VENEER

Again in keeping with trends throughout the Midsouth, Arkansas has increased its pine plywood plants by three since 1968, and has seen a net decrease of three hardwood veneer plants. Of the 13 veneer plants operating during 1971, seven manufactured southern pine plywood and one produced only green pine veneer.

Arkansas forests yielded 259 million board feet of veneer logs in 1971, a 14-percent increase over 1968. Softwood logs accounted for this increase and also made up for a 20-percent decline in hardwood veneer logs. Softwoods represented 94 percent of the State's veneer log harvest in 1971. Less than 10 years ago, hardwoods accounted for all of it.

OTHER PRODUCTS

The volume of roundwood used for all other products increased by 42 percent since 1968

2

and accounted for almost 8 percent of the total harvest. Southern pine poles were the leading item in this category, with charcoal wood second. The two combined used 23 million cubic feet of wood. Another 12 million cubic feet were cut for miscellaneous products such as commercial posts, piling, furniture stock, handlestock, excelsior, miscellaneous dimension, and cooperage.

PLANT RESIDUES

In the conversion of roundwood into primary products, more than 170 million cubic feet of wood residues was generated. Two-thirds of this volume was in coarse items such as slabs, edgings, cull pieces, and other material suitable for conversion into pulp chips. The rest was comprised of finer particles such as sawdust and shavings.

Over 104 million cubic feet of such plant byproducts went into pulp. Fourteen million cubic feet were burned for domestic and industrial fuel. And 17 million cubic feet were used for miscellaneous purposes such as charcoal, animal bedding, and soil mulch.

Thus, Arkansas forest industries converted 79 percent of their wood residues into plant byproducts in 1971. The unused 35 million cubic feet was mostly fine particles with no present market. In 1968, 65 percent of residues were utilized. Decline of small sawmills, with consequently greater aggregation of residues at large sawmills with chipping equipment, explains most of the improvement in utilization.

While converting roundwood during 1971, Arkansas forest industries accumulated 1.5 million tons of bark. Somewhat less than two-thirds of this material was burned as industrial fuel or—in smaller amounts—utilized for charcoal, domestic fuel, animal bedding, and soil mulch. Over one-half million tons of bark was unused in the State.

Bark presently has little value, but a tremendous amount is generated annually. A major need is to devise ways of using it to advantage.

Table 1. *Volume of industrial roundwood, 1971*

Product	Standard units	Volume in standard units			Roundwood volume		
		All species	Softwood	Hardwood	All species	Softwood	Hardwood
					- - - - - -M cu.ft.- - - - -		
Saw logs	M bd. ft.[1]	1,341,352	919,632	421,720	221,581	151,280	70,301
Veneer logs	M bd. ft.[1]	258,581	242,323	16,258	42,590	39,862	2,728
Pulpwood	Std. cords	1,884,564	1,236,179	648,385	152,001	100,130	51,871
Piling	M linear ft.	1,142	1,142	...	855	855	...
Poles	M pieces	1,142	1,142	...	12,044	12,044	...
Posts	M pieces	7,240	7,240	...	4,065	4,065	...
Misc. products[2]	M cu. ft.	18,189	1,701	16,488	18,189	1,701	16,488
Total					451,325	309,937	141,388

[1]International 1/4-inch rule.
[2]Includes chemical wood, furntiure stock, handlestock, excelsior, cooperage, misc. dimension, mine timbers, and other industrial products.

Table 2. *Industrial roundwood, by species, 1971*

Species group	Saw logs	Veneer logs	Pulpwood	Piling	Poles	Posts	Miscellaneous products
	- - - -M bd.ft.[1]- - - -		Std. cords	M linear ft.	- -M pieces- -		M cu.ft.
Softwood:							
Pines	908,664	242,323	1,236,179	1,142	1,142	7,189	1,701
Cypress	9,895	...	...	...	...	...	...
Other softwoods	1,073	...	...	...	...	51	...
Total	919,632	242,323	1,236,179	1,142	1,142	7,240	1,701
Hardwood:							
Black and tupelo gums	61,158	4,422	[2] 221,364	...	...	...	770
Sweetgum	14,491	1,207	...	...	...	...	1,470
Red oaks	188,298	3,876	[3] 275,303	...	...	...	3,651
White oaks	74,857	2,682	...	...	...	...	3,138
Other hardwoods	82,916	4,071	151,718	...	...	...	7,459
Total	421,720	16,258	648,385	...	...	...	16,488
All species	1,341,352	258,581	1,884,564	1,142	1,142	7,240	18,189

[1]International 1/4-inch rule.
[2]Black and tupelo combined with sweetgum.
[3]Red and white oaks combined.

Table 3. *Residues produced by primary wood-using plants, 1971*

Type of industry [1]	All species			Softwood			Hardwood		
	Total	Fine[2]	Coarse[3]	Total	Fine[2]	Coarse[3]	Total	Fine[2]	Coarse[3]
	- - - - - - - - - - - - - - - - - - - -M cu.ft. - - - - - - - - - - - - - - - -								
Lumber	134,844	45,350	89,494	101,516	30,694	70,822	33,328	14,656	18,672
Veneer	20,173	840	19,333	19,113	796	18,317	1,060	44	1,016
Piling, poles, and posts	3,916	2,435	1,481	3,916	2,435	1,481	...	...	...
Miscellaneous products	11,695	6,805	4,890	869	521	348	10,826	6,284	4,542
All products	170,628	55,430	115,198	125,414	34,446	90,968	45,214	20,984	24,230

[1]Excludes woodpulp industry.
[2]Fine residues includes sawdust, screenings, and other material generally too small for chipping.
[3]Coarse residues include slabs, edgings, trimmings, and other material generally suitable for chipping.

4

Table 4. *Volume of primary plant byproducts, 1971*

Source industry[1]	Type of use	All species	Softwood	Hardwood
		- - - - - - - -M cu. ft.- - - - - -		
Lumber	Fuel[2]	13,052	9,237	3,815
	Fiber[3]	87,149	75,201	11,948
	Other[4]	12,606	8,532	4,074
	Total	112,807	92,970	19,837
Veneer	Fuel	578	422	156
	Fiber	16,953	16,085	868
	Other	2,326	2,326	...
	Total	19,857	18,833	1,024
Piling, poles,	Fuel	3	3	
and posts	Fiber	301	301	...
	Other	27	27	...
	Total	331	331	...
Miscellaneous	Fuel	442	131	311
industries	Fiber	...	...	...
	Other	2,182	68	2,114
	Total	2,624	199	2,425
All industries	Fuel	14,075	9,793	4,282
	Fiber	104,403	91,587	12,816
	Other	17,141	10,953	6,188
	Total	135,619	112,333	23,286

[1]Excludes woodpulp industry.
[2]Includes all residues used as fuel by industrial plants and domestic fuel either sold or given away.
[3]Includes all residues used in manufa ture of fiber products, such as pulp or hardboard.
[4]Includes residues used as livestock bedding, mulch, floor sweepings, and specialty items.

Table 5. *Movement of industrial roundwood, by product, 1971*

Product	Unit	Out of State receipts	Logged and remained in State	Logged and shipped out of State	Total receipts	Total production
		- - - - - - - - - - - - - - Standard units- - - - - - - - - - - - - -				
Saw logs	M bd. ft.[1]	67,106	1,317,683	23,669	1,384,789	1,341,352
Veneer	M bd. ft.[1]	52,746	258,581	...	311,327	258,581
Pulpwood	Std. cords	184,917	1,672,361	212,203	1,857,278	1,884,564
Piling	M linear ft.	4	1,142	...	1,146	1,142
Poles	M pieces	71	1,141	1	1,212	1,142
Posts	M pieces	2,921	7,202	38	10,123	7,240
Misc. products	M cu. ft.	712	18,091	98	18,803	18,189

[1]International 1/4-inch rule.

Table 6. *Saw-log production by county, 1971*

County	All species	Softwood	Hardwood	County	All species	Softwood	Hardwood
	- - - - - M bd. ft.[1] - - - - -				- - - - - M bd. ft.[1] - - - - -		
Arkansas	24,529	746	23,783	Lincoln	11,324	4,981	6,343
Ashley	18,182	2,805	15,377	Little River	22,618	19,903	2,715
				Logan	13,506	13,080	426
Baxter	1,666	376	1,290	Lonoke	5,335	15	5,320
Benton	2,268	98	2,170				
Boone	1,432	3	1,429	Madison	6,869	73	6,796
Bradley	49,073	45,202	3,871	Marion	2,361	768	1,593
				Miller	7,297	5,849	1,448
Calhoun	57,128	38,974	18,154	Mississippi	6,429	1,257	5,172
Carroll	1,296	291	1,005	Monroe	9,612	182	9,430
Chicot	1,114	6	1,108	Montgomery	19,635	19,622	13
Clark	69,115	55,452	13,663				
Clay	3,609	503	3,106	Nevada	35,929	29,207	6,722
Cleburne	2,658	1,230	1,428	Newton	7,780	3,686	4,094
Cleveland	77,206	46,648	30,558				
Columbia	19,732	16,250	3,482	Ouachita	38,249	17,608	20,641
Conway	1,133	424	709				
Craighead	2,111	265	1,846	Perry	16,822	14,781	2,041
Crawford	1,495	13	1,482	Phillips	5,451	78	5,373
Crittenden	317	...	317	Pike	53,811	51,688	2,123
Cross	2,239	...	2,239	Poinsett	3,991	13	3,978
				Polk	11,849	10,797	1,052
Dallas	60,420	45,147	15,273	Pope	16,289	12,873	3,416
Desha	17,253	1,806	15,447	Prairie	3,527	72	3,455
Drew	13,080	2,126	10,954	Pulaski	19,869	16,651	3,218
Faulkner	1,379	370	1,009	Randolph	4,787	108	4,679
Franklin	5,816	1,978	3,838				
Fulton	377	...	377	St. Francis	4,204	42	4,162
				Saline	24,193	20,457	3,736
Garland	11,064	10,705	359	Scott	26,357	24,577	1,780
Grant	78,032	54,963	23,069	Searcy	12,409	5,531	6,878
Greene	692	102	590	Sebastian	707	707	...
				Sevier	22,453	16,942	5,511
Hempstead	27,526	24,396	3,130	Sharp	1,783	...	1,783
Hot Spring	43,373	39,211	4,162	Stone	12,111	2,989	9,122
Howard	98,230	94,995	3,235				
				Union	79,974	56,972	23,002
Independence	2,620	189	2,431				
Izard	5,370	2,100	3,270	Van Buren	4,948	1,950	2,998
Jackson	1,615	127	1,488	Washington	3,148	...	3,148
Jefferson	12,979	7,940	5,039	White	12,314	380	11,934
Johnson	10,074	6,714	3,360	Woodruff	10,280	538	9,742
Lafayette	12,976	10,579	2,397	Yell	50,826	49,328	1,498
Lawrence	8,449	3,172	5,277				
Lee	4,677	21	4,656	All counties	1,341,352	919,632	421,720

[1] International 1/4-inch rule.

Table 7. *Sawlog movement, 1971*

County [1]	Logged and remained in county	Outgoing shipments	Incoming shipments	Total log receipts
	- - - - -*Million board feet*[2] - - - -			
Arkansas	6,036	18,493	1,066	7,102
Baxter	671	995	...	671
Benton	2,086	182	980	3,066
Boone	295	1,137	188	483
Bradley	21,580	27,493	76,179	97,759
Carroll	798	498	7	805
Clark	40,859	28,256	27,414	68,273
Cleburne	2,658	...	3,954	6,612
Cleveland	15,174	62,032	5,555	20,729
Columbia	13,741	5,991	19,850	33,591
Conway	170	963	30	200
Crawford	30	1,465	496	526
Dallas	16,238	44,182	26,840	43,078
Drew	12,452	628	676	13,128
Franklin	580	5,236	3	583
Grant	57,011	21,021	62,898	119,909
Hempstead	6,728	20,798	3,827	10,555
Hot Spring	10,621	32,752	17,301	27,922
Howard	93,431	4,799	34,159	127,590
Independence	2,620	...	8,326	10,946
Izard	4,780	590	4,411	9,191
Johnson	7,616	2,458	2,659	10,275
Lawrence	4,554	3,895	1,780	6,334
Little River	4,676	17,942	5,292	9,968
Lonoke	5,223	112	1,636	6,859
Madison	4,451	2,418	5,731	10,182
Marion	712	1,649	6	718
Miller	4,693	2,604	5,284	9,977

Table 7. *Sawlog movement, 1971* (Continued)

County[1]	Logged and remained in county	Outgoing shipments	Incoming shipments	Total log receipts
	- - - - - Million board feet[2] - - - -			
Monroe	8,805	807	8,920	17,725
Montgomery	9,793	9,842	12,398	22,191
Nevada	16,669	19,260	42,982	59,651
Newton	3,894	3,886	1,566	5,460
Ouachita	26,164	12,085	39,861	66,025
Phillips	4,963	488	6,469	11,432
Pike	17,507	36,304	14,552	32,059
Polk	6,353	5,496	10,890	17,243
Pope	14,681	1,608	11,816	26,497
Pulaski	2,878	16,992	13,653	16,531
Randolph	3,999	788	111	4,110
St. Francis	2,990	1,214	5,023	8,013
Saline	11,418	12,775	7,249	18,667
Scott	18,796	7,561	9,256	28,052
Searcy	12,409	...	5,680	18,089
Sevier	5,669	16,784	49	5,718
Sharp	1,008	775	84	1,092
Stone	7,948	4,163	1,195	9,143
Union	76,904	3,070	81,482	158,386
Van Buren	2,322	2,626	85	2,407
Washington	2,902	246	2,439	5,341
White	10,116	2,198	...	10,116
Yell	39,056	11,770	14,858	53,914
All other counties	49,089	165,208	80,806	129,895
Total	696,817	644,535	687,972	1,384,789

[1] Counties with less than three plants are omitted.
[2] International 1/4-inch rule

8

Table 8. *Round pulpwood production, 1971*

County [1]	All species	Softwood	Hardwood	County [1]	All species	Softwood	Hardwood
	- - - *Standard cords* - - -				- - - *Standard cords* - - -		
Arkansas	4	4	...	Logan	9,713	8,834	879
Ashley	91,025	51,631	39,394	Lonoke	2,628	12	2,616
Boone	3	3	...	Miller	26,845	18,012	8,833
Bradley	26,072	13,368	12,704	Mississippi	1,039	...	1,039
				Monroe	3	...	3
Calhoun	88,497	64,409	24,088	Montgomery	18,143	14,809	3,334
Chicot	7,456	...	7,456				
Clark	69,615	46,457	23,158	Nevada	92,492	77,647	14,845
Cleburne	21,469	19,025	2,444	Newton	8	8	...
Cleveland	57,475	29,682	27,793				
Columbia	71,324	57,480	13,844	Ouachita	76,238	53,930	22,308
Conway	25,779	20,166	5,613				
Crawford	3,589	720	2,869	Perry	11,679	10,111	1,568
Crittenden	721	...	721	Phillips	3,797	...	3,797
				Pike	52,771	43,817	8,954
Dallas	100,241	59,310	40,931	Polk	28,422	23,959	4,463
Desha	18,143	11	18,132	Pope	22,295	18,714	3,581
Drew	100,775	50,430	50,345	Prairie	23	...	23
				Pulaski	14,000	6,392	7,608
Faulkner	257	...	257				
Franklin	2,370	2,005	365	St. Francis	7	4	3
				Saline	44,168	27,806	16,362
Garland	12,904	9,560	3,344	Scott	13,007	11,826	1,181
Grant	126,285	62,801	63,484	Searcy	8	4	4
				Sebastian	880	750	130
Hempstead	56,450	45,566	10,884	Sevier	37,920	22,016	15,904
Hot Spring	60,609	37,539	23,070	Stone	1,375	1,200	175
Howard	43,042	33,118	9,924				
				Union	171,958	120,829	51,129
Independence	7,587	3,878	3,709				
Izard	2,725	2,264	461	Van Buren	19,298	16,578	2,720
Jackson	828	78	750	White	12,251	1,626	10,625
Jefferson	55,467	33,505	21,962	Woodruff	65	10	55
Johnson	14,546	10,395	4,151				
				Yell	30,346	23,022	7,324
Lafayette	57,213	43,943	13,270				
Lee	3,902	24	3,878				
Lincoln	24,083	7,269	16,814	All counties	1,884,564	1,236,179	648,385
Little River	42,729	29,622	13,107				

[1]Counties with no pulpwood production are omitted.

9

Table 9. *Veneer-log production by county, 1971*

County[1]	All species	County[1]	All species
	M. bd. ft.[2]		M. bd. ft.[2]
Arkansas	758	Lee	102
Ashley	107,087	Lincoln	153
		Little River	17,511
Bradley	4,597	Lonoke	613
Calhoun	17,145	Nevada	615
Clark	9,219		
Cleveland	21,182	Ouachita	2,794
Columbia	615		
		Perry	306
Dallas	27,936	Phillips	692
Drew	3,978	Pike	1,644
		Polk	615
Faulkner	306	Pulaski	613
Grant	3,751	St. Francis	45
		Saline	1,534
Hempstead	1,056	Sevier	1,644
Hot Spring	615		
Howard	15,128	Union	15,254
Jefferson	1,073	Total	258,581

[1]Counties with negligible output are omitted.
[2]International 1/4-inch rule.

Table 10. *Piling production by county, 1971*

County[1]	All species (softwood)	County	All species (softwood)
	M linear feet		M linear feet
Clark	10	Ouachita	
Cleveland	28		
		Pike	5
Dallas	15	Pulaski	200
Garland	200	Saline	200
Grant	221		
		Union	10
Hot Spring	200		
		Yell	22
Jefferson	20		
Lincoln	4	Total	1,142

[1]Counties with negligible output are omitted.

Table 11. *Pole production by county, 1971*

County[1]	All species (softwood)	County[1]	All species (softwood)
	M pieces		M pieces
Cleburne	60	Ouachita	1
Cleveland	156		
		Perry	7
Dallas	54	Pike	33
		Polk	90
Grant	119		
		Scott	203
Hot Spring	26	Sevier	55
Howard	98	Stone	18
Jefferson	112	Union	2
Johnson	10		
		Yell	33
Lincoln	22		
Little River	4		
Logan	39	Total	1,142

[1] Counties with negligible output are omitted.

Table 12. *Commercial post production by county, 1971*

County[1]	All species (softwood)	County[1]	All species (softwood)
	M pieces		M pieces
Baxter	33	Nevada	25
Boone	30	Newton	17
Bradley	106		
		Ouachita	30
Carroll	6		
Clark	90	Perry	100
Cleburne	280	Pike	40
Columbia	3	Polk	2,512
Crawford	4	Pope	17
Franklin	18	Scott	1,766
Fulton	65	Searcy	50
		Sevier	108
Hot Spring	40	Stone	63
Howard	370		
		Union	11
Izard	196		
		Van Buren	30
Johnson	423		
		Yell	519
Logan	167		
Marion	11		
Montgomery	110	Total	7,240

[1] Counties with negligible output are omitted.

Table 13. *Output of miscellaneous products by county, 1971*

County[1]	All species	Softwood	Hardwood	County[1]	All species	Softwood	Hardwood
	- - - M cubic feet- - -				- - -M cubic feet- - -		
Arkansas	40	...	40	Logan	955	...	955
				Lonoke	15	...	15
Benton	14	...	14				
Boone	897	...	897	Madison	2,793	...	2,793
Bradley	10	...	10	Marion	4	...	4
				Mississippi	5	...	5
Calhoun	7	...	7	Monroe	489	...	489
Carroll	2,120	...	2,120	Montgomery	137	92	45
Clark	635	599	36				
Clay	7	...	7	Nevada	77	19	58
Cleburne	16	...	16	Newton	3,460	...	3,460
Cleveland	82	...	82				
Columbia	28	...	28	Ouachita	62	...	62
Craighead	84	...	84				
Crawford	12	...	12	Phillips	94	...	94
Cross	52	...	52	Pike	29	...	29
				Poinsett	20	...	20
Dallas	404	26	378	Polk	445	445	...
Desha	28	...	28	Prairie	352	...	352
Drew	7		7	Pulaski	168	61	107
Faulkner	342	...	342	Randolph	170	...	170
Franklin	1,016	47	969				
				St. Francis	93	...	93
Garland	34	15	19	Saline	55	23	32
Grant	203	15	188	Scott	772	2	770
Greene	68	...	68	Searcy	323	14	309
				Sebastian	43	35	8
Hempstead	37	...	37	Sevier	28	...	28
Hot Spring	330	199	131	Stone	64	...	64
Howard	28	...	28				
				Union	-		-
Independence	14	...	14				
Izard	14	...	14	Van Buren	.	...	.
Jackson	4	...	4	Washington	234	49	185
Jefferson	258	60	198	White	161	...	161
Johnson	24	...	24	Woodruff	272	...	272
Lafayette	7		7	Yell	8	...	8
Lawrence	7		7				
Lee	22	...	22				
				All counties	18,189	1,701	16,488

[1]Counties with negligible output are omitted.

Table 14. *Industrial roundwood production by county, 1971*

County	All species	Softwood	Hardwood	County	All species	Softwood	Hardwood
	- - - M cubic feet- - -				- - - M cubic feet - - -		
Arkansas	4,254	123	4,131	Lincoln	4,071	1,643	2,428
Ashley	27,974	22,259	5,715	Little River	10,096	8,521	1,575
				Logan	4,469	3,372	1,097
Baxter	296	81	215	Lonoke	1,218	4	1,214
Benton	391	16	375				
Boone	1,153	18	1,135	Madison	3,938	12	3,926
Bradley	11,021	8,578	2,443	Marion	402	132	270
				Miller	3,369	2,421	948
Calhoun	19,410	14,386	5,024	Mississippi	1,157	207	950
Carroll	2,339	51	2,288	Monroe	2,091	30	2,061
Chicot	782	1	781	Montgomery	4,896	4,582	314
Clark	19,225	15,058	4,167				
Clay	607	83	524	Nevada	13,594	11,228	2,366
Cleburne	2,983	2,533	450	Newton	4,759	617	4,142
Cleveland	22,629	15,191	7,438				
Columbia	9,148	7,432	1,716	Ouachita	13,049	7,761	5,288
Conway	2,270	1.703	567				
Craighead	436	44	392	Perry	3,898	3,381	517
Crawford	552	63	489	Phillips	1,423	13	1,410
Crittenden	110	...	110	Pike	13,797	12,624	1,173
Cross	425	...	425	Poinsett	685	2	683
				Polk	7,152	6,619	533
Dallas	23,634	17,435	6,199	Pope	4,499	3,643	856
Desha	4,351	298	4,053	Prairie	942	12	930
Drew	10,957	4,711	6,246	Pulaski	4,823	3,468	1,355
Faulkner	643	61	582	Randolph	968	18	950
Franklin	2,183	545	1,638				
Fulton	100	37	63	St.Francis	801	7	794
				Saline	8,010	5,892	2,118
Garland	3,047	2,700	347	Scott	9,288	8,127	1,161
Grant	25,294	16,021	9,273	Searcy	2,408	952	1,456
Greene	184	17	167	Sebastian	230	212	18
				Sevier	7,702	5,409	2,293
Hempstead	9,309	7,805	1,504	Sharp	297	...	297
Hot Spring	12,912	10,242	2,670	Stone	2,409	810	1,599
Howard	23,402	21,967	1,435				
				Union	29,635	21,703	7,932
Independence	1,061	345	716				
Izard	1,236	640	596	Van Buren	2,401	1,681	720
Jackson	339	27	312	Washington	759	49	710
Jefferson	8,251	5,276	2,975	White	3,195	194	3,001
Johnson	3,205	2,289	916	Woodruff	1,990	89	1,901
Lafayette	6,768	5,300	1,468	Yell	11,483	10,639	844
Lawrence	1,409	522	887				
Lee	1,131	5	1,126	All counties	451,325	309,937	141,388

13

Table 15. *Plant byproducts by county, 1971*

County[1]	All species		Softwood		Hardwood	
	Fine	Coarse	Fine	Coarse	Fine	Coarse
- - - - - - - - -M cubic feet- - - - - - - - -						
Arkansas	...	219	...	1	....	218
Ashley	675	9,043	376	8,649	299	394
Baxter	5	16	...	...	5	16
Benton	92	71	3	4	89	67
Boone	26	131	...	...	26	131
Bradley	2,974	6,489	2,100	4,888	874	1,601
Carroll	22	25	7	7	15	18
Clark	1,484	6,141	968	5,138	516	1,003
Cleburne	38	194	15	55	23	139
Cleveland	...	390	...	216	...	174
Columbia	893	2,088	893	2,084	...	4
Conway	2	3	1	...	1	3
Craighead	45	69	3	5	42	64
Crawford	22	11	4	1	18	10
Cross	59	45	...	...	59	45
Dallas	873	6,536	781	6,239	92	297
Drew	439	646	69	160	370	486
Faulkner	...	5	...	...	...	5
Franklin	276	210	16	13	260	197
Garland	900	2,095	898	2,094	2	1
Grant	3,343	7,898	2,916	6,807	427	1,091
Greene	3	35	...	2	3	33
Hempstead	433	841	321	748	112	93
Hot Spring	754	1,894	754	1,894	...	...
Howard	3,716	10,178	3,710	9,743	6	435
Independence	7	480	2	399	5	81
Izard	41	316	10	270	31	46
Jefferson	626	1,443	616	1,436	10	7
Johnson	3	529	1	521	2	8
Lawrence	...	12	...	...	...	12
Little River	154	479	154	479	...	...
Logan	276	824	1	640	275	184

Table 15. *Plant byproducts by county, 1971* (Continued)

County[1]	All species		Softwood		Hardwood	
	Fine	Coarse	Fine	Coarse	Fine	Coarse
	- - - - - - - - M cubic feet- - - - - - - -					
Madison	671	424	2	...	669	424
Marion	...	1	...	...	...	1
Miller	158	538	158	374	...	164
Monroe	555	740	5	13	550	727
Montgomery	457	1,400	457	1,400	...	...
Nevada	1,749	4,085	1,749	4,082	...	3
Newton	4	121	...	...	4	121
Ouachita	720	2,433	346	1,592	374	841
Phillips	6	534	...	2	6	532
Pike	873	2,024	873	2,024	...	...
Polk	670	1,398	666	1,376	4	22
Pope	732	1,644	705	1,625	27	19
Prairie	...	221	...	7	...	214
Pulaski	286	752	38	143	248	609
Randolph	9	14	...	...	9	14
St. Francis	80	185	...	...	80	185
Saline	442	1,275	435	1,258	7	17
Scott	554	1,898	363	1,745	191	153
Searcy	74	671	25	147	49	524
Sevier	32	440	32	315	...	125
Sharp	3	4	...	...	3	4
Stone	576	655	...	...	576	655
Union	4,314	12,045	3,742	10,742	572	1,303
Washington	195	231	14	9	181	222
White	64	206	1	11	63	195
Woodruff	...	5	...	...	...	5
Yell	1,558	4,690	1,504	4,625	54	65
All other counties	1,282	3,384	747	1,869	535	1,515
Total	34,245	101,374	26,481	85,852	7,764	15,522

[1] Omitted counties have either negligible volume or less than three plants.

15

Table 16. *Unused plant residues by county, 1971*

County[1]	All species		Softwood		Hardwood	
	Fine	Coarse	Fine	Coarse	Fine	Coarse
			- - - - - - - *M cubic feet* - - - - - - -			
Arkansas	245	97	2	3	243	94
Baxter	17	11	...	...	17	11
Benton	38	79	23	10	15	69
Boone	397	161	36	20	361	161
Bradley	138	187	87	122	51	65
Carroll	215	151	2	6	213	145
Clark	956	16	624	16	332	...
Cleburne	312	205	205	175	107	30
Cleveland	690	446	126	...	564	446
Columbia	145	180	...	...	145	180
Conway	5	6	1	2	4	4
Craighead	40	13	1	1	39	12
Crawford	1	15	...	5	1	10
Cross	...	39	...	...	...	39
Dallas	1,800	1,486	1,013	591	787	895
Faulkner	98	63	...	...	98	63
Franklin	19	16	2	3	17	13
Garland	...	2	...	...	...	2
Grant	538	92	64	46	474	46
Greene	59	49	4	5	55	44
Hempstead	30	4	1	2	29	2
Hot Spring	136	79	91	22	45	57
Howard	383	165	58	67	325	98
Independence	345	150	212	61	133	89
Izard	268	230	210	164	58	66
Jefferson	68	45	...	...	68	45
Johnson	330	131	261	46	69	85
Lawrence	209	250	...	...	209	250
Little River	165	144	93	54	72	90
Logan	276	4	274	1	2	3
Lonoke	227	284	1	1	226	283
Madison	100	336	1	4	99	332

16

Table 16. *Unused plant residues by county, 1971* (Continued)

County[1]	All species		Softwood		Hardwood	
	Fine	Coarse	Fine	Coarse	Fine	Coarse
	— — — — — — — -M cubic feet - — — — — — —					
Marion	26	31	14	18	12	13
Miller	161	50	10	16	151	34
Monroe	56	60	1	...	55	60
Montgomery	277	218	268	200	9	18
Nevada	88	107	44	55	44	52
Newton	3,602	2,391	25	36	3,577	2,355
Ouachita	1,369	1,683	1,029	1,591	340	92
Phillips	428	154	3	5	425	149
Pike	196	269	101	149	95	120
Polk	642	423	592	375	50	48
Pope	97	151	46	72	51	79
Prairie	335	136	9	13	326	123
Pulaski	435	434	220	178	215	256
Randolph	229	224	...	...	229	224
St. Francis	243	186	4	6	239	180
Saline	145	34	110	2	35	32
Scott	908	384	839	321	69	63
Searcy	547	282	178	261	369	21
Sevier	655	92	516	44	139	48
Sharp	33	41	...	...	33	41
Stone	86	161	56	80	30	81
Union	764	465	36	38	728	427
Van Buren	137	178	48	67	89	111
Washington	1	3	...	...	1	3
White	272	229	8	4	264	225
Woodruff	10	4	...	...	10	4
Yell	259	82	255	73	4	9
All other counties	934	196	161	85	773	111
Total	21,185	13,824	7,965	5,116	13,220	8,708

[1]Omitted counties have either negligible volume or less than three plants.

Table 17. *Bark used by county, 1971*

County[1]	All species	Softwood	Hardwood	County[1]	All species	Softwood	Hardwood
		- - - - - -*Tons*- - - - - -				- - - - - -*Tons*- - - - - -	
Ashley	152,301	103,268	49,033	Madison	8,818	...	8,818
				Marion	119	97	22
Baxter	144	...	144				
Benton	865	32	833	Nevada	21,027	20,991	36
Boone	11,997	1,845	10,152	Newton	5,574	...	5,574
Bradley	4,627	487	4,140				
				Ouachita	267,413	137,059	130,354
Carroll	103	57	46				
Clark	11,466	9,298	2,168	Phillips	1,016	...	1.016
Columbia	5,527	5,480	47	Pike	10,400	10,400	...
Conway	35,444	29,592	5,852	Polk	3,418	3,037	381
Craighead	902	41	861	Pope	8,648	8,382	266
Crawford	641	7	634	Pulaski	4,750	513	4,237
Cross	346	...	346				
				Randolph	31	...	31
Dallas	26,706	25,478	1,228				
				St. Francis	746	5	741
Faulkner	72	3	69	Saline	5,200	5,126	74
Franklin	378	37	341	Scott	3,036	2,666	370
				Searcy	563	195	368
Garland	10,765	10,765	...	Sevier	25,334	25,334	...
Grant	29,945	28,047	1,898	Sharp	50	...	50
Greene	394	12	382	Stone	2,630	...	2,630
Hempstead	4,003	3,845	158	Union	61,002	51,337	9,665
Hot Spring	9,740	9,740	...				
Howard	53,446	50,196	3,250	Washington	1,360	457	903
				White	1,941	23	1,918
Independence	1,566	...	1,566	Woodruff	2	...	2
Izard	866	222	644				
				Yell	9,227	8,338	889
Jefferson	14,130	13,111	1,019				
Johnson	24	1	23	All other			
				counties	16,920	1,148	15,772
Lawrence	165	...	165				
Little River	68,744	50,383	18,361	Total	911,739	617,055	294,684
Logan	7,207	...	7,207				

[1]Omitted counties have either negligible volume or
less than three plants.

18

Table 18. *Bark unused by county, 1971*

County[1]	All species	Softwood	Hardwood	County[1]	All species	Softwood	Hardwood
	- - - - - -Tons- - - - - -				- - - - - -Tons- - - - - -		
Arkansas	6,962	20	6,942	Madison	566	31	535
Ashley	5,057	...	5,057	Marion	284	98	186
				Miller	4,593	2,019	2,574
Baxter	241	...	241	Monroe	10,614	67	10,547
Benton	2,985	1,975	1,010	Montgomery	9,285	9,103	182
Boone	9,557	1,210	8,347				
Bradley	41,430	26,079	15,351	Nevada	1,646	919	727
				Newton	2,571	281	2,290
Carroll	605	73	532				
Clark	36,162	23,967	12,195	Ouachita	105,179	57,436	47,743
Cleburne	8,291	6,067	2,224				
Cleveland	11,063	1,510	9,553	Phillips	7,114	38	7,076
Columbia	7,718	5,232	2,486	Pike	2,876	1,214	1,662
Conway	3,997	3,304	693	Polk	25,376	24,781	595
Craighead	2,788	4	2,784	Pope	1,671	567	1,104
Crawford	204	58	146	Prairie	3,677	102	3,575
Cross	722	...	722	Pulaski	19,198	5,802	13,396
Dallas	46,810	32,910	13,900	Randolph	2,481	2	2,479
Drew	7,078	831	6,247				
				St. Francis	4,423	42	4,381
Faulkner	1,080	...	1,080	Slaine	2,048	1,456	592
Franklin	197	23	174	Scott	24,738	23,871	867
				Searcy	9,123	2,383	6,740
Garland	36	...	36	Sevier	2,971	559	2,412
Grant	21,715	8,858	12,857	Sharp	578	...	578
Greene	618	36	582	Stone	8,901	625	8,276
Hempstead	39	11	28	Union	18,316	5,907	12,409
Hot Spring	800	4	796				
Howard	4,776	1,228	3,548	Van Buren	2,212	657	1,555
Independence	4,860	2,530	2,330	Washington	2,276	...	2,276
Izard	4,580	3,668	912	White	3,817	79	3,738
				Woodruff	75	...	75
Jefferson	5,929	5,909	20				
Johnson	5,024	3,815	1,209	Yell	16,500	16,378	122
Lawrence	3,586	...	3,586	All other			
Little River	11,929	8,631	3,298	counties	24,085	9,734	14,351
Logan	3,348	3,296	52				
Lonoke	3,942	6	3,936	Total	581,323	305,406	275,917

[1] Omitted counties have either negligible volume or less than three plants.

19

Table 19. *Large sawmills*[1]

County	Firm	Plant Location	Plant Address[2]
Arkansas	C. P. Chaney Sawmill, Inc.[3]	Dewitt	Box 271
Ashley	P. E. Barnes Lumber Co.[3]	Hamburg	Rt. 3, Box 7
Bradley	Potlatch Forests, Inc.[3]	Warren	Box 390
Calhoun	Hampton Lumber Co.[3]	Hampton	Rt. 1, Fordyce
Chicot	J. H. Hamlen & Sons	Eudora	Box X
Clark	Barksdale Lumber Co.[3] J. A. Barringer & Sons[3] Johnnie & Curt Bean Lumber Co.[3] Milus Bean Lumber Co.[3] Daily Lumber Co.[3] Frizzell Lumber Co.[3] Gurdon Lumber Co.[3] Gurdon Lumber Co.[3]	Amity Whelen Springs Amity Amity Arkadelphia Gurdon Beirne Gurdon	 Box 56, Gurdon Box 97 Sparkman Box 207 Box 8 Box 160
Clay	J. W. Black Lumber Co.[3]	Corning	Box 107
Cleburne	Olivette Supply Co.[3]	Greers Ferry	Rt. 3, Higden
Cleveland	Kingsland Lumber Co., Inc.[3] Saline Hardwood Co.[3]	Kingsland Rison	Box 6
Columbia	Arkansas-Louisiana Lumber Co., Inc.[3] Magnolia Lumber Co., Inc.[3]	Emerson Magnolia	Box 286 Box 218
Crittenden	Dacus Lumber Co.	West Memphis	1105 North Missouri
Dallas	D. J. Barnes Lumber Co.[3] E. L. Bruce Co., Inc. Sparkman Lumber Co.[3]	Fordyce Fordyce Sparkman	Rt. 1 Box 312 North Commerce
Drew	J. P. Price Lumber Co.[3] Selma Timber Co.[3]	Monticello Selma	Box 536 Rt. 2, Box 62, Tillar
Garland	Bates Lumber Co.[3] B. G. Wilson Lumber Co., Inc.[3]	Hot Springs Hot Springs	Box 1265 Rt. 6, Box 515
Grant	John O. Brown Sawmill & Logging[3] A. L. English Mill[3] W. S. Fox & Sons[3] H. G. Toler & Son Lumber Co., Inc.[3] J. L. Williams & Son, Inc.[3] Herman Wilson Lumber Co.[3]	Sheridan Sheridan Sheridan Leola Sheridan Leola	Rt. 2, Box 17 C Rt. 4, Box 350 300 Long Bell Box 125 Box 68 Box 95
Hempstead	Hempstead Manufacturing Co.[3]	Hope	Box F
Hot Spring	Hot Spring County Lumber Co.[3]	Malvern	Box 158
Howard	Clearcreek Tie Co. J. D. Scott Lumber Co.[3] Weyerhaeuser Co., Dierks City Plant[3]	Nashville Nashville Dierks	Box 239 Box 98
Independence	Hiway Lumber Co.[3]	Batesville	Box 206
Izard	Hayes Bros. Lumber Co.	Calico Rock	Box 196
Jackson	Curtner Lumber Co.[3]	Newport	Box 617
Jefferson	W. S. Fox & Sons[3]	Pine Bluff	West 6th
Johnson	Ozark Box & Crating Co.[3]	Clarksville	Box 321
Lafayette	Fuller Lumber Co.[3]	Lewisville	
Lincoln	Floyds Sawmill, Inc.[3]	Star City	Box 36
Little River	Gunter Bros. Lumber Co.[3]	Wilton	
Logan	Simmons Lumber Co.[3]	Booneville	Box 398
Miller	Jones Lumber Co. Junkin Lumber Co., Inc.[3]	Texarkana Texarkana	Box 954 Box 59
Monroe	Potlatch Forests, Inc.[3]	Clarendon	
Montgomery	Arkansas Wood Products Co. Killian Lumber Co.[3] Scott Lumber Co.[3]	Norman Norman Mt. Ida	Fordyce Box 98 Box 275
Nevada	Potlatch Forests, Inc.[3]	Prescott	
Ouachita	Bearden Lumber Co., Inc.[3] Chidester Lumber Co.[3] Reynolds-White Lumber Co[3] Rogers Lumber Co., Inc.[3] Yellow Pine Lumber Co., Inc.[3]	Bearden Chidester Cullendale Camden Stephens	Box 155 Box 8 Box 366, Camden Rt. 3, Box 213 Box 486

20

Table 19. *Large sawmills*[1] (Continued)

County	Firm	Plant	
		Location	Address[2]
Perry	C. J. Pierce Lumber Co.[3]	Perry	
	B. H. Satterfield Mill	Perryville	Rt. 2
Phillips	Chicago Mill & Lumber Co.[3]	West Helena	Box 2517
	Faust Band Sawmill, Inc.[3]	West Helena	Box T
Pike	Murfreesboro Lumber Co.[3]	Murfreesboro	Box 338
Polk	Hatton Lumber Co.[3]	Hatton	
	Dale Rodgers Lumber Co.[3]	Mena	Box 232
Pope	Bibler Bros. Lumber & Supply Co., Inc.[3]	Russellville	Box 490
Prairie	Miller-Patterson Lumber & Timber, Inc.[3]	Des Arc	Box 310
Pulaski	J. H. Hamlen & Son, Inc.[3]	Little Rock	Box 327
	Koppers Co.	North Little Rock	Box 3185
	Pennington & Williams Sawmill Co.	Perryville	Rt. 2
Saline	Floyd Brown Lumber Co.[3]	Hensley	Rt. 1, Box 38
	Holicer & Jones-Lumber Co.[3]	Benton	Box 208
Scott	Big Pine Lumber Co.[3]	Waldron	Box 248
	Didier Lumber Co.[3]	Mansfield	Rt. 2, Box 190, Fort Smith
	Scott County Lumber Co.[3]	Waldron	Drawer G
	Waldron Lumber Co.	Waldron	
Searcy	Buffalo River Flooring Co.[3]	Marshall	Box 386
	Treadwell Lumber Co.	Morning Star	Marshall
Stone	Branscum & Harness Sawmill	Mountain View	Marshall
Union	Anthony Forest Products Co.[3]	Urbana	
	E. L. Bruce Co., Inc.[3]	Junction City	Box 370
	Calion Lumber Co.[3]	Calion	Box 348
	Georgia-Pacific Corp.[3]	Eldorado	Box 1511
	Gunnell Mill	New Hope	Rt. 5, Box 210, Magnolia
	Lewisville Flooring Co.[3]	Strong	Box 267
	Olinkraft Sawmill[3]	Huttig	Box 317
	Watson-Davis Lumber Co.	Mt. Holly	Box 122
White	Fred Beaman Sawmill	Searcy	Box 21
Yell	Deltic Farm & Timber Co.[3]	Ola	
	Plainview Lumber Co.[3]	Plainview	Box 156
	Wilson Wood Lumber Co., Inc.[3]	Ola	Box 194

[1]Output of 3 million board feet or more.
[2]Office address specified when different from plant location.
[3]Produced chips for sale to pulpmills.

Table 20. *Small sawmills*[1]

County	Firm	Plant	
		Location	Address[2]
Arkansas	A. G. Yarbrough Sawmill #1	Dewitt	Rt. 1, Humphrey
	A. G. Yarbrough Sawmill #2	Casscee	Rt. 1, Humphrey
Baxter	Alfred Lawson	Shady Grove	Rt. 2, Mountain Home
	H. L. Pool Mill	Mountain Home	Rt. 1
	Dave Tucker Mill	Gassville	
Benton	Ted DeGroff Sawmill	Bestwater	Rt. 4, Rogers
	J. G. Forriester	Gravette	Rt. 3
	Hurshel Keith	Hiwasse	Rt. 1
	Means & Eversole	Rogers	Box 183
	Jack Loyd	Bentonville	Rt. 2
	W. R. Moore	Springdale	Benton
	Ozark Hardwood Co.	Rogers	Box 423
	Elmer Rusher	Rogers	
	Chester Scott	Highfill	Rt. 1, Gentry
	Sullivan Sawmill	Highfill	Rt. 1, Siloam Springs
	Howard Todd	Gravette	Rt. 3
	James Todd	Sulphur Springs	
	Don W. Webb	Gravette	
	White & Haden	Healing Springs	Rt. 2, Bentonville
Boone	N. B. Cantwell	Alpena	
	Kenneth Greenhaw	Harrison	Rt. 2
	Schaeffer Tie & Lumber	Omaha	Box 66
Bradley	Braham-Sevier Co.	Banks	Box 471, Fordyce
Carroll	Dale Buell Lumber Co.	Green Forest	
	Lepley Sawmill	Dry Fork	Rt. 3, Berryville
	Andrew McNeill Sawmill	Eureka Springs	Rt. 1
	Carroll Minick Sawmill	Green Forest	Rt. 3
	Gary Morrell Sawmill	Eureka Springs	Rt. 1
	J. E. Parker Sawmill	Grandview	Rt. 5, Berryville
	Homer Price Sawmill	Eureka Springs	Rt. 1
	Ted Scates Sawmill	Eureka Springs	Rt. 1
	Troy Sietz Sawmill	Berryville	Rt. 3
	Joe Wilson Sawmill	Metalton	Rt. 4, Huntsville
Clark	Billy McKa Hardwood Mill[3]	Arkadelphia	Box 474
Clay	Octo Smith Sawmill	Corning	409 N. Hope
Cleburne	Cleburne County Post Co.	Herber Springs	Rt. 3, Box 53
	Martin Lumber Co.	Concord	
	Randy Smith Mill	Greers Ferry	Edgemont
	Lisle Turney Sawmill	Quitman	Box 3
Cleveland	Troy Miller Tie Co.	Kingsland	Rt, 1, Box 199
Columbia	H. F. Efird	Village	R. 2, Box 449, Camden
	S. L. Smith Sawmill	Waldo	Box 191
	Tucker Lumber Co.	Taylor	Box 515, Springhill, La.
	Frank E. Williams Lumber Co.	Macedonia	Box 715, Springhill, La.
Conway	Aurbon Heflin Sawmill	Atkins	Rt. 3
	Willie T. Howard Sawmill	Jerusalem	Star Route, Hattieville
	E. E. Vaughn Sawmill	Jerusalem	Rt. 3, Atkins
Craighead	Slavens Sawmill	Jonesboro	Rt. 2, Bono
	Tinsley Sawmill	Jonesboro	Box 1166
Crawford	Ben Brewers Sawmill	Mulberry	Rt. 2
	M. C. Hopkins Sawmill	Natural Dam	
	Glenn Kimes Sawmill	Chester	
	Southwestern Manufacturing Co.	Van Buren	113 Lafayette St.
Cross	Roy Richardson & Son	Wynne	Box 124
	J. H. Sherman Mill	Wynne	Rt. 1
Dallas	Homer & Gean Brazeale Sawmill	Sparkman	Rt. 1
	Henry Draper Mill	Willow	Rt. 2, Box 240, Malvern
	Garland Gaston Mill[3]	Sparkman	
	Dale Givens Sawmill	Sparkman	Rt. 1
	Henry Jackson Sawmill	Manning	Box 22
	Tedsco	Fordyce	Box 471
Drew	Herman Wilson Lumber Co.[3]	Monticello	Box 577
Faulkner	Fred Aycock Sawmill	Mayflower	
	B.B. Heffington Sawmill	Vilonia	815 Arum St., Conway
Franklin	John Gosset	Ozark	
	James Jones Sawmill	Cass	Star Route 1, Ozark
	Everett Owen Sawmill	Ozark	Rt. 2
	Gavin Patterson Sawmill	Mulberry	Rt. 2, Box 241
	O. B. Sturdivant Sawmill	Ozark	Star Route 2

22

Table 20. *Small sawmills*[1] (Continued)

County	Firm	Plant Location	Plant Address[2]
Fulton	Edward Baldridge Mill	Hardy	Rt. 1
	Bill McCradic Mill	Mammoth Spring	Rt. 2
Grant	Donald Davis Sawmill	Poyen	
	S. W. Main Mill	Sheridan	Rt. 3, Box 200A
	Walker Lumber Co.	Poyen	Rt. 1, Malvern
Greene	Cox Sawmill	Paragould	Rt. 7
	Cupples Sawmill	Marmaduke	Box 131
Hempstead	Lester Fincher Lumber Co.	Washington	Rt. 1
	Verdo Hollis Sawmill	Patmos	
Hot Spring	H. A. Chandler	Glen Rose	Rt. 3, Box 346, Malvern
	Kidder Lumber Co.	Malvern	Box 115
	James Tuggle	Glen Rose	Rt. 3, Malvern
Howard	Cohen Davis Tie Mill	Athens	
	Foag Lumber Co.	Dierks	Hwy. 70 W, DeQueen
	Doyle Tollett Lumber Co.	Athens	
	Terry Wax Sawmill	Dierks	Gillham
Independence	Benton Hardwood Inc.	Batesville	Box 21
	Alfred Heyde Mill	Cord	
	Wesley Hipp Lumber Co.	Batesville	Hwy 14 W.
	C. E. Trotter Sawmill	Batesville	Newport Rt.
Izard	Carl Bailey Mill	Sidney	
	Bandmill Gin Co.	Melborne	Box 35
	Woodrow Cook Mill	Forty Four	
	Clifton Dockins Lumber Co.	Brockwell	
	Moss American	Melbourne	Box 25861, Oklahoma City, Oklahoma
	James Sanders Mill	Dolph	
Jefferson	K. M. Watson	Sulphur Springs	Rt. 1, Box 312, Pine Bluff
Johnson	R. L. Curtis Sawmill	Hagarville	
	Willis Grace Sawmill	Lamar	Rt. 1
	Arch Griffin Sawmill	Clarksville	Rt. 2, Box 178
	Vaughn Selby Sawmill	Ozone	Rt. 1, Lamar
Lafayette	Tyco Lumber Co.	Lewisville	Box 10
Lawrence	Lee Edwards & Son Sawmill	Hoxie	Box 1
	Dewey Ellis	Ravenden	Box 19
	Ronald Morse Tie Mill	Dowdy	Saffell
	Moss American	Lynn	Box 25861, Oklahoma City, Oklahoma
	Murphy Sawmill	Ravenden	
	H. T. Saffell	Strawberry	Saffell
	Smith & Son Mill	Ravenden	Rt. 1
	Ray Swartzlander Mill	Ravenden	Rt. 1
Lee	Dale Bennett Sawmill	Aubrey	
Little River	Ryman Bowman Sawmill	Ogden	1420 Rankin, Ashdown
	John Bristow Sawmill	Gravely	Rt. 2, Box 81, Foreman
	Brown Sawmill	Arden	Rt. 3, Box 175, Ashdown
	D & M Sawmill	Alleene	Box 54
	Alvin Ferrell Sawmill	Richmond	Rt. 3, Ashdown
	George Garrett Sawmill	Arden	Rt. 3, Box 165, Ashdown
	Junior Green Sawmill	Arkinda	
	M. F. Lisenby & Son Mill	Wilton	Rt. 1, Ashdown
	Scarborough Mill	Wallace	Rt. 3, Ashdown
	Jack Scott Sawmill	Arden	Rt. 3, Ashdown
Logan	Raggio Sawmill	Chismville	Rt. 2, Magazine
Lonoke	W. W. Chrisp	Lonoke	Rt. 2, Beebe
	Bille Lynxviler Sawmill	Lonoke	Rt. 2, Beebe
	Mitchell Bros.	Lonoke	Bald Knob
	Allen Neal Tie Mill	Lonoke	Rt. 2, Box 3
	C. W. Owens & Son	Lonoke	Carlisle
	W. E. White Tie Mill	Carlisle	Cabot
Madison	J. R. Banks Sawmill	Marble	Harrison
	Delbert Clark Sawmill	Forum	Rt. 3, Huntsville
	Clarksville Wood Products	Combs	Clarksville
	Combs Mill	Combs	
	DHM Lumber Co.	Huntsville	Rt. 1
	Ozark Forest Products	Pettigrew	
	Richland Handle Co.	Wesley	
	C. L. Thacker Sawmill	Pettigrew	
	Alfred Thompson Sawmill	Huntsville	Rt. 4
	Andy Todd Sawmill	Hindsville	Rt. 1
	Ralph White Sawmill	Forum	
	Willhite Sawmill	Boston	

Table 20. *Small sawmills*[1] (Continued)

County	Firm	Plant	
		Location	Address[2]
Marion	Beal Halliday	Yellville	
	Humphrey Sawmill	Flippin	
	H. C. Ormand Supply Co.	Summit	Harrison
	A. L. Pilgrim	Flippin	
	Art Purdom	Dodge City Hollow	Rt. 1, Yellville
Miller	Bryant & Horn Sawmill	Texarkana	1121 Prince
Monroe	Farrell-Cooper Lumber Co.	Brinkley	103 W. Pine St.
	Roy & Octie Pledger Tie Mill	Monroe	
Nevada	Acorn Lumber Co.	Rosston	Box 341, Camden
	Gulley Lumber Co.	Prescott	Box 143
	John L. Saunders Sawmill	Sutton	Rt. 2, Emmett
	D. A. Wicker Sawmill	Prescott	Rt. 4
Newton	Bowling Sawmill	Fallsville	Salus
	Campbell Bros.	Fallsville	Mt. Judea
	Lawrence Carlton	Fallsville	Oark
	A. L. Casey Sawmill	Boxley	Ponca
	Gordon Day Sawmill	Piercetown	Rt. 1, box 17, Jasper
	Fowler Lumber Co.	Ponca	
	Harold Greenhaw	Vendor	
	Turney Hughes	Murray	Parthenon
	Bill James Sawmill	Fallsville	Star Route, Salus
	Lackey Sawmill	Low Gap	Rt. 2, Jasper
	Lane Bros. Sawmill	Jasper	Mt. Judea
	Etzel Mack	Fallsville	Oark
Ouachita	Amy Lumber Co.	Amy	Rt. 3, Box 134B, Camden
	T. J. Belt Sawmill	Amy	Eagle Mills
	Eli Charles	Buena Vista	Rt. 2, Box 96, Stephens
	Goodwin-White Co.[3]	Cullendale	Box 366, Camden
	P. W. Strickland Sawmill	Smackover	Rt. 4, Box 368, Camden
	Joe Walker Sawmill	Camden	619 Crestwood
Phillips	Bill Gulledge Lumber Co.	Marvell	Box 132
	Pearson Lumber Co.[3]	Clarendon	Box 3385, Memphis, Tenn.
	J. D. Sweeney	Marvell	Box 662, Brinkley
Pike	G. D. Brewer Sawmill	New Hope	DeQueen
	Elbert Davis Lumber Co.	Murfreesboro	Box 201
	Inell Jones Sawmill	Langley	Box 311, Glenwood
	Pinkerton Lumber Co.	Glenwood	
Polk	Bowden Sawmill	Board Camp	
	Lewis Lumber Co.[3]	Cove	Box 95
	C. E. Martin	Hatfield	
	Reese Tie Co.	Cove	
	Rosson Sawmill	Ink	Star Rt. 9, Box 82
	Sanderson Sawmill	Mena	Rt. 2, Box 216
Pope	Jess Austin Sawmill	Dover	Rt. 1
	Duvall Sawmill	Hector	Rt. 4, Russellville
	Ennis Sawmill	Buttermilk	Rt. 3, Atkins
	Leon Ford Sawmill	Dover	Pelsor
	Robert L. Johnson Sawmill	Ben Hur	
	Loyon Langford Sawmill	Hector	
	Elmer Middleton Sawmill	Sand Gap	Vendor
	Garrison Standridge SAwmill	Scottsville	Ben Hur
	Treadwell SAwmill	Scottsville	Rt. 1, Hector
Prairie	Jimmie Don Green Tie Mill	Hickory Plains	Des Arc
Pulaski	Eschbach Bros. Sawmill Co.	Bigelow	Rt. 1
Randolph	Walter Agnew Mill	Ravenden Springs	Rt. 2
	Emory Blevins	Pocahontas	Rt. 3
	I. M. Bounds Mill	Warm Springs	
	Hubert Casady Mill	Maynard	
	L. R. Haney Timber Works	Pocahontas	Rt. 2
	Ralph Hill Mill	Maynard	
	George Jones Mill	Maynard	Rt. 1
	Hubert Lynxwiller	Warm Springs	
	Wayne Moore	Warm Springs	
	Arnold Rapport	Warm Springs	Rt. 1, Maynard
	Jerry Sullivan	Maynard	
	Bill Turner Mill	Warm Springs	
	Wilkerson-Lynxwiller	Ravenden Springs	

24

Table 20. *Small sawmills*[1] (Continued)

County	Firm	Plant	
		Location	Address [2]
St. Francis	Alderson Lumber Co.	Forrest City	
	A. P. DeMange Lumber Co.	Madison	Box 171
	Griffith Lumber Co.[3]	Madison	Box 151
	Donnie R. Jones Mill	Palestine	
	T. C. Ridings Sawmill	Hunter	
	Bill Smith Tie Mill	Palestine	
	Herman Young Enterprises	Forrest City	Hwy. 1
Saline	D. B. Beck	Benton	Box 21
	Ralph Johnson Sawmill Co.	Paron	
	Kling Sawmill	Mabelvale	9800 Kling Road
	Arthur Lindsey	Avilla	Rt. 1, Box 137, Alexander
	George Price	Benton	Rt. 2, Box 323
Scott	Terry Edwards Sawmill	Bates	Rt. 1, Heavener, Okla.
	Goddard Bros. Sawmill	Waldron	Rt. 3
	Ted Metcalf	Abbott	Rt. 2, Booneville
	Sanders Sawmill	Bates	Rt. 1, Heavener, Okla.
	J. W. Vaught Sawmill	Mountainburg	
	Waltreak Tie Co.	Parks	
	Rufus Williams Sawmill	Abbott	
Searcy	Branscum & Harness Sawmill [3]	Marshall	Box 14
	Bobby Bratton Sawmill	Snowball	Box 434, Marshall
	Passmore Sawmill	Leslie	Rt. 6, Box 27
	D. C. Still Sawmill	Morning Star	Rt. 4, Box 47
	White Wood Treating Co.	St. Joe.	
Sevier	Horatio Lumber Co.	Horatio	Box 155
	Poag Lumber Co.	Horatio	Hwy. 70 W., DeQueen
	Poag Lumber Co.	Lockesburg	Hwy. 70 W., DeQueen
	C. C. Smith Sawmill	Central	Winthrop
Sharp	Bailey Sawmill	Ash Flat	
	V. L. Baldridge Mill	Hardy	Rt. 1
	Collins Bros.	Hardy	Rt. 2, Mammoth Spring
	Earnest Green Mill	Hardy	Rt. 1
	Alfred Oakes Mills	Hardy	Rt. 1
	C. B. Oaks	Hardy	Rt. 1
	Harry Ratliff	Williford	
	Dwane Young Mill	Williford	Rt. 1
Stone	Cartwright Sawmill	Fifty Six	
	W. H. Cartwright Pine Sawmill	Mountain View	Hwy. 14 E.
	Chitwood & Adams Sawmill	St. James	Mountain View
	Olis Gammell Sawmill	Timbo	
Union	E. L. Goodwin Tie Mill	Calion	Box 2
Van Buren	Arkwood, Inc.	Clinton	
	Conway Manufacturing Co.	Clinton	Box G
	Jerl Hefner Sawmill	Clinton	Rt. 3
Washington	Roy Lee Drummond	Winslow	Rt. 1
	Alvis Hampton	Winslow	Rt. 1
	Hayes Industries	Winslow	
	Tremon Henson	Winslow	Rt. 2
	Lawrence Lyons	Winslow	Rt. 1
	Nations Hardwood Co.	Prairie Grove	
	Ozark Forest Products, Inc.	Fayetteville	1819 W. 6 St.
	Fay Reed	Winslow	Rt. 1
White	Wallace Bell Sawmill	Albion	Rt. 5, Searcy
	Calvin Davis Sawmill	Judsonia	
	Ralph Davis Sawmill	Bald Knob	
	Bill Giles Sawmill	Searcy	
	Jack Moore Sawmill	Griffithville	
	Porter & Bratcher Sawmill	Griffithville	
	Roy Rettig Sawmill	Beebe	Rt. 2
	Ronald Root Sawmill	Bald Knob	
	E. D. Strickland Sawmill	Bald Knob	Box 374
	Elmo Usery Tie Mill	Higginson	
	J. W. Wallace Mill	Bald Knob	Rt. 2, Box 385
Woodruff	Lolon C. Risler Sawmill	Pangburn	Rt. 1
	Clarence C. Shue	Morton	
Yell	Elmer Gist Sawmill	Mt. George	Danville
	Dick H. Jewell Sawmill	Ola	Box 186
	Vester Neeley Sawmill	Ola	
	Plainview Wood Products	Plainview	
	Otto Potter Mill	Onyx	Star Route, Steve
	Bruce Stewart Sawmill	Danville	Box 368
	J. D. Winters Sawmill	Dardanelle	814 East J, Russellville

[1] Output of less than 3 million board feet.
[2] Office address specified when different from plant location.
[3] Produced chips for sale to pulpmills.

25

Table 21. *Wood pulpmills*

County	Firm	Location
Ashley	Georgia-Pacific Corp., Crossett Division-Paper	Crossett
Conway	Arkansas Kraft Corp.	Morrilton
Jefferson	Weyerhaeuser Co., Dierks Division	Pine Bluff
	International Paper Co.	Pine Bluff
Little River	Nekoosa-Edwards Paper Co.	Ashdown
Ouachita	International Paper Co.	Camden
Pulaski	Superwood Corp. of Arkansas	Little Rock

Table 22. *Veneer plants*

County	Firm	Plant		Type[2]
		Location	Address[1]	
Ashley	Georgia-Pacific Corp.*#1[3]	Crossett	Box 520	O
	Georgia-Pacific Corp.*#2[3]	Crossett	Box 520	O
Bradley	Sykes & Wilson Flooring Co., Inc.[3]	Warren	Drawer 520	O
Clark	Arkla Chemical Corp.*[3]	Gurdon	Box 43	O
Dallas	Georgia-Pacific Corp.*[3]	Fordyce	Box 660	O
Garland	Weyerhaeuser Co.*	Mountain Pine		O
Howard	Nashville Crate Co.[3]	Nashville	Box 29	C
	Umpire Timber Products[3]	Umpire		O
	Weyerhaeuser Co.*	Dierks		O
Phillips	Beisel Veneer Hoop Co.[3]	West Helena	Box 2338	O
	McKnight Veneer & Plywoods Inc.	West Helena	Box M	C
Pulaski	Little Rock Crate & Basket Co.[3]	Little Rock	1623 E. 14th	C
Union	Olinkraft Plywood*[3]	Huttig	Box 317	O

[1] Office address specified when different from plant location.
[2] C = plants producing chiefly container veneer.
O = plants producing chiefly commercial and other veneer.
[3] Produces chips for sale to pulpmills.
* Produces southern pine plywood.

Table 23. *Post, pole, and piling plants*

County	Firm	Plant	
		Location	Address[1]
Benton	Timber Treated Products Co.	Rogers	Box 183
Boone	Arkwood Inc.	Omaha	Box 199
	G. H. Widner Post Yard	Omaha	Rt. 5, Harrison
Bradley	Post & Pole Co.	Hermitage	Box 707, Camden
Carroll	Earl Clifton Post Yard	Berryville	Rt. 4
Cleburne	Cleburne County Post Co.	Herber Springs	Rt. 3, Box 53
Crawford	Sherman Martindale	Van Buren	804 Federal Road
Dallas	Elrod Co.	Fordyce	Mt. Elbo Road, Rison
Grant	International Paper Co., Wood Preserving Div.	Leola	Box 121
Izard	Sentinel of Arkansas	Calico Rock	Box 376
Johnson	Arkwood Inc.	Lamar	
Little River	Francies Hubrel Pole Operation	Allene	Rt. 1, Ashdown
Marion	Burleson & Son	Yellville	
Montgomery	Tidwell Co.	Caddo Gap	
Nevada	Ouachita-Nevada County Treating Co.	Reader	Reader Station, Chidester
	R. & A. Post Plant	Laneburg	Rt. 2, Emmett
Pike	International Paper Co., Wood Preserving Div.	Delight	Box 116
Polk	Cimarron Lumber Co.	Hatfield	Box 10
	International Paper Co., Wood Preserving Div.	Mena	Box 125
	Mena Products Co.	Mena	Box 736
	Reese Tie Co.	Cove	
	Three States Lumber Co.	Mena	Box 70
Pulaski	Kroppers Co.	North Little Rock	Box 3185
Scott	Sarratt Lumber & Post	Waldron	Box 172
	Southwestern Wood Preserving Co.	Waldron	Box 129
	Southwestern Wood Preserving Co.	Bates	
	Three States Lumber Co.	Waldron	
Searcy	White Wood Treating Co.	St. Joe	
Sevier	Weyerhaeuser Co., Dierks Div., DeQueen Treating Plant	DeQueen	
Union	Eldorado Pole & Piling Co., Inc.	Eldorado	Box 7
Van Buren	Arkwood Inc.	Clinton	
Yell	Midland Supply Co., Inc.	Ola	Box 128
	Wood Treating Co.	Ola	Box 206

[1]Office address specified when different from plant location.

Table 24. *Miscellaneous plants*

County	Firm	Plant Location	Plant Address
Arkansas	Spraton Square Mill [6]	Tichnor	702 West 3, DeWitt
Benton	Eversole & Son [3]	Rogers	Box 183
Boone	Flexsteel Industries, Inc. [6] Independent Stave Co. [3] Keeter Charcoal Co. [2] Sutton Products, Inc. [5]	Harrison Harrison Omaha Harrison	Box 1059 Box 176 Box 191
Carroll	Keeter Charcoal Co. [2]	Green Forest	Branson, Mo.
Clark	National Gypsum Co. [4]	Arkadelphia	Box 39
Craighead	Angelo Manufacturing Co., Inc. [6] Arkansas Dimensions, Inc. [6] B & T Dimension Mill [6] Clems Sawmill [6] Hill Lumber Co. [6] Tinsley Sawmill [6]	Jonesboro Jonesboro Jonesboro Jonesboro Lake City Jonesboro	1106 Hope Box 846 Rt. 5 213-1/2 S. Main Box 1166
Crawford	Nolen Handle Co. [5]	Mountainburg	
Cross	Richardson & Son Stave Mill [3]	Wynne	Box 124
Dallas	Bruner & Ivory Handle Co. [5] L. W. Clark, Inc. [3]	Sparkman Fordyce	Box 283 Box 728
Faulkner	Foster Oar Co. [6]	Conway	Box 1185
Franklin	Earmon Ellison Stave Mill [3] Ozark Charcoal Co. [2]	Cass Ozark	Rt. 2, Ozark Rt. 2
Grant	The LaPierre Sawyer Handle Co. [5]	Sheridan	Box 32
Greene	J. H. Hamlen & Son, Inc. [3] Paragould Wood Products Co., Inc. [6]	Paragould Paragould	709 S. 3rd Ave. Box 31
Hempstead	Bruner-Ivory Handle Co. [5] Split Hickory Co., Inc. [5]	Hope Hope	Box 647 Box 625
Hot Spring	Bray Lumber Co. [6] Joe Robbins [6]	Malvern Malvern	531 Sunset Rt. 2, Box 49
Independence	Bowman Handle Mill [5]	Batesville	Newport Rt.
Jefferson	Brown Furniture Manufacturing Co. [6] Wilbanks Wood Products [5]	Pine Bluff Pine Bluff	Box 5699 3rd & Willow
Johnson	Clarksville Wood Products [3]	Clarksville	Box 529
Lawrence	Kifer Mill [6]	O'Kean	
Lee	Jose Luis Pineda [6]	Monroe	
Logan	Arkansas Charcoal Co. [2] Scranton Charcoal Co. [2]	Paris Scranton	Box 66 Rt. 1, Box 1178
Madison	Keeter Charcoal Co. [2] Keeter Shavings Mill [4] Willhite Industries [5] Wood Shaving Corp. [4]	Huntsville Huntsville Pettigrew Huntsville	Rt. 5 Box 537 Rt. 5
Marion	Burleson & Son [6]	Yellville	
Monroe	H. L. Patrick [5] Volner Square Mill [6]	Brinkley Brinkley	Rt. 1, Box 106 Rt. 1
Montgomery	Mt. Ida Stave Co. [3] O. J. Tubbs [6]	Mt. Ida Mt. Ida	 Box 32
Newton	A. L. Casey Sawmill [5] Fowler Lumber Co. [6] George Charcoal Co. [2] Jasper Charcoal [2]	Boxley Ponca George Pruitt	Ponca Osage Jasper
Ouachita	Monarch Wedge Co. [6]	Cullendale	Box 2155, Camden
Phillips	Earl Bartlett Square Mill [6] Lonnie Moore Square Mill [6]	Marvell Marvell	Rt. 2, Box 249 Box 458
Poinsett	Lairson Square Mill [6]	Trumann	Box 191
Polk	Arkansas Charcoal Co. [2]	Hatfield	
Prairie	Treat Bros. Stave Co. [3] White River Square Co. [6]	Des Arc Des Arc	Box 556 Box 214

28

Table 24. *Miscellaneous plants* (Continued)

County	Firm	Plant	
		Location	Address[1]
Pulaski	American Excelsior Co.[4]	North Little Rock	
	L. D. Johnson Stave Mill[3]	Little Rock	11420 Southridge
Randolph	Hubert Allison Mill[5]	Pocahontas	Rt. 5
	Charles Griffin[5]	Warm Springs	
	Roy Orbarts Mill[5]	Pocahontas	
	Sallee Bros.[5]	Pocahontas	Box 91
St. Francis	Overtus Brinker Handle & Square Mill[5]	Caldwell	Box 39
	True Temper Corp., Wheatley Plant[6]	Wheatley	Box 95
Saline	J. W. Mashburn[6]	East End	Rt. 1, Hensley
Scott	Waldron Charcoal Co.[2]	Waldron	Box 303
	Williams & Son Moulding Co.[6]	Abbott	
Searcy	Treat Bros. Stave Co.[3]	Marshall	Box 217
Sebastian	Sutton Products, Inc.[6]	Ft. Smith	Rt. 4, Box 219
Stone	Hinesley & Everett Enterprises, Inc.[2]	Mountain View	
	E. W. Stewart Mill[3]	Mountain View	Webb St.
	Ed Younger Stave Co.[3]	St. James	Mountain View
Washington	Acme Handle Co.[5]	Greenland	Box 208, Fayetteville
	Nations Hardwood Co.[4]	Prairie Grove	
Woodruff	Clarence C. Shue[6]	Morton	
Yell	Plainview Wood Products[3]	Plainview	

[1]Office address specified when different from plant location.
[2]Charcoal.
[3]Cooperage.
[4]Excelsior.
[5]Handlestock.
[6]Miscellaneous dimension mill.

Bertelson, Daniel F.

    1973. Arkansas forest industries, 1971. South. For.
        Exp. Stn., New Orleans, La. 29 p. (USDA
        For. Serv. Resour. Bull. SO-38)

Arkansas forests supplied more than 451 million cubic feet
of roundwood to forest industries in 1971. Total timber
harvest has increased 15 percent since 1968. Saw logs and
pulpwood, ranking first and second, accounted for 83 percent of the roundwood harvest. The total number of sawmills declined, but average receipts per mill increased.

Forest Statistics
for
Alabama Counties

Arnold Hedlund

and

J. M. Earles

Southern Forest Experiment Station
New Orleans, Louisiana
Forest Service, U. S. Department of Agriculture

Acknowledgments

Generous assistance from public and private organizations made it possible to keep the field work for the latest forest inventory of Alabama ahead of the schedule that could have been maintained with regularly allotted funds. The very material aid of the organizations listed below, and of the individuals in them, is gratefully acknowledged:

Alabama Forestry Commission

Cooperative Extension Service

Tennessee Valley Authority

Alabama Power Company

American Can Company

Champion International

Container Corporation of America

Hammermill Paper Company

International Paper Company

Kimberly-Clark Corporation

MacMillan Bloedel Products, Inc.

Scotch Lumber Company

Scott Paper Company

Tennessee River Pulp & Paper Company

Weyerhaeuser Company

Forest Statistics
for
Alabama Counties

Arnold Hedlund

and

J. M. Earles

Southern Forest Experiment Station
New Orleans, Louisiana
Forest Service, U. S. Department of Agriculture

LAUDERDALE LIMESTONE MADISON JACKSON

Florence■ *TENNESSEE*

COLBERT

NORTH

LAWRENCE

DE KALB

FRANKLIN

MORGAN

MARSHALL

MARION WINSTON CULLMAN

CHEROKEE

ETOWAH

BLOUNT

Gadsden■

CALHOUN

LAMAR

WALKER

ST. CLAIR

CLEBURNE

FAYETTE

JEFFERSON

NORTH CENTRAL

TALLADEGA

PICKENS TUSCALOOSA

Birmingham■

SHELBY

CLAY

RANDOLPH

WEST CENTRAL

Tuscaloosa■

BIBB

COOSA

TALLAPOOSA CHAMBERS

GREENE

HALE

CHILTON

SUMTER

PERRY

ELMORE

LEE

AUTAUGA

MACON

RUSSELL

Demopolis■

MARENGO

DALLAS

RIVER

Montgomery■

MONTGOMERY

CHOCTAW

Naheola■

WILCOX

LOWNDES

SOUTHEAST

BULLOCK

BARBOUR

CLARKE

SOUTHWEST-NORTH

MONROE

BUTLER

PIKE

CRENSHAW

HENRY

WASHINGTON

■Jackson

CONECUH

COFFEE DALE

ALABAMA

COVINGTON

HOUSTON

MOBILE

BALDWIN ESCAMBIA

Brewton■

GENEVA

SOUTHWEST-SOUTH

PJ 11-53

Mobile■

MILES

0 10 20 30 40 50

Forest Resource regions in Alabama.

ii

Forest Statistics
for
Alabama Counties

This report tabulates information from a new forest survey of Alabama, completed in 1972 by the Forest Resources Research Unit of the Southern Forest Experiment Station. The tables are intended for use as source data in compiling estimates for groups of counties. Because the sampling procedure is intended primarily to furnish inventory data for the State as a whole, estimates for individual counties have limited and variable accuracy.

The data on forest acreage and timber volume were secured by a systematic sampling method involving a forest-nonforest classification on aerial photographs and on-the-ground measurements of trees at sample locations. The sample locations were at the intersections of a grid of lines spaced 3 miles apart. At each forested location, 10 small plots were uniformly distributed on an area of about 1 acre.

The sampling errors to which the State area and volume totals are liable (on a probability of two chances out of three) are indicated in table 1.

Table 1.—*Sampling errors for forest land and volume estimates*

Item	Sampling error
	Percent
Commercial forest land	0.2
Growing-stock volume	1.2
Sawtimber volume [1]	1.8
Growth on growing stock	2.3
Growth on sawtimber [1]	3.4
Removals from growing stock	1.8
Removals from sawtimber [1]	4.1

[1] International ¼-inch rule.

Detailed sampling errors are shown in tables 33-37. An approximation of sampling errors for groups of counties may be obtained from the formula:

$$e = \frac{(SE) \sqrt{\text{(Specified volume or area)}}}{\sqrt{\text{(Volume or area total in question)}}}$$

Where: e = Estimated sampling error of the volume or area total in question

SE = Specified sampling error for the State.

When data for two or more counties are grouped the error decreases. Conversely, as data for individual counties are broken down by various subdivisions, the possibility of error increases and is greatest for the smallest items.

Because of differences in standards of tree measurement, direct comparisons cannot be made between the estimates in this report and those from a prior inventory in 1963. In table 2, changes between the two surveys are summarized in terms of current measurement standards.

DEFINITIONS OF TERMS

Acceptable trees.—Growing-stock trees of commercial species that meet specified standards of size and quality but do not qualify as desirable trees.

Commercial forest land.—Forest land producing or capable of producing crops of industrial wood and not withdrawn from timber utilization.

Desirable trees.—Growing-stock trees that are of commercial species, have no defects in quality for timber products, are of relatively high vigor, and contain no pathogens that may result in death or serious deterioration before rotation age.

Table 2. *Commercial forest land, growing-stock, and sawtimber volume, 1972, and change since 1963*

Resource region	Commercial forest		Growing stock				Sawtimber			
			Softwood		Hardwood		Softwood		Hardwood	
	Volume	Change	Volume	Change [1]	Volume	Change [1]	Volume	Change [1]	Volume	Change [1]
	Thousand acres	*Per-cent*	*Million cu. ft.*	*Per-cent*	*Million cu. ft.*	*Per-cent*	*Million bd. ft.*	*Per-cent*	*Million bd. ft.*	*Per-cent*
Southwest-South	2,787.4	−3	1,724.0	+ 6	896.2	+ 1	7,227.7	+ 8	2,245.4	− 2
Southwest-North	3,378.6	+3	2,240.8	+14	1,666.2	+ 2	9,848.2	+19	4,579.9	([2])
Southeast	5,348.4	−2	2,825.0	+43	2,122.1	+22	10,664.9	+45	4,747.7	+30
West Central	3,165.8	−2	1,691.1	+37	1,480.9	+31	5,928.3	+31	3,418.2	+38
North Central	4,535.9	−4	2,286.6	+45	1,454.5	+19	7,160.3	+44	3,149.1	+22
North	2,117.0	−3	515.1	+71	1,309.2	+12	1,454.0	+85	3,093.4	+10
All regions	21,333.1	−2	11,282.2	+30	8,929.1	+15	42,283.4	+30	21,233.7	+15

[1] Based on current measurement standards.
[2] Negligible.

Forest type.—A classification of forest land based upon the species forming a plurality of live-tree stocking.

Growing-stock trees.—Live trees that are of commercial species and qualify as desirable or acceptable trees.

Growing-stock volume.—Net volume in cubic feet (or meters) of growing-stock trees at least 5.0 inches in diameter at breast height, from a 1-foot stump to a minimum 4.0-inch top diameter outside bark of the central stem, or to the point where the central stem breaks into limbs.

Mortality.—Sound-wood volume of live trees dying from natural causes during a specified period.

Net annual growth.—The increase in volume of a specified size class for a specific year.

Poletimber trees.—Growing-stock trees of commercial species at least 5.0 inches in diameter at breast height, but smaller than sawtimber size.

Sawtimber trees.—Live trees that are of commercial species, contain at least a 12-foot saw log, and meet regional specifications for freedom from defect. Softwoods must be at least 9.0 inches in diameter at breast height and hardwoods at least 11.0 inches.

Sawtimber volume.—Net volume of the saw-log portion of live sawtimber in board feet, International ¼-inch rule.

Site class.—A classification of forest land in terms of inherent capacity to grow crops of industrial wood.

Stand-size class.—A classification of forest land based upon the size class of growing-stock trees on the area; that is, sawtimber, poletimber, or seedlings and saplings.

Timber removals.—The net volume of growing-stock trees removed from the inventory by harvesting, cultural operations such as timber-stand improvement, land clearing, or changes in land use.

2

Table 3. *Total area, commercial forest land, and proportion of total area, 1972, and change since 1963*

County	Total area[1]	Commercial forest			County	Total area[1]	Commercial forest		
		Area	Pro-portion	Change since 1963			Area	Pro-portion	Change since 1963
	Thousand acres	*Thousand acres*	- - *Percent*- -			*Thousand acres*	*Thousand acres*	- -*Percent*- -	
AuLauga	386.6	253.7	66	+ 1	Jackson	727.0	436.8	60	- 1
Baldwin	1,068.1	702.1	66	- 8	Jefferson	717.5	459.2	64	- 8
Barbour	575.4	385.0	67	+ 1	Lamar	387.2	285.0	74	- 5
Bibb	400.0	332.8	83	- 3	Lauderdale	460.2	154.0	33	-12
Blount	411.5	245.7	60	(2)	Lawrence	453.8	203.5	45	- 7
Bullock	393.6	232.2	59	+ 1	Lee	395.5	264.0	67	- 2
Butler	494.7	371.2	75	(2)	Limestone	380.2	77.9	20	-21
Calhoun	391.7	241.9	62	- 5	Lowndes	460.2	224.0	49	- 9
Chambers	383.4	270.0	70	+ 4	Macon	394.2	218.4	55	- 8
Cherokee	384.0	214.6	56	-12	Madison	518.4	180.0	35	+ 2
Chilton	451.2	296.4	66	- 7	Marengo	626.0	402.6	64	+ 1
Choctaw	590.7	504.0	85	(2)	Marion	475.5	348.1	73	- 2
Clarke	802.5	722.4	90	+ 4	Marshall	401.2	173.6	43	- 1
Clay	385.9	313.2	81	- 1	Mobile	817.9	522.9	64	-10
Cleburne	367.4	312.7	85	(2)	Monroe	666.9	508.8	76	(2)
Coffee	433.3	241.5	56	+ 2	Montgomery	508.8	171.1	34	-17
Colbert	403.8	222.3	55	(2)	Morgan	380.2	157.5	41	+ 5
Conecuh	544.0	428.4	79	+ 6	Perry	469.8	286.2	61	- 6
Coosa	421.8	354.0	84	- 2	Pickens	567.7	427.5	75	+ 1
Covington	662.4	450.0	68	+ 2	Pike	430.7	250.8	58	+ 4
Crenshaw	391.0	274.5	70	+ 7	Randolph	371.8	270.3	73	+ 2
Cullman	475.5	256.5	54	- 5	Russell	409.6	268.4	66	+ 9
Dale	358.4	225.5	63	+ 9	St. Clair	414.0	311.1	75	+ 1
Dallas	629.7	313.5	50	- 7	Shelby	516.5	400.2	77	- 1
De Kalb	497.9	246.4	49	- 2	Sumter	589.5	390.6	66	+ 9
Elmore	421.8	243.0	58	- 4	Talladega	484.5	291.2	60	- 2
Escambia	615.7	490.2	80	+ 1	Tallapoosa	492.1	369.6	75	- 2
Etowah	355.2	176.9	50	-12	Tuscaloosa	863.3	696.2	81	+ 1
Fayette	401.3	307.4	77	- 2	Walker	518.4	369.2	71	- 7
Franklin	412.2	265.0	64	- 6	Washington	687.4	622.2	91	+ 3
Geneva	369.9	159.0	43	-10	Wilcox	581.1	421.8	73	+ 2
Greene	420.5	234.6	56	-11	Winston	405.1	319.2	79	- 2
Hale	424.3	248.0	58	- 1					
Henry	361.6	209.1	58	(2)					
Houston	370.6	107.5	29	-23	All counties	33,029.8	21,333.1	65	- 2

[1]Source: United States Bureau of the Census, Land and Water Area of the United States, 1960.
[2]Negligible.

Table 4. *Commercial forest land by ownership class, 1972*

County	All ownerships	National forest	Other public	Forest industry	Farmer	Misc. private
			- - - - - - - - - -Thousand acres- - - - - - - - - -			
Autauga	253.7	...	1.8	94.4	82.5	75.0
Baldwin	702.1	...	5.7	286.0	114.5	295.9
Barbour	385.0	...	15.8	60.5	109.9	198.8
Bibb	332.8	60.6	3.9	98.8	42.3	127.2
Blount	245.7	...	6.8	...	87.6	151.3
Bullock	232.2	...	...	10.8	64.8	156.6
Butler	371.2	...	.3	150.8	121.7	98.4
Calhoun	241.9	15.1	52.2	53.1	76.2	45.3
Chambers	270.0	...	.6	10.8	113.3	145.3
Cherokee	214.6	...	...	63.8	57.6	93.2
Chilton	296.4	21.4	.6	52.0	103.9	118.5
Choctaw	504.0	...	3.9	150.0	102.0	248.1
Clarke	722.4	...	8.2	291.2	112.0	311.0
Clay	313.2	65.2	1.6	27.0	91.2	128.2
Cleburne	312.7	79.4	1.9	88.5	52.8	90.1
Coffee	241.5	...	10.2	41.4	117.2	72.7
Colbert	222.3	...	11.3	11.4	91.9	107.7
Conecuh	428.4	...	(^{1})	170.1	132.3	126.0
Coosa	354.0	...	5.0	90.0	59.6	199.4
Covington	450.0	54.2	2.1	156.0	158.5	79.2
Crenshaw	274.5	...	.2	42.7	115.8	115.8
Cullman	256.5	...	1.2	22.8	141.6	90.9
Dale	225.5	...	33.8	...	87.9	103.8
Dallas	313.5	5.0	1.9	60.5	126.4	119.7
De Kalb	246.4	...	5.8	22.4	135.4	82.8
Elmore	243.0	...	1.8	5.4	75.6	160.2
Escambia	490.2	32.0	4.0	216.6	61.3	176.3
Etowah	176.9	...	1.4	6.1	97.0	72.4
Fayette	307.4	...	7.5	68.9	86.2	144.8
Franklin	265.0	1.6	1.4	60.0	125.9	76.1
Geneva	159.0	...	7.2	5.3	79.5	67.0
Greene	234.6	...	2.3	35.7	103.7	92.9
Hale	248.0	27.7	2.9	55.8	56.7	104.9
Henry	209.1	...	.9	30.6	81.5	96.1
Houston	107.5	...	1.4	...	34.4	71.7

Table 4. *Commercial forest land by ownership class, 1972* (Continued)

County	All ownerships	National forest	Other public	Forest industry	Farmer	Misc. private
			- - - - - - - - - -*Thousand acres*- - - - - - - - - -			
Jackson	436.8	...	14.9	44.8	259.5	117.6
Jefferson	459.2	...	11.6	...	44.5	403.1
Lamar	285.0	...	.1	39.9	92.7	152.3
Lauderdale	154.0	...	4.0	11.0	110.8	28.2
Lawrence	203.5	88.7	1.8	...	88.6	24.4
Lee	264.0	...	5.1	22.0	71.5	165.4
Limestone	77.9	...	5.6	...	53.7	18.6
Lowndes	224.0	...	1.5	50.4	89.5	82.6
Macon	218.4	9.8	1.5	31.2	98.7	77.2
Madison	180.0	...	17.9	6.0	84.6	71.5
Marengo	402.6	...	1.0	79.2	165.0	157.4
Marion	348.1	...	2.5	94.4	95.9	155.3
Marshall	173.6	...	12.6	22.4	73.3	65.3
Mobile	522.9	...	24.4	50.4	92.5	355.6
Monroe	508.8	...	3.3	164.3	196.0	145.2
Montgomery	171.1	...	1.3	...	100.2	69.6
Morgan	157.5	...	7.8	...	122.4	27.3
Perry	286.2	32.9	.4	53.0	102.3	97.6
Pickens	427.5	...	...	136.8	127.4	163.3
Pike	250.8	...	.4	22.8	159.5	68.1
Randolph	270.3	...	.3	10.2	157.1	102.7
Russell	268.4	...	8.2	36.6	61.0	162.6
St. Clair	311.1	...	.9	66.3	86.2	157.7
Shelby	400.2	...	12.8	133.4	92.2	161.8
Sumter	390.6	...	1.4	124.0	155.0	110.2
Talladega	291.2	41.6	9.2	22.4	44.5	173.5
Tallapoosa	369.6	...	1.2	44.8	78.4	245.2
Tuscaloosa	696.2	8.5	10.2	153.4	138.0	386.1
Walker	369.2	...	15.5	46.8	67.2	239.7
Washington	622.2	...	1.4	79.3	107.4	434.1
Wilcox	421.8	...	4.3	57.0	153.9	206.6
Winston	319.2	85.8	2.3	62.7	62.3	106.1
All counties	21,333.1	629.5	391.0	4,204.9	6,732.5	9,375.2

[1]Negligible.

Table 5. *Commercial forest land by forest type, 1972*

County	All types	Longleaf-slash pine	Loblolly-shortleaf pine	Oak-pine	Oak-hickory	Oak-gum cypress	Elm-ash-cottonwood
			- - - - - - - - - - -*Thousand acres*- - - - - - - - - - -				
Autauga	253.7	41.3	94.4	47.2	59.0	11.8	...
Baldwin	702.1	283.9	58.5	156.0	47.7	156.0	...
Barbour	385.0	22.0	170.5	66.0	88.0	38.5	...
Bibb	332.8	26.0	130.0	104.0	67.6	5.2	...
Blount	245.7	...	81.9	81.9	69.3	12.6	...
Bullock	232.2	...	97.2	27.0	64.8	43.2	...
Butler	371.2	5.8	145.0	87.0	87.0	40.6	5.8
Calhoun	241.9	...	76.7	82.6	82.6	...	...
Chambers	270.0	...	145.8	43.2	70.2	10.8	...
Cherokee	214.6	...	98.6	58.0	46.4	11.6	...
Chilton	296.4	10.4	72.8	88.4	119.6	5.2	...
Choctaw	504.0	...	186.0	132.0	108.0	72.0	6.0
Clarke	722.4	...	308.0	151.2	117.6	134.4	11.2
Clay	313.2	5.4	102.6	86.4	118.8	...	...
Cleburne	312.7	5.9	129.8	82.6	94.4	...	...
Coffee	241.5	13.8	48.3	62.1	82.8	34.5	...
Colbert	222.3	...	17.1	57.0	136.8	5.7	5.7
Conecuh	428.4	12.6	119.7	94.5	163.8	37.8	...
Coosa	354.0	24.0	138.0	102.0	84.0	6.0	...
Covington	450.0	144.0	72.0	84.0	102.0	48.0	...
Crenshaw	274.5	18.3	54.9	79.3	48.8	73.2	...
Cullman	256.5	...	96.9	85.5	74.1	...	...
Dale	225.5	5.5	66.0	44.0	88.0	22.0	...
Dallas	313.5	5.5	99.0	71.5	93.5	38.5	5.5
De Kalb	246.4	...	84.0	50.4	112.0	...	...
Elmore	243.0	...	81.0	48.6	91.8	21.6	...
Escambia	490.2	245.1	22.8	119.7	39.9	62.7	...
Etowah	176.9	...	61.0	36.6	73.2	6.1	...
Fayette	307.4	...	127.2	53.0	79.5	42.4	5.3
Franklin	265.0	...	55.0	65.0	145.0	...	...
Geneva	159.0	37.1	...	15.9	53.0	53.0	...
Greene	234.6	...	61.2	40.8	40.8	91.8	...
Hale	248.0	6.2	68.2	86.8	31.0	55.8	...
Henry	209.1	5.1	81.6	45.9	56.1	20.4	...
Houston	107.5	25.8	21.5	8.6	21.5	30.1	...

6

Table 5. *Commercial forest land by forest type, 1972* (Continued)

County	All types	Longleaf-slash pine	Loblolly-shortleaf pine	Oak-pine	Oak-hickory	Oak-gum-cypress	Elm-ash-cottonwood
				Thousand acres			
Jackson	436.8	...	16.8	28.0	369.6	22.4	...
Jefferson	459.2	11.2	207.2	134.4	95.2	5.6	5.6
Lamar	285.0	...	62.7	85.5	57.0	74.1	5.7
Lauderdale	154.0	...	5.5	22.0	115.5	11.0	...
Lawrence	203.5	...	38.5	16.5	132.0	16.5	...
Lee	264.0	11.0	143.0	44.0	44.0	22.0	...
Limestone	77.9	...	4.1	4.1	45.1	24.6	...
Lowndes	224.0	...	61.6	50.4	61.6	44.8	5.6
Macon	218.4	...	57.2	57.2	52.0	52.0	...
Madison	180.0	...	18.0	12.0	102.0	48.0	...
Marengo	402.6	...	151.8	99.0	59.4 .	92.4	...
Marion	348.1	...	100.3	82.6	159.3	...	5.9
Marshall	173.6	...	50.4	39.2	84.0	...	...
Mobile	522.9	201.6	31.5	126.0	81.9	81.9	...
Monroe	508.8	21.2	111.3	137.8	148.4	84.8	5.3
Montgomery	171.1	...	47.2	23.6	41.3	59.0	...
Morgan	157.5	...	36.0	31.5	58.5	31.5	...
Perry	286.2	15.9	90.1	74.2	63.6	31.8	10.6
Pickens	427.5	...	176.7	102.6	74.1	68.4	5.7
Pike	250.8	22.8	62.7	51.3	62.7	51.3	...
Randolph	270.3	5.1	117.3	71.4	71.4	5.1	...
Russell	268.4	12.2	183.0	30.5	18.3	24.4	...
St. Clair	311.1	5.1	102.0	76.5	96.9	30.6	...
Shelby	400.2	29.0	116.0	116.0	116.0	17.4	5.8
Sumter	390.6	...	117.8	55.8	124.0	86.8	6.2
Talladega	291.2	11.2	89.6	95.2	95.2	...	...
Tallapoosa	369.6	...	117.6	128.8	106.4	16.8	...
Tuscaloosa	696.2	23.6	247.8	194.7	141.6	88.5	...
Walker	369.2	...	171.6	93.6	104.0	...	...
Washington	622.2	158.6	103.7	176.9	85.4	97.6	...
Wilcox	421.8	11.4	131.1	125.4	91.2	62.7	...
Winston	319.2	...	136.8	85.5	96.9	...	...
All counties	21,333.1	1,483.6	6,380.1	5,016.9	5,913.1	2,443.5	95.9

Table 6. *Commercial forest land by stand-size class, 1972*

County	All classes	Sawtimber	Poletimber	Sapling and seedling	Nonstocked areas
- - - - - - - Thousand acres- - - - - - -					
Autauga	253.7	118.0	64.9	70.8	...
Baldwin	702.1	268.7	112.7	312.0	8.7
Barbour	385.0	132.0	132.0	110.0	11.0
Bibb	332.8	83.2	130.0	119.6	...
Blount	245.7	94.5	69.3	81.9	...
Bullock	232.2	75.6	97.2	59.4	...
Butler	371.2	156.6	69.6	139.2	5.8
Calhoun	241.9	64.9	94.4	82.6	...
Chambers	270.0	43.2	97.2	129.6	...
Cherokee	214.6	40.6	63.8	110.2	...
Chilton	296.4	57.2	109.2	130.0	...
Choctaw	504.0	180.0	174.0	150.0	...
Clarke	722.4	386.4	168.0	168.0	...
Clay	313.2	59.4	140.4	113.4	...
Cleburne	312.7	88.5	135.7	88.5	...
Coffee	241.5	75.9	75.9	82.8	6.9
Colbert	222.3	22.8	96.9	102.6	...
Conecuh	428.4	182.7	107.1	132.3	6.3
Coosa	354.0	72.0	144.0	138.0	...
Covington	450.0	168.0	114.0	162.0	6.0
Crenshaw	274.5	97.6	103.7	67.1	6.1
Cullman	256.5	62.7	142.5	51.3	...
Dale	225.5	66.0	82.5	71.5	5.5
Dallas	313.5	99.0	93.5	121.0	...
De Kalb	246.4	56.0	100.8	89.6	...
Elmore	243.0	43.2	81.0	118.8	...
Escambia	490.2	216.6	96.9	176.7	...
Etowah	176.9	36.6	54.9	85.4	...
Fayette	307.4	68.9	137.8	95.4	5.3
Franklin	265.0	15.0	155.0	95.0	...
Geneva	159.0	37.1	47.7	74.2	...
Greene	234.6	122.4	66.3	45.9	...
Hale	248.0	105.4	68.2	74.4	...
Henry	209.1	61.2	102.0	45.9	...
Houston	107.5	25.8	25.8	55.9	...

Table 6. *Commercial forest land by stand-size class, 1972*
(Continued)

County	All classes	Sawtimber	Poletimber	Sapling and seedling	Nonstocked areas
			-Thousand acres-		
Jackson	436.8	156.8	173.6	106.4	...
Jefferson	459.2	100.8	162.4	196.0	...
Lamar	285.0	57.0	165.3	62.7	...
Lauderdale	154.0	44.0	55.0	55.0	...
Lawrence	203.5	38.5	88.0	77.0	...
Lee	264.0	82.5	99.0	77.0	5.5
Limestone	77.9	32.8	32.8	12.3	...
Lowndes	224.0	89.6	61.6	67.2	5.6
Macon	218.4	57.2	78.0	83.2	...
Madison	180.0	48.0	90.0	42.0	...
Marengo	402.6	158.4	118.8	125.4	...
Marion	348.1	47.2	153.4	147.5	...
Marshall	173.6	67.2	67.2	39.2	...
Mobile	522.9	126.0	126.0	252.0	18.9
Monroe	508.8	201.4	143.1	164.3	...
Montgomery	171.1	64.9	64.9	41.3	...
Morgan	157.5	45.0	58.5	54.0	...
Perry	286.2	127.2	95.4	63.6	...
Pickens	427.5	148.2	131.1	148.2	...
Pike	250.8	79.8	85.5	79.8	5.7
Randolph	270.3	76.5	61.2	132.6	...
Russell	268.4	85.4	109.8	67.1	6.1
St. Clair	311.1	66.3	122.4	122.4	...
Shelby	400.2	116.0	156.6	121.8	5.8
Sumter	390.6	192.2	68.2	130.2	...
Talladega	291.2	72.8	128.8	89.6	...
Tallapoosa	369.6	89.6	89.6	190.4	...
Tuscaloosa	696.2	206.5	236.0	253.7	...
Walker	369.2	114.4	166.4	88.4	...
Washington	622.2	250.1	164.7	207.4	...
Wilcox	421.8	216.6	108.3	96.9	...
Winston	319.2	96.9	125.4	96.9	...
All counties	21,333.1	6,839.5	7,141.9	7,242.5	109.2

Table 7. *Commercial forest land by site class, 1972*

County	All classes	165 cu.ft. or more	120-165 cu.ft.	85-120 cu.ft.	50-85 cu.ft.	Less than 50 cu.ft.
		- - - - - - - - *Thousand acres* - - - - - - - -				
Autauga	253.7	...	23.6	94.4	112.1	23.6
Baldwin	702.1	...	19.5	188.5	444.2	49.9
Barbour	385.0	5.5	110.0	187.0	82.5	...
Bibb	332.8	...	10.4	124.8	166.4	31.2
Blount	245.7	...	18.9	37.8	163.8	25.2
Bullock	232.2	10.8	27.0	108.0	86.4	...
Butler	371.2	...	81.2	156.6	127.6	5.8
Calhoun	241.9	...	11.8	82.6	106.2	41.3
Chambers	270.0	...	21.6	102.6	140.4	5.4
Cherokee	214.6	...	5.8	40.6	156.6	11.6
Chilton	296.4	10.4	52.0	88.4	124.8	20.8
Choctaw	504.0	30.0	84.0	276.0	114.0	...
Clarke	722.4	39.2	190.4	291.2	184.8	16.8
Clay	313.2	...	10.8	86.4	172.8	43.2
Cleburne	312.7	...	5.9	41.3	236.0	29.5
Coffee	241.5	6.9	27.6	131.1	69.0	6.9
Colbert	222.3	...	11.4	51.3	153.9	5.7
Conecuh	428.4	50.4	207.9	157.5	12.6	...
Coosa	354.0	...	18.0	108.0	198.0	30.0
Covington	450.0	30.0	102.0	162.0	150.0	6.0
Crenshaw	274.5	...	12.2	115.9	140.3	6.1
Cullman	256.5	...	...	68.4	171.0	17.1
Dale	225.5	5.5	22.0	66.0	121.0	11.0
Dallas	313.5	22.0	77.0	170.5	44.0	...
De Kalb	246.4	...	...	16.8	168.0	61.6
Elmore	243.0	...	16.2	102.6	113.4	10.8
Escambia	490.2	...	45.6	176.7	245.1	22.8
Etowah	176.9	...	6.1	48.8	97.6	24.4
Fayette	307.4	...	10.6	111.3	164.3	21.2
Franklin	265.0	5.0	15.0	105.0	115.0	25.0
Geneva	159.0	...	5.3	68.9	68.9	15.9
Greene	234.6	...	20.4	137.7	61.2	15.3
Hale	248.0	12.4	31.0	136.4	68.2	...
Henry	209.1	5.1	20.4	132.6	45.9	5.1
Houston	107.5	...	8.6	38.7	51.6	8.6

Table 7. *Commercial forest land by site class, 1972* (Continued)

County	All classes	165 cu.ft. or more	120-165 cu.ft.	80-120 cu.ft.	50-85 cu.ft.	Less than 50 cu.ft.
		- - - - - - - - -Thousand acres- - - - - - - - -				
Jackson	436.8	5.6	...	61.6	252.0	117.6
Jefferson	459.2	5.6	72.8	246.4	128.8	5.6
Lamar	285.0	...	17.1	91.2	148.2	28.5
Lauderdale	154.0	...	...	66.0	71.5	16.5
Lawrence	203.5	...	...	33.0	137.5	33.0
Lee	264.0	11.0	33.0	71.5	115.5	33.0
Limestone	77.9	...	12.3	36.9	28.7	...
Lowndes	224.0	22.4	22.4	140.0	39.2	...
Macon	218.4	10.4	26.0	72.8	109.2	...
Madison	180.0	6.0	24.0	30.0	78.0	42.0
Marengo	402.6	6.6	118.8	204.6	72.6	...
Marion	348.1	5.9	17.7	123.9	182.9	17.7
Marshall	173.6	...	11.2	61.6	84.0	16.8
Mobile	522.9	...	12.6	107.1	296.1	107.1
Monroe	508.8	10.6	90.1	164.3	164.3	79.5
Montgomery	171.1	...	17.7	106.2	41.3	5.9
Morgan	157.5	...	4.5	90.0	49.5	13.5
Perry	286.2	15.9	58.3	100.7	100.7	10.6
Pickens	427.5	5.7	11.4	205.2	176.7	28.5
Pike	250.8	...	...	165.3	79.8	5.7
Randolph	270.3	5.1	5.1	96.9	147.9	15.3
Russell	268.4	6.1	30.5	122.0	97.6	12.2
St. Clair	311.1	...	35.7	117.3	142.8	15.3
Shelby	400.2	11.6	40.6	174.0	150.8	23.2
Sumter	390.6	18.6	80.6	173.6	99.2	18.6
Talladega	291.2	...	...	50.4	190.4	50.4
Tallapoosa	369.6	...	28.0	100.8	190.4	50.4
Tuscaloosa	696.2	...	64.9	224.2	324.5	82.6
Walker	369.2	15.6	57.2	145.6	145.6	5.2
Washington	622.2	6.1	48.8	250.1	298.9	18.3
Wilcox	421.8	11.4	51.3	188.1	165.3	5.7
Winston	319.2	...	11.4	114.0	188.1	5.7
All counties	21,333.1	413.4	2,334.2	7,947.7	9,175.6	1,462.2

Table 8. *Cordage of growing stock on commercial forest land by species group, 1972*

County	All species	Softwood			Hardwood			
		Total	Pine	Other	Total	Oak	Gum	Other
			- - - - - - - - - - -*Thousand cords* - - - - - - - - - - - - -					
Autauga	3,577	2,273	2,264	9	1,304	433	507	364
Baldwin	10,382	6,127	5,472	655	4,255	775	2,149	1,331
Barbour	5,405	3,364	3,360	4	2,041	696	791	554
Bibb	5,004	3,183	3,168	15	1,821	864	515	442
Blount	3,466	1,575	1,572	3	1,891	990	270	631
Bullock	2,790	1,750	1,733	17	1,040	260	364	416
Butler	5,334	3,231	3,195	36	2,103	736	582	785
Calhoun	2,485	1,473	1,473	...	1,012	579	118	315
Chambers	2,754	1,464	1,464	...	1,290	378	479	433
Cherokee	1,778	937	937	...	841	612	51	178
Chilton	3,732	1,792	1,789	3	1,940	733	425	782
Choctaw	7,897	5,067	4,914	153	2,830	1,188	884	758
Clarke	12,910	7,740	7,560	180	5,170	1,763	1,703	1,704
Clay	3,250	1,809	1,809	...	1,441	709	235	497
Cleburne	3,895	2,491	2,491	...	1,404	825	155	424
Coffee	2,254	1,226	1,221	5	1,028	585	185	258
Colbert	2,247	340	337	3	1,907	1,030	176	701
Conecuh	6,632	3,256	3,245	11	3,376	1,221	1,136	1,019
Coosa	3,577	1,979	1,979	...	1,598	737	358	503
Covington	5,856	4,087	4,068	19	1,769	506	703	560
Crenshaw	3,883	1,835	1,827	8	2,048	727	687	634
Cullman	3,527	1,847	1,844	3	1,680	951	140	589
Dale	2,985	1,332	1,316	16	1,653	497	613	543
Dallas	4,754	2,744	2,744	...	2,010	575	872	563
De Kalb	2,560	1,260	1,260	...	1,300	825	145	330
Elmore	2,346	962	931	31	1,384	424	476	484
Escambia	6,562	4,823	4,815	8	1,739	515	436	788
Etowah	1,585	888	888	...	697	448	76	173
Fayette	3,743	1,730	1,727	3	2,013	860	616	537
Franklin	3,131	1,127	1,118	9	2,004	1,010	169	825
Geneva	1,656	642	635	7	1,014	236	385	393
Greene	4,197	1,709	1,600	109	2,488	685	864	939
Hale	4,198	2,334	2,331	3	1,864	831	561	472
Henry	2,591	1,615	1,615	...	976	467	206	303
Houston	1,224	637	637	...	587	166	184	237

Table 8. *Cordage of growing stock on commercial forest land by species group, 1972* (Continued)

County	All species	Softwood			Hardwood			
		Total	Pine	Other	Total	Oak	Gum	Other
				- - - - - - - - - - -Thousand cords - - - - - - - - - - -				
Jackson	6,140	533	390	143	5,607	2,830	431	2,346
Jefferson	4,992	3,676	3,676	...	1,316	679	215	422
Lamar	4,015	1,343	1,319	24	2,672	946	1,108	618
Lauderdale	1,772	165	165	...	1,607	1,005	96	506
Lawrence	2,180	679	603	76	1,501	964	154	383
Lee	3,541	2,129	2,129	...	1,412	264	545	603
Limestone	1,204	189	185	4	1,015	545	149	321
Lowndes	3,392	1,465	1,465	...	1,927	493	518	916
Macon	2,850	1,227	1,219	8	1,623	570	401	652
Madison	2,259	428	360	68	1,831	706	170	955
Marengo	5,866	3,247	3,163	84	2,619	1,066	534	1,019
Marion	3,414	1,578	1,573	5	1,836	1,097	173	566
Marshall	2,816	1,429	1,393	36	1,387	657	194	536
Mobile	5,169	3,121	2,884	237	2,048	349	1,051	648
Monroe	7,683	3,659	3,580	79	4,024	1,434	1,212	1,378
Montgomery	2,323	980	964	16	1,343	366	549	428
Morgan	2,096	717	702	15	1,379	585	315	479
Perry	4,285	2,509	2,468	41	1,776	590	501	685
Pickens	5,820	3,335	3,323	12	2,485	1,058	878	549
Pike	3,440	1,616	1,604	12	1,824	616	687	521
Randolph	2,822	1,668	1,668	...	1,154	543	145	466
Russell	4,387	3,032	3,032	...	1,355	296	722	337
St. Clair	3,381	1,917	1,911	6	1,464	785	285	394
Shelby	4,074	2,323	2,323	...	1,751	852	281	618
Sumter	6,348	3,208	3,152	56	3,140	1,270	816	1,054
Talladega	3,222	1,768	1,768	...	1,454	739	240	475
Tallapoosa	4,122	2,351	2,348	3	1,771	637	479	655
Tuscaloosa	9,975	4,827	4,800	27	5,148	2,306	1,635	1,207
Walker	5,585	3,433	3,433	...	2,152	1,055	294	803
Washington	8,395	4,829	4,689	140	3,566	1,180	1,001	1,385
Wilcox	7,410	3,701	3,678	23	3,709	1,550	987	1,172
Winston	4,558	2,704	2,700	4	1,854	1,181	112	561
All counties	283,703	150,435	148,006	2,429	133,268	54,051	35,094	44,123

Table 9. *Growing-stock volume on commercial forest land by species group, 1972* [1]

County	All species	Softwood			Hardwood			
		Total	Pine	Other	Total	Oak	Gum	Other

- - - - - - - - - - - - -Million cubic feet- - - - - - - - - - - - -

County	All species	Total	Pine	Other	Total	Oak	Gum	Other
Autauga	257.9	170.5	169.8	0.7	87.4	29.0	34.0	24.4
Baldwin	744.6	459.5	410.4	49.1	285.1	51.9	144.0	89.2
Barbour	389.0	252.3	252.0	.3	136.7	46.6	53.0	37.1
Bibb	360.7	238.7	237.6	1.1	122.0	57.9	34.5	29.6
Blount	244.8	118.1	117.9	.2	126.7	66.3	18.1	42.3
Bullock	201.0	131.3	130.0	1.3	69.7	17.4	24.4	27.9
Butler	383.2	242.3	239.6	2.7	140.9	49.3	39.0	52.6
Calhoun	178.3	110.5	110.5	...	67.8	38.8	7.9	21.1
Chambers	196.2	109.8	109.8	...	86.4	25.3	32.1	29.0
Cherokee	126.6	70.3	70.3	...	56.3	41.0	3.4	11.9
Chilton	264.4	134.4	134.2	.2	130.0	49.1	28.5	52.4
Choctaw	569.6	380.0	368.5	11.5	189.6	79.6	59.2	50.8
Clarke	926.9	580.5	567.0	13.5	346.4	118.1	114.1	114.2
Clay	232.2	135.7	135.7	...	96.5	47.5	15.7	33.3
Cleburne	280.9	186.8	186.8	...	94.1	55.3	10.4	28.4
Coffee	160.9	92.0	91.6	.4	68.9	39.2	12.4	17.3
Colbert	153.3	25.5	25.3	.2	127.8	69.0	11.8	47.0
Conecuh	470.4	244.2	243.4	.8	226.2	81.8	76.1	68.3
Coosa	255.5	148.4	148.4	...	107.1	49.4	24.0	33.7
Covington	425.0	306.5	305.1	1.4	118.5	33.9	47.1	37.5
Crenshaw	274.8	137.6	137.0	.6	137.2	48.7	46.0	42.5
Cullman	251.1	138.5	138.3	.2	112.6	63.7	9.4	39.5
Dale	210.7	99.9	98.7	1.2	110.8	33.3	41.1	36.4
Dallas	340.4	205.8	205.8	...	134.6	38.5	58.4	37.7
De Kalb	181.6	94.5	94.5	...	87.1	55.3	9.7	22.1
Elmore	164.8	72.1	69.8	2.3	92.7	28.4	31.9	32.4
Escambia	478.2	361.7	361.1	.6	116.5	34.5	29.2	52.8
Etowah	113.3	66.6	66.6	...	46.7	30.0	5.1	11.6
Fayette	264.6	129.7	129.5	.2	134.9	57.6	41.3	36.0
Franklin	218.8	84.5	83.8	.7	134.3	67.7	11.3	55.3
Geneva	116.0	48.1	47.6	.5	67.9	15.8	25.8	26.3
Greene	294.9	128.2	120.0	8.2	166.7	45.9	57.9	62.9
Hale	299.9	175.0	174.8	.2	124.9	55.7	37.6	31.6
Henry	186.5	121.1	121.1	...	65.4	31.3	13.8	20.3
Houston	87.1	47.8	47.8	...	39.3	11.1	12.3	15.9

14

Table 9. *Growing-stock volume on commercial forest land by species group, 1972* [1](Continued)

County	All species	Softwood			Hardwood			
		Total	Pine	Other	Total	Oak	Gum	Other
				-*Million cubic feet*-				
Jackson	415.7	40.0	29.3	10.7	375.7	189.6	28.9	157.2
Jefferson	363.9	275.7	275.7	...	88.2	45.5	14.4	28.3
Lamar	279.7	100.7	98.9	1.8	179.0	63.4	74.2	41.4
Lauderdale	120.1	12.4	12.4	...	107.7	67.4	6.4	33.9
Lawrence	151.5	50.9	45.2	5.7	100.6	64.6	10.3	25.7
Lee	254.3	159.7	159.7	...	94.6	17.7	36.5	40.4
Limestone	82.2	14.2	13.9	.3	68.0	36.5	10.0	21.5
Lowndes	239.0	109.9	109.9	...	129.1	33.0	34.7	61.4
Macon	200.8	92.0	91.4	.6	108.8	38.2	26.9	43.7
Madison	154.8	32.1	27.0	5.1	122.7	47.3	11.4	64.0
Marengo	419.0	243.5	237.2	6.3	175.5	71.4	35.8	68.3
Marion	241.4	118.4	118.0	.4	123.0	73.5	11.6	37.9
Marshall	200.1	107.2	104.5	2.7	92.9	44.0	13.0	35.9
Mobile	371.3	234.1	216.3	17.8	137.2	23.4	70.4	43.4
Monroe	544.0	274.4	268.5	5.9	269.6	96.1	81.2	92.3
Montgomery	163.5	73.5	72.3	1.2	90.0	24.5	36.8	28.7
Morgan	146.2	53.8	52.7	1.1	92.4	39.2	21.1	32.1
Perry	307.2	188.2	185.1	3.1	119.0	39.5	33.6	45.9
Pickens	416.6	250.1	249.2	.9	166.5	70.9	58.8	36.8
Pike	243.4	121.2	120.3	.9	122.2	41.3	46.0	34.9
Randolph	202.4	125.1	125.1	...	77.3	36.4	9.7	31.2
Russell	318.2	227.4	227.4	...	90.8	19.8	48.4	22.6
St. Clair	241.9	143.8	143.3	.5	98.1	52.6	19.1	26.4
Shelby	291.5	174.2	174.2	...	117.3	57.1	18.8	41.4
Sumter	451.0	240.6	236.4	4.2	210.4	85.1	54.7	70.6
Talladega	230.0	132.6	132.6	...	97.4	49.5	16.1	31.8
Tallapoosa	295.0	176.3	176.1	.2	118.7	42.7	32.1	43.9
Tuscaloosa	707.0	362.1	360.1	2.0	344.9	154.5	109.5	80.9
Walker	401.7	257.5	257.5	...	144.2	70.7	19.7	53.8
Washington	601.1	362.2	351.7	10.5	238.9	79.0	67.1	92.8
Wilcox	526.1	277.6	275.9	1.7	248.5	103.9	66.1	78.5
Winston	327.0	202.8	202.5	.3	124.2	79.1	7.5	37.6
All counties	20,211.7	11,282.6	11,100.6	182.0	8,929.1	3,621.3	2,351.3	2,956.5

[1] Detailed county statistics by species and diameter class are available upon request.

Table 10. *Sawtimber volume on commercial forest land by species group, 1972*[1]

County	All species	Softwood			Hardwood			
		Total	Pine	Other	Total	Oak	Gum	Other

- - - - - - - - - - - *Million board feet* - - - - - - - - - - - -

County	All species	Total	Pine	Other	Total	Oak	Gum	Other
Autauga	889.0	670.7	666.8	3.9	218.3	74.1	95.2	49.0
Baldwin	2,911.1	2,078.6	1,857.4	221.2	832.5	173.1	417.5	241.9
Barbour	1,213.6	929.4	929.4	...	284.2	127.4	68.9	87.9
Bibb	1,155.2	902.6	901.5	1.1	252.6	146.3	58.2	48.1
Blount	704.1	352.8	352.8	...	351.3	208.2	53.4	89.7
Bullock	641.7	487.3	486.1	1.2	154.4	54.4	42.3	57.7
Butler	1,482.8	1,081.4	1,069.7	11.7	401.4	148.3	91.4	161.7
Calhoun	470.3	318.9	318.9	...	151.4	104.9	13.6	32.9
Chambers	561.7	381.9	381.9	...	179.8	68.5	58.8	52.5
Cherokee	341.7	210.5	210.5	...	131.2	108.4	5.0	17.8
Chilton	730.5	517.7	517.7	...	212.8	111.1	23.2	78.5
Choctaw	2,105.6	1,683.6	1,616.4	67.2	422.0	238.8	84.2	99.0
Clarke	3,639.4	2,732.2	2,670.4	61.8	907.2	376.8	262.0	268.4
Clay	603.4	447.4	447.4	...	156.0	97.8	17.8	40.4
Cleburne	724.9	569.5	569.5	...	155.4	103.4	12.3	39.7
Coffee	434.8	274.0	274.0	...	160.8	118.8	13.1	28.9
Colbert	310.3	46.9	46.9	...	263.4	182.1	6.2	75.1
Conecuh	1,734.0	1,127.2	1,123.3	3.9	606.8	274.3	194.5	138.0
Coosa	676.4	455.3	455.3	...	221.1	113.5	35.5	72.1
Covington	1,475.3	1,279.3	1,272.1	7.2	196.0	66.2	64.5	65.3
Crenshaw	970.5	629.9	628.0	1.9	340.6	161.8	91.0	87.8
Cullman	590.3	367.3	367.3	...	223.0	125.4	17.7	79.9
Dale	651.4	400.4	398.8	1.6	251.0	91.3	71.7	88.0
Dallas	1,084.6	862.0	862.0	...	222.6	72.8	77.2	72.6
De Kalb	418.6	223.9	223.9	...	194.7	132.6	21.2	40.9
Elmore	424.6	222.7	212.3	10.4	201.9	74.1	61.2	66.6
Escambia	1,850.6	1,545.8	1,545.8	...	304.8	124.9	67.4	112.5
Etowah	270.3	153.3	153.3	...	117.0	93.2	7.1	16.7
Fayette	635.6	380.8	380.8	...	254.8	131.3	56.0	67.5
Franklin	372.6	131.4	131.4	...	241.2	147.1	8.1	86.0
Geneva	288.2	164.0	161.3	2.7	124.2	47.5	37.8	38.9
Greene	1,073.8	552.0	509.0	43.0	521.8	151.0	213.3	157.5
Hale	1,085.5	794.4	794.4	...	291.1	164.7	65.8	60.6
Henry	499.8	388.1	388.1	...	111.7	69.4	14.3	28.0
Houston	247.1	135.8	135.8	...	111.3	41.9	34.6	34.8

16

Table 10. *Sawtimber volume on commercial forest land by species group, 1972*[1] (Continued)

County	All species	Softwood			Hardwood			
		Total	Pine	Other	Total	Oak	Gum	Other
		- - - - - - - - - - - - *Million board feet* - - - - - - - - - - - - - -						
Jackson	1,164.9	123.9	108.9	15.0	1,041.0	634.6	53.7	352.7
Jefferson	1,195.6	999.3	999.3	...	196.3	117.5	13.2	65.6
Lamar	599.7	223.9	219.3	4.6	375.8	163.7	132.6	79.5
Lauderdale	268.2	25.1	25.1	...	243.1	166.9	7.6	68.6
Lawrence	387.4	170.2	156.0	14.2	217.2	156.4	18.5	42.3
Lee	749.5	508.3	508.3	...	241.2	57.3	49.1	134.8
Limestone	270.8	73.0	73.0	...	197.8	131.4	16.8	49.6
Lowndes	853.0	486.6	486.6	...	366.4	114.3	94.5	157.6
Macon	607.7	371.3	368.1	3.2	236.4	86.8	56.0	93.6
Madison	345.1	94.9	90.2	4.7	250.2	124.2	21.5	104.5
Marengo	1,475.5	939.8	910.8	29.0	535.7	243.3	101.9	190.5
Marion	480.6	262.0	260.8	1.2	218.6	147.3	13.4	57.9
Marshall	633.8	414.9	414.9	...	218.9	125.1	27.8	66.0
Mobile	1,192.5	890.3	818.2	72.1	302.2	79.4	170.2	52.6
Monroe	1,865.0	1,087.6	1,057.9	29.7	777.4	368.4	164.2	244.8
Montgomery	451.6	259.8	254.0	5.8	191.8	51.0	88.0	52.8
Morgan	375.7	149.8	144.4	5.4	225.9	94.6	54.1	77.2
Perry	1,066.1	796.7	780.6	16.1	269.4	116.5	72.7	80.2
Pickens	1,219.5	821.4	818.2	3.2	398.1	196.6	123.5	78.0
Pike	792.6	465.0	459.7	5.3	327.6	123.3	109.1	95.2
Randolph	569.2	387.4	387.4	...	181.8	109.5	9.5	62.8
Russell	1,040.0	867.5	867.5	...	172.5	39.0	88.7	44.8
St. Clair	629.4	397.7	397.7	...	231.7	141.3	38.3	52.1
Shelby	743.6	502.3	502.3	...	241.3	136.0	41.6	63.7
Sumter	1,837.5	1,224.4	1,216.9	7.5	613.1	319.9	120.3	172.9
Talladega	643.4	445.4	445.4	...	198.0	117.7	21.9	58.4
Tallapoosa	797.9	561.1	561.1	...	236.8	112.1	33.0	91.7
Tuscaloosa	2,030.5	1,194.5	1,189.1	5.4	836.0	453.5	213.6	168.9
Walker	1,189.2	905.7	905.7	...	283.5	136.1	29.5	117.9
Washington	2,043.6	1,433.7	1,386.7	47.0	609.9	225.2	182.5	202.2
Wilcox	1,771.1	1,053.4	1,053.4	...	717.7	343.4	167.2	207.1
Winston	957.6	647.5	647.5	...	310.1	232.7	10.1	67.3
All counties	63,517.1	42,283.4	41,575.2	708.2	21,233.7	10,190.4	4,806.6	6,236.7

[1] Detailed county statistics by species and diameter class are available upon request.

17

Table 11. *Sawtimber volume on commercial forest land by species group and diameter class, 1972*

County	All species	Softwood			Hardwood		
		Total	9.0-14.9 inches	15.0 inches and up	Total	11.0-14.9 inches	15.0 inches and up

- - - - - - - - - - - - - *Million board feet-* - - - - - - - - - - - -

County	All species	Total	9.0-14.9 inches	15.0 inches and up	Total	11.0-14.9 inches	15.0 inches and up
Autauga	889.0	670.7	438.2	232.5	218.3	116.7	101.6
Baldwin	2,911.1	2,078.6	1,492.3	586.3	832.5	272.3	560.2
Barbour	1,213.6	929.4	630.7	298.7	284.2	147.9	136.3
Bibb	1,155.2	902.6	562.2	340.4	252.6	139.4	113.2
Blount	704.1	352.8	301.1	51.7	351.3	165.6	185.7
Bullock	641.7	487.3	337.2	150.1	154.4	79.4	75.0
Butler	1,482.8	1,081.4	518.8	562.6	401.4	164.3	237.1
Calhoun	470.3	318.9	242.1	76.8	151.4	84.2	67.2
Chambers	561.7	381.9	256.8	125.1	179.8	81.5	98.3
Cherokee	341.7	210.5	148.4	62.1	131.2	62.6	68.6
Chilton	730.5	517.7	326.1	191.6	212.8	147.2	65.6
Choctaw	2,105.6	1,683.6	1,047.5	636.1	422.0	211.5	210.5
Clarke	3,639.4	2,732.2	1,570.2	1,162.0	907.2	374.3	532.9
Clay	603.4	447.4	329.6	117.8	156.0	98.5	57.5
Cleburne	724.9	569.5	398.0	171.5	155.4	106.7	48.7
Coffee	434.8	274.0	213.0	61.0	160.8	77.3	83.5
Colbert	310.3	46.9	39.7	7.2	263.4	181.0	82.4
Conecuh	1,734.0	1,127.2	615.0	512.2	606.8	349.9	256.9
Coosa	676.4	455.3	359.2	96.1	221.1	112.7	108.4
Covington	1,475.3	1,279.3	884.8	394.5	196.0	134.4	61.6
Crenshaw	970.5	629.9	407.6	222.3	340.6	182.6	158.0
Cullman	590.3	367.3	319.5	47.8	223.0	122.4	100.6
Dale	651.4	400.4	246.4	154.0	251.0	112.5	138.5
Dallas	1,084.6	862.0	507.5	354.5	222.6	140.3	82.3
De Kalb	418.6	223.9	163.8	60.1	194.7	98.6	96.1
Elmore	424.6	222.7	157.7	65.0	201.9	147.0	54.9
Escambia	1,850.6	1,545.8	1,103.2	442.6	304.8	112.1	192.7
Etowah	270.3	153.3	129.3	24.0	117.0	59.2	57.8
Fayette	635.6	380.8	279.0	101.8	254.8	163.8	91.0
Franklin	372.6	131.4	116.9	14.5	241.2	158.9	82.3
Geneva	288.2	164.0	129.6	34.4	124.2	77.2	47.0
Greene	1,073.8	552.0	322.1	229.9	521.8	159.0	362.8
Hale	1,085.5	794.4	418.0	376.4	291.1	127.1	164.0
Henry	499.8	388.1	226.4	161.7	111.7	56.0	55.7
Houston	247.1	135.8	64.3	71.5	111.3	57.9	53.4

Table 11. *Sawtimber volume on commercial forest land by species group and diameter class, 1972* (Continued)

County	All species	Softwood			Hardwood		
		Total	9.0-14.9 inches	15.0 inches and up	Total	11.0-14.9 inches	15.0 inches and up
				-Million board feet-			
Jackson	1,164.9	123.9	99.8	24.1	1,041.0	557.5	483.5
Jefferson	1,195.6	999.3	571.4	427.9	196.3	85.9	110.4
Lamar	599.7	223.9	182.3	41.6	375.8	241.4	134.4
Lauderdale	268.2	25.1	25.1	...	243.1	122.8	120.3
Lawrence	387.4	170.2	76.3	93.9	217.2	70.6	146.6
Lee	749.5	508.3	379.0	129.3	241.2	83.4	157.8
Limestone	270.8	73.0	21.2	51.8	197.8	60.2	137.6
Lowndes	853.0	486.6	270.0	216.6	366.4	178.1	188.3
Macon	607.7	371.3	213.0	158.3	236.4	116.1	120.3
Madison	345.1	94.9	70.4	24.5	250.2	123.1	127.1
Marengo	1,475.5	939.8	603.4	336.4	535.7	189.6	346.1
Marion	480.6	262.0	223.5	38.5	218.6	153.7	64.9
Marshall	633.8	414.9	171.1	243.8	218.9	113.3	105.6
Mobile	1,192.5	890.3	651.3	239.0	302.2	118.8	183.4
Monroe	1,865.0	1,087.6	739.6	348.0	777.4	324.8	452.6
Montgomery	451.6	259.8	215.4	44.4	191.8	101.0	90.8
Morgan	375.7	149.8	115.6	34.2	225.9	84.3	141.6
Perry	1,066.1	796.7	494.9	301.8	269.4	104.7	164.7
Pickens	1,219.5	821.4	585.3	236.1	398.1	221.6	176.5
Pike	792.6	465.0	314.3	150.7	327.6	183.1	144.5
Randolph	569.2	387.4	262.5	124.9	181.8	86.2	95.6
Russell	1,040.0	867.5	636.3	231.2	172.5	102.2	70.3
St. Clair	629.4	397.7	305.7	92.0	231.7	111.8	119.9
Shelby	743.6	502.3	333.6	168.7	241.3	117.3	124.0
Sumter	1,837.5	1,224.4	666.7	557.7	613.1	249.1	364.0
Talladega	643.4	445.4	303.9	141.5	198.0	106.1	91.9
Tallapoosa	797.9	561.1	344.7	216.4	236.8	135.2	101.6
Tuscaloosa	2,030.5	1,194.5	775.9	418.6	836.0	408.2	427.8
Walker	1,189.2	905.7	703.2	202.5	283.5	173.4	110.1
Washington	2,043.6	1,433.7	890.8	542.9	609.9	220.7	389.2
Wilcox	1,771.1	1,053.4	690.9	362.5	717.7	307.9	409.8
Winston	957.6	647.5	397.5	250.0	310.1	156.9	153.2
All counties	63,517.1	42,283.4	27,636.8	14,646.6	21,233.7	10,291.0	10,942.7

Table 12. *Growing-stock volume of softwoods on commercial forest land by forest type, 1972*

County	All types	Longleaf-slash pine	Loblolly-shortleaf pine	Oak-pine	Oak-hickory	Oak-gum-cypress	Elm-ash-cottonwood
				- - - - - - - *Million cubic feet* - - - - - - - - -			
Autauga	170.5	36.8	88.0	27.0	13.7	5.0	...
Baldwin	459.5	272.2	34.3	77.0	11.7	64.3	...
Barbour	252.3	13.5	169.6	47.4	17.6	4.2	...
Bibb	238.7	27.1	129.0	74.6	8.0	...	...
Blount	118.1	...	81.4	31.4	4.5	.8	...
Bullock	131.3	...	96.5	19.1	10.0	5.7	...
Butler	242.3	16.0	149.4	52.1	14.1	10.7	...
Calhoun	110.5	...	59.4	41.6	9.5	...	...
Chambers	109.8	...	70.2	15.6	17.6	6.4	...
Cherokee	70.3	...	52.9	12.7	3.2	1.5	...
Chilton	134.4	10.5	63.2	43.4	17.3	...	...
Choctaw	380.0	...	235.9	101.7	23.5	18.9	...
Clarke	580.5	...	390.0	141.2	26.3	17.3	5.7
Clay	135.7	...	75.8	42.3	17.6	...	...
Cleburne	186.8	3.3	137.1	32.7	13.7	...	...
Coffee	92.0	9.0	37.5	20.6	20.5	4.4	...
Colbert	25.5	...	3.2	14.5	7.8	...	...
Conecuh	244.2	13.0	113.8	88.4	24.9	4.1	...
Coosa	148.4	17.2	80.1	41.1	9.4	.6	...
Covington	306.5	145.8	87.6	52.2	12.0	8.9	...
Crenshaw	137.6	25.7	38.7	42.8	16.2	14.2	...
Cullman	138.5	...	95.9	33.9	8.7	...	...
Dale	99.9	9.8	46.7	31.9	8.3	3.2	...
Dallas	205.8	4.1	128.0	50.6	20.6	2.5	...
De Kalb	94.5	...	57.1	23.7	13.7	...	...
Elmore	72.1	...	41.2	19.3	8.5	3.1	...
Escambia	361.7	252.9	12.8	69.7	4.3	22.0	...
Etowah	66.6	...	45.8	10.3	9.2	1.3	...
Fayette	129.7	...	93.8	24.4	8.7	2.8	...
Franklin	84.5	...	51.9	24.9	7.7	...	...
Geneva	48.1	43.2	...	1.4	2.0	1.5	...
Greene	128.2	...	67.8	31.3	7.4	21.7	...
Hale	175.0	20.3	69.9	72.5	3.0	9.3	...
Henry	121.1	6.9	81.1	24.7	6.9	1.5	...
Houston	47.8	33.1	10.3	1.6	1.4	1.4	...

20

Table 12. *Growing-stock volume of softwoods on commercial forest land by forest type, 1972* (Continued)

County	All types	Longleaf-slash pine	Loblolly-shortleaf pine	Oak-pine	Oak-hickory	Oak-gum-cypress	Elm-ash-cottonwood
			-*Million cubic feet*-				
Jackson	40.0	...	11.4	12.2	16.4	...	...
Jefferson	275.7	15.0	204.9	45.5	9.9	...	.4
Lamar	100.7	...	63.1	24.7	8.0	4.9	...
Lauderdale	12.4	...	1.1	7.0	4.3	...	...
Lawrence	50.9	...	26.0	3.5	21.0	.4	...
Lee	159.7	4.7	126.8	23.0	2.5	2.7	...
Limestone	14.2	...	4.2	6.0	.7	3.3	...
Lowndes	109.9	...	69.1	29.7	8.3	2.8	...
Macon	92.0	...	51.7	21.5	10.9	7.9	...
Madison	32.1	...	12.3	6.3	2.0	11.5	...
Marengo	243.5	...	164.5	62.3	8.4	8.3	...
Marion	118.4	...	79.5	25.1	13.4	...	.4
Marshall	107.2	...	73.8	27.1	6.3	...	...
Mobile	234.1	124.2	26.0	49.3	7.0	27.6	...
Monroe	274.4	13.4	101.8	103.8	38.8	16.6	...
Montgomery	73.5	...	55.8	8.0	7.2	2.5	...
Morgan	53.8	...	36.1	12.0	5.7	...	...
Perry	188.2	10.2	90.7	68.2	9.8	7.6	1.7
Pickens	250.1	...	170.2	64.4	7.5	8.0	...
Pike	121.2	19.3	46.5	34.7	9.5	11.2	...
Randolph	125.1	7.8	62.5	50.6	4.2	...	...
Russell	227.4	4.1	200.6	18.4	3.7	.6	...
St. Clair	143.8	7.1	90.6	26.6	11.2	8.3	...
Shelby	174.2	18.4	91.6	44.9	19.3	...	...
Sumter	240.6	...	181.8	31.6	22.0	5.2	...
Talladega	132.6	9.6	62.7	48.0	12.3	...	...
Tallapoosa	176.3	...	97.8	65.5	11.1	1.9	...
Tuscaloosa	362.1	23.9	200.2	97.9	27.1	13.0	...
Walker	257.5	...	185.5	55.3	16.7	...	...
Washington	362.2	134.6	87.4	105.0	12.5	22.7	...
Wilcox	277.6	4.5	155.5	87.1	23.9	6.6	...
Winston	202.8	...	139.5	41.3	22.0	...	...
All counties	11,282.6	1,357.2	5,967.1	2,746.1	793.1	410.9	8.2

21

Table 13. *Growing-stock volume of hardwoods on commercial forest land by forest type, 1972*

County	All types	Longleaf-slash pine	Loblolly-shortleaf pine	Oak-pine	Oak-hickory	Oak-gum-cypress	Elm-ash-cottonwood
			- - - - - - - - - -*Million cubic feet*- - - - - - - - - -				
Autauga	87.4	...	8.5	18.0	34.1	26.8	...
Baldwin	285.1	12.5	2.9	22.5	13.1	234.1	...
Barbour	136.7	.2	23.9	33.4	44.4	34.8	...
Bibb	122.0	2.9	23.4	54.5	33.7	7.5	...
Blount	126.7	...	12.3	31.1	67.8	15.5	...
Bullock	69.7	...	7.2	8.7	22.4	31.4	...
Butler	140.9	1.3	30.1	20.1	64.8	24.6	...
Calhoun	67.8	...	6.2	17.2	44.4	...	...
Chambers	86.4	...	9.6	11.3	51.7	13.8	...
Cherokee	56.3	...	10.8	8.4	24.9	12.2	...
Chilton	130.0	1.4	6.6	33.5	85.5	3.0	...
Choctaw	189.6	...	30.7	43.0	50.0	65.4	0.5
Clarke	346.4	...	60.3	77.4	51.6	149.8	7.3
Clay	96.5	...	9.7	32.5	54.3	...	...
Cleburne	94.1	...	16.8	24.5	52.8	...	...
Coffee	68.9	...	2.2	11.8	33.9	21.0	...
Colbert	127.8	...	1.1	16.0	97.8	8.4	4.5
Conecuh	226.2	1.2	24.3	61.6	80.5	58.6	...
Coosa	107.1	1.5	17.4	36.9	44.4	6.9	...
Covington	118.5	9.1	10.5	14.6	28.6	55.7	...
Crenshaw	137.2	.4	5.0	31.6	29.1	71.1	...
Cullman	112.6	...	15.0	37.2	60.4	...	...
Dale	110.8	...	10.1	25.3	58.4	17.0	...
Dallas	134.6	.7	19.4	22.9	48.7	38.5	4.4
De Kalb	87.1	...	8.8	17.7	60.6	...	...
Elmore	92.7	...	7.7	10.6	46.6	27.8	...
Escambia	116.5	10.1	2.0	22.4	10.5	71.5	...
Etowah	46.7	...	4.2	6.5	33.6	2.4	...
Fayette	134.9	...	13.0	22.9	54.2	43.0	1.8
Franklin	134.3	...	15.6	22.5	96.2	...	...
Geneva	67.9	4.1	...	1.7	12.8	49.3	...
Greene	166.7	...	7.1	22.6	27.6	109.4	...
Hale	124.9	1.4	15.2	28.2	6.7	73.4	...
Henry	65.4	...	5.2	11.9	27.9	20.4	...
Houston	39.3	3.2	.3	.8	1.7	33.3	...

Table 13. *Growing-stock volume of hardwoods on commercial forest land by forest type, 1972* (Continued)

County	All types	Longleaf-slash pine	Loblolly-shortleaf pine	Oak-pine	Oak-hickory	Oak-gum-cypress	Elm-ash-cottonwood
			-Million cubic feet-				
Jackson	375.7	...	1.7	8.7	332.6	32.7	...
Jefferson	88.2	.7	19.4	29.6	34.2	.6	3.7
Lamar	179.0	...	3.8	26.4	45.3	101.5	2.0
Lauderdale	107.7	...	.3	3.9	92.7	10.8	...
Lawrence	100.6	...	4.1	3.5	84.8	8.2	...
Lee	94.6	.4	16.9	17.2	35.1	25.0	...
Limestone	68.0	...	1.7	2.1	39.5	24.7	...
Lowndes	129.1	...	11.6	15.4	28.6	67.1	6.4
Macon	108.8	...	8.1	10.9	18.1	71.7	...
Madison	122.7	...	1.5	1.3	79.9	40.0	...
Marengo	175.5	...	23.6	40.9	36.8	74.2	...
Marion	123.0	...	8.8	18.4	92.3	...	3.5
Marshall	92.9	...	6.9	26.0	60.0	...	...
Mobile	137.2	7.5	10.4	30.3	5.4	83.6	...
Monroe	269.6	1.1	13.0	61.5	106.3	85.3	2.4
Montgomery	90.0	...	1.9	1.4	21.3	65.4	...
Morgan	92.4	...	8.4	10.5	40.0	33.5	...
Perry	119.0	.8	7.5	34.2	32.9	24.6	19.0
Pickens	166.5	...	19.2	38.3	34.0	71.5	3.5
Pike	122.2	...	5.4	17.4	42.3	57.1	...
Randolph	77.3	...	9.0	29.9	36.2	2.2	...
Russell	90.8	...	33.9	7.9	20.0	29.0	...
St. Clair	98.1	...	10.5	19.4	50.4	17.8	...
Shelby	117.3	1.2	15.8	30.1	47.7	11.8	10.7
Sumter	210.4	...	32.0	22.9	63.6	87.5	4.4
Talladega	97.4	1.1	6.8	33.9	55.6	...	...
Tallapoosa	118.7	...	12.4	47.9	40.8	17.6	...
Tuscaloosa	344.9	3.3	35.5	64.9	111.1	130.1	...
Walker	144.2	...	39.6	31.5	73.1	...	...
Washington	238.9	6.1	15.3	58.7	39.6	119.2	...
Wilcox	248.5	.1	22.1	63.6	63.4	99.3	...
Winston	124.2	...	19.4	34.2	70.6	...	...
All counties	8,929.1	72.3	869.6	1,704.6	3,489.9	2,718.6	74.1

Table 14. *Sawtimber volume of softwoods on commercial forest land by forest type, 1972*

County	All types	Longleaf-slash pine	Loblolly-shortleaf pine	Oak-pine	Oak-hickory	Oak-gum-cypress	Elm-ash-cottonwood
			-Million board feet-				
Autauga	670.7	113.4	352.0	120.3	55.6	29.4	...
Baldwin	2,078.6	1,224.0	146.2	352.5	52.1	303.8	...
Barbour	929.4	6.2	631.4	198.9	76.2	16.7	...
Bibb	902.6	95.5	485.5	295.7	25.9	...	...
Blount	352.8	...	271.3	68.4	13.1	...	...
Bullock	487.3	...	347.8	65.8	47.5	26.2	...
Butler	1,081.4	57.9	663.2	234.2	58.7	67.4	...
Calhoun	318.9	...	154.1	138.1	26.7	...	...
Chambers	381.9	...	219.6	44.9	75.5	41.9	...
Cherokee	210.5	...	152.9	42.1	10.8	4.7	...
Chilton	517.7	57.5	252.7	146.7	60.8	...	...
Choctaw	1,683.6	...	1,007.1	463.7	106.9	105.9	...
Clarke	2,732.2	...	1,807.1	704.8	112.5	83.3	24.5
Clay	447.4	...	224.9	153.2	69.3	...	...
Cleburne	569.5	11.3	406.2	102.6	49.4	...	...
Coffee	274.0	11.6	104.3	63.5	81.0	13.6	...
Colbert	46.9	...	1.9	33.6	11.4	...	...
Conecuh	1,127.2	46.0	440.2	494.2	125.1	21.7	...
Coosa	455.3	70.1	256.1	98.1	26.5	4.5	...
Covington	1,279.3	575.5	401.3	205.6	51.1	45.8	...
Crenshaw	629.9	115.4	158.7	191.7	91.6	72.5	...
Cullman	367.3	...	269.9	74.5	22.9	...	...
Dale	400.4	21.4	192.7	144.6	32.4	9.3	...
Dallas	862.0	...	507.0	260.0	83.2	11.8	...
De Kalb	223.9	...	111.6	68.4	43.9	...	...
Elmore	222.7	...	121.0	55.7	28.9	17.1	...
Escambia	1,545.8	994.4	50.5	362.7	22.7	115.5	...
Etowah	153.3	...	91.8	28.6	24.6	8.3	...
Fayette	380.8	...	247.0	101.0	25.0	7.8	...
Franklin	131.4	...	73.5	44.2	13.7	...	...
Geneva	164.0	144.4	...	2.5	7.7	9.4	...
Greene	552.0	...	244.0	147.6	39.6	120.8	...
Hale	794.4	122.2	275.3	324.8	14.7	57.4	...
Henry	388.1	.3	262.2	92.6	25.8	7.2	...
Houston	135.8	85.9	37.7	3.5	3.7	5.0	...

Table 14. *Sawtimber volume of softwoods on commercial forest land by forest type, 1972* (Continued)

County	All types	Longleaf-slash pine	Loblolly shortleaf pine	Oak-pine	Oak-hickory	Oak-gum-cypress	Elm-ash-cottonwood
					Million board feet		
Jackson	123.9	...	39.2	52.0	32.7	...	...
Jefferson	999.3	54.6	773.0	141.6	28.3	...	1.8
Lamar	223.9	...	127.5	52.7	28.8	14.9	...
Lauderdale	25.1	...	2.8	20.3	2.0	...	...
Lawrence	170.2	...	80.0	5.9	83.1	1.2	...
Lee	508.3	18.7	385.2	83.1	12.7	8.6	...
Limestone	73.0	...	18.3	32.2	3.9	18.6	...
Lowndes	486.6	...	308.2	131.9	30.6	15.9	...
Macon	371.3	...	201.4	76.0	48.5	45.4	...
Madison	94.9	...	29.0	20.5	1.5	43.9	...
Marengo	939.8	...	591.8	273.0	34.3	40.7	...
Marion	262.0	...	184.5	50.3	26.0	...	1.2
Marshall	414.9	...	297.0	106.5	11.4	...	...
Mobile	890.3	444.8	91.8	212.5	15.1	126.1	...
Monroe	1,087.6	60.5	296.1	470.8	173.5	86.7	...
Montgomery	259.8	...	198.1	24.8	25.9	11.0	...
Morgan	149.8	...	96.7	37.1	16.0	...	...
Perry	796.7	40.9	330.0	327.2	42.8	46.6	9.2
Pickens	821.4	...	465.2	294.8	19.7	41.7	...
Pike	465.0	21.0	194.0	144.8	39.3	65.9	...
Randolph	387.4	17.6	151.1	205.8	12.9	...	...
Russell	867.5	4.6	774.1	69.0	16.0	3.8	...
St. Clair	397.7	34.7	198.9	86.8	36.7	40.6	...
Shelby	502.3	47.7	240.3	130.1	84.2	...	...
Sumter	1,224.4	...	934.4	155.4	103.9	30.7	...
Talladega	445.4	28.9	188.1	183.0	45.4	...	...
Tallapoosa	561.1	...	232.0	272.3	46.7	10.1	...
Tuscaloosa	1,194.5	103.0	583.5	323.5	102.3	82.2	...
Walker	905.7	...	661.9	195.4	48.4	...	...
Washington	1,433.7	472.1	333.6	462.1	53.0	112.9	...
Wilcox	1,053.4	8.5	569.6	354.4	98.6	22.3	...
Winston	647.5	...	413.2	134.4	99.9	...	...
All counties	42,283.4	5,110.6	20,959.2	11,059.5	3,040.6	2,076.8	36.7

25

Table 15. *Sawtimber volume of hardwoods on commercial forest land by forest type, 1972*

County	All types	Longleaf-slash pine	Loblolly-shortleaf pine	Oak-pine	Oak-hickory	Oak-gum-cypress	Elm-ash-cottonwood
				- - - - - *Million board feet* - - - - - - -			
Autauga	218.3	...	20.0	30.1	77.5	90.7	...
Baldwin	832.5	35.5	1.7	53.6	31.5	710.2	...
Barbour	284.2	...	47.8	50.0	92.4	94.0	...
Bibb	252.6	5.0	63.5	111.0	51.0	22.1	...
Blount	351.3	...	36.3	82.2	182.9	49.9	...
Bullock	154.4	...	19.5	20.1	61.6	53.2	...
Butler	401.4	...	56.1	57.8	197.1	90.4	...
Calhoun	151.4	...	13.3	38.6	99.5	...	...
Chambers	179.8	...	4.0	16.5	104.8	54.5	...
Cherokee	131.2	...	16.7	13.4	64.7	36.4	...
Chilton	212.8	1.7	6.7	39.8	162.7	1.9	...
Choctaw	422.0	...	53.1	103.7	97.7	167.5	...
Clarke	907.2	...	99.6	205.7	124.5	453.0	24.4
Clay	156.0	...	10.9	38.8	106.3	...	...
Cleburne	155.4	...	37.9	45.2	72.3	...	...
Coffee	160.8	...	1.9	34.3	80.6	44.0	...
Colbert	263.4	...	2.2	20.4	222.6	10.7	7.5
Conecuh	606.8	2.0	73.0	183.8	202.2	145.8	...
Coosa	221.1	2.8	29.6	58.4	106.4	23.9	...
Covington	196.0	22.5	18.2	29.0	33.1	93.2	...
Crenshaw	340.6	1.7	7.4	58.2	69.8	203.5	...
Cullman	223.0	...	29.1	68.3	125.6	...	...
Dale	251.0	...	34.1	59.2	133.9	23.8	...
Dallas	222.6	...	25.6	46.5	92.6	52.8	5.1
De Kalb	194.7	...	8.6	41.1	145.0	...	...
Elmore	201.9	...	17.5	13.5	104.1	66.8	...
Escambia	304.8	34.3	5.8	45.4	24.2	195.1	...
Etowah	117.0	...	6.9	11.5	90.8	7.8	...
Fayette	254.8	...	24.4	42.5	113.8	71.5	2.6
Franklin	241.2	...	28.5	35.8	176.9	...	...
Geneva	124.2	...	...	...	25.3	98.9	...
Greene	521.8	...	17.5	41.6	74.4	388.3	....
Hale	291.1	...	40.9	51.7	9.7	188.8	...
Henry	111.7	...	2.3	15.4	55.9	38.1	...
Houston	111.3	9.9	1.4	...	...	100.0	...

Table 15. *Sawtimber volume of hardwoods on commercial forest land by forest type, 1972*
(Continued)

County	All types	Longleaf-slash pine	Loblolly-shortleaf pine	Oak-pine	Oak-hickory	Oak-gum-cypress	Elm-ash-cottonwood
			- - - - - - - - - - -Million board feet- - - - - - - - - - -				
Jackson	1,041.0	...	2.7	13.1	941.7	83.5	...
Jefferson	196.3	2.2	40.0	69.5	66.9	...	17.7
Lamar	375.8	...	7.5	47.8	100.3	220.2	...
Lauderdale	243.1	...	...	4.9	219.2	19.0	...
Lawrence	217.2	...	9.5	1.8	193.6	12.3	...
Lee	241.2	...	21.9	33.5	106.5	79.3	...
Limestone	197.8	...	2.6	6.7	119.3	69.2	...
Lowndes	366.4	...	27.0	41.2	50.3	235.6	12.3
Macon	236.4	...	18.7	26.0	33.4	158.3	...
Madison	250.2	...	4.4	2.2	155.7	87.9	...
Marengo	535.7	...	54.5	85.7	146.3	249.2	...
Marion	218.6	...	9.0	22.6	182.7	...	4.3
Marshall	218.9	...	11.8	74.3	132.8	...	...
Mobile	302.2	13.8	32.2	61.1	8.9	186.2	...
Monroe	777.4	2.0	20.0	141.3	321.4	283.8	8.9
Montgomery	191.8	...	3.2	1.6	32.6	154.4	...
Morgan	225.9	...	7.1	14.1	96.6	108.1	...
Perry	269.4	...	13.4	57.5	82.6	65.9	50.0
Pickens	398.1	...	32.1	92.0	70.4	197.5	6.1
Pike	327.6	...	7.8	36.4	92.1	191.3	...
Randolph	181.8	...	10.3	69.3	95.5	6.7	...
Russell	172.5	...	62.0	9.7	35.1	65.7	...
St. Clair	231.7	...	19.2	43.4	109.9	59.2	...
Shelby	241.3	1.2	24.0	68.6	112.9	30.8	3.8
Sumter	613.1	...	69.5	83.6	186.9	257.8	15.3
Talladega	198.0	1.6	6.1	49.2	141.1	...	...
Tallapoosa	236.8	...	16.9	86.5	103.7	29.7	...
Tuscaloosa	836.0	2.3	56.7	130.6	293.0	353.4	...
Walker	283.5	...	82.9	56.8	143.8	...	...
Washington	609.9	9.8	32.3	111.2	99.7	356.9	...
Wilcox	717.7	...	36.6	158.1	172.8	350.2	...
Winston	310.1	...	43.2	87.4	179.5	...	...
All counties	21,233.7	148.3	1,647.1	3,550.8	8,240.6	7,488.9	158.0

27

Table 16. *Growing-stock volume of softwoods on commercial forest land by stand-size class, 1972*

County	All classes	Sawtimber	Poletimber	Sapling and seedling	Nonstocked areas
			- - - - - -*Million cubic feet*- - - - - - - -		
Autauga	170.5	118.4	36.5	15.6	...
Baldwin	459.5	326.7	61.6	70.8	0.4
Barbour	252.3	131.5	93.4	27.4	...
Bibb	238.7	133.6	73.3	31.8	...
Blount	118.1	72.6	26.2	19.3	...
Bullock	131.3	65.5	55.7	10.1	...
Butler	242.3	175.8	45.3	21.2	...
Calhoun	110.5	33.0	59.5	18.0	...
Chambers	109.8	40.3	38.6	30.9	...
Cherokee	70.3	18.6	24.0	27.7	...
Chilton	134.4	47.1	60.2	27.1	...
Choctaw	380.0	240.9	91.7	47.4	...
Clarke	580.5	465.3	80.9	34.3	...
Clay	135.7	59.5	57.6	18.6	...
Cleburne	186.8	97.8	70.3	18.7	...
Coffee	92.0	38.4	39.0	14.6	...
Colbert	25.5	.5	10.5	14.5	...
Conecuh	244.2	163.7	61.0	19.5	...
Coosa	148.4	54.0	72.3	22.1	...
Covington	306.5	231.4	48.1	27.0	...
Crenshaw	137.6	87.3	36.6	13.7	...
Cullman	138.5	60.6	68.7	9.2	...
Dale	99.9	45.5	39.9	14.1	.4
Dallas	205.8	134.2	46.1	25.5	...
De Kalb	94.5	24.7	58.1	11.7	...
Elmore	72.1	19.4	28.4	24.3	...
Escambia	361.7	258.4	75.7	27.6	...
Etowah	66.6	14.5	38.9	13.2	...
Fayette	129.7	63.5	50.0	16.2	...
Franklin	84.5	8.0	64.0	12.5	...
Geneva	48.1	22.0	19.0	7.1	...
Greene	128.2	80.7	34.1	13.4	...
Hale	175.0	132.2	23.8	19.0	...
Henry	121.1	54.6	52.8	13.7	...
Houston	47.8	19.2	19.1	9.5	...

Table 16. *Growing-stock volume of softwoods on commercial forest land by stand-size class, 1972* (Continued)

County	All classes	Sawtimber	Poletimber	Salping and seedling	Nonstocked areas
- - - - - - -Million cubic feet- - - - - - - - -					
Jackson	40.0	2.2	29.4	8.4	
Jefferson	275.7	126.4	108.7	40.6	...
Lamar	100.7	35.5	54.9	10.3	...
Lauderdale	12.4	...	5.3	7.1	
Lawrence	50.9	29.8	15.2	5.9	
Lee	159.7	79.1	65.8	14.8	...
Limestone	14.2	13.9	.3	...	
Lowndes	109.9	78.3	21.7	9.9	
Macon	92.0	42.8	27.3	21.9	...
Madison	32.1	17.1	11.0	4.0	
Marengo	243.5	137.4	80.9	25.2	...
Marion	118.4	27.0	59.2	32.2	...
Marshall	107.2	83.1	17.5	6.6	...
Mobile	234.1	126.2	57.7	49.4	.8
Monroe	274.4	136.1	97.0	41.3	...
Montgomery	73.5	53.7	14.6	5.2	
Morgan	53.8	24.4	18.9	10.5	...
Perry	188.2	128.0	54.1	6.1	
Pickens	250.1	135.6	79.1	35.4	...
Pike	121.2	64.0	42.5	14.7	...
Randolph	125.1	64.8	39.3	21.0	...
Russell	227.4	126.0	84.4	16.8	.2
St. Clair	143.8	67.0	50.0	26.8	...
Shelby	174.2	62.8	86.3	24.9	.2
Sumter	240.6	206.9	18.4	15.3	...
Talladega	132.6	49.2	70.7	12.7	...
Tallapoosa	176.3	74.7	71.3	30.3	...
Tuscaloosa	362.1	162.8	142.8	56.5	...
Walker	257.5	131.8	98.2	27.5	...
Washington	362.2	208.9	117.5	35.8	...
Wilcox	277.6	201.3	63.4	12.9	...
Winston	202.8	89.8	97.8	15.2	...
All counties	11,282.6	6,326.0	3,562.1	1,392.5	2.0

Table 17. *Growing-stock volume of hardwoods on commercial forest land by stand-size class, 1972*

County	All classes	Sawtimber	Poletimber	Sapling and seedling	Nonstocked areas
			- - - - - - - -*Million cubic feet*- - - - - - - - - -		
Autauga	87.4	60.9	17.2	9.3	...
Baldwin	285.1	201.6	58.6	24.9	...
Barbour	136.7	71.6	49.5	15.4	0.2
Bibb	122.0	32.9	76.5	12.6	...
Blount	126.7	68.6	47.8	10.3	...
Bullock	69.7	29.6	32.6	7.5	...
Butler	140.9	102.1	24.1	14.0	.7
Calhoun	67.8	27.0	30.4	10.4	...
Chambers	86.4	29.3	43.1	14.0	...
Cherokee	56.3	31.1	14.1	11.1	...
Chilton	130.0	43.7	59.2	27.1	...
Choctaw	189.6	90.7	83.3	15.6	...
Clarke	346.4	242.6	86.2	17.6	...
Clay	96.5	20.1	59.9	16.5	...
Cleburne	94.1	21.9	57.0	15.2	...
Coffee	68.9	33.7	29.2	6.0	...
Colbert	127.8	24.2	85.2	18.4	...
Conecuh	226.2	136.8	70.5	18.9	...
Coosa	107.1	25.0	66.3	15.8	...
Covington	118.5	45.0	61.0	12.5	...
Crenshaw	137.2	75.9	53.2	7.7	.4
Cullman	112.6	26.7	80.7	5.2	...
Dale	110.8	47.9	44.2	18.7	...
Dallas	134.6	52.7	60.0	21.9	...
De Kalb	87.1	44.5	27.9	14.7	...
Elmore	92.7	38.9	36.4	17.4	...
Escambia	116.5	76.5	34.8	5.2	...
Etowah	46.7	19.8	13.9	13.0	...
Fayette	134.9	39.5	81.9	13.5	...
Franklin	134.3	15.4	90.0	28.9	...
Geneva	67.9	25.3	34.7	7.9	...
Greene	166.7	124.3	36.2	6.2	...
Hale	124.9	58.5	57.0	9.4	...
Henry	65.4	26.1	32.2	7.1	...
Houston	39.3	26.5	3.6	9.2	...

Table 17. *Growing-stock volume of hardwoods on commercial forest land by stand-size class, 1972*   (Continued)

County	All classes	Sawtimber	Poletimber	Sapling and seedling	Nonstocked areas
- - - - - - -Million cubic feet- - - - - - - - -					
Jackson	375.7	213.1	124.0	38.6	...
Jefferson	88.2	31.5	37.3	19.4	...
Lamar	179.0	57.0	107.4	14.6	...
Lauderdale	107.7	48.5	42.0	17.2	...
Lawrence	100.6	25.8	62.2	12.6	...
Lee	94.6	48.2	36.5	9.4	.5
Limestone	68.0	36.6	28.7	2.7	...
Lowndes	129.1	81.2	31.9	16.0	...
Macon	108.8	40.5	58.4	9.9	...
Madison	122.7	47.8	66.5	8.4	...
Marengo	175.5	108.4	50.5	16.6	...
Marion	123.0	28.5	74.5	20.0	...
Marshall	92.9	40.1	47.2	5.6	...
Mobile	137.2	81.9	45.2	10.1	...
Monroe	269.6	186.1	63.8	19.7	...
Montgomery	90.0	41.6	43.0	5.4	...
Morgan	92.4	44.7	36.9	10.8	...
Perry	119.0	70.2	39.7	9.1	...
Pickens	166.5	95.7	56.6	14.2	...
Pike	122.2	62.4	47.7	12.1	...
Randolph	77.3	39.7	16.7	20.9	...
Russell	90.8	33.9	48.8	8.1	...
St. Clair	98.1	30.5	51.4	16.2	...
Shelby	117.3	54.8	51.1	11.4	...
Sumter	210.4	140.7	43.3	26.4	...
Talladega	97.4	53.3	33.4	10.7	...
Tallapoosa	118.7	53.5	31.4	33.8	...
Tuscaloosa	344.9	155.8	149.9	39.2	...
Walker	144.2	56.1	75.8	12.3	...
Washington	238.9	154.9	62.0	22.0	...
Wilcox	248.5	190.3	37.2	21.0	...
Winston	124.2	61.3	37.6	25.3	...
All counties	8,929.1	4,451.5	3,477.0	998.8	1.8

Table 18. *Sawtimber volume of softwoods on commercial forest land by stand-size class, 1972*

County	All classes	Sawtimber	Poletimber	Sapling and seedling	Nonstocked areas
			- - - - - - - *Million board feet-* - - - - - -		
Autauga	670.7	540.1	97.5	33.1	...
Baldwin	2,078.6	1,666.0	137.9	274.7	...
Barbour	929.4	558.6	254.3	116.5	...
Bibb	902.6	667.5	154.9	80.2	·...
Blount	352.8	281.5	35.8	35.5	...
Bullock	487.3	307.6	135.1	44.6	...
Butler	1,081.4	895.8	129.3	56.3	...
Calhoun	318.9	116.8	143.7	58.4	...
Chambers	381.9	198.1	97.2	86.6	...
Cherokee	210.5	82.4	40.1	88.0	...
Chilton	517.7	269.2	173.8	74.7	...
Choctaw	1,683.6	1,208.7	285.8	189.1	...
Clarke	2,732.2	2,373.0	237.5	121.7	...
Clay	447.4	267.3	135.7	44.4	...
Cleburne	569.5	376.9	170.8	21.8	...
Coffee	274.0	152.0	86.5	35.5	...
Colbert	46.9	2.5	17.5	26.9	...
Conecuh	1,127.2	879.4	169.5	78.3	...
Coosa	455.3	242.5	164.0	48.8	...
Covington	1,279.3	1,074.7	117.0	87.6	...
Crenshaw	629.9	435.9	146.0	48.0	...
Cullman	367.3	229.6	122.8	14.9	...
Dale	400.4	224.1	133.4	41.0	1.9
Dallas	862.0	686.1	98.0	77.9	...
De Kalb	223.9	108.1	94.8	21.0	...
Elmore	222.7	90.9	58.5	73.3	...
Escambia	1,545.8	1,251.9	214.0	79.9	...
Etowah	153.3	58.8	64.9	29.6	...
Fayette	380.8	260.4	96.6	23.8	...
Franklin	131.4	22.6	80.3	28.5	...
Geneva	164.0	103.3	38.6	22.1	...
Greene	552.0	411.1	95.1	45.8	...
Hale	794.4	664.7	65.6	64.1	...
Henry	388.1	230.9	104.8	52.4	...
Houston	135.8	105.9	6.7	23.2	...

Table 18. *Sawtimber volume of softwoods on commercial forest land by stand-size class, 1972* (Continued)

County	All classes	Sawtimber	Poletimber	Sapling and seedling	Nonstocked areas
			- - - - - - - Million board feet - - - - - - -		
Jackson	123.9	11.4	90.7	21.8	...
Jefferson	999.3	619.2	270.6	109.5	...
Lamar	223.9	115.5	90.4	18.0	...
Lauderdale	25.1	...	2.8	22.3	...
Lawrence	170.2	130.7	32.3	7.2	
Lee	508.3	333.0	152.9	22.4	...
Limestone	73.0	73.0	...	...	
Lowndes	486.6	403.7	52.7	30.2	...
Macon	371.3	211.2	84.3	75.8	...
Madison	94.9	73.7	9.8	11.4	...
Marengo	939.8	625.5	230.6	83.7	...
Marion	262.0	110.9	97.1	54.0	...
Marshall	414.9	384.9	22.7	7.3	...
Mobile	890.3	602.0	142.7	142.7	2.9
Monroe	1,087.6	679.5	288.3	119.8	...
Montgomery	259.8	204.0	47.0	8.8	
Morgan	149.8	73.7	43.2	32.9	...
Perry	796.7	638.7	151.5	6.5	...
Pickens	821.4	588.3	103.0	130.1	...
Pike	465.0	316.6	100.6	47.8	...
Randolph	387.4	264.1	70.4	52.9	...
Russell	867.5	583.3	224.0	60.2	...
St. Clair	397.7	255.8	77.0	64.9	...
Shelby	502.3	282.9	161.6	56.9	.9
Sumter	1,224.4	1,095.9	61.4	67.1	...
Talladega	445.4	226.0	185.1	34.3	...
Tallapoosa	561.1	333.5	173.0	54.6	...
Tuscaloosa	1,194.5	759.6	318.1	116.8	...
Walker	905.7	597.3	227.5	80.9	...
Washington	1,433.7	993.7	344.5	95.5	...
Wilcox	1,053.4	864.8	146.0	42.6	...
Winston	647.5	427.8	187.8	31.9	...
All counties	42,283.4	29,925.1	8,393.6	3,959.0	5.7

Table 19. *Sawtimber volume of hardwoods on commercial forest land by stand-size class, 1972*

County	All classes	Sawtimber	Poletimber	Sapling and seedling	Nonstocked areas
- - - - - - -Million board feet- - - - - - -					
Autauga	218.3	185.2	22.7	10.4	...
Baldwin	832.5	655.4	108.9	68.2	...
Barbour	284.2	213.8	54.5	15.9	...
Bibb	252.6	79.6	149.9	23.1	...
Blount	351.3	228.2	101.8	21.3	...
Bullock	154.4	85.2	45.2	24.0	...
Butler	401.4	332.3	47.0	22.1	...
Calhoun	151.4	92.2	47.8	11.4	...
Chambers	179.8	88.7	73.1	18.0	...
Cherokee	131.2	97.5	10.1	23.6	...
Chilton	212.8	109.0	55.2	48.6	...
Choctaw	422.0	274.6	127.3	20.1	...
Clarke	907.2	752.1	128.3	26.8	...
Clay	156.0	48.4	80.2	27.4	...
Cleburne	155.4	57.0	76.5	21.9	...
Coffee	160.8	118.2	36.7	5.9	...
Colbert	263.4	93.1	143.2	27.1	...
Conecuh	606.8	427.7	150.4	28.7	...
Coosa	221.1	80.9	121.4	18.8	...
Covington	196.0	115.0	66.6	14.4	...
Crenshaw	340.6	259.8	65.3	15.5	...
Cullman	223.0	78.0	139.9	5.1	
Dale	251.0	160.3	62.2	28.5	...
Dallas	222.6	121.1	59.8	41.7	...
De Kalb	194.7	128.4	30.3	36.0	...
Elmore	201.9	115.2	56.1	30.6	...
Escambia	304.8	251.8	40.2	12.8	...
Etowah	117.0	75.0	19.1	22.9	...
Fayette	254.8	115.3	119.7	19.8	...
Franklin	241.2	43.3	161.6	36.3	...
Geneva	124.2	74.5	38.2	11.5	...
Greene	521.8	444.5	64.6	12.7	...
Hale	291.1	190.1	88.3	12.7	...
Henry	111.7	61.2	36.7	13.8	...
Houston	111.3	88.8	6.0	16.5	...

Table 19. *Sawtimber volume of hardwoods on commercial forest land by stand-size class, 1972* (Continued)

County	All classes	Sawtimber	Poletimber	Sapling and seedling	Nonstocked areas
	- - - - - - -*Million board feet*- - - - - -				
Jackson	1,041.0	759.0	213.3	68.7	...
Jefferson	196.3	97.9	59.6	38.8	...
Lamar	375.8	191.0	153.6	31.2	...
Lauderdale	243.1	175.9	48.8	18.4	...
Lawrence	217.2	81.5	122.4	13.3	...
Lee	241.2	149.7	58.1	31.7	1.7
Limestone	197.8	138.8	56.6	2.4	...
Lowndes	366.4	273.9	66.7	25.8	...
Macon	236.4	121.4	100.4	14.6	...
Madison	250.2	142.4	96.4	11.4	...
Marengo	535.7	415.1	92.7	27.9	...
Marion	218.6	73.1	114.6	30.9	...
Marshall	218.9	107.2	102.6	9.1	...
Mobile	302.2	235.8	48.7	17.7	...
Monroe	777.4	622.6	116.3	38.5	...
Montgomery	191.8	121.0	61.7	9.1	...
Morgan	225.9	161.6	51.0	13.3	...
Perry	269.4	200.7	55.9	12.8	...
Pickens	398.1	282.6	97.0	18.5	...
Pike	327.6	207.9	94.0	25.7	...
Randolph	181.8	123.3	14.5	44.0	...
Russell	172.5	87.2	71.0	14.3	...
St. Clair	231.7	112.7	92.5	26.5	...
Shelby	241.3	167.4	61.7	12.2	...
Sumter	613.1	480.3	64.2	68.6	...
Talladega	198.0	139.9	46.6	11.5	...
Tallapoosa	236.8	139.3	44.2	53.3	...
Tuscaloosa	836.0	475.7	283.9	76.4	...
Walker	283.5	160.3	108.6	14.6	...
Washington	609.9	471.4	102.7	35.8	...
Wilcox	717.7	623.6	52.9	41.2	...
Winston	310.1	198.5	64.6	47.0	...
All counties	21,233.7	14,080.1	5,452.6	1,699.3	1.7

Table 20. *Net annual growth of growing stock on commercial forest land by species group, 1971*

County	All species	Softwood			Hardwood			
		Total	Pine	Other	Total	Oak	Gum	Other

- - - - - - - - - - *Million cubic feet-* - - - - - - - - -

County	All species	Total	Pine	Other	Total	Oak	Gum	Other
Autauga	16.2	12.6	12.6	([1])	3.6	1.3	1.0	1.3
Baldwin	31.5	22.3	20.9	1.4	9.2	2.2	3.9	3.1
Barbour	24.6	18.1	18.1	([1])	6 5	1.9	2.9	1.7
Bibb	20.6	15.3	15.2	.1	5 3	2.2	1.5	1.6
Blount	16.5	9.8	9.8	([1])	6.7	3.7	.5	2.5
Bullock	14.1	10.2	10.1	.1	3.9	1.1	1.5	1.3
Butler	20.6	14.9	14.7	.2	5.7	2.1	1.5	2.1
Calhoun	14.5	10.7	10.7	...	3.8	2.4	.3	1.1
Chambers	12.5	8.9	8.9	...	3.6	1.2	1.0	1.4
Cherokee	8.8	6.0	6.0	...	2.8	2.1	.1	.6
Chilton	17.8	11.4	11.4	([1])	6.4	2.5	1.4	2.5
Choctaw	35.9	24.5	24.2	.3	11.4	4.7	3.4	3.3
Clarke	49.0	32.1	31.6	.5	16.9	6.3	4.2	6.4
Clay	14.7	9.6	9.6	...	5.1	2.8	.7	1.6
Cleburne	15.2	10.6	10.6	...	4.6	2.9	.4	1.3
Coffee	11.0	7.8	7.8	([1])	3.2	1.9	.5	.8
Colbert	5.0	1.1	1.1	([1])	3.9	2.2	.1	1.6
Conecuh	27.7	16.8	16.8	([1])	10.9	5.0	2.9	3.0
Coosa	19.0	12.9	12.9	...	6.1	2.8	1.6	1.7
Covington	22.3	17.3	17.2	.1	5.0	1.9	1.4	1.7
Crenshaw	13.3	8.3	8.3	([1])	5.0	1.8	1.6	1.6
Cullman	17.1	11.0	11.0	([1])	6.1	3.6	.8	1.7
Dale	13.0	7.9	7.8	.1	5.1	1.8	1.5	1.8
Dallas	19.9	14.0	14.0	...	5.9	2.4	2.1	1.4
De Kalb	8.4	5.5	5.5	...	2.9	2.2	.2	.5
Elmore	11.5	6.7	6.5	.2	4.8	1.8	1.5	1.5
Escambia	23.5	18.6	18.6	([1])	4.9	1.3	.9	2.7
Etowah	9.0	6.8	6.8	...	2.2	1.3	.3	.6
Fayette	18.1	11.4	11.4	([1])	6.7	2.7	1.7	2.3
Franklin	8.7	4.2	4.2	([1])	4.5	2.8	.2	1.5
Geneva	6.3	3.2	3.2	([1])	3.1	.8	1.1	1.2
Greene	14.6	7.6	7.5	.1	7.0	1.5	2.3	3.2
Hale	15.0	9.8	9.8	([1])	5.2	2.2	1.4	1.6
Henry	13.6	10.4	10.4	...	3.2	1.5	.6	1.1
Houston	6.4	4.4	4.4	...	2.0	.5	.6	.9

36

Table 20. *Net annual growth of growing stock on commercial forest land by species group, 1971* (Continued)

County	All species	Softwood			Hardwood			
		Total	Pine	Other	Total	Oak	Gum	Other
				- - - - - - - - - - *Million cubic feet* - - - - - - - - -				
Jackson	10.0	1.8	1.3	.5	8.2	5.0	.7	2.5
Jefferson	27.7	21.9	21.9	...	5.8	3.4	.9	1.5
Lamar	18.8	10.1	9.9	.2	8.7	2.8	3.5	2.4
Lauderdale	6.5	1.1	1.1	...	5.4	3.8	.8	.8
Lawrence	5.5	1.8	1.7	.1	3.7	2.7	.4	.6
Lee	17.0	12.5	12.5	...	4.5	1.1	2.0	1.4
Limestone	2.6	.4	.4	(1)	2.2	1.1	.5	.6
Lowndes	13.0	7.5	7.5	...	5.5	1.7	1.4	2.4
Macon	11.8	7.2	7.1	.1	4.6	1.7	1.0	1.9
Madison	5.2	1.7	1.4	.3	3.5	1.6	.5	1.4
Marengo	24.7	16.4	16.0	.4	8.3	4.2	1.5	2.6
Marion	19.2	12.0	12.0	(1)	7.2	4.1	.8	2.3
Marshall	7.2	3.9	3.7	.2	3.3	1.6	.7	1.0
Mobile	22.6	17.4	16.4	1.0	5.2	.9	2.2	2.1
Monroe	31.0	19.3	19.0	.3	11.7	4.4	3.5	3.8
Montgomery	10.2	5.1	5.0	.1	5.1	1.9	1.2	2.0
Morgan	6.2	2.9	2.9	(1)	3.3	1.9	.7	.7
Perry	17.8	11.4	11.3	.1	6.4	1.9	1.5	3.0
Pickens	27.2	19.8	19.7	.1	7.4	3.2	2.3	1.9
Pike	14.7	8.5	8.4	.1	6.2	2.7	2.0	1.5
Randolph	15.8	11.9	11.9	...	3.9	2.0	.6	1.3
Russell	19.7	15.0	15.0	...	4.7	1.1	2.0	1.6
St. Clair	21.0	15.9	15.8	.1	5.1	2.9	.7	1.5
Shelby	21.1	14.7	14.7	...	6.4	3.3	.9	2.2
Sumter	23.8	13.2	12.8	.4	10.6	4.2	2.9	3.5
Talladega	15.7	11.1	11.1	...	4.6	2.6	.8	1.2
Tallapoosa	21.5	15.5	15.5	(1)	6.0	2.0	1.5	2.5
Tuscaloosa	43.2	29.7	29.6	.1	13.5	5.3	4.8	3.4
Walker	27.9	19.4	19.4	...	8.5	5.0	1.0	2.5
Washington	31.9	22.1	21.9	.2	9.8	4.0	1.9	3.9
Wilcox	28.4	18.0	17.7	.3	10.4	5.4	2.3	2.7
Winston	22.6	16.1	16.1	(1)	6.5	4.1	.5	1.9
All counties	1,187.4	788.0	780.3	7.7	399.4	175.0	95.6	128.8

[1] Negligible.

37

Table 21. *Net annual growth of sawtimber on commercial forest land by species group, 1971*

County	All species	Softwood			Hardwood			
		Total	Pine	Other	Total	Oak	Gum	Other
				- - -Million board feet- - - - - - - - - - -				
Autauga	53.2	46.2	46.0	0.2	7.0	2.2	3.1	1.7
Baldwin	142.1	114.1	108.0	6.1	28.0	7.6	10.7	9.7
Barbour	99.4	80.2	80.2	...	19.2	5.3	4.8	9.1
Bibb	81.3	66.2	65.1	1.1	15.1	7.5	5.8	1.8
Blount	47.7	32.8	32.8	...	14.9	10.0	1.0	3.9
Bullock	53.2	44.1	44.0	..1	9.1	3.9	1.8	3.4
Butler	83.3	67.4	66.6	.8	15.9	8.1	2.4	5.4
Calhoun	39.4	31.2	31.2	...	8.2	3.4	.3	4.5
Chambers	40.6	31.4	31.4	...	9.2	3.8	2.3	3.1
Cherokee	20.5	12.0	12.0	...	8.5	8.0	.1	.4
Chilton	49.2	36.0	36.0	...	13.2	6.9	1.7	4.6
Choctaw	152.6	124.7	122.9	1.8	27.9	15.3	5.8	6.8
Clarke	192.4	154.4	152.0	2.4	38.0	17.7	7.7	12.6
Clay	40.1	31.5	31.5	...	8.6	4.8	1.8	2.0
Cleburne	61.9	51.6	51.6	...	10.3	8.6	.3	1.4
Coffee	36.8	30.9	30.9	...	5.9	4.0	.5	1.4
Colbert	20.7	3.6	3.6	(^{1})	17.1	12.2	.1	4.8
Conecuh	93.5	66.9	66.8	.1	26.6	14.4	7.5	4.7
Coosa	64.8	48.2	48.2	...	16.6	11.0	2.8	2.8
Covington	86.7	75.4	75.0	.4	11.3	3.9	3.0	4.4
Crenshaw	67.7	47.4	45.4	2.0	20.3	11.4	2.6	6.3
Cullman	48.5	34.2	34.2	...	14.3	8.3	.5	5.5
Dale	39.0	28.7	28.5	.2	10.3	5.6	1.7	3.0
Dallas	69.4	56.7	56.7	...	12.7	5.9	4.5	2.3
De Kalb	19.0	12.7	12.7	...	6.3	3.9	.4	2.0
Elmore	39.6	23.7	23.0	.7	15.9	6.8	2.8	6.3
Escambia	95.8	80.8	80.8	...	15.0	7.6	3.6	3.8
Etowah	25.0	15.6	15.6	...	9.4	8.7	.2	.5
Fayette	54.0	36.5	36.5	...	17.5	8.8	4.5	4.2
Franklin	21.0	10.7	10.7	...	10.3	5.2	2.5	2.6
Geneva	19.0	12.5	12.4	.1	6.5	2.6	1.6	2.3
Greene	58.0	39.5	38.9	.6	18.5	7.0	5.3	6.2
Hale	62.8	51.8	51.8	...	11.0	5.8	1.8	3.4
Henry	47.4	42.2	42.2	...	5.2	3.4	.6	1.2
Houston	15.6	9.1	9.1	...	6.5	2.5	1.1	2.9

38

Table 21. *Net annual growth of sawtimber on commercial forest land by species group, 1971* (Continued)

County	All species	Softwood			Hardwood			
		Total	Pine	Other	Total	Oak	Gum	Other
				-*Million board feet*-				
Jackson	34.4	4.6	2.9	1.7	29.8	17.7	.5	11.6
Jefferson	91.5	77.8	77.8	...	13.7	6.6	1.8	5.3
Lamar	45.9	27.1	26.7	.4	18.8	8.8	4.1	5.9
Lauderdale	21.3	4.2	4.2	...	17.1	11.5	1.3	4.3
Lawrence	9.6	5.3	5.1	.2	4.3	3.6	.1	.6
Lee	94.3	82.6	82.6	...	11.7	2.0	2.5	7.2
Limestone	6.5	2.3	2.3	...	4.2	3.2	.2	.8
Lowndes	60.1	41.7	41.7	...	18.4	5.8	5.2	7.4
Macon	38.7	27.5	27.2	.3	11.2	4.0	3.8	3.4
Madison	14.7	4.7	3.2	1.5	10.0	4.8	1.9	3.3
Marengo	100.6	74.4	72.9	1.5	26.2	18.0	2.5	5.7
Marion	39.2	25.3	25.2	.1	13.9	9.5	.4	4.0
Marshall	27.2	19.2	19.1	.1	8.0	4.2	2.3	1.5
Mobile	75.0	64.0	61.1	2.9	11.0	4.4	3.4	3.2
Monroe	135.3	96.2	94.3	1.9	39.1	20.3	10.0	8.8
Montgomery	35.6	25.8	25.6	.2	9.8	2.7	2.8	4.3
Morgan	15.9	8.0	7.9	.1	7.9	4.5	1.9	1.5
Perry	61.2	50.9	50.1	.8	10.3	3.5	2.2	4.6
Pickens	96.2	75.5	75.4	.1	20.7	14.3	3.1	3.3
Pike	53.6	37.8	37.5	.3	15.8	5.4	3.2	7.2
Randolph	45.4	35.9	35.9	...	9.5	5.9	.2	3.4
Russell	81.2	72.7	72.7	...	8.5	1.5	4.1	2.9
St. Clair	48.5	38.8	38.8	...	9.7	5.2	2.4	2.1
Shelby	76.0	53.3	53.3	...	22.7	17.7	2.1	2.9
Sumter	119.5	81.0	80.4	.6	38.5	18.9	10.6	9.0
Talladega	50.3	37.1	37.1	...	13.2	8.5	.8	3.9
Tallapoosa	66.5	49.4	49.4	...	17.1	4.3	3.9	8.9
Tuscaloosa	125.7	94.2	94.0	.2	31.5	12.9	7.4	11.2
Walker	93.9	72.6	72.6	...	21.3	10.4	3.7	7.2
Washington	126.6	94.8	93.4	1.4	31.8	16.7	5.1	10.0
Wilcox	110.6	77.9	77.9	(1)	32.7	14.8	8.4	9.5
Winston	59.5	40.0	40.0	...	19.5	14.8	.4	4.3
All counties	4,201.7	3,153.5	3,122.6	30.9	1,048.2	538.5	199.5	310.2

[1]Negligible.

39

Table 22. *Timber removals from growing stock on commercial forest land by species group and county, 1971*

County	All species	Softwood			Hardwood			
		Total	Pine	Other	Total	Oak	Gum	Other
				- - - - - - - - *Million cubic feet-* - - - - - - -				
Autauga	6.7	4.1	4.1	...	2.6	0.5	1.2	0.9
Baldwin	28.7	22.5	22.4	.1	6.2	.6	2.8	2.8
Barbour	15.7	11.8	11.8	...	3.9	1.9	.7	1.3
Bibb	14.2	10.4	10.4	...	3.8	.8	1.0	2.0
Blount	4.6	3.8	3.8	...	.8	.3	.2	.3
Bullock	5.7	4.3	4.3	...	1.4	.3	.7	.4
Butler	21.9	15.5	15.5	...	6.4	3.2	1.9	1.3
Calhoun	5.5	4.5	4.5	...	1.0	.7	.1	.2
Chambers	7.9	5.9	5.9	...	2.0	.4	.7	.9
Cherokee	7.4	3.3	3.3	...	4.1	3.0	...	1.1
Chilton	10.1	7.2	7.2	...	2.9	1.3	.8	.8
Choctaw	30.6	19.5	19.3	.2	11.1	4.1	3.2	3.8
Clarke	36.2	25.8	25.8	...	10.4	5.4	2.7	2.3
Clay	10.2	7.1	7.1	...	3.1	2.2	...	.9
Cleburne	7.0	5.4	5.4	...	1.6	1.1	.1	.4
Coffee	4.8	3.3	3.3	...	1.5	.9	...	.6
Colbert	2.9	1.0	.9	.1	1.9	1.1	.2	.6
Conecuh	19.3	14.9	14.9	...	4.4	2.3	1.4	.7
Coosa	12.1	8.7	8.7	...	3.4	1.1	.5	1.8
Covington	17.2	15.1	15.1	...	2.1	.9	.9	.3
Crenshaw	12.0	8.4	8.1	.3	3.6	1.2	.9	1.5
Cullman	7.2	5.9	5.9	...	1.3	.8	...	.5
Dale	9.8	6.8	6.8	...	3.0	1.3	1.5	.2
Dallas	13.2	8.4	8.4	...	4.8	1.9	1.6	1.3
De Kalb	2.6	1.6	1.6	...	1.0	.5	.1	.4
Elmore	6.2	4.6	4.6	...	1.6	.3	.8	.5
Escambia	17.3	14.9	14.9	...	2.4	.4	.6	1.4
Etowah	3.7	3.1	3.1	...	.6	.3	.1	.2
Fayette	5.0	3.6	3.6	...	1.4	.9	.2	.3
Franklin	4.3	2.3	2.3	...	2.0	1.0	.2	.8
Geneva	5.5	4.5	4.5	...	1.0	.2	.7	.1
Greene	9.5	5.4	5.4	...	4.1	1.6	1.5	1.0
Hale	10.8	6.6	6.6	...	4.2	3.2	.2	.8
Henry	6.8	4.8	4.8	...	2.0	.6	.5	.9
Houston	4.9	2.8	2.8	...	2.1	.6	1.0	.5

40

Table 22. *Timber removals from growing stock on commercial forest land by species group and county, 1971* (Continued)

County	All species	Softwood			Hardwood			
		Total	Pine	Other	Total	Oak	Gum	Other
		- - - - - - - - - *Million cubic feet* - - - - - - - -						
Jackson	5.0	2.6	.7	1.9	2.4	1.5	.3	.6
Jefferson	14.0	11.8	11.8	...	2.2	1.6	.1	.5
Lamar	7.4	5.1	5.1	...	2.3	1.3	.8	.2
Lauderdale	2.2	.7	.7	...	1.5	.6	.2	.7
Lawrence	2.7	.8	.7	.1	1.9	1.6	.1	.2
Lee	9.6	8.4	8.4	...	1.2	.3	.5	.4
Limestone	1.7	.1	.1	...	1.6	.6	.2	.8
Lowndes	12.1	8.7	8.7	...	3.4	1.4	1.0	1.0
Macon	6.4	4.8	4.8	...	1.6	.2	.7	.7
Madison	1.2	.2	...	.2	1.0	.3	.1	.6
Marengo	19.3	11.3	11.3	...	8.0	2.7	1.3	4.0
Marion	7.8	5.1	5.1	...	2.7	2.0	...	.7
Marshall	2.4	1.6	1.0	.6	.8	.8	...	...
Mobile	15.0	11.9	11.7	.2	3.1	1.0	1.2	.9
Monroe	22.6	15.9	15.9	...	6.7	2.9	2.0	1.8
Montgomery	8.3	5.6	5.6	...	2.7	.4	1.3	1.0
Morgan	2.4	1.1	.8	.3	1.3	.5	.3	.5
Perry	12.4	8.7	8.7	...	3.7	.2	3.0	.5
Pickens	16.3	9.8	9.7	.1	6.5	3.7	1.1	1.7
Pike	13.8	8.2	8.2	...	5.6	1.0	2.1	2.5
Randolph	9.0	6.7	6.7	...	2.3	1.8	.4	.1
Russell	7.8	6.9	6.9	...	.9	.2	.4	.3
St. Clair	6.8	5.1	5.1	...	1.7	.8	.3	.6
Shelby	9.1	7.5	7.5	...	1.6	.9	.2	.5
Sumter	19.5	13.8	13.8	...	5.7	2.7	.8	2.2
Talladega	12.8	11.2	11.2	...	1.6	.1	.5	1.0
Tallapoosa	15.3	11.3	11.3	...	4.0	2.0	.4	1.6
Tuscaloosa	17.2	11.0	11.0	...	6.2	3.3	1.3	1.6
Walker	15.6	12.4	12.4	...	3.2	1.5	.1	1.6
Washington	22.3	17.2	17.1	.1	5.1	1.1	3.1	.9
Wilcox	24.8	16.6	16.5	.1	8.2	3.2	1.7	3.3
Winston	9.3	6.0	6.0	...	3.3	2.1	...	1.2
All counties	739.6	525.9	521.6	4.3	213.7	91.2	54.5	68.0

Table 23. *Timber removals from sawtimber on commercial forest land by species group and county, 1971*

County	All species	Softwood			Hardwood			
		Total	Pine	Other	Total	Oak	Gum	Other

– – – – – – – – – – – *Million board feet* – – – – – – – – – – –

County	All species	Total	Pine	Other	Total	Oak	Gum	Other
Autauga	24.8	16.5	16.5	...	8.3	1.9	1.9	4.5
Baldwin	101.3	80.9	80.0	.9	20.4	1.7	8.2	10.5
Barbour	61.1	46.2	46.2	...	14.9	6.7	1.6	6.6
Bibb	57.9	44.5	44.5	...	13.4	3.1	4.8	5.5
Blount	17.1	14.2	14.2	...	2.9	.8	...	2.1
Bullock	22.5	17.4	17.4	...	5.1	1.0	2.8	1.3
Butler	89.7	72.0	72.0	...	17.7	10.1	4.8	2.8
Calhoun	20.2	17.1	17.1	...	3.1	2.0	1.1	...
Chambers	28.0	21.5	21.5	...	6.5	1.1	1.2	4.2
Cherokee	19.0	11.4	11.4	...	7.6	7.6	...	...
Chilton	37.4	27.4	27.4	...	10.0	6.7	1.0	2.3
Choctaw	116.4	89.3	88.1	1.2	27.1	10.9	5.9	10.3
Clarke	161.7	125.4	125.4	...	36.3	19.7	8.3	8.3
Clay	34.8	25.4	25.4	...	9.4	7.2	...	2.2
Cleburne	22.0	17.6	17.6	...	4.4	3.1	...	1.3
Coffee	15.5	11.0	11.0	...	4.5	2.1	...	2.4
Colbert	11.2	4.3	3.3	1.0	6.9	3.1	.6	3.2
Conecuh	78.3	64.7	64.7	...	13.6	6.6	4.3	2.7
Coosa	36.9	27.9	27.9	...	9.0	2.4	1.6	5.0
Covington	70.0	64.9	64.9	...	5.1	2.1	1.9	1.1
Crensahw	47.3	34.9	32.8	2.1	12.4	4.6	3.1	4.7
Cullman	26.7	21.7	21.7	...	5.0	2.8	...	2.2
Dale	33.9	26.1	26.1	...	7.8	3.4	3.6	.8
Dallas	48.5	35.0	35.0	...	13.5	6.5	4.2	2.8
De Kalb	9.0	5.1	5.1	...	3.9	2.0	.7	1.2
Elmore	20.4	16.0	16.0	...	4.4	1.0	2.3	1.1
Escambia	63.3	56.0	56.0	...	7.3	1.6	2.1	3.6
Etowah	11.9	9.9	9.9	...	2.0	1.2	.3	.5
Fayette	20.1	13.9	13.9	...	6.2	3.9	1.2	1.1
Franklin	16.1	8.0	8.0	...	8.1	4.5	.4	3.2
Geneva	20.9	17.3	17.3	...	3.6	.6	2.7	.3
Greene	39.3	23.6	23.6	...	15.7	5.4	7.1	3.2
Hale	45.3	29.1	29.1	...	16.2	11.9	1.0	3.3
Henry	24.5	18.2	18.2	...	6.3	1.6	1.4	3.3
Houston	12.8	8.3	8.3	...	4.5	2.3	.8	1.4

Table 23. *Timber removals from sawtimber on commercial forest land by species group and county, 1971* (Continued)

County	All species	Softwood			Hardwood			
		Total	Pine	Other	Total	Oak	Gum	Other
				-Million board feet-				
Jackson	24.2	13.2	8.3	4.9	11.0	7.7	.6	2.7
Jefferson	68.4	59.0	59.0	...	9.4	7.7	.4	1.3
Lamar	28.1	18.7	18.7	...	9.4	3.0	5.6	.8
Lauderdale	8.1	2.0	2.0	...	6.1	2.3	.9	2.9
Lawrence	10.1	3.8	3.8	...	6.3	5.5	.2	.6
Lee	35.6	31.1	31.1	...	4.5	.4	1.9	2.2
Limestone	7.2	.6	.6	...	6.6	3.4	.6	2.6
Lowndes	47.6	36.6	36.6	...	11.0	5.6	2.4	3.0
Macon	23.3	17.3	17.3	...	6.0	1.6	1.7	2.7
Madison	4.2	.7	...	.7	3.5	1.8	.3	1.4
Marengo	66.3	42.6	42.6	...	23.7	9.6	2.1	12.0
Marion	28.2	18.2	18.2	...	10.0	9.4	...	.6
Marshall	8.9	5.6	3.6	2.0	3.3	3.3	...	...
Mobile	52.9	43.2	42.6	.6	9.7	3.8	3.4	2.5
Monroe	86.7	66.5	66.5	...	20.2	9.3	5.2	5.7
Montgomery	26.7	18.8	18.8	...	7.9	.8	3.9	3.2
Morgan	9.9	5.0	5.0	...	4.9	1.6	1.3	2.0
Perry	49.3	37.2	37.2	...	12.1	...	10.9	1.2
Pickens	66.6	42.6	42.2	.4	24.0	13.3	2.6	8.1
Pike	59.7	33.0	33.0	...	26.7	5.9	9.6	11.2
Randolph	28.8	21.9	21.9	...	6.9	5.2	1.3	.4
Russell	30.8	27.1	27.1	...	3.7	.8	1.7	1.2
St. Clair	22.9	16.7	16.7	...	6.2	3.2	1.7	1.3
Shelby	34.4	31.4	31.4	...	3.0	2.0	.2	.8
Sumter	83.4	66.5	66.5	...	16.9	8.7	2.0	6.2
Talladega	55.3	49.7	49.7	...	5.6	...	3.5	2.1
Tallapoosa	50.5	37.2	37.2	...	13.3	5.3	1.1	6.9
Tuscaloosa	71.2	48.0	48.0	...	23.2	10.9	5.6	6.7
Walker	64.8	51.2	51.2	...	13.6	5.3	...	8.3
Washington	87.6	72.0	72.0	...	15.6	3.6	9.6	2.4
Wilcox	105.5	77.7	77.2	.5	27.8	9.5	6.4	11.9
Winston	39.4	25.6	25.6	...	13.8	7.1	...	6.7
All counties	2,852.4	2,143.4	2,129.1	14.3	709.0	310.8	167.6	230.6

Table 24. *Mortality of growing stock and sawtimber on commercial forest land by species group, 1971*

County	Growing stock			Sawtimber		
	All species	Softwood	Hardwood	All species	Softwood	Hardwood
	- - *Million cubic feet*- -			- - *Million board feet*- -		
Autauga	1.4	0.6	0.8	4.6	2.9	1.7
Baldwin	4.0	1.5	2.5	14.8	6.7	8.1
Barbour	1.7	.7	1.0	5.4	2.6	2.8
Bibb	1.9	1.5	.4	3.5	3.1	.4
Blount	.8	.5	.3	1.9	1.4	.5
Bullock	1.0	.4	.6	.9	...	.9
Butler	1.3	.4	.9	1.8	.5	1.3
Calhoun	.5	.3	.2	1.7	1.7	...
Chambers	1.0	.7	.3	2.0	1.7	.3
Cherokee	.5	.5	...	3.4	3.4	...
Chilton	.5	.2	.3	1.0	.4	.6
Choctaw	2.0	.9	1.1	5.2	.7	4.5
Clarke	4.8	1.8	3.0	14.1	6.0	8.1
Clay	1.5	1.0	.5	5.3	3.1	2.2
Cleburne	1.3	1.1	.2	5.3	4.7	.6
Coffee	1.8	.1	1.7	3.1	...	3.1
Colbert	.8	.2	.6	2.5	.4	2.1
Conecuh	2.3	.6	1.7	4.3	.4	3.9
Coosa	1.5	1.0	.5	3.2	1.9	1.3
Covington	1.4	1.2	.2	4.1	3.9	.2
Crenshaw	2.0	.6	1.4	5.7	2.1	3.6
Cullman	1.1	.5	.6	2.8	.7	2.1
Dale	1.6	.5	1.1	5.3	2.0	3.3
Dallas	3.6	.9	2.7	6.8	1.2	5.6
De Kalb	.4	.1	.3	.6	.3	.3
Elmore	1.1	.8	.3	3.2	2.6	.6
Escambia	2.2	1.2	1.0	8.0	4.9	3.1
Etowah	.3	.2	.1	.4	.4	...
Fayette	.8	.7	.1	2.2	2.2	...
Franklin	1.7	.8	.9	3.2	1.7	1.5
Geneva	1.0	.2	.8	1.6	.4	1.2
Greene	1.9	.6	1.3	7.2	2.9	4.3
Hale	2.0	1.5	.5	5.6	4.8	.8
Henry	.7	.1	.6	1.2	...	1.2
Houston	1.0	.1	.9	4.0	.8	3.2

Table 24. *Mortality of growing stock and sawtimber on commercial forest land by species group, 1971* (Continued)

County	Growing stock			Sawtimber		
	All species	Softwood	Hardwood	All species	Softwood	Hardwood
	- - *Million cubic feet*- -			- -*Million board feet*- -		
Jackson	3.2	.1	3.1	7.6	...	7.6
Jefferson	2.6	2.2	.4	5.7	5.0	.7
Lamar	3.1	1.9	1.2	9.7	5.9	3.8
Lauderdale	.4	.1	.3	1.3	.4	.9
Lawrence	1.0	.3	.7	3.1	.7	2.4
Lee	1.2	1.0	.2	2.6	2.6	...
Limestone	.4	...	.4	1.5	...	1.5
Lowndes	1.6	.3	1.3	2.6	.3	2.3
Macon	1.0	.8	.2	2.6	2.3	.3
Madison	.2	...	.2	.2	...	.2
Marengo	1.1	.4	.7	1.4	...	1.4
Marion	1.2	.8	.4	1.7	1.3	.4
Marshall	.9	.4	.5	2.2	1.2	1.0
Mobile	1.4	.7	.7	3.2	2.2	1.0
Monroe	2.6	1.0	1.6	6.4	1.6	4.8
Montgomery	.3	.1	.2	.6	.3	.3
Morgan	.5	.1	.4	1.1	.2	.9
Perry	2.5	1.7	.8	10.2	8.3	1.9
Pickens	2.1	.9	1.2	5.5	2.5	3.0
Pike	1.3	.2	1.1	2.5	...	2.5
Randolph	.9	.3	.6	1.9	.7	1.2
Russell	.3	.2	.1	1.0	.4	.6
St. Clair	1.5	.9	.6	3.3	1.4	1.9
Shelby	1.8	1.3	.5	3.5	2.4	1.1
Sumter	.9	.6	.3	3.9	3.0	.9
Talladega	1.3	.8	.5	2.3	1.5	.8
Tallapoosa	1.8	1.4	.4	4.1	3.8	.3
Tuscaloosa	5.6	3.0	2.6	14.2	7.7	6.5
Walker	1.4	1.0	.4	3.4	2.6	.8
Washington	2.4	1.3	1.1	5.8	3.8	2.0
Wilcox	2.2	.8	1.4	7.0	2.8	4.2
Winston	1.4	1.2	.2	3.2	2.5	.7
All counties	103.5	49.8	53.7	271.2	139.9	131.3

Table 25. *Net annual change in growing stock and sawtimber on commercial forest land by species group, 1971*

County	Growing stock			Sawtimber		
	All species	Softwood	Hardwood	All species	Softwood	Hardwood
	- -Million cubic feet- -			- - Million board feet- -		
Autauga	+ 9.5	+ 8.5	+ 1.0	+ 28.4	+ 29.7	− 1.3
Baldwin	+ 2.8	− .2	+ 3.0	+ 40.8	+ 33.2	+ 7.6
Barbour	+ 8.9	+ 6.3	+ 2.6	+ 38.3	+ 34.0	+ 4.3
Bibb	+ 6.4	+ 4.9	+ 1.5	+ 23.4	+ 21.7	+ 1.7
Blount	+ 11.9	+ 6.0	+ 5.9	+ 30.6	+ 18.6	+ 12.0
Bullock	+ 8.4	+ 5.9	+ 2.5	+ 30.7	+ 26.7	+ 4.0
Butler	− 1.3	− .6	− .7	− 6.4	− 4.6	− 1.8
Calhoun	+ 9.0	+ 6.2	+ 2.8	+ 19.2	+ 14.1	+ 5.1
Chambers	+ 4.6	+ 3.0	+ 1.6	+ 12.6	+ 9.9	+ 2.7
Cherokee	+ 1.4	+ 2.7	− 1.3	+ 1.5	+ .6	+ .9
Chilton	+ 7.7	+ 4.2	+ 3.5	+ 11.8	+ 8.6	+ 3.2
Choctaw	+ 5.3	+ 5.0	+ .3	+ 36.2	+ 35.4	+ .8
Clarke	+ 12.8	+ 6.3	+ 6.5	+ 30.7	+ 29.0	+ 1.7
Clay	+ 4.5	+ 2.5	+ 2.0	+ 5.3	+ 6.1	− .8
Cleburne	+ 8.2	+ 5.2	+ 3.0	+ 39.9	+ 34.0	+ 5.9
Coffee	+ 6.2	+ 4.5	+ 1.7	+ 21.3	+ 19.9	+ 1.4
Colbert	+ 2.1	+ .1	+ 2.0	+ 9.5	− .7	+ 10.2
Conecuh	+ 8.4	+ 1.9	+ 6.5	+ 15.2	+ 2.2	+ 13.0
Coosa	+ 6.9	+ 4.2	+ 2.7	+ 27.9	+ 20.3	+ 7.6
Covington	+ 5.1	+ 2.2	+ 2.9	+ 16.7	+ 10.5	+ 6.2
Crenshaw	+ 1.3	− .1	+ 1.4	+ 20.4	+ 12.5	+ 7.9
Cullman	+ 9.9	+ 5.1	+ 4.8	+ 21.8	+ 12.5	+ 9.3
Dale	+ 3.2	+ 1.1	+ 2.1	+ 5.1	+ 2.6	+ 2.5
Dallas	+ 6.7	+ 5.6	+ 1.1	+ 20.9	+ 21.7	− .8
De Kalb	+ 5.8	+ 3.9	+ 1.9	+ 10.0	+ 7.6	+ 2.4
Elmore	+ 5.3	+ 2.1	+ 3.2	+ 19.2	+ 7.7	+ 11.5
Escambia	+ 6.2	+ 3.7	+ 2.5	+ 32.5	+ 24.8	+ 7.7
Etowah	+ 5.3	+ 3.7	+ 1.6	+ 13.1	+ 5.7	+ 7.4
Fayette	+ 13.1	+ 7.8	+ 5.3	+ 33.9	+ 22.6	+ 11.3
Franklin	+ 4.4	+ 1.9	+ 2.5	+ 4.9	+ 2.7	+ 2.2
Geneva	+ .8	− 1.3	+ 2.1	− 1.9	− 4.8	+ 2.9
Greene	+ 5.1	+ 2.2	+ 2.9	+ 18.7	+ 15.9	+ 2.8
Hale	+ 4.2	+ 3.2	+ 1.0	+ 17.5	+ 22.7	− 5.2
Henry	+ 6.8	+ 5.6	+ 1.2	+ 22.9	+ 24.0	− 1.1
Houston	+ 1.5	+ 1.6	− .1	+ 2.8	+ .8	+ 2.0

46

Table 25. *Net annual change in growing stock and sawtimber on commercial*
forest land by species group, 1971 (Continued)

County	Growing stock			Sawtimber		
	All species	Softwood	Hardwood	All species	Softwood	Hardwood
	- - *Million cubic feet*- -			- - *Million board feet*- -		
Jackson	+ 5.0	- .8	+ 5.8	+ 10.2	- 8.6	+ 18.8
Jefferson	+ 13.7	+ 10.1	+ 3.6	+ 23.1	+ 18.8	+ 4.3
Lamar	+ 11.4	+ 5.0	+ 6.4	+ 17.8	+ 8.4	+ 9.4
Lauderdale	+ 4.3	+ .4	+ 3.9	+ 13.2	+ 2.2	+ 11.0
Lawrence	+ 2.8	+ 1.0	+ 1.8	- .5	+ 1.5	- 2.0
Lee	+ 7.4	+ 4.1	+ 3.3	+ 58.7	+ 51.5	+ 7.2
Limestone	+ .9	+ .3	+ .6	- .7	+ 1.7	- 2.4
Lowndes	+ .9	- 1.2	+ 2.1	+ 12.5	+ 5.1	+ 7.4
Macon	+ 5.4	+ 2.4	+ 3.0	+ 15.4	+ 10.2	+ 5.2
Madison	+ 4.0	+ 1.5	+ 2.5	+ 10.5	+ 4.0	+ 6.5
Marengo	+ 5.4	+ 5.1	+ .3	+ 34.3	+ 31.8	+ 2.5
Marion	+ 11.4	+ 6.9	+ 4.5	+ 11.0	+ 7.1	+ 3.9
Marshall	+ 4.8	+ 2.3	+ 2.5	+ 18.3	+ 13.6	+ 4.7
Mobile	+ 7.6	+ 5.5	+ 2.1	+ 22.1	+ 20.8	+ 1.3
Monroe	+ 8.4	+ 3.4	+ 5.0	+ 48.6	+ 29.7	+ 18.9
Montgomery	+ 1.9	- .5	+ 2.4	+ 8.9	+ 7.0	+ 1.9
Morgan	+ 3.8	+ 1.8	+ 2.0	+ 6.0	+ 3.0	+ 3.0
Perry	+ 5.4	+ 2.7	+ 2.7	+ 11.9	+ 13.7	- 1.8
Pickens	+ 10.9	+ 10.0	+ .9	+ 29.6	+ 32.9	- 3.3
Pike	+ .9	+ .3	+ .6	- 6.1	+ 4.8	- 10.9
Randolph	+ 6.8	+ 5.2	+ 1.6	+ 16.6	+ 14.0	+ 2.6
Russell	+ 11.9	+ 8.1	+ 3.8	+ 50.4	+ 45.6	+ 4.8
St. Clair	+ 14.2	+ 10.8	+ 3.4	+ 25.6	+ 22.1	+ 3.5
Shelby	+ 12.0	+ 7.2	+ 4.8	+ 41.6	+ 21.9	+ 19.7
Sumter	+ 4.3	- .6	+ 4.9	+ 36.1	+ 14.5	+ 21.6
Talladega	+ 2.9	- .1	+ 3.0	- 5.0	- 12.6	+ 7.6
Tallapoosa	+ 6.2	+ 4.2	+ 2.0	+ 16.0	+ 12.2	+ 3.8
Tuscaloosa	+ 26.0	+ 18.7	+ 7.3	+ 54.5	+ 46.2	+ 8.3
Walker	+ 12.3	+ 7.0	+ 5.3	+ 29.1	+ 21.4	+ 7.7
Washington	+ 9.6	+ 4.9	+ 4.7	+ 39.0	+ 22.8	+ 16.2
Wilcox	+ 3.6	+ 1.4	+ 2.2	+ 5.1	+ .2	+ 4.9
Winston	+ 13.3	+ 10.1	+ 3.2	+ 20.1	+ 14.4	+ 5.7
All counties	+447.8	+262.1	+185.7	+1,349.3	+1,010.1	+339.2

Table 26. *Growing-stock volume on commercial forest land by Resource region and species, Alabama, 1972*

Species	State	Southwest-south	Southwest-north	Southeast	West central	North central	North
			- - - - - - - - - - - - *Million cubic feet* - - - - - - - - - - -				
Softwood:							
Longleaf pine	1,280.3	744.8	80.9	185.0	103.4	166.2	...
Slash pine	730.6	530.2	41.0	148.1	6.7	4.6	...
Shortleaf pine	2,532.3	45.2	599.3	756.5	382.6	599.1	149.6
Loblolly pine	5,962.0	310.3	1,358.6	1,666.7	1,107.9	1,268.4	250.1
Virginia pine	408.2	...	...	3.5	68.7	247.1	88.9
Spruce pine	186.8	13.7	117.1	52.1	3.9	...	...
Redcedar	56.4	13.3	8.4	5.4	3.7	.9	24.7
Cypress	125.1	66.1	35.5	7.7	14.2	...	1.6
Other softwoods	.9	.4	...	...	...	.3	.2
Total	11,282.6	1,724.0	2,240.8	2,825.0	1,691.1	2,286.6	515.1
Hardwood:							
Select white oaks[1]	782.7	15.2	126.2	114.6	118.0	183.9	224.8
Select red oaks [2]	282.1	9.8	65.3	34.2	40.9	57.5	74.4
Other white oaks	649.5	24.7	74.8	80.7	111.4	204.9	153.0
Other red oaks	1,907.0	173.0	369.7	450.7	348.6	336.6	228.4
Pecan	29.9	18.4	7.4	3.5	.6	...	...
Other hickories	970.3	11.7	119.6	185.4	140.7	246.5	266.4
Persimmon	30.7	1.1	5.4	12.9	3.4	3.5	4.4
Hard maple	16.9	.3	2.2	1.9	.4	.2	11.9
Soft maple	174.2	25.8	28.0	43.9	34.7	19.3	22.5
Boxelder	5.9	...	.9	3.7	...	.3	1.0
Beech	76.1	2.7	31.7	15.0	10.1	12.5	4.1
Sweetgum	1,449.9	63.9	356.9	468.2	307.8	159.2	93.9
Blackgum	560.1	135.2	89.7	161.3	93.8	40.1	40.0
Other gums	341.3	158.7	40.6	84.6	57.4	...	...
White ash	91.0	15.9	11.3	22.6	5.2	9.0	27.0
Other ashes	148.5	16.9	53.4	36.5	14.3	9.9	17.5
Sycamore	47.4	3.1	15.4	18.9	3.9	.9	5.2
Cottonwood	30.6	3.9	3.8	10.2	.3	11.2	1.2
Basswood	29.7	...	10.6	8.5	1.0	4.7	4.9
Yellow-poplar	564.5	49.3	87.4	178.7	69.0	126.1	54.0
Magnolia (*Magnolia* spp.)	35.0	2.4	9.6	17.8	1.1	1.4	2.7
Sweetbay	256.6	116.8	35.2	70.4	32.9	1.3	...
Willow	15.9	1.1	5.2	3.3	3.6	1.0	1.7
Black walnut	8.4	...	1.4	...	...	...	7.0
Black cherry	19.6	...	3.5	4.4	2.9	4.0	4.8
American elm	86.6	6.3	25.0	17.7	21.7	4.5	11.4
Other elms	95.6	6.6	20.9	27.7	14.3	8.7	17.4
Birch	37.5	...	4.3	9.7	14.6	1.8	7.1
Hackberry	116.5	21.5	42.8	21.4	20.4	.9	9.5
Black locust	4.5	...	...	.4	...	...	4.1
Other locusts	2.9	...	...	.6	.7	.3	1.3
Sassafras	5.0	.3	.4	.7	2.1	...	...
Dogwood	30.2	5.4	8.8	6.4	3.3	3.7	2.6
Holly	11.4	3.9	2.9	4.1	.3	.2	...
Other hardwoods	15.1	2.3	5.9	1.5	1.5	.4	3.5
Total	8,929.1	896.2	1,666.2	2,122.1	1,480.9	1,454.5	1,309.2
All species	20,211.7	2,620.2	3,907.0	4,947.1	3,172.0	3,741.1	1,824.3

[1] Includes white, swamp chestnut, swamp white, and chinkapin oaks.
[2] Includes northern red, Shumard, and cherrybark oaks.

Table 27. *Sawtimber volume on commercial forest land by Resource region and species, Alabama, 1972*

Species	State	Southwest-south	Southwest-north	Southeast	West central	North central	North
			-Million board feet-				
Softwood:							
Longleaf pine	5,384.8	3,166.1	355.9	764.1	460.4	638.3	...
Slash pine	2,593.1	2,119.6	159.7	269.5	22.2	22.1	...
Shortleaf pine	7,904.7	164.3	2,387.8	2,489.6	1,125.5	1,383.7	353.8
Loblolly pine	24,013.2	1,378.4	6,217.1	6,868.7	4,095.1	4,551.2	902.7
Virginia pine	860.6	...	...	6.3	131.1	565.0	158.2
Spruce pine	818.8	51.8	528.6	219.0	19.4	...	...
Redcedar	96.5	36.0	10.9	7.0	3.3	...	39.3
Cypress	611.7	311.5	188.2	40.7	71.3	...	...
Total	42,283.4	7,227.7	9,848.2	10,664.9	5,928.3	7,160.3	1,454.0
Hardwood:							
Select white oaks[1]	2,383.1	41.9	464.3	352.8	314.2	558.3	651.6
Select red oaks[2]	1,036.2	41.9	277.2	126.1	136.3	188.4	266.3
Other white oaks	1,544.5	72.5	234.3	195.5	282.9	400.5	358.8
Other red oaks	5,226.6	512.5	1,189.1	1,170.8	937.5	798.4	618.3
Pecan	96.4	63.0	21.8	8.1	3.5	...	...
Other hickories	2,001.9	28.1	339.2	404.8	305.6	399.1	525.1
Persimmon	30.1	...	1.6	10.8	3.0	9.7	5.0
Hard maple	23.5	...	3.1	1.0	...	...	19.4
Soft maple	266.9	24.8	35.9	70.0	56.7	31.8	47.7
Beech	234.3	9.0	99.0	48.8	33.6	33.4	10.5
Sweetgum	2,837.5	185.2	820.0	773.2	661.4	254.2	143.5
Blackgum	1,104.5	282.2	163.2	325.6	169.2	72.3	92.0
Other gums	864.6	434.7	111.1	200.3	118.5	...	...
White ash	262.1	67.8	30.0	59.6	12.3	26.3	66.1
Other ashes	321.4	44.2	118.4	79.1	35.8	26.3	17.6
Sycamore	149.2	4.4	45.2	62.1	17.9	...	19.6
Cottonwood	81.4	17.8	16.6	37.4	...	6.4	3.2
Basswood	79.8	...	34.3	25.6	3.2	11.1	5.6
Yellow-poplar	1,479.6	144.0	275.4	485.4	150.1	299.5	125.2
Magnolia (*Magnolia* spp.)	57.9	1.2	19.7	29.7	...	...	7.3
Sweetbay	386.2	171.7	58.5	125.4	30.6	...	...
Willow	13.3	1.8	3.7	1.8	1.5	3.5	1.0
Black walnut	18.7	...	3.6	...	...	...	15.1
Black cherry	15.3	...	2.7	2.1	...	4.6	5.9
American elm	215.4	19.0	61.0	56.5	45.7	9.0	24.2
Other elms	135.9	22.1	30.6	32.0	21.4	10.2	19.6
Birch	84.4	...	15.7	11.4	27.6	6.1	23.6
Hackberry	251.2	52.4	100.0	43.0	47.5	...	8.3
Other hardwoods	31.8	3.2	4.7	8.8	2.2	...	12.9
Total	21,233.7	2,245.4	4,579.9	4,747.7	3,418.2	3,149.1	3,093.4
All species	63,517.1	9,473.1	14,428.1	15,412.6	9,346.5	10,309.4	4,547.4

[1]Includes white, swamp chestnut, swamp white, and chinkapin oaks.
[2]Includes northern red, Shumard, and cherrybark oaks.

Table 28. *Average volume per acre of growing stock and sawtimber on commercial forest land by species group and ownership class, 1972*

Ownership class	Growing stock			Sawtimber		
	All species	Softwood	Hardwood	All species	Softwood	Hardwood
	- - - *Cubic feet* - - -			- - - *Board feet* - - -		

STATE OF ALABAMA

National forest	1,159	798	361	4,360	3,521	839
Other public	950	537	413	3,249	2,170	1,079
Forest industry	1,087	706	381	3,813	2,845	968
Farmer	911	441	470	2,648	1,567	1,081
Misc. private	896	493	403	2,735	1,782	953
All ownerships	948	529	419	2,977	1,982	995

SOUTHWEST-SOUTH

National forest	1,134	994	140	4,606	4,340	266
Other public	707	707	...	3,362	3,362	...
Forest industry	1,205	836	369	4,638	3,689	949
Farmer	825	493	332	2,730	1,973	757
Misc. private	824	514	310	2,860	2,062	798
All ownerships	940	618	322	3,399	2,593	806

SOUTHWEST-NORTH

National forest	...	...	...	...	...	...
Other public	1,796	710	1,086	7,131	2,932	4,199
Forest industry	1,239	808	431	5,090	3,904	1,186
Farmer	1,082	553	529	3,782	2,345	1,437
Misc. private	1,138	633	505	3,953	2,574	1,379
All ownerships	1,156	663	493	4,271	2,915	1,356

SOUTHEAST

National forest	1,583	895	688	6,235	4,528	1,707
Other public	1,281	913	368	5,199	4,375	824
Forest industry	1,144	766	378	3,936	2,941	995
Farmer	891	441	450	2,626	1,659	967
Misc. private	860	503	357	2,617	1,836	781
All ownerships	925	528	397	2,882	1,994	888

WEST CENTRAL

National forest	1,369	1,138	231	5,942	5,496	446
Other public	913	440	473	2,252	1,292	960
Forest industry	1,019	634	385	2,996	2,057	939
Farmer	933	465	468	2,646	1,620	1,026
Misc. private	1,003	471	532	2,855	1,610	1,245
All ownerships	1,002	534	468	2,953	1,873	1,080

NORTH CENTRAL

National forest	1,085	724	361	3,821	2,948	873
Other public	708	350	358	2,019	1,021	998
Forest industry	776	513	263	1,985	1,465	520
Farmer	861	516	345	2,193	1,466	727
Misc. private	792	474	318	2,220	1,529	691
All ownerships	825	504	321	2,273	1,579	694

NORTH

National forest	949	320	629	2,812	1,319	1,493
Other public	827	294	533	2,092	898	1,194
Forest industry	933	323	610	2,704	1,161	1,543
Farmer	872	222	650	2,125	598	1,527
Misc. private	813	241	572	1,941	594	1,347
All ownerships	861	243	618	2,148	687	1,461

Table 29. *Net annual growth per acre of growing stock and sawtimber on commercial forest land by species and ownership class, 1971*

Ownership class	Growing stock			Sawtimber		
	All species	Softwood	Hardwood	All species	Softwood	Hardwood
	- - - Cubic feet - - -			- - - Board feet - - -		
STATE OF ALABAMA						
National forest	53	39	14	207	172	35
Other public	51	34	17	196	148	48
Forest industry	58	42	16	234	189	45
Farmer	54	33	21	175	120	55
Misc. private	57	38	19	195	147	48
All ownerships	56	37	19	197	148	49
SOUTHWEST-SOUTH						
National forest	51	48	3	268	262	6
Other public	37	37	...	250	250	...
Forest industry	53	40	13	215	187	28
Farmer	45	32	13	151	120	31
Misc. private	45	33	12	181	138	43
All ownerships	47	35	12	189	154	35
SOUTHWEST-NORTH						
National forest	...	...	...	...	...	...
Other public	77	32	45	267	118	149
Forest industry	67	45	22	297	236	61
Farmer	63	37	26	249	170	79
Misc. private	65	42	23	259	196	63
All ownerships	66	42	24	268	200	68
SOUTHEAST						
National forest	60	41	19	293	221	72
Other public	57	42	15	294	256	38
Forest industry	67	52	15	249	211	38
Farmer	55	34	21	188	135	53
Misc. private	57	40	17	219	175	44
All ownerships	57	39	18	214	167	47
WEST CENTRAL						
National forest	60	48	12	279	250	29
Other public	47	30	17	158	81	77
Forest industry	66	50	16	220	181	39
Farmer	57	35	22	195	137	58
Misc. private	62	38	24	180	129	51
All ownerships	61	40	21	198	148	50
NORTH CENTRAL						
National forest	55	40	15	189	147	42
Other public	59	40	19	135	87	48
Forest industry	37	27	10	207	150	57
Farmer	68	48	20	162	123	39
Misc. private	61	43	18	181	138	43
All ownerships	59	42	17	179	135	44
NORTH						
National forest	35	11	24	65	30	35
Other public	33	14	19	145	99	46
Forest industry	30	12	18	63	26	37
Farmer	31	11	20	96	36	60
Misc. private	29	11	18	82	30	52
All ownerships	31	12	19	90	36	54

51

Table 30. *Metric area of commercial forest land by ownership class, 1972*

County	All ownerships	National forest	Other public	Forest industry	Farmer	Misc. private
			-Thousand hectares - - - - - - - -			
Autauga	102.7	...	0.7	38.2	33.4	30.4
Baldwin	284.1	...	2.3	115.7	46.3	119.8
Barbour	155.8	...	6.4	24.5	44.5	80.4
Bibb	134.7	24.5	1.6	40.0	17.1	51.5
Blount	99.4	...	2.8	...	35.4	61.2
Bullock	94.0	...	...	4.4	26.2	63.4
Butler	150.2	...	.1	61.0	49.3	39.8
Calhoun	97.9	6.1	21.2	21.5	30.8	18.3
Chambers	109.3	...	.2	4.4	45.9	58.8
Cherokee	86.8	...	...	25.8	23.3	37.7
Chilton	120.0	8.7	.2	21.0	42.0	48.1
Choctaw	204.0	...	1.6	60.7	41.3	100.4
Clarke	292.4	...	3.3	117.9	45.3	125.9
Clay	126.8	26.4	.6	10.9	36.9	52.0
Cleburne	126.5	32.1	.8	35.8	21.4	36.4
Coffee	97.7	...	4.1	16.8	47.4	29.4
Colbert	90.0	...	4.6	4.6	37.2	43.6
Conecuh	173.4	...	(¹)	68.8	53.6	51.0
Coosa	143.3	...	2.0	36.5	24.1	80.7
Covington	182.1	21.9	.8	63.1	64.2	32.1
Crenshaw	111.1		.1	17.3	46.9	46.8
Cullman	103.8	...	.5	9.2	57.3	36.8
Dale	91.3	...	13.7	...	35.6	42.0
Dallas	126.9	2.0	.8	24.5	51.2	48.4
De Kalb	99.7	...	2.3	9.1	54.8	33.5
Elmore	98.3	...	.7	2.2	30.6	64.8
Escambia	198.4	13.0	1.6	87.7	24.8	71.3
Etowah	71.6	...	.6	2.5	39.2	29.3
Fayette	124.4	...	3.0	27.9	34.9	58.6
Franklin	107.3	.6	.6	24.3	51.0	30.8
Geneva	64.3	...	2.9	2.1	32.2	27.1
Greene	94.9	...	.9	14.4	42.0	37.6
Hale	100.4	11.2	1.2	22.6	22.9	42.5
Henry	84.6	...	.4	12.4	33.0	38.8
Houston	43.5	...	.6	...	13.9	29.0

Table 30. *Metric area of commercial forest land by ownership class, 1972*
(Continued)

County	All ownerships	National forest	Other public	Forest industry	Farmer	Misc. private
	- - - - - - - -*Thousand hectares*- - - - - - - -
Jackson	176.8	...	6.0	18.1	105.1	47.6
Jefferson	185.8		4.7	...	18.0	163.1
Lamar	115.3	...	(1)	16.1	37.5	61.7
Lauderdale	62.3	...	1.6	4.5	44.8	11.4
Lawrence	82.4	35.9	.7	...	35.9	9.9
Lee	106.8	...	2.1	8.9	28.9	66.9
Limestone	31.5	...	2.3	...	21.7	7.5
Lowndes	90.6	...	.6	20.4	36.2	33.4
Macon	88.3	4.0	.6	12.6	39.9	31.2
Madison	72.8	...	7.2	2.4	34.2	29.0
Marengo	162.9		.4	32.1	66.8	63.6
Marion	140.9	...	1.0	38.2	38.8	62.9
Marshall	70.3	...	5.1	9.1	29.7	26.4
Mobile	211.6	...	9.9	20.4	37.4	143.9
Monroe	205.9	...	1.3	66.5	79.3	58.8
Montgomery	69.2	...	.5	...	40.5	28.2
Morgan	63.7	...	3.2	...	49.5	11.0
Perry	115.8	13.3	.2	21.4	41.4	39.5
Pickens	173.1	...	...	55.4	51.6	66.1
Pike	101.5		.2	9.2	64.5	27.6
Randolph	109.4	...	.1	4.1	63.6	41.6
Russell	108.6	...	3.3	14.8	24.7	65.8
St. Clair	125.9		.4	26.8	34.9	63.8
Shelby	162.0	...	5.2	54.0	37.3	65.5
Sumter	158.1	...	.6	50.2	62.7	44.6
Talladega	117.8	16.8	3.7	9.1	18.0	70.2
Tallapoosa	149.6	...	.5	18.1	31.7	99.3
Tuscaloosa	281.8	3.4	4.1	62.1	55.9	156.3
Walker	149.4	...	6.3	18.9	27.2	97.0
Washington	251.8	...	.6	32.1	43.5	175.6
Wilcox	170.7	...	1.7	23.1	62.3	83.6
Winston	129.2	34.8	.9	25.4	25.2	42.9
All counties	8,633.4	254.7	158.2	1,701.8	2,724.6	3,794.1

1 Negligible.

53

Table 31. *Metric volume of growing stock on commercial forest land by species group, 1972*

County	All species	Softwood			Hardwood			
		Total	Southern pine	Other	Total	Oak	Gum	Other
				- - - - - - - - - - *Thousand cubic meters*- - - - - - - - - - -				
Autauga	7,303	4,828	4,808	20	2,475	821	963	691
Baldwin	21,085	13,012	11,621	1,391	8,073	1,470	4,078	2,525
Barbour	11,015	7,144	7,136	8	3,871	1,320	1,500	1,051
Bibb	10,214	6,759	6,728	31	3,455	1,640	977	838
Blount	6,932	3,344	3,338	6	3,588	1,877	513	1,198
Bullock	5,692	3,718	3,681	37	1,974	493	691	790
Butler	10,851	6,861	6,785	76	3,990	1,396	1,104	1,490
Calhoun	5,049	3,129	3,129	...	1,920	1,099	224	597
Chambers	5,556	3,109	3,109	...	2,447	716	910	821
Cherokee	3,585	1,991	1,991	...	1,594	1,161	96	337
Chilton	7,487	3,806	3,800	6	3,681	1,390	807	1,484
Choctaw	16,128	10,760	10,434	326	5,368	2,254	1,676	1,438
Clarke	26,248	16,439	16,056	383	9,809	3,344	3,231	3,234
Clay	6,576	3,843	3,843	...	2,733	1,345	445	943
Cleburne	7,955	5,290	5,290	...	2,665	1,567	294	804
Coffee	4,556	2,605	2,594	11	1,951	1,110	351	490
Colbert	4,341	722	716	6	3,619	1,954	334	1,331
Conecuh	13,320	6,915	6,892	23	6,405	2,316	2,155	1,934
Coosa	7,235	4,202	4,202	...	3,033	1,399	680	954
Covington	12,035	8,679	8,639	40	3,356	960	1,334	1,062
Crenshaw	7,781	3,896	3,879	17	3,885	1,379	1,303	1,203
Cullman	7,110	3,922	3,916	6	3,188	1,803	266	1,119
Dale	5,967	2,829	2,795	34	3,138	943	1,164	1,031
Dallas	9,639	5,828	5,828	...	3,811	1,090	1,653	1,068
De Kalb	5,142	2,676	2,676	...	2,466	1,565	275	626
Elmore	4,667	2,042	1,977	65	2,625	804	903	918
Escambia	13,541	10,242	10,225	17	3,299	977	827	1,495
Etowah	3,208	1,886	1,886	...	1,322	850	144	328
Fayette	7,493	3,673	3,667	6	3,820	1,632	1,169	1,019
Franklin	6,196	2,393	2,373	20	3,803	1,917	320	1,566
Geneva	3,285	1,362	1,348	14	1,923	447	731	745
Greene	8,350	3,630	3,398	232	4,720	1,300	1,640	1,780
Hale	8,492	4,955	4,949	6	3,537	1,577	1,065	895
Henry	5,281	3,429	3,429	...	1,852	886	391	575
Houston	2,467	1,354	1,354	...	1,113	314	348	451

Table 31. *Metric volume of growing stock on commercial forest land by species group, 1972*
(Continued)

County	All species	Softwood			Hardwood			
		Total	Southern pine	Other	Total	Oak	Gum	Other
				- - Thousand cubic meters - - - - - - - - - -				
Jackson	11,771	1,133	830	303	10,638	5,368	818	4,452
Jefferson	10,305	7,807	7,807	...	2,498	1,289	408	801
Lamar	7,921	2,852	2,801	51	5,069	1,795	2,102	1,172
Lauderdale	3,401	351	351	...	3,050	1,909	181	960
Lawrence	4,290	1,441	1,280	161	2,849	1,829	292	728
Lee	7,201	4,522	4,522	...	2,679	501	1,034	1,144
Limestone	2,328	402	394	8	1,926	1,034	283	609
Lowndes	6,768	3,112	3,112	...	3,656	934	983	1,739
Macon	5,686	2,605	2,588	17	3,081	1,082	762	1,237
Madison	4,383	909	765	144	3,474	1,339	323	1,812
Marengo	11,864	6,895	6,717	178	4,969	2,021	1,014	1,934
Marion	6,836	3,353	3,342	11	3,483	2,082	328	1,073
Marshall	5,667	3,036	2,960	76	2,631	1,246	368	1,017
Mobile	10,515	6,630	6,125	505	3,885	663	1,993	1,229
Monroe	15,404	7,770	7,603	167	7,634	2,721	2,299	2,614
Montgomery	4,630	2,081	2,047	34	2,549	694	1,042	813
Morgan	4,139	1,523	1,492	31	2,616	1,110	597	909
Perry	8,699	5,329	5,241	88	3,370	1,119	951	1,300
Pickens	11,796	7,082	7,057	25	4,714	2,007	1,665	1,042
Pike	6,892	3,432	3,407	25	3,460	1,169	1,303	988
Randolph	5,731	3,542	3,542	...	2,189	1,031	275	883
Russell	9,010	6,439	6,439	...	2,571	561	1,370	640
St. Clair	6,850	4,072	4,058	14	2,778	1,489	541	748
Shelby	8,255	4,933	4,933	...	3,322	1,618	532	1,172
Sumter	12,771	6,813	6,694	119	5,958	2,410	1,549	1,999
Talladega	6,513	3,755	3,755	...	2,758	1,402	456	900
Tallapoosa	8,353	4,992	4,986	6	3,361	1,209	909	1,243
Tuscaloosa	20,020	10,254	10,197	57	9,766	4,375	3,100	2,291
Walker	11,375	7,292	7,292	...	4,083	2,002	558	1,523
Washington	17,021	10,256	9,959	297	6,765	2,237	1,900	2,628
Wilcox	14,898	7,861	7,813	48	7,037	2,942	1,872	2,223
Winston	9,260	5,743	5,735	8	3,517	2,240	212	1,065
All counties	572,335	319,490	314,336	5,154	252,845	102,544	66,582	83,719

55

Table 32. *Average volume per hectare of growing stock on commercial forest land by species group and ownership class, 1972*

Ownership class	Growing stock		
	All species	Softwood	Hardwood
	- - - -*Cubic meters*- - - -		
ALABAMA			
National forest	81	56	25
Other public	67	38	29
Forest industry	76	49	27
Farmer	64	31	33
Misc. private	63	35	28
All ownerships	66	37	29
SOUTHWEST-SOUTH			
National forest	80	70	10
Other public	50	50	...
Forest industry	84	58	26
Farmer	58	35	23
Misc. private	58	36	22
All ownerships	66	43	23
SOUTHWEST-NORTH			
National forest	...	...	...
Other public	126	50	76
Forest industry	87	57	30
Farmer	76	39	37
Misc. private	79	44	35
All ownerships	81	46	35

56

Table 32. *Average volume per hectare of growing stock*
on commercial forest land by species
group and ownership class, 1972 (Continued)

Ownership class	Growing stock		
	All species	Softwood	Hardwood
	- - - - *Cubic meters*- - - -		
SOUTHEAST			
National forest	111	63	48
Other public	90	64	26
Forest industry	80	54	26
Farmer	62	31	31
Misc. private	60	35	25
All ownerships	65	37	28
WEST CENTRAL			
National forest	96	80	16
Other public	64	31	33
Forest industry	71	44	27
Farmer	66	33	33
Misc. private	70	33	37
All ownerships	70	37	33
NORTH CENTRAL			
National forest	76	51	25
Other public	50	25	25
Forest industry	54	36	18
Farmer	60	36	24
Misc. private	55	33	22
All ownerships	57	35	22
NORTH			
National forest	66	22	44
Other public	58	21	37
Forest industry	66	23	43
Farmer	61	16	45
Misc. private	57	17	40
All ownerships	60	17	43

Table 33. *Sampling errors for commercial forest land, growing stock, and sawtimber volume by species group, 1972*

County	Commercial forest land	Growing stock			Sawtimber		
		All species	Soft-wood	Hard-wood	All species	Soft-wood	Hard-wood
				- - - - - - - - - - Percent - - - - - - - - - -			
Autauga	2	12	13	28	16	17	42
Baldwin	2	9	12	18	10	14	20
Barbour	2	8	10	17	10	12	24
Bibb	2	10	13	14	15	18	18
Blount	2	13	23	19	18	31	22
Bullock	3	12	18	18	18	23	·21
Butler	2	11	14	17	14	16	23
Calhoun	2	10	15	18	13	17	28
Chambers	3	12	12	20	19	18	33
Cherokee	2	12	16	26	20	25	41
Chilton	2	10	16	15	18	24	21
Choctaw	1	8	11	13	11	13	18
Clarke	1	6	8	9	8	10	14
Clay	2	11	16	15	16	21	23
Cleburne	2	9	14	14	14	17	16
Coffee	1	12	16	22	16	16	29
Colbert	1	11	21	14	16	33	19
Conecuh	1	10	13	15	13	16	17
Coosa	2	10	12	16	14	19	24
Covington	1	10	13	19	14	16	23
Crenshaw	2	11	18	16	15	19	26
Cullman	2	8	14	16	14	19	22
Dale	3	10	17	14	16	20	21
Dallas	2	10	15	16	15	18	20
De Kalb	2	11	17	17	17	23	24
Elmore	2	11	15	18	17	24	24
Escambia	1	10	12	23	12	13	27
Etowah	2	14	22	23	20	24	36
Fayette	2	9	16	14	16	24	18
Franklin	2	8	19	11	12	22	16
Geneva	2	17	33	24	24	40	32
Greene	2	10	15	17	14	16	25
Hale	2	11	17	16	16	22	23
Henry	1	11	17	20	18	24	28
Houston	2	19	28	33	33	50	39

Table 33. *Sampling errors for commercial forest land, growing stock, and sawtimber volume by species group, 1972* (Continued)

County	Commercial forest land	Growing stock			Sawtimber		
		All species	Soft-wood	Hard-wood	All species	Soft-wood	Hard-wood
- - - - - - - - -Percent- - - - - - - - -							
Jackson	1	6	22	8	9	28	11
Jefferson	2	10	13	12	16	19	18
Lamar	3	9	18	15	14	25	21
Lauderdale	2	11	41	13	20	(^{1})	22
Lawrence	1	12	23	15	20	32	23
Lee	2	12	16	23	16	21	33
Limestone	1	11	(^{1})	12	19	(^{1})	21
Lowndes	2	12	21	18	17	26	25
Macon	3	13	18	20	16	20	24
Madison	1	11	32	14	21	43	22
Marengo	2	8	14	15	12	17	21
Marion	2	8	16	13	14	24	19
Marshall	2	15	28	16	24	37	17
Mobile	1	12	12	21	15	15	26
Monroe	1	7	10	11	10	12	14
Montgomery	2	13	27	22	18	31	29
Morgan	2	11	23	16	17	26	30
Perry	1	9	13	14	13	17	20
Pickens	2	8	11	15	12	15	18
Pike	2	12	16	18	17	21	24
Randolph	3	10	14	17	16	21	27
Russell	3	11	15	22	14	16	26
St. Clair	2	8	14	14	14	18	22
Shelby	2	7	10	14	13	14	22
Sumter	2	10	17	13	14	20	16
Talladega	1	11	12	20	16	17	31
Tallapoosa	2	10	14	13	14	18	17
Tuscaloosa	1	7	10	12	10	14	15
Walker	2	8	12	10	13	16	16
Washington	1	8	10	14	10	13	19
Wilcox	2	8	12	13	10	15	17
Winston	2	9	13	14	14	18	21
All counties	0.2	1.2	1.9	2.0	1.8	2.4	3.0

[1]Exceeds 50 percent.

Table 34. *Sampling errors for growth on growing stock and sawtimber on commercial forest land by species group, 1971*

County	Growing stock			Sawtimber		
	All species	Softwood	Hardwood	All species	Softwood	Hardwood
- - - - - - - - - - - Percent- - - - - - - - - - - -

Autauga	11	12	23	14	15	39
Baldwin	7	9	13	12	13	27
Barbour	8	9	15	11	12	25
Bibb	10	11	19	15	17	35
Blount	13	17	20	16	20	29
Bullock	11	13	21	17	19	42
Butler	10	12	19	16	18	36
Calhoun	13	15	26	20	22	43
Chambers	10	12	18	16	18	33
Cherokee	10	12	18	26	33	40
Chilton	9	12	16	15	18	29
Choctaw	7	8	12	10	11	24
Clarke	6	7	9	7	8	17
Clay	10	12	17	18	20	38
Cleburne	9	11	17	17	19	42
Coffee	13	15	23	20	22	(1)
Colbert	12	26	14	33	(1)	36
Conecuh	8	11	13	13	15	24
Coosa	10	13	18	15	17	29
Covington	8	9	16	11	12	32
Crenshaw	8	10	13	14	17	26
Cullman	9	11	14	18	21	33
Dale	10	13	16	13	15	26
Dallas	10	12	18	13	15	31
De Kalb	16	20	27	19	23	33
Elmore	10	13	16	18	23	28
Escambia	8	9	18	11	12	28
Etowah	19	22	39	22	28	36
Fayette	9	11	14	16	20	29
Franklin	11	16	15	26	37	37
Geneva	16	23	23	24	30	42
Greene	10	14	14	14	16	24
Hale	11	13	18	16	18	39
Henry	11	12	22	16	17	49
Houston	17	21	31	25	32	38

Table 34. *Sampling errors for growth on growing stock and sawtimber on commercial forest land by species group, 1971* (Continued)

County	Growing stock			Sawtimber		
	All species	Softwood	Hardwood	All species	Softwood	Hardwood
- - - - - - - - - - -Percent- - - - - - - - - - - -						
Jackson	11	25	12	17	47	18
Jefferson	8	9	18	14	15	35
Lamar	9	12	13	14	18	22
Lauderdale	16	39	18	23	([1])	26
Lawrence	13	23	16	22	30	33
Lee	9	11	18	29	31	([1])
Limestone	15	39	17	22	38	28
Lowndes	8	11	13	18	22	33
Macon	10	12	16	16	19	29
Madison	15	26	18	28	49	33
Marengo	7	9	13	12	14	23
Marion	8	10	13	14	18	24
Marshall	13	17	19	20	24	37
Mobile	8	10	18	13	14	35
Monroe	7	9	11	10	12	18
Montgomery	9	13	13	20	23	37
Morgan	13	19	18	18	25	25
Perry	9	11	15	13	15	32
Pickens	8	9	16	12	13	25
Pike	9	12	14	·16	19	29
Randolph	10	11	20	15	17	33
Russell	9	11	19	13	14	40
St. Clair	13	15	26	18	20	40
Shelby	9	10	16	16	19	30
Sumter	8	11	12	13	15	22
Talladega	11	13	20	14	17	28
Tallapoosa	9	11	17	16	19	32
Tuscaloosa	7	9	13	10	12	20
Walker	7	8	12	11	13	24
Washington	6	7	11	10	11	19
Wilcox	7	9	12	9	11	17
Winston	12	14	23	14	17	24
All counties	2.3	2.8	4.0	3.4	3.9	6.8

[1]Exceeds 50 percent.

Table 35. *Sampling errors for timber removals from growing stock and saw-timber on commercial forest land by species group, 1971*

County	Growing stock			Sawtimber		
	All species	Softwood	Hardwood	All species	Softwood	Hardwood
	- - - - - - - - Percent- - - - - - - - - - - -					
Autauga	16	21	22	45	(1)	38
Baldwin	8	9	13	23	27	26
Barbour	10	13	18	29	37	29
Bibb	12	15	16	25	33	25
Blount	31	38	40	(1)	(1)	(1)
Bullock	17	21	30	48	(1)	49
Butler	9	11	14	24	30	26
Calhoun	29	35	36	(1)	(1)	(1)
Chambers	15	18	25	43	(1)	44
Cherokee	25	41	18	(1)	(1)	35
Chilton	13	16	21	37	48	35
Choctaw	8	12	9	17	21	24
Clarke	8	10	9	15	18	21
Clay	21	28	20	44	(1)	32
Cleburne	25	32	29	(1)	(1)	46
Coffee	19	24	29	(1)	(1)	(1)
Colbert	26	(1)	27	(1)	(1)	27
Conecuh	10	13	14	21	25	33
Coosa	19	25	20	43	(1)	32
Covington	10	11	22	28	30	(1)
Crenshaw	12	15	18	33	43	32
Cullman	25	30	32	(1)	(1)	43
Dale	13	17	20	39	49	40
Dallas	11	15	16	32	43	30
De Kalb	27	40	37	(1)	(1)	35
Elmore	17	20	28	(1)	(1)	(1)
Escambia	10	11	21	30	33	44
Etowah	35	42	47	(1)	(1)	(1)
Fayette	20	26	27	43	(1)	36
Franklin	21	34	26	42	(1)	25
Geneva	18	21	35	49	(1)	(1)
Greene	14	21	16	31	46	23
Hale	13	19	16	28	41	22
Henry	16	20	25	46	(1)	44
Houston	19	26	24	(1)	(1)	44

Table 35. *Sampling errors for timber removals from growing stock and saw-timber on commercial forest land by species group, 1971* (Continued)

County	Growing stock			Sawtimber		
	All species	Softwood	Hardwood	All species	Softwood	Hardwood
	- - - - - - - - - -Percent- - - - - - - - - -					
Jackson	19	31	24	34	(^{1})	21
Jefferson	18	22	24	31	38	32
Lamar	16	22	21	36	(^{1})	29
Lauderdale	29	(^{1})	30	(^{1})	(^{1})	28
Lawrence	26	(^{1})	27	(^{1})	(^{1})	28
Lee	13	15	32	38	45	(^{1})
Limestone	33	(^{1})	29	(^{1})	(^{1})	27
Lowndes	12	15	19	33	42	33
Macon	16	20	28	47	(^{1})	45
Madison	40	(^{1})	37	(^{1})	(^{1})	37
Marengo	10	15	10	23	31	25
Marion	16	22	19	36	(^{1})	29
Marshall	28	40	41	(^{1})	(^{1})	38
Mobile	11	12	19	32	37	38
Monroe	10	13	11	20	25	27
Montgomery	14	18	21	44	(^{1})	39
Morgan	28	49	32	(^{1})	(^{1})	32
Perry	13	17	17	27	36	26
Pickens	11	16	13	23	34	18
Pike	11	15	15	29	44	21
Randolph	22	29	24	48	(^{1})	37
Russell	15	17	37	41	49	(^{1})
St. Clair	26	33	28	(^{1})	(^{1})	39
Shelby	22	27	29	44	(^{1})	(^{1})
Sumter	10	14	12	20	25	30
Talladega	19	22	29	36	41	41
Tallapoosa	11	13	18	32	41	30
Tuscaloosa	11	15	13	23	32	19
Walker	17	21	20	32	40	26
Washington	9	10	14	25	29	30
Wilcox	9	13	10	18	23	23
Winston	22	30	20	41	(^{1})	26
All counties	1.8	2.3	2.3	4.1	5.3	3.9

[1]Exceeds 50 percent.

Table 36. *Sampling errors for growing-stock volume on commercial forest land by Resource region and species, 1972*

Species	State	Southwest-south	Southwest-north	South-east	West central	North central	North
				Percent			
Softwood:							
Longleaf pine	6	9	16	15	22	13	...
Slash pine	8	10	37	19	[1]	[1]	...
Shortleaf pine	3	32	8	6	8	6	12
Loblolly pine	3	14	6	5	6	6	13
Virginia pine	8	...	...	41	17	10	19
Spruce pine	14	38	18	23	[1]	...	...
Redcedar	19	[1]	35	32	40	46	21
Cypress	25	41	41	39	46	...	[1]
Other softwoods	[1]	...	...	...	...	[1]	[1]
All softwoods	1.9	5.3	4.4	3.6	4.6	3.7	8.7
Hardwood:							
Select white oaks	4	29	12	10	10	9	9
Select red oaks	7	38	16	17	16	16	14
Other white oaks	5	22	14	12	10	8	11
Other red oaks	3	10	7	6	7	6	8
Pecan	28	42	35	41	[1]	...	...
Other hickories	4	30	10	9	9	7	8
Persimmon	13	[1]	30	18	35	[1]	31
Hard maple	27	[1]	[1]	41	[1]	[1]	36
Soft maple	8	22	15	14	14	21	30
Boxelder	34	...	[1]	49	...	[1]	[1]
Beech	12	[1]	21	22	24	27	39
Sweetgum	4	18	8	7	10	10	14
Blackgum	7	15	18	11	20	12	14
Other gums	17	27	41	32	35	...	...
White ash	13	[1]	22	22	[1]	28	16
Other ashes	14	36	25	22	33	33	[1]
Sycamore	18	47	32	33	[1]	[1]	41
Cottonwood	39	[1]	[1]	37	[1]	[1]	[1]
Basswood	17	...	29	34	[1]	35	40
Yellow-poplar	6	21	13	12	12	12	13
Magnolia (*Magnolia* spp.)	15	42	26	24	[1]	45	[1]
Sweetbay	10	17	22	16	25	[1]	...
Willow	24	[1]	44	48	[1]	[1]	[1]
Black walnut	28	...	[1]	...	...	...	31
Black cherry	15	...	34	29	31	32	35
American elm	11	[1]	18	23	23	31	24
Other elms	9	38	21	15	24	28	17
Birch	22	...	[1]	40	33	[1]	[1]
Hackberry	15	49	24	27	35	[1]	34
Black locust	45	...	...	[1]	...	...	48
Other locusts	47	...	...	[1]	[1]	[1]	[1]
Sassafras	39	[1]	[1]	[1]	[1]	...	[1]
Dogwood	10	24	20	19	24	23	41
Holly	22	39	37	39	[1]	[1]	...
Other hardwoods	16	[1]	32	43	49	[1]	34
All hardwoods	2.0	8.6	4.7	4.2	5.0	4.2	4.0
All species	1.2	4.3	3.0	2.5	3.0	2.5	3.4

[1] Exceeds 50 percent.

Table 37. *Sampling errors for sawtimber volume on commercial forest land by Resource region and species, 1972*

Species	State	Southwest-south	Southwest-north	South-east	West central	North central	North
				- -Percent- -			
Softwood:							
Longleaf pine	7	10	18	16	25	14	...
Slash pine	10	11	36	32	(1)	(1)	...
Shortleaf pine	4	35	9	8	11	8	17
Loblolly pine	3	17	7	6	8	7	17
Virginia pine	11	...	...	(1)	26	14	24
Spruce pine	15	39	20	25	(1)	...	...
Redcedar	29	(1)	47	45	(1)	...	34
Cypress	27	44	43	40	50	...	...
All softwoods	2.4	6.4	5.4	4.6	6.4	5.3	13.0
Hardwood:							
Select white oaks	6	40	14	14	13	12	12
Select red oaks	8	40	18	19	19	21	16
Other white oaks	7	32	19	18	14	12	16
Other red oaks	4	13	9	8	10	10	10
Pecan	31	45	39	(1)	(1)	...	...
Other hickories	5	42	12	12	12	11	11
Persimmon	32	...	(1)	40	(1)	(1)	(1)
Hard maple	47	...	(1)	(1)	...	...	(1)
Soft maple	13	39	34	27	19	28	46
Beech	13	(1)	24	21	28	29	43
Sweetgum	7	23	13	11	18	16	26
Blackgum	8	17	17	14	18	18	21
Other gums	19	28	42	39	48	...	...
White ash	19	(1)	33	24	(1)	34	21
Other ashes	15	40	27	30	49	46	(1)
Sycamore	21	(1)	38	34	(1)	...	45
Cottonwood	32	(1)	(1)	44	...	(1)	(1)
Basswood	22	...	36	39	(1)	(1)	(1)
Yellow-poplar	7	24	16	15	16	14	17
Magnolia (*Magnolia* spp.)	22	(1)	44	27	...	...	(1)
Sweetbay	14	24	27	22	30	...	...
Willow	37	(1)	(1)	(1)	(1)	(1)	(1)
Black walnut	37	...	(1)	...	...	...	43
Black cherry	35	...	(1)	(1)	...	(1)	(1)
American elm	14	(1)	22	27	26	50	33
Other elms	15	46	37	28	32	42	31
River birch	27	...	(1)	50	36	(1)	(1)
Hackberry	20	(1)	33	31	36	...	49
Other hardwoods	(1)	(1)	(1)	...	(1)	...	(1)
All hardwoods	3.0	10.7	6.3	6.0	6.9	6.2	6.1
All species	1.8	5.3	4.1	3.6	4.6	4.1	5.6

[1]Exceeds 50 percent.

Forest Area Statistics
for
Midsouth Counties

OCT 1 1973

U. S. DEPARTMENT OF AGRICULTURE
FOREST SERVICE RESOURCE BULLETIN SO-40

1973

Forest Area Statistics for Midsouth Counties

J. M. Earles

U. S. DEPARTMENT OF AGRICULTURE
FOREST SERVICE

SOUTHERN FOREST EXPERIMENT STATION
New Orleans, Louisiana

1973

Counties of the Midsouth

Forest Area Statistics
for Midsouth Counties

J. M. Earles

This report summarizes acreage data on commercial forest land in counties of the seven States of the Midsouth. It includes some data that have been issued previously and some that have never been published at the county level. The information was gathered during 1963-1972 by the Forest Resources Research Unit of the Southern Forest Experiment Station.

Published for the first time are acreage statistics on Louisiana, Texas, and Oklahoma—States that were inventoried early in the current cycle. Also added are tables on stand size and site class for most Midsouth States. In the future, all State statistical bulletins will contain tables similar in format to those printed here.

The data were secured by a systematic sampling method involving a forest-nonforest classification on aerial photographs and on-the-ground measurements at approximately 35,000 sample locations. The sample locations were at the intersections of a grid of lines spaced 3 miles apart. At each forested location, 10 small plots were uniformly distributed on an area of about 1 acre.

The sampling errors to which the county area totals are liable (on a probability of two chances out of three) are shown in the last table of the sequence for each State. An approximation of sampling errors for groups of counties may be obtained by using the following formula:

$$e = \frac{(SE)\sqrt{\text{Specified area}}}{\sqrt{\text{Area total in question}}}$$

Where: e = Estimated sampling error of the area total in question

SE = Specified sampling error for the State.

When data for two or more counties are grouped the error decreases. Conversely, as data for individual counties are broken down by various subdivisions, the possibility of error increases and is greatest for the smallest items.

DEFINITIONS OF TERMS

Commercial forest land.—Forest land producing or capable of producing crops of industrial wood and not withdrawn from timber utilization.

Forest type.—A classification of forest land based upon the species forming a plurality of live-tree stocking.

Poletimber trees.—Merchantable trees of commercial species at least 5.0 inches in diameter at breast height, but smaller than sawtimber size.

Sawtimber trees.—Live trees that are of commercial species, contain at least a 12-foot saw log, and meet regional specifications for freedom from defect. Softwoods must be at least 9.0 inches in diameter at breast height and hardwoods at least 11.0 inches.

Site class.—A classification of forest land in terms of inherent capacity (expressed in cubic feet per acre annually) to grow crops of industrial wood.

Stand-size class.—A classification of forest land based on the size class of merchantable trees on the area; that is, sawtimber, poletimber, or seedlings and saplings.

Table 1. *Total area and forest area, Alabama, 1972*

County	Total area	Commercial forest	Commercial forest	Noncommercial forest	County	Total area	Commercial forest	Commercial forest	Noncommercial forest
	Thousand acres	*Thousand acres*	*Percent*	*Thousand acres*		*Thousand acres*	*Thousand acres*	*Percent*	*Thousand acres*
Autauga	386.6	253.7	66	...	Jackson	727.0	436.8	60	...
Baldwin	1,068.1	702.1	66	...	Jefferson	717.5	459.2	64	...
Barbour	575.4	385.0	67	...	Lamar	387.2	285.0	74	...
Bibb	400.0	332.8	83	...	Lauderdale	460.2	154.0	33	1.2
Blount	411.5	245.7	60	...	Lawrence	453.8	203.5	45	.4
Bullock	393.6	232.2	59	...	Lee	395.5	264.0	67	...
Butler	494.7	371.2	75	...	Limestone	380.2	77.9	20	...
Calhoun	391.7	241.9	62	4.8	Lowndes	460.2	224.0	49	...
Chambers	383.4	270.0	70	...	Macon	394.2	218.4	55	...
Cherokee	384.0	214.6	56	...	Madison	518.4	180.0	35	...
Chilton	451.2	296.4	66	...	Marengo	626.0	402.6	64	...
Choctaw	590.7	504.0	85	...	Marion	475.5	348.1	73	...
Clarke	802.5	722.4	90	(2)	Marshall	401.2	173.6	43	...
Clay	385.9	313.2	81	...	Mobile	817.9	522.9	64	...
Cleburne	367.4	312.7	85	.2	Monroe	666.9	508.8	76	...
Coffee	433.3	241.5	56	3.0	Montgomery	508.8	171.1	34	...
Colbert	403.8	222.3	55	2.5	Morgan	380.2	157.5	41	...
Conecuh	544.0	428.4	79	...	Perry	469.8	286.2	61	(2)
Coosa	421.8	354.0	84	...	Pickens	567.7	427.5	75	...
Covington	662.4	450.0	68	(2)	Pike	430.7	250.8	58	...
Crenshaw	391.0	274.5	70	...	Randolph	371.8	270.3	73	...
Cullman	475.5	256.5	54	(2)	Russell	409.6	268.4	66	...
Dale	358.4	225.5	63	2.0	St. Clair	414.0	311.1	75	...
Dallas	629.7	313.5	50	...	Shelby	516.5	400.2	77	...
De Kalb	497.9	246.4	49	...	Sumter	589.5	390.6	66	...
Elmore	421.8	243.0	58	...	Talladega	484.5	291.2	60	...
Escambia	615.7	490.2	80	...	Tallapoosa	492.1	369.6	75	.1
Etowah	355.2	176.9	50	...	Tuscaloosa	863.3	696.2	81	1.7
Fayette	401.3	307.4	77	...	Walker	518.4	369.2	71	(2)
Franklin	412.2	265.0	64	...	Washington	687.4	622.2	91	...
Geneva	369.9	159.0	43	.1	Wilcox	581.1	421.8	73	...
Greene	420.5	234.6	56	...	Winston	405.1	319.2	79	.4
Hale	424.3	248.0	58	.6					
Henry	361.6	209.1	58	...					
Houston	370.6	107.5	29	...	All counties	33,029.8	21,333.1	65	17.0

[1] Source: United States Bureau of the Census, Land and Water Area of the United States, 1960.
[2] Negligible.

Table 2. *Commercial forest land by ownership class, Alabama, 1972*

County	All ownerships	National forest	Other public	Forest industry	Farmer	Misc. private
		- - - - - - - - *Thousand acres* - - - - - - - -				
Autauga	253.7	...	1.8	94.4	82.5	75.0
Baldwin	702.1	...	5.7	286.0	114.5	295.9
Barbour	385.0	...	15.8	60.5	109.9	198.8
Bibb	332.8	60.6	3.9	98.8	42.3	127.2
Blount	245.7	...	6.8	...	87.6	151.3
Bullock	232.2	...	...	10.8	64.8	156.6
Butler	371.2	...	.3	150.8	121.7	98.4
Calhoun	241.9	15.1	52.2	53.1	76.2	45.3
Chambers	270.0	...	.6	10.8	113.3	145.3
Cherokee	214.6	...	...	63.8	57.6	93.2
Chilton	296.4	21.4	.6	52.0	103.9	118.5
Choctaw	504.0	...	3.9	150.0	102.0	248.1
Clarke	722.4	...	8.2	291.2	112.0	311.0
Clay	313.2	65.2	1.6	27.0	91.2	128.2
Cleburne	312.7	79.4	1.9	88.5	52.8	90.1
Coffee	241.5	...	10.2	41.4	117.2	72.7
Colbert	222.3	...	11.3	11.4	91.9	107.7
Conecuh	428.4	...	(¹)	170.1	132.3	126.0
Coosa	354.0	...	5.0	90.0	59.6	199.4
Covington	450.0	54.2	2.1	156.0	158.5	79.2
Crenshaw	274.5		.2	42.7	115.8	115.8
Cullman	256.5	...	1.2	22.8	141.6	90.9
Dale	225.5	...	33.8	...	87.9	103.8
Dallas	313.5	5.0	1.9	60.5	126.4	119.7
De Kalb	246.4	...	5.8	22.4	135.4	82.8
Elmore	243.0	...	1.8	5.4	75.6	160.2
Escambia	490.2	32.0	4.0	216.6	61.3	176.3
Etowah	176.9	...	1.4	6.1	97.0	72.4
Fayette	307.4	...	7.5	68.9	86.2	144.8
Franklin	265.0	1.6	1.4	60.0	125.9	76.1
Geneva	159.0	...	7.2	5.3	79.5	67.0
Greene	234.6	...	2.3	35.7	103.7	92.9
Hale	248.0	27.7	2.9	55.8	56.7	104.9
Henry	209.1	...	.9	30.6	81.5	96.1
Houston	107.5	...	1.4	...	34.4	71.7

Table 2. *Commercial forest land by ownership class, Alabama, 1972* (Continued)

County	All ownerships	National forest	Other public	Forest industry	Farmer	Misc. private
			-Thousand acres-			
Jackson	436.8	...	14.9	44.8	259.5	117.6
Jefferson	459.2		11.6	...	44.5	403.1
Lamar	285.0	...	.1	39.9	92.7	152.3
Lauderdale	154.0	...	4.0	11.0	110.8	28.2
Lawrence	203.5	88.7	1.8	...	88.6	24.4
Lee	264.0	...	5.1	22.0	71.5	165.4
Limestone	77.9	...	5.6	...	53.7	18.6
Lowndes	224.0	...	1.5	50.4	89.5	82.6
Macon	218.4	9.8	1.5	31.2	98.7	77.2
Madison	180.0	...	17.9	6.0	84.6	71.5
Marengo	402.6	...	1.0	79.2	165.0	157.4
Marion	348.1	...	2.5	94.4	95.9	155.3
Marshall	173.6	...	12.6	22.4	73.3	65.3
Mobile	522.9	...	24.4	50.4	92.5	355.6
Monroe	508.8	...	3.3	164.3	196.0	145.2
Montgomery	171.1	...	1.3	...	100.2	69.6
Morgan	157.5	...	7.8	...	122.4	27.3
Perry	286.2	32.9	.4	53.0	102.3	97.6
Pickens	427.5	...	...	136.8	127.4	163.3
Pike	250.8		.4	22.8	159.5	68.1
Randolph	270.3	...	.3	10.2	157.1	102.7
Russell	268.4	...	8.2	36.6	61.0	162.6
St. Clair	311.1	...	.9	66.3	86.2	157.7
Shelby	400.2	...	12.8	133.4	92.2	161.8
Sumter	390.6	...	1.4	124.0	155.0	110.2
Talladega	291.2	41.6	9.2	22.4	44.5	173.5
Tallapoosa	369.6	...	1.2	44.8	78.4	245.2
Tuscaloosa	696.2	8.5	10.2	153.4	138.0	386.1
Walker	369.2	...	15.5	46.8	67.2	239.7
Washington	622.2	...	1.4	79.3	107.4	434.1
Wilcox	421.8	...	4.3	57.0	153.9	206.6
Winston	319.2	85.8	2.3	62.7	62.3	106.1
All counties	21,333.1	629.5	391.0	4,204.9	6,732.5	9,375.2

[1] Negligible.

Table 3. *Commercial forest land by forest type, Alabama, 1972*

County	All types	Longleaf-slash pine	Loblolly-shortleaf pine	Oak-pine	Oak-hickory	Oak-gum-cypress	Elm-ash-cottonwood
			- - - - - - - - - - - *Thousand acres* - - - - - - - - - - -				
Autauga	253.7	41.3	94.4	47.2	59.0	11.8	...
Baldwin	702.1	283.9	58.5	156.0	47.7	156.0	...
Barbour	385.0	22.0	170.5	66.0	88.0	38.5	...
Bibb	332.8	26.0	130.0	104.0	67.6	5.2	....
Blount	245.7	...	81.9	81.9	69.3	12.6	...
Bullock	232.2	...	97.2	27.0	64.8	43.2	...
Butler	371.2	5.8	145.0	87.0	87.0	40.6	5.8
Calhoun	241.9	...	76.7	82.6	82.6	...	...
Chambers	270.0	...	145.8	43.2	70.2	10.8	...
Cherokee	214.6	...	98.6	58.0	46.4	11.6	...
Chilton	296.4	10.4	72.8	88.4	119.6	5.2	...
Choctaw	504.0	...	186.0	132.0	108.0	72.0	6.0
Clarke	722.4	...	308.0	151.2	117.6	134.4	11.2
Clay	313.2	5.4	102.6	86.4	118.8	...	...
Cleburne	312.7	5.9	129.8	82.6	94.4	...	...
Coffee	241.5	13.8	48.3	62.1	82.8	34.5	...
Colbert	222.3	...	17.1	57.0	136.8	5.7	5.7
Conecuh	428.4	12.6	119.7	94.5	163.8	37.8	...
Coosa	354.0	24.0	138.0	102.0	84.0	6.0	...
Covington	450.0	144.0	72.0	84.0	102.0	48.0	...
Crenshaw	274.5	18.3	54.9	79.3	48.8	73.2	...
Cullman	256.5	...	96.9	85.5	74.1	...	....
Dale	225.5	5.5	66.0	44.0	88.0	22.0	...
Dallas	313.5	5.5	99.0	71.5	93.5	38.5	5.5
De Kalb	246.4	...	84.0	50.4	112.0	...	...
Elmore	243.0	...	81.0	48.6	91.8	21.6	...
Escambia	490.2	245.1	22.8	119.7	39.9	62.7	...
Etowah	176.9	...	61.0	36.6	73.2	6.1	...
Fayette	307.4	...	127.2	53.0	79.5	42.4	5.3
Franklin	265.0	...	55.0	65.0	145.0	...	...
Geneva	159.0	37.1	...	15.9	53.0	53.0	...
Greene	234.6	...	61.2	40.8	40.8	91.8	...
Hale	248.0	6.2	68.2	86.8	31.0	55.8	...
Henry	209.1	5.1	81.6	45.9	56.1	20.4	...
Houston	107.5	25.8	21.5	8.6	21.5	30.1	...

Table 3. *Commercial forest land by forest type, Alabama, 1972* (Continued)

County	All types	Longleaf-slash pine	Loblolly-shortleaf pine	Oak-pine	Oak-hickory	Oak-gum-cypress	Elm-ash-cottonwood
				— — — — Thousand acres — — — —			
Jackson	436.8	...	16.8	28.0	369.6	22.4	....
Jefferson	459.2	11.2	207.2	134.4	95.2	5.6	5.6
Lamar	285.0	...	62.7	85.5	57.0	74.1	5.7
Lauderdale	154.0	...	5.5	22.0	115.5	11.0	...
Lawrence	203.5	...	38.5	16.5	132.0	16.5	...
Lee	264.0	11.0	143.0	44.0	44.0	22.0	...
Limestone	77.9	...	4.1	4.1	45.1	24.6	...
Lowndes	224.0	...	61.6	50.4	61.6	44.8	5.6
Macon	218.4	...	57.2	57.2	52.0	52.0	...
Madison	180.0	...	18.0	12.0	102.0	48.0	...
Marengo	402.6	...	151.8	99.0	59.4	92.4	...
Marion	348.1	...	100.3	82.6	159.3	...	5.9
Marshall	173.6	...	50.4	39.2	84.0	...	...
Mobile	522.9	201.6	31.5	126.0	81.9	81.9	...
Monroe	508.8	21.2	111.3	137.8	148.4	84.8	5.3
Montgomery	171.1	...	47.2	23.6	41.3	59.0	...
Morgan	157.5	...	36.0	31.5	58.5	31.5	...
Perry	286.2	15.9	90.1	74.2	63.6	31.8	10.6
Pickens	427.5	...	176.7	102.6	74.1	68.4	5.7
Pike	250.8	22.8	62.7	51.3	62.7	51.3	...
Randolph	270.3	5.1	117.3	71.4	71.4	5.1	...
Russell	268.4	12.2	183.0	30.5	18.3	24.4	...
St. Clair	311.1	5.1	102.0	76.5	96.9	30.6	...
Shelby	400.2	29.0	116.0	116.0	116.0	17.4	5.8
Sumter	390.6	...	117.8	55.8	124.0	86.8	6.2
Talladega	291.2	11.2	89.6	95.2	95.2	...	...
Tallapoosa	369.6	...	117.6	128.8	106.4	16.8	...
Tuscaloosa	696.2	23.6	247.8	194.7	141.6	88.5	...
Walker	369.2	...	171.6	93.6	104.0	...	...
Washington	622.2	158.6	103.7	176.9	85.4	97.6	...
Wilcox	421.8	11.4	131.1	125.4	91.2	62.7	...
Winston	319.2	...	136.8	85.5	96.9	...	...
All counties	21,333.1	1,483.6	6,380.1	5,016.9	5,913.1	2,443.5	95.9

6

Table 4. *Commercial forest land by stand-size class, Alabama, 1972*

County	All classes	Sawtimber	Poletimber	Sapling and seedling	Nonstocked areas
- - - - - - - - -Thousand acres- - - - - - - - -					
Autauga	253.7	118.0	64.9	70.8	...
Baldwin	702.1	268.7	112.7	312.0	8.7
Barbour	385.0	132.0	132.0	110.0	11.0
Bibb	332.8	83.2	130.0	119.6	...
Blount	245.7	94.5	69.3	81.9	
Bullock	232.2	75.6	97.2	59.4	...
Butler	371.2	156.6	69.6	139.2	5.8
Calhoun	241.9	64.9	94.4	82.6	...
Chambers	270.0	43.2	97.2	129.6	
Cherokee	214.6	40.6	63.8	110.2	
Chilton	296.4	57.2	109.2	130.0	
Choctaw	504.0	180.0	174.0	150.0	
Clarke	722.4	386.4	168.0	168.0	
Clay	313.2	59.4	140.4	113.4	
Cleburne	312.7	88.5	135.7	88.5	
Coffee	241.5	75.9	75.9	82.8	6.9
Colbert	222.3	22.8	96.9	102.6	...
Conecuh	428.4	182.7	107.1	132.3	6.3
Coosa	354.0	72.0	144.0	138.0	...
Covington	450.0	168.0	114.0	162.0	6.0
Crenshaw	274.5	97.6	103.7	67.1	6.1
Cullman	256.5	62.7	142.5	51.3	...
Dale	225.5	66.0	82.5	71.5	5.5
Dallas	313.5	99.0	93.5	121.0	...
De Kalb	246.4	56.0	100.8	89.6	
Elmore	243.0	43.2	81.0	118.8	
Escambia	490.2	216.6	96.9	176.7	...
Etowah	176.9	36.6	54.9	85.4	...
Fayette	307.4	68.9	137.8	95.4	5.3
Franklin	265.0	15.0	155.0	95.0	...
Geneva	159.0	37.1	47.7	74.2	
Greene	234.6	122.4	66.3	45.9	
Hale	248.0	105.4	68.2	74.4	
Henry	209.1	61.2	102.0	45.9	...
Houston	107.5	25.8	25.8	55.9	...

Table 4. *Commercial forest land by stand-size class, Alabama, 1972* (Continued)

County	All classes	Sawtimber	Poletimber	Sapling and seedling	Nonstocked areas
			- - - - - - - - - -Thousand acres- - - - - - - - - -		
Jackson	436.8	156.8	173.6	106.4	
Jefferson	459.2	100.8	162.4	196.0	
Lamar	285.0	57.0	165.3	62.7	
Lauderdale	154.0	44.0	55.0	55.0	
Lawrence	203.5	38.5	88.0	77.0	
Lee	264.0	82.5	99.0	77.0	5.5
Limestone	77.9	32.8	32.8	12.3	...
Lowndes	224.0	89.6	61.6	67.2	5.6
Macon	218.4	57.2	78.0	83.2	...
Madison	180.0	48.0	90.0	42.0	
Marengo	402.6	158.4	118.8	125.4	
Marion	348.1	47.2	153.4	147.5	...
Marshall	173.6	67.2	67.2	39.2	...
Mobile	522.9	126.0	126.0	252.0	18.9
Monroe	508.8	201.4	143.1	164.3	...
Montgomery	171.1	64.9	64.9	41.3	
Morgan	157.5	45.0	58.5	54.0	
Perry	286.2	127.2	95.4	63.6	...
Pickens	427.5	148.2	131.1	148.2	...
Pike	250.8	79.8	85.5	79.8	5.7
Randolph	270.3	76.5	61.2	132.6	...
Russell	268.4	85.4	109.8	67.1	6.1
St. Clair	311.1	66.3	122.4	122.4	...
Shelby	400.2	116.0	156.6	121.8	5.8
Sumter	390.6	192.2	68.2	130.2	...
Talladega	291.2	72.8	128.8	89.6	
Tallapoosa	369.6	89.6	89.6	190.4	
Tuscaloosa	696.2	206.5	236.0	253.7	
Walker	369.2	114.4	166.4	88.4	
Washington	622.2	250.1	164.7	207.4	
Wilcox	421.8	216.6	108.3	96.9	...
Winston	319.2	96.9	125.4	96.9	...
All counties	21,333.1	6,839.5	7,141.9	7,242.5	109.2

Table 5. *Commercial forest land by site class, Alabama, 1972*

County	All classes	165 cu.ft. or more	120-165 cu. ft.	85-120 cu.ft.	50-85 cu.ft.	Less than 50 cu.ft.
		- - - - - - - - - - *Thousand acres* - - - - - - - - - -				
Autauga	253.7	...	23.6	94.4	112.1	23.6
Baldwin	702.1	...	19.5	188.5	444.2	49.9
Barbour	385.0	5.5	110.0	187.0	82.5	...
Bibb	332.8	...	10.4	124.8	166.4	31.2
Blount	245.7	...	18.9	37.8	163.8	25.2
Bullock	232.2	10.8	27.0	108.0	86.4	...
Butler	371.2	...	81.2	156.6	127.6	5.8
Calhoun	241.9	...	11.8	82.6	106.2	41.3
Chambers	270.0		21.6	102.6	140.4	5.4
Cherokee	214.6		5.8	40.6	156.6	11.6
Chilton	296.4	10.4	52.0	88.4	124.8	20.8
Choctaw	504.0	30.0	84.0	276.0	114.0	...
Clarke	722.4	39.2	190.4	291.2	184.8	16.8
Clay	313.2	...	10.8	86.4	172.8	43.2
Cleburne	312.7		5.9	41.3	236.0	29.5
Coffee	241.5	6.9	27.6	131.1	69.0	6.9
Colbert	222.3	...	11.4	51.3	153.9	5.7
Conecuh	428.4	50.4	207.9	157.5	12.6	...
Coosa	354.0	...	18.0	108.0	198.0	30.0
Covington	450.0	30.0	102.0	162.0	150.0	6.0
Crenshaw	274.5	...	12.2	115.9	140.3	6.1
Cullman	256.5	...	...	68.4	171.0	17.1
Dale	225.5	5.5	22.0	66.0	121.0	11.0
Dallas	313.5	22.0	77.0	170.5	44.0	...
De Kalb	246.4	...	...	16.8	168.0	61.6
Elmore	243.0	...	16.2	102.6	113.4	10.8
Escambia	490.2		45.6	176.7	245.1	22.8
Etowah	176.9	...	6.1	48.8	97.6	24.4
Fayette	307.4	...	10.6	111.3	164.3	21.2
Franklin	265.0	5.0	15.0	105.0	115.0	25.0
Geneva	159.0	...	5.3	68.9	68.9	15.9
Greene	234.6	...	20.4	137.7	61.2	15.3
Hale	248.0	12.4	31.0	136.4	68.2	...
Henry	209.1	5.1	20.4	132.6	45.9	5.1
Houston	107.5	...	8.6	38.7	51.6	8.6

9

Table 5. *Commercial forest land by site class, Alabama, 1972* (Continued)

County	All classes	165 cu.ft. or more	120-165 cu. ft.	85-120 cu. ft.	50-85 cu.ft.	Less than 50 cu. ft.
			- - - - - - - - - - -*Thousand acres*- - - - - - - - - - -			
Jackson	436.8	5.6	...	61.6	252.0	117.6
Jefferson	459.2	5.6	72.8	246.4	128.8	5.6
Lamar	285.0	...	17.1	91.2	148.2	28.5
Lauderdale	154.0		...	66.0	71.5	16.5
Lawrence	203.5		...	33.0	137.5	33.0
Lee	264.0	11.0	33.0	71.5	115.5	33.0
Limestone	77.9	...	12.3	36.9	28.7	...
Lowndes	224.0	22.4	22.4	140.0	39.2	...
Macon	218.4	10.4	26.0	72.8	109.2	...
Madison	180.0	6.0	24.0	30.0	78.0	42.0
Marengo	402.6	6.6	118.8	204.6	72.6	...
Marion	348.1	5.9	17.7	123.9	182.9	17.7
Marshall	173.6	...	11.2	61.6	84.0	16.8
Mobile	522.9	...	12.6	107.1	296.1	107.1
Monroe	508.8	10.6	90.1	164.3	164.3	79.5
Montgomery	171.1	...	17.7	106.2	41.3	5.9
Morgan	157.5	...	4.5	90.0	49.5	13.5
Perry	286.2	15.9	58.3	100.7	100.7	10.6
Pickens	427.5	5.7	11.4	205.2	176.7	28.5
Pike	250.8	...	...	165.3	79.8	5.7
Randolph	270.3	5.1	5.1	96.9	147.9	15.3
Russell	268.4	6.1	30.5	122.0	97.6	12.2
St. Clair	311.1	...	35.7	117.3	142.8	15.3
Shelby	400.2	11.6	40.6	174.0	150.8	23.2
Sumter	390.6	18.6	80.6	173.6	99.2	18.6
Talladega	291.2		...	50.4	190.4	50.4
Tallapoosa	369.6	...	28.0	100.8	190.4	50.4
Tuscaloosa	696.2	...	64.9	224.2	324.5	82.6
Walker	369.2	15.6	57.2	145.6	145.6	5.2
Washington	622.2	6.1	48.8	250.1	298.9	18.3
Wilcox	421.8	11.4	51.3	188.1	165.3	5.7
Winston	319.2	...	11.4	114.0	188.1	5.7
All counties	21,333.1	413.4	2,334.2	7,947.7	9,175.6	1,462.2

Table 6. *Sampling errors*[1] *for commercial forest land,*
Alabama, 1972

County	Percent	County	Percent
Autauga	2	Jackson	1
Baldwin	2	Jefferson	2
Barbour	2	Lamar	3
Bibb	2	Lauderdale	2
Blount	2	Lawrence	1
Bullock	3	Lee	2
Butler	2	Limestone	1
Calhoun	2	Lowndes	2
Chambers	3	Macon	3
Cherokee	2	Madison	1
Chilton	2	Marengo	2
Choctaw	1	Marion	2
Clarke	1	Marshall	2
Clay	2	Mobile	1
Cleburne	2	Monroe	1
Coffee	1	Montgomery	2
Colbert	1	Morgan	2
Conecuh	1	Perry	1
Coosa	2	Pickens	2
Covington	1	Pike	2
Crenshaw	2	Randolph	3
Cullman	2	Russell	3
Dale	3	St. Clair	2
Dallas	2	Shelby	2
De Kalb	2	Sumter	2
Elmore	2	Talladega	1
Escambia	1	Tallapoosa	2
Etowah	2	Tuscaloosa	1
Fayette	2	Walker	2
Franklin	2	Washington	1
Geneva	2	Wilcox	2
Greene	2	Winston	2
Hale	2		
Henry	1		
Houston	2	All counties	0.2

[1]By random-sampling formula.

11

Table 7. *Total area and forest area, Arkansas, 1969*

County	Total area[1] (Thousand acres)	Commercial forest (Thousand acres)	Commercial forest (Percent)	Noncommercial forest (Thousand acres)	County	Total area[1] (Thousand acres)	Commercial forest (Thousand acres)	Commercial forest (Percent)	Noncommercial forest (Thousand acres)
Arkansas	666.9	207.2	31	...	Lincoln	364.8	142.8	39	(2)
Ashley	597.8	410.4	69	...	Little River	359.0	192.5	54	...
					Logan	468.5	254.2	54	4.4
Baxter	369.9	254.8	69	...	Lonoke	512.7	91.8	18	...
Benton	567.1	219.6	39	2.4					
Boone	386.6	195.5	51	...	Madison	532.5	356.4	67	.4
Bradley	417.3	354.0	85	...	Marion	407.6	282.0	69	6.9
					Miller	410.9	217.0	53	...
Calhoun	404.5	348.0	86	...	Mississippi	596.5	34.8	6	...
Carroll	405.7	239.4	59	...	Monroe	394.9	150.4	38	...
Chicot	437.1	75.6	17	...	Montgomery	512.6	410.4	80	8.6
Clark	561.9	423.4	75	...					
Clay	409.6	65.0	16	...	Nevada	394.2	300.0	76	.2
Cleburne	380.8	240.7	63	...	Newton	526.1	478.0	91	.2
Cleveland	384.6	319.0	83	...					
Columbia	491.5	379.5	77	...	Ouachita	473.0	384.3	81	.3
Conway	364.2	137.5	38	...					
Craighead	458.9	45.5	10	.5	Perry	359.0	273.6	76	1.6
Crawford	388.5	208.0	54	5.1	Phillips	465.9	81.6	18	...
Crittenden	414.7	32.0	8	...	Pike	393.6	319.0	81	...
Cross	400.6	49.5	12	...	Poinsett	487.7	65.0	13	(2)
					Polk	550.4	435.0	79	16.2
Dallas	430.1	372.6	87	...	Pope	526.0	338.4	64	...
Desha	515.2	143.0	28	...	Prairie	435.8	140.4	32	...
Drew	535.0	387.6	72	...	Pulaski	515.2	252.0	49	...
Faulkner	422.4	156.8	37	...	Randolph	414.1	186.2	45	(2)
Franklin	398.7	211.2	53	...					
Fulton	391.0	247.0	63	...	St. Francis	408.3	65.0	16	.1
					Saline	466.6	372.6	80	.6
Garland	470.4	335.5	71	3.5	Scott	574.7	448.2	78	4.9
Grant	403.8	346.8	86	...	Searcy	425.0	310.6	73	...
Greene	370.6	53.3	14	.2	Sebastian	343.7	134.4	39	1.8
					Sevier	374.4	269.5	72	...
Hempstead	474.9	286.7	60	...	Sharp	382.7	255.3	67	...
Hot Spring	398.7	294.8	74	...	Stone	391.7	322.0	82	...
Howard	384.0	254.8	66	...					
					Union	674.0	572.4	85	...
Independence	486.4	244.8	50	...					
Izard	369.3	240.0	65	...	Van Buren	457.0	303.8	66	...
Jackson	407.7	65.0	16	...	Washington	616.3	318.8	52	12.2
Jefferson	580.5	193.5	33	...	White	667.5	222.6	33	...
Johnson	435.2	298.1	68	...	Woodruff	379.5	77.4	20	...
Lafayette	352.6	212.8	60	...	Yell	606.7	403.2	66	1.0
Lawrence	378.9	108.8	29	.1					
Lee	403.2	87.4	22	...	All counties	33,985.9	18,206.7	54	71.2

[1]Source: United States Bureau of the Census, Land and Water Area of the United States, 1960.
[2]Negligible.

12

Table 8. *Commercial forest land by ownership class, Arkansas, 1969*

County	All ownerships	National forest	Other public	Forest industry	Farmer	Misc. private
- - - - - - - - - -Thousand acres - - - - - - - - - -						
Arkansas	207.2	...	72.1	11.8	57.7	65.6
Ashley	410.4	...	3.5	268.1	51.3	87.5
Baxter	254.8	60.4	21.5	...	30.0	142.9
Benton	219.6	6.4	3.6	...	87.2	122.4
Boone	195.5	...	5.4	...	82.2	107.9
Bradley	354.0	...	...	194.9	76.8	82.3
Calhoun	348.0	...	(1)	232.2	5.8	110.0
Carroll	239.4		3.0	...	116.4	120.0
Chicot	75.6	...	...	31.1	25.9	18.6
Clark	423.4	...	10.3	151.0	98.7	163.4
Clay	65.0	...	11.0	10.8	12.9	30.3
Cleburne	240.7	...	3.1	25.4	84.7	127.5
Cleveland	319.0	...	...	145.2	75.5	98.3
Columbia	379.5	...	.2	82.9	89.7	206.7
Conway	137.5	6.9	3.2	...	38.3	89.1
Craighead	45.5	...	...	...	17.4	28.1
Crawford	208.0	81.9	.1	...	53.6	72.4
Crittenden	32.0	...	7.8	5.3	12.7	6.2
Cross	49.5		...	...	43.9	5.6
Dallas	372.6	...	(1)	237.9	70.3	64.4
Desha	143.0	...	20.2	96.9	25.9	...
Drew	387.6	...	9.3	137.8	81.6	158.9
Faulkner	156.8	...	11.5	...	57.2	88.1
Franklin	211.2	100.3	4.3	...	42.3	64.3
Fulton	247.0	...	1.5	...	159.2	86.3
Garland	335.5	99.4	17.9	121.4	10.6	86.2
Grant	346.8	...	...	240.0	56.2	50.6
Greene	53.3		.4	...	40.8	12.1
Hempstead	286.7	...	7.2	79.4	97.7	102.4
Hot Spring	294.8	.4	6.2	154.3	53.7	80.2
Howard	254.8	1.2	9.0	165.6	63.8	15.2
Independence	244.8		1.2	...	73.5	170.1
Izard	240.0		(1)	...	98.0	142.0
Jackson	65.0	...	...	...	32.4	32.6
Jefferson	193.5	...	18.6	38.0	50.9	86.0
Johnson	298.1	173.5	.1	...	52.6	71.9
Lafayette	212.8	...	(1)	61.7	56.1	95.0
Lawrence	108.8	...	8.5	...	57.4	42.9
Lee	87.4	9.4	...	4.9	42.6	30.5
Lincoln	142.8	...	.3	10.8	31.5	100.2

13

Table 8. *Commercial forest land by ownership class, Arkansas, 1969* (Continued)

County	All ownerships	National forest	Other public	Forest industry	Farmer	Misc. private
			- - - - - - - - - -*Thousand acres* - - - - - - - - - -			
Little River	192.5	...	4.7	71.6	49.6	66.6
Logan	254.2	86.6	9.1	5.9	59.5	93.1
Lonoke	91.8	...	(¹)	...	61.1	30.7
Madison	356.4	45.3	8.9	...	176.3	125.9
Marion	282.0	1.7	20.6	...	57.6	202.1
Miller	217.0	...	8.9	21.0	77.1	110.0
Mississippi	34.8	...	14.4	10.2	10.2	...
Monroe	150.4	...	22.1	48.6	75.2	4.5
Montgomery	410.4	290.3	10.9	54.7	10.9	43.6
Nevada	300.0	...	7.2	90.1	90.1	112.6
Newton	478.0	193.2	9.2	...	139.2	136.4
Ouachita	384.3	...	9.9	103.8	85.5	185.1
Perry	273.6	94.3	1.9	65.6	60.2	51.6
Phillips	81.6	8.8	8.8	10.8	26.2	27.0
Pike	319.0	2.2	6.8	220.6	81.3	8.1
Poinsett	65.0	...	3.9	...	34.8	26.3
Polk	435.0	178.0	1.5	100.2	33.4	121.9
Pope	338.4	181.3	4.1	...	80.8	72.2
Prairie	140.4	...	13.7	16.5	56.2	54.0
Pulaski	252.0	...	28.1	21.5	43.0	159.4
Randolph	186.2		6.6	...	95.0	84.6
St. Francis	65.0	...	9.6	4.2	29.9	21.3
Saline	372.6	51.5	1.6	171.0	15.5	133.0
Scott	448.2	349.9	(¹)	25.9	46.6	25.8
Searcy	310.6	29.5	1.7	...	76.0	203.4
Sebastian	134.4	9.5	37.1	...	43.0	44.8
Sevier	269.5	...	9.3	137.3	68.7	54.2
Sharp	255.3	...	...	...	181.2	74.1
Stone	322.0	57.8	.8	...	122.1	141.3
Union	572.4	...	.9	194.6	54.0	322.9
Van Buren	303.8	30.5	2.1	10.0	80.0	181.2
Washington	318.8	17.2	1.8	...	138.6	161.2
White	222.6	...	15.1	10.8	97.4	99.3
Woodruff	77.4		(¹)	...	42.8	34.6
Yell	403.2	210.8	18.0	48.4	86.0	40.0
All counties	18,206.7	2,378.2	560.3	3,950.7	4,800.0	6,517.5

¹ Negligible.

Table 9. *Commercial forest land by forest type, Arkansas, 1969*

County	All types	Loblolly-shortleaf pine	Oak-pine	Oak-hickory	Oak-gum-cypress	Elm-ash-cottonwood
			- - - *Thousand acres* - - -			
Arkansas	207.2	...	...	44.8	145.6	16.8
Ashley	410.4	205.2	79.8	57.0	68.4	...
Baxter	254.8	...	9.8	245.0	...	
Benton	219.6	...	...	219.6	...	
Boone	195.5	...	...	195.5	...	
Bradley	354.0	123.9	76.7	76.7	76.7	
Calhoun	348.0	133.4	69.6	63.8	81.2	...
Carroll	239.4	11.4	22.8	205.2	...	...
Chicot	75.6	...	...	4.2	50.4	21.0
Clark	423.4	116.0	127.6	110.2	69.6	...
Clay	65.0	...	...	19.5	45.5	...
Cleburne	240.7	33.2	58.1	141.1	8.3	...
Cleveland	319.0	110.2	58.0	75.4	69.6	5.8
Columbia	379.5	144.9	96.6	55.2	82.8	...
Conway	137.5	12.5	25.0	87.5	12.5	...
Craighead	45.5	...	...	14.0	24.5	7.0
Crawford	208.0	29.2	8.2	170.6	...	...
Crittenden	32.0	...	...	...	19.2	12.8
Cross	49.5		...	22.0	27.5	...
Dallas	372.6	118.8	102.6	70.2	81.0	...
Desha	143.0	...	...	...	117.0	26.0
Drew	387.6	91.8	81.6	112.2	96.9	5.1
Faulkner	156.8	...	...	156.8	...	
Franklin	211.2	22.2	30.6	158.4	...	
Fulton	247.0	26.0	...	221.0	...	
Garland	335.5	115.5	115.5	104.5	...	...
Grant	346.8	76.5	96.9	81.6	91.8	...
Greene	53.3	...	4.1	36.9	8.2	4.1
Hempstead	286.7	109.8	79.3	42.7	54.9	...
Hot Spring	294.8	80.4	87.1	107.2	20.1	...
Howard	254.8	93.1	88.2	49.0	19.6	4.9
Independence	244.8	14.4	14.4	216.0	...	
Izard	240.0	19.2	19.2	192.0	9.6	...
Jackson	65.0	...	...	39.0	26.0	...
Jefferson	193.5	31.5	31.5	49.5	72.0	9.0
Johnson	298.1	36.6	31.8	222.0	7.7	...
Lafayette	212.8	78.4	56.0	22.4	44.8	11.2
Lawrence	108.8	...	...	64.0	44.8	...
Lee	87.4	...	...	9.2	55.2	23.0

Table 9. *Commercial forest land by forest type, Arkansas, 1969*(Continued)

County	All types	Loblolly-shortleaf pine	Oak-pine	Oak-hickory	Oak-gum-cypress	Elm-ash-cottonwood
			Thousand acres			
Lincoln	142.8	20.4	15.3	61.2	35.7	10.2
Little River	192.5	38.5	77.0	33.0	38.5	5.5
Logan	254.2	80.6	49.6	111.6	12.4	...
Lonoke	91.8	...	...	32.4	59.4	
Madison	356.4	...	10.8	345.6	...	...
Marion	282.0	14.1	...	267.9	...	...
Miller	217.0	56.0	56.0	21.0	63.0	21.0
Mississippi	34.8	...	...	...	17.4	17.4
Monroe	150.4	...	4.7	18.8	126.9	...
Montgomery	410.4	165.3	114.0	131.1	...	
Nevada	300.0	102.0	54.0	90.0	54.0	...
Newton	478.0	32.4	32.4	413.2	...	
Ouachita	384.3	85.4	109.8	85.4	103.7	
Perry	273.6	102.6	119.7	45.6	5.7	...
Phillips	81.6	...	...	15.3	61.2	5.1
Pike	319.0	139.2	110.2	63.8	...	5.8
Poinsett	65.0	...	...	20.0	20.0	25.0
Polk	435.0	104.4	168.2	162.4	...	...
Pope	338.4	54.7	44.6	239.1	...	...
Prairie	140.4	...	...	46.8	93.6	...
Pulaski	252.0	22.4	50.4	117.6	56.0	5.6
Randolph	186.2		...	172.9	13.3	...
St. Francis	65.0	...	...	...	60.0	5.0
Saline	372.6	81.0	91.8	167.4	27.0	5.4
Scott	448.2	226.8	75.6	140.4	5.4	...
Searcy	310.6	...	14.9	295.7	...	...
Sebastian	134.4	6.4	6.4	96.0	19.2	6.4
Sevier	269.5	78.4	39.2	78.4	58.8	14.7
Sharp	255.3	11.1	11.1	233.1	...	...
Stone	322.0	27.6	27.6	266.8	...	
Union	572.4	199.8	118.8	118.8	135.0	...
Van Buren	303.8	39.2	34.3	230.3	...	
Washington	318.8	...	10.2	308.6	...	...
White	222.6	...	21.2	159.0	42.4	...
Woodruff	77.4		...	...	73.1	4.3
Yell	403.2	145.6	100.8	95.2	61.6	...
All counties	18,206.7	3,668.0	3,039.6	8,446.3	2,774.7	278.1

Table 10. *Commercial forest land by stand-size class, Arkansas, 1969*

County	All classes	Sawtimber	Poletimber	Sapling and seedling	Nonstocked areas
		- - - - -*Thousand acres*- - - - - - - -			
Arkansas	207.2	134.4	39.2	33.6	...
Ashley	410.4	188.1	51.3	171.0	...
Baxter	254.8	29.4	68.6	156.8	...
Benton	219.6	36.6	48.8	134.2	...
Boone	195.5	46.0	34.5	103.5	11.5
Bradley	354.0	171.1	53.1	123.9	5.9
Calhoun	348.0	116.0	63.8	168.2	...
Carroll	239.4	57.0	57.0	125.4	...
Chicot	75.6	37.8	21.0	8.4	8.4
Clark	423.4	226.2	87.0	104.4	5.8
Clay	65.0	19.5	19.5	26.0	...
Cleburne	240.7	16.6	66.4	157.7	...
Cleveland	319.0	150.8	75.4	92.8	...
Columbia	379.5	103.5	75.9	193.2	6.9
Conway	137.5	25.0	25.0	87.5	...
Craighead	45.5	17.5	7.0	21.0	...
Crawford	208.0	56.1	37.4	114.5	...
Crittenden	32.0	25.6	...	6.4	...
Cross	49.5	22.0	5.5	22.0	...
Dallas	372.6	156.6	91.8	124.2	...
Desha	143.0	97.5	13.0	32.5	...
Drew	387.6	163.2	76.5	142.8	5.1
Faulkner	156.8	...	11.2	134.4	11.2
Franklin	211.2	47.4	69.6	94.2	...
Fulton	247.0	13.0	52.0	182.0	...
Garland	335.5	126.5	93.5	115.5	...
Grant	346.8	137.7	86.7	122.4	...
Greene	53.3	28.7	8.2	16.4	...
Hempstead	286.7	103.7	85.4	97.6	...
Hot Spring	294.8	80.4	120.6	93.8	...
Howard	254.8	98.0	83.3	73.5	...
Independence	244.8	14.4	43.2	187.2	...
Izard	240.0	48.0	28.8	163.2	...
Jackson	65.0	6.5	19.5	39.0	...
Jefferson	193.5	81.0	49.5	63.0	...
Johnson	298.1	66.0	80.9	151.2	...
Lafayette	212.8	72.8	56.0	84.0	...
Lawrence	108.8	12.8	44.8	51.2	...
Lee	87.4	59.8	23.0	4.6	...

Table 10. *Commercial forest land by stand-size class, Arkansas, 1969*
(Continued)

County	All classes	Sawtimber	Poletimber	Sapling and seedling	Nonstocked areas
			-*Thousand acres*-		
Lincoln	142.8	51.0	45.9	45.9	...
Little River	192.5	55.0	60.5	77.0	...
Logan	254.2	55.8	68.2	130.2	...
Lonoke	91.8	37.8	16.2	37.8	...
Madison	356.4	37.8	102.6	216.0	...
Marion	282.0	28.2	84.6	169.2	...
Miller	217.0	84.0	49.0	84.0	...
Mississippi	34.8	17.4	11.6	5.8	...
Monroe	150.4	89.3	32.9	28.2	...
Montgomery	410.4	148.2	159.6	102.6	...
Nevada	300.0	102.0	108.0	90.0	...
Newton	478.0	58.0	187.4	232.6	...
Ouachita	384.3	146.4	152.5	85.4	...
Perry	273.6	96.9	74.1	102.6	...
Phillips	81.6	35.7	25.5	20.4	...
Pike	319.0	92.8	121.8	104.4	...
Poinsett	65.0	30.0	25.0	10.0	...
Polk	435.0	145.0	127.6	162.4	...
Pope	338.4	64.8	109.6	164.0	...
Prairie	140.4	70.2	31.2	39.0	...
Pulaski	252.0	44.8	72.8	128.8	5.6
Randolph	186.2	13.3	66.5	106.4	...
St. Francis	65.0	30.0	15.0	20.0	...
Saline	372.6	108.0	113.4	151.2	...
Scott	448.2	151.2	167.4	129.6	...
Searcy	310.6	50.2	55.7	204.7	...
Sebastian	134.4	...	12.8	121.6	...
Sevier	269.5	107.8	63.7	98.0	...
Sharp	255.3	22.2	66.6	155.4	11.1
Stone	322.0	36.8	73.6	211.6	...
Union	572.4	280.8	91.8	199.8	...
Van Buren	303.8	19.6	83.3	200.9	...
Washington	318.8	23.6	81.6	203.4	10.2
White	222.6	63.6	42.4	116.6	...
Woodruff	77.4	34.4	17.2	25.8	...
Yell	403.2	117.6	168.0	117.6	...
All counties	18,206.7	5,443.4	4,759.5	7,922.1	81.7

Table 11. *Commercial forest land by site class, Arkansas, 1969*

County	All sites	165 cu.ft. or more	120-165 cu.ft.	85-120 cu.ft.	50-85 cu.ft.	Less than 50 cu.ft.

- - - - - - - - - - *Thousand acres-* - - - - - - - - -

County	All sites	165 cu.ft. or more	120-165 cu.ft.	85-120 cu.ft.	50-85 cu.ft.	Less than 50 cu.ft.
Arkansas	207.2	5.6	22.4	95.2	56.0	28.0
Ashley	410.4	5.7	74.1	205.2	114.0	11.4
Baxter	254.8	...	...	...	19.6	235.2
Benton	219.6	...	...	...	97.6	122.0
Boone	195.5	...	...	11.5	80.5	103.5
Bradley	354.0	...	17.7	218.3	118.0	...
Calhoun	348.0	...	52.2	121.8	174.0	...
Carroll	239.4	...	...	...	125.4	114.0
Chicot	75.6	...	8.4	21.0	33.6	12.6
Clark	423.4	5.8	46.4	168.2	203.0	...
Clay	65.0	...	6.5	32.5	19.5	6.5
Cleburne	240.7	...	...	8.3	157.7	74.7
Cleveland	319.0	5.8	23.2	145.0	145.0	...
Columbia	379.5	...	27.6	151.8	186.3	13.8
Conway	137.5	12.5	...	12.5	62.5	50.0
Craighead	45.5	3.5	3.5	14.0	17.5	7.0
Crawford	208.0	...	...	8.2	66.6	133.2
Crittenden	32.0	19.2	...	...	12.8	...
Cross	49.5	...	...	...	44.0	5.5
Dallas	372.6	...	48.6	172.8	140.4	10.8
Desha	143.0	19.5	39.0	39.0	45.5	...
Drew	387.6	15.3	76.5	137.7	122.4	35.7
Faulkner	156.8	...	...	...	33.6	123.2
Franklin	211.2	...	...	...	42.0	169.2
Fulton	247.0	...	...	...	156.0	91.0
Garland	335.5	...	...	16.5	242.0	77.0
Grant	346.8	15.3	61.2	142.8	127.5	...
Greene	53.3	...	...	4.1	28.7	20.5
Hempstead	286.7	...	24.4	103.7	146.4	12.2
Hot Spring	294.8	...	6.7	60.3	167.5	60.3
Howard	254.8	...	29.4	93.1	127.4	4.9
Independence	244.8	...	...	...	100.8	144.0
Izard	240.0	...	...	9.6	134.4	96.0
Jackson	65.0	...	...	6.5	13.0	45.5
Jefferson	193.5	4.5	4.5	40.5	144.0	...
Johnson	298.1	...	...	5.3	183.0	109.8
Lafayette	212.8	5.6	5.6	78.4	112.0	11.2
Lawrence	108.8	...	12.8	12.8	57.6	25.6
Lee	87.4	18.4	23.0	27.6	13.8	4.6

Table **11.** *Commercial forest land by site class, Arkansas, 1969* (Continued)

County	All sites	165 cu.ft. or more	120-165 cu.ft.	85-120 cu.ft.	50-85 cu.ft.	Less than 50 cu.ft.
	- - - - - - - - - - *Thousand acres-* - - - - - - - - - - -					
Lincoln	142.8	...	10.2	20.4	91.8	20.4
Little River	192.5	...	5.5	99.0	82.5	5.5
Logan	254.2		...	...	124.0	130.2
Lonoke	91.8			10.8	54.0	27.0
Madison	356.4	...	...	...	86.4	270.0
Marion	282.0	...	...	14.1	141.0	126.9
Miller	217.0	14.0	14.0	77.0	98.0	14.0
Mississippi	34.8	5.8	5.8	...	11.6	11.6
Monroe	150.4	...	14.1	61.1	75.2	...
Montgomery	410.4		...	68.4	222.3	119.7
Nevada	300.0	6.0	36.0	150.0	108.0	...
Newton	478.0	...	...	...	174.2	303.8
Ouachita	384.3	6.1	42.7	170.8	158.6	6.1
Perry	273.6	...	...	28.5	193.8	51.3
Phillips	81.6	10.2	5.1	25.5	30.6	10.2
Pike	319.0	...	11.6	98.6	185.6	23.2
Poinsett	65.0	10.0	15.0	30.0	...	10.0
Polk	435.0	...	...	58.0	232.0	145.0
Pope	338.4	...		10.0	223.9	104.5
Prairie	140.4	...		7.8	85.8	46.8
Pulaski	252.0	5.6	...	33.6	140.0	72.8
Randolph	186.2			13.3	53.2	119.7
St. Francis	65.0	...	10.0	20.0	35.0	...
Saline	372.6	...	5.4	59.4	226.8	81.0
Scott	448.2		...	5.4	259.2	183.6
Searcy	310.6	...	...	...	105.9	204.7
Sebastian	134.4	...	...	...	32.0	102.4
Sevier	269.5	14.7	19.6	107.8	117.6	9.8
Sharp	255.3	...	...	11.1	88.8	155.4
Stone	322.0			...	119.6	202.4
Union	572.4	5.4	75.6	232.2	259.2	
Van Buren	303.8			...	151.9	151.9
Washington	318.8		...	...	51.0	267.8
White	222.6	...	21.2	10.6	127.2	63.6
Woodruff	77.4	...	4.3	34.4	38.7	...
Yell	403.2	...	...	28.0	246.4	128.8
All counties	18,206.7	214.5	909.8	3,650.0	8,303.4	5,129.0

Table 12. *Sampling errors[1] for commercial forest land, Arkansas, 1969*

County	Percent	County	Percent
Arkansas	2	Lee	1
Ashley	4	Lincoln	2
Baxter	3	Little River	3
Benton	3	Logan	2
Boone	3	Lonoke	2
Bradley	2	Madison	2
Calhoun	2	Marion	2
Carroll	3	Miller	4
Chicot	2	Mississippi	1
Clark	4	Monroe	2
Clay	2	Montgomery	1
Cleburne	4	Nevada	2
Cleveland	1	Newton	2
Columbia	2	Ouachita	2
Conway	3	Perry	2
Craighead	2	Phillips	1
Crawford	3	Pike	1
Crittenden	1	Poinsett	1
Cross	1	Polk	2
Dallas	1	Pope	1
Desha	2	Prairie	3
Drew	2	Pulaski	3
Faulkner	4	Randolph	3
Franklin	3	St. Francis	1
Fulton	3	Saline	2
Garland	2	Scott	1
Grant	1	Searcy	2
Greene	2	Sebastian	3
Hempstead	3	Sevier	2
Hot Spring	3	Sharp	3
Howard	2	Stone	2
Independence	2	Union	2
Izard	2	Van Buren	3
Jackson	1	Washington	2
Jefferson	2	White	3
Johnson	2	Woodruff	2
Lafayette	.4	Yell	2
Lawrence	3	All counties	0.3

[1]By random-sampling formula.

Table 13. *Total area and forest area, Louisiana, 1964*

Parish	Total area[1] Thousand acres	Commercial forest Thousand acres	Commercial forest Percent	Noncommercial forest Thousand acres
Acadia	424.3	71.5	17	...
Allen	496.0	367.2	74	...
Ascension	197.1	103.7	53	...
Assumption	243.2	143.0	59	...
Avoyelles	544.0	313.5	58	...
Beauregard	757.8	661.2	87	...
Bienville	536.3	437.4	82	...
Bossier	556.8	414.0	74	...
Caddo	603.6	352.8	58	...
Calcasieu	714.9	244.2	34	...
Caldwell	352.6	305.0	87	...
Cameron [2]	480.0	..	..	...
Catahoula	480.0	345.0	72	...
Claiborne	490.2	365.8	75	0.2
Concordia	480.0	313.6	65	...
De Soto	581.1	428.4	74	...
East Baton Rouge	302.1	130.9	43	...
East Carroll	291.8	109.2	37	...
East Feliciana	290.6	161.0	55	...
Evangeline	435.2	219.6	50	...
Franklin	414.7	144.0	35	...
Grant	435.8	359.9	83	.6
Iberia	414.1	115.0	28	...
Iberville	411.5	280.8	68	...
Jackson	373.1	335.0	90	...
Jefferson [3]	382.8	..	..	...
Jefferson Davis	423.0	81.9	19	...
Lafayette	181.1	14.1	8	...
Lafourche	865.9	156.0	18	...
La Salle	427.5	374.0	87	...
Lincoln	300.2	218.4	73	...
Livingston	443.5	358.4	81	...
Madison	435.9	244.8	56	...
Morehouse	514.6	291.5	57	...
Natchitoches	849.9	616.0	72	.9
Orleans [3]	232.3	..	..	...
Ouachita	411.5	300.8	73	...
Plaquemines [3]	895.4	..	..	...
Pointe Coupee	376.3	194.7	52	...
Rapides	849.3	621.6	73	.6
Red River	265.0	174.0	66	...
Richland	369.3	149.1	40	...
Sabine	658.6	540.0	82	...
St. Bernard [3]	517.1	..	..	...
St. Charles	269.4	68.8	26	...
St. Helena	268.8	203.0	76	...
St. James	165.8	85.5	52	...
St. John Baptist	250.2	93.8	37	...
St. Landry	598.4	255.0	43	...
St. Martin	514.6	310.0	60	...
St. Mary	453.8	143.0	32	...
St. Tammany	762.2	404.7	53	...
Tangipahoa	531.2	345.6	65	...
Tensas	413.4	230.1	56	...
Terrebonne	1,144.3	122.4	11	...
Union	579.8	489.7	84	...
Vermilion [2]	1,932.2	31.6	4	..
Vernon	870.4	736.7	85	35.0
Washington	425.6	280.8	66	...
Webster	401.9	295.8	74	.7
West Baton Rouge	135.7	69.3	51	...
West Carroll	227.8	67.5	30	...
West Feliciana	272.6	179.2	66	...
Winn	610.6	567.0	93	.2
All parishes	31,054.7	16,036.5	52	38.2

[1] Source: United States Bureau of the Census, Land and Water Area of the United States, 1960.
[2] Cameron included with Vermilion.
[3] Urban area.

Table 14. *Commercial forest land by ownership class, Louisiana, 1964*

Parish	All ownerships	National forest	Other public	Forest industry	Farmer	Misc. private
	- - - - - - - - - *Thousand acres* - - - - - - - - -					
Acadia	71.5	...	0.1	...	5.6	65.8
Allen	367.2	...	.2	44.7	22.3	300.0
Ascension	103.7	...	3.9	...	43.3	56.5
Assumption	143.0	...	3.4	...	19.8	119.8
Avoyelles	313.5	...	7.1	69.2	34.7	202.5
Beauregard	661.2	...	.1	89.9	149.9	421.3
Bienville	437.4	...	.2	181.1	27.4	228.7
Bossier	414.0	...	43.3	...	48.8	321.9
Caddo	352.8	...	7.0	...	11.4	334.4
Calcasieu	244.2	...	1.0	15.3	7.7	220.2
Caldwell	305.0	...	.8	111.6	31.0	161.6
Cameron [1]	...	...	...	...	...	...
Catahoula	345.0	...	4.8	80.2	29.2	230.8
Claiborne	365.8	17.0	.2	...	24.0	324.6
Concordia	313.6	...	6.3	53.3	59.2	194.8
De Soto	428.4	...	1.3	83.3	121.6	222.2
East Baton Rouge	130.9	...	2.6	...	31.1	97.2
East Carroll	109.2	...	2.1	16.5	11.0	79.6
East Feliciana	161.0	...	1.2	14.1	70.6	75.1
Evangeline	219.6	...	4.9	75.7	69.4	69.6
Franklin	144.0	...	1.9	19.0	66.6	56.5
Grant	359.9	138.3	1.8	100.9	6.3	112.6
Iberia	115.0	...	2.6	...	10.1	102.3
Iberville	280.8	...	4.9	65.6	32.8	177.5
Jackson	335.0	...	.1	147.4	35.6	151.9
Jefferson [2]	...	...	...	...	...	...
Jefferson Davis	81.9	...	...	...	45.6	36.3
Lafayette	14.1	...	...	...	4.8	9.3
Lafourche	156.0	...	2.0	...	36.9	117.1
La Salle	374.0	...	2.6	130.8	11.4	229.2
Lincoln	218.4	...	...	...	105.7	112.7
Livingston	358.4	...	.7	141.2	28.2	188.3
Madison	244.8	...	.6	91.3	45.7	107.2

Table 14. *Commercial forest land by ownership class, Louisiana, 1964* (Continued)

Parish	All ownerships	National forest	Other public	Forest industry	Farmer	Misc. private
	- - - - - - - - - - - *Thousand acres* - - - - - - - - - -						
Morehouse	291.5	...	6.8	116.3	17.4	151.0
Natchitoches	616.0	125.6	7.7	113.7	51.2	317.8
Orleans [2]	...	...	...	...	...	...
Ouachita	300.8	...	14.8	52.0	58.6	175.4
Plaquemines [2]	...	...	...	...	...	...
Pointe Coupee	194.7	...	1.0	11.9	77.6	104.2
Rapides	621.6	100.3	23.7	81.0	28.9	387.7
Red River	174.0	...	.1	42.7	36.6	94.6
Richland	149.1	...	2.9	7.5	105.0	33.7
Sabine	540.0	...	11.0	256.8	89.3	182.9
St. Bernard [2]	...	...	...	...	...	...
St. Charles	68.8	...	3.8	...	8.7	56.3
St. Helena	203.0	...	.1	77.7	21.2	104.0
St. James	85.5	...	...	...	11.6	73.9
St. John Baptist	93.8	...	2.6	...	27.2	64.0
St. Landry	255.0	...	3.4	25.8	51.7	174.1
St. Martin	310.0	...	29.0	...	25.1	255.9
St. Mary	143.0	...	4.6	...	33.4	105.0
St. Tammany	404.7	...	3.6	11.5	17.3	372.3
Tangipahoa	345.6	...	3.3	76.3	70.8	195.2
Tensas	230.1	...	.1	49.9	18.7	161.4
Terrebonne	122.4	...	1.6	...	65.6	55.2
Union	489.7	...	.4	131.9	30.0	327.4
Vermilion [1]	31.6	...	.6	...	31.0	...
Vernon	736.7	72.5	55.3	104.1	71.2	433.6
Washington	280.8	...	1.1	110.2	68.2	101.3
Webster	295.8	10.9	17.3	17.7	17.7	232.2
West Baton Rouge	69.3	...	1.3	38.9	...	29.1
West Carroll	67.5	...	.1	7.9	39.6	19.9
West Feliciana	179.2	...	4.4	19.4	32.4	123.0
Winn	567.0	110.2	.1	296.5	65.9	94.3
All parishes	16,036.5	574.8	308.4	3,180.8	2,419.6	9,552.9

1 Cameron included with Vermilion.
2 Urban area.

Table ·15、 *Commercial forest land by forest type, Louisiana, 1964*

Parish	All types	Longleaf-slash pine	Loblolly-shortleaf pine	Oak-pine	Oak-hickory	Oak-gum-cypress	Elm-ash-cottonwood
				- - - - *Thousand acres* - - - -			
Acadia	71.5	...	16.5	5.5	...	49.5	...
Allen	367.2	86.4	102.6	64.8	21.6	91.8	...
Ascension	103.7	...	12.2	...	...	91.5	...
Assumption	143.0	...	...	...	...	136.5	6.5
Avoyelles	313.5	...	11.4	5.7	5.7	262.2	28.5
Beauregard	661.2	353.8	87.0	92.8	63.8	63.8	...
Bienville	437.4	...	259.2	81.0	70.2	27.0	...
Bossier	414.0	...	144.0	72.0	108.0	84.0	6.0
Caddo	352.8	...	106.4	95.2	78.4	67.2	5.6
Calcasieu	244.2	74.0	66.6	37.0	...	66.6	...
Caldwell	305.0	...	103.7	36.6	54.9	103.7	6.1
Cameron 1	...	...	...	...	...	...	...
Catahoula	345.0	...	13.8	48.3	20.7	255.3	6.9
Claiborne	365.8	...	230.1	64.9	29.5	41.3	...
Concordia	313.6	...	...	...	...	274.4	39.2
De Soto	428.4	...	245.7	88.2	50.4	44.1	...
East Baton Rouge	130.9	...	...	...	77.0	53.9	...
East Carroll	109.2	...	...	...	...	88.4	20.8
East Feliciana	161.0	...	56.0	42.0	28.0	35.0	...
Evangeline	219.6	24.4	73.2	36.6	24.4	61.0	...
Franklin	144.0	...	...	...	18.0	126.0	...
Grant	359.9	30.5	183.0	30.5	54.9	61.0	...
Iberia	115.0	...	...	...	...	70.0	45.0
Iberville	280.8	...	...	...	...	194.4	86.4
Jackson	335.0	15.0	160.0	95.0	40.0	25.0	...
Jefferson[2]	...	...	...	...	...	...	...
Jefferson Davis	81.9	12.6	37.8	18.9	12.6	...	...
Lafayette	14.1	...	...	...	...	14.1	...
Lafourche	156.0	...	...	...	...	124.8	31.2
La Salle	374.0	5.5	165.0	71.5	11.0	121.0	...
Lincoln	218.4	...	109.2	41.6	57.2	10.4	...
Livingston	358.4	...	145.6	67.2	22.4	123.2	...
Madison	244.8	...	...	...	...	208.8	36.0

Table 15. *Commercial forest land by forest type, Louisiana, 1964* (Continued)

Parish	All types	Longleaf-slash pine	Loblolly-shortleaf pine	Oak-pine	Oak-hickory	Oak-gum-cypress	Elm-ash-cottonwood
				Thousand acres			
Morehouse	291.5	...	27.5	44.0	33.0	181.5	5.5
Natchitoches	616.0	44.0	220.0	137.5	66.0	121.0	27.5
Orleans [2]	...	...	...	...	...	...	...
Ouachita	300.8	...	70.4	70.4	25.6	134.4	...
Plaquemines [2]	...	...	...	...	...	...	...
Pointe Coupee	194.7	...	...	...	...	182.9	11.8
Rapides	621.6	78.4	173.6	112.0	84.0	173.6	...
Red River	174.0	6.0	36.0	66.0	12.0	30.0	24.0
Richland	149.1	...	...	7.1	...	134.9	7.1
Sabine	540.0	5.4	280.8	91.8	113.4	48.6	...
St. Bernard [2]	...	...	...	...	...	...	...
St. Charles	68.8	...	...	...	...	55.9	12.9
St. Helena	203.0	14.0	126.0	28.0	35.0	...	...
St. James	85.5	...	...	...	...	79.8	5.7
St. John Baptist	93.8	...	...	...	...	73.7	20.1
St. Landry	255.0	...	5.1	...	...	219.3	30.6
St. Martin	310.0	...	...	...	...	173.6	136.4
St. Mary	143.0	...	...	...	...	132.0	11.0
St. Tammany	404.7	114.0	96.9	22.8	39.9	125.4	5.7
Tangipahoa	345.6	48.6	91.8	43.2	75.6	86.4	...
Tensas	230.1	...	...	...	...	200.6	29.5
Terrebonne	122.4	...	...	...	...	115.2	7.2
Union	489.7	5.9	253.7	41.3	82.6	106.2	...
Vermilion [1]	31.6	...	...	...	...	31.6	...
Vernon	736.7	222.6	196.1	148.4	100.7	63.6	5.3
Washington	280.8	62.4	83.2	88.4	...	46.8	...
Webster	295.8	5.8	127.6	69.6	46.4	46.4	...
West Baton Rouge	69.3	...	...	...	...	53.9	15.4
West Carroll	67.5	...	...	...	...	67.5	...
West Feliciana	179.2	...	19.2	6.4	51.2	89.6	12.8
Winn	567.0	10.8	302.4	97.2	86.4	70.2	...
All parishes	16,036.5	1,220.1	4,439.3	2,169.4	1,700.5	5,820.5	686.7

[1] Cameron included with Vermilion.
[2] Urban area.

26

Table 16. *Commercial forest land by stand-size class, Louisiana, 1964*

Parish	All classes	Sawtimber	Poletimber	Sapling and seedling	Nonstocked areas
			-Thousand acres-			
Acadia	71.5	60.5	5.5	5.5	
Allen	367.2	189.0	32.4	145.8	
Ascension	103.7	79.3	24.4	...	...
Assumption	143.0	136.5	...	6.5	...
Avoyelles	313.5	245.1	39.9	22.8	5.7
Beauregard	661.2	214.6	87.0	324.8	34.8
Bienville	437.4	232.2	54.0	140.4	10.8
Bossier	414.0	210.0	78.0	120.0	6.0
Caddo	352.8	156.8	33.6	156.8	5.6
Calcasieu	244.2	111.0	7.4	118.4	7.4
Caldwell	305.0	231.8	30.5	42.7	...
Cameron [1]	...	...	...	...	...
Catahoula	345.0	296.7	20.7	20.7	6.9
Claiborne	365.8	165.2	64.9	135.7	...
Concordia	313.6	280.0	16.8	16.8	
De Soto	428.4	207.9	100.8	119.7	
East Baton Rouge	130.9	84.7	30.8	15.4	...
East Carroll	109.2	46.8	31.2	26.0	5.2
East Feliciana	161.0	98.0	28.0	35.0	...
Evangeline	219.6	85.4	24.4	103.7	6.1
Franklin	144.0	99.0	9.0	36.0	
Grant	359.9	262.3	24.4	73.2	
Iberia	115.0	75.0	20.0	15.0	5.0
Iberville	280.8	232.2	16.2	32.4	...
Jackson	335.0	240.0	50.0	45.0	
Jefferson [2]	...	...	...	...	
Jefferson Davis	81.9	69.3	12.6		
Lafayette	14.1	14.1	...	...	...
Lafourche	156.0	114.4	10.4	26.0	5.2
La Salle	374.0	231.0	33.0	110.0	...
Lincoln	218.4	72.8	36.4	109.2	
Livingston	358.4	291.2	39.2	28.0	
Madison	244.8	216.0	14.4	14.4	...

27

Table **16**. *Commercial forest land by stand-size class, Louisiana, 1964* (Continued)

Parish	All classes	Sawtimber	Poletimber	Sapling and seedling	Nonstocked areas
			-Thousand acres-		
Morehouse	291.5	181.5	27.5	82.5	
Natchitoches	616.0	379.5	104.5	132.0	
Orleans[2]	...	...	...	...	
Ouachita	300.8	172.8	38.4	89.6	
Plaquemines[2]	...	...	...	...	
Pointe Coupee	194.7	165.2	17.7	11.8	
Rapides	621.6	347.2	50.4	212.8	11.2
Red River	174.0	84.0	18.0	72.0	...
Richland	149.1	71.0	21.3	49.7	7.1
Sabine	540.0	345.6	108.0	81.0	5.4
St. Bernard[2]	...	...	...	...	...
St. Charles	68.8	51.6	8.6	8.6	...
St. Helena	203.0	119.0	28.0	56.0	...
St. James	85.5	62.7	11.4	5.7	5.7
St. John Baptist	93.8	67.0	13.4	6.7	6.7
St. Landry	255.0	219.3	20.4	15.3	...
St. Martin	310.0	210.8	80.6	12.4	6.2
St. Mary	143.0	77.0	16.5	44.0	5.5
St. Tammany	404.7	159.6	57.0	176.7	11.4
Tangipahoa	345.6	194.4	37.8	113.4	
Tensas	230.1	188.8	23.6	17.7	
Terrebonne	122.4	108.0	14.4	...	
Union	489.7	241.9	70.8	177.0	
Vermilion[1]	31.6	31.6	...	...	...
Vernon	736.7	371.0	42.4	291.5	31.8
Washington	280.8	182.0	46.8	52.0	...
Webster	295.8	121.8	92.8	75.4	5.8
West Baton Rouge	69.3	69.3	...	...	...
West Carroll	67.5	45.0	...	22.5	
West Feliciana	179.2	128.0	32.0	19.2	...
Winn	567.0	426.6	59.4	81.0	...
All parishes	16,036.5	9,871.0	2,017.6	3,952.4	195.5

[1] Cameron included with Vermilion.
[2] Urban area.

Table 17. *Commercial forest land by site class, Louisiana, 1964*

Parish	All classes	165 cu.ft. or more	120-165 cu. ft.	85-120 cu.ft.	50-85 cu.ft.	Less than 50 cu. ft.
	- - - - - - - - - *Thousand acres* - - - - - - - - -					
Acadia	71.5	...	5.5	49.5	11.0	5.5
Allen	367.2	10.8	27.0	178.2	59.4	91.8
Ascension	103.7	6.1	...	61.0	6.1	30.5
Assumption	143.0	...	...	130.0	...	13.0
Avoyelles	313.5	5.7	11.4	205.2	...	91.2
Beauregard	661.2	...	23.2	197.2	394.4	46.4
Bienville	437.4	10.8	97.2	216.0	102.6	10.8
Bossier	414.0	12.0	30.0	306.0	42.0	24.0
Caddo	352.8	5.6	16.8	218.4	106.4	5.6
Calcasieu	244.2	...	7.4	88.8	118.4	29.6
Caldwell	305.0	12.2	48.8	158.6	48.8	36.6
Cameron [1]	...	...	...	...	...	...
Catahoula	345.0	...	6.9	151.8	20.7	165.6
Claiborne	365.8	5.9	47.2	265.5	41.3	5.9
Concordia	313.6	16.8	...	179.2	...	117.6
De Soto	428.4	...	12.6	151.2	214.2	50.4
East Baton Rouge	130.9	...	...	115.5	15.4	...
East Carroll	109.2	10.4	...	83.2	...	15.6
East Feliciana	161.0	14.0	35.0	98.0	14.0	...
Evangeline	219.6	6.1	12.2	85.4	103.7	12.2
Franklin	144.0	...	...	72.0	9.0	63.0
Grant	359.9	12.2	36.6	195.2	79.3	36.6
Iberia	115.0	20.0	...	85.0	...	10.0
Iberville	280.8	10.8	...	248.4	...	21.6
Jackson	335.0	...	70.0	170.0	95.0	...
Jefferson [2]	...	...	...	...	...	...
Jefferson Davis	81.9	...	...	25.2	50.4	6.3
Lafayette	14.1	...	...	9.4	...	4.7
Lafourche	156.0	...	...	104.0	...	52.0
La Salle	374.0	...	44.0	126.5	99.0	104.5
Lincoln	218.4	...	46.8	145.6	26.0	...
Livingston	358.4	39.2	106.4	151.2	33.6	28.0
Madison	244.8	21.6	...	223.2	...	...

Table 17. *Commercial forest land by site class, Louisiana, 1964* (Continued)

Parish	All classes	165 cu.ft. or more	120-165 cu. ft.	85-120 cu.ft.	50-85 cu.ft.	Less than 50 cu.ft.
			- - - -Thousand acres- - - - - - - -			
Morehouse	291.5	...	60.5	198.0	...	33.0
Natchitoches	616.0	27.5	77.0	313.5	154.0	44.0
Orleans[2]	...	...	...	...	...	...
Ouachita	300.8	6.4	64.0	153.6	12.8	64.0
Plaquemines[2]	...		...	...	...	...
Pointe Coupee	194.7	...	...	171.1	...	23.6
Rapides	621.6	11.2	33.6	336.0	145.6	95.2
Red River	174.0	12.0	12.0	108.0	36.0	6.0
Richland	149.1	...	...	120.7	...	28.4
Sabine	540.0	10.8	81.0	280.8	156.6	10.8
St. Bernard[2]	...	...	...	...	...	...
St. Charles	68.8	4.3	...	60.2	...	4.3
St. Helena	203.0	21.0	56.0	35.0	84.0	7.0
St. James	85.5	...	...	74.1	...	11.4
St. John Baptist	93.8	6.7	...	73.7	...	13.4
St. Landry	255.0	15.3	5.1	214.2	...	20.4
St. Martin	310.0	74.4	...	217.0	...	18.6
St. Mary	143.0	11.0	...	115.5	...	16.5
St. Tammany	404.7	...	28.5	159.6	96.9	119.7
Tangipahoa	345.6	5.4	32.4	151.2	86.4	70.2
Tensas	230.1	11.8	...	206.5	...	11.8
Terrebonne	122.4	...	...	100.8	...	21.6
Union	489.7	5.9	76.7	330.4	64.9	11.8
Vermilion[1]	31.6	...	...	31.6	...	...
Vernon	736.7	21.2	42.4	291.5	355.1	26.5
Washington	280.8	...	46.8	83.2	52.0	98.8
Webster	295.8	11.6	75.4	174.0	34.8	...
West Baton Rouge	69.3	7.7	...	61.6	...	...
West Carroll	67.5	...	...	67.5	...	...
West Feliciana	179.2	38.4	19.2	76.8	38.4	6.4
Winn	567.0	5.4	91.8	302.4	145.8	21.6
All parishes	16,036.5	528.2	1,487.4	9,002.9	3,154.0	1,864.0

1 Cameron included with Vermilion.
2 Urban area.

Table 18. *Sampling errors[1] for commercial forest land, Louisiana, 1964*

Parish	Percent	Parish	Percent
Acadia	2	Morehouse	2
Allen	2	Natchitoches	2
Ascension	6	Orleans [3]	...
Assumption	2	Ouachita	3
Avoyelles	2	Plaquemines [3]	...
Beauregard	2	Pointe Coupee	1
Bienville	3	Rapides	2
Bossier	3	Red River	4
Caddo	4	Richland	3
Calcasieu	2	Sabine	2
Caldwell	2	St. Bernard [3]	...
Cameron [2]	...	St. Charles	4
Catahoula	2	St. Helena	3
Claiborne	3	St. James	2
Concordia	3	St. John Baptist	4
De Soto	4	St. Landry	2
East Baton Rouge	4	St. Martin	2
East Carroll	3	St. Mary	2
East Feliciana	4	St. Tammany	2
Evangeline	3	Tangipahoa	2
Franklin	3	Tensas	2
Grant	3	Terrebonne	2
Iberia	2	Union	3
Iberville	2	Vermilion [2]	2
Jackson	2	Vernon	1
Jefferson [3]	...	Washington	2
Jefferson Davis	1	Webster	4
Lafayette	1	West Baton Rouge	2
Lafourche	2	West Carroll	3
La Salle	2	West Feliciana	3
Lincoln	4	Winn	2
Livingston	2		
Madison	3	All counties	0.4

[1]By random-sampling formula.
[2]Cameron included with Vermilion.
[3]Urban area.

Table 19. *Total area and forest area, Mississippi, 1967*

County	Total area[1]	Commercial forest		Noncommercial forest	County	Total area[1]	Commercial forest		Noncommercial forest
	Thousand acres	*Thousand acres*	*Percent*	*Thousand acres*		*Thousand acres*	*Thousand acres*	*Percent*	*Thousand acres*
Adams	305.9	209.0	68	0.2	Lowndes	325.1	130.0	40	...
Alcorn	259.2	126.0	49	...					
Amite	466.6	319.0	68	(2)	Madison	480.6	189.0	39	3.4
Attala	463.4	313.2	68	1.8	Marion	352.0	214.5	61	...
					Marshall	454.4	212.2	47	.1
Benton	263.7	167.0	63	(2)	Monroe	492.2	254.2	52	...
Bolivar	601.6	75.6	13	.1	Montgomery	257.9	139.7	62	...
Calhoun	378.9	210.8	56	...	Neshoba	363.5	202.4	56	...
Carroll	408.3	217.8	53	...	Newton	371.2	245.0	66	...
Chickasaw	323.8	132.2	41	2.2	Noxubee	444.8	225.5	51	...
Choctaw	266.9	188.7	71	1.3					
Claiborne	317.5	221.0	70	2.5	Oktibbeha	290.6	148.8	51	...
Clarke	446.1	347.2	78	...					
Clay	265.0	112.0	42	.1	Panola	450.6	147.1	33	...
Coahoma	379.5	68.6	18	...	Pearl River	530.0	359.6	68	...
Copiah	499.8	345.0	69	...	Perry	417.9	347.2	83	.1
Covington	266.2	151.2	57	...	Pike	262.4	144.9	55	....
					Pontotoc	320.6	143.5	45	.5
De Soto	312.3	75.8	24	...	Prentiss	267.5	133.4	50	...
Forrest	300.2	216.2	72	.1	Quitman	263.7	42.7	16	...
Franklin	363.5	300.0	83	(2)					
					Rankin	512.0	353.8	69	(2)
George	307.8	235.2	76	...					
Greene	465.9	408.0	88	...	Scott	393.6	261.0	66	.2
Grenada	286.1	161.4	56	...	Sharkey	279.0	95.4	34	.2
					Simpson	375.7	248.0	66	...
Hancock	313.0	236.8	76	1.8	Smith	410.9	278.4	68	(2)
Harrison	384.6	285.6	74	(2)	Stone	286.7	243.0	85	...
Hinds	561.3	208.8	37	1.6	Sunflower	444.2	36.9	8	...
Holmes	493.4	214.7	44	...					
Humphreys	270.1	68.0	25	...	Tallahatchie	412.8	127.5	31	...
					Tate	263.0	86.4	33	...
Issaquena	285.5	128.0	45	...	Tippah	297.0	161.1	54	...
Itawamba	346.2	225.6	65	...	Tishomingo	289.9	188.1	65	1.0
					Tunica	304.6	72.0	24	...
Jackson	487.0	378.0	78	...					
Jasper	437.1	308.0	70	...	Union	270.1	128.7	48	...
Jefferson	336.0	239.4	71	.8					
Jefferson Davis	265.0	135.0	51	...	Walthall	257.9	122.4	47	...
Jones	451.8	297.6	66	(2)	Warren	385.3	193.2	50	...
					Washington	487.7	70.8	15	...
Kemper	484.5	347.7	72	...	Wayne	529.3	436.6	82	(2)
					Webster	266.2	165.2	62	1.0
Lafayette	434.5	259.2	60	(2)	Wilkinson	437.1	329.0	75	...
Lamar	320.0	235.2	74	...	Winston	387.8	253.7	65	...
Lauderdale	462.1	345.6	75	...					
Lawrence	277.1	187.0	67	...	Yalobusha	322.6	184.5	57	(2)
Leake	375.0	230.0	61	1.4	Yazoo	600.9	234.4	39	...
Lee	291.2	75.4	26	.9					
Leflore	380.2	66.0	17	...					
Lincoln	375.1	249.6	67	...	All counties	30,538.2	16,891.9	55	21.3

[1] Source: United States Bureau of the Census, Land and Water Area of the United States, 1960.
[2] Negligible.

Table 20. *Commercial forest land by ownership class, Mississippi, 1967*

County	All ownerships	National forest	Other public	Forest industry	Farmer	Misc. private
			- - - - - - - - - Thousand acres - - - - - - - - -			
Adams	209.0	15.0	8.0	5.5	82.6	97.9
Alcorn	126.0	...	...	3.6	67.9	54.5
Amite	319.0	34.5	8.6	33.1	99.1	143.7
Attala	313.2	...	4.5	26.2	110.2	172.3
Benton	167.0	50.5	...	...	95.0	21.5
Bolivar	75.6	...	2.5	12.2	20.6	40.3
Calhoun	210.8	...	9.2	94.3	94.7	12.6
Carroll	217.8	...	5.6	10.7	131.7	69.8
Chickasaw	132.2	25.1	...	6.2	47.9	53.0
Choctaw	188.7	11.0	3.1	15.2	76.0	83.4
Claiborne	221.0	...	7.4	32.5	104.1	77.0
Clarke	347.2	...	11.6	92.5	59.8	183.3
Clay	112.0	...	1.3	22.2	38.9	49.6
Coahoma	68.6	...	3.9	23.3	41.4	...
Copiah	345.0	7.1	16.5	30.0	140.2	151.2
Covington	151.2	...	4.7	10.7	90.7	45.1
De Soto	75.8	..	3.4	...	62.9	9.5
Forrest	216.2	49.7	10.1	18.6	27.9	109.9
Franklin	300.0	93.7	8.8	48.1	84.1	65.3
George	235.2	8.8	12.2	66.4	60.9	86.9
Greene	408.0	33.2	13.5	146.2	105.8	109.3
Grenada	161.4	...	21.6	17.0	56.6	66.2
Hancock	236.8	...	20.7	50.6	63.2	102.3
Harrison	285.6	60.5	7.5	75.6	70.6	71.4
Hinds	208.8	...	7.2	5.8	133.6	62.2
Holmes	214.7	...	6.2	15.9	151.6	41.0
Humphreys	68.0	...	2.2	6.6	33.4	25.8
Issaquena	128.0	...	5.2	68.3	12.6	41.9
Itawamba	225.6	...	.1	42.9	114.4	68.2
Jackson	378.0	19.0	13.6	100.8	53.4	191.2
Jasper	308.0	16.9	7.4	65.3	59.8	158.6
Jefferson	239.4	7.8	5.3	28.5	125.5	72.3
Jefferson Davis	135.0	...	3.9	39.5	54.3	37.3
Jones	297.6	32.7	5.4	12.3	73.5	173.7
Kemper	347.7	...	10.0	83.1	177.3	77.3
Lafayette	259.2	35.5	18.6	10.5	139.1	55.5
Lamar	235.2	...	5.0	55.3	71.9	103.0
Lauderdale	345.6	...	17.1	42.0	178.4	108.1
Lawrence	187.0	...	3.4	65.2	81.5	36.9
Leake	230.0	...	7.7	29.1	97.2	96.0
Lee	75.4	...	.4	...	40.3	34.7
Leflore	66.0	...	3.7	...	62.3	...
Lincoln	249.6	7.7	6.8	12.8	121.7	100.6

Table 20. *Commercial forest land by ownership class, Mississippi, 1967* (Continued)

County	All ownerships	National forest	Other public	Forest industry	Farmer	Misc. private
	- - - - - - - - - *Thousand acres* - - - - - - - - --					
Lowndes	130.0	...	4.7	5.0	89.4	30.9
Madison	189.0	...	7.4	16.2	102.7	62.7
Marion	214.5	(¹)	13.7	38.0	65.2	97.6
Marshall	212.2	19.6	16.2	...	104.0	72.4
Monroe	254.2	...	4.6	30.8	12.3	206.5
Montgomery	159.7	...	4.3	11.5	78.7	65.2
Neshoba	202.4	...	12.0	25.7	59.8	104.9
Newton	245.0	3.1	7.6	24.3	77.7	132.3
Noxubee	225.5	...	13.5	32.1	106.9	73.0
Oktibbeha	148.8	.1	23.1	14.3	23.8	87.5
Panola	147.1	...	15.4	20.6	79.5	31.6
Pearl River	359.6	5.2	11.7	67.4	42.9	232.4
Perry	347.2	158.9	10.1	44.3	49.8	84.1
Pike	144.9	...	6.4	6.9	82.9	48.7
Pontotoc	143.5	.5	.4	4.4	112.4	25.8
Prentiss	133.4	...	...	9.1	59.4	64.9
Quitman	42.7	...	5.9	...	36.8	...
Rankin	353.8	...	13.8	22.5	146.5	171.0
Scott	261.0	85.9	8.0	11.3	95.8	60.0
Sharkey	95.4	57.8	4.0	...	20.8	12.8
Simpson	248.0	...	6.3	60.2	78.3	103.2
Smith	278.4	67.8	7.4	28.2	56.4	118.6
Stone	243.0	39.4	20.6	57.8	17.8	107.4
Sunflower	36.9	...	1.5	...	35.4	...
Tallahatchie	127.5	...	5.1	...	106.6	15.8
Tate	86.4	...	3.4	7.0	59.6	16.4
Tippah	161.1	7.6	.2	...	97.3	56.0
Tishomingo	188.1	...	7.6	34.0	22.6	123.9
Tunica	72.0	...	1.8	17.5	31.0	21.7
Union	128.7	7.8	(¹)	...	52.2	68.7
Walthall	122.4	...	3.4	...	53.8	65.2
Warren	193.2	...	10.1	35.6	81.4	66.1
Washington	70.8	...	13.4	11.5	29.1	16.8
Wayne	436.6	89.2	12.8	119.5	77.7	137.4
Webster	165.2	...	2.3	22.7	92.2	48.0
Wilkinson	329.0	20.6	9.5	140.2	49.1	109.6
Winston	253.7	27.7	22.9	40.1	97.4	65.6
Yalobusha	184.5	18.9	18.2	8.9	98.3	40.2
Yazoo	234.4	...	8.2	12.9	6.5	206.8
All counties	16,891.9	1,118.8	651.4	2,505.1	6,204.6	6,412.0

1 Negligible.

Table 21. *Commercial forest land by forest type, Mississippi, 1967*

County	All types	Longleaf- slash pine	Loblolly- shortleaf pine	Oak- pine	Oak- hickory	Oak- gum- cypress	Elm- ash- cottonwood
				-Thousand acres - - - - - - - - - - -			
Adams	209.0	...	16.5	33.0	93.5	27.5	38.5
Alcorn	126.0	...	28.8	18.0	57.6	21.6	...
Amite	319.0	5.5	165.0	88.0	27.5	33.0	...
Attala	313.2	...	91.8	37.8	108.0	75.6	...
Benton	167.0	...	38.5	48.3	66.3	4.1	9.8
Bolivar	75.6	...	...	...	...	21.0	54.6
Calhoun	210.8	...	81.6	61.2	61.2	6.8	...
Carroll	217.8	...	42.9	42.6	96.6	30.6	5.1
Chickasaw	132.2	...	25.3	53.7	50.1	3.1	...
Choctaw	188.7	...	81.6	66.3	30.6	10.2	...
Claiborne	221.0	...	32.5	13.0	84.5	91.0	...
Clarke	347.2	5.6	162.4	44.8	78.4	50.4	5.6
Clay	112.0	...	28.0	...	33.6	50.4	...
Coahoma	68.6	...	...	...	...	39.2	29.4
Copiah	345.0	...	110.0	90.0	75.0	70.0	...
Covington	151.2	5.4	37.8	32.4	37.8	37.8	...
De Soto	75.8	...	...	7.5	32.5	33.3	2.5
Forrest	216.2	98.7	47.0	32.9	14.1	23.5	...
Franklin	300.0	...	162.0	54.0	48.0	36.0	...
George	235.2	67.2	44.8	44.8	16.8	61.6	...
Greene	408.0	56.1	102.0	96.9	76.5	76.5	...
Grenada	161.4	...	39.9	22.8	62.7	36.0	...
Hancock	236.8	128.0	19.2	25.6	...	64.0	...
Harrison	285.6	183.6	20.4	45.9	10.2	25.5	...
Hinds	208.8	...	52.2	34.8	75.4	46.4	...
Holmes	214.7	...	16.4	58.7	83.5	45.9	10.2
Humphreys	68.0	...	...	...	...	68.0	...
Issaquena	128.0	...	...	...	6.4	108.8	12.8
Itawamba	225.6	...	48.0	57.6	76.8	38.4	4.8
Jackson	378.0	192.0	18.0	54.0	...	114.0	...
Jasper	308.0	...	140.0	39.2	89.6	39.2	...
Jefferson	239.4	...	34.2	39.9	108.3	34.2	22.8
Jefferson Davis	135.0	...	55.0	20.0	45.0	15.0	...
Jones	297.6	55.8	105.4	68.2	43.4	24.8	...
Kemper	347.7	...	119.7	102.6	57.0	68.4	...
Lafayette	259.2	...	75.2	27.1	135.3	21.6	...
Lamar	235.2	112.0	39.2	39.2	28.0	16.8	...
Lauderdale	345.6	5.4	172.8	48.6	70.2	48.6	...
Lawrence	187.0	5.5	77.0	38.5	16.5	49.5	...
Leake	230.0	...	90.0	60.0	55.0	25.0	...
Lee	75.4	...	11.6	23.2	29.0	11.6	...
Leflore	66.0	...	...	...	11.0	55.0	...
Lincoln	249.6	6.4	115.2	32.0	76.8	19.2	...

Table 21. *Commercial forest land by forest type, Mississippi, 1967* (Continued)

County	All types	Longleaf-slash pine	Loblolly-shortleaf pine	Oak-pine	Oak-hickory	Oak-gum-cypress	Elm-ash-cottonwood
			-Thousand acres-				
Lowndes	130.0	...	10.0	35.0	25.0	60.0	...
Madison	189.0	5.4	59.4	32.4	37.8	54.0	...
Marion	214.5	11.0	27.5	71.5	55.0	49.5	...
Marshall	212.2	...	34.9	20.2	103.8	53.3	...
Monroe	254.2	...	31.0	18.6	117.8	86.8	...
Montgomery	159.7	...	38.4	53.6	57.2	10.5	...
Neshoba	202.4	...	70.4	44.0	52.8	35.2	...
Newton	245.0	5.0	100.0	50.0	65.0	25.0	...
Noxubee	225.5	...	49.5	55.0	55.0	66.0	...
Oktibbeha	148.8	4.8	38.4	24.0	57.6	24.0	...
Panola	147.1	...	17.8	5.3	93.7	17.8	12.5
Pearl River	359.6	130.2	43.4	80.6	24.8	80.6	...
Perry	347.2	84.0	78.4	89.6	56.0	39.2	...
Pike	144.9	...	48.3	62.1	13.8	20.7	...
Pontotoc	143.5	...	32.5	29.8	66.6	14.6	...
Prentiss	133.4	...	41.4	36.8	41.4	9.2	4.6
Quitman	42.7	...	...	...	...	36.6	6.1
Rankin	353.8	...	110.2	121.8	63.8	58.0	...
Scott	261.0	5.8	116.0	63.8	58.0	17.4	...
Sharkey	95.4	...	...	...	5.3	90.1	...
Simpson	248.0	...	80.6	74.4	49.6	43.4	...
Smith	278.4	5.8	116.0	87.0	63.8	5.8	...
Stone	243.0	94.5	31.5	63.0	13.5	40.5	...
Sunflower	36.9	...	...	...	...	24.6	12.3
Tallahatchie	127.5	...	4.3	12.9	43.0	67.3	...
Tate	86.4	...	3.4	...	67.0	8.0	8.0
Tippah	161.1	...	49.7	32.5	70.3	8.6	...
Tishomingo	188.1	...	51.3	51.3	51.3	34.2	...
Tunica	72.0	...	...	...	...	31.5	40.5
Union	128.7	...	24.6	22.4	63.8	17.9	...
Walthall	122.4	20.4	27.2	20.4	20.4	34.0	...
Warren	193.2	...	...	...	105.8	55.2	32.2
Washington	70.8	...	...	...	...	53.1	17.7
Wayne	436.6	35.4	100.3	182.9	82.6	35.4	...
Webster	165.2	...	59.4	26.0	73.0	6.8	...
Wilkinson	329.0	...	98.0	56.0	91.0	77.0	7.0
Winston	253.7	5.9	64.9	94.4	70.8	17.7	...
Yalobusha	184.5	...	36.0	45.0	94.5	9.0	...
Yazoo	234.4	...	...	6.6	126.8	85.8	15.2
All counties	16,891.9	1,335.4	4,242.6	3,372.0	4,306.3	3,283.4	352.2

36

Table 22. *Commercial forest land by stand-size class, Mississippi, 1967*

County	All classes	Sawtimber	Poletimber	Sapling and seedling	Nonstocked areas
- - - - - - - *Thousand acres* - - - - - - - -					
Adams	209.0	71.5	33.0	99.0	5.5
Alcorn	126.0	14.4	25.2	86.4	...
Amite	319.0	88.0	104.5	121.0	5.5
Attala	313.2	43.2	86.4	178.2	5.4
Benton	167.0	41.7	60.6	64.7	
Bolivar	75.6	54.6	12.6	8.4	
Calhoun	210.8	81.6	34.0	95.2	...
Carroll	217.8	21.0	31.5	165.3	
Chickasaw	132.2	19.8	28.4	84.0	
Choctaw	188.7	35.7	45.9	107.1	
Claiborne	221.0	78.0	65.0	78.0	
Clarke	347.2	72.8	112.0	162.4	
Clay	112.0	33.6	33.6	44.8	
Coahoma	68.6	29.4	29.4	9.8	
Copiah	345.0	130.0	100.0	115.0	
Covington	151.2	43.2	21.6	86.4	
De Soto	75.8	17.5	17.5	40.8	
Forrest	216.2	51.7	32.9	131.6	...
Franklin	300.0	174.0	36.0	84.0	6.0
George	235.2	72.8	39.2	123.2	...
Greene	408.0	102.0	76.5	219.3	10.2
Grenada	161.4	34.2	41.7	85.5	...
Hancock	236.8	83.2	25.6	121.6	6.4
Harrison	285.6	96.9	45.9	137.7	5.1
Hinds	208.8	34.8	58.0	104.4	11.6
Holmes	214.7	11.3	41.9	161.5	...
Humphreys	68.0	27.2	6.8	34.0	...
Issaquena	128.0	70.4	25.6	32.0	...
Itawamba	225.6	28.8	52.8	139.2	4.8
Jackson	378.0	144.0	96.0	120.0	18.0
Jasper	308.0	84.0	67.2	156.8	...
Jefferson	239.4	45.6	79.8	114.0	
Jefferson Davis	135.0	40.0	25.0	70.0	
Jones	297.6	86.8	55.8	155.0	
Kemper	347.7	68.4	119.7	159.6	
Lafayette	259.2	54.2	21.8	183.2	...
Lamar	235.2	56.0	33.6	134.4	11.2
Lauderdale	345.6	113.4	108.0	124.2	...
Lawrence	187.0	66.0	27.5	93.5	
Leake	230.0	60.0	80.0	90.0	
Lee	75.4	11.6	29.0	34.8	
Leflore	66.0	11.0	22.0	33.0	...
Lincoln	249.6	76.8	57.6	108.8	6.4

Table 22. *Commercial forest land by stand-size class, Mississippi, 1967* (continued)

County	All classes	Sawtimber	Poletimber	Sapling and seedling	Nonstocked areas
			- - - - - - - -Thousand acres - - - - - - - -		
Lowndes	130.0	20.0	35.0	75.0	
Madison	189.0	37.8	54.0	97.2	...
Marion	214.5	82.5	16.5	115.5	...
Marshall	212.2	29.4	45.0	133.2	4.6
Monroe	254.2	37.2	86.8	130.2	...
Montgomery	159.7	38.4	37.3	84.0	
Neshoba	202.4	74.8	66.0	57.2	4.4
Newton	245.0	55.0	75.0	115.0	...
Noxubee	225.5	55.0	49.5	121.0	
Oktibbeha	148.8	38.4	33.6	76.8	
Panola	147.1	12.5	45.6	89.0	...
Pearl River	359.6	93.0	62.0	198.4	6.2
Perry	347.2	117.6	16.8	212.8	...
Pike	144.9	34.5	6.9	103.5	
Pontotoc	143.5	7.9	33.3	102.3	
Prentiss	133.4	23.0	23.0	87.4	
Quitman	42.7	6.1	18.3	18.3	
Rankin	353.8	81.2	81.2	191.4	
Scott	261.0	81.2	46.4	133.4	
Sharkey	95.4	53.0	5.3	37.1	
Simpson	248.0	43.4	62.0	142.6	...
Smith	278.4	115.2	69.6	93.6	...
Stone	243.0	72.0	27.0	139.5	4.5
Sunflower	36.9	24.6	...	12.3	...
Tallahatchie	127.5	12.9	69.7	44.9	...
Tate	86.4	12.0	27.0	47.4	...
Tippah	161.1	11.0	39.2	106.6	4.3
Tishomingo	188.1	28.5	39.9	119.7	...
Tunica	72.0	22.5	18.0	31.5	
Union	128.7	5.6	33.6	89.5	
Walthall	122.4	13.6	47.6	61.2	...
Warren	193.2	96.6	41.4	41.4	13.8
Washington	70.8	23.6	17.7	29.5	...
Wayne	436.6	106.2	59.0	271.4	
Webster	165.2	26.0	56.3	82.9	
Wilkinson	329.0	196.0	7.0	126.0	
Winston	253.7	59.0	53.1	141.6	
Yalobusha	184.5	18.0	49.5	117.0	...
Yazoo	234.4	111.6	70.0	52.8	...
All counties	16,891.9	4,557.9	3,772.2	8,427.9	133.9

Table **23.** *Commercial forest land by site class, Mississippi, 1967*

County	All classes	165 cu.ft. or more	120-165 cu.ft.	85-120 cu.ft.	50-85 cu.ft.	Less than 50 cu.ft.
			- - - - - - - -Thousand acres - - - - - - - - -			
Adams	209.0	38.5	16.5	99.0	49.5	5.5
Alcorn	126.0	3.6	7.2	10.8	72.0	32.4
Amite	319.0	38.5	55.0	148.5	77.0	...
Attala	313.2	5.4	32.4	81.0	167.4	27.0
Benton	167.0	9.8	9.8	66.3	77.0	4.1
Bolivar	75.6	46.2	12.6	12.6	4.2	...
Calhoun	210.8	...	20.4	88.4	81.6	20.4
Carroll	217.8	10.5	10.5	41.4	106.8	48.6
Chickasaw	132.2	29.6	10.5	32.7	53.2	6.2
Choctaw	188.7	...	15.3	45.9	112.2	15.3
Claiborne	221.0	...	13.0	162.5	45.5	...
Clark	347.2	5.6	61.6	156.8	89.6	33.6
Clay	112.0	11.2	22.4	39.2	33.6	5.6
Coahoma	68.6	9.8	...	34.3	19.6	4.9
Copiah	345.0	...	15.0	135.0	195.0	...
Covington	151.2	...	21.6	54.0	70.2	5.4
De Soto	75.8	...	...	30.8	32.5	12.5
Forrest	216.2	...	...	70.5	145.7	...
Franklin	300.0	18.0	42.0	144.0	96.0	...
George	235.2	5.6	16.8	72.8	123.2	16.8
Greene	408.0	...	20.4	168.3	219.3	...
Grenada	161.4	5.7	17.1	22.8	110.1	5.7
Hancock	236.8	...	...	76.8	153.6	6.4
Harrison	285.6	...	5.1	61.2	163.2	56.1
Hinds	208.8	...	23.2	69.6	110.2	5.8
Holmes	214.7	...	...	53.2	138.9	22.6
Humphreys	68.0	13.6	6.8	27.2	13.6	6.8
Issaquena	128.0	19.2	19.2	57.6	19.2	12.8
Itawamba	225.6	...	14.4	24.0	129.6	57.6
Jackson	378.0	...	24.0	90.0	204.0	60.0
Jasper	308.0	11.2	67.2	106.4	117.6	5.6
Jefferson	239.4	28.5	11.4	125.4	68.4	5.7
Jefferson Davis	135.0	5.0	10.0	45.0	55.0	20.0
Jones	297.6	6.2	18.6	117.8	136.4	18.6
Kemper	347.7	...	17.1	182.4	125.4	22.8
Lafayette	259.2	5.5	16.1	65.0	134.9	37.7
Lamar	235.2	5.6	5.6	56.0	156.8	11.2
Lauderdale	345.6	10.8	54.0	124.2	129.6	27.0
Lawrence	187.0	22.0	44.0	82.5	38.5	...
Leake	230.0	5.0	45.0	125.0	55.0	...
Lee	75.4	5.8	11.6	17.4	23.2	17.4
Leflore	66.0	...	...	...	55.0	11.0
Lincoln	249.6	...	25.6	57.6	140.8	25.6

39

Table 23. *Commercial forest land by site class, Mississippi, 1967* (Continued)

County	All classes	165 cu.ft. or more	120-165 cu.ft.	85-120 cu.ft.	50-85 cu.ft.	Less than 50 cu.ft.
	- - - - - - - - - -Thousand acres - - - - - - - - - - -					
Lowndes	130.0	...	...	55.0	70.0	5.0
Madison	189.0	5.4	21.6	54.0	102.6	5.4
Marion	214.5	...	22.0	77.0	93.5	22.0
Marshall	212.2	...	13.8	83.6	101.0	13.8
Monroe	254.2	...	24.8	80.6	142.6	6.2
Montgomery	159.7	...	9.4	24.6	89.5	36.2
Neshoba	202.4	...	22.0	123.2	52.8	4.4
Newton	245.0	5.0	40.0	85.0	115.0	...
Noxubee	225.5	11.0	16.5	126.5	71.5	...
Oktibbeha	148.8	4.8	4.8	38.4	91.2	9.6
Panola	147.1	5.3	27.8	21.2	58.7	34.1
Pearl River	359.6	...	18.6	55.8	279.0	6.2
Perry	347.2	...	11.2	106.4	212.8	16.8
Pike	144.9	...	13.8	48.3	75.9	6.9
Pontotoc	143.5	...	4.4	24.0	80.3	34.8
Prentiss	133.4	4.6	18.4	27.6	64.4	18.4
Quitman	42.7	...	6.1	...	24.4	12.2
Rankin	353.8	...	34.8	139.2	168.2	11.6
Scott	261.0	...	46.4	87.0	121.8	5.8
Sharkey	95.4	15.9	15.9	26.5	26.5	10.6
Simpson	248.0	...	24.8	74.4	105.4	43.4
Smith	278.4	11.6	58.0	121.8	81.2	5.8
Stone	243.0	...	9.0	117.0	103.5	13.5
Sunflower	36.9	...	...	...	36.9	...
Tallahatchie	127.5	...	...	33.9	89.3	4.3
Tate	86.4	...	...	24.0	43.0	19.4
Tippah	161.1	...	...	41.6	98.0	21.5
Tishomingo	188.1	...	...	34.2	142.5	11.4
Tunica	72.0	18.0	...	27.0	22.5	4.5
Union	128.7	...	5.6	40.3	66.0	16.8
Walthall	122.4	...	6.8	47.6	61.2	6.8
Warren	193.2	18.4	...	55.2	119.6	...
Washington	70.8	11.8	5.9	23.6	29.5	...
Wayne	436.6	...	17.7	135.7	247.8	35.4
Webster	165.2	...	6.8	36.5	112.0	9.9
Wilkinson	329.0	56.0	84.0	140.0	49.0	...
Winston	253.7	...	11.8	64.9	129.8	47.2
Yalobusha	184.5	...	18.0	81.0	76.5	9.0
Yazoo	234.4	...	6.6	151.2	72.3	4.3
All counties	16,891.9	544.2	1,466.3	5,815.7	7,877.8	1,187.9

Table 24. *Sampling errors[1] for commercial forest land, Mississippi, 1967*

County	Percent	County	Percent
Adams	3	Lincoln	3
Alcorn	4	Lowndes	4
Amite	3	Madison	3
Attala	3	Marion	3
Benton	3	Marshall	3
Bolivar	4	Monroe	3
Calhoun	3	Montgomery	3
Carroll	3	Neshoba	3
Chickasaw	3	Newton	3
Choctaw	3	Noxubee	3
Claiborne	3	Oktibbeha	3
Clarke	3	Panola	3
Clay	4	Pearl River	2
Coahoma	4	Perry	2
Copiah	2	Pike	4
Covington	4	Pontotoc	3
De Soto	5	Prentiss	3
Forrest	3	Quitman	5
Franklin	3	Rankin	3
George	3	Scott	3
Greene	2	Sharkey	3
Grenada	3	Simpson	3
Hancock	3	Smith	3
Harrison	3	Stone	3
Hinds	3	Sunflower	6
Holmes	2	Tallahatchie	3
Humphreys	4	Tate	4
Issaquena	3	Tippah	3
Itawamba	3	Tishomingo	3
Jackson	2	Tunica	4
Jasper	3	Union	4
Jefferson	3	Walthall	4
Jefferson Davis	4	Warren	2
Jones	3	Washington	4
Kemper	3	Wayne	2
Lafayette	2	Webster	3
Lamar	3	Wilkinson	3
Lauderdale	3	Winston	3
Lawrence	3	Yalobusha	3
Leake	3	Yazoo	2
Lee	5		
Leflore	4	All counties	0.3

[1]By random-sampling formula.

Table 25. *Total area and forest area, Oklahoma, 1966*

County	Total area[1]	Commercial forest		Noncommercial forest
	Thousand acres	*Thousand acres*	*Percent*	*Thousand acres*
Adair	364.8	237.9	65	...
Atoka	634.9	328.3	52	40.2
Cherokee	501.8	256.2	51	57.8
Choctaw	508.8	261.0	51	(2)
Coal	336.6	108.0	32	36.0
Delaware	498.6	254.2	51	(2)
Haskell	397.4	127.6	32	29.0
Latimer	471.7	305.0	65	50.9
Le Flore	1,012.5	661.2	65	5.4
McCurtain	1,199.4	874.5	73	21.9
McIntosh	460.8	102.6	22	33.9
Mayes	440.3	118.0	27	(2)
Muskogee	538.2	77.9	14	25.0
Ottawa	309.1	78.4	25	(2)
Pittsburg	876.2	217.6	25	213.2
Pushmataha	910.7	693.0	76	33.4
Sequoyah	456.3	116.0	25	105.4
All counties	9,918.1	4,817.4	49	652.1

[1]Source: United States Bureau of the Census, Land and Water Area of the United States, 1960.
[2]Negligible.

Table 26. *Commercial forest land by ownership class, Oklahoma, 1966*

County	All ownerships	National forest	Other public	Forest industry	Farmer	Misc. private
			Thousand acres			
Adair	237.9	...	25.9	...	70.0	142.0
Atoka	328.3	...	19.1	...	112.2	197.0
Cherokee	256.2	...	69.9	...	127.3	59.0
Choctaw	261.0	...	8.5	...	62.9	189.6
Coal	108.0	...	2.8	...	85.1	20.1
Delaware	254.2	...	29.1	...	161.8	63.3
Haskell	127.6	...	6.3	...	51.4	69.9
Latimer	305.0	...	8.1	6.0	96.2	194.7
Le Flore	661.2	187.6	16.9	80.0	154.3	222.4
McCurtain	874.5	34.3	47.8	511.7	83.6	197.1
McIntosh	102.6	...	20.9	...	56.4	25.3
Mayes	118.0	...	10.0	...	24.6	83.4
Muskogee	77.9	...	19.9	...	47.1	10.9
Ottawa	78.4	...	2.7	...	40.9	34.8
Pittsburg	217.6	...	17.9	...	69.4	130.3
Pushmataha	693.0	...	28.5	271.0	119.2	274.3
Sequoyah	116.0	...	9.6	...	48.4	58.0
All counties	4,817.4	221.9	343.9	868.7	1,410.8	1,972.1

42

Table 27. *Commercial forest land by forest type, Oklahoma, 1966*

County	All types	Longleaf-slash pine	Loblolly-shortleaf pine	Oak-pine	Oak-hickory	Oak-gum-cypress	Elm-ash-cottonwood
			-Thousand acres - - - - - - - - -				
Adair	237.9		6.1	12.2	207.4	12.2	...
Atoka	328.3		26.8	33.5	187.6	73.7	6.7
Cherokee	256.2		6.1	...	225.7	12.2	12.2
Choctaw	261.0		5.8	11.6	191.4	29.0	23.2
Coal	108.0		...	...	93.6	...	14.4
Delaware	254.2		...	...	254.2	...	...
Haskell	127.6		...	23.2	69.6	29.0	5.8
Latimer	305.0		30.5	67.1	201.3	6.1	...
Le Flore	661.2	...	121.8	121.8	382.8	23.2	11.6
McCurtain	874.5	...	344.5	222.6	227.9	68.9	10.6
McIntosh	102.6	...	...	...	86.4	5.4	10.8
Mayes	118.0		5.9	...	100.3	5.9	5.9
Muskogee	77.9		...	...	61.5	12.3	4.1
Ottawa	78.4		...	...	78.4	...	
Pittsburg	217.6	...	...	12.8	166.4	38.4	
Pushmataha	693.0	...	242.0	159.5	264.0	27.5	...
Sequoyah	116.0	...	5.8	...	92.8	5.8	11.6
All counties	4,817.4	...	795.3	664.3	2,891.3	349.6	116.9

Table 28. *Commercial forest land by stand-size class, Oklahoma, 1966*

County	All classes	Sawtimber	Poletimber	Sapling and seedling	Nonstocked areas
		- - - - - - - - Thousand acres - - - - - - - -			
Adair	237.9	18.3	61.0	158.6	...
Atoka	328.3	40.2	46.9	234.5	6.7
Cherokee	256.2	42.7	24.4	189.1	...
Choctaw	261.0	63.8	52.2	139.2	5.8
Coal	108.0	21.6	14.4	64.8	7.2
Delaware	254.2	37.2	43.4	173.6	...
Haskell	127.6	17.4	23.2	87.0	...
Latimer	305.0	61.0	61.0	170.8	12.2
Le Flore	661.2	174.0	156.6	319.0	11.6
McCurtain	874.5	439.9	196.1	238.5	...
McIntosh	102.6	21.6	...	75.6	5.4
Mayes	118.0	41.3	35.4	17.7	23.6
Muskogee	77.9	8.2	28.7	41.0	...
Ottawa	78.4	39.2	22.4	11.2	5.6
Pittsburg	217.6	25.6	44.8	128.0	19.2
Pushmataha	693.0	192.5	115.5	379.5	5.5
Sequoyah	116.0	17.4	17.4	69.6	11.6
All counties	4,817.4	1,261.9	943.4	2,497.7	114.4

43

Table 29. *Commercial forest land by site class, Oklahoma, 1966*

County	All classes	165 cu.ft. or more	120-165 cu. ft.	85-120 cu.ft.	50-85 cu.ft.	Less than 50 cu.ft.
	- - - - - - - - - - *Thousand acres-* - - - - - - - - -					
Adair	237.9	...	...	42.7	146.4	48.8
Atoka	328.3	...	...	13.4	120.6	194.3
Cherokee	256.2	...	...	12.2	12.2	231.8
Choctaw	261.0	...	...	29.0	63.8	168.2
Coal	108.0	...	...	21.6	7.2	79.2
Delaware	254.2	...		...	130.2	124.0
Haskell	127.6	5.8		5.8	...	116.0
Latimer	305.0	...		...	24.4	280.6
Le Flore	661.2	...	...	11.6	191.4	458.2
McCurtain	874.5	...	...	143.1	450.5	280.9
McIntosh	102.6	...		...	10.8	91.8
Mayes	118.0	...	...	5.9	...	112.1
Muskogee	77.9	...	...	4.1	8.2	65.6
Ottawa	78.4	...		...	22.4	56.0
Pittsburg	217.6	...	...	12.8	32.0	172.8
Pushmataha	693.0	...	...	11.0	99.0	583.0
Sequoyah	116.0	11.6	...	5.8	11.6	87.0
All counties	4,817.4	17.4	...	319.0	1,330.7	3,150.3

Table 30. *Sampling errors[1] for commercial forest land, Oklahoma, 1966*

County	Percent	County	Percent
Adair	2	McCurtain	2
Atoka	3	McIntosh	1
Cherokee	2	Mayes	2
Choctaw	3	Muskogee	2
Coal	4	Ottawa	3
Delaware	2	Pittsburg	3
Haskell	2	Pushmataha	1
Latimer	2	Sequoyah	2
Le Flore	2	All counties	0.8

[1]By random-sampling formula.

Table 31. *Total area and forest area, Tennessee, 1971*

County	Total area[1] Thousand acres	Commercial forest Thousand acres	Commercial forest Percent	Noncommercial forest Thousand acres	County	Total area[1] Thousand acres	Commercial forest Thousand acres	Commercial forest Percent	Noncommercial forest Thousand acres
Anderson	218.2	140.3	64	3.4	Lauderdale	325.8	88.5	27	...
					Lawrence	405.8	182.7	45	1.4
Bedford	308.5	76.0	25	...	Lewis	182.4	144.9	79	2.7
Benton	279.0	168.2	60	...	Lincoln	371.2	116.6	31	.3
Bledsoe	258.6	173.6	67	5.5	Loudon	159.4	53.3	33	...
Blount	373.8	125.6	34	95.0					
Bradley	216.3	107.2	50	...	McMinn	278.4	145.5	52	...
					McNairy	364.2	197.6	54	...
Campbell	299.5	225.5	75	2.5	Macon	194.6	73.6	38	...
Cannon	173.4	86.4	50	...	Madison	358.4	112.8	31	...
Carroll	381.4	153.0	40	...	Marion	329.6	247.5	75	...
Carter	227.2	145.0	64	2.3	Marshall	241.3	78.1	32	...
Cheatham	197.1	108.8	55	...	Maury	393.0	126.0	32	...
Chester	182.4	97.2	53	.2	Meigs	139.5	80.6	58	...
Claiborne	291.2	166.4	57	2.0	Monroe	424.9	295.8	70	.3
Clay	169.0	99.0	59	...	Montgomery	347.5	116.2	33	...
Cocke	278.4	168.0	60	18.3	Moore	79.4	30.8	39	...
Coffee	278.4	117.6	42	...	Morgan	345.0	291.6	85	...
Crockett	172.2	12.4	7	...					
Cumberland	434.5	324.5	75	1.4	Obion	359.0	72.8	20	...
					Overton	282.9	174.2	62	.9
Davidson	341.1	104.0	30	...					
Decatur	225.3	149.1	66	...	Perry	270.7	212.8	79	...
De Kalb	202.9	88.2	43	...	Pickett	111.4	67.0	60	.8
Dickson	311.0	160.0	51	3.7	Polk	281.0	227.7	81	.5
Dyer	345.6	65.5	19	...	Putnam	261.1	140.3	54	.3
Fayette	450.5	108.0	24	...	Rhea	217.6	134.6	62	.1
Fentress	319.4	246.4	77	...	Roane	248.3	131.2	53	9.5
Franklin	358.4	187.0	52	...	Robertson	304.6	59.0	19	...
					Rutherford	403.2	117.6	29	.3
Gibson	388.5	49.0	13	...					
Giles	396.1	160.0	40	...	Scott	351.4	308.0	88	...
Grainger	199.7	94.6	47	...	Sequatchie	174.7	140.0	80	...
Greene	396.1	135.2	34	(2)	Sevier	387.2	159.2	41	123.7
Grundy	229.1	186.0	81	.1	Shelby	492.1	73.0	15	13.0
					Smith	208.0	72.0	35	...
Hamblen	111.4	25.2	23	...	Stewart	314.9	221.1	70	.1
Hamilton	375.7	180.2	48	3.5	Sullivan	273.9	109.2	40	.4
Hancock	147.2	85.4	58	...	Sumner	351.4	98.1	28	...
Hardeman	419.8	222.0	53	.3					
Hardin	386.6	225.6	58	2.4	Tipton	303.4	55.8	18	...
Hawkins	316.2	167.4	53	...	Trousdale	74.2	23.8	32	...
Haywood	332.2	73.6	22	...					
Henderson	329.6	170.5	52	.7	Unicoi	118.4	94.4	80	.4
Henry	384.0	124.3	32	1.2	Union	154.2	84.6	55	3.6
Hickman	392.3	269.5	69	...					
Houston	133.1	91.0	68	...	Van Buren	163.2	124.2	76	12.8
Humphreys	357.8	248.0	69	...					
					Warren	283.5	114.0	40	...
Jackson	209.3	110.5	53	...	Washington	209.3	61.6	29	...
Jefferson	206.1	58.5	28	...	Wayne	474.2	378.0	80	2.0
Johnson	191.4	124.2	65	(2)	Weakley	368.6	76.5	21	...
					White	246.4	127.2	52	...
Knox	337.9	106.2	31	...	Williamson	379.5	145.0	38	...
					Wilson	371.2	109.0	29	.8
Lake	122.9	16.0	13	.1	All counties	27,036.2	12,819.8	47	316.5

[1]Source: United States Bureau of the Census, Land and Water Area of the United States, 1960.
[2]Negligible.

45

Table 32. *Commercial forest land by ownership class, Tennessee, 1971*

County	All ownerships	National forest	Other public	Forest industry	Farmer	Misc. private
	- - - - - - - - - Thousand acres - - - - - - - -					
Anderson	140.3	...	10.1	...	30.3	99.9
Bedford	76.0	...	(^{1})	...	60.0	16.0
Benton	168.2	...	14.9	...	69.5	83.8
Bledsoe	173.6	...	5.8	47.4	35.5	84.9
Blount	125.6		.2	17.9	94.9	12.6
Bradley	107.2		.2	26.6	39.9	40.5
Campbell	225.5	...	12.9	33.7	16.9	162.0
Cannon	86.4	...	(^{1})	...	56.8	29.6
Carroll	153.0	...	19.5	...	85.6	47.9
Carter	145.0	78.9	(1)	...	23.0	43.1
Cheatham	108.8	...	21.2	...	13.4	74.2
Chester	97.2		6.3	...	32.0	58.9
Claiborne	166.4	...	6.4	...	95.3	64.7
Clay	99.0	...	9.8	...	16.3	72.9
Cocke	168.0	42.2	.1	...	72.3	53.4
Coffee	117.6	...	22.2	9.7	67.7	18.0
Crockett	12.4		...	...	12.4	...
Cumberland	324.5	...	49.9	39.3	106.8	128.5
Davidson	104.0		6.1	...	20.5	77.4
Decatur	149.1	...	3.4	11.4	74.0	60.3
De Kalb	88.2		17.6	...	12.4	58.2
Dickson	160.0		.3	...	74.0	85.7
Dyer	65.5	...	6.3	12.8	13.0	33.4
Fayette	108.0		9.0	...	66.8	32.2
Fentress	246.4	...	3.8	74.4	34.3	133.9
Franklin	187.0		13.8	5.6	50.6	117.0
Gibson	49.0		3.4	...	45.6	...
Giles	160.0	...	.1	4.9	88.8	66.2
Grainger	94.6	...	3.4	4.3	81.1	5.8
Greene	135.2	35.7	.1	...	92.9	6.5
Grundy	186.0	...	.7	19.0	19.0	147.3
Hamblen	25.2		1.9	...	18.8	4.5
Hamilton	180.2		13.8	5.3	57.9	103.2
Hancock	85.4		...	...	84.8	.6
Hardeman	222.0		5.5	5.9	77.1	133.5
Hardin	225.6	...	2.9	38.3	91.1	93.3
Hawkins	167.4		6.4	5.4	118.0	37.6
Haywood	73.6		8.2	...	27.3	38.1
Henderson	170.5		24.2	...	73.3	73.0
Henry	124.3		20.0	...	78.2	26.1
Hickman	269.5	...	...	83.2	117.5	68.8
Houston	91.0		.9	13.0	38.9	38.2
Humphreys	248.0	...	7.3	24.8	86.7	129.2
Jackson	110.5	...	3.0	...	83.8	23.7
Jefferson	58.5	...	.9	...	49.1	8.5
Johnson	124.2	49.0	.1	...	32.2	42.9
Knox	106.2		1.7	...	41.0	63.5
Lake	16.0	...	6.6	...	9.4	...

Table 32. *Commercial forest land by ownership class, Tennessee, 1971* (Continued)

County	All ownerships	National forest	Other public	Forest industry	Farmer	Misc. private
			- - - - - - - - - -Thousand acres- - - - - - - - - -			
Lauderdale	88.5	...	.2	51.9	...	36.4
Lawrence	182.7	...	12.6	6.3	100.6	63.2
Lewis	144.9	...	1.4	25.2	25.2	93.1
Lincoln	116.6	...	...	...	62.7	53.9
Loudon	53.3	...	1.0	4.1	28.5	19.7
McMinn	145.5	2.1	.5	22.2	55.6	65.1
McNairy	197.6	...	2.1	25.4	77.1	93.0
Macon	73.6	...	...	...	54.4	19.2
Madison	112.8	...	([1])	...	102.2	10.6
Marion	247.5	...	34.9	28.1	28.1	156.4
Marshall	78.1	...	([1])	...	42.0	36.1
Maury	126.0	...	...	...	65.1	60.9
Meigs	80.6	...	1.6	12.3	43.1	23.6
Monroe	295.8	138.1	.8	17.3	86.4	53.2
Montgomery	116.2	...	21.2	...	40.9	54.1
Moore	30.8	...	...	...	30.4	.4
Morgan	291.6	...	44.3	11.0	82.7	153.6
Obion	72.8	...	9.6	10.2	41.1	11.9
Overton	174.2	...	9.1	6.8	89.0	69.3
Perry	212.8	...	2.5	39.1	111.8	59.4
Pickett	67.0	...	14.5	...	13.7	38.8
Polk	227.7	148.8	2.3	5.4	21.7	49.5
Putnam	140.3	...	1.1	6.2	37.4	95.6
Rhea	134.6	...	...	36.1	71.8	26.7
Roane	131.2	...	27.7	...	73.3	30.2
Robertson	59.0	...	...	...	11.6	47.4
Rutherford	117.6	...	4.5	...	87.0	26.1
Scott	308.0	...	5.5	17.2	91.5	193.8
Sequatchie	140.0	...	.1	28.6	5.7	105.6
Sevier	159.2	...	.8	...	70.9	87.5
Shelby	73.0	...	5.5	...	21.7	45.8
Smith	72.0	...	1.8	...	35.5	34.7
Stewart	221.1	...	86.2	40.1	53.5	41.3
Sullivan	109.2	36.9	2.9	...	29.2	40.2
Sumner	98.1	...	1.3	...	43.0	53.8
Tipton	55.8	...	...	...	55.2	.6
Trousdale	23.8	...	.3	...	11.7	11.8
Unicoi	94.4	51.5	.1	11.8	...	31.0
Union	84.6	...	28.5	...	23.3	32.8
Van Buren	124.2	...	.4	93.8	11.0	19.0
Warren	114.0	...	...	...	58.2	55.8
Washington	61.6	16.5	([1])	...	33.4	11.7
Wayne	378.0	...	.2	106.9	138.4	132.5
Weakley	76.5	...	([1])	...	30.3	46.2
White	127.2	...	1.2	32.5	32.5	61.0
Williamson	145.0	...	.6	...	88.8	55.6
Wilson	109.0	...	8.3	...	75.2	25.5
All counties	12,819.8	599.7	686.5	1,121.4	5,079.1	5,333.1

[1]Negligible.

47

Table 33. *Commercial forest land by forest type, Tennessee, 1971*

County	All types	White pine	Loblolly-shortleaf pine	Oak-pine	Cedar	Oak-hickory	Maple-beech-birch	Elm-ash-cotton-wood	Oak-gum-cypress
				- - - *Thousand acres* - - -					
Anderson	140.3	...	6.1	18.3	12.2	103.7	...	...	...
Bedford	76.0	...	...	...	30.4	·38.0	...	...	7.6
Benton	168.2	...	11.6	5.8	11.6	121.8	...	...	17.4
Bledsoe	173.6	...	23.1	17.4	...	133.1	...	...	...
Blount	125.6	6.0	12.0	47.8	...	59.8	...	...	...
Bradley	107.2	...	67.0	...	...	40.2	...	...	...
Campbell	225.5	...	38.5	16.5	...	170.5	...	...	...
Cannon	86.4	...	...	9.6	9.6	67.2	...	...	...
Carroll	153.0	...	10.2	5.1	5.1	102.0	...	5.1	25.5
Carter	145.0	5.8	11.6	11.6	...	110.2	5.8	...	...
Cheatham	108.8	...	...	...	13.6	95.2	...	...	...
Chester	97.2	...	10.8	16.2	...	59.4	...	...	10.8
Claiborne	166.4	...	6.4	12.8	12.8	128.0	6.4	...	...
Clay	99.0	...	...	...	16.5	82.5	....	...	...
Cocke	168.0	...	11.2	39.2	...	112.0	5.6	...	...
Coffee	117.6	...	...	...	9.8	98.0	...	...	9.8
Crockett	12.4	...	...	...	...	...	...	...	12.4
Cumberland	324.5	...	27.5	71.5	...	225.5	...	...	...
Davidson	104.0	...	...	...	10.4	93.6	...	...	...
Decatur	149.1	...	5.8	5.7	5.8	131.8	...	...	...
De Kalb	88.2	...	...	...	31.5	50.4	...	...	6.3
Dickson	160.0	...	...	...	...	160.0	...	...	...
Dyer	65.5	...	...	...	...	26.2	...	13.1	26.2
Fayette	108.0	...	13.5	...	...	81.0	...	...	13.5
Fentress	246.4	...	39.2	50.4	5.6	145.6	5.6	...	...
Franklin	187.0	...	...	...	5.5	176.0	5.5	...	...
Gibson	49.0	...	...	...	...	39.2	...	...	9.8
Giles	160.0	...	...	5.0	...	150.0	...	...	5.0
Grainger	94.6	...	...	...	8.6	86.0	...	...	...
Greene	135.2	...	5.2	10.4	10.4	109.2	...	...	...
Grundy	186.0	...	12.4	24.8	...	148.8	...	...	...
Hamblen	25.2	...	6.3	...	6.3	12.6	...	...	...
Hamilton	180.2	...	21.2	58.3	...	100.7	...	...	...
Hancock	85.4	...	...	...	...	85.4	...	...	...
Hardeman	222.0	...	30.0	...	...	156.0	...	6.0	30.0
Hardin	225.6	...	28.8	43.2	...	115.2	...	...	38.4
Hawkins	167.4	...	21.6	16.2	10.8	118.8	...	...	...
Haywood	73.6	...	...	...	9.2	9.2	...	9.2	46.0
Henderson	170.5	...	22.7	5.7	17.1	108.0	...	...	17.0
Henry	124.3	...	...	...	...	79.1	...	...	45.2
Hickman	269.5	...	4.9	...	...	264.6	...	...	...
Houston	91.0	...	...	...	6.5	84.5	...	...	...
Humphreys	248.0	...	...	...	12.4	235.6	...	...	...
Jackson	110.5	...	...	...	25.5	85.0	...	...	...
Jefferson	58.5	...	13.5	4.5	13.5	27.0	...	...	....
Johnson	124.2	...	...	16.2	...	102.6	5.4	...	...
Knox	106.2	...	11.8	17.7	11.8	64.9	...	...	...
Lake	16.0	...	...	...	...	...	...	8.0	8.0

Table 33. *Commercial forest land by forest type, Tennessee, 1971* (Continued)

County	All types	White pine	Loblolly-shortleaf pine	Oak-pine	Cedar	Oak-hickory	Maple-beech-birch	Elm-ash-cotton-wood	Oak-gum-cypress
				-Thousand acres-					
Lauderdale	88.5	...	...	...	...	17.7	...	17.7	53.1
Lawrence	182.7	...	...	...	...	176.4	...	6.3	...
Lewis	144.9	...	...	6.3	...	138.6	...	...	...
Lincoln	116.6	...	...	...	53.0	42.4	...	10.6	10.6
Loudon	53.3	...	12.3	12.3	4.1	24.6	...	...	...
McMinn	145.5	...	56.0	22.3	5.6	61.6	...	...	...
McNairy	197.6	...	31.2	26.0	...	124.8	...	...	15.6
Macon	73.6	...	...	...	...	73.6	...	...	...
Madison	112.8	...	...	...	9.4	75.2	...	9.4	18.8
Marion	247.5	...	5.5	55.0	...	176.0	5.5	5.5	...
Marshall	78.1	...	...	...	28.4	49.7	...	...	...
Maury	126.0	...	...	...	6.0	114.0	...	...	6.0
Meigs	80.6	...	12.4	31.0	...	37.2	...	...	...
Monroe	295.8	5.8	92.8	58.0	5.8	121.8	11.6	...	...
Montgomery	116.2	...	...	8.3	8.3	74.7	...	...	24.9
Moore	30.8	...	...	...	...	30.8	...	...	...
Morgan	291.6	...	10.8	48.6	...	232.2	...	...	...
Obion	72.8	...	...	...	...	31.2	...	10.4	31.2
Overton	174.2	...	6.7	13.4	...	154.1	...	...	...
Perry	212.8	...	...	...	11.2	196.0	...	...	5.6
Pickett	67.0	...	6.7	6.7	...	53.6	...	...	...
Polk	227.7	...	92.3	70.6	...	64.8	...	...	...
Putnam	140.3	...	...	6.1	6.1	122.0	6.1	...	...
Rhea	134.6	...	15.5	36.3	...	82.8	...	...	...
Roane	131.2	...	16.4	16.4	8.2	90.2	...	...	...
Robertson	59.0	...	...	...	...	59.0	...	...	...
Rutherford	117.6	...	...	...	68.6	49.0	...	...	...
Scott	308.0	11.2	28.0	28.0	...	224.0	16.8	...	...
Sequatchie	140.0	...	16.8	44.8	...	78.4	...	...	...
Sevier	159.2	...	36.0	41.0	...	82.2	...	...	...
Shelby	73.0	...	...	...	...	29.2	...	21.9	21.9
Smith	72.0	...	...	...	18.0	54.0	...	...	...
Stewart	221.1	...	...	...	6.7	214.4	...	...	...
Sullivan	109.2	4.2	16.8	4.2	4.2	75.6	4.2	...	...
Sumner	98.1	...	...	...	10.9	76.3	...	10.9	...
Tipton	55.8	...	...	...	...	55.8	...	...	...
Trousdale	23.8	...	...	...	...	23.8	...	...	...
Unicoi	94.4	5.9	...	23.6	...	59.0	5.9	...	...
Union	84.6	...	9.4	23.5	14.1	37.6	...	...	...
Van Buren	124.2	...	10.8	32.4	...	81.0	...	...	...
Warren	114.0	...	5.7	...	5.7	102.6	...	...	...
Washington	61.6	...	...	16.8	...	44.8	...	...	...
Wayne	378.0	...	12.6	31.5	6.3	321.3	...	6.3	...
Weakley	76.5	...	15.3	...	...	30.6	...	...	30.6
White	127.2	...	15.9	...	5.3	100.7	...	5.3	...
Williamson	145.0	...	...	5.0	30.0	105.0	...	5.0	...
Wilson	109.0	...	...	...	65.4	43.6	...	...	...
All counties	12,819.8	38.9	998.8	1,198.0	693.8	9,108.0	84.4	150.7	547.2

49

Table 34. *Commercial forest land by stand-size class, Tennessee, 1971*

County	All classes	Sawtimber	Poletimber	Sapling and seedling	Nonstocked areas
- - - - - - - *Thousand acres* - - - - - - -					
Anderson	140.3	36.6	42.7	61.0	...
Bedford	76.0	15.2	7.6	53.2	...
Benton	168.2	23.2	92.8	52.2	...
Bledsoe	173.6	5.8	57.8	110.0	...
Blount	125.6	36.0	47.8	41.8	...
Bradley	107.2	13.4	80.4	13.4	...
Campbell	225.5	88.0	110.0	27.5	...
Cannon	86.4	9.6	48.0	28.8	...
Carroll	153.0	35.7	81.6	35.7	...
Carter	145.0	75.4	52.2	17.4	...
Cheatham	108.8	40.8	40.8	27.2	...
Chester	97.2	27.0	37.8	32.4	...
Claiborne	166.4	38.4	51.2	70.4	6.4
Clay	99.0	33.0	49.5	16.5	...
Cocke	168.0	50.4	72.8	44.8	...
Coffee	117.6	39.2	58.8	19.6	...
Crockett	12.4	12.4	...	...	...
Cumberland	324.5	93.5	126.5	104.5	...
Davidson	104.0	20.8	31.2	52.0	...
Decatur	149.1	51.6	63.1	34.4	...
De Kalb	88.2	12.6	18.9	56.7	...
Dickson	160.0	60.0	70.0	30.0	...
Dyer	65.5	65.5	...	...	...
Fayette	108.0	13.5	27.0	67.5	...
Fentress	246.4	78.4	78.4	89.6	...
Franklin	187.0	82.5	60.5	44.0	...
Gibson	49.0	19.6	19.6	9.8	...
Giles	160.0	20.0	60.0	75.0	5.0
Grainger	94.6	30.1	21.5	43.0	...
Greene	135.2	26.0	20.8	88.4	...
Grundy	186.0	49.6	49.6	86.8	...
Hamblen	25.2	6.3	12.6	6.3	...
Hamilton	180.2	58.3	31.8	90.1	...
Hancock	85.4	18.3	30.5	36.6	...
Hardeman	222.0	54.0	114.0	54.0	...
Hardin	225.6	62.4	91.2	72.0	...
Hawkins	167.4	27.0	81.0	59.4	...
Haywood	73.6	46.0	18.4	9.2	...
Henderson	170.5	28.4	79.5	62.6	...
Henry	124.3	33.9	67.8	11.3	11.3
Hickman	269.5	44.1	127.4	98.0	...
Houston	91.0	32.5	32.5	26.0	...
Humphreys	248.0	31.0	130.2	86.8	...
Jackson	110.5	17.0	59.5	34.0	...
Jefferson	58.5	13.5	9.0	36.0	...
Johnson	124.2	32.4	64.8	27.0	...
Knox	106.2	29.5	17.7	59.0	...
Lake	16.0	16.0	...	...	...

Table 34. *Commercial forest land by stand-size class, Tennessee, 1971*
(Continued)

County	All classes	Sawtimber	Poletimber	Sapling and seedling	Nonstocked areas
- - - - - - - *Thousand acres* - - - - - - -					
Lauderdale	88.5	70.8	17.7	...	...
Lawrence	182.7	31.5	69.3	81.9	...
Lewis	144.9	25.2	75.6	44.1	...
Lincoln	116.6	10.6	42.4	63.6	...
Loudon	53.3	16.4	16.4	20.5	...
McMinn	145.5	33.6	44.8	67.1	...
McNairy	197.6	20.8	78.0	98.8	...
Macon	73.6	9.2	55.2	9.2	...
Madison	112.8	47.0	37.6	28.2	...
Marion	247.5	77.0	71.5	99.0	...
Marshall	78.1	14.2	14.2	49.7	...
Maury	126.0	24.0	36.0	66.0	...
Meigs	80.6	6.2	37.2	37.2	...
Monroe	295.8	81.2	98.6	116.0	...
Montgomery	116.2	24.9	24.9	66.4	...
Moore	30.8	7.7	23.1	...	...
Morgan	291.6	102.6	75.6	113.4	...
Obion	72.8	31.2	10.4	31.2	...
Overton	174.2	40.2	87.1	46.9	...
Perry	212.8	33.6	128.8	50.4	...
Pickett	67.0	13.4	33.5	20.1	...
Polk	227.7	102.7	76.1	48.9	...
Putnam	140.3	48.8	61.0	30.5	...
Rhea	134.6	15.5	51.9	67.2	...
Roane	131.2	20.5	36.9	73.8	...
Robertson	59.0	23.6	11.8	23.6	...
Rutherford	117.6	...	49.0	58.8	9.8
Scott	308.0	89.6	123.2	95.2	...
Sequatchie	140.0	22.4	50.4	67.2	...
Sevier	159.2	36.0	51.3	71.9	...
Shelby	73.0	21.9	29.2	21.9	...
Smith	72.0	...	36.0	36.0	...
Stewart	221.1	87.1	87.1	46.9	...
Sullivan	109.2	29.4	29.4	50.4	...
Sumner	98.1	32.7	...	65.4	...
Tipton	55.8	18.6	...	37.2	...
Trousdale	23.8	...	11.9	11.9	...
Unicoi	94.4	47.2	17.7	29.5	...
Union	84.6	28.2	37.6	18.8	...
Van Buren	124.2	21.6	32.4	70.2	...
Warren	114.0	22.8	51.3	39.9	...
Washington	61.6	28.0	16.8	16.8	...
Wayne	378.0	37.8	277.2	63.0	...
Weakley	76.5	15.3	30.6	30.6	...
White	127.2	42.4	42.4	42.4	...
Williamson	145.0	30.0	25.0	90.0	...
Wilson	109.0	...	32.7	76.3	...
All counties	12,819.8	3,297.8	4,893.6	4,595.9	32.5

Table 35. *Commercial forest land by site class, Tennessee, 1971*

County	All classes	165 cu.ft. or more	120-165 cu. ft.	85-120 cu.ft.	50-85 cu.ft.	Less than 50 cu.ft.
			- - - - Thousand acres- - - - - - - -			
Anderson	140.3	...	12.2	24.4	67.1	36.6
Bedford	76.0	...		7.6	22.8	45.6
Benton	168.2	...	...	29.0	63.8	75.4
Bledsoe	173.6	...	...	11.6	98.3	63.7
Blount	125.6	12.0	12.0	11.9	71.7	18.0
Bradley	107.2	...	...	13.4	67.0	26.8
Campbell	225.5	11.0	11.0	77.0	110.0	16.5
Cannon	86.4	...	...	...	38.4	48.0
Carroll	153.0	...	10.2	40.8	76.5	25.5
Carter	145.0	...	...	23.2	63.8	58.0
Cheatham	108.8	...	...	13.6	81.6	13.6
Chester	97.2	5.4	16.2	43.2	21.6	10.8
Claiborne	166.4	...	...	51.2	76.8	38.4
Clay	99.0	...	...	49.5	...	49.5
Cocke	168.0	...	5.6	28.0	95.2	39.2
Coffee	117.6	...	...	19.6	58.8	39.2
Crockett	12.4	...	...	12.4	...	...
Cumberland	324.5	...	5.5	22.0	148.5	148.5
Davidson	104.0	...	...	...	62.4	41.6
Decatur	149.1	...	40.3	28.6	74.5	5.7
De Kalb	88.2	...	...	18.9	25.2	44.1
Dickson	160.0	...	...	30.0	85.0	45.0
Dyer	65.5	...	13.1	26.2	26.2	...
Fayette	108.0	...	...	40.5	40.5	27.0
Franklin	187.0	...	...	16.5	77.0	93.5
Fentress	246.4	5.6	5.6	67.2	128.8	39.2
Gibson	49.0	...	9.8	...	39.2	...
Giles	160.0	...	...	40.0	90.0	30.0
Grainger	94.6	...	4.3	25.8	25.8	38.7
Greene	135.2	...	10.4	15.6	57.2	52.0
Grundy	186.0	...	...	31.0	86.8	68.2
Hamblen	25.2	...	...	6.3	18.9	...
Hamilton	180.2	...	...	26.5	121.9	31.8
Hancock	85.4	...	...	18.3	48.8	18.3
Hardeman	222.0	...	...	30.0	168.0	24.0
Hardin	225.6	...	28.8	52.8	110.4	33.6
Hawkins	167.4	...	10.8	16.2	86.4	54.0
Haywood	73.6	...	9.2	27.6	36.8	...
Henderson	170.5	5.7	22.7	85.1	51.3	5.7
Henry	124.3	...	...	45.2	33.9	45.2
Hickman	269.5	...	4.9	24.5	181.3	58.8
Houston	91.0	...	...	19.5	58.5	13.0
Humphreys	248.0	...	...	49.6	80.6	117.8
Jackson	110.5	...	...	25.5	51.0	34.0
Jefferson	58.5	...	...	13.5	18.0	27.0
Johnson	124.2	...	...	16.2	81.0	27.0
Knox	106.2	...	11.8	29.5	47.2	17.7
Lake	16.0	8.0	...	...	8.0	...

52

Table 35. *Commercial forest land by site class, Tennessee, 1971* (Continued)

County	All classes	165 cu.ft. or more	120-165 cu. ft.	85-120 cu. ft.	50-85 cu.ft.	Less than 50 cu.ft.
			- - Thousand acres- -			
Lauderdale	88.5	53.1	17.7	...	17.7	...
Lawrence	182.7	...	...	31.5	88.2	63.0
Lewis	144.9	...	...	...	94.5	50.4
Lincoln	116.6	...	...	10.6	74.2	31.8
Loudon	53.3	...	4.1	4.1	36.9	8.2
McMinn	145.5	...	11.2	33.6	78.3	22.4
McNairy	197.6	...	...	31.2	109.2	57.2
Macon	73.6	...	...	18.4	55.2	...
Madison	112.8	9.4	...	37.6	47.0	18.8
Marion	247.5	...	11.0	11.0	154.0	71.5
Marshall	78.1	...	...	...	42.6	35.5
Maury	126.0	...	...	42.0	42.0	42.0
Meigs	80.6	...	6.2	6.2	62.0	6.2
Monroe	295.8	5.8	11.6	75.4	127.6	75.4
Montgomery	116.2	8.3	...	49.8	49.8	8.3
Moore	30.8	...		...	23.1	7.7
Morgan	291.6	...	...	75.6	167.4	48.6
Obion	72.8	10.4	...	20.8	20.8	20.8
Overton	174.2	...	...	20.1	127.3	26.8
Perry	212.8	...	...	11.2	128.8	72.8
Pickett	67.0	...	6.7	33.5	13.4	13.4
Polk	227.7	5.4	16.4	64.9	103.1	37.9
Putnam	140.3	...	...	12.2	103.7	24.4
Rhea	134.6	...	...	30.8	62.2	41.6
Roane	131.2	...	...	32.8	86.1	12.3
Robertson	59.0	...		...	59.0	...
Rutherford	117.6	...	...	...	19.6	98.0
Scott	308.0	...	11.2	84.0	168.0	44.8
Sequatchie	140.0	...	...	11.2	112.0	16.8
Sevier	159.2	...	...	20.5	66.9	71.8
Shelby	73.0	14.6	...	36.5	21.9	...
Smith	72.0	...	...	9.0	54.0	9.0
Stewart	221.1	...	...	20.1	140.7	60.3
Sullivan	109.2	4.2	...	16.8	50.4	37.8
Sumner	98.1	...	...	10.9	65.4	21.8
Tipton	55.8	...	18.6	18.6	18.6	
Trousdale	23.8	...	...	...	23.8	...
Unicoi	94.4	...	...	29.5	53.1	11.8
Union	84.6	...	...	28.2	37.6	18.8
Van Buren	124.2	...	...	27.0	64.8	32.4
Warren	114.0	...	...	28.5	51.3	34.2
Washington	61.6	...	...	16.8	28.0	16.8
Wayne	378.0	6.3	...	63.0	144.9	163.8
Weakley	76.5	...	15.3	15.3	15.3	30.6
White	127.2	...	5.3	10.6	84.8	26.5
Williamson	145.0	...	...	50.0	65.0	30.0
Wilson	109.0	...	...	10.9	54.5	43.6
All counties	12,819.8	165.2	379.7	2,465.7	6,497.2	3,312.0

Table 36. *Sampling errors[1] for commercial forest land, Tennessee, 1971*

County	Percent	County	Percent
Anderson	2	Lauderdale	3
Bedford	2	Lawrence	1
Benton	4	Lewis	5
Bledsoe	4	Lincoln	2
Blount	3	Loudon	9
Bradley	7	McMinn	3
Campbell	3	McNairy	1
Cannon	2	Macon	4
Carroll	2	Madison	3
Carter	2	Marion	2
Cheatham	2	Marshall	3
Chester	5	Maury	2
Claiborne	3	Meigs	4
Clay	2	Monroe	1
Cocke	2	Montgomery	3
Coffee	4	Moore	3
Crockett	4	Morgan	2
Cumberland	2	Obion	2
Davidson	1	Overton	3
Decatur	3	Perry	1
De Kalb	3	Pickett	2
Dickson	1	Polk	2
Dyer	3	Putnam	3
Fayette	2	Rhea	3
Fentress	2	Roane	4
Franklin	3	Robertson	1
Gibson	3	Rutherford	2
Giles	2	Scott	3
Grainger	3	Sequatchie	5
Greene	2	Sevier	3
Grundy	1	Shelby	2
Hamblen	4	Smith	5
Hamilton	3	Stewart	3
Hancock	2	Sullivan	1
Hardeman	1	Sumner	3
Hardin	2	Tipton	4
Hawkins	3	Trousdale	3
Haywood	1	Unicoi	5
Henderson	4	Union	5
Henry	3	Van Buren	4
Hickman	2	Warren	2
Houston	2	Washington	1
Humphreys	2	Wayne	2
Jackson	4	Weakley	2
Jefferson	5	White	4
Johnson	4	Williamson	3
Knox	2	Wilson	4
Lake	2	All counties	0.3

[1] By random-sampling formula.

Table 37. *Total area and forest area, Texas, 1965*

County	Total area Thousand acres	Commercial forest Thousand acres	Commercial forest Percent	Noncommercial forest Thousand acres
Anderson	687.4	396.9	58	0.6
Angelina	551.7	359.9	65	.2
Austin	426.2	62.0	15	...
Bastrop	570.2	38.4	7	163.2
Bowie	590.7	300.9	51	...
Brazos	375.7	23.9	6	47.8
Burleson	437.1	38.8	9	77.6
Caldwell	348.2	12.8	4	64.0
Camp	123.5	53.2	43	...
Cass	617.6	383.4	62	...
Chambers	560.0	35.4	6	...
Cherokee	675.2	386.4	57	1.1
Colorado	613.1	44.4	7	81.4
Delta	176.6	16.8	10	...
Fayette	601.6	28.2	5	122.2
Franklin	187.5	74.4	40	...
Freestone	554.2	166.4	30	10.4
Gonzales	677.1	46.2	7	138.6
Gregg	181.8	84.0	46	...
Grimes	513.3	115.5	23	22.0
Guadalupe	458.2	10.8	2	75.6
Hardin	574.1	501.6	87	...
Harris	1,129.6	185.0	16	...
Harrison	576.0	360.0	62	...
Henderson	604.8	193.8	32	...
Hopkins	508.2	68.6	13	...
Houston	792.3	442.4	56	.3
Jasper	624.7	541.8	87	.1
Jefferson	643.8	54.4	8	(2)
Lamar	581.8	94.6	16	...
Lavaca	624.0	13.2	2	158.4
Lee	412.8	...	...	118.0
Leon	706.6	211.2	30	81.6
Liberty	757.1	453.6	60	...

County	Total area Thousand acres	Commercial forest Thousand acres	Commercial forest Percent	Noncommercial forest Thousand acres
Limestone	596.5	(2)	(2)	73.6
Madison	307.2	47.5	15	9.5
Marion	266.2	192.0	72	...
Milam	659.2	14.6	2	116.8
Montgomery	697.6	564.3	81	...
Morris	169.0	84.5	50	...
Nacogdoches	617.6	400.4	65	...
Newton	609.9	560.0	92	...
Orange	240.6	145.0	60	(2)
Panola	567.7	353.8	62	...
Polk	704.0	592.8	84	...
Rains	150.4	37.8	25	...
Red River	662.4	338.0	51	...
Robertson	561.9	27.2	5	122.4
Rusk	604.2	303.8	50	...
Sabine	363.5	295.8	81	.3
San Augustine	391.7	285.2	73	.3
San Jacinto	399.4	313.5	78	1.2
Shelby	525.4	363.0	69	.1
Smith	601.6	237.9	40	2.7
Titus	267.5	105.6	39	...
Trinity	453.1	347.7	77	.1
Tyler	597.8	552.0	92	...
Upshur	377.0	220.0	58	...
Van Zandt	547.2	94.6	17	...
Walker	505.6	360.4	71	(2)
Waller	327.0	61.2	19	...
Washington	393.0	...	...	...
Wood	462.7	226.8	49	42.0
All counties	32,089.6	12,924.3	40	1,532.1

[1]Source: United States Bureau of the Census, Land and Water Area of the United States, 1960.
[2] Negligible.

Table 38. *Commercial forest land by ownership class, Texas, 1965*

County	All ownerships	National forest	Other public	Forest industry	Farmer	Misc. private
			- - - - - - - -*Thousand acres* - - - - - - - -			
Anderson	396.9	...	10.7	68.9	112.9	204.4
Angelina	359.9	52.1	13.7	207.2	...	86.9
Austin	62.0	...	...	...	62.0	...
Bastrop	38.4	...	2.7	...	...	35.7
Bowie	300.9	...	51.2	17.6	76.4	155.7
Brazos	23.9	...	...	...	...	23.9
Burleson	38.8	...	...	...	20.1	18.7
Caldwell	12.8	...	...	...	12.8	...
Camp	53.2	...	.3	...	7.6	45.3
Cass	383.4	...	19.5	48.4	64.5	251.0
Chambers	35.4	...	...	...	35.4	...
Cherokee	386.4	...	2.7	94.7	39.0	250.0
Colorado	44.4	...	...	...	15.4	29.0
Delta	16.8	...	...	...	...	16.8
Fayette	28.2	...	...	...	28.2	...
Franklin	74.4	...	.1	...	74.0	.3
Freestone	166.4	...	.2	...	108.1	58.1
Gonzales	46.2	...	...	...	24.0	22.2
Gregg	84.0	...	.6	...	...	83.4
Grimes	115.5	...	.1	22.1	55.1	38.2
Guadalupe	10.8	...	...	...	10.8	...
Hardin	501.6	...	.3	314.5	17.2	169.6
Harris	185.0	...	2.9	10.0	40.1	132.0
Harrison	360.0	...	7.9	...	49.7	302.4
Henderson	193.8	...	.3	5.1	30.7	157.7
Hopkins	68.6	...	...	...	30.5	38.1
Houston	442.4	92.0	.8	61.8	84.3	203.5
Jasper	541.8	19.7	4.3	360.3	63.2	94.3
Jefferson	54.4	...	.8	...	13.6	40.0
Lamar	94.6	...	5.0	...	62.5	27.1
Lavaca	13.2	...	.1	...	13.1	...
Lee	...	...	...	...	...	...
Leon	211.2	...	2.6	...	67.3	141.3
Liberty	453.6	...	.5	134.8	61.8	256.5

Table 38. *Commercial forest land by ownership class, Texas, 1965*(Continued)

County	All ownerships	National forest	Other public	Forest industry	Farmer	Misc. private
				- - - -*Thousand acres*- - - - - - -		
Limestone	...	...	...	...		
Madison	47.5	...	.4	...	28.6	18.5
Marion	192.0	...	8.8	17.9	17.9	147.4
Milam	14.6	...	(1)	...	...	14.6
Montgomery	564.3	45.4	2.4	51.5	103.0	362.0
Morris	84.5	...	1.3	...	32.3	50.9
Nacogdoches	400.4	2.1	19.4	93.1	119.0	166.8
Newton	560.0	...	1.9	348.3	22.5	187.3
Orange	145.0	...	.2	29.1	17.5	98.2
Panola	353.8	...	.1	57.7	23.1	272.9
Polk	592.8	...	6.6	457.5	22.9	105.8
Rains	37.8	...	...	...	6.5	31.3
Red River	338.0	...	.1	77.6	226.4	33.9
Robertson	27.2	...	.5	...	...	26.7
Rusk	303.8	...	.6	18.5	30.8	253.9
Sabine	295.8	110.5	2.7	117.7	15.3	49.6
San Augustine	285.2	58.9	16.0	124.4	74.6	11.3
San Jacinto	313.5	55.4	.3	74.3	22.9	160.6
Shelby	363.0	66.7	.1	52.5	131.4	112.3
Smith	237.9	...	1.2	...	30.3	206.4
Titus	105.6	(1)	...	...	52.5	53.1
Trinity	347.7	67.3	.8	183.6	...	96.0
Tyler	552.0	...	4.5	409.4	6.0	132.1
Upshur	220.0	...	.9	...	10.9	208.2
Van Zandt	94.6	...	(1)	...	34.5	60.1
Walker	360.4	52.2	7.0	26.6	58.5	216.1
Waller	61.2	...	(1)	5.1	25.6	30.5
Washington	...	...	...	...	...	...
Wood	226.8	...	.1	6.3	12.5	207.9
All counties	12,924.3	622.3	203.2	3,496.5	2,405.8	6,196.5

[1] Negligible.

Table 39. *Commercial forest land by forest type, Texas, 1965*

County	All types	Longleaf-slash pine	Loblolly-shortleaf pine	Oak-pine	Oak-hickory	Oak-gum-cypress	Elm-ash-cottonwood
			- - - - *Thousand acres-* - - - -				
Anderson	396.9	...	88.2	31.5	189.0	88.2	...
Angelina	359.9	5.9	206.5	100.3	11.8	35.4	...
Austin	62.0	...	...	...	31.0	31.0	...
Bastrop	38.4		9.6	9.6	19.2	...	...
Bowie	300.9		59.0	59.0	112.1	59.0	11.8
Brazos	23.9		...	...	...	23.9	...
Burleson	38.8		...	...	...	38.8	...
Caldwell	12.8	...	...	...	12.8	...	...
Camp	53.2	...	15.2	22.8	7.6	7.6	...
Cass	383.4	5.4	113.4	64.8	108.0	86.4	5.4
Chambers	35.4	...	35.4	...	...	...	...
Cherokee	386.4	11.2	100.8	106.4	128.8	39.2	...
Colorado	44.4	...	14.8	...	22.2	7.4	...
Delta	16.8		...	...	...	16.8	...
Fayette	28.2		...	9.4	9.4	9.4	...
Franklin	74.4		9.3	37.2	18.6	9.3	...
Freestone	166.4		...	10.4	104.0	52.0	...
Gonzales	46.2		...	...	...	23.1	23.1
Gregg	84.0		21.0	7.0	28.0	21.0	7.0
Grimes	115.5	...	49.5	...	49.5	16.5	...
Guadalupe	10.8	...	...	...	10.8	...	...
Hardin	501.6	74.1	165.3	108.3	28.5	125.4	...
Harris	185.0	...	65.0	35.0	25.0	60.0	...
Harrison	360.0	...	130.0	80.0	105.0	45.0	...
Henderson	193.8		20.4	5.1	127.5	30.6	10.2
Hopkins	68.6		...	...	39.2	29.4	...
Houston	442.4	...	229.6	100.8	50.4	50.4	11.2
Jasper	541.8	56.7	270.9	107.1	31.5	75.6	...
Jefferson	54.4	...	6.8	6.8	6.8	34.0	...
Lamar	94.6		...	...	77.4	17.2	...
Lavaca	13.2		...	...	13.2	...	...
Lee	...		...	...	...	...	...
Leon	211.2	...	4.8	4.8	163.2	38.4	...
Liberty	453.6	...	89.6	95.2	28.0	235.2	5.6

Table 39. *Commercial forest land by forest type, Texas, 1965* (Continued)

County	All types	Longleaf-slash pine	Loblolly-shortleaf pine	Oak-pine	Oak-hickory	Oak-gum-cypress	Elm-ash-cottonwood
			-Thousand acres-				
Limestone			...	...	...	...	...
Madison	47.5	...	...	...	9.5	38.0	...
Marion	192.0	6.0	54.0	36.0	66.0	30.0	...
Milam	14.6	...	...	...	...	14.6	...
Montgomery	564.3	...	313.5	165.3	34.2	51.3	...
Morris	84.5	...	32.5	32.5	6.5	13.0	...
Nacogdoches	400.4	10.4	202.8	78.0	62.4	46.8	...
Newton	560.0	95.2	257.6	78.4	50.4	78.4	...
Orange	145.0	11.6	46.4	40.6	5.8	40.6	...
Panola	353.8	...	145.0	87.0	63.8	58.0	...
Polk	592.8	...	450.3	79.8	22.8	39.9	...
Rains	37.8	...	...	...	18.9	18.9	...
Red River	338.0	...	71.5	32.5	149.5	84.5	...
Robertson	27.2	...	...	...	...	27.2	...
Rusk	303.8	...	148.8	55.8	74.4	24.8	...
Sabine	295.8	5.1	183.6	51.0	51.0	5.1	...
San Augustine	285.2	...	179.8	37.2	6.2	62.0	...
San Jacinto	313.5	...	210.9	22.8	34.2	45.6	...
Shelby	363.0	...	145.2	105.6	66.0	39.6	6.6
Smith	237.9	12.2	48.8	30.5	97.6	42.7	6.1
Titus	105.6	...	...	19.8	59.4	26.4	...
Trinity	347.7	12.2	286.7	30.5	6.1	12.2	...
Tyler	552.0	36.0	246.0	186.0	42.0	42.0	...
Upshur	220.0	16.5	55.0	55.0	71.5	22.0	...
Van Zandt	94.6		...	8.6	77.4	8.6	...
Walker	360.4	...	180.2	100.7	58.3	21.2	...
Waller	61.2	...	30.6	...	15.3	15.3	...
Washington	...	...	...	...	...	...	...
Wood	226.8	...	44.1	18.9	113.4	50.4	...
All counties	12,924.3	358.5	5,038.4	2,354.0	2,821.1	2,265.3	87.0

59

Table 40. *Commercial forest land by stand-size class, Texas, 1965*

County	All classes	Sawtimber	Poletimber	Sapling and seedling	Nonstocked areas
		- - - - - - - -Thousand acres - - - - - - - -			
Anderson	396.9	220.5	50.4	113.4	12.6
Angelina	359.9	265.5	53.1	41.3	...
Austin	62.0	31.0	15.5	15.5	...
Bastrop	38.4	9.6	...	28.8	...
Bowie	300.9	141.6	53.1	106.2	...
Brazos	23.9	23.9	...	...	...
Burleson	38.8	...	19.4	19.4	...
Caldwell	12.8	...	...	12.8	...
Camp	53.2	15.2	15.2	22.8	...
Cass	383.4	167.4	64.8	151.2	...
Chambers	35.4	11.8	...	23.6	...
Cherokee	386.4	212.8	56.0	117.6	...
Colorado	44.4	14.8	22.2	...	7.4
Delta	16.8	16.8		...	...
Fayette	28.2	18.8	...	9.4	...
Franklin	74.4	37.2	9.3	27.9	...
Freestone	166.4	31.2	52.0	83.2	...
Gonzales	46.2	46.2	...	...	...
Gregg	84.0	49.0	7.0	28.0	...
Grimes	115.5	44.0	49.5	16.5	5.5
Guadalupe	10.8	10.8	...	...	...
Hardin	501.6	319.2	51.3	131.1	...
Harris	185.0	90.0	30.0	55.0	10.0
Harrison	360.0	120.0	55.0	185.0	...
Henderson	193.8	35.7	51.0	102.0	5.1
Hopkins	68.6	29.4	29.4	9.8	...
Houston	442.4	240.8	95.2	100.8	5.6
Jasper	541.8	308.7	50.4	176.4	6.3
Jefferson	54.4	47.6	...	6.8	...
Lamar	94.6	25.8	34.4	34.4	...
Lavaca	13.2	...	...	13.2	...
Lee	...	...	...	...	...
Leon	211.2	81.6	62.4	67.2	...
Liberty	453.6	347.2	50.4	39.2	16.8

Table 40. *Commercial forest land by stand-size class, Texas, 1965* (Continued)

County	All classes	Sawtimber	Poletimber	Sapling and seedling	Nonstocked areas
	- - - - - - - - *Thousand acres* - - - - - - - -				
Limestone					
Madison	47.5	28.5	9.5	9.5	. . .
Marion	192.0	84.0	18.0	90.0	. . .
Milam	14.6	14.6	. . .	. . .	
Montgomery	564.3	319.2	125.4	119.7	. . .
Morris	84.5	26.0	6.5	52.0	. . .
Nacogdoches	400.4	187.2	78.0	130.0	5.2
Newton	560.0	380.8	61.6	112.0	5.6
Orange	145.0	104.4	17.4	23.2	. . .
Panola	353.8	197.2	52.2	104.4	. . .
Polk	592.8	456.0	45.6	91.2	. . .
Rains	37.8	12.6	. . .	25.2	. . .
Red River	338.0	117.0	123.5	97.5	. . .
Robertson	27.2	. . .	27.2	. . .	
Rusk	303.8	99.2	86.8	117.8	. . .
Sabine	295.8	249.9	30.6	15.3	. . .
San Augustine	285.2	210.8	49.6	24.8	. . .
San Jacinto	313.5	182.4	91.2	39.9	. . .
Shelby	363.0	191.4	85.8	79.2	6.6
Smith	237.9	85.4	42.7	109.8	. . .
Titus	105.6	26.4	26.4	52.8	. . .
Trinity	347.7	268.4	36.6	36.6	6.1
Tyler	552.0	384.0	48.0	120.0	. . .
Upshur	220.0	60.5	33.0	126.5	. . .
Van Zandt	94.6	17.2	25.8	51.6	. . .
Walker	360.4	201.4	58.3	100.7	. . .
Waller	61.2	30.6	10.2	15.3	5.1
Washington	. . .	. . .	. . .	. . .	. . .
Wood	226.8	69.3	18.9	138.6	. . .
All counties	12,924.3	7,018.5	2,185.8	3,622.1	97.9

Table 41. *Commercial forest land by site class, Texas, 1965*

County	All classes	165 cu. ft. or more	120-165 cu. ft.	85-120 cu.ft.	50-85 cu.ft.	Less than 50 cu.ft.
				Thousand acres		
Anderson	396.9	...	6.3	144.9	157.5	88.2
Angelina	359.9	5.9	23.6	283.2	47.2	...
Austin	62.0	...	...	15.5	31.0	15.5
Bastrop	38.4	...	...	...	...	38.4
Bowie	300.9	5.9	11.8	47.2	212.4	23.6
Brazos	23.9	...	...	...	23.9	...
Burleson	38.8	...	...	...	...	38.8
Caldwell	12.8	...	...	...	...	12.8
Camp	53.2	...	...	22.8	30.4	...
Cass	383.4	...	10.8	140.4	210.6	21.6
Chambers	35.4	...	...	11.8	23.6	...
Cherokee	386.4	...	22.4	196.0	168.0	...
Colorado	44.4	...	...	...	14.8	29.6
Delta	16.8	...	...	...	...	16.8
Fayette	28.2	...	...	9.4	18.8	...
Franklin	74.4	...	...	...	18.6	55.8
Freestone	166.4	...	...	41.6	20.8	104.0
Gonzales	46.2	...	...	46.2	...	...
Gregg	84.0	...	...	28.0	42.0	14.0
Grimes	115.5	...	...	22.0	44.0	49.5
Guadalupe	10.8	...	...	10.8	...	...
Hardin	501.6	...	5.7	342.0	153.9	...
Harris	185.0	...	5.0	70.0	105.0	5.0
Harrison	360.0	...	5.0	95.0	260.0	...
Henderson	193.8	...	...	35.7	56.1	102.0
Hopkins	68.6	...	...	...	...	68.6
Houston	442.4	...	16.8	145.6	252.0	28.0
Jasper	541.8	18.9	119.7	283.5	107.1	12.6
Jefferson	54.4	...	...	34.0	20.4	...
Lamar	94.6	...	...	...	51.6	43.0
Lavaca	13.2	...	...	...	...	13.2
Lee	...	...	...	...	...	...
Leon	211.2	...	...	38.4	57.6	115.2
Liberty	453.6	...	28.0	252.0	173.6	...

Table 41. *Commercial forest land by site class, Texas, 1965* (Continued)

County	All classes	165 cu. ft. or more	120-165 cu.ft.	85-120 cu.ft.	50-85 cu.ft.	Less than 50 cu.ft.
	- - - - - - - - - - -Thousand acres- - - - - - - - - - -					
Limestone	...	...	...	...	...	...
Madison	47.5	...	...	19.0	9.5	19.0
Marion	192.0	...	...	84.0	102.0	6.0
Milam	14.6	...	...	...	14.6	...
Montgomery	564.3	...	34.2	228.0	302.1	...
Morris	84.5	...	...	13.0	71.5	...
Nacogdoches	400.4	5.2	26.0	197.6	156.0	15.6
Newton	560.0	...	22.4	252.0	257.6	28.0
Orange	145.0	...	5.8	104.4	34.8	...
Panola	353.8	...	11.6	208.8	110.2	23.2
Polk	592.8	5.7	68.4	347.7	165.3	5.7
Rains	37.8	...	...	18.9	18.9	...
Red River	338.0	...	...	45.5	253.5	39.0
Robertson	27.2	...	...	13.6	...	13.6
Rusk	303.8	...	6.2	117.8	167.4	12.4
Sabine	295.8	...	10.2	255.0	30.6	...
San Augustine	285.2	6.2	12.4	173.6	86.8	6.2
San Jacinto	313.5	...	28.5	176.7	96.9	11.4
Shelby	363.0	...	...	118.8	217.8	26.4
Smith	237.9	...	...	164.7	67.1	6.1
Titus	105.6	...	...	6.6	59.4	39.6
Trinity	347.7	...	6.1	109.8	225.7	6.1
Tyler	552.0	12.0	54.0	342.0	126.0	18.0
Upshur	220.0	...	5.5	121.0	82.5	11.0
Van Zandt	94.6	...	...	43.0	43.0	8.6
Walker	360.4	...	10.6	132.5	201.4	15.9
Waller	61.2	...	...	10.2	45.9	5.1
Washington	...	...	...	...	...	...
Wood	226.8	...	...	88.2	107.1	31.5
All counties	12,924.3	59.8	557.0	5,708.4	5,354.5	1,244.6

Table 42. *Sampling errors[1] for commercial forest land, Texas, 1965*

County	Percent	County	Percent
Anderson	2	Liberty	1
Angelina	4	Limestone	...
Austin	4	Madison	4
Bastrop	20	Marion	4
Bowie	2	Milam	18
Brazos	8	Montgomery	2
Burleson	13	Morris	7
Caldwell	22	Nacogdoches	3
Camp	2	Newton	2
Cass	2	Orange	3
Chambers	1	Panola	3
Cherokee	3	Polk	2
Colorado	11	Rains	2
Delta	1	Red River	2
Fayette	8	Robertson	17
Franklin	18	Rusk	4
Freestone	4	Sabine	2
Gonzales	12	San Augustine	2
Gregg	7	San Jacinto	2
Grimes	4	Shelby	3
Guadalupe	21	Smith	3
Hardin	2	Titus	1
Harris	1	Trinity	3
Harrison	3	Tyler	1
Henderson	3	Upshur	4
Hopkins	3	Van Zandt	3
Houston	3	Walker	3
Jasper	2	Waller	2
Jefferson	1	Washington	...
Lamar	2	Wood	3
Lavaca	25		
Lee	...		
Leon	5	All counties	1.0

[1] By random-sampling formula.

64

Earles, J. M.

    1973. Forest area statistics for Midsouth counties. South. For. Exp. Stn., New Orleans, La. 64 p. (USDA For. Serv. Resour. Bull. SO-40)

Brings together acreage statistics for the seven Midsouth States, as of the most recent forest survey. Includes first published acreage data for Louisiana, Texas, and Oklahoma, plus information on stand size and site class for most States.

Additional keywords: Area, forest type, ownership, site class, stand size.

Southern Pulpwood Production, 1972

Daniel F. Bertelson

Southern Forest Experiment Station
New Orleans, Louisiana
Forest Service, U. S. Department of Agriculture

1973

Southern Pulpwood Production, 1972

Daniel F. Bertelson

SOUTHERN FOREST EXPERIMENT STATION
New Orleans, Louisiana

and

SOUTHEASTERN FOREST EXPERIMENT STATION
Asheville, North Carolina

of the

Forest Service, U. S. Department of Agriculture

in cooperation with the

AMERICAN PULPWOOD ASSOCIATION

1973

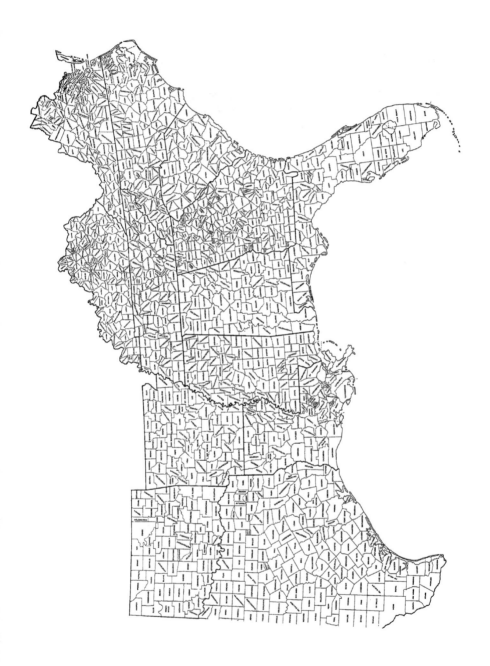

The South harvested a record high of 44,-279,487 cords of pulpwood in 1972. Roundwood output and residue use expanded in both softwoods and hardwoods for a total gain of 2,-365,671 cords. Through the 1960's southern pulpwood production averaged a 6-percent increase per year. In 1970, the rise was 3 percent, and in 1971 a slight decline occurred. With a 6-percent increase in 1972, the South is again in pace with the trend set in the sixties.

Production was up in 10 States (table 1). Alabama had the largest gain, about 708,000

Table 1. *Pulpwood production in the South during 1972, and change since 1971*

State	Pulpwood	Change
	Thousand cords	*Percent*
Alabama	6,991.8	+ 11
Arkansas	3,393.9	+ 7
Florida	3,393.3	+ 1
Georgia	7,565.1	+ 4
Louisiana	4,137.7	+ 4
Mississippi	4,584.4	− 2
North Carolina	4,106.2	+ 12
Oklahoma	469.6	+108
South Carolina	3,473.9	+ 8
Tennessee	633.9	+ 1
Texas	3,323.1	+ 6
Virginia	2,206.6	− 4
All States	44,279.5	+ 6

cords. North Carolina was second with an increase of 452,000 cords, and Georgia's output rose 307,000 cords. Mississippi and Virginia were the only States that recorded a decline in total output. Oklahoma accounted for only 1 percent of the South's total output, but more than doubled its production.

Georgia is still the region's top producer, with about 7.6 million cords. Alabama is second with just under 7 million cords. Mississippi remains third with about 4.6 million cords, despite declines for the last 3 years.

Roundwood production in 1972 increased 5 percent, with most Southern States showing gains (table 2). Softwood roundwood rose by 3 percent, hardwood by 12 percent. Oklahoma had the largest percentage increase, 212; the gain was ascribable to recent expansion of pulpmill capacity in the State. Alabama was the leader in volume with an increase of 600,000 cords. Five States recorded an increase in both softwood and hardwood output, Tennessee being the only State down in both categories. Virginia's softwood roundwood harvest fell for the seventh consecutive year and is now only 58 percent of the 1965 peak.

Species composition changed very little as softwood roundwood decreased slightly to just under three-fourths of the total production

Table 2. *Roundwood production in the South, 1972 and 1971*

State	Change from 1971	1972			1971		
		All species	Softwood	Hardwood	All species	Softwood	Hardwood
	Percent	— — — — — — — — — — — — — — *Thousand cords* — — — — — — — — — — — — —
Alabama	+ 12	5,458.3	3,819.3	1,639.0	4,858.7	3,430.0	1,428.7
Arkansas	+ 13	2,132.1	1,343.3	788.8	1,884.6	1,236.2	648.4
Florida	(¹)	2,896.1	2,687.2	208.9	2,886.5	2,662.1	224.4
Georgia	+ 5	6,003.6	5,317.0	686.6	5,720.9	5,116.6	604.3
Louisiana	(²)	3,164.8	2,351.2	813.6	3,164.9	2,348.3	816.6
Mississippi	− 2	3,545.5	2,367.6	1,177.9	3,599.8	2,624.6	975.2
North Carolina	+ 7	3,031.6	1,892.9	1,138.7	2,827.5	1,854.1	973.4
Oklahoma	+212	285.7	190.8	94.9	91.5	54.1	37.4
South Carolina	+ 7	2,547.6	1,991.0	556.6	2,376.1	1,801.2	574.9
Tennessee	− 5	453.2	180.8	272.4	475.7	195.8	279.9
Texas	+ 1	2,198.6	1,836.1	362.5	2,177.2	1,883.9	293.3
Virginia	− 2	1,674.6	827.7	846.9	1,711.9	873.8	838.1
All States	+ 5	33,391.7	24,804.9	8,586.8	31,775.3	24,080.7	7,694.6

¹ Less than 0.5 percent increase.
² Less than 0.5 percent decrease.

(table 3). The hardwood cut was made up of 42 percent oaks, 31 percent gums, and 27 percent other species. The volume of gums declined as oaks and other hardwoods increased.

Choctaw County in Alabama, which has been one of the top producers of round pulpwood in the past, was again the leader with 279,470 cords. McCurtain County, Oklahoma, was second, followed by Sabine and Vernon Parishes in Louisiana. In 1972, there were 68 counties which produced over 100,000 cords of roundwood. Alabama led with 18 counties and Louisiana was next with 11 parishes.

As a special feature, figures 1-4 have been prepared to depict regionwide patterns of pro-

duction and competition for roundwood (competition has been defined in terms of the number of pulpmills buying wood in a county). The last previous maps of this kind presented data for 1967. As might be expected from silvicultural considerations, areas of concentration are much the same as they were 6 years ago. The most notable changes have been the general intensification of activity and a broadening of interest in hardwood.

The use of plant byproducts increased by some 749,000 cords, or 7 percent over the previous year (table 4). Softwood residue use rose 9 percent while hardwoods gained 2 percent. More than 81 percent of the residues

Table 3. *Roundwood production in the South, by species group, 1972*

State	All species	Softwood	Hardwood			
			Total	Gums	Oaks	Other hardwoods
			- - - - - - - - - - - - - - Thousand cords - - - - - - - - - - - - - - -			
Alabama	5,458.3	3,819.3	1,639.0	460.7	721.2	457.1
Arkansas	2,132.1	1,343.3	788.8	185.0	404.6	199.2
Florida	2,896.1	2,687.2	208.9	74.0	72.9	62.0
Georgia	6,003.6	5,317.0	686.6	255.0	263.1	168.5
Louisiana	3,164.8	2,351.2	813.6	220.3	335.6	257.7
Mississippi	3,545.5	2,367.6	1,177.9	381.1	396.7	400.1
North Carolina	3,031.6	1,892.9	1,138.7	526.2	398.9	213.6
Oklahoma	285.7	190.8	94.9	18.3	29.8	46.8
South Carolina	2,547.6	1,991.0	556.6	225.2	233.8	97.6
Tennessee	453.2	180.8	272.4	30.7	176.6	65.1
Texas	2,198.6	1,836.1	362.5	107.6	170.1	84.8
Virginia	1,674.6	827.7	846.9	186.8	404.7	255.4
All States	33,391.7	24,804.9	8,586.8	2,670.9	3,608.0	2,307.9

Table 4. *Southern output of wood residues for pulp manufacture, by species group, 1972 and 1971*

State	Change from 1971	1972			1971		
		All species	Softwood	Hardwood	All species	Softwood	Hardwood
	Percent	- - - - - - - - - - - - - - Thousand cords - - - - - - - - - - - - - - -					
Alabama	+ 8	1,533.5	1,258.8	274.7	1,424.9	1,157.3	267.6
Arkansas	− 2	1,261.8	1,113.9	147.9	1,290.9	1,130.7	160.2
Florida	+ 2	497.2	397.6	99.6	488.3	401.0	87.3
Georgia	+ 2	1,561.5	1,346.5	215.0	1,537.2	1,314.5	222.7
Louisiana	+ 17	972.9	802.9	170.0	830.9	687.1	143.8
Mississippi	− 4	1,038.9	793.8	245.1	1,079.9	830.9	249.0
North Carolina	+ 30	1,074.6	861.3	213.3	826.9	608.2	218.7
Oklahoma	+ 36	183.9	182.6	1.3	134.8	131.0	3.8
South Carolina	+ 12	926.3	750.9	175.4	829.5	668.8	160.7
Tennessee	+ 17	180.7	14.8	165.9	154.0	12.8	141.2
Texas	+ 18	1,124.5	1,064.6	59.9	952.2	880.7	71.5
Virginia	− 10	532.0	293.4	238.6	589.0	351.8	237.2
All States	+ 7	10,887.8	8,881.1	2,006.7	10,138.5	8,174.8	1,963.7

were softwood and more than 93 percent were received at the mill in the form of chips. Residues accounted for just under one-fourth of total pulpwood receipts, a slight increase over the 1971 ratio.

Volume of residues going to pulpmills is determined by the amount of lumber and plywood manufactured, and by the percentage of sawmills that are equipped with residue chippers or chipping headrigs. Residue utilization made large gains throughout the 1960's, partly because small mills were closing down and lumber production was being concentrated at plants large enough to afford equipment for converting waste portions of saw logs to chips. The process of concentration is now well advanced, and it is likely that most coarse residues are being used.

Daily pulping capacity at the South's 109 pulpmills (fig. 5, p. 21) was 88,124 tons in 1972, an increase of 1 percent. By the end of the year four new mills were under construction, one each in Florida, Georgia, Louisiana, and Texas. Southern pulpwood also went to 15 mills in seven States outside the region.

3

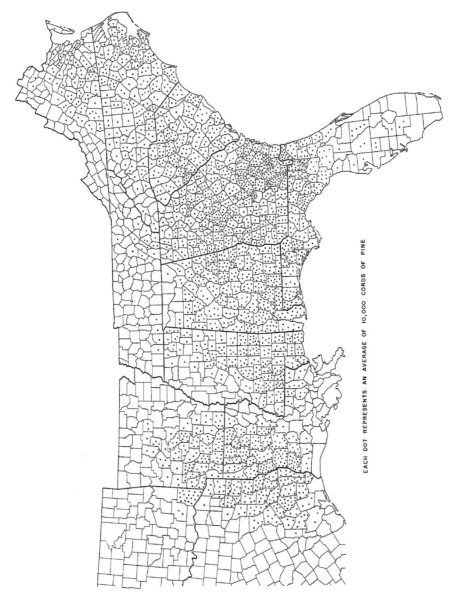

EACH DOT REPRESENTS AN AVERAGE OF 10,000 CORDS OF PINE

4

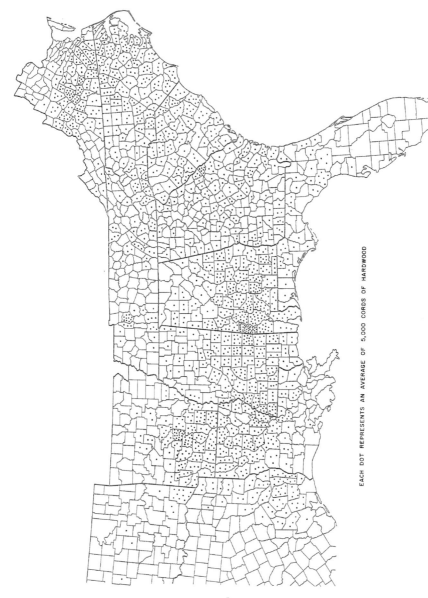

EACH DOT REPRESENTS AN AVERAGE OF 5,000 CORDS OF HARDWOOD

Figure 2. *Hardwood roundwood production, 1972.*

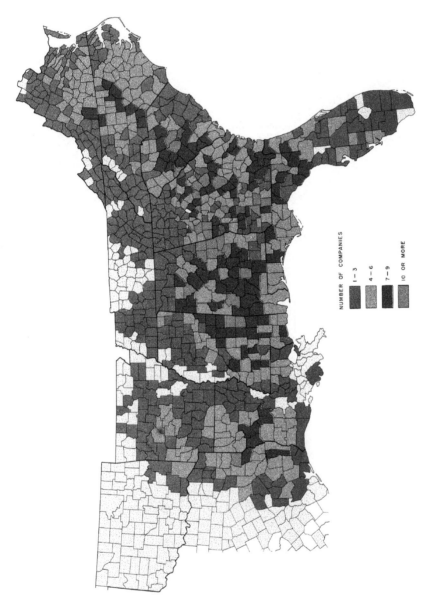

NUMBER OF COMPANIES

1 – 3

4 – 6

7 – 9

10 OR MORE

6

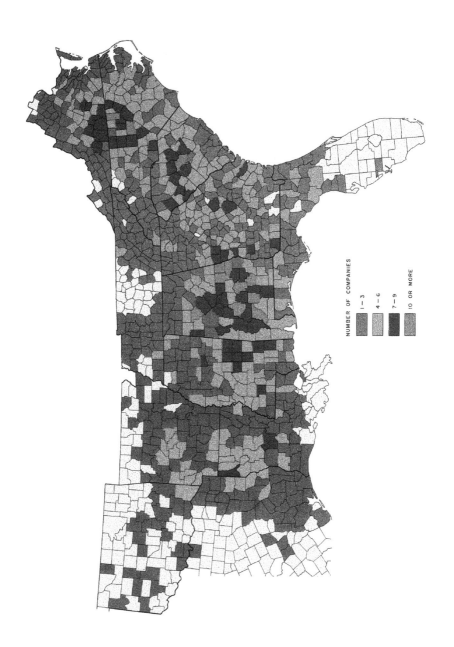

NUMBER OF COMPANIES

1 – 3
4 – 6
7 – 9
10 OR MORE

Table 5. *Southern output of wood residues for pulp manufacture, by type of residue, 1972*

State	All types	Chips			Other residues[1]		
		All species	Softwood	Hardwood	All species	Softwood	Hardwood
				-Thousand cords-			
Alabama	1,533.5	1,397.6	1,129.3	268.3	135.9	129.5	6.4
Arkansas	1,261.8	1,163.5	1,031.0	132.5	98.3	82.9	15.4
Florida	497.2	479.6	380.0	99.6	17.6	17.6	...
Georgia	1,561.5	1,530.3	1,317.3	213.0	31.2	29.2	2.0
Louisiana	972.9	909.3	761.7	147.6	63.6	41.2	22.4
Mississippi	1,038.9	989.8	749.7	240.1	49.1	44.1	5.0
North Carolina	1,074.6	1,008.7	809.4	199.3	65.9	51.9	14.0
Oklahoma	183.9	171.1	169.8	1.3	12.8	12.8	...
South Carolina	926.3	853.2	677.8	175.4	73.1	73.1	...
Tennessee	180.7	180.7	14.8	165.9	...	...	...
Texas	1,124.5	995.4	935.5	59.9	129.1	129.1	...
Virginia	532.0	456.2	241.5	214.7	75.8	51.9	23.9
All States	10,887.8	10,135.4	8,217.8	1,917.6	752.4	663.3	89.1

[1]Veneer cores, pole and piling trim, cull crossties, sawdust and secondary residues.

Table 6. *Southern pulpwood production by Experiment Station territory, 1972*

Station and source of wood	All species	Softwood	Hardwood
	- - - - Standard cords- - - -		
Southeastern:[1]			
Roundwood	16,153,507	12,715,847	3,437,660
Residues	4,591,565	3,649,686	941,879
Total	20,745,072	16,365,533	4,379,539
Southern:[2]			
Roundwood	17,238,239	12,089,082	5,149,157
Residues	6,296,176	5,231,418	1,064,758
Total	23,534,415	17,320,500	6,213,915
Both Stations:			
Roundwood	33,391,746	24,804,929	8,586,817
Residues	10,887,741	8,881,104	2,006,637
Total	44,279,487	33,686,033	10,593,454

[1]States of Florida, Georgia, North and South Carolina, Virginia.
[2]States of Alabama, Arkansas, Louisiana, Mississippi, Oklahoma, Tennessee, Texas.

able 7. *Round pulpwood production in Alabama, 1972*

County	All species	Softwood	Hardwood	County	All species	Softwood	Hardwood
	- - - *Standard cords-* - -				- - - *Standard cords-* - -		
utauga	68,207	31,501	36,706	Jackson	9,020	6,536	2,484
				Jefferson	35,531	32,453	3,078
aldwin	182,494	138,778	43,716				
arbour	92,819	73,060	19,759	Lamar	50,276	40,263	10,013
ibb	111,599	76,663	34,936	Lauderdale	9,611	4,052	5,559
lount	25,151	23,823	1,328	Lawrence	8,494	2,348	6,146
ullock	48,140	35,328	12,812	Lee	103,296	88,362	14,934
utler	163,077	94,140	68,937	Limestone	2,067	2,050	17
				Lowndes	97,750	68,124	29,626
alhoun	46,656	40,870	5,786				
hambers	92,655	65,723	26,932	Macon	59,418	45,428	13,990
herokee	36,420	33,066	3,354	Madison	616	392	224
hilton	72,762	53,614	19,148	Marengo	161,638	81,253	80,385
hoctaw	279,470	106,256	173,214	Marion	56,747	44,621	12,126
larke	209,593	125,501	84,092	Marshall	18,522	18,392	130
lay	126,763	107,814	18,949	Mobile	78,625	64,164	14,461
leburne	47,401	40,425	6,976	Monroe	164,808	105,309	59,499
offee	92,688	63,026	29,662	Montgomery	77,446	43,885	33,561
olbert	4,648	3,150	1,498	Morgan	4,308	1,542	2,766
onecuh	185,346	133,133	52,213				
oosa	143,425	108,215	35,210	Perry	75,664	48,337	27,327
ovington	173,795	149,299	24,496	Pickens	88,430	49,227	39,203
renshaw	105,224	72,656	32,568	Pike	93,403	68,445	24,958
ullman	64,505	56,144	8,361				
				Randolph	108,037	88,348	19,689
ale	84,554	49,858	34,696	Russell	64,582	57,855	6,727
allas	85,605	45,491	40,114				
e Kalb	18,207	15,758	2,449	St. Clair	71,910	65,458	6,452
				Shelby	59,541	50,205	9,336
lmore	53,833	35,491	18,342	Sumter	90,689	44,260	46,429
scambia	164,201	139,889	24,312				
towah	27,703	25,925	1,778	Talladega	61,552	52,844	8,708
				Tallapoosa	144,128	114,360	29,768
ayette	40,686	35,210	5,476	Tuscaloosa	72,085	61,914	10,171
ranklin	39,458	20,352	19,106				
				Walker	80,560	71,038	9,522
eneva	69,467	51,497	17,970	Washington	158,892	99,158	59,734
reene	53,550	28,439	25,111	Wilcox	126,543	58,195	68,348
				Winston	56,755	49,197	7,558
ale	44,050	25,104	18,946				
enry	58,932	42,778	16,154				
ouston	54,297	43,319	10,978	All counties	5,458,325	3,819,311	1,639,014

Table 8. *Round pulpwood production in Arkansas, 1972*

County[1]	All species	Softwood	Hardwood	County[1]	All species	Softwood	Hardwood
	- - - Standard cords- - -				- - - Standard cords- - -		
Arkansas	153	...	153	Little River	68,104	50,194	17,910
Ashley	117,490	61,478	56,012	Logan	4,256	3,675	581
				Lonoke	4,954	88	4,866
Baxter	130	130	...				
Boone	4	4	...	Miller	34,815	24,618	10,197
Bradley	20,364	9,968	10,396	Mississippi	81	...	81
				Monroe	2	2	...
Calhoun	78,488	52,554	25,934	Montgomery	14,275	9,912	4,363
Chicot	4,822	4	4,818				
Clark	58,713	34,535	24,178	Nevada	98,251	75,554	22,697
Cleburne	20,792	18,721	2,071	Newton	357	4	353
Cleveland	63,586	33,600	29,986				
Columbia	93,493	72,443	21,050	Ouachita	80,555	52,859	27,696
Conway	43,265	32,346	10,919				
Craighead	11	3	8	Perry	15,888	14,619	1,269
Crawford	3,945	2,230	1,715	Phillips	3,376	4	3,372
Cross	221	...	221	Pike	116,669	90,578	26,091
				Poinsett	23	23	...
Dallas	114,465	60,609	53,856	Polk	29,060	19,139	9,921
Desha	18,473	14	18,459	Pope	32,861	23,052	9,809
Drew	80,954	28,704	52,250	Prairie	44	...	44
				Pulaski	29,275	6,137	23,138
Faulkner	942	574	368				
Franklin	7	7	...	Randolph			
Garland	45,556	40,683	4,873	St. Francis	171	...	171
Grant	144,539	65,602	78,937	Saline	61,293	45,983	15,310
				Scott	16,306	14,889	1,417
Hempstead	51,870	35,700	16,170	Sebastian	43	41	2
Hot Spring	56,185	33,573	22,612	Sevier	40,841	30,102	10,739
Howard	78,677	55,563	23,114				
				Union	168,804	119,376	49,428
Independence	6,534	3,342	3,192				
Izard	1,313	1,082	231	Van Buren	16,521	13,147	3,374
Jackson	492	20	472	White	14,121	3,062	11,059
Jefferson	45,852	19,084	26,768	Woodruff	203	7	196
Johnson	4,498	2,969	1,529				
				Yell	44,872	37,424	7,448
Lafayette	49,696	35,385	14,311				
Lee	9,353	...	9,353	All counties	2,132,138	1,343,265	788,873
Lincoln	21,231	7,849	13,382				

[1]Counties with no pulpwood production are omitted.

County[1]	All species	Softwood	Hardwood	County[1]	All species	Softwood	Hardwood
	- - - *Standard cords*- - -				- - - *Standard cords*- - -		
chua	50,145	45,145	5,000	Lake	8,234	8,234	...
				Lee	493	493	...
er	106,356	105,756	600	Leon	31,954	31,524	430
'	99,212	98,678	534	Levy	119,998	87,630	32,368
dford	71,053	68,568	2,485	Liberty	49,254	43,789	5,465
vard	168	168	...				
ward	21	21	...	Madison	82,207	74,436	7,771
				Manatee	933	933	...
houn	102,806	99,903	2,903	Marion	86,001	71,174	14,827
rlotte	850	805	45				
rus	5,699	5,212	487	Nassau	178,965	164,722	14,243
y	55,844	53,858	1,986				
lier	1,924	1,924	...	Okaloosa	31,338	26,173	5,165
umbia	120,759	116,896	3,863	Okeechobee	1,598	1,598	...
				Orange	144	144	...
e	1,616	1,616	...	Osceola	45,703	45,703	...
Soto	288	288	...				
ie	93,177	85,423	7,754	Palm Beach	669	669	...
al	58,064	56,576	1,488	Pasco	13,790	11,234	2,556
				Pinellas	48	48	...
ambia	89,830	85,267	4,563	Polk	15,718	15,718	...
				Putnam	69,139	60,165	8,974
gler	33,544	30,544	3,000				
nklin	51,254	51,244	10	St. Johns	89,852	77,786	12,066
				St. Lucie	124	124	...
sden	29,119	28,267	852	Santa Rosa	90,000	85,778	4,222
christ	25,108	17,669	7,439	Sarasota	1,811	1,811	...
des	5,906	5,906	...	Seminole	4,430	4,430	...
f	23,699	18,208	5,491	Suwannee	63,034	57,962	5,072
ilton	54,575	53,518	1,057	Taylor	203,867	203,229	638
dee	23,283	23,283	...				
dry	16,012	16,012	...	Union	43,947	43,787	160
nando	4,141	2,427	1,714				
hlands	3,980	3,980	...	Volusia	28,135	27,545	590
lsborough	5,532	5,532	...				
mes	73,532	65,813	7,719	Wakulla	43,601	42,013	1,588
				Walton	73,250	61,431	11,819
ian River	2,704	2,704	...	Washington	65,088	60,867	4,221
kson	127,762	113,584	14,178				
ferson	34,978	31,397	3,581				
ayette	79,893	79,893	...	All counties	2,896,159	2,687,235	208,924

unties with no pulpwood production are omitted.

Table 10. *Round pulpwood production in Georgia, 1972*

County[1]	All species	Softwood	Hardwood	County[1]	All species	Softwood	Hardwood
	- - - *Standard cords* - - -				- - - *Standard cords* - - -		
Appling	130,394	111,978	18,416	Fannin	19,132	9,613	9,519
Atkinson	104,366	103,871	495	Fayette	9,526	8,902	624
				Floyd	22,238	19,188	3,050
Bacon	65,561	64,712	849	Forsyth	15,165	14,920	245
Baker	18,488	17,546	942	Franklin	24,110	18,909	5,201
Baldwin	26,741	25,182	1,559	Fulton	20,722	20,035	687
Banks	9,353	8,799	554				
Barrow	22,131	19,730	2,401	Gilmer	9,603	7,325	2,278
Bartow	22,201	21,745	456	Glascock	49	49	...
Ben Hill	76,701	72,269	4,432	Glynn	62,790	45,093	17,697
Berrien	30,471	26,538	3,933	Gordon	23,307	20,920	2,387
Bibb	17,694	15,155	2,539	Grady	46,149	33,215	12,934
Bleckley	21,777	14,200	7,577	Greene	49,360	42,162	7,198
Brantley	130,075	118,417	11,658	Gwinnett	19,879	19,507	372
Brooks	37,606	32,056	5,550				
Bryan	73,657	69,845	3,812	Habersham	8,045	4,786	3,259
Bulloch	21,905	20,709	1,196	Hall	24,881	24,286	595
Burke	92,827	70,689	22,138	Hancock	71,650	55,631	16,019
Butts	24,764	23,836	928	Haralson	41,085	34,598	6,487
				Harris	59,938	55,612	4,326
Calhoun	21,357	17,929	3,428	Hart	3,402	3,352	50
Camden	81,900	68,741	13,159	Heard	59,078	55,018	4,060
Candler	21,289	18,447	2,842	Henry	30,626	26,861	3,765
Carroll	55,499	51,292	4,207	Houston	48,158	41,440	6,718
Catoosa	6,128	4,224	1,904				
Charlton	120,846	116,084	4,762	Irwin	1.700	1,600	100
Chatham	21,956	18,239	3,717				
Chattahoochee	65,576	51,182	14,394	Jackson	27,554	25,460	2,094
Chattooga	21,213	19,079	2,134	Jasper	51,941	46,790	5,151
Cherokee	32,201	30,781	1,420	Jeff Davis	33,446	30,543	2,903
Clarke	6,705	6,555	150	Jefferson	31,474	27,174	4,300
Clay	52,728	38,381	14,347	Jenkins	35,031	30,460	4,571
Clayton	5,429	5,162	267	Johnson	28,122	22,593	5,529
Clinch	168,572	168,572	...	Jones	55,365	47,634	7,731
Cobb	20,362	20,078	284				
Coffee	70,249	68,476	1,773	Lamar	24,985	22,624	2,361
Colquitt	33,437	26,437	7,000	Lanier	8,734	8,634	100
Columbia	40,643	26,931	13,712	Laurens	57,117	45,465	11,652
Cook	9,100	9,063	37	Lee	6,565	6,411	154
Coweta	47,203	46,151	1,052	Liberty	100,518	80,602	19,916
Crawford	52,233	45,437	6,796	Lincoln	15,751	14,553	1,198
Crisp	6,732	6,669	63	Long	46,139	42,436	3,703
				Lowndes	26,067	26,067	...
Dade	1,063	943	120	Lumpkin	5,238	5,229	9
Dawson	7,539	7,443	96				
Decatur	75,322	60,991	14,331	McDuffie	15,676	10,751	4,925
De Kalb	3,041	3,013	28	McIntosh	70,582	67,184	3,398
Dodge	101,209	88,754	12,455	Macon	35,944	27,072	8,872
Dooly	10,564	6,637	3,927	Madison	22,715	20,903	1,812
Dougherty	45,734	42,340	3,394	Marion	24,487	21,298	3,189
Douglas	22,603	22,006	597	Meriwether	60,292	57,730	2,562
				Miller	23,796	19,835	3,961
Early	40,400	33,096	7,304	Mitchell	67,924	65,306	2,618
Echols	61,061	61,039	22	Monroe	57,643	54,405	3,238
Effingham	45,679	41,578	4,101	Montgomery	45,195	40,527	4,668
Elbert	31,685	29,116	2,569	Morgan	15,186	13,490	1,696
Emanuel	71,256	67,171	4,085	Murray	23,418	21,130	2,288
Evans	20,391	17,642	2,749	Muscogee	6,494	5,407	1,087

12

Table 10. *Round pulpwood production in Georgia, 1972* (Continued)

County[1]	All species	Softwood	Hardwood	County[1]	All species	Softwood	Hardwood
	- - - *Standard cords* - - -				- - - *Standard cords* - - -		
Newton	15,991	15,114	877	Taylor	30,430	26,962	3,468
				Telfair	78,166	66,805	11,361
Oconee	28,561	24,897	3,664	Terrell	36,645	36,063	582
Oglethorpe	44,122	38,691	5,431	Thomas	74,476	62,357	12,119
				Tift	15,652	14,320	1,332
Paulding	30,825	27,072	3,753	Toombs	59,109	58,132	977
Peach	7,493	7,109	384	Towns	1,227	1,079	148
Pickens	27,765	24,895	2,870	Treutlen	14,973	13,773	1,200
Pierce	47,721	47,048	673	Troup	64,180	58,303	5,877
Pike	8,806	8,462	344	Turner	12,962	12,962	...
Polk	28,149	25,760	2,389	Twiggs	26,960	23,113	3,847
Pulaski	17,677	15,771	1,906				
Putnam	30,949	25,244	5,705	Union	7,826	5,836	1,990
				Upson	57,654	53,485	4,169
Quitman	11,804	10,480	1,324				
				Walker	21,840	18,705	3,135
Rabun	6,600	2,435	4,165	Walton	10,337	9,653	684
Randolph	50,097	36,311	13,786	Ware	189,898	185,839	4,059
Richmond	40,024	9,515	30,509	Warren	19,146	16,157	2,989
				Washington	56,896	49,230	7,666
Schley	6,840	6,571	269	Wayne	119,731	111,388	8,343
Screven	27,466	23,917	3,549	Webster	21,549	19,814	1.735
Seminole	20,226	18,413	1,813	Wheeler	43,818	35,542	8,276
Spalding	12,567	12,297	270	White	2,516	2,513	3
Stephens	10,291	6,277	4,014	Whitfield	11,965	9,933	2,032
Stewart	87,654	76,643	11,011	Wilcox	46,550	44,229	2,321
Sumter	27,075	25,611	1,464	Wilkes	41,529	34,165	7,364
				Wilkinson	69,230	59,376	9,854
Talbot	53,723	48,569	5,154	Worth	43,564	42,274	1,290
Taliaferro	9,601	8,151	1,450				
Tattnall	53,096	46,037	7,059	All counties	6,003,561	5,316,989	686,572

[1]Counties with no pulpwood production are omitted.

13

Table 11. *Round pulpwood production in Louisiana, 1972*

Parish[1]	All species	Softwood	Hardwood	Parish[1]	All species	Softwood	Hardwood
	- - - *Standard cords*- - -				- - - *Standard cords*- - -		
Acadia	7,974	7,903	71	Madison	21,559	78	21,481
Allen	92,980	78,971	14,009	Morehouse	61,546	30,682	30,864
Ascension	812	...	812				
Avoyelles	28,347	5,074	23,273	Natchitoches	151,707	113,878	37,829
Beauregard	197,174	193,558	3,616	Orleans	18	6	12
Bienville	143,732	120,190	23,542	Ouachita	60,119	42,629	17,490
Bossier	90,044	63,065	26,979				
				Pointe Coupee	36,135	102	36,033
Caddo	52,917	39,891	13,026				
Calcasieu	34,999	33,624	1,375	Rapides	186,823	142,311	44,512
Caldwell	46,643	32,239	14,404	Red River	49,827	41,226	8,601
Cameron	7	5	2	Richland	6,554	375	6,179
Catahoula	75,280	22,393	52,887				
Claiborne	98,659	76,889	21,770	Sabine	214,616	197,802	16,814
Concordia	30,889	...	30,889	St. Helena	63,141	54,793	8,348
				St. James	469	...	469
De Soto	111,127	90,933	20,194	St. Landry	5,381	...	5,381
				St. Martin	113	81	32
East Baton Rouge	4,784	204	4,580	St. Tammany	38,629	33,214	5,415
East Carroll	11,915	86	11,829				
East Feliciana	22,722	17,594	5,128	Tangipahoa	55,260	44,446	10,814
Evangeline	33,861	30,062	3,799	Tensas	24,463	62	24,401
				Terrebonne	6	6	...
Franklin	1,227	50	1,177				
				Union	170,964	117,920	53,044
Grant	106,434	74,425	32,009				
				Vermilion	11	11	...
Iberia	9,564	...	9,564	Vernon	213,309	200,542	12,767
Iberville	2,581	112	2,469				
				Washington	25,258	20,921	4,337
Jackson	80,556	61,832	18,724	Webster	79,111	62,652	16,459
Jefferson Davis	6,327	5,157	1,170	West Baton Rouge	624	54	570
				West Carroll	119	38	81
La Salle	101,605	85,245	16,360	West Feliciana	5,488	1,759	3,729
Lincoln	93,284	75,332	17,952	Winn	156,859	100,479	56,380
Livingston	50,211	30,332	19,879	All parishes	3,164,764	2,351,233	813,531

[1]Parishes with no pulpwood production are omitted.

14

Table 12. *Round pulpwood production in Mississippi, 1972*

County[1]	All species	Softwood	Hardwood	County[1]	All species	Softwood	Hardwood
	- - - Standard cords- - -				- - - Standard cords- - -		
Adams	34,619	1,645	32,974	Madison	39,692	18,687	21,005
Alcorn	10,355	8,816	1,539	Marion	69,549	46,837	22,712
Amite	84,426	71,004	13,422	Marshall	17,407	11,365	6,042
Attala	76,385	57,650	18,735	Monroe	16,114	10,960	5,154
				Montgomery	37,334	25,712	11,622
Benton	11,826	9,437	2,389				
Bolivar	14,024	...	14,024	Neshoba	61,191	41,815	19,376
				Newton	94,056	55,261	38,795
Calhoun	9,577	8,099	1,478	Noxubee	35,912	15,852	20,060
Carroll	13,133	8,002	5,131				
Chickasaw	21,939	16,134	5,805	Oktibbeha	16,869	11,745	5,124
Choctaw	42,761	28,069	14,692				
Claiborne	47,911	14,454	33,457	Panola	6,838	890	5,948
Clarke	159,201	96,795	62,406	Pearl River	57,213	45,484	11,729
Clay	7,437	5,019	2,418	Perry	62,572	52,368	10,204
Coahoma	4,302	...	4,302	Pike	93,612	80,280	13,332
Copiah	125,303	91,397	33,906	Pontotoc	8,851	4,509	4,342
Covington	66,067	51,043	15,024	Prentiss	26,171	20,786	5,385
Forrest	37,458	27,064	10,394	Quitman	319	290	29
Franklin	60,576	29,908	30,668				
				Rankin	119,344	77,130	42,214
George	54,547	45,273	9,274				
Greene	94,642	57,966	36,676	Scott	65,943	45,273	20,670
Grenada	5,077	2,527	2,550	Sharkey	4,074	70	4,004
				Simpson	64,271	51,455	12,816
Hancock	54,789	50,716	4,073	Smith	37,816	25,025	12,791
Harrison	55,686	50,046	5,640	Stone	36,481	26,041	10,440
Hinds	37,231	15,124	22,107	Sunflower	267	3	264
Holmes	48,597	23,118	25,479				
Humphreys	3,782	...	3,782	Tallahatchie	3,579	1,261	2,318
				Tate	4,361	...	4,361
Issaquena	11,039	...	11,039	Tippah	32,960	26,485	6,475
Itawamba	40,112	31,780	8,332	Tishomingo	50,536	41,153	9,383
				Tunica	12	9	3
Jackson	98,953	89,668	9,285				
Jasper	111,281	78,580	32,701	Union	12,348	9,876	2,472
Jefferson	63,295	25,296	37,999				
Jefferson Davis	51,552	47,024	4,528	Walthall	52,721	39,096	13,625
Jones	71,052	37,152	33,900	Warren	23,558	1,147	22,411
				Washington	3,628	...	3,628
Kemper	56,958	34,726	22,232	Wayne	89,584	54,649	34,935
				Webster	42,745	30,488	12,257
Lafayette	19,098	9,879	9,219	Wilkinson	73,224	26,265	46,959
Lamar	27,006	19,521	7,485	Winston	57,019	40,395	16,624
Lauderdale	96,822	60,491	36,331				
Lawrence	58,974	49,221	9,753	Yalobusha	13,445	8,481	4,964
Leake	80,959	62,532	18,427	Yazoo	16,314	517	15,797
Lee	6,430	5,273	1,157				
Leflore	1,409	410	999				
Lincoln	105,259	86,646	18,613				
Lowndes	15,719	12,402	3,317	All counties	3,545,499	2,367,567	1,177,932

[1]Counties with no pulpwood production are omitted.

15

Table 13. *Round pulpwood production in North Carolina, 1972*

County[1]	All species	Softwood	Hardwood	County[1]	All species	Softwood	Hardwood
	- - -	Standard cords	- - -		- - -	Standard cords	- - -
Alamance	9,357	3,654	5,703	Lee	20,209	10,728	9,481
Alexander	12,774	11,156	1,618	Lenoir	48,088	33,477	14,611
Alleghany	3	3	...	Lincoln	11,536	8,598	2,938
Anson	77,907	48,479	29,428				
Avery	1,213	...	1,213	McDowell	17,136	8,644	8,492
				Macon	5,742	544	5,198
Beaufort	158,815	108,358	50,457	Madison	4,739	2,692	2,047
Bertie	60,143	24,999	35,144	Martin	54,920	38,709	16,211
Bladen	66,130	45,955	20,175	Mecklenburg	15,822	10,477	5,345
Brunswick	112,562	93,112	19,450	Mitchell	1,116	...	1,116
Buncombe	33,086	10,039	23,047	Montgomery	46,456	27,626	18,830
Burke	39,682	23,972	15,710	Moore	45,483	26,146	19,337
Cabarrus	11,416	6,485	4,931	Nash	45,655	25,404	20,251
Caldwell	11,426	7,714	3,712	New Hanover	11,359	7,711	3,648
Camden	5,591	3,133	2,458	Northampton	45,042	20,483	24,559
Carteret	38,207	27,319	10,888				
Caswell	10,962	5,147	5,815	Onslow	102,837	82,055	20,782
Catawba	10,928	8,812	2,116	Orange	27,708	19,246	8,462
Chatham	60,328	36,780	23,548				
Cherokee	40,963	17,200	23,763	Pamlico	27,400	18,162	9,238
Chowan	12,748	5,058	7,690	Pasquotank	8,920	3,875	5,045
Clay	3,997	3,558	439	Pender	52,357	35,568	16,789
Cleveland	14,747	10,592	4,155	Perquimans	13,186	3,623	9,563
Columbus	78,539	50,524	28,015	Person	20,645	7,193	13,452
Craven	112,311	77,022	35,289	Pitt	39,169	26,436	12,733
Cumberland	32,938	25,712	7,226	Polk	16,012	5,385	10,627
Currituck	6,807	2,099	4,708				
				Randolph	23,381	9,028	14,353
Dare	8,548	8,174	374	Richmond	49,417	36,309	13,108
Davidson	14,053	10,617	3,436	Robeson	42,990	22,662	20,328
Davie	9,021	5,062	3,959	Rockingham	20,038	15,510	4,528
Duplin	67,647	39,524	28,123	Rowan	6,841	5,232	1,609
Durham	22,095	11,550	10,545	Rutherford	44,338	29,386	14,952
Edgecombe	29,474	19,588	9,886	Sampson	63,095	35,570	27,525
				Scotland	48,736	43,768	4,968
Forsyth	12,431	8,614	3,817	Stanly	19,745	10,451	9,294
Franklin	72,505	46,698	25,807	Stokes	10,629	6,874	3,755
				Surry	17,200	13,607	3,593
Gaston	10,757	7,883	2,874	Swain	11,064	6,787	4,277
Gates	26,395	11,420	14,975				
Graham	203	...	203	Transylvania	19,192	2,565	16,627
Granville	30,605	14,350	16,255	Tyrrell	45,603	34,079	11,524
Greene	13,144	8,902	4,242				
Guilford	12,178	7,091	5,087	Union	29,782	17,573	12,209
Halifax	58,356	36,892	21,464	Vance	5,574	2,100	3,474
Harnett	16,116	11,393	4,723				
Haywood	14,543	2,209	12,334	Wake	43,899	24,917	18,982
Henderson	31,075	7,781	23,294	Warren	56,563	33,783	22,780
Hertford	36,771	14,584	22,187	Washington	24,200	15,600	8,600
Hoke	26,551	22,514	4,037	Wayne	20,439	12,006	8,433
Hyde	44,664	33,002	11,662	Wilkes	15,625	7,715	7,910
				Wilson	18,273	14,090	4,183
Iredell	26,885	21,338	5,547				
				Yadkin	9,831	7,634	2,197
Jackson	19,521	1,863	17,658				
Johnston	18,852	9,375	9,477				
Jones	57,667	45,617	12,050	All counties	3,031,629	1,892,951	1,138,678

[1]Counties with no pulpwood production are omitted.

16

Table 14. *Round pulpwood production in Oklahoma, 1972*

County[1]	All species	Softwood	Hardwood	County[1]	All species	Softwood	Hardwood
	- - - *Standard cords* - - -				- - - *Standard cords* - - -		
Alfalfa	1,148	...	1,148	Kiowa	847	...	847
Beckham	2,455	...	2,455	Le Flore	9,158	2,614	6,544
Blaine	3,045	...	3,045	Lincoln	4,393	...	4,393
				Love	185	...	185
Caddo	303	...	303				
Carter	971	...	971	McCurtain	215,241	165,168	50,073
Choctaw	2,752	1,866	886				
Creek	4,147	...	4,147	Okfuskee	990	...	990
Custer	1,876	...	1,876	Oklahoma	869	...	869
				Okmulgee	126	...	126
Ellis	1,709	...	1,709				
				Pittsburg	2,188	...	2,188
Haskell	2,057	200	1,857	Pontotoc	45	...	45
Hughes	2,016	...	2,016	Pushmataha	28,872	20,943	7,929
Jefferson	261	...	261	All counties	285,654	190,791	94,863

[1]Counties with no pulpwood production are omitted.

Table 15. *Round pulpwood production in South Carolina, 1972*

County	All species	Softwood	Hardwood	County	All species	Softwood	Hardwood
	- - - *Standard cords* - - -				- - - *Standard cords* - - -		
Abbeville	39,972	32,020	7,952	Jasper	35,754	31,604	4,150
Aiken	94,511	80,009	14,502	Kershaw	130,326	106,582	23,744
Allendale	33,163	24,607	8,556				
Anderson	41,731	36,876	4,855	Lancaster	49,077	31,696	17,381
				Laurens	70,497	58,857	11,640
Bamberg	24,303	17,882	6,421	Lee	24,511	17,511	7,000
Barnwell	42,604	41,986	618	Lexington	58,441	53,519	4,922
Beaufort	14,461	13,923	538				
Berkeley	74,754	54,764	19,990	McCormick	92,448	78,135	14,313
				Marion	38,552	15,102	23,450
Calhoun	7,608	7,256	352	Marlboro	35,603	17,749	17,854
Charleston	45,521	36,072	9,449				
Cherokee	17,033	13,287	3,746	Newberry	95,569	85,020	10,549
Chester	90,209	68,186	22,023				
Chesterfield	71,839	52,494	19,345	Oconee	34,108	20,979	13,129
Clarendon	35,311	26,009	9,302	Orangeburg	60,130	53,506	6,624
Colleton	81,989	63,619	18,370				
				Pickens	22,455	15,182	7,273
Darlington	28,280	18,780	9,500				
Dillon	42,142	27,053	15,089	Richland	73,022	63,547	9,475
Dorchester	30,611	20,963	9,648				
				Saluda	56,188	43,071	13,117
Edgefield	61,959	51,823	10,136	Spartanburg	39,076	30,939	8,137
				Sumter	31,705	23,857	7,848
Fairfield	127,457	107,055	20,402				
Florence	27,884	14,195	13,689	Union	57,092	50,496	6,596
Georgetown	140,120	106,635	33,485	Williamsburg	84,261	56,218	28,043
Greenville	16,110	13,890	2,220				
Greenwood	85,636	71,540	14,096	York	61,425	44,296	17,129
Hampton	44,278	35,642	8,636				
Horry	77,864	56,557	21,307	All counties	2,547,590	1,990,989	556,601

Table 16. *Round pulpwood production in Tennessee, 1972*

County[1]	All species	Softwood	Hardwood	County[1]	All species	Softwood	Hardwood
	- - - *Standard cords* - - -				- - - *Standard cords* - - -		
Anderson	3,689	1,733	1,956	Johnson	2,952	108	2,844
Benton	17,168	1,504	15,664	Knox	5,403	4,113	1,290
Bledsoe	8,204	6,413	1.791				
Blount	12,182	8,951	3,231	Lawrence	5,268	1,393	3,875
Bradley	16,760	15,102	1,658	Lewis	3,927	4	3,923
				Lincoln	553	...	553
Campbell	11,582	3,766	7,816	Loudon	4,336	1,726	2,610
Carroll	2,506	207	2,299				
Carter	2,393	87	2,306	McMinn	23,897	20,707	3,190
Chester	1,412	1,189	223	McNairy	9,006	5,908	3,098
Claiborne	2	...	2	Madison	118	61	57
Cocke	9,617	4,185	5,432	Marion	14	14	...
Coffee	3,281	3,281	...	Meigs	11,285	5,609	5,676
Cumberland	18,073	5,522	12,551	Monroe	23,577	14,021	9,556
				Montgomery	307	...	307
Decatur	595	536	59	Morgan	6,139	4,290	1,849
Dickson	4	...	4				
Dyer	55	...	55	Obion	45	...	45
Fayette	1,246	756	490	Perry	301	16	285
Fentress	4,573	2,972	1,601	Polk	9,720	6,580	3,140
				Putnam	10,523	3,221	7,302
Gibson	112	5	107				
Giles	2,405	8	2,397	Rhea	19,784	6,716	13,068
Grainger	273	...	273	Roane	9,895	5,864	4,031
Greene	3,776	756	3,020				
Grundy	6,859	3,682	3,177	Scott	19,071	5,421	13,650
				Sequatchie	4,234	1,476	2,758
Hamblen	108	108	...	Sevier	873	648	225
Hamilton	14,978	6,832	8,146	Shelby	34	32	2
Hancock	194	7	187	Stewart	556	...	556
Hardeman	10,431	6,238	4,193	Sullivan	9,076	332	8,744
Hardin	24,840	8,285	16,555				
Hawkins	2,407	88	2,319	Unicoi	1,957	71	1,886
Haywood	5	5	...	Union	1,126	98	1,028
Henderson	1,088	875	213				
Henry	5,253	47	5,206	Warren	2,534	2,114	420
Hickman	3,789	98	3,691	Washington	1,398	51	1,347
Houston	1,343	...	1,343	Wayne	20,686	6,927	13,759
Humphreys	48,790	...	48,790	Weakley	4,624	32	4,592
Jefferson	12	...	12	All counties	453,224	180,791	272,433

[1]Counties with no pulpwood production are omitted.

Table 17. *Round pulpwood production in Texas, 1972*

County[1]	All species	Softwood	Hardwood	County[1]	All species	Softwood	Hardwood
	- - - Standard cords - - -				- - - Standard cords - - -		
Anderson	38,330	36,605	1,725	Morris	13,365	11,857	1,508
Angelina	92,820	77,818	15,002				
				Nacogdoches	103,810	93,673	10,137
Bowie	39,683	31,445	8,238	Newton	127,749	87,990	39,759
Brazoria	33	...	33				
Burleson	908	...	908	Orange	41,007	38,134	2,873
Camp	9,863	9,651	212	Panola	88,441	81,946	6,495
Cass	54,089	46,400	7,689	Polk	152,477	133,321	19,156
Chambers	1,726	1,698	28				
Cherokee	83,568	75,801	7,767	Red River	11,757	10,816	941
Cooke	890	...	890	Robertson	83	...	83
				Rusk	61,322	50,001	11,321
Franklin	8,229	4,499	3,730				
				Sabine	44,247	39,313	4,934
Gregg	27,706	25,648	2,058	San Augustine	77,090	64,376	12,714
Grimes	9,653	8,930	723	San Jacinto	33,097	27,861	5,236
				Shelby	116,303	107,840	8,463
Hardin	97,759	72,417	25,342	Smith	31,517	31,342	175
Harris	29,786	24,752	5,034				
Harrison	81,885	74,206	7,679	Titus	2,295	1,953	342
Houston	68,137	64,434	3,703	Trinity	92,793	81,801	10,992
				Tyler	97,073	62,619	34,454
Jasper	142,367	102,898	39,469				
Jefferson	1,533	967	566	Upshur	69,435	66,855	2,580
Lee	26	...	26	Walker	37,165	26,173	10,992
Leon	4,780	4,780	...	Waller	861	...	861
Liberty	50,607	25,253	25,354	Wood	9,665	9,112	553
Marion	63,236	54,887	8,349				
Montgomery	79,469	66,052	13,417	All counties	2,198,635	1,836,124	362,511

[1]Counties with no pulpwood production are omitted.

Table 18. *Round pulpwood production in Virginia, 1972*

County[1]	All species	Softwood	Hardwood	County[1]	All species	Softwood	Hardwood
	- - - Standard cords - - -				- - - Standard cords - - -		
Accomack	8,883	8,655	228	Lancaster	2,615	2,447	168
Albemarle	33,571	14,592	18,979	Lee	759	28	731
Alleghany	21,712	3,014	18,698	Louisa	21,065	12,603	8,462
Amelia	18,252	11,954	6,298	Lunenburg	30,563	14,819	15,744
Amherst	27,952	10,671	17,281				
Appomattox	53,908	24,607	29,301	Madison	176	125	51
Augusta	23,711	2,409	21,302	Mathews	1,190	1,145	45
				Mecklenburg	32,215	17,106	15,109
Bath	26,584	2,746	23,838	Middlesex	2,998	1,836	1,162
Bedford	54,255	20,282	33,973	Montgomery	82	39	43
Bland	7	...	7				
Botetourt	27,995	2,455	25,540	Nansemond	17,098	5,598	11,500
Brunswick	98,126	58,984	39,142	Nelson	37,705	17,039	20,666
Buchanan	33	18	15	New Kent	14,234	11,009	3,225
Buckingham	89,514	33,247	56,267	Newport News	625	413	212
				Northampton	2,093	2,058	35
Campbell	63,102	29,453	33,649	Northumberland	2,613	2,588	25
Caroline	20,398	15,955	4,443	Nottoway	59,297	26,458	32,839
Carroll	2,629	1,400	1,229				
Charles City	17,787	5,911	11,876	Orange	2,344	1,259	1,085
Charlotte	33,089	17,671	15,418				
Chesapeake	2,320	512	1,808	Page	2,346	1,379	967
Chesterfield	21,868	14,293	7,575	Patrick	7,033	4,477	2,556
Craig	10,225	1,518	8,707	Pittsylvania	67,871	48,386	19,485
Culpeper	4,685	4,108	577	Powhatan	9,381	4,814	4,567
Cumberland	5,708	2,338	3,370	Prince Edward	59,000	34,677	24,323
				Prince George	31,992	16,846	15,146
Dinwiddie	32,491	20,188	12,303	Prince William	11,004	9,767	1,237
				Pulaski	477	217	260
Essex	7,606	6,462	1,144				
				Rappahannock	27	20	7
Fairfax	171	151	20	Richmond	6,620	6,338	282
Fauquier	9,058	8,239	819	Roanoke	2,443	638	1,805
Floyd	164	119	45	Rockbridge	50,989	9,905	41,084
Fluvanna	30,970	14,161	16,809	Rockingham	4,405	1,525	2,880
Franklin	29,827	15,014	14,813	Russell	241	9	232
Frederick	5,095	4,423	672				
				Scott	3,038	111	2,927
Giles	53	28	25	Shenandoah	4,275	1,260	3,015
Gloucester	5,770	4,049	1,721	Smyth	3,292	121	3,171
Goochland	23,979	13,056	10,923	Southampton	53,165	14,367	38,798
Grayson	33	6	27	Spotsylvania	17,248	13,843	3,405
Greene	1,565	872	693	Stafford	70	61	9
Greensville	59,892	41,474	18,418	Surry	26,417	4,564	21,853
				Sussex	51,070	24,360	26,710
Halifax	15,112	5,574	9,538				
Hanover	15,228	11,752	3,476	Virginia Beach	1,409	382	1,027
Henrico	3,918	2,564	1,354				
Henry	20,181	15,441	4,740	Warren	1,025	313	712
Highland	2,409	64	2,345	Washington	6,082	222	5,860
				Westmoreland	4,019	3,988	31
Isle of Wight	11,838	2,818	9,020	Wise	3,511	129	3,382
				Wythe	3,635	1,216	2,419
James City	11,400	6,322	5,078				
				York	1,943	1,218	725
King and Queen	38,560	30,760	7,800				
King George	19	19	...				
King William	21,215	15,611	5,604	All counties	1,674,568	827,683	846,885

[1]Counties with no pulpwood production are omitted.

20

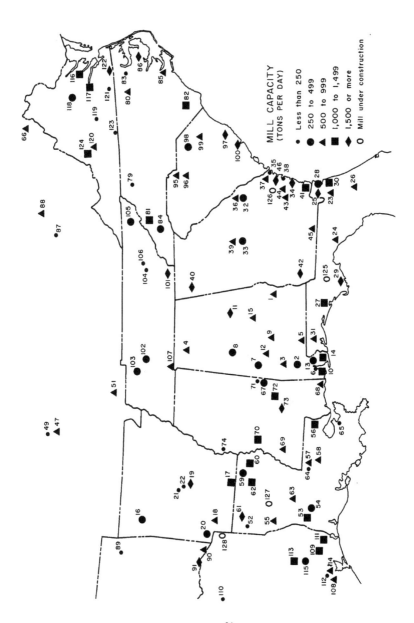

Figure 5. *Mills using southern pulpwood in 1972, and mills under construction.*
Numbers at mill locations correspond to numbers in tables 19 and 20.

MILL CAPACITY
(TONS PER DAY)

• Less than 250
● 250 to 499
▲ 500 to 999
■ 1,000 to 1,499
◆ 1,500 or more
○ Mill under construction

Location	Map code[1]	Company	All processes	Sulfate	Groundwood and other mechanical	Semi-chemical	Soda and sulfite
					- - - - - - -*Tons* - - - - - - -		
ALABAMA							
Mahrt	(1)	Alabama Kraft Co., Div. Ga. Kraft Co.	975	975	...	...	...
Jackson	(2)	Allied Paper Inc.	470	470	...	...	...
Naheola	(3)	American Can Co.	900	900	...	...	...
Courtland	(4)	Champion International	500	500	...	...	...
Brewton	(5)	Container Corp. of America	800	800	...	...	...
Mobile	(6)	General Aniline and Film Corp.	48	...	48	...	...
Demopolis	(7)	Gulf States Paper Corp.	400	400	...	...	...
Tuscaloosa	(8)	Gulf States Paper Corp.	450	450	...	...	...
Riverdale	(9)	Hammermill Paper Co., Riverdale Div.	500	500	...	...	...
Mobile	(10)	International Paper Co.	1,315	1,015	300	...	...
Coosa Pines	(11)	Kimberly-Clark Corp., Coosa River Newsprint Div.	1,590	650	940	...	...
Pine Hill	(12)	McMillan Bloedel United, Inc.	925	925	...	...	...
Mobile	(13)	National Gypsum Co.	400	...	200	200	...
Mobile	(14)	Scott Paper Co.	1,400	1,400	...	...	...
Montgomery	(15)	Union Camp Corp.	870	870	...	...	...
		Total	11,543	9,855	1,488	200	...
ARKANSAS							
Morrilton	(16)	Arkansas Kraft Corp.	380	380	...	...	...
Crossett	(17)	Georgia-Pacific Corp., Crossett Division-Paper	1,220	1,220	...	...	...
Camden	(18)	International Paper Co.	750	750	...	...	...
Pine Bluff	(19)	International Paper Co.	1,700	1,300	400	...	...
Ashdown	(20)	Nekoosa-Edwards Paper Co., Inc.	400	400	...	...	...
Little Rock	(21)	Superwood Corp.	140	...	140	...	...
Pine Bluff	(22)	Weyerhaeuser Co., Pine Bluff Operation	150	150	...	...	...
		Total	4,740	4,200	540	...	...
FLORIDA							
Jacksonville	(23)	Alton Box Board Co.	625	625	...	...	...
Foley	(24)	The Buckeye Cellulose Corp.	923	923	...	...	...
Fernandina Beach	(25)	Container Corp. of America	1,700	1,700	...	...	...
Palatka	(26)	Hudson Pulp and Paper Corp.	950	950	...	...	...
Panama City	(27)	International Paper Co.	1,375	1,375	...	...	...
Fernandina Beach	(28)	I.T.T. Rayonier Inc.	375	...	...	...	375
Port St. Joe	(29)	St. Joe Paper Co.	1,700	1,700	...	...	...
Jacksonville	(30)	St. Regis Paper Co.	1,400	1,400	...	...	...
Pensacola	(31)	St. Regis Paper Co.	900	900	...	...	...
		Total	9,948	9,573	...	...	375
GEORGIA							
Augusta	(32)	Abitibi Southern Corp.	375	...	375	...	...
Macon	(33)	Armstrong Cork Co.	400	...	400	...	...
Brunswick	(34)	Brunswick Pulp and Paper Co.	1,520	1,520	...	...	...
Savannah	(35)	Certain-teed Products Corp.	65	...	...	65	...
Augusta	(36)	Continental Can Co., Inc.	700	700	...	...	...
Port Wentworth	(37)	Continental Can Co., Inc.	600	600	...	...	...
Savannah	(38)	General Aniline and Film Corp.	48	...	48	...	...
Macon	(39)	Georgia Kraft Co., Mead Div.	850	850	...	...	...
Rome	(40)	Georgia Kraft Co., Krannert Div.	1,600	1,600	...	...	...
St. Marys	(41)	Gilman Paper Co., St. Marys Kraft Div.	1,000	1,000	...	...	...
Cedar Springs	(42)	Great Northern Paper Co., Southern Div.	2,025	1,700	...	325	...
Jesup	(43)	I.T.T. Rayonier Inc.	675	675	...	...	...
Riceboro	(44)	Interstate Paper Corp.	500	500	...	...	...
Valdosta	(45)	Owens-Illinois, Forest Products Div.	875	875	...	...	...
Savannah	(46)	Union Camp Corp.	3,000	2,600	...	400	...
		Total	14,233	12,620	823	790	...

Table 19. *Mills using southern pulpwood in 1972, by process and capacity* (Continued)

Location	Map code[1]	Company	Pulping capacity, 24 hours[2]				
			All processes	Sulfate	Groundwood and other mechanical	Semi-chemical	Soda and sulfite
			- - - - - - -*Tons*- - - - - - -				
ILLINOIS							
Alton	(47)	Alton Box Board Co.	800	...	...	800	...
Peoria	(48)	The Celotex Corp.	110	...	110	...	...
East St. Louis	(49)	Certain-teed Products Corp.	100	...	100	...	...
Wilmington	(50)	Philip Carey Corp.	150	...	150	...	...
		Total	1,160	...	360	800	...
KENTUCKY							
Wickliffe	(51)	Westvaco Corp.	600	600	...	...	...
		Total	600	600	...	...	...
LOUISIANA							
Shreveport	(52)	Bird and Son, Inc.	150	...	...	150	...
DeRidder	(53)	Boise Southern Co.	1,300	950	350	...	...
Elizabeth	(54)	Calkraft Paper Co., Inc.	305	305	...	...	...
Hodge	(55)	Continental Can Co., Inc.	750	550	...	200	...
Bogalusa	(56)	Crown Zellerbach Corp.	1,435	1,300	...	135	...
St. Francisville	(57)	Crown Zellerbach Corp.	500	500	...	...	...
Port Hudson	(58)	Georgia-Pacific Corp., Crossett Division	600	600	...	...	...
Bastrop	(59)	International Paper Co. (Bastrop Mill)	485	...	...	485	...
Bastrop	(60)	International Paper Co. (Louisiana Mill)	1,100	1,100	...	...	...
Springhill	(61)	International Paper Co.	1,625	1,625	...	...	...
West Monroe	(62)	Olinkraft, Inc.	1,385	1,135	...	250	...
Pineville	(63)	Pineville Kraft Corp.	750	750	...	...	...
St. Francisville	(64)	St. Francisville Paper Co.	235	...	235	...	...
New Orleans	(65)	Southern Johns-Manville Products Corp.	130	...	130	...	...
		Total	10,750	8,815	715	1,220	...
MARYLAND							
Luke	(66)	Westvaco Corp.	743	743	...	...	...
		Total	743	743	...	...	...
MISSISSIPPI							
Meridian	(67)	The Flintkote Co.	250	...	200	50	...
Moss Point	(68)	International Paper Co.	725	725	...	...	...
Natchez	(69)	International Paper Co.	950	950	...	...	...
Vicksburg	(70)	International Paper Co.	1,000	1,000	...	...	...
Meridian	(71)	Kroehler Mfg. Co. of Miss., Inc.	80	...	80	...	...
Laurel	(72)	Masonite Corp.	1,200	...	1,200	...	...
Monticello	(73)	St. Regis Paper Co.	1,620	1,620	...	...	...
Greenville	(74)	United States Gypsum Co.	225	...	225	...	...
		Total	6,050	4,295	1,705	50	...
MISSOURI							
Kansas City	(75)	General Aniline and Film Corp.	100	...	100	...	...
		Total	100	...	100	...	...
NEW JERSEY							
Perth Amboy	(76)	The Celotex Corp.	50	...	50	...	...
Gloucester	(77)	General Aniline and Film Corp.	192	...	192	...	...
Manville	(78)	Johns-Manville Products Corp.	200	...	200	...	...
		Total	442	...	442	...	...

Table 19. *Mills using southern pulpwood in 1972, by process and capacity*

Location	Map code[1]	Company	Pulping capacity, 24 hours[2]				
			All processes	Sulfate	Groundwood and other mechanical	Semi-chemical	Soda and sulfite
			- - - - - - -Tons - - - - - - -				
ALABAMA							
Mahrt	(1)	Alabama Kraft Co., Div. Ga. Kraft Co.	975	975	...	...	...
Jackson	(2)	Allied Paper Inc.	470	470	...	...	...
Naheola	(3)	American Can Co.	900	900	...	...	...
Courtland	(4)	Champion International	500	500	...	...	...
Brewton	(5)	Container Corp. of America	800	800	...	...	...
Mobile	(6)	General Aniline and Film Corp.	48	...	48	...	...
Demopolis	(7)	Gulf States Paper Corp.	400	400	...	...	...
Tuscaloosa	(8)	Gulf States Paper Corp.	450	450	...	...	...
Riverdale	(9)	Hammermill Paper Co., Riverdale Div.	500	500	...	...	...
Mobile	(10)	International Paper Co.	1,315	1,015	300	...	...
Coosa Pines	(11)	Kimberly-Clark Corp., Coosa River Newsprint Div.	1,590	650	940	...	...
Pine Hill	(12)	McMillan Bloedel United, Inc.	925	925	...	...	...
Mobile	(13)	National Gypsum Co.	400	...	200	200	...
Mobile	(14)	Scott Paper Co.	1,400	1,400	...	...	...
Montgomery	(15)	Union Camp Corp.	870	870	...	...	...
		Total	11,543	9,855	1,488	200	...
ARKANSAS							
Morrilton	(16)	Arkansas Kraft Corp.	380	380	...	...	...
Crossett	(17)	Georgia-Pacific Corp., Crossett Division-Paper	1,220	1,220	...	...	...
Camden	(18)	International Paper Co.	750	750	...	...	...
Pine Bluff	(19)	International Paper Co.	1,700	1,300	400	...	...
Ashdown	(20)	Nekoosa-Edwards Paper Co., Inc.	400	400	...	...	...
Little Rock	(21)	Superwood Corp.	140	...	140	...	...
Pine Bluff	(22)	Weyerhaeuser Co., Pine Bluff Operation	150	150	...	...	...
		Total	4,740	4,200	540	...	...
FLORIDA							
Jacksonville	(23)	Alton Box Board Co.	625	625	...	...	...
Foley	(24)	The Buckeye Cellulose Corp.	923	923	...	...	...
Fernandina Beach	(25)	Container Corp. of America	1,700	1,700	...	...	...
Palatka	(26)	Hudson Pulp and Paper Corp.	950	950	...	...	...
Panama City	(27)	International Paper Co.	1,375	1,375	...	...	...
Fernandina Beach	(28)	I.T.T. Rayonier Inc.	375	...	...	...	375
Port St. Joe	(29)	St. Joe Paper Co.	1,700	1,700	...	...	...
Jacksonville	(30)	St. Regis Paper Co.	1,400	1,400	...	...	...
Pensacola	(31)	St. Regis Paper Co.	900	900	...	...	...
		Total	9,948	9,573	...	...	375
GEORGIA							
Augusta	(32)	Abitibi Southern Corp.	375	...	375	...	...
Macon	(33)	Armstrong Cork Co.	400	...	400	...	...
Brunswick	(34)	Brunswick Pulp and Paper Co.	1,520	1,520	...	...	...
Savannah	(35)	Certain-teed Products Corp.	65	...	...	65	...
Augusta	(36)	Continental Can Co., Inc.	700	700	...	...	...
Port Wentworth	(37)	Continental Can Co., Inc.	600	600	...	...	...
Savannah	(38)	General Aniline and Film Corp.	48	...	48	...	...
Macon	(39)	Georgia Kraft Co., Mead Div.	850	850	...	...	...
Rome	(40)	Georgia Kraft Co., Krannert Div.	1,600	1,600	...	...	...
St. Marys	(41)	Gilman Paper Co., St. Marys Kraft Div.	1,000	1,000	...	...	...
Cedar Springs	(42)	Great Northern Paper Co., Southern Div.	2,025	1,700	...	325	...
Jesup	(43)	I.T.T. Rayonier Inc.	675	675	...	...	...
Riceboro	(44)	Interstate Paper Corp.	500	500	...	...	...
Valdosta	(45)	Owens-Illinois, Forest Products Div.	875	875	...	...	...
Savannah	(46)	Union Camp Corp.	3,000	2,600	...	400	...
		Total					

Location	Map code[1]	Company	Pulping capacity, 24 hours[2]				
			All processes	Sulfate	Groundwood and other mechanical	Semi-chemical	Soda and sulfite
					- - - - - - *Tons* - - - - - - - -			
ILLINOIS							
Alton	(47)	Alton Box Board Co.	800	...	...	800	...
Peoria	(48)	The Celotex Corp.	110	...	110	...	...
East St. Louis	(49)	Certain-teed Products Corp.	100	...	100	...	...
Wilmington	(50)	Philip Carey Corp.	150	...	150	...	...
		Total	1,160	...	360	800	...
KENTUCKY							
Wickliffe	(51)	Westvaco Corp.	600	600	...	...	...
		Total	600	600	...	...	...
LOUISIANA							
Shreveport	(52)	Bird and Son, Inc.	150	...	...	150	...
DeRidder	(53)	Boise Southern Co.	1,300	950	350	...	...
Elizabeth	(54)	Calkraft Paper Co., Inc.	305	305	...	...	...
Hodge	(55)	Continental Can Co., Inc.	750	550	...	200	...
Bogalusa	(56)	Crown Zellerbach Corp.	1,435	1,300	...	135	...
St. Francisville	(57)	Crown Zellerbach Corp.	500	500	...	...	...
Port Hudson	(58)	Georgia-Pacific Corp., Crossette Division	600	600	...	...	...
Bastrop	(59)	International Paper Co. (Bastrop Mill)	485	...	...	485	...
Bastrop	(60)	International Paper Co. (Louisiana Mill)	1,100	1,100	...	...	...
Springhill	(61)	International Paper Co.	1,625	1,625	...	...	...
West Monroe	(62)	Olinkraft, Inc.	1,385	1,135	...	250	...
Pineville	(63)	Pineville Kraft Corp.	750	750	...	...	...
St. Francisville	(64)	St. Francisville Paper Co.	235	...	235	...	...
New Orleans	(65)	Southern Johns-Manville Products Corp.	130	...	130	...	...
		Total	10,750	8,815	715	1,220	...
MARYLAND							
Luke	(66)	Westvaco Corp.	743	743	...	...	...
		Total	743	743	...	...	...
MISSISSIPPI							
Meridian	(67)	The Flintkote Co.	250	...	200	50	...
Moss Point	(68)	International Paper Co.	725	725	...	...	...
Natchez	(69)	International Paper Co.	950	950	...	...	...
Vicksburg	(70)	International Paper Co.	1,000	1,000	...	...	...
Meridian	(71)	Kroehler Mfg. Co. of Miss., Inc.	80	...	80	...	...
Laurel	(72)	Masonite Corp.	1,200	...	1,200	...	...
Monticello	(73)	St. Regis Paper Co.	1,620	1,620	...	...	...
Greenville	(74)	United States Gypsum Co.	225	...	225	...	...
		Total	6,050	4,295	1,705	50	...
MISSOURI							
Kansas City	(75)	General Aniline and Film Corp.	100	...	100	...	...
		Total	100	...	100	...	...
NEW JERSEY							
Perth Amboy	(76)	The Celotex Corp.	50	...	50	...	...
Gloucester	(77)	General Aniline and Film Corp.	192	...	192	...	...
Manville	(78)	Johns-Manville Products Corp.	200	...	200	...	...
		Total	442	...	442	...	...

Location	Map code[1]	Company	Pulping capacity, 24 hours[2]				
			All processes	Sulfate	Groundwood and other mechanical	Semi-chemical	Soda and sulfite
			- - - - - - -Tons - - - - - - -				
NORTH CAROLINA							
Roaring River	(79)	Abitibi Corp.	120	...	120	...	...
Roanoke Rapides	(80)	Albemarle Paper Co.	940	940	...	...	...
Canton	(81)	Champion International	1,325	1,325	...	...	...
Riegelwood	(82)	Federal Paper Board Co., Inc.	1,100	1,100	...	...	...
Conway	(83)	Georgia-Pacific Corp.	200	...	200	...	...
Sylva	(84)	The Mead Corp.	290	...	...	290	...
New Bern	(85)	Weyerhaeuser Co., N.C. Div.	800	800	...	...	...
Plymouth	(86)	Weyerhaeuser Co., N.C. Div.	1,500	1,250	...	250	...
		Total	6,275	5,415	320	540	...
OHIO							
Cincinnati	(87)	The Celotex Corp.	100	...	100	...	...
Chillicothe	(88)	The Mead Corp.	600	600	...	...	...
		Total	700	600	100	...	...
OKLAHOMA							
Pryor	(89)	Georgia-Pacific, Gypsum Division	150	...	150	...	...
Broken Bow	(90)	Weyerhaeuser Co., Craig Plant	520	...	520	...	...
Valliant	(91)	Weyerhaeuser Co., Valliant Operation	1,600	1,200	...	400	...
		Total	2,270	1,200	670	400	...
PENNSYLVANIA							
Roaring Spring	(92)	Appleton Papers Inc.	180	180	...	...	...
Philadelphia	(93)	The Celotex Corp.	160	...	...	160	...
York	(94)	Certain-teed Products Corp.	75	...	...	75	...
		Total	415	180	...	235	...
SOUTH CAROLINA							
Catawba	(95)	Bowaters Carolina Corp.	700	600	100	...	...
Catawba	(96)	Catawba Newsprint Co.	500	...	500	...	...
Georgetown	(97)	International Paper Co.	2,130	1,650	...	480	...
Hartsville	(98)	Sonoco Products Co.	320	...	...	320	...
Florence	(99)	South Carolina Industries, Inc.	600	600	...	...	...
Charleston	(100)	Westvaco Corp.	1,950	1,950	...	...	...
		Total	6 200	4 800	600	800	...
TENNESSEE							
Calhoun	(101)	Bowaters Southern Paper Corp.	1,625	500	925	·200	...
New Johnsonville	(102)	Inland Container Corp.	450	...	...	450	...
Paris	(103)	Celotex Corp.	300	...	...	300	...·
Harriman	(104)	The Mead Corp.	190	...	...	190	...
Kingsport	(105)	Mead Papers	300	...	...	...	300
Knoxville	(106)	Southern Extract Co.	140	...	...	140	...
Counce	(107)	Tennessee River Pulp and Paper Co.	775	775	...	...	...
		Total					
TEXAS							
Pasadena	(108)	Champion International	930	850	80	...	...
Evadale	(109)	EasTex, Inc.	1,200	1,200	...	...	...
Dallas	(110)	General Aniline and Film Corp.	50	...	50	...	...
Orange	(111)	Owens-Illinois, Forest Products Div.	1,000	1,000	...	...	...
Houston	(112)	Celotex Corp.	25	...	25	...	...
Lufkin	(113)	Southland Paper Mills, Inc.	1,250	400	850	...	...
Sheldon	(114)	Southland Paper Mills, Inc.	860	500	360	...	...
Diboll	(115)	Temple Industries, Fiber Products Div.	350	...	...	350	...
		Total					

Table 19. *Mills using southern pulpwood in 1972, by process and capacity* (Continued)

Location	Map code[1]	Company	All processes	Sulfate	Groundwood and other mechanical	Semi-chemical	Soda and sulfite
					- - - - - - -*Tons* - - - - - - -		
VIRGINIA							
West Point	(116)	The Chesapeake Corp. of Virginia	1,150	1,150	...	...	...
Hopewell	(117)	Continental Can Co., Inc.	1,100	900	...	200	...
Doswell	(118)	Evans Products Co.	300	...	300	...	...
Lynchburg	(119)	The Mead Corp.	190	...	...	190	...
Big Island	(120)	Owens-Illinois, Forest Products Div.	500	...	...	500	...
Jarratt	(121)	Southern Johns-Manville Products Corp.	200	...	200	...	...
Franklin	(122)	Union Camp Corp.	1,750	1,750	...	...	...
Danville	(123)	United States Gypsum Co.	225	...	225	...	...
Covington	(124)	Westvaco Corp.	1,255	1,058	...	197	...
		Total	6,670	4,858	725	1,087	...
		All States	92,284	72,979	10,878	7,752	675

[1]Corresponds to numbers at locations on mill capacity map, page 21.
[2]Southern Pulp and Paper Manufacturer, vol. 35, No. 10 (Oct. 1, 1972); and other sources.

Table 20. *Pulpmills under construction in the South*

Location	Map code[1]	Company	Pulping capacity, 24 hours
			Tons
FLORIDA			
Blountstown	(125)	Abitibi Corp.	100
GEORGIA			
Jesup	(126)	I.T.T. Rayonier Inc.	591
LOUISIANA			
Campti	(127)	Western Kraft Corp.	300
TEXAS			
Texarkana	(128)	International Paper Co.	610

[1]Corresponds to numbers at locations on mill capacity map, page 21.

Bertelson, Daniel F.

    1973. Southern pulpwood production, 1972. South.
    For. Exp. Stn., New Orleans, La. 25 p. (USDA
    For. Serv. Resour. Bull. SO-41).

The South harvested a record 44,279,487 cords of pulpwood
in 1972. Roundwood and residue use expanded in both
softwoods and hardwoods for a total gain of 6 percent over
1971. Daily pulping capacity of the region's 109 mills was
88,124 tons, an increase of 1 percent.

Bertelson, Daniel F.

1973. Southern pulpwood production, 1972. South. For. Exp. Stn., New Orleans, La. 25 p. (USDA For. Serv. Resour. Bull. SO-41).

The South harvested a record 44,279,487 cords of pulpwood in 1972. Roundwood and residue use expanded in both softwoods and hardwoods for a total gain of 6 percent over 1971. Daily pulping capacity of the region's 109 mills was 88,124 tons, an increase of 1 percent.

Alabama Forests: Trends and Prospects

Paul A. Murphy

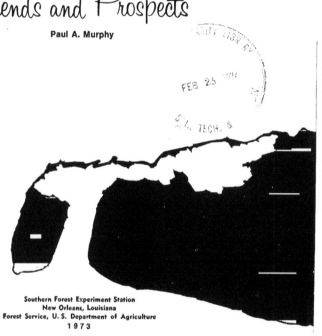

Southern Forest Experiment Station
New Orleans, Louisiana
Forest Service, U. S. Department of Agriculture
1973

Highlights

This report contains the principal findings of the latest forest survey of Alabama. Data for growth and cut are given for 1971, and the inventory is reported for January 1, 1972. A canvass of forest products output for 1971 also provided information.

Forest area declined 2 percent since 1963 and now totals 21.3 million acres. The loss was principally due to woodland clearing for pasture.

The only noteworthy change in ownership was a decline in farmer-owned forest land due to clearing for pasture and shifts by farmers to other occupations. Most forest land is still owned by individuals, but forest industries have a substantial amount—4.2 million acres.

The volume of softwood growing stock is currently 11.3 billion cubic feet, an increase of 30 percent over 1963. All size classes experienced an increase, but most of the rise occurred in trees 14 inches and less in diameter. About 93 percent of the softwood growing stock is in the four major southern pines.

The softwood sawtimber inventory also increased 30 percent and now totals 42.3 billion board feet. Concomitant with this improvement in sawtimber inventory was an increase in timber quality.

In contrast, hardwood growing stock increased 15 percent, resulting in a 1972 inventory of 8.9 billion cubic feet. About three-fourths of this volume increase was in trees 14 inches in diameter and less. The most important species groups in order of volume are oak, sweetgum, hickories, and tupelo and blackgum.

Hardwood sawtimber volume is presently 21.2 billion board feet, an increase of 15 percent. However, no improvement in hardwood sawtimber quality was detected.

Net growth in 1971 was 1.2 billion cubic feet or 56 cubic feet per acre; 1962 growth was 45 cubic feet per acre. However, growth is still below its potential of 90 cubic feet per acre because 65 percent of Alabama's forests are less than fully stocked.

After deducting the 1971 timber removals from net growth, 448 million cubic feet remained

to add to the State's timber inventory in 1971. These removals—such as from timber harvesting and land clearing—totaled 739.6 million cubic feet. Thus, Alabama enjoys a comfortable margin of timber growth over cut.

About 718 million cubic feet of roundwood were supplied to forest industries from Alabama's forests. Two products, sawtimber and pulpwood, accounted for 91 percent of the total output.

Between 1962 and 1971 softwood saw-log production rose 46 percent to 1.1 billion board feet. Many pine saw logs are now being processed by the 11 chipping headrigs in Alabama. Hardwood saw-log cutting increased only 13 percent, to 386 million board feet.

Pulpwood production reached 4.8 million cords in 1971, making pulpwood Alabama's leading roundwood product. Pulping capacity has more than doubled since 1962, but roundwood requirements have been moderated somewhat by the increased utilization of residue in pulp manufacture.

There are now six pine plywood plants in Alabama, and they account for most of the veneer-log consumption. From virtually nothing in 1962, softwood veneer-log output rose to 221 million board feet in 1971. By contrast, hardwood veneer-log production dropped 44 percent to 57 million board feet in 1971. Most of the hardwood mills produced veneer for containers.

Although Alabama's forests have improved in volume, stocking, and growth, problems still remain. Almost 10 million acres suitable for growing pine are currently supporting pure or mixed hardwood stands. Moreover, one of every five hardwood trees 5 inches d.b.h. and larger is a cull.

The expansion of the forest products industry in the last decade indicates that more industrial growth may be in the offing. Improving hardwood stands and converting unproductive upland hardwood stands to pine can help Alabama's forests meet the increased resource demands of the years ahead.

Figure 1.—*Forest resource regions of Alabama.*

2

Resource Trends

FOREST AREA

Less Forest Area

Occupying 65 percent of the State, forests are a dominant feature of Alabama's landscape (fig. 1). Some 21.3 million acres (table I) are capable of and available for growing commercial crops of timber, and an additional 17,000 are reserved for nontimber uses. The present commercial forest area represents a 2 percent decline from that of 1963.

Table I. *Commercial forest land in 1972 and change since 1963*

Region	Commercial forest	Change since last survey	Proportion of region forested[1]
	Thousand acres	*Percent*	*Percent*
North	9,818.7	−3	63
Southeast	5,348.4	−2	59
Southwest	6,166.0	(²)	75
All regions	21,333.1	−2	65

[1] Total forest, including noncommercial, as a proportion of total area in the region.
² Negligible.

Of the 67 counties in Alabama, 37 lost significant forest area since the last survey in 1963 (fig. 2). The remainder had either no change or an increase. The counties experiencing losses were mostly in the North and Southeast regions.

Most of the decline was attributable to agriculture. Since the last survey, about 696,000 acres of forest were cleared for agriculture, mostly pasture (table II). An additional 216,000 were diverted to other uses. Although 503,000 acres reverted to forest, they were insufficient to offset the losses from land clearing.

The modest decline in forest acreage reverses a trend of increasing forest area documented in early 1960's.[1] Recent surveys in other Midsouth States also have revealed losses in timbered acreage. As agriculture and other uses continue to claim forest land, further declines are anticipated for the future.

No Big Changes in Ownership

Ownership patterns did not change substantially since 1963. Forest ownership in Alabama is overwhelmingly private; only 5 percent is publicly owned. Most of the public forest land is in national forests.

Forest industries own 4.2 million acres and lease an additional 372,000. As large tracts suitable for acquisition have become more scarce, forest industries have turned to leasing to assure a raw material supply.

About 16.1 million acres are held by private owners other than forest industries. Corporations in this category have some 1.7 million acres; the remainder is owned by farmers or other individuals. Farmer-owned forest land has declined as some operators switched to other occupations and others cleared timber for pasture and cropland. This category was the only one that changed appreciably in the last 9 years.

[1] Sternitzke, H. S. Alabama forests. USDA For. Serv. Resour. Bull. SO-3, 32 p. South. For. Exp. Stn., New Orleans, La. 1963.

Table II. *Changes in commercial forest land, 1963-1972*

Region	Net change	Additions from:			Diversions to:		
		Total	Nonforest	Noncommercial forest	Total	Agriculture	Other
				Thousand acres			
North	−315.3	123.2	122.6	0.6	438.5	301.7	136.8
Southeast	−104.4	155.5	149.3	6.2	259.9	210.9	49.0
Southwest	+ 10.6	224.6	218.0	6.6	214.0	183.7	30.3
All regions	−409.1	503.3	489.9	13.4	912.4	696.3	216.1

Figure 2.—*Alabama counties with a loss in commercial forest area from 1963 to 1972.*

4

About 7.7 million acres are owned by other private individuals, a heterogeneous category that includes professionals, retirees, housewives, and others.

Forest Type

Forest land in Alabama was classified according to its suitability for growing certain species groups—pines, upland hardwoods, or bottomland hardwoods (table III). These site classes do not necessarily indicate what species are presently growing on an area.

Most of Alabama's forest land is suited for southern pine. Such areas, comprising 17.4 million acres, occur in the Coastal Plain and in the uplands on dry sites. Some are already occupied by the longleaf-slash or loblolly-shortleaf pine forest types, but more than half are currently supporting pure or mixed stands of hardwoods. Oak-pine and oak-hickory forests collectively oc-

Table III. *Commercial forest land by forest type and site, 1972*

Forest type	All sites	Southern pine	Upland hardwood	Bottom-land hardwood
	— — — *Thousand acres* — — —			
Longleaf-slash pine	1,483.6	1,365.2	....	118.4
Loblolly-shortleaf pine	6,380.1	6,272.6	....	107.5
Oak-pine	5,016.9	4,682.9	....	334.0
Oak-hickory	5,913.1	5,036.4	876.7	....
Oak-gum-cypress	2,443.5	....	....	2,443.5
Elm-ash-cottonwood	95.9	....	....	95.9
All types	21,333.1	17,357.1	876.7	3,099.8

cupy 9.7 million acres or more than half of the pine sites.

There are 877,000 acres of uplands that are suitable for growing cove-type hardwoods such as yellow-poplar. An additional 3.1 million acres of hardwood sites are in bottom lands, principally along the Mobile, Tombigbee, Black Warrior, and other rivers.

TIMBER VOLUME

In 1972 there were 22.4 billion cubic feet of wood in Alabama's forests. Volume in growing stock—that is, in trees presently or prospectively suitable for sawtimber—totaled 20.2 billion cubic feet. Because methods for computing tree volume were changed since the 1963 survey, the volumes from 1963 were adjusted to conform to the 1972 standards.

Softwood Increases Moderately

Softwood growing stock composes 98 percent of the softwood volume (fig. 3). Almost all is in the four major southern pines. For example, loblolly pine alone makes up 53 percent of the softwood (fig. 4).

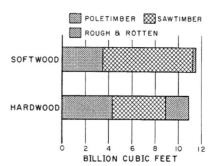

Figure 3.—*Volume of softwoods and hardwoods by class of timber.*

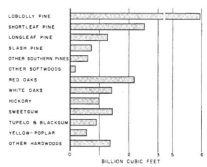

Figure 4.—*Growing stock by species.*

The 11.3 billion cubic feet in softwoods represents a 30-percent increase over 1963 (table IV). An upward trend in softwood volume was also documented in the previous survey. Although the most sizable gain was in trees in the 14-inch class and less, all diameter classes grew in volume (fig. 5). The sizable growth in the small sizes is encouraging to the pulp industry, and the increase in the sawtimber sizes bodes well for sawmills and plywood mills.

5

Table IV. *Growing-stock volume in 1972 and change since 1963*

Region	Softwood		Hardwood	
	Volume	Change	Volume	Change
	Million cu. ft.	*Percent*	*Million cu. ft.*	*Percent*
North	4,492.8	+44	4,244.6	+21
Southeast	2,825.0	+43	2,122.1	+22
Southwest	3,964.8	+11	2,562.4	+ 2
All regions	11,282.6	+30	8,929.1	+15

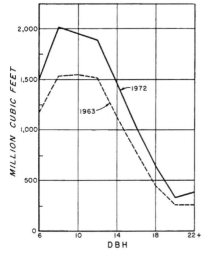

Figure 5.—*Softwood growing stock by tree diameter, 1963 and 1972.*

About 69 percent of the growing stock volume is in sawtimber trees. The percentage increases in sawtimber resemble those of growing stock (table V). The overall gain was 30 percent, with

Table V. *Sawtimber volume in 1972 and change since 1963*

Region	Softwood		Hardwood	
	Volume	Change	Volume	Change
	Million bd. ft.	*Percent*	*Million bd. ft.*	*Percent*
North	14,542.6	+42	9,660.7	+22
Southeast	10,664.9	+45	4,747.7	+30
Southwest	17,075.9	+14	6,825.3	− 1
All regions	42,283.4	+30	21,233.7	+15

the North and Southeast regions posting the largest increases. Most sawtimber is in private nonindustrial ownership (fig. 6). Associated with the increase in volume was some improvement in quality.

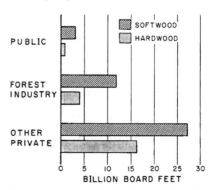

Figure 6.—*Sawtimber volume by class of ownership.*

The smaller volume gains for growing stock and sawtimber in the Southwest region are probably the result of larger initial volumes per acre and greater removals. This region has the largest per-acre volumes (table VI). As stand volume increases, annual growth becomes proportionately less of the standing inventory. With a high concentration of forest industry in the Southwest, there is a relatively large drain on the forest resource. Despite the heavy removals in the Southwest, its inventory continues to increase.

Table VI. *Average volume per acre of growing stock and sawtimber by species group and region, 1972*

Region	Growing stock			Sawtimber		
	Total	Soft-wood	Hard-wood	Total	Soft-wood	Hard-wood
	— Cubic feet —			— — Board feet — —		
North	890	458	432	2,465	1,481	984
Southeast	925	528	397	2,882	1,994	888
Southwest	1,059	643	416	3,876	2,769	1,107
All regions	948	529	419	2,977	1,982	995

Hardwood Increases Some

Hardwood growing stock presently totals 8.9 billion cubic feet (table IV). Species groups with greatest volumes were oaks, sweetgum, hickories, and tupelo and blackgum.

The present volume represents a 15-percent increase over the 1963 inventory (table IV). At that time a volume increase in the Southwest region compensated for inventory declines in the remainder of the State. Since 1963, however, the North and Southeast regions had gains of over 20 percent, while the Southwest region's hardwood volume remained relatively stable.

About 52 percent of the growing-stock volume is in sawtimber-size trees. The present sawtimber volume is 21.2 billion board feet; its increase was the same as for growing stock—15 percent (table V). However, sawtimber volume in the Southwest region declined slightly, mainly due to a reduction of the blackgum and tupelo inventory in that region. This soft-textured species group is much in demand, but its diameter growth is slow.

The distribution of the volume increase was uneven. While growing-stock volume in the lower diameter classes increased considerably, the absolute gain in diameter classes 18 inches and greater was small (fig. 7).

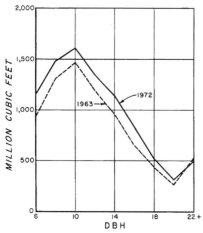

Figure 7.—*Hardwood growing stock by tree diameter, 1963 and 1972.*

Concomitant with the small increase in large trees was a lack of improvement in timber qual-ity. These two trends are not good for hardwood industries that depend upon factory lumber logs. These mills may have to buy smaller and poorer quality logs to maintain or increase production. If they do, the yield of high-quality lumber will decline. Moreover, supplies will not increase much in the future unless management of hardwood stands is improved.

In contrast, low quality material suitable for pulpwood is plentiful. Much of this volume is currently on pine sites where growth is slower for hardwoods. About 5.2 billion cubic feet or over half of the hardwood growing stock falls in this category.

GROWTH AND REMOVALS

Gross growth for Alabama's forests was 1.3 billion cubic feet in 1971 (table VII). The components of gross growth are: (1) survivor growth—the increment in net volume of growing stock trees at the beginning of the specified year and surviving to its end; (2) ingrowth—the net volume of trees at the time they grew into growing stock during a specified year; (3) growth on ingrowth—the increment in net volume of trees after they grew into growing stock in a specified year; (4) growth on removals—the increment in net volume of growing-stock trees that were cut during the year; (5) mortality—the net volume in growing-stock trees that died during the year.

Survivor growth comprised 78 percent of gross growth in 1971, ingrowth and growth on ingrowth contributed 12 percent, growth on removals took up 2 percent of gross growth, and mortality claimed 8 percent. These percentages did not vary significantly between regions, but differences between hardwoods and softwoods did occur.

The relative importance of each growth component was the same for both species groups, but mortality claimed a bigger percentage of gross growth in hardwoods. This bigger mortality also reduced the percentage contribution of hardwood survivor growth. The difference in species groups was least pronounced in the North resource region.

Net growth, gross growth minus mortality, was 1.2 billion cubic feet in 1971 (table VII). About 44 percent of this net growth was in the North region, 26 percent occurred in the Southeast, and the remaining 30 percent was in the

Table VII. *Growth components of growing stock on commercial forest land, by species group and resource region, Alabama, 1971*

Resource region	Species group	Growth components					Total	
		Survivor growth	Ingrowth	Growth on ingrowth	Growth on removals	Mortality	Gross growth	Net growth
		— — — — — — — — — Million cubic feet — — — — — — — — —						
North	Softwood	287.7	44.2	1.1	6.9	27.5	367.4	339.9
	Hardwood	161.2	23.2	.3	1.8	21.5	208.0	186.5
	Total	448.9	67.4	1.4	8.7	49.0	575.4	526.4
Southeast	Softwood	174.4	29.6	.8	5.3	10.3	220.4	210.1
	Hardwood	82.1	15.0	.2	1.3	16.9	115.5	98.6
	Total	256.5	44.6	1.0	6.6	27.2	335.9	308.7
Southwest	Softwood	206.1	25.4	.7	5.8	12.0	250.0	238.0
	Hardwood	93.3	19.0	.3	1.7	15.3	129.6	114.3
	Total	299.4	44.4	1.0	7.5	27.3	379.6	352.3
All regions	Softwood	668.2	99.2	2.6	18.0	49.8	837.8	788.0
	Hardwood	336.6	57.2	.8	4.8	53.7	453.1	399.4
	Total	1,004.8	156.4	3.4	22.8	103.5	1,290.9	1,187.4

Southwest. The percentage contribution of each region to growth followed the distribution of the State's growing stock.

Nearly all the softwood growth is in southern pine, and sweetgum and the oaks comprise almost two-thirds of the growth of hardwood growing stock. The growth in hardwoods, however, is not so well distributed in desirable species as in softwood. For example, only 25 percent of oak growth is in preferred species.

In 1962, annual net growth was 972.7 million cubic feet or 45 cubic feet per acre. By 1971, growth had increased to 56 cubic feet per acre. But annual net growth has not reached its capacity.

Alabama's forests are capable of producing an average annual net growth of 90 cubic feet per acre. Thus, growth was only 62 percent of its potential in 1971. Stocking and stand structure provide clues as to why commercial forests in Alabama are not producing at capacity.

Stocking is an indication of how much the productive capacity of a site is being utilized by trees, and it is usually measured by comparing the number of trees or basal area with some standard. Full or 100 percent stocking is the relative density at which there is no increase in growth with any further increase in stocking.

About 65 percent of Alabama's forests are less than fully occupied by growing-stock trees. In some stands growing space is being preempted by less desirable trees or competing vegetation; until this material is removed, growing stock cannot fully occupy these sites. In other stands the growing space is not fully occupied by any trees, good or bad.

Stand structure also affects net volume growth. Nonstocked and seedling and sapling stands contribute little volume growth, and there are 7.4 million acres of these stands in Alabama.

Growing stock in Alabama increased by 448 million cubic feet in 1971, while the sawtimber inventory grew by 1.3 billion board feet (table VIII). These increases are the residual after subtracting the year's timber removals from net growth. Growing stock increased for all species in 1971. Likewise, the sawtimber inventory grew except for tupelo and sweetgum. Cutting in excess of growth in the Southeast and Southwest regions reduced the statewide sawtimber inventory in these species.

Of the 739.6 million cubic feet of removals, 92 percent left the woods as roundwood products, 5 percent remained as logging residue, and 3 percent was destroyed in operations such as land clearing and timber stand improvement.

8

Table VIII. *Summary of volume-change statistics, 1971*

Resource region	Species group	Growing stock			Sawtimber		
		Net growth	Removals	Net change	Net growth	Removals	Net change
		— — — Million cubic feet — — —			— — — Million board feet — — —		
North	Softwood	339.9	180.2	+159.7	1,154.9	724.8	+ 430.1
	Hardwood	186.5	82.1	+104.4	472.7	292.7	+ 180.0
	All species	526.4	262.3	+264.1	1,627.6	1,017.5	+ 610.1
Southeast	Softwood	210.1	146.3	+ 63.8	894.0	568.9	+ 325.1
	Hardwood	98.6	58.2	+ 40.4	249.4	192.6	+ 56.8
	All species	308.7	204.5	+104.2	1,143.4	761.5	+ 381.9
Southwest	Softwood	238.0	199.4	+ 38.6	1,104.6	849.7	+ 254.9
	Hardwood	114.3	73.4	+ 40.9	326.1	223.7	+ 102.4
	All species	352.3	272.8	+ 79.5	1,430.7	1,073.4	+ 357.3
All regions	Softwood	788.0	525.9	+262.1	3,153.5	2,143.4	+1,010.1
	Hardwood	399.4	213.7	+185.7	1,048.2	709.0	+ 339.2
	All species	1,187.4	739.6	+447.8	4,201.7	2,852.4	+1,349.3

Timber Products Output

About 718 million cubic feet of wood were supplied to industry from Alabama's forests in 1971.[2] Saw logs and pulpwood together comprised 91 percent of the industrial roundwood output. An additional 17 million cubic feet were cut for nonindustrial or domestic consumption, mostly for firewood.

The last 9 years have witnessed many changes in forest industries and timber harvesting in Alabama. These developments have expanded the resource by increasing its utilization.

TRENDS IN TECHNOLOGY

There have been two major developments in forest industries. Improvements in peeling equipment have made it practical to produce veneer from relatively small southern pine logs. A new sawmill headrig has been developed.

The southern pine plywood industry began in Arkansas in 1963. By 1969, there were 34 plywood plants located throughout the Midsouth. The industry owes its growth to three factors—an available timber supply, nearness to populous markets, and the development of high-speed peeling equipment with low unit operating cost for small diameter logs. To be profitable, logs for plywood should be at least 12 inches in diameter, and the region's supply in these sizes is ample.

The other new technology is the chipping headrig. Instead of producing slabs and sawdust like a conventional headrig, the chipping headrig, as its name implies, produces chips while forming a cant, which is subsequently sawn into dimension lumber. In this operation, only about 5 percent of the log is ultimately converted into sawdust versus the 22 percent for a conventional operation.[3] Moreover, chipping headrigs can profitably process logs as small as 6 inches in diameter, and they can be used to convert veneer cores into chips and studs.

Time has also wrought changes in timber harvesting. Because the trees can be more complete-ly utilized, shears are being used to sever the tree stems. The lower stump height means less waste.

The need for more complete utilization has stimulated tree-length and multiproduct logging. For example, in 1964 about 6 percent of the softwood pulpwood came from multiproduct logging operations, but by 1972 this proportion had increased to 20 percent.[4]

Forest industries have improved utilization through lateral integration—manufacturing of several products at single locations. Logs can be hauled tree length to these locations. Sections less than 6 inches in diameter can be completely chipped, and 6- to 12-inch portions can be processed by a chipping headrig. Logs at least 12 inches in diameter can be made into plywood if the quality is sufficient. Otherwise, they too may be processed by the chipping headrig.

The effect of these new technologies can be seen in the 1971 timber harvest for Alabama.

TIMBER HARVEST

Saw Logs

About 1.5 billion board feet of saw logs were harvested in Alabama during 1971, which is an increase of 36 percent over 1962. Softwoods, mainly pine, made up three-fourths of the production.

Softwood volume has risen by 46 percent since 1962. The advent of the chipping headrig has made the processing of once marginal log sizes profitable. Lumber production has risen accordingly. Eleven of the 323 sawmills in Alabama had chipping headrigs in 1971. They accounted for 28 percent of all the softwood saw logs produced.

In contrast to softwood, hardwood saw-log production has risen only 13 percent to 386 million board feet. Oak comprises over one-half of the volume; yellow-poplar, sweetgum, and tupelo and blackgum are the other principal species.

Attrition continues to reduce the ranks of sawmills. There were 323 in 1971 (fig. 8), 555 in 1962, and 3,030 in 1946. Although the number

[2] Bertelson, D. F. Alabama forest industries. USDA For. Serv. Resour. Bull. SO-36, 29 p. South. For. Exp. Stn., New Orleans, La. 1972.
[3] Koch, P. Technological developments in the southern pine industry. For. Farmer 30(7):16-20. 1971.

[4] Beltz, R. C., and Chappell, T. W. Trends in product logging and tree utilization in Alabama. For. Prod. J. 23(8):15-16. 1973.

Figure 8.—*Primary wood-using industries in Alabama, 1971.*

11

has decreased, average size has increased, and 43 mills cut over 10 million board feet in 1971. Most of the large plants—those processing at least 3 million board feet per year—use pine. With a potential processing rate of 100 or more lineal feet per minute, the 11 mills with chipping headrigs have large raw material requirements. Consequently, their occurrence has raised average production significantly.

The supply radius for the State's mill is large; half of the saw logs cut in Alabama cross county lines before primary processing. Alabama's sawmills get most of their logs from inside the State. Only 84 million board feet of logs are imported, and only 3 percent of the logs cut in the State are exported.

Pulpwood

With a 1971 production of more than 4.8 million cords, pulpwood is Alabama's leading roundwood product (fig. 9). Only Georgia led Alabama in pulpwood production in 1971, and these States together accounted for one-third of the South's output.[5]

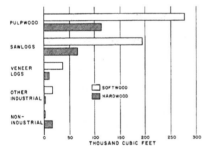

Figure 9.—*Output of Alabama roundwood by product, 1971.*

Softwood pulpwood cutting has risen 71 percent since 1962, and the hardwood share has risen from 24 to 29 percent of the total. Roundwood production — especially pine — increased briskly until about 1968, when residue use started growing rapidly (fig. 10). Roundwood output has subsequently remained at a plateau as softwood residue has assumed a larger share of the pulpwood output.

[5] Bellamy, T. R. Southern pulpwood production, 1971. USDA For. Serv. Resour. Bull. SE-23, 20 p. Southeast. For. Exp. Stn., Asheville, N. C. 1972.

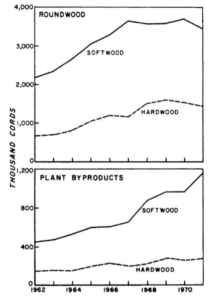

Figure 10.—*Pulpwood production in Alabama, 1962-1971.*

About 1.4 million cords of Alabama wood were processed in other States, and 800,000 cords were imported. Hence, 71 percent of the roundwood produced in Alabama is also processed there.

Several pulpmills have been expanded, and six pulpmills have been built since 1962, raising the daily capacity from 5,093 to 11,443 tons. The State's 15 pulpmills (fig. 8) now have an average daily capacity of 764 tons—up from 556 tons in 1962.

Veneer Logs

About 278 million board feet of veneer logs were removed from Alabama's forests in 1971, and pine comprised almost four-fifths of this total. In 1962, the southern pines made up a minuscule portion of the veneer-log harvest; today they dominate it. Virtually all this pine volume finds its way into plywood.

With six plants located now in Alabama, the nascent southern pine plywood industry has grown and matured. Production of logs for plywood has zoomed. From virtually nothing in 1962, harvest of pine peeler logs reached 137 million board feet in 1969 and 220 million in 1971.

Three of the six plants also have a sawmill with a chipping headrig. Thus, these firms can allocate logs for the greatest financial return. Logs that are submarginal for veneer can be processed by the chipping headrig.

Hardwood veneer-log production has been waning because of a declining resource base. Even in Alabama, which leads the other Midsouth States in hardwood veneer-log production, the harvest went from 101 million board feet in 1962 to 57 million in 1971—a drop of 44 percent. Soft-textured hardwoods, such as tupelo and blackgum, have been preferred by the industry, but their proportion of the harvest has been declining as large trees of these species have become scarcer. Others, such as oaks, now make up a larger portion of the harvest.

The number of hardwood veneer mills has declined from 34 to 26 since 1963. Seventeen of the 26 produce veneer for containers, and these mills can utilize smaller and lower quality logs than producers of standard veneer.

Other Products

Alabama is one of the leading producers of poles in the Midsouth. In 1971, its forests produced over 1 million poles, which represents about 2 percent of the industrial roundwood har-

vest. Pole production has been increasing—from 820,000 in 1962 and 836,000 in 1964 to the present amount.

Other roundwood products comprised less than 1 percent of the total industrial roundwood output. These products include commercial posts, cooperage, excelsior, furniture stock, handlestocks, miscellaneous dimension, piling, and shuttleblocks.

PLANT RESIDUES AND BYPRODUCTS

About 179 million cubic feet of residues were generated by the forest industries in Alabama in 1971. About two-thirds was coarse material, such as slabs, edgings, and cull pieces, which can be converted into chips for pulping. The rest was in fines like sawdust, which cannot be chipped.

Some 115 million cubic feet of residues were used in pulp and particleboard, 29 million were burned for fuel, and 7.8 million were used for other purposes like charcoal, animal bedding, or mulch. In total, 87 percent of all the plant residue was used in some manner.

About 97 percent of coarse residues are being utilized versus only 70 percent of the fines. About 24 million cubic feet, mostly fine, were wasted. Chipping headrigs have reduced the proportion of fine residue that might have ordinarily occurred.

About 2 million tons of bark were also generated by Alabama industries. Currently about two-thirds of it is being utilized.

Timber Supply Outlook

Although future demand for timber is difficult to predict, it will almost certainly increase. Timber supply too is unpredictable, but projections can be made to see what might happen under different assumptions about future conditions.

Two such projections, called prospective cut and potential cut, were made for Alabama. In the prospective cut, present trends in forest management were assumed to continue, and the cut was adjusted to balance with growth by the end of the projection period. In the potential cut, more intensive management was assumed so that there would be a better balance of tree sizes in 30 years, the length of the projection period.

PROSPECTIVE CUT

The annual cut in this projection was adjusted each year so that it balanced with the growth on growing stock for the last year of the projection period (figs. 11 and 12). The other assumptions were that commercial forest area will remain constant, and that growth, mortality, and cutting rates for each diameter class will not change.

The margin of growth over cut for softwood was 1.5 for both growing stock and sawtimber at the start. This margin decreased as annual removals were increased until the year 2001, when they balanced. The growth in 2001 would be approximately 1 billion cubic feet—an increase of 27 percent over the growth for 1971. Sawtimber cut for softwood also increased throughout the projection period. In 2001, the cut for sawtimber would be slightly less than the growth of 4.4 billion board feet (fig. 11). Most of the increase in volume would be in the smaller classes (fig. 13). The growing-stock volume in 2002 would be 15.1 billion cubic feet.

The growth-cut ratios for hardwoods in 1971 were 1.9 for growing stock and 1.5 for sawtimber. Growing stock growth and cut both increased during the projection period and balanced in 2001, when they equalled 599 million cubic feet (fig. 12). Growing-stock growth in

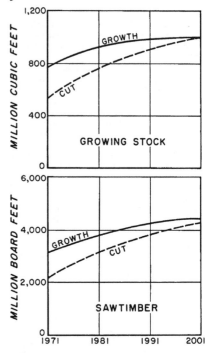

Figure 11.—*Prospective growth and cut of softwood, 1971-2001.*

fact increased 50 percent during the projection period.

Hardwood sawtimber growth and cut are a different matter. Although growth exceeded cut in 1971, sawtimber removals equaled growth in 1979 and exceeded it by an increasing margin for the remainder of the projection period. Growth would be only 81 percent of removals in 2001.

This persistent excess of removals over growth would reduce the hardwood sawtimber inventory from 21.2 billion board feet in 1971

14

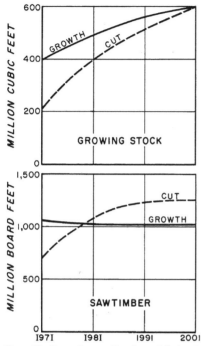

Figure 12.—*Prospective growth and cut of hardwood, 1971-2001.*

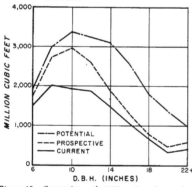

Figure 13.—*Comparison of 1972 softwood growing stock with prospective and potential inventories of 2002.*

to 17.7 billion in 2002. Graphically, this reduction is even more dramatic (fig. 14). There would be a volume loss in every diameter class over 12 inches.

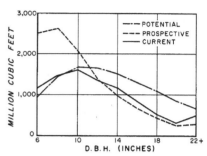

Figure 14.—*Comparison of 1972 hardwood growing stock with prospective and potential inventories of 2002.*

The reason for this reduction is the high cutting rates in the upper diameter classes. Growth on the remaining trees and ingrowth from trees moving from lower diameters cannot compensate for the large removals. The consequence is a reduction in the inventory.

In computing prospective hardwood cut, no cognizance was given to the insufficient number of trees of large diameter. However, size distribution and other variables were considered in the potential cut.

POTENTIAL CUT

For this projection, it was assumed that the commercial forest area will be the same, but that the oak-pine type will be converted to pure pine. With this conversion there will be 12.9 million acres in softwood forest types and 8.4 million in hardwoods. Mortality and growth rates were not adjusted.

Specific goals for softwood stands are a basal area of 90 square feet per acre for all live trees —rough and rotten as well as growing stock— and a reduction of the cull tree proportion from 7 to 3 percent. For the hardwoods, a basal area of 90 square feet is the desired density. The present cull proportion is relatively high, 28 percent. The goal, 14 percent, would result in a significant increase in the growing-stock inventory.

To correct the deficit of trees in the larger diameter classes, a goal for both types is to improve the distribution of trees by adjusting the annual cut. With the 1972 inventory and the desired inventory of 2002 as the bases, stand tables for each year of the projection period were found by interpolation. The cut each year was adjusted so that the interpolated stand structure was left. In the early years of the projection period the cut is reduced, but as the stand structure is rehabilitated by growth the removals increase toward the end. The annual removals are concentrated in lower diameters so that the deficit in large trees is gradually ameliorated.

If the goals for the potential cut projection were attained, Alabama would have a growing-stock inventory in 2002 of 32.1 billion cubic feet —versus 20.2 billion for the current inventory and 26.3 billion for the prospective cut. Softwoods would comprise 65 percent of the total.

About 1.6 billion cubic feet in annual growth would be available for harvest in 2001. This growth is 76 cubic feet per acre versus the 1971 growth of 56 cubic feet.

The increase in sawtimber growth is even more dramatic. It would be 328 board feet per acre versus the 197 board feet of current growth and 252 board feet for the prospective cut in 2001. The inventory needed for this growth may be seen in figures 13 and 14.

The volume and growth for both species groups in the potential cut is much greater than for 1971. Consequently, Alabama's forests are capable of supporting more than they now do.

Management Opportunities

Extensive acreages of mixed and pure hardwood types cover sites in Alabama that can support southern pine. Often the hardwood growth is small and concentrated on trees of little or no commercial value. Because most suitable non-stocked areas have been planted to pine, converting these low-potential hardwood stands is now the best means of increasing the pine timber supply.

The magnitude of the conversion task is enormous. Of the 17.4 million acres of pine sites in Alabama, some 9.7 million are now growing oak-pine or oak-hickory stands. Some of these stands have enough potential to be managed and regenerated to pine after the hardwoods are harvested. Others, however, have no potential value and are candidates for immediate conversion.

There are 2 million acres of pine sites that are poorly stocked with growing stock trees. Of these about 635,000 have an adequate pine seed source. Although control of competing hardwoods and some site preparation may be needed, natural regeneration may be relied upon to convert these sites. On the remaining areas, seed sources are either inadequate or absent, and artificial regeneration—either by seeding or planting—must be relied upon. About 1.3 million acres fall into this category.

Priorities for type conversion on pine sites can be outlined on the basis of cost and technical difficulty.

The first priority would be those sites which can be naturally regenerated. In some cases adequate pine reproduction already exists, and it can be released by harvesting or deadening the competing overstory. If an adequate seed source is present, reproduction can be established naturally prior to overstory removal.

Pine sites needing planting or seeding are next in priority. Some areas may have an overstory of a few large trees, which can be deadened economically. Most, however, are composed of many trees of different sizes, and site preparation with heavy machinery is necessary. Hence, conversion can be quite expensive for these areas.

Almost 4 million acres of forest land in Alabama are suited for hardwoods. Most of this acreage in bottom lands, which are some of the most potentially productive in the United States. The condition of a great many of these stands, however, bears witness to years of neglect. One of every five hardwood trees 5 inches or larger in Alabama has defects or rot that make it unsuitable for sawtimber now or in the future.

How serious are the conditions of these stands, and what can be done to improve them? The proportion of desirable trees provides clues.

A desirable tree is growing stock that is vigorous, has no defects that would seriously limit its present or prospective use, and contains no pathogens that would cause death or serious degrade before rotation age. Growing stock not classed as desirable is called acceptable. Forest land in Alabama was classified according to the amount of desirable trees present.

There are about 726,000 acres of hardwood sites that are poorly stocked with growing stock trees. These stands are the poorest, and restocking will take a long time. Improvement may be facilitated in some cases by removing cull trees. Some locations may be suitable for prompt restocking by planting such species as yellow-poplar in coves and cottonwood on good quality bottom land.

An additional 2.7 million acres are poorly stocked with desirable trees but are at least medium stocked with growing stock. There is enough growing stock on these areas to maintain periodic removals. These stands can be improved by killing culls and favoring desirable trees in improvement cuts.

There are 500,000 acres that are medium stocked with desirable trees. On about 118,000 acres there is not much competition from less desirable trees or unwanted vegetation; hence no special treatment is necessary. On the remainder, desirable trees have significant competition; and cull tree removal and thinning acceptable trees can improve the proportion of desirables.

17

About 76,000 acres of hardwoods are well stocked with desirable trees. No stand treatments are necessary except for thinning to reduce overstocking in some stands.

In total, over 3.5 million acres of hardwood sites need some form of stand treatment. Because of the magnitude of the hardwood stand treatment task, priorities need to be assigned. Although the economic values of treatments in hardwood stands are hard to measure, a preliminary list of priorities may be made on the basis of cost.

First would be the harvesting of undesirable but merchantable trees. Growing space would be freed while furnishing a net return. Next would be the deadening of large culls. The cost of girdling a tree is proportional to its diameter, but the growing space it occupies is proportional to its basal area. Hence, the greatest return will come by concentrating on large stems.

Clumps of small weed or cull trees should be treated last. Blanket treatment by chemical spraying or clearing with heavy machinery is needed. There are problems associated with blanket treatment—sprouting may occur or seedlings of desirable species may not appear promptly. Nevertheless, blanket treatment may be the only way to rehabilitate these stands.

RESOURCE OUTLOOK

Despite the increase in timber products output during the last 9 years, timber volume increased. Can Alabama's forests sustain expansion in the State's timber industries in the future? The answer is a qualified yes.

The outlook for the softwood supply is good. The excess of growth over removals in 1971 suggests that a moderate increase in pine timber removals will not deplete the resource. However, Alabama's forests could furnish more softwood than indicated by growth-cut ratios alone, if measures like type conversion were undertaken.

The prospect for hardwoods is mixed. Pulpwood and sawtimber were the leading roundwood products in 1971. The balance of growth over cut for growing stock is favorable for an increase in hardwood pulpwood removals. However, as indicated by the prospective cut, a substantial increase in the hardwood sawtimber harvest is not feasible. The supply of quality large-diameter hardwoods has not increased much since 1963, and the sawtimber cut in tupelo and blackgum is already exceeding growth. However, with hardwood stand improvement, the sawtimber supply for the future could be increased. Removals from improvement cuttings could furnish pulpwood while the stands were being rehabilitated.

Only by improving the resource now can Alabama's forests fully provide for industrial expansion in the years ahead.

Appendix

SURVEY METHODS

The data on forest acreage and timber volume in this report were secured by a sampling method involving a forest-nonforest classification on aerial photographs and on-the-ground measurements of trees at sample locations. The sample locations were at the intersections of a grid of lines spaced 3 miles apart. In Alabama, 151,673 photographic classifications were made and 5,724 ground sample locations were visited.

The initial estimates of forest area that were obtained with the aerial photographs were adjusted on the basis of the ground check.

A cluster of 10 variable-radius plots were installed at each ground sample location. Each sample tree on the variable-radius plots represented 3.75 square feet of basal area per acre. Trees less than 5.0 inches in diameter were tallied on fixed-radius plots around the plot centers. Together, these samples provided most of the information for the new inventory. A subsample of trees on the plots was measured in detail to obtain data for calculating timber volumes.

The plots established by the prior survey were remeasured to determine the elements of change and were the basis for estimating growth, mortality, removals, and changes in land use.

A special study was made to determine product output. It consisted of a canvass of all primary wood-using plants active in Alabama during 1971. Out-of-State firms known to use Alabama roundwood were also contacted. Additionally, fuelwood and other domestic uses were determined from an area sample.

RELIABILITY OF THE DATA

Reliability of the estimates may be affected by two types of errors. The first stems from the use of a sample to estimate the whole and from variability of the items being sampled. This type is termed sampling error; it is susceptible to a mathematical evaluation of the probability of error. The second type—often referred to as reporting or estimating error—derives from mistakes in measurement, judgment, or recording, and from limitations of method or equipment. Its effects cannot be appraised mathematically, but the Forest Service constantly attempts to hold it to a minimum by proper training and good supervision, and by emphasis on careful work.

Statistical analysis of the data indicates a sampling error of plus or minus 0.2 percent for the estimate of total commercial forest area, 1.2 percent for total cubic volume, and 1.8 percent for total board-foot volume. As these totals are broken down by forest type, species, tree diameter, and other subdivisions, the possibility of error increases and is greatest for the smallest items. The order of this increase is suggested in the following tabulation, which shows the sampling error to which the timber volume and area estimates are liable, two chances out of three:

Sampling errors for commercial forest area, growing-stock and sawtimber volumes, Alabama, 1972

Commercial forest area	Sampling error[1]	Cubic volume[2]	Sampling error[1]	Board-foot volume[3]	Sampling error[1]
Thousand acres	*Percent*	*Million cubic feet*	*Percent*	*Million board feet*	*Percent*
21,333.1	0.2				
853.3	1.0	20,211.7	1.2	63,517.1	1.8
213.3	2.0	7,276.2	2.0	51,448.8	2.0
94.8	3.0	3,433.9	3.0	22,866.2	3.0
53.3	4.0	1,819.1	4.0	12,862.2	4.0
34.1	5.0	1,164.2	5.0	8,231.8	5.0
8.5	10.0	291.0	10.0	2,058.0	10.0
3.8	15.0	129.4	15.0	914.6	15.0
2.1	20.0	72.8	20.0	514.5	20.0
1.4	25.0	46.6	25.0	329.3	25.0

[1] By random-sampling formula.
[2] Growing-stock volume on commercial forest land.
[3] Sawtimber volume on commercial forest land.

The sampling error to which the estimates of growth, mortality, and removals are liable, on a probability of two chances out of three, are:

Net annual growth and timber removals sampling error, Alabama, 1971

Net annual growth				Annual removals			
Cubic volume	Sampling error[1]	Board-foot volume	Sampling error[1]	Cubic volume	Sampling error[1]	Board-foot volume	Sampling error[1]
Million cubic feet	*Percent*	*Million board feet*	*Percent*	*Million cubic feet*	*Percent*	*Million board feet*	*Percent*
				739.6	1.8		
1,187.4	2.3			599.1	2.0		
697.9	3.0	4,201.7	3.4	266.3	3.0		
392.6	4.0	3,035.7	4.0	149.8	4.0	2,852.4	4.1
251.3	5.0	1,942.9	5.0	95.9	5.0	1,918.0	5.0
62.8	10.0	485.7	10.0	24.0	10.0	479.5	10.0
27.9	15.0	215.9	15.0	10.7	15.0	213.1	15.0
15.7	20.0	121.4	20.0	6.0	20.0	119.9	20.0
10.1	25.0	77.7	25.0	3.8	25.0	76.7	25.0

[1] By random-sampling formula.

DEFINITIONS OF TERMS

Forest Land Class

Forest land.—Land at least 16.7 percent stocked by forest trees of any size, or formerly having such tree cover and not currently developed for nonforest use.

Commercial forest land.—Forest land that is producing or is capable of producing crops of industrial wood and not withdrawn from timber utilization.

Nonstocked land.—Commercial forest land less than 16.7 percent stocked with growing-stock trees.

Productive-reserved forest land.—Productive public forest land withdrawn from timber utilization through statute or administrative regulation.

Unproductive forest land.—Forest land incapable of yielding crops of industrial wood because of adverse site conditions.

Tree Species

Commercial species.—Tree species presently or prospectively suitable for industrial wood products; excludes so-called weed species such as blackjack oak and blue beech.

Hardwoods.—Dicotyledonous trees, usually broadleaved and deciduous.

Softwoods.—Coniferous trees, usually evergreen, having needle or scale-like leaves.

Forest Type

Longleaf-slash pine.—Forests in which longleaf or slash pine, singly or in combination, comprise a plurality of the stocking. Common associates include other southern pines, oak, and gum.

Loblolly-shortleaf pine.—Forests in which southern pine and eastern redcedar except longleaf or slash pine, singly or in combination, comprise a plurality of the stocking. Common associates include oak, hickory, and gum.

Oak-pine.—Forests in which hardwoods (usually upland oaks) comprise a plurality of the stocking but in which softwoods, except cypress, comprise 25-50 percent of the stocking. Common associates include gum, hickory, and yellow-poplar.

Oak-hickory.—Forests in which upland oaks or hickory, singly or in combination, comprise a plurality of the stocking except where pines comprise 25-50 percent, in which case the stand would be classified oak-pine. Common associates include yellow-poplar, elm, maple, and black walnut.

Oak-gum-cypress.—Bottomland forests in which tupelo, blackgum, sweetgum, oaks, or southern cypress, singly or in combination, comprise a plurality of the stocking except where pines comprise 25-50 percent, in which case the stand would be classified oak-pine. Common associates include cottonwood, willow, ash, elm, hackberry, and maple.

Elm-ash-cottonwood.—Forests in which elm, ash, or cottonwood, singly or in combination, comprise a plurality of the stocking. Common associates include willow, sycamore, beech, and maple.

Class of Timber

Growing stock trees.—Sawtimber trees, poletimber trees, saplings, and seedlings; that is, all live trees except rough and rotten trees.

Desirable trees.—Growing-stock trees that have no serious defects to limit present or prospective use, are of relatively high vigor, and contain no pathogens that may result in death or serious deterioration before rotation age. They comprise the type of trees that forest managers aim to grow; that is, the trees favored in silvicultural operations.

Acceptable trees.—Trees meeting the specifications for growing stock but not qualifying as desirable trees.

Sawtimber trees.—Live trees of commercial species, 9.0 inches and larger in diameter at breast height for softwoods and 11.0 inches and larger for hardwoods, and containing at least one 12-foot saw log.

Poletimber trees.—Live trees of commercial species 5.0 to 9.0 inches in d.b.h. for softwoods and 5.0 to 11.0 inches for hardwoods, and of good form and vigor.

20

Saplings.—Live trees of commercial species, 1.0 inch to 5.0 inches in d.b.h. and of good form and vigor.

Rough and rotten trees.—Live trees that are unmerchantable for saw logs now or prospectively because of defect, rot, or species.

Salvable dead trees.—Standing or down dead trees that are considered currently or potentially merchantable.

Stand-Size Class

Sawtimber stands.—Stands at least 16.7 percent stocked with growing-stock trees, with half or more of this stocking in sawtimber or poletimber trees, and with sawtimber stocking at least equal to poletimber stocking.

Poletimber stands.—Stands at least 16.7 percent stocked with growing-stock trees, with half or more of this stocking in sawtimber or poletimber trees, and with poletimber stocking exceeding that of sawtimber stocking.

Sapling-seedling stands.—Stands at least 16.7 percent stocked with growing-stock trees, with more than half of this stocking in saplings or seedlings.

Nonstocked areas.—Commercial forest lands less than 16.7 percent stocked with growing-stock trees.

Stocking

Stocking is a measure of the extent to which the growth potential of the site is utilized by trees or preempted by vegetative cover. Stocking is determined by comparing the stand density in terms of number of trees or basal area with a specified standard. Full stocking is assumed to range from 100 to 133 percent of the stocking standard.

The tabulation below shows the density standard in terms of trees per acre, by size class, required for full stocking:

D.b.h. (inches)	Number of trees	D.b.h. (inches)	Number of trees
Seedlings	600	16	72
2	560	18	60
4	460	20	51
6	340	22	42
8	240	24	36
10	155	26	31
12	115	28	27
14	90	30	24

Volume

Volume of sawtimber.—Net volume of the saw-log portion of live sawtimber trees in board feet of the International rule, ¼-inch kerf.

Volume of growing stock.—Volume of sound wood in the bole of sawtimber and poletimber trees from stump to a minimum 4.0-inch top outside bark or to the point where the central stem breaks into limbs.

Volume of timber.—The volume of sound wood in the bole of growing stock, rough, rotten, and salvable dead trees 5.0 inches and larger in d.b.h. from stump to a

minimum 4.0-inch top outside bark or to the point where the central stem breaks into limbs.

Area Condition Class

A classification of commercial forest land based upon stocking by desirable trees and other conditions affecting current and prospective timber growth.

Class 10.—Areas 100 percent or more stocked with desirable trees and not overstocked.

Class 20.—Areas 100 percent or more stocked with desirable trees and overstocked with all live trees.

Class 30.—Areas 60 to 100 percent stocked with desirable trees and with less than 30 percent of the area controlled by other trees, inhibiting vegetation, slash, or nonstockable conditions.

Class 40.—Areas 60 to 100 percent stocked with desirable trees and with 30 percent or more of the area controlled by other trees, or conditions that ordinarily prevent occupancy by desirable trees.

Class 50.—Areas less than 60 percent stocked with desirable trees, but with 100 percent or more stocking of growing-stock trees.

Class 60.—Areas less than 60 percent stocked with desirable trees, but with 60 to 100 percent stocking of growing-stock trees.

Class 70.—Areas less than 60 percent stocked with desirable trees and with less than 60 percent stocking of growing-stock trees.

Miscellaneous Definitions

Basal area.—The area in square feet of the cross section at breast height of a single tree or of all the trees in a stand, usually expressed as square feet per acre.

D.b.h. (Diameter breast high).—Tree diameter in inches, outside bark, measured at 4½ feet above ground.

Diameter classes.—The 2-inch diameter classes extend from 1.0 inch below to 0.9 inch above the stated midpoint. Thus, the 12-inch class includes trees 11.0 inches through 12.9 inches d.b.h.

Site classes.—A classification of forest land in terms of inherent capacity to grow crops of industrial wood.

Log grades.—A classification of logs based on external characteristics as indicators of quality or value.

Gross growth.—Annual increase in net volume of trees in the absence of cutting and mortality.

Net annual growth.—The increase in volume of a specified size class for a specific year. Components of net annual growth include the increment in net volume of trees at the beginning of the specific year surviving to its end plus volume of trees reaching the size class during the year minus the volume of trees that died during the year minus the net volume of trees that become rough or rotten during the year.

Mortality.—Number or sound-wood volume of live trees dying from natural causes during a specified period.

Timber removals.—The net volume of growing-stock trees removed from the inventory by harvesting, cultural operations such as timber-stand improvement, land clearing, or changes in land use.

21

Timber products.—Roundwood products and plant by-products. Timber products output includes roundwood products cut from growing stock on commercial forest land; from other sources, such as cull trees, salvable dead trees, limbs, and saplings; from trees on noncommercial and nonforest lands; and from plant byproducts.

Roundwood products.—Logs, bolts, or other round sections cut from trees for industrial or consumer uses. Included are saw logs, veneer logs and bolts, cooperage logs and bolts, pulpwood, fuelwood, piling, poles and posts, hewn ties, mine timbers, and various other round, split, or hewn products.

Logging residues.—The unused portions of trees cut or killed by logging.

Plant byproducts.—Wood products, such as pulp chips, obtained incidental to manufacture of other products.

Plant residues.—Wood materials from manufacturing plants not utilized for some product. Included are slabs, edgings, trimmings, miscuts, sawdust, shavings, veneer cores and clippings, and pulp screening.

STANDARD TABLES

NOTE: Regional tables, identical in format to standard State tables 1-22, are available for each of the six forest resource regions in Alabama. They are free on request to the Southern Forest Experiment Station.

Table 1. *Area by land classes, Alabama, 1972*

Land class	Area
	Thousand acres
Forest:	
Commercial	21,333.1
Productive-reserved	17.0
Unproductive	...
Total forest	21,350.1
Nonforest:	
Cropland[1]	5,118.6
Pasture and range[1]	2,555.0
Other[2]	3,521.7
Total nonforest	11,195.3
All land[3]	32,545.4

[1] Source: Census of Agriculture.
[2] Includes swampland, industrial and urban areas, other nonforest land, and 113,100 acres, classed as water by Forest Survey standards, but defined by the Bureau of the Census as land.
[3] Source: United States Bureau of the Census, Land and Water Area of the United States.

Table 2. *Area of commercial forest land by ownership classes, Alabama, 1972*

Ownership class	Area
	Thousand acres
Public:	
National forest	629.5
Other federal	182.0
State	155.6
County and municipal	53.4
Total public	1,020.5
Private:	
Forest industry[1]	4,204.9
Farmer	6,732.5
Miscellaneous private:	
Individual	7,675.8
Corporate	1,699.4
Total private	20,312.6
All ownerships	21,333.1

[1] Not including 371,800 acres of farmer-owned and miscellaneous private lands leased to forest industry.

Table 3. *Area of commercial forest land by stand-size and ownership classes, Alabama, 1972*

Stand-size class	All ownerships	National forest	Other public	Forest industry	Farmer and misc. private
	— — — — — *Thousand acres* — — — — —				
Sawtimber	6,839.5	302.6	113.9	1,517.7	4,905.3
Poletimber	7,141.9	203.7	122.1	1,214.0	5,602.1
Sapling and seedling	7,242.5	123.2	155.0	1,449.8	5,514.5
Nonstocked areas	109.2	...	...	23.4	85.8
All classes	21,333.1	629.5	391.0	4,204.9	16,107.7

Table 4. *Area of commercial forest land by stand-volume and ownership classes, Alabama, 1972*

Stand-volume per acre[1]	All ownerships	National forest	Other public	Forest industry	Farmer and misc. private
	— — — — *Thousand acres* — — — —				
Less than 1,500 board feet	9,398.6	175.9	143.7	1,618.9	7,460.1
1,500 to 5,000 board feet	7,644.3	248.3	154.3	1,386.0	5,855.7
More than 5,000 board feet	4,290.2	205.3	93.0	1,200.0	2,791.9
All classes	21,333.1	629.5	391.0	4,204.9	16,107.7

[1] International ¼-inch rule.

24

Table 5. *Area of commercial forest land by stocking classes based on selected stand components, Alabama, 1972*

Stocking percentage	All trees	Stocking classified in terms of				
		Growing-stock trees			Rough and rotten trees	Inhibiting vegetation
		Total	Desirable	Acceptable		
— — — — — — *Thousand acres* — — — — — —						
160 or more	10.8	...	...	...		
150 to 160	258.9	74.8	28.9	...	...	
140 to 150	713.6	266.9	28.3	22.5	...	
130 to 140	1,591.1	553.2	43.6	29.8	6.3	
120 to 130	3,173.3	1,209.2	71.8	27.6	...	...
110 to 120	4,248.1	2,201.8	201.8	95.7	...	...
100 to 110	4,249.0	3,089.2	299.7	288.1	16.9	6.3
90 to 100	3,156.1	3,473.0	494.1	634.0	12.3	...
80 to 90	1,883.5	3,269.6	897.5	1,121.0	45.6	...
70 to 80	978.5	2,870.8	1,110.9	1,880.2	67.9	6.3
60 to 70	495.4	1,633.0	1,782.7	2,758.1	200.2	...
50 to 60	250.8	1,134.9	2,050.0	3,270.5	405.0	12.0
40 to 50	145.1	705.9	2,613.4	3,146.7	949.4	22.2
30 to 40	77.3	518.4	2,784.5	2,842.6	2,227.5	12.4
20 to 30	29.4	158.3	3,152.9	2,584.4	3,804.8	120.0
10 to 20	29.9	97.0	3,006.0	1,492.9	6,102.3	251.3
Less than 10	42.3	77.1	2,767.0	1,139.0	7,494.9	20,902.6
All areas	21,333.1	21,333.1	21,333.1	21,333.1	21,333.1	21,333.1

Table 6. *Area of commercial forest land by area-condition and ownership classes, Alabama, 1972*

Area-condition class	All ownerships	National forest	Other public	Forest industry	Farmer and misc. private
— — — — — — *Thousand acres* — — — — — —					
10	462.5	6.0	...	92.9	363.6
20	211.6	5.7	12.3	56.7	136.9
30	1,136.6	33.0	4.7	333.1	765.8
40	3,148.6	54.0	53.8	886.8	2,154.0
50	4,004.6	157.7	86.9	896.0	2,864.0
60	9,677.6	286.1	189.1	1,595.6	7,606.8
70	2,691.6	87.0	44.2	343.8	2,216.6
All classes	21,333.1	629.5	391.0	4,204.9	16,107.7

Table 7. *Area of commercial forest land by site and ownership classes, Alabama, 1972*

Site class	All ownerships	National forest	Other public	Forest industry	Farmer and misc. private
			Thousand acres		
165 cu. ft. or more	413.4	...	11.4	87.5	314.5
120 to 165 cu. ft.	2,334.2	17.5	22.6	677.0	1,617.1
85 to 120 cu. ft.	7,947.7	145.5	95.6	1,581.0	6,125.6
50 to 85 cu. ft.	9,175.6	378.1	202.8	1,624.5	6,970.2
Less than 50 cu. ft.	1,462.2	88.4	58.6	234.9	1,080.3
All classes	21,333.1	629.5	391.0	4,204.9	16,107.7

Table 8. *Area of commercial forest land by forest types and ownership classes, Alabama, 1972*

Type	All ownerships	National forest	Other public	Forest industry	Farmer and misc. private
			Thousand acres		
Longleaf-slash pine	1,483.6	88.5	39.1	545.2	810.8
Loblolly-shortleaf pine	6,380.1	162.1	101.2	1,394.5	4,722.3
Oak-pine	5,016.9	185.1	103.9	1,065.3	3,662.6
Oak-hickory	5,913.1	187.8	103.6	813.6	4,808.1
Oak-gum-cypress	2,443.5	6.0	43.2	381.0	2,013.3
Elm-ash-cottonwood	95.9	...	...	5.3	90.6
All types	21,333.1	629.5	391.0	4,204.9	16,107.7

Table 9. *Area of noncommercial forest land by forest types, Alabama, 1972*

Type	All areas	Productive-reserved areas	Unproductive areas
		Thousand acres	
Longleaf-slash pine	1.0	1.0	
Loblolly-shortleaf pine	8.8	8.8	
Oak-pine	4.4	4.4	...
Oak-hickory	2.8	2.8	...
All types	17.0	17.0	...

26

Table 10. *Number of growing-stock trees on commercial forest land by species and diameter classes, Alabama, 1972*

Species	All classes	5.0- 6.9	7.0- 8.9	9.0- 10.9	11.0- 12.9	13.0- 14.9	15.0- 16.9	17.0- 18.9	19.0- 20.9	21.0- 28.9	29.0 and larger
						Thousand trees					
Softwood:											
Longleaf pine	115,522	38,735	28,329	21,231	14,936	8,215	3,022	791	225	38	...
Slash pine	98,884	48,184	27,481	11,971	5,840	2,876	1,514	678	236	104	...
Shortleaf pine	351,841	177,709	88,610	46,541	24,365	9,315	3,904	1,005	290	102	...
Loblolly pine	653,817	299,366	163,157	82,432	48,503	28,398	16,430	8,867	3,653	2,924	87
Virginia pine	83,602	49,487	21,522	7,845	3,450	1,030	208	60	...	...	...
Spruce pine	12,365	4,798	2,536	1,158	1,225	1,200	614	477	212	132	13
Cypress	6,343	1,849	1,481	838	647	387	381	232	172	335	21
Other softwoods[1]	16,359	9,687	4,930	1,226	312	142	32	13	8	9	...
Total	1,338,733	629,815	338,046	173,242	99,278	51,563	26,105	12,123	4,796	3,644	121
Hardwood:											
Select white oaks[2]	83,660	33,241	20,119	12,789	7,073	5,253	2,523	1,387	633	601	41
Select red oaks[3]	21,333	7,345	4,230	3,327	2,511	1,285	1,057	685	319	516	58
Other white oaks	89,143	37,785	24,771	12,737	6,592	3,797	1,725	887	437	384	28
Other red oaks	223,098	97,381	51,061	34,130	16,746	11,141	6,134	3,180	1,422	1,663	240
Pecan	2,144	622	504	384	202	222	51	39	47	65	8
Other hickories	121,236	51,096	30,469	19,525	9,936	5,702	2,526	961	503	506	12
Sweetgum	215,765	118,327	50,571	24,266	11,445	5,905	2,818	1,306	586	528	13
Tupelo and blackgum	107,786	41,272	28,226	19,298	8,782	5,183	2,985	1,125	486	418	11
Hard maple	2,590	1,273	539	426	213	119	12	...	...	8	...
Soft maple	31,152	17,803	6,555	3,602	1,234	756	714	186	217	81	4
Beech	5,883	1,915	870	966	636	501	403	242	194	138	18
Ash	26,639	12,539	5,833	3,210	1,875	1,740	750	261	257	170	4
Cottonwood	2,388	929	781	225	173	105	51	13	41	64	6
Basswood	2,664	1,101	662	294	221	160	156	48	10	7	5
Yellow-poplar	45,310	16,454	10,628	7,182	4,406	2,886	1,741	1,111	482	382	38
Black walnut	1,002	509	178	108	108	76	14	9	...	...	...
Black cherry	4,339	2,518	1,373	241	140	61	...	...	...	6	...
Willow	2,680	1,202	801	445	194	23	15	...	...	...	...
Magnolia (*Magnolia* spp.)	41,483	18,733	10,124	6,757	3,545	1,368	512	294	93	57	...
American elm	9,609	3,652	2,215	1,575	873	621	368	196	74	19	16
Other elms	15,490	7,521	4,199	2,245	877	242	270	69	38	29	...
Hackberry	13,679	4,735	3,408	2,971	1,050	464	576	286	98	87	4
Sycamore	3,143	1,123	749	356	260	237	128	133	57	92	8
Other hardwoods	43,713	33,222	6,544	2,305	781	353	316	109	51	28	4
Total	1,115,929	512,298	265,410	159,364	79,873	48,200	25,845	12,527	6,045	5,849	518
All species	2,454,662	1,142,113	603,456	332,606	179,151	99,763	51,950	24,650	10,841	9,493	639

[1] Includes redcedar, hemlock, and sand pine.
[2] Includes white, swamp chestnut, swamp white, and chinkapin oaks.
[3] Includes northern red, Shumard, and cherrybark oaks.

27

Table 11. *Volume of timber on commercial forest land by class of timber and by softwoods and hardwoods, Alabama, 1972*

Class of Timber	All species	Soft-wood	Hard-wood
	— — Million cubic feet — —		
Sawtimber trees:			
Saw-log portion	10,402.1	6,782.7	3,619.4
Upper-stem portion	2,021.0	969.4	1,051.6
Total	12,423.1	7,752.1	4,671.0
Poletimber trees	7,788.6	3,530.5	4,258.1
All growing stock	20,211.7	11,282.6	8,929.1
Rough trees	1,514.3	138.4	1,375.9
Rotten trees	698.1	117.4	580.7
Salvable dead trees	13.6	9.3	4.3
All timber	22,437.7	11,547.7	10,890.0

Table 12. *Volume of growing stock and sawtimber on commercial forest land by ownership classes and by softwoods and hardwoods, Alabama, 1972*

Ownership class	Growing stock			Sawtimber		
	All species	Soft-wood	Hard-wood	All species	Soft-wood	Hard-wood
	— Million cubic feet —			— Million board feet —		
National forest	729.7	502.5	227.2	2,744.3	2,216.3	528.0
Other public	371.6	210.1	161.5	1,270.2	848.3	421.9
Forest industry	4,572.3	2,969.2	1,603.1	16,035.0	11,962.6	4,072.4
Farmer and misc. private	14,538.1	7,600.8	6,937.3	43,467.6	27,256.2	16,211.4
All ownerships	20,211.7	11,282.6	8,929.1	63,517.1	42,283.4	21,233.7

Table 13. *Volume of growing stock on commercial forest land by species and diameter classes, Alabama, 1972*

Species	All classes	Diameter class (inches at breast height)									
		5.0-6.9	7.0-8.9	9.0-10.9	11.0-12.9	13.0-14.9	15.0-16.9	17.0-18.9	19.0-20.9	21.0-28.9	29.0 and larger
	— — — — — — — — — — Million cubic feet — — — — — — — — — —										
Softwood:											
Longleaf pine	1,280.3	103.4	210.9	271.8	301.7	229.6	110.5	36.1	13.0	3.3	...
Slash pine	730.6	112.4	164.3	141.2	116.4	80.1	59.8	33.1	14.8	8.5	...
Shortleaf pine	2,532.3	438.3	555.2	526.3	478.7	278.4	165.0	60.1	20.1	10.2	...
Loblolly pine	5,962.0	701.9	924.0	907.8	903.9	815.0	660.2	481.5	256.2	293.3	18.2
Virginia pine	408.2	119.8	119.4	79.6	55.5	25.6	6.1	2.2	...	...	...
Spruce pine	186.8	11.4	18.0	13.0	21.9	36.7	27.3	26.6	17.0	12.5	2.4
Cypress	125.1	3.4	9.0	9.0	11.0	11.0	15.5	11.5	13.1	37.1	4.5
Other softwoods	57.3	18.6	20.5	8.3	4.7	2.4	1.2	.4	.3	.9	...
Total	11,282.6	1,509.2	2,021.3	1,957.0	1,893.8	1,478.8	1,045.6	651.5	334.5	365.8	25.1
Hardwood:											
Select white oaks	782.7	78.0	109.8	125.9	123.9	126.5	79.8	58.9	31.4	41.9	6.6
Select red oaks	282.1	18.0	25.6	36.1	40.6	30.9	34.0	28.9	18.1	41.0	8.9
Other white oaks	649.5	90.3	129.4	116.5	101.5	80.6	50.0	33.5	19.3	23.4	5.0
Other red oaks	1,907.0	236.7	286.0	328.7	269.7	252.8	187.9	127.5	69.8	114.8	33.1
Pecan	29.9	.8	2.5	3.7	4.3	6.4	1.7	1.7	2.2	5.6	1.0
Other hickories	970.3	110.8	161.1	192.7	166.1	140.0	86.6	43.0	28.1	39.8	2.1
Sweetgum	1,449.9	267.8	299.2	272.4	216.1	156.1	100.1	59.5	33.3	44.0	1.4
Tupelo and blackgum	901.4	89.7	158.9	207.7	143.0	118.5	89.9	42.9	23.7	25.4	1.7
Hard maple	16.9	3.2	2.6	3.9	3.6	2.9	.3	...	...	.4	...
Soft maple	174.2	38.5	30.7	32.4	17.1	15.8	19.0	5.7	8.9	5.8	.3
Beech	76.1	3.5	4.1	8.5	9.3	10.1	11.9	8.3	9.6	8.0	2.8
Ash	239.5	29.0	35.7	33.1	32.8	44.9	26.2	12.0	13.0	12.1	.7
Cottonwood	30.6	3.3	5.5	2.9	3.4	3.0	1.7	.7	2.9	5.6	1.6
Basswood	29.7	2.6	4.5	3.7	4.3	4.6	6.1	2.4	.6	.4	.5
Yellow-poplar	564.5	45.5	71.2	83.8	86.5	82.2	68.0	58.3	31.1	32.7	5.2
Black walnut	8.4	1.2	1.2	1.1	2.2	1.7	.5	.5	...	...	...
Black cherry	19.6	6.0	6.9	2.3	2.3	1.6	...	...	...	.5	...
Willow	15.9	3.3	4.3	4.1	3.3	.5	.4	...	...	...	...
Magnolia (*Magnolia* spp.)	291.6	46.4	55.3	63.9	58.2	30.6	16.2	11.2	4.9	3.9	...
American elm	86.6	7.6	12.2	14.1	12.1	15.3	11.4	7.4	3.7	1.3	1.5
Other elms	95.6	16.0	23.4	22.2	13.8	5.6	7.8	2.9	1.7	2.2	...
Hackberry	116.5	9.8	16.8	24.8	16.4	10.4	16.0	10.1	5.2	6.6	.4
Sycamore	47.4	3.5	5.6	3.7	4.8	5.9	4.8	6.3	3.9	7.5	1.4
Other hardwoods	143.2	53.8	29.7	21.4	11.5	8.9	9.4	4.0	2.4	1.8	.3
Total	8,929.1	1,165.3	1,483.2	1,609.6	1,346.8	1,155.8	829.7	525.7	313.8	424.7	74.5
All species	20,211.7	2,674.5	3,504.5	3,566.6	3,240.6	2,634.6	1,875.3	1,177.2	648.3	790.5	99.6

28

Table 14. *Volume of sawtimber on commercial forest land by species and diameter classes, Alabama, 1972*

Species	Diameter class (inches at breast height)								
	All classes	9.0-10.9	11.0-12.9	13.0-14.9	15.0-16.9	17.0-18.9	19.0-20.9	21.0-28.9	29.0 and larger
	Million board feet								
Softwood:									
Longleaf pine	5,384.8	1,220.0	1,719.2	1,401.1	701.3	233.3	86.4	23.5	...
Slash pine	2,593.1	635.8	691.3	499.5	390.3	219.7	98.8	57.7	...
Shortleaf pine	7,904.7	2,597.3	2,497.7	1,467.1	870.8	314.3	102.5	55.0	...
Loblolly pine	24,013.2	3,881.9	4,855.5	4,748.2	3,988.3	2,997.2	1,607.1	1,824.2	110.8
Virginia pine	860.6	396.8	292.2	130.3	30.4	10.9	...	...	...
Spruce pine	818.8	63.9	111.0	191.3	143.6	144.7	90.6	60.9	12.8
Cypress	611.7	40.3	55.9	58.6	85.6	62.2	75.2	211.3	22.6
Other softwoods	96.5	44.0	24.3	13.6	6.4	2.2	1.0	5.0	...
Total	42,283.4	8,880.0	10,247.1	8,509.7	6,216.7	3,984.5	2,061.6	2,237.6	146.2
Hardwood:									
Select white oaks	2,383.1	...	540.9	637.9	424.1	322.6	180.7	240.2	36.7
Select red oaks	1,036.2	...	160.5	153.5	176.6	151.3	104.1	241.0	49.2
Other white oaks	1,544.5	...	431.9	395.6	263.3	182.2	108.9	130.2	32.4
Other red oaks	5,226.6	...	1,103.9	1,230.5	973.1	698.8	383.3	644.3	192.7
Pecan	96.4	...	15.2	25.0	8.6	6.6	9.9	26.7	4.4
Other hickories	2,001.9	...	568.4	560.8	365.3	186.5	126.5	183.9	10.5
Sweetgum	2,837.5	...	828.7	741.8	514.6	318.8	181.9	244.9	6.8
Tupelo and blackgum	1,969.1	...	516.6	531.1	438.3	218.0	124.0	132.1	9.0
Hard maple	23.5	...	10.4	10.2	.9	...	...	2.0	...
Soft maple	266.9	...	49.5	57.1	71.2	22.9	40.9	24.2	1.1
Beech	234.3	...	29.4	36.5	46.9	29.2	43.7	36.8	11.8
Ash	583.5	...	103.8	188.9	116.6	54.3	61.1	55.6	3.2
Cottonwood	81.4	...	11.6	11.5	7.6	2.9	13.0	27.4	7.4
Basswood	79.8	...	14.0	19.7	28.3	10.4	2.0	1.8	3.6
Yellow-poplar	1,479.6	...	265.7	336.8	293.4	265.4	143.5	150.9	23.9
Black walnut	18.7	...	7.9	6.2	2.0	2.6	...	...	...
Black cherry	15.3	...	7.8	5.5	...	...	...	2.0	...
Willow	13.3	...	9.8	1.5	2.0	...	...	...	...
Magnolia (*Magnolia* spp.)	444.1	...	180.5	113.0	63.1	49.4	19.3	18.8	...
American elm	215.4	...	37.6	64.3	48.8	35.5	15.3	6.3	7.6
Other elms	135.9	...	49.6	21.2	33.5	12.3	8.7	10.6	...
Hackberry	251.2	...	50.9	39.8	63.9	43.5	23.3	28.2	1.6
Sycamore	149.2	...	15.0	21.3	20.3	28.4	19.7	38.1	6.4
Other hardwoods	146.3	...	36.2	35.5	39.2	16.9	9.1	7.9	1.5
Total	21,233.7	...	5,045.8	5,245.2	4,001.6	2,658.5	1,618.9	2,253.9	409.8
All species	63,517.1	8,880.0	15,292.9	13,754.9	10,218.3	6,643.0	3,680.5	4,491.5	556.0

Table 15. *Volume of sawtimber on commercial forest land by species and log grade, Alabama, 1972*

Species	All grades	Grade 1	Grade 2	Grade 3	Grade 4
	— — — — — *Million board feet* — — — — — —				
Softwood:					
Yellow pines[1]	41,575.2	4,539.2	4,909.6	32,126.4	...
Cypress	611.7	198.9	110.7	302.1	...
Redcedar[2]	96.5	96.5	...	...	...
Total	42,283.4	4,834.6	5,020.3	32,428.5	...
Hardwood:[3]					
Select white and red oaks	3,419.3	405.8	644.7	1,667.7	701.1
Other white and red oaks	6,771.1	431.9	875.3	3,242.6	2,221.3
Hickory	2,098.3	147.2	326.8	1,136.2	488.1
Hard maple	23.5	...	2.3	7.7	13.5
Sweetgum	2,837.5	290.9	401.5	1,433.8	711.3
Ash, walnut, and black cherry	617.5	79.2	111.8	332.4	94.1
Yellow-poplar	1,479.6	136.7	178.9	649.8	514.2
Other hardwoods	3,986.9	340.5	621.4	2,154.6	870.4
Total	21,233.7	1,832.2	3,162.7	10,624.8	5,614.0
All species	63,517.1	6,666.8	8,183.0	43,053.3	5,614.0

[1] Based on **Southern Pine Log Grades for Yard and Structural Lumber**, Research Paper SE-39, published by the Southeastern Forest Experiment Station in 1968.
[2] All redcedar saw logs are graded as No. 1.
[3] Grades 1-3 are based on **Hardwood Log Grades for Standard Lumber**, issued by the U.S. Forest Products Laboratory under the designation D1737A in 1961. Grade-4 tie and timber log specifications are based chiefly on knot size and log soundness.

Table 16. *Annual growth and removals of growing stock on commercial forest land by species, Alabama, 1971*

Species	Net annual growth	Annual removals
	Million cubic feet	
Softwood:		
Yellow pines	780.3	521.6
Cypress	4.0	.8
Other softwoods	3.7	3.5
Total	788.0	525.9
Hardwood:		
Select white and red oaks	44.3	23.3
Other white and red oaks	130.7	67.9
Hickory	35.4	21.4
Hard maple	.4	...
Sweetgum	67.6	30.9
Tupelo and blackgum	28.0	23.6
Ash, walnut, and black cherry	11.6	5.3
Yellow-poplar	26.1	11.4
Other hardwoods	55.3	29.9
Total	399.4	213.7
All species	1,187.4	739.6

Table 17. *Annual growth and removals of growing stock on commercial forest land by ownership classes and by softwoods and hardwoods, Alabama, 1971*

Ownership class	Net annual growth			Annual removals		
	All species	Soft-wood	Hard-wood	All species	Soft-wood	Hard-wood
	— — — — — — *Million cubic feet* — — — — — — —					
National forest	33.5	24.4	9.1	14.6	10.4	4.2
Other public	19.9	13.1	6.8	14.5	10.7	3.8
Forest industry	259.0	188.1	70.9	179.7	139.1	40.6
Farmer and misc. private	875.0	562.4	312.6	530.8	365.7	165.1
All ownerships	1,187.4	788.0	399.4	739.6	525.9	213.7

Table 18. *Annual growth and removals of sawtimber on commercial forest land by species, Alabama, 1971*

Species	Net annual growth	Annual removals
	— *Million board feet* —	
Softwood:		
Yellow pines	3,122.6	2,129.1
Cypress	22.8	4.0
Other softwoods	8.1	10.3
Total	3,153.5	2,143.4
Hardwood:		
Select white and red oaks	163.8	92.2
Other white and red oaks	374.7	218.6
Hickory	97.7	72.6
Hard maple	2.0	1.0
Sweetgum	136.1	90.5
Tupelo and blackgum	62.4	77.1
Ash, walnut, and black cherry	30.0	12.9
Yellow-poplar	81.6	52.7
Other hardwoods	99.9	91.4
Total	1,048.2	709.0
All species	4,201.7	2,852.4

Table 19. *Annual growth and removals of sawtimber on commercial forest land by ownership classes and by softwoods and hardwoods, Alabama, 1971*

Ownership class	Net annual growth			Annual removals		
	All species	Soft-wood	Hard-wood	All species	Soft-wood	Hard-wood
	— — — — — — *Million board feet* — — — — — — —					
National forest	130.1	108.0	22.1	73.5	55.9	17.6
Other public	76.7	57.8	18.9	63.9	51.3	12.6
Forest industry	985.3	796.8	188.5	726.2	601.1	125.1
Farmer and misc. private	3,009.6	2,190.9	818.7	1,988.8	1,435.1	553.7
All ownerships	4,201.7	3,153.5	1,048.2	2,852.4	2,143.4	709.0

Table 20. *Mortality of growing stock and sawtimber on commercial forest land by species, Alabama, 1971*

Species	Growing stock	Sawtimber
	Million cubic feet	*Million board feet*
Softwood:		
Yellow pines	49.3	138.9
Other softwoods	.5	1.0
Total	49.8	139.9
Hardwood:		
Select white and red oaks	2.4	8.5
Other white and red oaks	11.6	29.3
Hickory	6.3	15.6
Hard maple	.1	.3
Sweetgum	9.8	17.4
Tupelo and blackgum	6.7	17.9
Ash, walnut, and black cherry	2.4	5.5
Yellow-poplar	1.6	5.3
Other hardwoods	12.8	31.5
Total	53.7	131.3
All species	103.5	271.2

Table 21. *Mortality of growing stock and sawtimber on commercial forest land by ownership classes and by softwoods and hardwoods, Alabama, 1971*

Ownership class	Growing stock			Sawtimber		
	All species	Soft-wood	Hard-wood	All species	Soft-wood	Hard-wood
	— — — — — — Million cubic feet — — — — — —					
National forest	3.1	2.6	0.5	12.8	11.0	1.8
Other public	2.0	1.5	.5	7.4	6.0	1.4
Forest industry	20.3	10.7	9.6	51.5	30.8	20.7
Farmer and misc. private	78.1	35.0	43.1	199.5	92.1	107.4
All ownerships	103.5	49.8	53.7	271.2	139.9	131.3

Table 22. *Mortality of growing stock and sawtimber on commercial forest land by causes and by softwoods and hardwoods, Alabama, 1971*

Cause of death	Growing stock			Sawtimber		
	All species	Soft-wood	Hard-wood	All species	Soft-wood	Hard-wood
	— — — — — — Million cubic feet — — — — — —					
Fire	2.9	2.0	0.9	5.2	3.2	2.0
Insects	6.1	6.1	...	22.2	22.2	...
Disease	4.7	4.0	.7	13.1	10.6	2.5
Other	15.8	4.9	10.9	42.9	10.2	32.7
Unknown	74 0	32.8	41.2	187.8	93.7	94.1
All causes	103.5	49.8	53.7	271.2	139.9	131.3

Table 23. *Total output of timber products by product, by type of material used, and by softwoods and hardwoods, Alabama, 1971*

Product and species group	Standard unit	Total output		Roundwood products		Plant byproducts	
		Number	M cu. ft.	Number	M cu. ft.	Number	M cu. ft.
Saw logs:							
Softwood	M bd. ft.[1]	1,139,317	198,987	1,095,586	195,343	43,731	3,644
Hardwood	M bd. ft.[1]	385,929	66,418	385,929	66,418	...	...
Total	M bd. ft.[1]	1,525,246	265,405	1,481,515	261,761	43,731	3,644
Veneer logs and bolts:							
Softwood	M bd. ft.	221,031	35,719	221,031	35,719	...	...
Hardwood	M bd. ft.	57,019	9,568	57,019	9,568	...	...
Total	M bd. ft.	278,050	45,287	278,050	45,287	...	...
Pulpwood:							
Softwood	Std. cords[2]	4,587,240	371,566	3,429,940	277,825	1,157,300	93,741
Hardwood	Std. cords[2]	1,696,331	135,675	1,428,731	114,301	267,600	21,374
Total	Std. cords[2]	6,283,571	507,241	4,858,671	392,126	1,424,900	115,115
Cooperage:							
Softwood	M bd. ft.	3,633	596	3,633	596	...	...
Hardwood	M bd. ft.	1,826	263	1,826	263	...	...
Total	M bd. ft.	5,459	859	5,459	859	...	...
Piling:							
Softwood	M linear ft.	805	645	805	645	...	...
Hardwood	M linear ft.	...	...	...	...	...	...
Total	M linear ft.	805	645	805	645	...	...
Poles:							
Softwood	M pieces	1,002	14,231	1,002	14,231	...	...
Hardwood	M pieces	...	...	...	...	...	...
Total	M pieces	1,002	14,231	1,002	14,231	...	...
Commercial posts (round and split):							
Softwood	M pieces	1,974	1,146	1,974	1,146	...	...
Hardwood	M pieces	1	1	1	1	...	...
Total	M pieces	1,975	1,147	1,975	1,147	...	...
Other[3]:							
Softwood	M cu. ft.	4,232	4,232	108	108	4,124	4,124
Hardwood	M cu. ft.	5,650	5,650	1,971	1,971	3,679	3,679
Total	M cu. ft.	9,882	9,882	2,079	2,079	7,803	7,803
Total industrial products:							
Softwood		...	...	...	525,613	...	101,509
Hardwood		...	...	...	192,522	...	25,053
Total		...	...	...	718,135	...	126,562
Noncommercial posts (round and split):							
Softwood	M pieces	326	207	326	207	...	...
Hardwood	M pieces	2,008	1,288	2,008	1,288	...	...
Total	M pieces	2,334	1,495	2,334	1,495	...	...
Fuelwood:							
Softwood	Std. cords	290,780	21,809	11,367	853	[4]279,413	[4]20,956
Hardwood	Std. cords	299,947	22,496	192,000	14,400	[4]107,947	[4] 8,096
Total	Std. cords	590,727	44,305	203,367	15,253	[4]387,360	[4]29,052
All products:							
Softwood		...	...	...	526,673	...	122,465
Hardwood	...	...	...	...	208,210	...	33,149
Total	...	...	...	...	734,883	...	155,614

[1] International ¼-inch rule.
[2] Rough wood basis (for example, chips converted to equivalent standard cords).
[3] Includes chemical wood, handle stock, miscellaneous dimension and other minor industrial products. Additionally, byproducts include material used for livestock bedding, mulch, etc.
[4] Includes plant byproducts used for industrial and domestic fuel.

Table 24. *Output of roundwood products by source and by softwoods and hardwoods, Alabama, 1971*

Product and species group	All sources	Growing stock trees[1]			Rough and rotten trees[1]	Salvable dead trees[1]	Other sources[2]
		Total	Saw-timber	Pole-timber			
				Thousand cubic feet			
Industrial products:							
Saw logs:							
Softwood	195,343	191,290	190,303	987	658	438	2,957
Hardwood	66,418	64,064	63,408	656	1,891	...	463
Total	261,761	255,354	253,711	1,643	2,549	438	3,420
Veneer logs and bolts:							
Softwood	35,719	34,658	34,658	...	...	...	1,061
Hardwood	9,568	9,402	9,402	...	126	...	40
Total	45,287	44,060	44,060	...	126	...	1,101
Pulpwood:							
Softwood	277,825	256,910	188,046	68,864	3,256	333	17,326
Hardwood	114,301	96,100	57,040	39,060	9,862	49	8,290
Total	392,126	353,010	245,086	107,924	13,118	382	25,616
Misc. industrial products:							
Cooperage:							
Softwood	596	588	566	22	...	2	6
Hardwood	263	259	259	...	2	...	2
Total	859	847	825	22	2	2	8
Piling:							
Softwood	645	642	642	...	...	...	3
Hardwood	...	...	...	...	...	...	...
Total	645	642	642	...	...	...	3
Poles:							
Softwood	14,231	14,126	12,494	1,632	...	...	105
Hardwood	...	...	...	...	...	...	...
Total	14,231	14,126	12,494	1,632	...	...	105
Commercial posts (round and split):							
Softwood	1,146	1,045	...	1,045	...	...	101
Hardwood	1	1	...	1	...	...	...
Total	1,147	1,046	...	1,046	...	...	101
Other:							
Softwood	108	102	52	50	...	...	6
Hardwood	1,971	1,967	1,847	120	1	...	3
Total	2,079	2,069	1,899	170	1	...	9
All misc. industrial products:							
Softwood	16,726	16,503	13,754	2,749	...	2	221
Hardwood	2,235	2,227	2,106	121	3	...	5
Total	18,961	18,730	15,860	2,870	3	2	226
All industrial products:							
Softwood	525,613	499,361	426,761	72,600	3,914	773	21,565
Hardwood	192,522	171,793	131,956	39,837	11,882	49	8,798
Total	718,135	671,154	558,717	112,437	15,796	822	30,363
Noncommercial posts (round and split):							
Softwood	207	151	38	113	...	...	56
Hardwood	1,288	945	45	900	...	...	343
Total	1,495	1,096	83	1,013	...	...	399
Fuelwood:							
Softwood	853	524	66	458	96	38	195
Hardwood	14,400	8,855	1,851	7,004	1,613	649	3,283
Total	15,253	9,379	1,917	7,462	1,709	687	3,478
All products:							
Softwood	526,673	500,036	426,865	73,171	4,010	811	21,816
Hardwood	208,210	181,593	133,852	47,741	13,495	698	12,424
Total	734,883	681,629	560,717	120,912	17,505	1,509	34,240

[1] On commercial forest land.
[2] Includes noncommercial forest land, nonforest land such as fence rows, trees less than 5.0 inches in diameter, and treetops and limbs.

Table 25. *Timber removals from growing stock on commercial forest land by items and by softwoods and hardwoods, Alabama, 1971*

Item	All species	Soft-wood	Hard-wood
	— *Thousand cubic feet* —		
Roundwood products:			
Saw logs	255,354	191,290	64,064
Veneer logs and bolts	44,060	34,658	9,402
Pulpwood	353,010	256,910	96,100
Cooperage logs and bolts	847	588	259
Piling	642	642	...
Poles	14,126	14,126	...
Posts	2,142	1,196	946
Other	2,069	102	1,967
Fuelwood	9,379	524	8,855
All products	681,629	500,036	181,593
Logging residues	32,918	17,235	15,683
Other removals	25,111	8,677	16,434
Total removals	739,658	525,948	213,710

Table 26. *Timber removals from live sawtimber on commercial forest lands by items and by softwoods and hardwoods, Alabama, 1971*

Item	All species	Soft-wood	Hard-wood
	— *Thousand board feet* —		
Roundwood products:			
Saw logs	1,384,482	1,037,301	347,181
Veneer logs and bolts	263,355	208,035	55,320
Pulpwood	886,949	697,149	189,800
Cooperage logs and bolts	4,924	3,179	1,745
Piling	3,808	3,808	...
Poles	72,197	72,197	...
Posts	325	150	175
Other	11,630	284	11,346
Fuelwood	9,388	333	9,055
All products	2,637,058	2,022,436	614,622
Logging residues	141,436	78,134	63,302
Other removals	73,895	42,820	31,075
Total removals	2,852,389	2,143,390	708,999

Table 27. *Volume of plant residues by industrial source and type of residue and by softwoods and hardwoods, Alabama, 1971*

Species group and type	All industries	Lumber	Veneer and plywood	Other
	— — — — — *Thousand cubic feet* — — — — —			
Softwood:				
Coarse[1]	1,855	1,792	9	54
Fine[2]	10,513	10,266	90	157
Total	12,368	12,058	99	211
Hardwood:				
Coarse	1,946	1,478	437	31
Fine	9,528	9,212	129	187
Total	11,474	10,690	566	218
All species:				
Coarse	3,801	3,270	446	85
Fine	20,041	19,478	219	344
All types	23,842	22,748	665	429

[1] Unused material suitable for chipping, such as slabs, edgings, and veneer cores.
[2] Unused material not suitable for chipping, such as sawdust and shavings.

Table 28. *Projections of net annual growth, available cut, and inventory of growing stock and sawtimber on commercial forest land, Alabama, 1971-2001[1]*

Species group	Growing stock				Sawtimber			
	1971	1981	1991	2001	1971	1981	1991	2001
	— — — — *Thousand cubic feet* — — — —				— — — — *Thousand board feet* — — — —			
Softwood:								
Cut	525,900	754,500	901,300	1,002,600	2,143,400	3,188,000	3,824,000	4,281,000
Growth	788,000	926,900	989,900	1,002,600	3,153,500	3,831,000	4,243,000	4,382,000
Inventory[2]	11,282,600	13,425,000	14,687,700	15,111,900	42,283,400	49,665,000	54,930,000	57,454,000
Hardwood:								
Cut	213,700	397,100	511,100	598,600	709,000	1,086,000	1,238,000	1,251,000
Growth	399,400	497,300	565,900	598,600	1,048,200	1,011,000	1,020,000	1,009,000
Inventory[2]	8,929,100	10,144,200	10,900,200	11,182,800	21,233,700	21,776,000	20,118,000	17,745,000
Total:								
Cut	739,600	1,151,600	1,412,400	1,601,200	2,852,400	4,274,000	5,062,000	5,532,000
Growth	1,187,400	1,424,200	1,555,800	1,601,200	4,201,700	4,842,000	5,263,000	5,391,000
Inventory[2]	20,211,700	23,569,200	25,587,900	26,294,700	63,517,100	71,441,000	75,048,000	75,199,000

[1] Based on the assumption that the cut of growing stock will be in balance with growth by the year 2001, and that forestry progress will continue at the rate indicated by recent trends.
[2] Inventory as of January 1 of the following year.

USDA Forest Service
Resource Bulletin SO-43

1973

Mississippi Forest Industries, 1972

USDA Forest Service
Resource Bulletin SO-43

Mississippi Forest Industries, 1972

Daniel F. Bertelson

Southern Forest Experiment Station
New Orleans, Louisiana
Forest Service, U.S. Department of Agriculture

1973

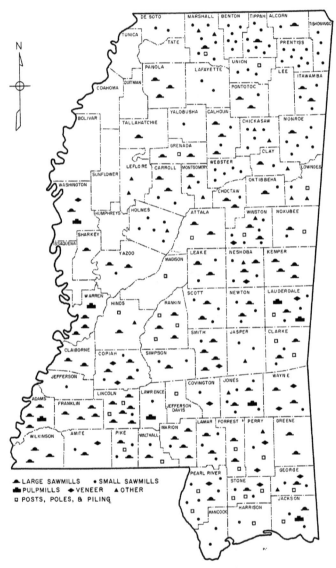

Primary wood-using plants in Mississippi, 1972.

ii

MISSISSIPPI FOREST INDUSTRIES, 1972

Daniel F. Bertelson

Mississippi forests supplied more than 559 million cubic feet of roundwood to forest industries in 1972, an increase of over 39 percent since 1966. Softwoods, mainly pine, made up more than two-thirds of the total. Pulpwood and saw logs were the major products, accounting for 85 percent of the harvest. Veneer logs added 11 percent, and poles and piling made up more than half the remainder. Figure 1 shows recent trends in output of these products.

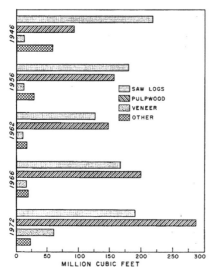

Figure 1.—*Output of industrial roundwood in Mississippi, 1946-1972.*

A total of 315 wood-using plants were in operation in 1972, 40 percent less than in 1966. The numbers of sawmills, hardwood veneer plants, post, pole, and piling plants, and miscellaneous plants decreased, while numbers of pulpmills and pine plywood plants increased.

These are among the major findings of a canvass of all primary forest industries in Mississippi. Past surveys of Mississippi forest industries were made in 1946, 1956, 1962, and 1966. The Mississippi Forestry Commission saw a need for a 1972 survey in conjunction with the interim forest inventory by 3P sampling. Under supervision of Oscar Tissue, Commission personnel visited all primary wood-using plants in the State. Their data were compiled and analyzed by the Forest Resources Research Unit of the Southern Forest Experiment Station.

This report tabulates total State production and shows softwood and hardwood output by county. It also lists names and addresses of all primary forest industries; plant locations are mapped on page ii. For readers who need greater detail, a supplementary report, "Mississippi Product Output and Timber Removals by County," is available without charge from the Southern Forest Experiment Station.

PULPWOOD

In 1972, Mississippi forests produced 3.5 million cords of round pulpwood, which accounted for 51 percent of the State's timber harvest. Although the roundwood production was almost twice that of 1962, it declined some 14 percent since the 1969 record year (fig. 2).

Hardwoods were the main pulpwood species in Mississippi in 1962. Since then hardwood pro-

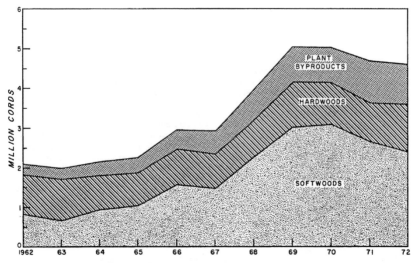

Figure 2.—*Pulpwood production in Mississippi, 1962-1972.*

duction has increased only 21 percent while the softwood harvest has risen 176 percent. Softwoods now make up two-thirds of the State's round pulpwood production.

Mississippi has always been a net exporter of pulpwood. In 1972, 1.3 million cords were sent to five neighboring States while some 0.2 million cords were imported from four adjacent States. Pulpmills in Mississippi processed 2.5 million cords of roundwood, of which 91 percent came from within the State.

Since 1966 two new pulpmills became operational, adding 2,620 tons per day to Mississippi's pulping capacity. With the two new mills and plant expansion at four other mills, Mississippi's pulping capability has risen from 3,605 tons in 1966 to 6,050 tons per day in 1972. Individual pulping capacity at the eight mills ranges from 80 to 1,620 tons daily.

In addition to the roundwood volume, the equivalent of 1 million cords of Mississippi plant byproducts were used by pulpmills. This volume is over one-fifth of the total pulpwood production. The amount of plant byproducts used in 1972 was almost four times that used in 1962. In three of Mississippi's eight pulpmills plant by-

products are the only source of fiber. Utilization of plant byproducts for pulp has increased greatly over the past decade and will continue to increase, though not as rapidly, in future years. Mississippi industries now sell over three-fourths of their coarse residues to pulpmills. This percentage should go up, and then the rate of increase will depend entirely on the volume of wood processed each year at the State's primary wood-using industries.

SAW LOGS

Mississippi produced 1.1 billion board feet of saw logs in 1972, an increase of 14 percent since 1966. Softwoods, mainly pine but including some cypress and redcedar, made up over three-fifths of the total volume. Oaks accounted for over half of the hardwoods cut for saw logs; gums were second in volume harvested.

The number of sawmills operating in Mississippi has been fluctuating greatly in the last two decades. In 1956, there were over 1,000 sawmills in the State. Six years later the number fell to 290. With an increase in lumber production in 1966, the number of mills rose to 350. In 1972,

2

Mississippi had 241 sawmills in operation, of which 103 were large (cutting at least 3 million board feet annually).

In 1966, the average sawmill produced under 3 million board feet annually. This average rose to almost 4.8 million in 1972. Individual mill production ranged from 2,000 to over 54 million board feet. Thirty-three mills each produced over 10 million board feet in 1972. Large sawmills processed 90 percent of the lumber in Mississippi; two-thirds of their production was softwood. Small sawmills processed almost one and a half times more hardwood than softwood.

Over half of the saw logs harvested in Mississippi crossed county lines before being sawn into lumber. This figure indicates the dominance of the large sawmills which reach into surrounding counties to obtain enough logs to maintain plant production. Small mills generally use logs from their own county. Five percent of the saw log harvest was shipped to surrounding States, while Mississippi sawmills imported 78 million board feet of logs.

All but 17 large sawmills reported selling wood chips to pulpmills in 1972, and 32 small mills disposed of their residues in the same manner. Over 65 million cubic feet of coarse residues were generated by the State's sawmills, and 88 percent of this volume was sold to the pulp industry.

VENEER

Mississippi forests produced 372 million board feet of veneer logs in 1972, almost four times the 1966 harvest. This great increase is due to the expansion of the southern pine plywood industry. In 1972, Mississippi had 16 veneer plants in operation. Seven produced pine plywood, five manufactured flat or face veneer, and four produced container veneer.

In 1962, Mississippi did not have a southern pine plywood plant. The State harvested 74 million board feet of veneer logs, of which softwoods accounted for less than 1 percent. By 1966, there were four plywood plants in operation, and softwoods made up almost half the harvest. The State's veneer-log production rose to 372 million board feet in 1972, with softwoods accounting for 92 percent of the total. The seven plywood plants processed 364 million board feet of pine veneer logs. They processed over 99 percent of all the softwood volume and 93 percent of the

total volume manufactured by the 16 veneer plants in the State. The average production of the seven plywood plants in 1972 was 52 million board feet.

Mississippi's hardwood veneer production hit its peak in the late 1940's, and the trend has been downward since then. The number of hardwood plants has dropped from 20 in 1962 to 18 in 1966 and only 9 in 1972. Like the number of plants, the volume harvested has declined. The 31 million board feet of hardwood veneer logs produced by Mississippi in 1972 was only 60 percent of the 1966 harvest.

Mississippi veneer plants imported 49 million board feet of veneer logs for their operations, while the State exported over 27 million feet to surrounding States. These plants converted 61 percent of their coarse residues into pulp chips and produced 26 million board feet of studs from veneer cores.

OTHER PRODUCTS

All other products accounted for 4 percent of the total Mississippi roundwood harvest. Over 800,000 Mississippi trees were cut for poles in 1972. The State also produced almost 8 million linear feet of piling and over 3 million commercial posts. The three products combined made up 3 percent of the harvest. The remaining 1 percent went into the manufacture of cooperage, furniture and handle stock, charcoal wood, excelsior, shuttleblocks, and miscellaneous dimension.

PLANT RESIDUES

Mississippi forest industries in converting roundwood into primary products generated 145 million cubic feet of various residues. Seven-tenths of this volume was in coarse items such as slabs, edgings, cull pieces, and other material suitable for conversion into pulp chips. The rest was comprised of finer particles such as saw dust and shavings.

Almost 84 million cubic feet of plant byproducts went into the production of pulp. Another 15 million cubic feet were burned for domestic and industrial fuel. And 18 million cubic feet were used for miscellaneous purposes such as charcoal, animal bedding, and soil mulch.

Mississippi forest industries converted 81 percent of their wood residues into plant byproducts in 1972. The remaining 27 million cubic feet of residues were mostly fine particles with no available market (fig. 3). Pulp chips are the most profitable byproduct, and Mississippi industries used over 78 percent of the coarse residues for this purpose.

Over 1.6 million tons of bark were accumulated by Mississippi forest industries in 1972. Only 57 percent of this volume was utilized. Industrial fuel accounted for 94 percent of bark use. Small amounts went into charcoal, domestic fuel, animal bedding, and soil mulch. The remaining 694,000 tons of bark went unused.

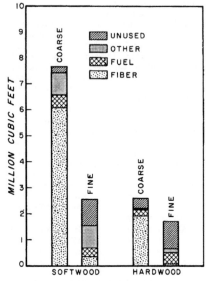

Figure 3.—*Use of Mississippi plant residues, 1972.*

4

Table 1. *Volume of industrial roundwood, 1972*

Product	Standard units	Volume in standard units			Roundwood volume		
		All species	Softwood	Hardwood	All species	Softwood	Hardwood
				—————— *M cu. ft.* ——————			
Saw logs	M bd. ft.[1]	1,146,673	714,421	432,252	189,579	117,523	72,056
Veneer logs	M bd. ft.[1]	372,680	341,491	31,189	61,409	56,175	5,234
Pulpwood	Std. cords	3,545,499	2,367,567	1,177,932	286,007	191,773	94,234
Piling	M linear ft.	7,882	7,882	...	5,642	5,642	...
Poles	M pieces	834	834	...	9,722	9,722	...
Posts	M pieces	3,026	3,026	...	1,740	1,740	...
Misc. products[2]	M cu. ft.	5,212	536	4,676	5,212	536	4,676
Total					559,311	383,111	176,200

[1] International ¼-inch rule.
[2] Includes chemical wood, furniture stock, handle stock, excelsior, cooperage, misc. dimension, and other industrial products.

Table 2. *Industrial roundwood, by species, 1972*

Species group	Saw logs	Veneer logs	Pulpwood	Piling	Poles	Posts	Miscellaneous products
	——*M bd. ft.[1]*——		Std. cords	*M linear ft.*	—*M pieces*—		*M cu. ft.*
Softwood:							
Pines	704,904	340,049	2,367,567	7,882	834	3,024	536
Cypress	9,463	1,442	...	...	...	2	...
Other softwoods	54	...	...	...	...	...	...
Total	714,421	341,491	2,367,567	7,882	834	3,026	536
Hardwood:							
Black and tupelo gums	9,513	2,558	[2]381,129	...	...	...	845
Sweetgum	56,187	8,013	...	...	...	...	1,081
Red oaks	169,042	982	[3]396,678	...	...	...	705
White oaks	68,171	492	...	...	...	...	495
Other hardwoods	129,339	19,144	400,125	...	...	...	1,550
Total	432,252	31,189	1,177,932	...	...	...	4,676
All species	1,146,673	372,680	3,545,499	7,882	834	3,026	5,212

[1] International ¼-inch rule.
[2] Black and tupelo combined with sweetgum.
[3] Red and white oaks combined.

Table 3. *Residues produced by primary wood-using plants, 1972*

Type of industry[1]	All species			Softwood			Hardwood		
	Type	Fine[2]	Coarse[3]	Total	Fine[2]	Coarse[3]	Total	Fine[2]	Coarse[3]
	——————————— *M cu. ft.* ———————————								
Lumber	102,975	37,468	65,507	65,275	21,742	43,533	37,700	15,726	21,974
Veneer	36,407	1,221	35,186	33,479	1,132	32,347	2,928	89	2,839
Piling, poles and posts	3,238	2,499	739	3,238	2,499	739	...	...	...
Miscellaneous products	2,467	1,340	1,127	246	148	98	2,221	1,192	1,029
All products	145,087	42,528	102,559	102,238	25,521	76,717	42,849	17,007	25,842

[1] Excludes woodpulp industry.
[2] Fine residues includes sawdust, screenings and other material generally too small for chipping.
[3] Coarse residues include slabs, edgings, trimmings, and other material generally suitable for chipping.

Table 4. *Volume of primary plant byproducts, 1972*

Source of industry[1]	Type of use	All species	Softwood	Hardwood
		— — — — — M cu. ft. — — — — —		
Lumber	Fuel[2]	8,778	3,027	5,751
	Fiber[3]	60,839	44,259	16,580
	Other[4]	9,880	8,387	1,493
	Total	79,497	55,673	23,824
Veneer	Fuel	5,951	5,248	703
	Fiber	21,779	19,590	2,189
	Other	8,526	8,526	...
	Total	36,256	33,364	2,892
Piling, poles and posts	Fuel	209	209	...
	Fiber	449	449	...
	Other	38	38	...
	Total	696	696	...
Miscellaneous industries	Fuel	576	35	541
	Fiber	839	...	839
	Other	155	...	155
	Total	1,570	35	1,535
All industries	Fuel	15,514	8,519	6,995
	Fiber	83,906	64,298	19,608
	Other	18,599	16,951	1,648
	Total	118,019	89,768	28,251

[1] Excludes woodpulp industry.
[2] Includes all residues used as fuel by industrial plants and domestic fuel either sold or given away.
[3] Includes all residues used in manufacture of fiber products, such as pulp or hardboard.
[4] Includes residues used as livestock bedding, mulch, floor sweepings, and specialty items.

Table 5. *Movement of industrial roundwood, by product, 1972*

Product	Unit	Out of State receipts	Logged and remained in State	Logged and shipped out of State	Total receipts	Total production
		— — — — — — — — — — Standard units — — — — — — — — — —				
Saw logs	M bd. ft.[1]	77,902	1,091,967	54,706	1,169,869	1,146,673
Veneer	M bd. ft.[1]	48,909	345,039	27,641	393,948	372,680
Pulpwood	Std. cords	214,442	2,256,047	1,289,452	2,470,489	3,545,499
Piling	M linear ft.	4,636	7,037	845	11,673	7,882
Poles	M pieces	169	805	29	974	834
Posts	M pieces	31	3,026	...	3,057	3,026
Misc. products	M cu. ft.	([2])	4,777	435	4,777	5,212

[1] International ¼-inch rule.
[2] Negligible.

Table 6. *Saw-log production by county, 1972*

County	All species	Softwood	Hardwood	County	All species	Softwood	Hardwood
	— — — *M bd. ft.¹* — — —				— — — *M bd. ft.¹* — — —		
Adams	22,583	11,145	11,438	Lowndes	6,010	2,792	3,218
Alcorn	3,773	372	3,401				
Amite	28,014	25,933	2,081	Madison	7,458	5,998	1,460
Attala	14,766	11,827	2,939	Marion	28,556	27,107	1,449
				Marshall	5,546	572	4,974
Benton	10,354	4,494	5,860	Monroe	15,029	7,097	7,932
Bolivar	1,496	17	1,479	Montgomery	6,658	3,022	3,636
Calhoun	10,530	4,197	6,333	Neshoba	22,811	17,103	5,708
Carroll	11,095	4,470	6,625	Newton	20,690	13,993	6,697
Chickasaw	6,392	900	5,492	Noxubee	15,887	8,642	7,245
Choctaw	9,365	5,159	4,206				
Claiborne	17,292	4,031	13,261	Oktibbeha	9,297	7,094	2,203
Clarke	27,138	23,210	3,928				
Clay	5,974	1,166	4,808	Panola	3,289	216	3,073
Coahoma	7,474	881	6,593	Pearl River	14,941	13,345	1,596
Copiah	33,859	28,493	5,366	Perry	15,967	14,185	1,782
Covington	8,642	6,543	2,099	Pike	6,180	5,832	348
				Pontotoc	7,587	1,539	6,048
De Soto	1,476	77	1,399	Prentiss	5,459	1,418	4,041
Forrest	14,339	13,539	800	Quitman	2,680	496	2,184
Franklin	49,502	44,923	4,579				
				Rankin	34,971	21,454	13,517
George	11,114	9,837	1,277				
Greene	15,025	13,903	1,122	Scott	21,416	14,489	6,927
Grenada	10,665	3,857	6,808	Sharkey	13,972	1,243	12,729
				Simpson	19,716	16,678	3,038
Hancock	4,276	3,918	358	Smith	24,570	20,445	4,125
Harrison	2,150	2,150	. . .	Stone	12,953	12,807	146
Hinds	7,286	2,186	5,100	Sunflower	180	. . .	180
Holmes	11,895	1,849	10,046				
Humphreys	2,569	191	2,378	Tallahatchie	4,052	598	3,454
				Tate	4,918	122	4,796
Issaquena	10,903	142	10,761	Tippah	6,354	1,416	4,938
Itawamba	17,986	3,867	14,119	Tishomingo	3,782	720	3,062
				Tunica	4,741	412	4,329
Jackson	12,617	11,134	1,483				
Jasper	20,720	18,398	2,322	Union	3,302	501	2,801
Jefferson	30,690	20,488	10,202				
Jefferson Davis	7,298	6,297	1,001	Walthall	6,656	6,150	506
Jones	19,270	14,735	4,535	Warren	37,767	1,809	35,958
				Washington	1,575	17	1,558
Kemper	47,722	36,543	11,179	Wayne	23,655	22,993	662
				Webster	6,380	3,683	2,697
Lafayette	11,247	6,391	4,856	Wilkinson	55,900	28,492	27,408
Lamar	11,724	10,860	864	Winston	17,702	9,224	8,478
Lauderdale	18,748	15,289	3,459				
Lawrence	8,086	4,156	3,930	Yalobusha	2,355	612	1,743
Leake	23,836	20,059	3,777	Yazoo	28,083	1,338	26,745
Lee	495	364	131				
Leflore	223	42	181	All counties	1,146,673	714,421	432,252
Lincoln	27,019	20,734	6,285				

¹ International ¼-inch rule.

7

Table 7. *Saw log movement, 1972*

County[1]	Logged and remained in county	Outgoing shipments	Incoming shipments	Total log receipts
		— — — — — — $M\ bd.\ ft.^2$ — — — — — — — —		
Adams	11,022	11,560	21,303	32,325
Benton	4,204	6,149	240	4,444
Calhoun	6,190	4,340	25,878	32,068
Carroll	6,836	4,259	2,718	9,554
Chickasaw	3,778	2,614	104	3,882
Choctaw	5,281	4,084	4,531	9,812
Clarke	15,415	11,722	16,620	32,035
Copiah	24,607	9,252	22,305	46,912
Franklin	20,452	29,050	22,092	42,544
George	3,116	7,998	2,338	5,454
Holmes	5,272	6,623	749	6,021
Itawamba	17,221	765	7,900	25,121
Jackson	7,578	5,039	1,390	8,968
Jones	9,526	9,744	19,106	28,632
Kemper	16,143	31,579	183	16,326
Lamar	7,047	4,678	23,170	30,217
Lauderdale	10,676	8,073	7,935	18,611
Leake	8,315	15,521	4,609	12,924
Lincoln	20,905	6,114	17,533	38,438
Marion	21,996	6,560	45,055	67,051
Marshall	4,993	553	6,484	11,477
Monroe	8,732	6,297	3,019	11,751
Neshoba	20,547	2,264	67,516	88,063
Newton	9,039	11,652	1,049	10,088
Panola	2,629	660	11,334	13,963
Pearl River	4,734	10,207	12,685	17,419
Pike	2,752	3,428	18,279	21,031
Pontotoc	6,108	1,478	5,483	11,591
Prentiss	2,746	2,713	416	3,162
Rankin	11,466	9,950	2,053	13,519
Scott	14,864	20,108	2,901	17,765
Simpson	9,192	10,524	947	10,139
Smith	18,694	5,876	6,924	25,618
Stone	4,127	8,827	20,200	24,327
Tippah	4,748	1,606	8,097	12,845
Tishomingo	1,972	1,810	...	1,972
Union	1,940	1,362	211	2,151
Warren	24,960	12,808	25,640	50,600
Wayne	13,096	10,558	24,268	37,364
Webster	2,249	4,131	501	2,750
Wilkinson	41,271	14,630	19,114	60,385
Winston	11,350	6,352	3,030	14,380
Yazoo	10,265	17,819	11,269	21,534
All other counties	83,472	253,819	131,164	214,636
All counties	541,526	605,156	628,343	1,169,869

[2] International ¼-inch rule.
[1] Counties with less than three sawmills are omitted.

8

Table 8. *Round pulpwood production, 1972*

County	All species	Softwood	Hardwood	County	All species	Softwood	Hardwood
	— — — *Standard cords* — — —				— — — *Standard cords* — — —		
Adams	34,619	1,645	32,974	Lowndes	15,719	12,402	3,317
Alcorn	10,355	8,816	1,539				
Amite	84,426	71,004	13,422	Madison	39,692	18,687	21,005
Attala	76,385	57,650	18,735	Marion	69,549	46,837	22,712
				Marshall	17,407	11,365	6,042
Benton	11,826	9,437	2,389	Monroe	16,114	10,960	5,154
Bolivar	14,024	...	14,024	Montgomery	37,334	25,712	11,622
Calhoun	9,577	8,099	1,478	Neshoba	61,191	41,815	19,376
Carroll	13,133	8,002	5,131	Newton	94,056	55,261	38,795
Chickasaw	21,939	16,134	5,805	Noxubee	35,912	15,852	20,060
Choctaw	42,761	28,069	14,692				
Claiborne	47,911	14,454	33,457	Oktibbeha	16,869	11,745	5,124
Clarke	159,201	96,795	62,406				
Clay	7,437	5,019	2,418	Panola	6,838	890	5,948
Coahoma	4,302	...	4,302	Pearl River	57,213	45,484	11,729
Copiah	125,303	91,397	33,906	Perry	62,572	52,368	10,204
Covington	66,067	51,043	15,024	Pike	93,612	80,280	13,332
				Pontotoc	8,851	4,509	4,342
De Soto	...	...	...	Prentiss	26,171	20,786	5,385
Forrest	37,458	27,064	10,394	Quitman	319	290	29
Franklin	60,576	29,908	30,668				
				Rankin	119,344	77,130	42,214
George	54,547	45,273	9,274				
Greene	94,642	57,966	36,676	Scott	65,943	45,273	20,670
Grenada	5,077	2,527	2,550	Sharkey	4,074	70	4,004
				Simpson	64,271	51,455	12,816
Hancock	54,789	50,716	4,073	Smith	37,816	25,025	12,791
Harrison	55,686	50,046	5,640	Stone	36,481	26,041	10,440
Hinds	37,231	15,124	22,107	Sunflower	267	3	264
Holmes	48,597	23,118	25,479				
Humphreys	3,782	...	3,782	Tallahatchie	3,579	1,261	2,318
				Tate	4,361	...	4,361
Issaquena	11,039	...	11,039	Tippah	32,960	26,485	6,475
Itawamba	40,112	31,780	8,332	Tishomingo	50,536	41,153	9,383
				Tunica	12	9	3
Jackson	98,953	89,668	9,285				
Jasper	111,281	78,580	32,701	Union	12,348	9,876	2,472
Jefferson	63,295	25,296	37,999				
Jefferson Davis	51,552	47,024	4,528	Walthall	52,721	39,096	13,625
Jones	71,052	37,152	33,900	Warren	23,558	1,147	22,411
				Washington	3,628	...	3,628
Kemper	56,958	34,726	22,232	Wayne	89,584	54,649	34,935
				Webster	42,745	30,488	12,257
Lafayette	19,098	9,879	9,219	Wilkinson	73,224	26,265	46,959
Lamar	27,006	19,521	7,485	Winston	57,019	40,395	16,624
Lauderdale	96,822	60,491	36,331				
Lawrence	58,974	49,221	9,753	Yalobusha	13,445	8,481	4,964
Leake	80,959	62,532	18,427	Yazoo	16,314	517	15,797
Lee	6,430	5,273	1,157				
Leflore	1,409	410	999				
Lincoln	105,259	86,646	18,613	All counties	3,545,499	2,367,567	1,177,932

Table 9. *Veneer-log production by county, 1972*

County[1]	All species	Softwood	Hardwood	County[1]	All species	Softwood	Hardwood
	— — —M bd. ft.[2] — — —				— — —M bd. ft.[2] — — —		
Adams	2,763	1,967	796	Lawrence	2,657	2,173	484
Alcorn	29	...	29	Leake	2,904	2,904	...
Amite	19,408	19,393	15	Lincoln	5,036	4,477	559
Attala	1,419	1,419	...				
				Madison	1,191	1,191	...
Bolivar	1,320	...	1,320	Marion	1,315	785	530
Calhoun	22	22	...	Neshoba	2,749	2,506	243
Choctaw	231	231	...	Newton	6,957	6,459	498
Claiborne	363	...	363	Noxubee	3,509	3,471	38
Clarke	14,278	12,952	1,326				
Coahoma	1,395	16	1,379	Oktibbeha	1,106	1,106	...
Copiah	7,650	4,844	2,806				
Covington	8,568	7,633	935	Pearl River	4,962	3,119	1,843
				Perry	13,934	13,321	613
Forrest	2,533	2,036	497	Pike	2,872	2,669	203
Franklin	12,899	12,758	141				
				Rankin	17,524	17,251	273
George	9,603	8,588	1,015				
Greene	13,673	11,479	2,194	Scott	9,646	9,646	...
				Sharkey	168	...	168
Hancock	5,362	5,259	103	Simpson	589	...	589
Harrison	2,789	2,774	15	Smith	14,068	13,619	449
Hinds	1,137	908	229	Stone	9,348	9,159	189
Issaquena	549	...	549	Tippah	1	...	1
Itawamba	41	33	8	Tunica	2,848	29	2,819
Jackson	14,164	14,158	6	Walthall	57	57	...
Jasper	16,614	16,006	608	Warren	616	...	616
Jefferson	2,298	1,833	465	Washington	1,520	...	1,520
Jefferson Davis	2,929	2,455	474	Wayne	27,867	27,021	846
Jones	8,778	7,488	1,290	Wilkinson	10,688	10,007	681
				Winston	12,890	12,890	...
Kemper	45,562	45,345	217				
				Yazoo	69	...	69
Lamar	6,502	6,058	444				
Lauderdale	12,710	11,976	734	All counties	372,680	341,491	31,189

[1] Counties with negligible output are omitted.

[2] International ¼-inch rule.

10

Table 10. *Piling production by county, 1972*

County[1]	All species (softwood)	County[1]	All species (softwood)	County[1]	All species (softwood)
	M linear feet		*M linear feet*		*M linear feet*
Amite	122	Jasper	1	Pearl River	2,411
Attala	5	Jefferson	5	Perry	84
Choctaw	4	Jones	8	Pike	151
Clarke	2	Kemper	82	Rankin	6
Copiah	108				
Covington	20	Lamar	324	Simpson	10
Forrest	307	Lauderdale	21	Stone	741
Franklin	110	Lawrence	57		
		Lincoln	46	Walthall	167
George	19			Warren	13
Hancock	1,448	Madison	10	Wayne	5
Harrison	331	Marion	142	Wilkinson	57
Hinds	39			Winston	5
		Neshoba	5		
Jackson	1,011	Noxubee	5	All counties	7,882

[1] Counties with negligible output are omitted.

Table 11. *Pole production by county, 1972*

County[1]	All species (softwood)	County[1]	All species (softwood)	County[1]	All species (softwood)
	M pieces		*M pieces*		*M pieces*
Amite	41	Jackson	106	Pearl River	21
		Jasper	6	Perry	65
Clarke	6	Jefferson Davis	52	Pike	4
Copiah	8	Jones	8		
Covington	4			Rankin	4
		Kemper	21		
Forrest	72			Stone	69
Franklin	4	Lamar	40		
		Lauderdale	14	Union	29
		Lawrence	4		
George	30	Lincoln	75		
Greene	59			Walthall	4
		Marion	5	Wayne	21
Hancock	8			Wilkinson	31
Harrison	14	Newton	1		
Hinds	3	Noxubee	5	All counties	834

[1] Counties with negligible output are omitted.

11

Table 12. *Commercial post production by county, 1972*

County[1]	All species (softwood)	County[1]	All species (softwood)	County[1]	All species (softwood)
	M pieces		*M pieces*		*M pieces*
Attala	32	Jasper	28	Pearl River	126
Choctaw	2	Jefferson	8	Perry	85
Claiborne	12	Jefferson Davis	217		
Clarke	35	Jones	56	Rankin	37
Copiah	70	Kemper	26	Scott	28
Covington	56	Lafayette	276	Simpson	9
Forrest	176	Lamar	276	Stone	165
Franklin	21	Lauderdale	83		
		Leake	158	Union	58
George	11	Lincoln	325		
Greene	219	Madison	4	Warren	4
Hancock	30	Marion	6	Winston	2
Harrison	7				
Hinds	80	Neshoba	35	Yalobusha	9
		Newton	33		
Jackson	151	Noxubee	70	All counties	3,026

[1] Counties with negligible output are omitted.

Table 13. *Output of miscellaneous products by county, 1972*

County[1]	All species	Softwood	Hardwood	County[1]	All species	Softwood	Hardwood
	— — — *M cubic feet* — — —				— — — *M cubic feet* — — —		
Alcorn	13	...	13	Lowndes	1,468	...	1,468
Benton	6	...	6	Marshall	67	...	67
Calhoun	155	...	155	Monroe	131	...	131
Chickasaw	224	...	224	Montgomery	75	2	73
Choctaw	96	...	96	Neshoba	50	...	50
Clarke	2	...	2	Newton	64	...	64
Clay	200	...	200	Noxubee	359	...	359
Copiah	19	19	...	Oktibbeha	129	...	129
De Soto	71	5	66	Panola	55	4	51
Forrest	3	...	3	Perry	5	...	5
George	2	...	2	Pontotoc	213	...	213
Greene	1	...	1	Prentiss	13	...	13
Grenada	89	...	89	Smith	2	...	2
Hinds	358	358	...	Stone	1	...	1
Holmes	9	...	9	Tate	60	4	56
Itawamba	37	...	37	Tishomingo	9	...	9
				Tunica	71	...	71
Jasper	7	...	7	Union	20	...	20
Jones	300	144	156	Wayne	11	...	11
Kemper	89	...	89	Webster	84	...	84
Lafayette	7	...	7	Winston	460	...	460
Lauderdale	33	...	33				
Leake	33	...	33	Yalobusha	34	...	34
Lee	20	...	20				
Leflore	57	...	57	All counties	5,212	536	4,676

[1] Counties with negligible output are omitted.

Table 14. *Industrial roundwood production by county, 1972*

County	All species	Softwood	Hardwood	County	All species	Softwood	Hardwood
	— — — M cubic feet — — —				— — — M cubic feet — — —		
Adams	6,968	2,290	4,678	Lowndes	3,733	1,464	2,269
Alcorn	1,484	776	708				
Amite	15,198	13,775	1,423	Madison	4,630	2,706	1,924
Attala	8,862	6,873	1,989	Marion	10,696	8,549	2,147
				Marshall	2,395	1,015	1,380
Benton	2,677	1,504	1,173	Monroe	3,921	2,055	1,866
Bolivar	1,593	3	1,590	Montgomery	4,191	2,583	1,608
Calhoun	2,679	1,350	1,329	Neshoba	9,232	6,639	2,593
Carroll	2,898	1,383	1,515	Newton	12,237	7,869	4,368
Chickasaw	3,059	1,455	1,604	Noxubee	6,559	3,381	3,178
Choctaw	5,139	3,167	1,972				
Claiborne	6,789	1,841	4,948	Oktibbeha	3,206	2,300	906
Clarke	19,754	13,882	5,872				
Clay	1,793	598	1,195	Panola	1,151	112	1,039
Coahoma	1,822	147	1,675	Pearl River	9,943	8,430	1,513
Copiah	17,195	13,117	4,078	Perry	10,843	9,622	1,221
Covington	8,273	6,564	1,709	Pike	9,218	8,060	1,158
				Pontotoc	2,186	618	1,568
De Soto	317	18	299	Prentiss	3,035	1,917	1,118
Forrest	6,961	5,910	1,051	Quitman	471	105	366
Franklin	15,289	12,049	3,240				
				Rankin	16,119	11,541	4,578
George	8,189	7,062	1,127				
Greene	13,172	9,682	3,490	Scott	12,706	8,799	3,907
Grenada	2,267	839	1,428	Sharkey	2,681	210	2,471
				Simpson	8,554	6,924	1,630
Hancock	7,172	6,769	403	Smith	9,419	7,630	1,789
Harrison	5,722	5,268	454	Stone	8,048	7,156	892
Hinds	4,858	2,201	2,657	Sunflower	51	...	51
Holmes	5,899	2,177	3,722				
Humphreys	730	31	699	Tallahatchie	962	201	761
				Tate	1,228	24	1,204
Issaquena	2,792	23	2,769	Tippah	3,720	2,379	1,341
Itawamba	6,275	3,216	3,059	Tishomingo	4,722	3,452	1,270
				Tunica	1,339	73	1,266
Jackson	14,460	13,469	991				
Jasper	15,220	12,109	3,111	Union	1,941	1,256	685
Jefferson	10,548	5,729	4,819				
Jefferson Davis	6,591	5,982	609	Walthall	5,526	4,352	1,174
Jones	10,780	6,940	3,840	Warren	8,293	402	7,891
				Washington	808	3	805
Kemper	20,369	16,602	3,767	Wayne	15,956	12,898	3,058
				Webster	4,590	3,075	1,515
Lafayette	3,564	2,010	1,554	Wilkinson	17,302	8,862	8,440
Lamar	6,036	5,218	818	Winston	10,120	6,917	3,203
Lauderdale	13,250	9,610	3,640				
Lawrence	6,636	5,120	1,516	Yalobusha	1,515	793	722
Leake	11,070	8,933	2,137	Yazoo	5,996	262	5,734
Lee	622	487	135				
Leflore	207	40	167				
Lincoln	14,889	12,258	2,631	All counties	559,311	383,111	176,200

13

Table 15. *Plant byproducts by county, 1972*

County[1]	All species		Softwood		Hardwood	
	Fine	Coarse	Fine	Coarse	Fine	Coarse
		— — — — — — — *M cubic feet* — — — — — — —				
Adams	19	1,296	19	87	...	1,209
Amite	587	8,790	587	8,790	...	...
Attala	192	432	122	232	70	200
Benton	...	14		10		4
Calhoun	829	1,193	15	23	814	1,170
Carroll	...	23	...	16	...	7
Chickasaw	139	253	5	31	134	222
Choctaw	...	141	...	...	...	141·
Clarke	762	1,790	762	1,498	...	292
Clay	320	533	61	114	259	419
Copiah	860	2,860	844	2,152	16	708
Forrest	377	547	377	547	...	...
Franklin	801	2,090	801	1,796	...	294
George	145	635	133	195	12	440
Grenada	947	1,692	490	1,038	457	654
Hinds	...	431	...	48	...	383
Holmes	...	319	...	33	...	286
Itawamba	768	1,220	250	476	518	744
Jackson	265	488	228	434	37	54
Jasper	137	268	116	228	21	40
Jones	881	1,559	670	1,273	211	286
Kemper	...	882	...	346	...	536
Lamar	347	1,681	168	1,398	179	283
Lauderdale	418	1,082	352	752	66	330
Leake	374	712	374	712	...	...
Lincoln	821	1,931	818	1,792	3	139
Lowndes	710	758	...	59	710	699
Marion	13	3,612	13	3,612	...	...

[1] Omitted counties have either negligible volume or less than three plants.

Table 15. *Plant byproducts by county, 1972* (Continued)

County[1]	All species		Softwood		Hardwood	
	Fine	Coarse	Fine	Coarse	Fine	Coarse
	— — — — — — — *M cubic feet* — — — — — — —					
Marshall	...	471	...	11	...	460
Monroe	...	376	...	108	...	268
Montgomery	...	196	...	106	...	90
Neshoba	2,352	6,549	2,346	6,039	6	510
Newton	102	541	102	234	...	307
Noxubee	162	517	162	326	...	191
Panola	254	370	13	25	241	345
Pearl River	34	1,501	34	1,163	...	338
Perry	144	4,479	144	4,479	...	...
Pike	581	1,148	581	1,102	...	46
Pontotoc	140	412	1	81	139	331
Prentiss	...	74	...	2	...	72
Rankin	164	742	155	561	9	181
Scott	585	982	254	476	331	506
Simpson	260	475	215	410	45	65
Smith	948	9,974	868	9,844	80	130
Stone	350	5,039	350	5,039	...	...
Tippah	...	431	...	266	...	165
Union		99		9		90
Walthall	203	518	203	518	...	...
Warren	1,225	2,217	84	142	1,141	2,075
Wayne	1,013	5,674	995	5,087	18	587
Webster	...	18	...	3	...	15
Wilkinson	...	2,901	...	2,093	...	808
Winston	170	5,377	170	5,336	...	41
Yazoo	483	1,145	18	47	465	1,098
All other counties	2,136	6,543	1,542	3,127	594	3,416
Total	22,018	96,001	15,442	74,326	6,576	21,675

Table 16. *Unused plant residues by county, 1972*

County[1]	All species		Softwood		Hardwood	
	Fine	Coarse	Fine	Coarse	Fine	Coarse
	— — — — — — — M cubic feet — — — — — — —					
Adams	1,159	306	46	28	1,113	278
Attala	70	...	1	...	69	...
Benton	154	189	48	61	106	128
Calhoun	347	375	32	49	315	326
Carroll	334	357	78	99	256	258
Chickasaw	233	149	12	...	221	149
Choctaw	338	299	85	124	253	175
Clarke	246	4	61	...	185	4
Clay	122	89	21	31	101	58
Copiah	577	188	310	34	267	154
Forrest	482	260	449	226	33	34
Franklin	481	194	277	194	204	...
George	76	1	6	...	70	
Grenada	141	31	141	31	...	...
Hinds	404	48	138	48	266	...
Holmes	217	44	28	15	189	29
Itawamba	89	114	22	31	67	83
Jackson	177	106	177	106	...	...
Jasper	21	8	7	...	14	8
Jones	82	88	41	27	41	61
Kemper	555	...	182	...	373	...
Lamar	569	6	569	4	...	2
Lauderdale	241	187	176	102	65	85
Leake	2	3	1	1	1	2
Lincoln	353	147	197	82	156	65
Lowndes	79	2	60	2	19	...
Marion	1,952	85	1,883	...	69	85
Marshall	426	126	24	25	402	101
Monroe	400	224	148	129	252	95
Montgomery	160	46	78	32	82	14
Neshoba	395	13	22	4	373	9
Newton	239	12	23	2	216	10
Noxubee	148	2	18	2	130	...
Panola	252	269	27	40	225	229
Pearl River	1,061	140	993	138	68	2
Perry	47	13	46	3	1	10
Pike	166	68	140	68	26	...
Pontotoc	277	148	45	4	232	144
Prentiss	113	89	15	20	98	69

[1] Omitted counties have either negligible volume or less than three plants.

16

Table 16. *Unused plant residues by county, 1972* (Continued)

County[1]	All species		Softwood		Hardwood	
	Fine	Coarse	Fine	Coarse	Fine	Coarse
	— — — — — — — M cubic feet — — — — — — —					
Rankin	259	1	143	1	116	...
Scott	1	9	1	7	...	2
Simpson	54	68	2	3	52	65
Smith	121	123	...	...	121	123
Stone	679	14	678	14	1	...
Tippah	431	231	170	42	261	189
Tishomingo	69	88	14	20	55	68
Union	112	29	44	9	68	20
Walthall	117	3	117	3	...	...
Warren	621	344	14	35	607	309
Wayne	192	42	192	42	...	...
Webster	93	109	44	59	49	50
Wilkinson	1,936	281	1,099	...	837	281
Winston	523	560	217	244	306	316
Yazoo	305	2	8	2	297	...
All other counties	1,812	224	709	148	1,103	76
Total	20,510	6,558	10,079	2,391	10,431	4,167

Table 17. *Bark used by county, 1972*

County	All species	Softwood	Hardwood	County	All species	Softwood	Hardwood
	— — — — Tons — — — —				— — — — Tons — — — —		
Adams	7,417	236	7,181	Newton	4,582	1,418	3,164
Amite	31,459	31,459	...				
				Panola	3,904	169	3,735
Calhoun	12,785	154	12,631	Pearl River	460	412	48
Carroll	164	100	64	Perry	10,731	10,262	469
Chickasaw	2,910	48	2,862	Prentiss	479	...	479
Clarke	11,208	9,901	1,307				
Copiah	1,644	...	1,644	Rankin	142	142	...
Forrest	3,623	3,623	...	Simpson	5	...	5
Franklin	4,998	4,998	...	Smith	33,321	33,321	...
				Stone	30,048	30,043	5
George	1,858	76	1,782				
Grenada	1,374	1,374	...	Warren	18,626	900	17,726
				Wilkinson	13,392	13,392	...
Hinds	4,188	49	4,139	Winston	20,112	20,112	...
Jackson	3,397	2,819	578				
Jasper	1,683	1,357	326	Yazoo	8,936	308	8,628
Jones	10,376	8,382	1,994				
				Other[1]	664,597	438,338	226,619
Lamar	5,024	5,024	...				
Lauderdale	10,931	8,321	2,610	Total	924,734	626,738	297,996

[1] Includes counties having either negligible volume or less than three plants.

17

Tabel 18. *Bark unusued by county, 1972*

County	All species	Softwood	Hardwood	County	All species	Softwood	Hardwood
	— — — *Tons* — — —				— — — *Tons* — — —		
Adams	10,705	584	10,121	Monroe	5,745	1,786	3,959
Amite	3,812	3,812	...	Montgomery	2,013	984	1,029
Attala	3,778	1,611	2,167				
				Neshoba	46,372	35,421	10,951
Benton	2,235	566	1,669	Newton	338	137	201
				Noxubee	4,722	2,699	2,023
Calhoun	5,337	406	4,931				
Carroll	4,782	865	3,917	Panola	3,832	346	3,486
Chickasaw	2,544	150	2,394	Pearl River	27,701	25,573	2,128
Choctaw	5,032	1,076	3,956	Perry	8,883	8,811	72
Clarke	3,253	1,653	1,600	Pike	12,628	12,210	418
Clay	6,321	1,013	5,308	Pontotoc	6,339	574	5,765
Copiah	19,685	14,527	5,158	Prentiss	1,239	176	1,063
Forrest	7,782	7,271	511	Rankin	5,695	3,744	1,951
Franklin	11,766	8,587	3,179				
				Scott	8,398	3,204	5,194
George	3,943	2,837	1,106	Simpson	4,270	2,744	1,526
Grenada	16,896	9,815	7,081	Smith	10,539	7,395	3,144
				Stone	2,158	2,153	5
Hinds	5,256	5,256	...				
Holmes	3,282	332	2,950	Tippah	6,196	2,098	4,098
				Tishomingo	1,042	163	879
Itawamba	12,513	3,408	9,105				
				Union	2,826	1,744	1,082
Jackson	6,326	6,326	...				
Jasper	135	78	57	Walthall	5,350	5,350	...
Jones	1,806	13	1,793	Warren	9,764	343	9,421
				Wayne	28,466	25,435	3,031
Kemper	8,089	2,292	5,797	Webster	1,289	516	773
				Wilkinson	13,475	467	13,008
Lamar	7,086	4,266	2,820	Winston	7,732	3,010	4,722
Lauderdale	1,755	1,133	622				
Leake	4,752	4,729	23	Yazoo	3,258	23	3,235
Lincoln	15,854	13,369	2,485				
Lowndes	3,115	1,578	1,537	Other[1]	254,010	182,540	71,147
Marion	24,999	23,916	1,083				
Marshall	6,610	291	6,319	Total	693,729	451,406	242,323

[1] Includes counties having either negligible volume or less than three plants.

Table 19. *Large sawmills*[1]

County	Firm	Plant	
		Location	Address[2]
Adams	Benbuck Lumber Co.	Natchez	Drawer B B
	J. M. Jones Lumber Co., Inc. [3]	Natchez	Drawer 1368
	W. S. Ricks Lumber Co., Inc. [3]	Natchez	Box 1323
Alcorn	Goodrum Sawmill[3]	Corinth	Rt. 1, Selmer, Tenn.
Amite	Sam Mabry Lumber Co. [3]	Liberty	Box 323
Attala	Attala Lumber Co. [3]	Ethel	Box 236
	Dendy Lumber Co. [3]	Kosciusko	Hwy. 35 North
Calhoun	Brown Contractors	Bruce	
	E. L. Bruce Co. [3]	Bruce	Box 337
	T. W. Plunk Sawmill	Bruce	
Carroll	Edwards Sawmill	Carrollton	Box 46, Winona
	George W. Fisackerly Sawmill	Carrollton	710 Shirley Ave., Winona
Choctaw	James Dewberry Lumber Co.	Eupora	RFD, Maben
	Fondren and McAdams	Sherwood	Mathiston
Claiborne	Hood Lumber Co. of Hermanville [3]	Hermanville	
	Pickens Bros. Lumber Co. [3]	Russum	Box 433, Port Gibson
Clarke	Hood Lumber Co. [3]	Quitman	
	Jones Bros. Lumber Co. [3]	Shubuta	Box 387
Clay	Seitz Lumber Co., Inc. [3]	West Point	Box 214
Copiah	Edward Hines Lumber Co.[3]	Hazlehurst	Box 767
	Hutchinson Lumber Co. [3]	Georgetown	
	R. C. Owen Co.	Hazlehurst	Box 533, Hopkinsville, Ky.
Forrest	Hood Lumber Co. of Hattiesburg [3]	Hattiesburg	Box 1922
	Richton Tie and Timber Co.	Petal	Box 606
Franklin	Franklin County Lumber Co. [3]	Roxie	Box 98
	Klumb Manufacturing Co. [3]	Bude	Box 147
	Koppers Co., Inc. [3]	Bude	Box 97
	Southern American Corp. [3]	Roxie	Box 87
George	J. M. Rogers and Sons [3]	Benndale	
Greene	Dickerson Sawmill Co. [3]	Leakesville	Rt. 4, Lucedale
	M. W. Hicks [3]	Leakesville	Rt. 5, Lucedale
Grenada	Hankins Lumber Co. [3]	Elliott	Box 8H
	Memphis Hardwood Flooring Co. [3]	Grenada	Box 837
Hinds	Kitchens Bros. Manufacturing Co. [3]	Utica	Box 217
Itawamba	Dura-Crates Inc. [3]	Fulton	500 W. Hill
	Evans Lumber Co. [3]	Evergreen	Rt. 4, Fulton
Jackson	Cumbest Manufacturing Co. [3]	Moss Point	Rt. 2, Pascagoula

Table 19. *Large sawmills*[1] (Continued)

County	Firm	Plant Location	Plant Address[2]
Jones	Bailey Lumber Co. [3]	Laurel	Box 125
	Hood Lumber Co. [3]	Laurel	Box 488
Kemper	Barnett Lumber Co.[3]	De Kalb	
	Fisher Bros. Lumber Co. [3]	De Kalb	
	McDade Lumber Co. [3]	Electric Mills	
	Weyerhaeuser Co. [3]	Electric Mills	De Kalb
Lamar	Joe N. Miles and Sons, Inc. [3]	Lumberton	Box 92
	Purvis Hardwood Lumber Co., Inc. [3]	Purvis	Box 266
Lauderdale	Sanders Lumber Co.[3]	Meridian	Box 2171
Leake	W. C. Croft, Jr., Lumber Co., Inc. [3]	Walnut Grove	Box 191
	Molpus Lumber Co. [3]	Carthage	1201 Hwy. 16 E
Lincoln	W. L. Byrd Lumber Co. [3]	Brookhaven	Rt. 5
	Columbus Lumber Co. [3]	Brookhaven	North 1st St.
	J. J. Meyers Lumber Co. [3]	Bogue Chitto	
	Gordan Redd Lumber Co. [3]	Brookhaven	Box 654
	Z. M. Redd Lumber Co. [3]	Bogue Chitto	Rt. 3
	Smith Bros. Lumber Co. [3]	Brookhaven	Box 257
Marion	Columbia Pulp and Paper Co. [3]	Goss	
	Jack Forbes Lumber Co.[3]	Sandy Hook	
	Georgia-Pacific Corp. [3]	Goss	Columbia
	Rogers Lumber Corp. [3]	Columbia	
Marshall	Memphis Hardwood Flooring Co. [3]	Potts Camp	
Monroe	Nickles Lumber Co. [3]	Aberdeen	Box 9
Montgomery	Pearson Bros. Sawmill[3]	Winona	
Neshoba	Molpus Lumber Co. [3]	Philadelphia	221 Gum St.
	Weyerhaeuser Co. [3]	Philadelphia	
Newton	Koppers Co., Inc. [3]	Hickory	Box 306, Decatur
	Prath Lumber C. [3]	Union	Box J
Noxubee	R. E. Prince Lumber Co. [3]	Shuqualak	
Oktibbeha	Sturgis Lumber Co. [3]	Sturgis	
Panola	A. A. Floyd and Sons	Batesville	Box 719
	Floyd Lumber Co. [3]	Sardis	
	Yount Lumber Co.	Askew	
Pearl River	Interpine [3]	Picayune	Box 1037
Pike	M. D. Hayles, Inc. [3]	Fernwood	Box A
	D. G. Seago Enterprises [3]	Summit	Hwy. 98 West, McComb
Pontotoc	Bankhead Lumber Co.	Pontotoc	Box 327
	Fergurson Sawmill [3]	Pontotoc	
Rankin	Kennedy Sawmill [3]	Brandon	Rt. 2, Box 4
	Price Paschal Lumber Co. [3]	Brandon	Box 127
	Brooks Vance Sawmill [3]	Koch	6106 White Stone Rd., Jackson

20

Table 19. *Large sawmills*[1]   (Continued)

County	Firm	Plant	
		Location	Address[2]
Scott	King Lumber Co. [3] .	Forest	Box 1479
	J. B. Wolfe Lumber Co. [3]	Lake	
Sharkey	Bellgrade Lumber Co. [3]	Cary	Box 437
Simpson	Broadhead Lumber and Mfg. Co., Inc. [3]	Mendenhall	513 W. Jackson Ave.
Smith	T. H. Luckey Lumber Co. [3]	Mize	Rt. 1
	Moss American Tie Co.	Raleigh	Box 487, Newton
	Raleigh Lumber Co., Inc. [3]	Raleigh	
	L. Vanderford Lumber Co. [3]	Raleigh	Rt. 1, Mendenhall
Stone	Hood Lumber of Wiggins [3]	Wiggins	Box 38
Tallahatchie	Tallahatchie Hardwood, Inc. [3]	Charleston	
Tippah	Robert Fryar Sawmill[3]	Dumas	Ripley
Walthall	Phillips-Lamb Lumber, Inc. [3]	Tylertown	Box 309
Warren	Anderson Tully Co., Mill D [3]	Vicksburg	Box 38
	Anderson Tully Co., Mill K [3]	Vicksburg	Box 38
	Houston Bros., Inc. [3]	Waltersville	Box 350, Vicksburg
Washington	Chicago Mill and Lumber Co.	Greenville	Box 1019
Wayne	M. S. Gatlin Lumber Co. [3]	Waynesboro	Box 407
	Longleaf Forest Products, Inc. [3]	Waynesboro	Box 637
Wilkinson	Hood Lumber Co. [3]	Crosby	
	Laurel Hill Lumber Co.	Woodville	
	Fred Netterville Lumber Co. [3]	Woodville	Rt. 1, Box 161
Winston	Quay Oswalt Sawmill	Louisville	Box 114, Sturgis
	Rivers and Reynolds Lumber Co., Inc.	Louisville	Box 184
Yazoo	Cathey-Williford-Jones Lumber Co. [3]	Bentonia	
	McGraw-Curran Lumber Co. [3]	Yazoo City	Box 450

[1] Output of 3 million board feet or more.
[2] Office address specified when different from plant location.
[3] Produced chips for sale to pulpmills.

21

Table 20. *Small sawmills*[1]

County	Firm	Plant	
		Location	Address[2]
Alcorn	Ray Crow Sawmill	Kossuth	Rt. 5, Corinth
Amite	O. R. and R. E. Williams	Smithdale	General Delivery
Benton	S. H. Childs, Jr., Sawmill	Ashland	Rt. 3, Ripley
	Robert Crawford Sawmill	Ashland	Rt. 2, Myrtle
	William Earl Matthews	Ashland	Rt. 1
	Billy Peeler Sawmill	Ashland	Rt. 1, Ripley
	Bobby Trainum Sawmill	Ashland	
	J. B. Ward and Son Sawmill [3]	Ashland	Rt. 1, Ripley
Calhoun	Hamiltons Sawmill	Vardaman	
	Hellums Sawmill	Sarepta	
Carroll	C. D. Whitfield Sawmill	Carrollton	Rt. 1
	Williams Lumber Co.	Carrollton	Box 137
Chickasaw	James Carter Sawmill	Houston	
	Lenard Funderburk Sawmill	Houston	
	Boots Pettit Sawmill	Thorn	Houston
	S & Y Inc. Sawmill [3]	Houston	
Choctaw	C. B. Ray and Sons Lbr. & Timber Co. [3]	Ackerman	RFD 1, Box 131
Clarke	Mayo Lumber Co. [3]	Quitman	Box 98
	Henry Stewart	Shubuta	Box 36
Clay	Trulove Lumber Co.	West Point	Rt. 1
Copiah	Copiah Manufacturing Co.	Hazlehurst	Box 637
	Allie Harris Sawmill	Gallman	Box 296
	Koppers Co., Inc. [3]	Georgetown	General Delivery
Covington	Rutland Lumber Co. [3]	Collins	Box 393
De Soto	Dudley R. Bumpous Sawmill	Engram Mills	Rt. 2, Box 327, Byhalia
	Trainum Lumber Co.	Lewisburg	Olive Branch
George	Cochran Lumber Co.	Central Community	Rt. 6, Lucedale
	James Davis Sawmill	Howell Community	Rt. 2, Box 111, Lucedale
Hancock	S. V. Jordan	Necaise Crossing	Rt. 2, Perkinston
	C. R. Moran	Lakeshore	Lower Bay Road
Harrison	West Creek Lumber Co. [3]	Saucier	Rt. 1, Box 300
Holmes	Allen Lumber Co.	Lexington	Durant Rd.
	W. H. Cooksey	Coxsburg	Lexington
	Fishers Mill	West	Rt. 3
	Koppers Co., Inc. [3]	Durant	Landrum
	S & G Lumber Co. [3]	Tehula	
Itawamba	Dow Brewer Sawmill	Tremont	
	F. J. Horn Sawmill	Belmont	Rt. 1, Golden
	Riley Lumber Co.	Fulton	Rt. 1
Jackson	Leo Nobles	Ft. Bayou	Rt. 2, Ocean Springs
	Kenneth Porter Sawmill Co.	Moss Point	Rt. 2, Pascagoula
Jasper	Georgia-Pacific Corp. [3]	Bay Springs	Box 570
	Heidleberg Lumber Co., Inc. [3]	Heidleberg	Drawer 280
Jefferson	C. M. Mangum Lumber Co.	Fayette	

Table 20. *Small sawmills*[1] (Continued)

County	Firm	Plant Location	Plant Address[2]
Jones	Buckhaults Pallet Mill	Ellisville	Rt. 1
	Gatlin Lumber Co. [3]	Laurel	2939 Audubon Dr.
	Gorman Lumber Co. [3]	Laurel	Box 261
	Laurel Lumber Co. [3]	Laurel	Compress Ave.
	Lightseys Crosstie Mill	Sandersville	Hwy. 11 North
Lafayette	J. D. Brown Sawmill	Old Dallas	Rt. 6, Oxford
	Pat Gandy Sawmill	Paris	Rt. 2
Lamar	Zeno Hickman	Oloh	Box 73, Sumrall
	Lamar County Development Corp. [3]	Purvis	Box 668
	Williamson and Williamson Lumber Co.	Sumrall	Rt. 1
Lauderdale	W. H. Cornish Lumber Co.	Marion	
	Covington Sawmill	Lockart	Rt. 4, Box 436, Meridian
	Haguewood Lumber Co.	Bailey	Rt. 1
Lawrence	Koppers Co., Inc. [3]	Monticello	Box 627
Leake	J. A. Biggett	Thomastown	Box 45
	T. F. Lacey	Thomastown	Rt. 2
Lincoln	Cullen Beeson Lumber Co.	Brookhaven	Rt. 1
Lowndes	McDill Bros. Lumber Co. [3]	Columbus	
Marion	W. F. Foxworth and Son	Foxworth	
Marshall	R. S. Bates	Potts Camp	Box 67
	Cheatwood and Johnson	Holly Springs	Rt. 2, Potts Camp
	Daniels and Hughes	Byhalia	Rt. 2
	L. D. Hutchens	Red Banks	Rt. 2, Potts Camp
	Roy Newsom	Waterford	Potts Camp
	G. R. Thompson Lumber Co.	Potts Camp	Rt. 1
Monroe	Atkins Sawmill	Amory	Rt. 2
	Grover Evans Sawmill	Aberdeen	Rt. 2
	Sam Frederick Sawmill	Smithville	
	Hollis Lumber Co.	Gatman	Box 35
	Jaudon Sawmill	Aberdeen	Rt. 2
	Gilmore Puckett Lumber Co. [3]	Amory	
Montgomery	McCrary Bros. Lumber Co.	Winona	McCarley
Neshoba	H. T. Barnes	Philadelphia	Rt. 6
	Gerald Branning	Philadelphia	Rt. 3
	Billy Irons	Philadelphia	Rt. 2
Newton	Decatur Lumber Co. [3]	Decatur	Box 313
	Jackie McMahan	Union	Rt. 4
	A. A. Wright Sawmill	Perdue	Rt. 2, Little Rock
Noxubee	Macon Lumber Co. [3]	Macon	
Oktibbeha	Robert Johnson Co.	Starkville	Rt. 3
Pearl River	Childs Sawmilll	Poplarville	Rt. 1
	Hemochitto Lumber Co. [3]	Picayune	Box 236
	Leon McQueen Lumber Co. [3]	Nicholson	Box 64, Picayune
	Redmond Mill	Lumberton	Rt. 3
	James J. Reyer and Son	Poplarville	Rt. 3
	Thomason Sawmill	Carriere	Rt. 2, Picayune
Perry	Joe Simmons Sawmill	New Augusta	Rt. 2, Hattiesburg

Table 20. *Small sawmills*[1] (Continued)

County	Firm	Plant Location	Plant Address[2]
Pike	Guy Holland Lumber Co. [3]	Osyka	
	Seller Forest Product Co. [3]	McComb	Hwy. 98 East
Pontotoc	Randolph Sawmill	Randolph	Rt. 5, Pontotoc
Prentiss	Gene Carroll Sawmill	Booneville	Rt. 1, Counce, Tenn.
	W. G. Cole Sawmill	Booneville	Rt. 5
	Hollis Davis Sawmill	Booneville	Rt. 6
	J. V. Hill	Baldwyn	Rt. 1
	Tulon L. Jackson Sawmill	Booneville	Rt. 6
	Garvin Lambert Sawmill	Tishomingo	Rt. 2
	Buster McElroy and Company	Baldwyn	
	Walden Sawmill	Booneville	Rt. 5
Scott	W. N. Jones, Jr., Sawmill	Forest	Rt. 2
	Morton Manufacturing Co., Inc.[3]	Morton	Drawer K
	M. L. Stewart Lumber Co.	Morton	Box 452
Simpson	Walter T. Davis Sawmill	Florence	Rt. 2
	C. D. Rhodes Tie and Timber Co.	Braxton	Elba, Ala.
Smith	J. B. Black Sawmill[3]	Homewood	Rt. 1, Pulaski
Stone	International Paper Co., Wiggins Complex[3]	Wiggins	Box 37
	Wade Parker Sawmill	Big Level	Rt. 1, Perkinston
Tippah	Corwin Childs Sawmill	Ripley	Hwy. 2
	Earnest Hodum	Walnut	Rt. 2
	Johnson Lumber Co.	Walnut	Hwy. 72
	Mathis and Jackson Sawmill	Tiplersville	Rt. 3, Walnut
	V. L. McElwain and Son Sawmill[3]	Ripley	
	A. Z. Nails Sawmill & Pallet Co.	Walnut	
	Rainey Wood Products	Ripley	
Tishomingo	Gene Caroll Sawmill	Holcut	Rt. 3, Iuka
	Chester Dawson	Tishomingo	Rt. 1
	L. O. Enlow Sawmill	Iuka	Rt. 1
	E. A. Wiggaton Sawmill	Golden	
Union	O. T. Hill	Myrtle	Rt. 2
	Clyde Langford Lumber Co.[3]	New Albany	Box 195
	M. W. Lancaster	New Albany	Rt. 3, Rienzi
Walthall	Lloyd Jones Lumber Co.[3]	Improve	Rt. 2, Sandy Hook
Wayne	A. L. Cooley Lumber Co.	Waynesboro	Rt. 3
Webster	T. H. Evans Sawmill	Bellefontaine	
	J. G. Hendrix Sawmill	Eupora	Rt. 2, Maben
	Forrest Herard Sawmill	Stewart	Rt. 2
	W. D. Long Sawmill	Cadaretta	Box 104, Sturgis
	Rodgers Bros. Sawmill	Eupora	Rt. 4
Winston	John Barton Sawmill[3]	Louisville	Box 44, Longview
	Koppers Co., Inc.	Louisville	Box 501
	Montgomery Bros. Sawmill	Louisville	Longview
	L. M. Shurden Sawmill	Louisville	Rt. 4
	Joseph Wray Sawmill	Louisville	Rt. 7
Yalobusha	Jack Wiggins Sawmill	Oakland	
Yazoo	Oliver Chisolm Sawmill	Yazoo City	Rt. 2

[1] Output of less than 3 million board feet.
[2] Office address specified when different from plant location.
[3] Produced chips for sale to pulpmills.

Table 21. *Wood pulpmills*

County	Firm	Location
Adams	International Paper Co.	Natchez
Jackson	International Paper Co.	Moss Point
Jones	Masonite Corp.	Laurel
Lauderdale	The Flintkote Co.	Meridian
	Kroehler Mfg. Co. of Miss., Inc.	Meridian
Lawrence	St. Regis Paper Co.	Monticello
Warren	International Paper Co.	Vicksburg
Washington	United States Gypsum Co.	Greenville

Table 22. *Veneer plants*

County	Firm	Plant		
		Location	Address[1]	Type
Amite	Georgia-Pacific Corp.[3]	Gloster	Box 400	P
Copiah	Central Box Co.[3]	Crystal Springs	Rt. 2, Box 129	C
	Hazlehurst Box Co.[3]	Hazlehurst	Box 506	C
Covington	Rhymes Veneers, Inc.	Collins	Box 345	O
George	Lucedale Veneer Co.[3]	Lucedale	Box 207	O
Lauderdale	Meridian Plywood, Inc.[3]	Meridian	Box 107	O
Neshoba	Weyerhaeuser Co.[3]	Philadelphia		P
Pearl River	St. Regis Paper Co., Wirebound Box Division	Picayune	Box 818	C
Perry	Delta Pine Plywood Co.[3]	Beaumont	Box 247	P
	Perry County Plywood Corp.	Beaumont		O
Smith	Georgia-Pacific Corp.[3]	Taylorsville	Box 627	P
Stone	International Paper Co., Wiggins Complex[3]	Wiggins	Box 37	P
Washington	Chicago Mill and Lumber Co.	Greenville	Box 1019	C
Wayne	The Day Co.[3]	Waynesboro	Box 151	O
	Scotch Plywood of Mississippi[3]	Waynesboro	Box 616	P
Winston	Georgia-Pacific Corp.[3]	Louisville	Box 309	P

[1] Office address specified when different from plant location.
[2] C = Plants producing chiefly container veneer.
O = Plants producing chiefly commercial and other hardwood veneer.
P = Plants producing southern pine plywood.
[3] Produces chips for sale to pulpmills.

Table 23. *Post, pole, and piling plants*

County	Firm	Plant Location	Plant Address[1]
Attala	Attala Wood Preservers	McCool	Rt. 3
Clarke	Koppers Co., Inc.	Stonewall	Box 555
	Bobby L. Rowell	De Soto	6634 W. Santos Dr., Mobile, Ala.
Forrest	Dixie Pole and Piling Co.	Hattiesburg	Box 1532
	Smith Wood Preserving	Hattiesburg	Box 1935
George	Southern Timber Co.	Evanston	Box 476, Lucedale
Grenada	Koppers Co., Inc.	Grenada	Box 160
Harrison	Gulfport Creosoting Co.	Gulfport	Box 1510
Hinds	Hinds Wood Preserving Co.	Learned	Box 41
Jackson	Delta Creosote Co., Inc.	Gautier	Drawer 7
Jefferson Davis	Prentiss Creosote and Forest Products, Inc.	Prentiss	Rt. 1, Box 19
Lauderdale	Moss American, Inc.	Meridian	Box 789
Lincoln	Brookhaven Piling Co.	Brookhaven	Box 387
	Mississippi Wood Preserving Co.	Brookhaven	Box 766
Lowndes	Moss American, Inc.	Columbus	
Madison	Dickson Treating Co.	Canton	Box 61
Marshall	Marshall H. Jacks Wood Preserving Co.	Byhalia	Rt. 1, Box 297A
Noxubee	Woody Jones Creosote Plant	Macon	Hwy. 45 North
Pearl River	Interpine	Picayune	Box 1037
	Arnold B. Smith Timber Co.	Poplarville	Box 445
Perry	Conway Pole and Piling Co.	New Augusta	Box 116
Pike	Fernwood Industries	Fernwood	
Rankin	H. A. Cole Products Co.	Pelahatchie	Box 9937, Jackson
	Willie Hicks Post Plant	Plain	Rt. 4, Box 472, Florence
	James Martin Post Operation	Johns	Rt. 2, Mendenhall
Stone	International Paper Co., Wiggins Complex	Wiggins	Box 37
	Southern Pine Wood Preserving Co., Inc.	Wiggins	Box 636
	Timco, Inc.	Wiggins	
Union	KGW Post and Wood Preserving Co., Inc.	New Albany	Box 851
Walthall	American Creosote Works, Inc.	Tylertown	Box 465
Winston	American Creosote Works, Inc.	Louisville	Box 311

[1] Office address specified when different from plant location.

Table 24. *Miscellaneous plants*

| County | Firm | Plant | |
		Location	Address[1]
Chickasaw	Chickasaw Handle Co.[6]	Houston	
	E. F. Dyer Handle Co.[5]	Pyland	Houston
Clay	Winters Hardwood Dimension Co., Inc.[5]	West Point	
George	Jim Havens Dogwood Mill[7]	Benndale	Star Route, Leaf
Hinds	Concrete Products, Inc.[4]	Terry	Box 338
Holmes	Leon Howard[5]	Cruger	
Jasper	B & T Handle Co.[6]	Bay Springs	Box 541
Jones	Shows Lumber Co.[8]	Ovett	
LeFlore	Solon Smith Sawmill[5]	Sidon	Rt. 1, Box 258
	Danny Weaver Sawmill[5]	Itta Bena	Williamson Road
Lowndes	Airline Manufacturing Co.[5]	Columbus	Box 2036
	Columbus Handle Co.[6]	Columbus	Box 702
Marshall	James E. Champion, Inc.[3]	Holly Springs	Rt. 2, Potts Camp
	Hubert Evans[5]	Bethlehem	Box 187
Montgomery	Bob Lancaster Excelsior[4]	Duck Hill	107 Cameron
	Winona Handle Co.[6]	Winona	
Neshoba	Weyerhaeuser Co.[6]	Philadelphia	
Perry	Ronnies Hickory Chips[2]	Beaumont	Box 306
Winston	Choctaw Stave and Heading Co.[3]	Louisville	Box 65

[1] Office address specified when different from plant location.
[2] Charcoal.
[3] Cooperage.
[4] Excelsior.
[5] Furniture stock.
[6] Handle stock.
[7] Shuttle blocks.
[8] Miscellaneous dimension mill.

Bertelson, Daniel F.

1973.   Mississippi forest industries, 1972. South.
For. Exp. Stn., New Orleans, La. 27 p. (USDA
For. Serv. Resour. Bull. SO-43)

Mississippi forests supplied more than 559 million cubic feet of
roundwood to forest industries in 1972. Pulpwood and saw logs
were the major products, accounting for 85 percent of the harvest.
A total of 315 primary wood-using plants were in operation in
1972.

Acknowledgments

Generous assistance from public and private organizations made it possible to expeditiously complete the field work for this midcycle inventory of Mississippi. The very material aid of the organization listed below, and of the individuals in them, is gratefully acknowledged:

MISSISSIPPI FORESTRY COMMISSION

YAZOO-LITTLE TALLAHATCHIE FLOOD PREVENTION PROJECT

EDWARD HINES LUMBER COMPANY

E. L. BRUCE COMPANY

CHAMPION INTERNATIONAL, INC.

CHICAGO MILL AND LUMBER COMPANY

CROWN ZELLERBACH CORPORATION

DELTA PINE PLYWOOD COMPANY

DURA-CRATES INC.

FUTORIAN MANUFACTURING COMPANY

GEORGIA-PACIFIC CORPORATION

HANKINS LUMBER COMPANY

HIWASSEE LAND COMPANY

INTERNATIONAL PAPER COMPANY

INTERPINE

KOPPERS COMPANY, INC.

LONGLEAF FOREST PRODUCTS, INC.

MASONITE CORPORATION

MEMPHIS HARDWOOD FLOORING CO.

SCOTT PAPER COMPANY

ST. REGIS PAPER COMPANY

SOUTHERN PINE SUPERIOR STUD CORPORATION

W. E. PARKS LUMBER COMPANY, INC.

WESTVACO CORPORATION

WEYERHAEUSER COMPANY

Midcycle Evaluation of Mississippi Timber Resources

Dwane D. Van Hooser

U.S. DEPARTMENT OF AGRICULTURE
FOREST SERVICE

Southern Forest Experiment Station
New Orleans, Louisiana

1973

Contents

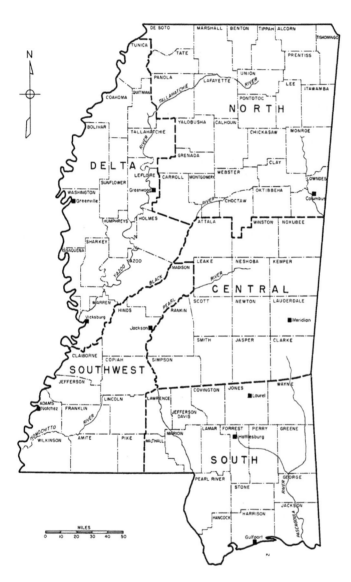

Forest Survey regions in Mississippi

iv

Midcycle Evaluation Of Mississippi Timber Resources

Dwane D. Van Hooser

The primary objective of the survey reported here was to quickly and accurately estimate growing-stock volume in Mississippi. This goal was accomplished through the relatively new technique of two-stage 3P sampling (3,4). The technique is described in Research Paper SO-77 (7).

The sample was of relatively low intensity. Only 2,300 of 42,000 trees measured in the 1967 survey were remeasured, and only one third of the original locations were revisited. It is impossible, therefore, to provide the detail that accompanies a full-scale forest survey of a State. Discussion related to area is confined to forest-nonforest classifications, and shifts that have taken place since 1967. Changes in volume are based on recomputed 1967 data. Volumes for that year were computed using program STX (4) and the second-stage 3P sample.

FOREST LAND

Although forest area has decreased 1 percent or 200,000 acres in the last 6 years, timber still occupies more than half of the State's land area (table I). In all, some 16.7 million acres are currently forested. The overall change was small, but substantial shifts in land use occurred within survey units.

Table I.—*Commercial forest land in 1973 and change since 1967*

Region	Commercial forest	Change since last survey	Proportion of region forested
	Thousand acres	*Percent*	*Percent*
Delta	1,306.7	− 13	23
North	4,141.5	− 1	49
Central	4,056.3	+ 2	68
South	4,446.9	− 1	72
Southwest	2,748.8	(1)	63
Total	16,700.2	− 1	55

[1] Negligible.

Four out of the five units experienced net losses in forest land. More than 14 percent of the Delta Unit's commercial forest was cleared and planted, primarily to soybeans or cotton. Here, the heavy losses through clearing have been taking place since the early 1960's. The Delta Unit, which is almost entirely on the alluvial plain of the Mississippi River, contains some of the State's most productive land. If widescale clearing continues, and all indications are that it will, the impact on the hardwood resource may become even more severe within the next decade.

The Northern Unit also lost more than 200,000 acres of commercial forest land to agriculture. More than 5 percent of the commercial forest in the unit was cleared.

Statewide, 4 percent or 655,000 acres of commercial forest land was converted to agricultural uses (table II). An additional 108,000 acres were lost to water and to urban uses, such as housing developments, parks, and interstate highways.

Idle lands reverted to forest in all units, but the Central Unit was the only one to show a net increase in forest land—97,000 acres. This unit has been gaining forest for some time, primarily due to reseeding of abandoned farmland.

For the State as a whole, some 570,000 acres have reverted to forest and have attained stocking levels sufficiently high to qualify as commercial forest.

Even though the changes in forest acreage were partly offsetting, timber growth suffered. Land removed from the forest usually contains trees that represent years of growth. Land reverting to forest is usually unproductive for a long time unless trees are artificially seeded or planted promptly.

Since this survey only determined changes in land use, shifts in forest type or ownership were not measured. However, much of the area lost

Table II.—*Change in commercial forest land, 1967-1973*

Region	Net change	Additions from: Nonforest	Conversions to: Total	Conversions to: Agriculture	Conversions to: Other [1]
		— — — — — — *Thousand acres* — — — — — —			
Delta	− 187.1	46.4	233.5	218.1	15.4
North	− 53.3	202.8	256.1	213.3	42.8
Central	+ 96.8	200.4	103.6	75.1	28.5
South	− 42.2	75.4	117.6	96.3	21.3
Southwest	− 5.9	46.7	52.6	52.6	...
Total	− 191.7	571.7	763.4	655.4	107.9

[1] Includes 38,400 acres that went to water impoundments and 69,500 acres transferred to urban and other uses.

in the Delta was in desirable bottom-land hardwood types. The gains made elsewhere were, for the most part, in the less productive upland hardwood types.

TIMBER VOLUME

Mississippi's forest contained more than 14 billion cubic feet of growing stock in 1973. The concepts of growing stock and sawtimber help to judge the quality of the inventory. Growing-stock trees have attributes that make them either presently or prospectively suitable for saw logs. Their volume is measured from a 1-foot stump to a 4-inch top. Sawtimber trees are growing-stock trees larger than a specified diameter.

Softwood Volume Still Increasing

Currently softwoods, primarily pine, account for more than half of the growing-stock volume. The State's forests contain slightly more than 7 billion cubic feet of softwood, 10 percent more than in 1967 (9) (table III).

Table III.—*Growing-stock volume in 1973 and change since 1967*

Region	Softwood Change	Softwood Volume	Hardwood Change	Hardwood Volume
	Million cu. ft.	*Percent*	*Million cu. ft.*	*Percent*
Delta	79.0	+ 55	1,290.3	+ 3
North	1,159.0	+ 31	1,874.5	+ 7
Central	2,187.5	+ 10	1,655.2	+ 6
South	2,066.3	− 5	1,034.4	− 5
Southwest	1,641.4	+ 16	1,187.5	+ 22
Total	7,133.2	+ 10	7,041.9	+ 6

The greatest overall gains, well over 200 million cubic feet, occurred in the North and Southwest regions. Loblolly pine accounts for half of the softwood inventory.

Volume increases by diameter class were greatest for trees between 8 and 16 inches (fig. 1). Volume gains through this range of diameters is a healthy sign. Because these trees are of the sizes most frequently harvested for pulpwood and other products, an adequate growth base must be maintained in this portion of the inventory.

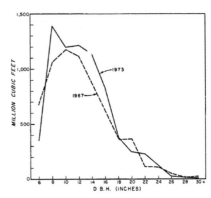

Figure 1.—*Softwood growing stock volume by tree diameter, 1967 and 1973.*

More than three-fourths of the softwood growing stock is in sawtimber-sized trees, i.e., trees at least 9 inches in diameter. The rest is classified as poletimber. Based on the 1967 distribution of volume into saw logs and upper

2

stems, some 90 percent of the 5.4 billion cubic feet in softwood sawtimber trees can be made into saw logs. This volume equates to nearly 30 billion board feet. The remaining 550 million plus cubic feet contained in upper stems is suitable for conversion to pulpwood and other products.

In all, the softwood sawtimber inventory increased 11 percent. The greatest gains were in the North and Central Units (table IV), as they had been between 1957-1967 (9).

Table IV.—*Sawtimber volume in 1973 and change since 1967*

Region	Softwood		Hardwood	
	Volume	Change	Volume	Change
	Million bd. ft.	*Percent*	*Million bd. ft.*	*Percent*
Delta	217.1	+ 16	4,301.9	+ 9
North	3,851.3	+ 58	4,635.3	+ 25
Central	8,932.0	+ 18	5,034.9	+ 43
South	9,098.2	− 10	2,630.9	+ 4
Southwest	7,814.4	+ 17	3,109.9	+ 35
Total	29,913.0	+ 11	19,712.9	+ 23

Hardwood Volume Increasing

The volume of hardwood growing stock has increased to 7 billion cubic feet, 6 percent more than in 1967. Trees from 10 to 17 inches d.b.h. were responsible for about half of the volume accretion (fig. 2). A significant gain was also registered by trees in the 20 inch class. As with softwood growing stock, the largest advances were in the North and Southwest regions of the State (table III).

The species composition of the hardwood inventory is changing somewhat, as it was between 1957-1967 (9). Oaks still dominate the stands, but now they comprise nearly 50 percent of the inventory as opposed to the 43 percent detected in 1967. The gums—sweetgum, black and other tupelos—account for some 21 percent of the hardwoods. The remaining inventory is made up of other hardwoods, i.e., hickory, ash, yellow-poplar, etc., in about the same proportion as they were in 1967.

The cubic foot volume in hardwood trees of sawtimber size, i.e., at least 11 inches d.b.h., has increased to 63 percent of the growing-stock inventory. If the 1967 ratio of saw-log volume to total volume remained constant, then four-

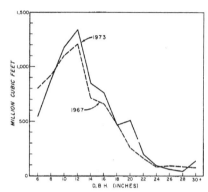

Figure 2.—*Hardwood growing stock volume by tree diameter, 1967 and 1973.*

fifths of the 4.4 billion cubic feet in sawtimber sized trees could be made into saw logs. This volume represents some 20 billion board feet, which is a 23 percent increase over 1967 board foot levels.

While the annual softwood gains are significant (about 2 percent/year) they are not nearly as substantial as those registered between the 1956 and 1967 surveys (9). During that time the softwood inventory had increased some 63 percent and was nearly equal to the hardwood sector of the forest. The apparent change in the softwood rate of increase is due primarily to the expansion of the primary wood-using industries within the State. Two industries in particular have gained significantly in producing capacity since 1966. These are, of course, the pulp and paper and southern pine plywood industries. The capacity of the State's pulp industry has increased 68 percent since 1966 and the number of mills has gone from seven to eight. The pine plywood industry, which was virtually nonexistant 10 years ago, now consumes more than 60 million cubic feet of pine logs. The hardwood veneer industry, once a major consumer of hardwood logs, has all but disappeared. Thus, it is easy to see why the gains in softwoods are increasing at a decreasing rate while hardwoods remain comparatively stable.

The inventory increased in four of the State's five units. Volumes declined in the Southern Unit. This area was damaged in 1969 by Hurricane Camille. At that time it was estimated that the volume of damaged material was equal to

3

nearly three-fourths of the State's total industrial cut for 1966 (8). A survey made in the damaged area immediately after the storm indicated that some 289 million cubic feet of growing stock had been either broken or damaged by wind. A subsequent resurvey revealed that 98 million cubic feet was salvaged (1). However, the growth base was reduced drastically in a fourth of the area, explaining the decline of the region's inventory. This loss represents a 5 percent volume reduction in a unit that gained more than 60 percent between 1957 and 1967(9). Hurricane Camille also partially explains the smaller than expected increase in the softwood inventory.

Growth, Mortality, and Removals

Mississippi's growing-stock inventory increased by 75.3 million cubic feet in 1972. This is the amount that growth added to the forests after deductions were made for mortality and removals.

The softwood inventory increased 7 percent in 1972, but 10 percent of this volume was offset by mortality (fig. 3). Although, fire, insects, and disease accounted for more than one third of the mortality from known causes, it was weather that killed more than half of the trees for which an actual cause of death was recorded. Virtually all of the mortality due to weather was confined to the Southern Unit. It was here that Hurricane Camille struck hardest in 1969.

Net growth of softwoods amounted to 453.8 million cubic feet. Timber removals offset 94 percent of this increment. Thus, growth exceeded cut by only 6 percent or 25.7 million cubic feet in 1972. Net growth on the sawtimber segment of the inventory exceeded cut by some 21 percent in 1972.

Hardwood net growth exceeded removals in 1972 by 15 percent. Some 49.6 million cubic feet of growing stock were added to this portion of the total stand (table V). Removals from the hardwood inventory amounted to 272 million cubic feet; more than two-thirds of this volume was manufactured into products. The remaining 84 million cubic feet were either left in the woods as logging residues or lost through land clearing or other operations, such as TSI, which remove trees from the stand but do not convert them to wood products.

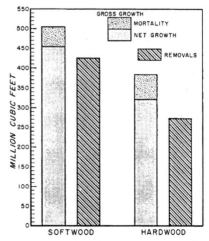

Figure 3.—Growth, mortality, and removals from growing stock, 1972.

Table V.—Summary of timber resource statistics, 1967-1973

. Item	Growing stock		Sawtimber	
	Soft-wood	Hard-wood	Soft-wood	Hard-wood
	Million cubic feet		Million board feet	
Inventory, 1967	6,512.9	6,631.1	26,946.8	16,023.8
Timber removals, 1972	428.1	272.1	1,752.4	817.0
Mortality, 1972	51.5	63.2	169.8	135.1
Net growth, 1972	453.8	321.7	2,227.5	1,488.8
Net change, 1972	+25.7	+49.6	+475.1	+671.8
Inventory, 1973	7,133.2	7,041.9	29,913.0	19,712.9

Hardwood mortality amounted to 16 percent of gross growth; its causes usually could not be identified. As with softwoods, however, weather killed most of the hardwoods for which a cause of death could be determined. Also, virtually all weather-killed trees were in the Southern Unit.

Net growth on the hardwood sawtimber inventory was nearly double the volume of removals. In total, this segment of the inventory had a net gain of 672 million board feet.

TIMBER HARVEST AND INDUSTRY

A 100-percent field canvass of Mississippi's primary wood-using industries (fig. 4) revealed

4

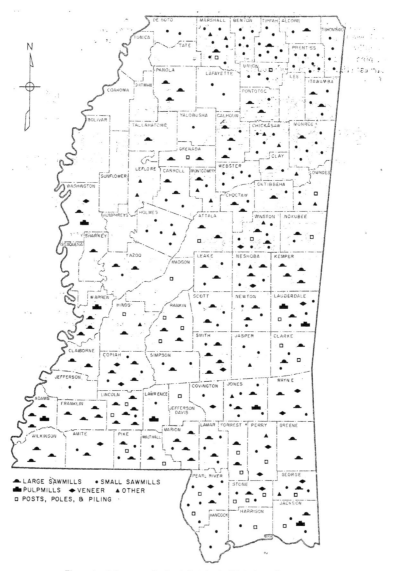

Figure 4.—*Primary wood-using industries in Mississippi, 1972.*

5

that the harvest for industrial roundwood products from the State's forests in 1972 was one of the largest on record. It amounted to more than ½-billion cubic feet. Softwood species, nearly all pine, made up more than two-thirds of the harvest (fig. 5). Hardwoods consisted primarily of oaks, gums, and hickories.

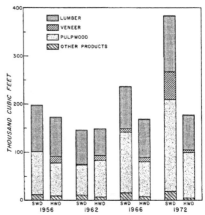

Figure 6.—*Output of roundwood by product, species group, and year.*

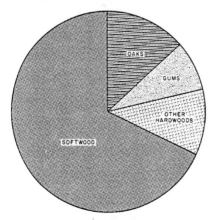

Figure 5.—*Distribution of roundwood output by species group.*

The major reason for the record production is the increased harvest of pulpwood and veneer bolts. Also, the demand for lumber has caused an increase in the cutting of saw logs, a continuation of the trend detected between 1962 and 1966 (*6*).

Pulpwood was the largest single product in 1972, accounting for more than half of the total roundwood output. The 3.5 million cords, though not a record high, were above 1966 production. Pulpwood production has generally trended upwards since 1946. Now, however, the harvest from Mississippi seems to have stabilized.

Saw-log production was second to pulpwood, and the margin appears to be growing wider (fig. 6). More than 1 billion board feet of saw logs were cut, with pine accounting for about two-thirds of the harvest. In total, logs cut for conversion to lumber made up one-third of the industrial harvest.

The thiːd ranking product was veneer logs. In 1956, the output was 90 million board feet (*5*),

all of which was hardwood. In 1966, the production rose to 98 million board feet; however, nearly half of this was pine (*6*). The total production of veneer logs in 1972 was 376 million board feet, nine-tenths of which was softwood— virtually all pine. Total production increased nearly threefold and softwood production 6.5 fold since 1966.

The harvest of pulpwood, lumber, and veneer made up 96 percent of the industrial roundwood production in 1972. The remaining 4 percent was comprised of poles, piling, posts, and miscellaneous products. Mississippi has long been a top ranking supplier of poles and piling. In 1972, more than 800,000 pines were cut for poles, and nearly 8 million linear feet of piling were harvested. These products accounted for about 3 percent of the total industrial removals in 1972. The remaining harvest was for other products such as posts, cooperage, handle and furniture stock, and miscellaneous dimension.

Mississippi continues to be a net exporter of wood. During 1972, resident plants processed 80 percent of the State's timber harvest. Pulpwood accounted for most of the interstate movement; 36 percent of the 3.5 million cords were shipped to out-of-State mills. More than two-thirds of the pulpwood exports were pine.

Eight pulpmills are on stream in Mississippi. Their combined capacity is 6,050 tons per day, a

68 percent increase over 1966 capacity. Although the net gain in number of mills is one, the two mills that began operating since the 1966 canvass have added more than 2,600 tons per day of capacity, while the one mill that no longer processed wood only removed 350 tons per day of pulping capability. In addition, three of the eight mills operate exclusively on residues. Although there are no mills currently under construction in the State, the future demand for pulpwood from Mississippi's forests should remain at current levels.

Even though the production of lumber exceeded the 1966 level, the number of firms cutting saw logs declined. In fact, the total number of sawmills now operating within the State, 241, is one less than the number of small sawmills that were in existance in 1966. Of these, 103 are each cutting more than 3 million board feet per year. These mills received 90 percent of the logs in 1972. Small sawmills have declined in number and they now total 138.

The southern pine plywood industry has expanded in Mississippi; at present seven mills are converting veneer logs to plywood. Four of these seven mills opened since 1966. In addition to these plants, nine others turn out container and other veneers. Mississippi lost 11 firms since 1966. The total number of plants producing veneer is 16.

The wood preserving industry in Mississippi consists of 31 plants, about three-fifths of which use pressure systems. They treat virtually all of the roundwood harvested in the State for poles, piling, and commercial posts. They also process some lumber, railroad ties, crossarms, and other sawn products.

Other plants using Mississippi roundwood manufacture miscellaneous dimension stock, handle stock, shuttleblocks, charcoal, cooperage, and excelsior. In all, these types of plants number 19. Most numerous are those producing miscellaneous dimension stock for use in furniture manufacture.

Plant Residues

Forest industries in Mississippi in 1972 produced more than 154 million cubic feet of residues while converting roundwood into primary products. About two-thirds of this material was coarse. Coarse residue is material, such as slabs, edgings, miscuts, and other items, that can be made into pulp chips. Fine residues consist mainly of sawdust and shavings and other material too small to be converted to chips.

More than 80 percent of the residues were utilized. Some 84 million cubic feet went into pulp and particleboard. Consumption by the pulp industry more than doubled since 1966. In fact, three pulpmills within the State are using residues exclusively in their operations. Of the remaining residues 25 million cubic feet were burned for fuel, and nearly 19 million cubic feet were used for other products such as lumber studs, animal bedding, and mulch.

Unused residues total 27 million cubic feet. More than three-fourths of this material was classified as fine.

The recovery and eventual sale of residues is becoming more and more a significant factor in forest industry operations. For example, in 1966, 68 percent of all residues were utilized (9), as compared to 82 percent in 1972. Only 24 percent of the sawmills operated some type of chipping facility in 1966; 49 percent now do.

RELIABILITY OF THE DATA

Reliability of the estimates may be affected by two types of errors. The first stems from the use of a sample to estimate the whole and from variability of the items being sampled. This type is termed sampling error; it is susceptible to a mathematical evaluation of the probability of error. The second type—often referred to as reporting or estimating error—derives from mistakes in measurement, judgment, or recording, and from limitations of method or equipment. Its effects cannot be appraised mathematically, but the Forest Survey constantly attempts to hold it to a minimum by proper training and good supervision, and by emphasis on careful work.

Since this survey involved two-stage sampling, it is necessary to combine the errors associated with each stage in order to determine overall variability. The sampling error associated with the first stage was determined to be ± 1.6 percent for growing-stock volume (9). The sampling error for the 3P second stage was ± 0.4 percent. Thus, by taking the square of the sum of the squared errors for each stage the combined sampling error is ± 1.6 percent. This ignores the covariance term which is usually negligible. As this total is broken down by species, tree diameter, county and other subdivisions, the possibility of error increases and is greatest for the smallest items.

In general, the sampling errors associated with the data in this report will be only slightly greater than those published for the 1967 survey of Mississippi (9).

DEFINITIONS OF TERMS

Forest Land Class

Forest land.—Land at least 16.7 percent stocked by forest trees of any size, or formerly having such tree cover and not currently developed for nonforest use.

Commercial forest land.—Forest land that is producing or is capable of producing crops of industrial wood and not withdrawn from timber utilization.

Tree Species

Commercial species.—Tree species presently or prospectively suitable for industrial wood products; excludes so-called weed species, such as blackjack oak and blue beech.

Hardwoods.—Dicotyledonous trees, usually broad-leaved and deciduous.

Softwoods.—Coniferous trees, usually evergreen, having needle or scale-like leaves.

Class of Timber

Growing stock trees.—Sawtimber trees, poletimber trees, saplings, and seedlings; that is, all live trees except rough and rotten trees.

Sawtimber trees.—Live trees of commercial species, 9.0 inches and larger in diameter at breast height for softwoods and 11.0 inches and larger for hardwoods, and containing at least one 12-foot saw log.

Poletimber trees.—Live trees of commercial species, 5.0 to 9.0 inches in d.b.h. for softwoods and 5.0 to 11.0 inches for hardwoods, and of good form and vigor.

Saplings.—Live trees of commercial species, 1.0 inch to 5.0 inches in d.b.h. and of good form and vigor.

Rough and rotten trees.—Live trees that are unmerchantable for saw logs now or prospectively because of defect, rot, or species.

Salvable dead trees.—Standing or down dead trees that are considered currently or potentially merchantable.

Volume

Volume of sawtimber.—Net volume of the saw-log portion of live sawtimber trees, in board feet, International 1/4-inch rule.

Volume of growing stock.—Volume of sound wood in the bole of sawtimber and poletimber trees from stump to a minimum 4.0-inch top outside bark or to the point where the central stem breaks into limbs.

Volume of timber.—The volume of sound wood in the bole of growing stock, rough, rotten, and salvable dead

trees 5.0 inches and larger in d.b.h. from stump to a minimum 4.0-inch top outside bark or to the point where the central stem breaks into limbs.

Miscellaneous Definitions

D.b.h. (diameter breast high).—Tree diameter in inches, outside bark, measured at 4½ feet above ground.

Diameter classes.—The 2-inch diameter classes extend from 1.0 inch below to 0.9 inch above the stated midpoint. Thus, the 12-inch class includes trees 11.0 inches through 12.9 inches d.b.h.

Gross growth.—Annual increase in net volume of trees in the absence of cutting and mortality.

Net annual growth.—The increase in volume of a specified size class for a given year.

Mortality.—Number or sound-wood volume of live trees dying from natural causes during a specified period.

Timber removals.—The net volume of growing stock trees removed from the inventory by harvesting, cultural operations such as timber-stand improvement, land clearing, or changes in land use.

Timber products.—Roundwood products and plant by-products. Timber products output includes roundwood products cut from growing stock on commercial forest land; from other sources, such as cull trees, salvable dead trees, limbs, and saplings; from trees on noncommercial and nonforest lands; and from plant byproducts.

Roundwood products.—Logs, bolts, or other round sections cut from trees for industrial or consumer uses. Included are saw logs, veneer logs and bolts, cooperage logs and bolts, pulpwood, fuelwood, piling, poles, and posts, hewn ties, mine timbers, and various other round, split, or hewn products.

Logging residues.—The unused portions of trees cut or killed by logging.

Plant byproducts.—Wood products, such as pulp chips, obtained incidentally to manufacture of other products.

Plant residues.—Wood materials not utilized for products. Included are slabs, edgings, trimmings, miscuts, sawdust, shavings, veneer cores and clippings, and pulp screenings.

LITERATURE CITED

1. Bertelson, D. F.
   1970. Timber salvage in Mississippi after Hurricane Camille. For. Farmer 29 (11) : 8.

2. Christopher, J. F.
   1963. Mississippi forest industry statistics, 1962. USDA For. Serv. Resour. Bull. SO-4, 24 p. South. For. Exp. Stn., New Orleans, La.

3. Grosenbaugh, L. R.
   1965. Three-pee sampling theory and program "THRP" for computer generation of selection criteria. USDA For. Serv. Res. Pap. PSW-21, 53 p. Pac. Southwest For. and Range Exp. Stn., Berkeley, Calif.

4. Grosenbaugh, L. R.
   1971. STX 1-11-71 for dendrometry of multistage 3P samples. USDA For. Serv. Publ. FS-277, 63 p.

5. Southern Forest Experiment Station.
   1958. Mississippi forests. U. S. For. Serv., South. For. Exp. Stn., For. Surv. Release 81, 52 p.

6. Van Hooser, D. D.
   1968. Mississippi forest industry. USDA For. Serv. Resour. Bull. SO-12, 25 p. South. For. Exp. Stn., New Orleans, La.

7. Van Hooser, D. D.
   1972. Evaluation of two-stage 3P sampling for forest surveys. USDA For. Serv. Res. Pap. SO-77, 9 p. South. For. Exp. Stn., New Orleans, La.

8. Van Hooser, D. D., and Hedlund, A.
   1969. Timber damaged by Hurricane Camille in Mississippi. USDA For. Serv. Res. Note SO-96, 5 p. South. For. Exp. Stn., New Orleans, La.

9. Van Sickle, C. C., and Van Hooser, D. D.
   1969. Forest resources of Mississippi. USDA For. Serv. Resour. Bull. SO-17, 34 p. South. For. Exp. Stn., New Orleans, La.

STANDARD TABLES

Table 1.—*Growing stock volume on commercial forest land by species and diameter class, Mississippi, 1973*

Species	All classes	6.0-7.9	8.0-9.9	10.0-11.9	12.0-13.9	14.0-15.9	16.0-17.9	18.0-19.9	20.0-21.9	22.0-23.9	24.0-25.9	26.0-27.9	28.0-29.9	30.0 and larger
						Million cubic feet								
Softwood:														
Longleaf	435.3	2.0	40.3	70.5	88.3	151.9	50.2	21.4	10.7	...	...	...	...	...
Slash	616.6	62.7	115.0	174.9	79.7	79.2	73.2	14.4	17.5	...	...	...	...	...
Loblolly	3,555.0	100.0	653.2	476.7	541.4	531.3	493.5	260.5	194.8	164.0	109.8	21.3	8.7	...
Other softwoods	2,526.3	190.9	579.0	473.8	509.6	367.9	202.5	80.6	27.0	67.0	14.0	...	...	14.0
Total	7,133.2	355.6	1,387.5	1,195.9	1,219.0	1,130.3	819.2	376.9	250.0	231.0	123.8	21.3	8.7	14.0
Hardwood:														
Gums	1,512.0	147.3	232.8	377.4	308.2	137.8	120.8	104.5	31.6	42.8	...	8.8	...	...
Oaks	3,451.3	205.1	453.0	516.3	527.3	467.8	436.4	286.9	321.3	82.3	34.1	38.5	25.2	57.1
Other hardwoods	2,078.6	192.6	202.0	283.3	500.0	242.0	206.6	76.0	149.5	69.6	58.0	8.8	13.4	76.8
Total	7,041.9	545.0	887.8	1,177.0	1,335.5	847.6	763.8	467.4	502.4	194.7	92.1	56.1	38.6	133.9
All species	14,175.1	900.6	2,275.3	2,372.9	2,554.5	1,977.9	1,583.0	844.3	752.4	425.7	215.9	77.4	47.3	147.9

Table 2.—*Sawtimber volume on commercial forest land by species and diameter class, Mississippi, 1973*

Species	All classes	9.0-10.9	11.0-12.9	13.0-14.9	15.0-16.9	17.0-18.9	19.0-20.9	21.0-22.9	23.0-24.9	25.0-26.9	27.0-28.9	29.0 and larger
						Million board feet						
Softwood:												
Longleaf pine	2,037.3	305.6	456.1	807.8	282.5	127.1	58.2	...	...	...	...	...
Slash pine	2,001.3	588.5	394.8	424.1	410.6	90.1	93.2	...	...	...	...	...
Loblolly pine	16,687.5	1,839.0	3,137.5	3,195.5	3,243.0	1,767.9	1,371.3	1,081.7	829.5	159.5	62.6	...
Other softwoods	9,186.9	1,731.6	2,591.6	2,229.0	1,263.0	490.5	190.1	493.4	105.7	...	...	92.0
Total	29,913.0	4,464.7	6,580.0	6,656.4	5,199.1	2,475.6	1,712.8	1,575.1	935.2	159.5	62.6	92.0
Hardwood:												
Gums	3,210.5	...	1,192.3	568.4	588.5	443.6	148.5	228.4	...	40.8	...	...
Oaks	10,100.4	...	2,064.8	1,985.1	2,043.0	1,441.5	1,384.1	388.6	191.0	192.4	126.9	283.0
Other hardwoods	6,402.0	...	1,987.1	1,094.0	1,098.6	378.5	787.6	357.2	235.3	44.1	55.3	364.3
Total	19,712.9	...	5,244.2	3,647.5	3,730.1	2,263.6	2,320.2	974.2	426.3	277.3	182.2	647.3
All species	49,625.9	4,464.7	11,824.2	10,303.9	8,929.2	4,739.2	4,033.0	2,549.3	1,361.5	436.8	244.8	739.3

Species	Net annual growth	Annual removals
	Million cubic feet	
Softwood:		
Longleaf pine	24.5	55.6
Slash pine	35.5	25.7
Loblolly pine	245.7	252.6
Other softwoods	148.2	94.2
Total	453.9	428.1
Hardwood:		
Gums	54.5	81.6
Oaks	169.9	100.7
Other hardwoods	97.3	89.8
Total	321.7	272.1
All species	775.6	700.2

Table 4.—*Annual growth and removals of sawtimber on commercial forest land by species, Mississippi, 1972*

Species	Net annual growth	Annual removals
	Million board feet	
Softwood:		
Longleaf pine	126.0	192.8
Slash pine	130.5	87.6
Loblolly pine	1,303.8	1,121.5
Other softwoods	667.2	350.5
Total	2,227.5	1,752.4
Hardwood:		
Gums	187.2	236.9
Oaks	801.2	310.5
Other hardwoods	500.4	269.6
Total	1,488.8	817.0
All species	3,716.3	2,569.4

Table 5.—*Mortality of growing stock and sawtimber on commercial forest land by species, Mississippi, 1972*

Species	Growing stock	Sawtimber
	Million cubic feet	*Million board feet*
Softwood:		
Longleaf pine	4.2	16.3
Slash pine	4.6	5.4
Loblolly pine	30.8	21.8
Other softwoods	11.9	26.3
Total	51.5	169.8
Hardwood:		
Gums	15.7	34.9
Oaks	15.6	39.1
Other softwoods	31.9	61.1
Total	63.2	135.1
All species	114.7	304.9

Table 6.—*Mortality of growing stock and sawtimber on commercial forest land by causes and by softwoods and hardwoods, Mississippi, 1972*

Cause	Growing stock			Sawtimber		
	All species	Softwood	Hardwood	All species	Softwood	Hardwood
	— — Million cubic feet — —			*— — Million board feet — —*		
Insect	6.5	6.5	...	14.2	14.2	...
Disease	3.9	3.2	0.7	6.1	6.1	...
Fire	4.5	3.9	.6	8.9	8.9	...
Animal	5.4	...	5.4	3.9	...	3.9
Weather	33.4	18.8	14.6	131.2	94.2	37.0
Other	3.7	3.7	...	...	...	...
Unknown	57.3	15.4	41.9	140.6	46.4	94.2
All causes	114.7	51.5	63.2	304.9	169.8	135.1

Table 7.—*Total output of timber products by product, by type of material used, and by softwoods and hardwoods, Mississippi, 1972*

Product and species group	Standard units	Total output		Roundwood products		Plant byproducts	
		Number	M cu. ft.	Number	M cu. ft.	Number	M cu. ft.
Saw logs:							
Softwood	M bd. ft. [1]	740,671	119,711	714,421	117,523	26,250	2,188
Hardwood	M bd. ft. [1]	432,252	72,056	432,252	72,056	...	...
Total	M bd. ft. [1]	1,172,923	191,767	1,146,673	189,579	26,250	2,188
Veneer logs and bolts:							
Softwood	M bd. ft.	341,491	56,175	341,491	56,175	...	...
Hardwood	M bd. ft.	31,189	5,234	31,189	5,234	...	...
Total	M bd. ft.	372,680	61,409	372,680	61,409	...	...
Pulpwood:							
Softwood	Std. cords [2]	3,161,367	256,071	2,367,567	191,773	793,800	64,298
Hardwood	Std. cords [2]	1,423,032	113,842	1,177,932	94,234	245,100	19,608
Total	Std. cords [2]	4,584,399	369,913	3,545,499	286,007	1,038,900	83,906
Cooperage:							
Softwood	M bd. ft.	...	...	...	...	...	...
Hardwood	M bd. ft.	1,275	184	1,275	184	...	...
Total	M bd. ft.	1,275	184	1,275	184	...	...
Piling:							
Softwood	M linear ft.	7,882	5,642	7,882	5,642	...	...
Hardwood	M linear ft.	...	...	...	...	...	...
Total	M linear ft.	7,882	5,642	7,882	5,642	...	...
Poles:							
Softwood	M pieces	834	9,722	834	9,722	...	...
Hardwood	M pieces	...	...	...	...	...	...
Total	M pieces	834	9,722	834	9,722	...	...
Commercial posts (round and split):							
Softwood	M pieces	3,026	1,740	3,026	1,740	...	...
Hardwood	M pieces	...	...	...	...	...	...
Total	M pieces	3,026	1,740	3,026	1,740	...	...
Other: [3]							
Softwood	M cu. ft.	15,299	15,299	536	536	14,763	14,763
Hardwood	M cu. ft.	6,140	6,140	4,492	4,492	1,648	1,648
Total	M cu. ft.	21,439	21,439	5,028	5,028	16,411	16,411
Total industrial products:							
Softwood		...	464,360	...	383,111	...	81,249
Hardwood		...	197,456	...	176,200	...	21,256
Total		...	661,816	...	559,311	...	102,505
Noncommercial posts [4] (round and split):							
Softwood	M pieces	2,111	1,351	2,111	1,351	...	...
Hardwood	M pieces	9,853	6,306	9,853	6,306	...	...
Total	M pieces	11,964	7,657	11,964	7,657	...	...
Fuelwood: [4]							
Softwood	Std. cords	253,550	19,016	58,897	4,417	[5] 194,653	[5] 14,599
Hardwood	Std. cords	663,961	49,797	526,588	39,494	[5] 137,373	[5] 10,303
Total	Std. cords	917,511	68,813	585,485	43,911	[5] 332,026	[5] 24,902
All products:							
Softwood		...	...	...	388,879	...	95,848
Hardwood	...	...	...	...	222,000	...	31,559
Total	...	...	...	...	610,879	...	127,407

[1] International ¼-inch rule.
[2] Rough wood basis (for example, chips converted to equivalent standard cords).
[3] Includes chemical wood, handle stock, miscellaneous dimension and other minor industrial products. Additionally, byproducts include material used for livestock bedding, mulch, etc.
[4] Based on data collected during the 1966 survey.
[5] Includes plant byproducts used for industrial and domestic fuel.

Table 8.—*Output of roundwood products by source and by softwoods and hardwoods, Mississippi, 1972*

Product and species group	All sources	Growing-stock trees [1]			Rough and rotten trees [1]	Salvable dead trees [1]	Other sources [2]
		Total	Saw-timber	Pole-timber			
	— — — — — — — *Thousand cubic feet* — — — — — — —						
Industrial products:							
Saw logs:							
Softwood	117,523	116,737	116,308	429	143	...	643
Hardwood	72,056	69,377	69,290	87	951	1,685	43
Total	189,579	186,114	185,598	516	1,094	1,685	686
Veneer logs and bolts:							
Softwood	56,175	55,800	55,595	205	68	...	307
Hardwood	5,234	5,143	5,143	...	69	...	22
Total	61,409	60,943	60,738	205	137	...	329
Pulpwood:							
Softwood	191,773	182,617	125,898	56,719	1,271	...	7,885
Hardwood	94,234	75,702	42,515	33,187	14,293	242	3,997
Total	286,007	258,319	168,413	89,906	15,564	242	11,882
Misc. industrial products:							
Cooperage:							
Softwood	...	...	...	...	...	...	...
Hardwood	184	181	181	...	1	...	2
Total	184	181	181	...	1	...	2
Piling:							
Softwood	5,642	5,617	5,617	...	...	...	25
Hardwood	...	...	...	...	...	...	...
Total	5,642	5,617	5,617	...	...	...	25
Poles:							
Softwood	9,722	9,650	8,535	1,115	...	...	72
Hardwood	...	...	...	...	...	...	...
Total	9,722	9,650	8,535	1,115	...	...	72
Commercial posts (round and split):							
Softwood	1,740	1,586	...	1,586	...	...	154
Hardwood	...	...	...	...	...	...	...
Total	1,740	1,586	...	1,586	...	...	154
Other:							
Softwood	536	505	271	234	...	...	31
Hardwood	4,492	4,477	4,234	243	6	1	8
Total	5,028	4,982	4,505	477	6	1	39
All misc. industrial products:							
Softwood	17,640	17,358	14,423	2,935	...	...	282
Hardwood	4,676	4,658	4,415	243	7	1	10
Total	22,316	22,016	18,838	3,178	7	1	292
All industrial products:							
Softwood	383,111	372,512	312,224	60,288	1,482	...	9,117
Hardwood	176,200	154,880	121,363	33,517	15,320	1,928	4,072
Total	559,311	527,392	433,587	93,805	16,802	1,928	13,189
Noncommercial posts [3] (round and split):							
Softwood	1,351	1,219	663	556	59	...	73
Hardwood	6,306	5,689	1,657	4,032	275	...	342
Total	7,657	6,908	2,320	4,588	334	...	415
Fuelwood: [3]							
Softwood	4,417	3,121	559	2,562	206	306	784
Hardwood	39,494	27,909	5,003	22,906	1,843	2,738	7,004
Total	43,911	31,030	5,562	25,468	2,049	3,044	7,788
All products:							
Softwood	388,879	376,852	313,446	63,406	1,747	306	9,974
Hardwood	222,000	188,478	128,023	60,454	17,438	4,666	11,418
Total	610,879	565,330	441,469	123,861	19,185	4,972	21,392

[1] On commercial forest land.
[2] Includes noncommercial forest land, nonforest land such as fence rows, trees less than 5.0 inches in diameter, and treetops and limbs.
[3] Based on data collected during 1966 survey.

13

Table 9.—*Timber removals from growing stock on commercial forest land by items and by softwoods and hardwoods, Mississippi, 1972*

Item	All species	Soft-wood	Hard-wood
	— Thousand cubic feet —		
Roundwood products:			
Saw logs	186,114	116,737	69,377
Veneer logs and bolts	60,943	55,800	5,143
Pulpwood	258,319	182,617	75,702
Cooperage logs and bolts	181	...	181
Piling	5,617	5,617	...
Poles	9,650	9,650	...
Posts[1]	8,494	2,805	5,689
Other	4,982	505	4,477
Fuelwood[2]	31,030	3,121	27,909
All products	565,330	376,852	188,478
Logging residues	64,915	29,632	35,283
Other removals	69,966	21,583	48,383
Total removals	700,211	428,067	272,144

[1] Includes 6,908 thousand cubic feet of noncommercial post, based on 1966 fuelwood survey.
[2] Based on 1966 fuelwood survey.

Table 10.—*Timber removals from sawtimber on commercial forest land by items and by softwoods and hardwoods, Mississippi, 1972*

Item	All species	Soft-wood	Hard-wood
	— Thousand board feet —		
Roundwood products:			
Saw logs	1,111,790	705,776	406,014
Veneer logs and bolts	367,618	337,358	30,260
Pulpwood	665,269	500,541	164,728
Cooperage logs and bolts	1,219	...	1,219
Piling	33,317	33,317	...
Poles	49,322	49,322	...
Posts	9,054	2,634	6,420
Other	27,623	1,347	26,276
Fuelwood	25,762	2,592	23,170
All products	2,290,974	1,632,887	658,087
Logging residues	127,455	51,125	76,330
Other removals	151,000	68,383	82,617
Total removals	2,569,429	1,752,395	817,034

Table 11.—*Volume of plant residues by industrial source and type of residue and by softwoods and hardwoods, Mississippi, 1972*

Species group and type	All industries	Lumber	Veneer and plywood	Other
	— — — — Thousand cubic feet — — — —			
Softwood:				
Coarse[1]	2,391	1,875	1	515
Fine[2]	10,079	7,727	114	2,238
Total	12,470	9,602	115	2,753
Hardwood:				
Coarse	4,167	3,891	28	248
Fine	10,431	9,985	8	438
Total	14,598	13,876	36	686
All species:				
Coarse	6,558	5,766	29	763
Fine	20,510	17,712	122	2,676
All types	27,068	23,478	151	3,439

[1] Unused material suitable for chipping, such as slabs, edging, and veneer cores.
[2] Unused material not suitable for chipping, such as sawdust and shavings.

14

COUNTY TABLES

Table 12.—*Total area and forest area, Mississippi, 1973*

County	Total area[1]	Commercial forest	Percent	Non-commercial forest	County	Total area[1]	Commercial forest	Percent	Non-commercial forest
	Thousand acres	*Thousand acres*	*Percent*	*Thousand acres*		*Thousand acres*	*Thousand acres*	*Percent*	*Thousand acres*
Adams	305.9	209.0	68	0.2	Lowndes	325.1	125.0	38	...
Alcorn	259.2	123.0	47	...					
Amite	466.6	319.0	68	([2])	Madison	480.6	189.7	39	3.4
Attala	463.4	309.3	67	1.8	Marion	352.0	203.5	58	...
					Marshall	454.4	215.0	47	.1
Benton	263.7	162.9	62	([2])	Monroe	492.2	248.0	50	...
Bolivar	601.6	73.7	12	.1	Montgomery	257.9	155.5	60	...
Calhoun	378.9	213.6	56	...	Neshoba	363.5	205.7	57	...
Carroll	408.3	209.5	51	...	Newton	371.2	268.2	72	...
Chickasaw	323.8	124.0	38	2.2	Noxubee	444.8	209.1	47	...
Choctaw	266.9	183.6	69	1.3					
Claiborne	317.5	226.5	71	2.5	Oktibbeha	290.6	148.5	51	...
Clarke	446.1	370.7	83	...					
Clay	265.0	100.9	38	.1	Panola	450.6	123.5	27	...
Coahoma	379.5	63.7	17	...	Pearl River	530.0	366.5	69	...
Copiah	499.8	335.1	67	...	Perry	417.9	336.0	80	.1
Covington	266.2	140.4	53	...	Pike	262.4	150.3	57	...
					Pontotoc	320.6	145.5	45	.5
De Soto	312.3	80.1	26	...	Prentiss	267.5	142.9	53	...
Forrest	300.2	216.1	72	.1					
Franklin	363.5	294.0	81	([2])	Quitman	263.7	18.4	7	...
George	307.8	236.8	77	...	Rankin	512.0	367.8	72	([2])
Greene	465.9	408.0	88	...					
Grenada	286.1	169.0	59	...	Scott	393.6	265.7	68	.2
					Sharkey	279.0	74.1	27	.2
Hancock	313.0	244.1	78	1.8	Simpson	375.7	248.0	66	...
Harrison	384.6	285.6	74	([2])	Smith	410.9	276.9	67	([2])
Hinds	561.3	196.8	35	1.6	Stone	286.7	238.5	83	...
Holmes	493.4	187.5	38	...	Sunflower	444.2	36.9	8	...
Humphreys	270.1	39.5	15	...					
					Tallahatchie	412.8	123.2	30	...
Issaquena	285.5	126.4	44	...	Tate	263.0	90.8	35	...
Itawamba	346.2	220.7	64	...	Tippah	297.0	166.5	56	...
					Tishomingo	289.9	198.7	69	1.0
Jackson	487.0	378.0	78	...	Tunica	304.6	58.4	19	...
Jasper	437.1	316.0	72	...					
Jefferson	336.0	248.1	74	.8	Union	270.1	115.5	43	...
Jefferson Davis	265.0	130.0	49	...					
Jones	451.8	290.4	64	([2])	Walthall	257.9	108.9	42	...
					Warren	385.3	184.0	48	...
Kemper	484.5	342.0	71	...	Washington	487.7	53.2	11	...
					Wayne	529.3	439.2	83	([2])
Lafayette	434.5	273.1	63	([2])	Webster	266.2	145.0	54	1.0
Lamar	320.0	235.2	74	...	Wilkinson	437.1	322.0	74	...
Lauderdale	462.1	340.2	74	...	Winston	387.8	277.6	72	...
Lawrence	277.1	189.7	68	...					
Leake	375.0	259.1	69	1.4	Yalobusha	322.6	175.4	54	([2])
Lee	291.2	85.3	29	.9	Yazoo	600.9	207.1	34	...
Leflore	380.2	60.6	16	...					
Lincoln	375.1	258.3	69	...	All counties	30,538.2	16,700.2	55	21.3

[1] Source: United States Bureau of the Census, Land and Water Area of the United States, 1960.
[2] Negligible.

15

Table 13.—*Growing-stock volume on commercial forest land by species group and county, Mississippi, 1973*

County	All species	Softwood	Hardwood	County	All species	Softwood	Hardwood
		——— Million cubic feet ———				*——— Million cubic feet ———*	
Adams	66.2	14.8	51.4	Lowndes	81.4	34.3	47.1
Alcorn	59.9	24.5	35.4				
Amite	388.0	282.9	105.1	Madison	165.4	87.1	78.3
Attala	217.8	126.1	91.7	Marion	164.9	101.6	63.3
				Marshall	107.7	41.0	66.7
Benton	161.1	23.1	138.0	Monroe	129.3	46.3	83.0
Bolivar	97.5	...	97.5	Montgomery	149.6	83.3	66.3
Calhoun	177.7	79.9	97.8	Neshoba	227.5	107.3	120.2
Carroll	121.0	29.1	91.9	Newton	257.6	168.9	88.7
Chickasaw	66.7	22.3	44.4	Noxubee	162.7	121.3	41.4
Choctaw	122.6	79.3	43.3				
Claiborne	240.7	36.7	204.0	Oktibbeha	115.6	49.5	66.1
Clarke	254.0	91.7	162.3				
Clay	91.3	21.0	70.3	Panola	55.6	...	55.6
Coahoma	51.6	4.0	47.6	Pearl River	123.9	68.6	55.3
Copiah	344.5	128.2	216.3	Perry	297.3	194.5	102.8
Covington	124.4	42.1	82.3	Pike	114.2	62.4	51.8
				Pontotoc	111.9	44.9	67.0
De Soto	46.8	3.1	43.7	Prentiss	102.5	31.8	70.7
Forrest	67.8	56.0	11.8	Quitman	4.2	...	4.2
Franklin	472.1	387.8	84.3				
				Rankin	414.6	244.0	170.6
George	173.8	104.5	69.3				
Greene	272.5	230.6	41.9	Scott	288.4	144.3	144.1
Grenada	146.2	64.6	81.6	Sharkey	76.3	...	76.3
				Simpson	144.0	81.6	62.4
Hancock	114.1	93.8	20.3	Smith	444.1	281.1	163.0
Harrison	248.9	177.3	71.6	Stone	157.2	105.5	51.7
Hinds	138.1	56.2	81.9	Sunflower	44.7	10.0	34.7
Holmes	77.5	18.4	59.1				
Humphreys	32.6	...	32.6	Tallahatchie	134.2	36.8	97.4
				Tate	76.8	...	76.8
Issaquena	138.3	...	138.3	Tippah	114.2	42.2	72.0
Itawamba	194.2	63.0	131.2	Tishomingo	170.3	68.7	101.6
				Tunica	18.9	...	18.9
Jackson	291.6	163.8	127.8				
Jasper	199.1	125.2	73.9	Union	125.5	41.3	84.2
Jefferson	226.4	135.8	90.6				
Jefferson Davis	87.0	54.5	32.5	Walthall	138.8	98.2	40.6
Jones	161.9	127.6	34.3	Warren	307.9	9.8	298.1
				Washington	34.3	...	34.3
Kemper	325.6	170.5	155.1	Wayne	407.7	266.4	141.3
				Webster	135.4	69.4	66.0
Lafayette	170.7	104.2	66.5	Wilkinson	406.4	259.5	146.9
Lamar	90.9	75.1	15.8	Winston	261.8	156.2	105.6
Lauderdale	402.6	276.4	126.2				
Lawrence	178.0	106.2	71.8	Yalobusha	164.8	92.2	72.6
Leake	242.9	92.9	150.0	Yazoo	270.7	...	270.7
Lee	34.7	...	34.7				
Leflore	80.6	...	80.6	All counties	14,175.1	7,133.2	7,041.9
Lincoln	266.9	190.0	76.9				

Table 14.—*Net change in growing-stock volume between 1967 and 1973, by species group and county, Mississippi*

County	All species	Softwood	Hardwood	County	All species	Softwood	Hardwood
	— — — *Million cubic feet* — — —				— — — *Million cubic feet* — — —		
Adams	− 95.8	− 46.3	− 49.5	Lowndes	+ 14.5	+ 12.0	+ 2.5
Alcorn	− 3.0	+ 3.7	− 6.7				
Amite	+ 85.3	+ 63.2	+ 22.1	Madison	+ 67.3	+ 36.2	+ 31.1
Attala	+ 15.2	+ 5.4	+ 9.8	Marion	+ 21.8	+ 6.6	+ 15.2
				Marshall	+ 24.5	+ 10.5	+ 14.0
Benton	+ 13.8	− .5	+ 14.3	Monroe	− 38.4	− 3.8	− 34.6
Bolivar	+ 10.7	− 1.9	+ 12.6	Montgomery	+ 4.6	+ 15.0	− 10.4
Calhoun	+ 30.1	+ 11.1	+ 19.0	Neshoba	+ 31.8	+ 2.7	+ 29.1
Carroll	− 5.3	+ 12.1	− 17.4	Newton	+ 42.7	+ 61.5	− 18.8
Chickasaw	− 12.1	− 8.0	− 4.1	Noxubee	− 41.5	+ 43.8	− 85.3
Choctaw	+ 4.1	+ 13.0	− 8.9				
Claiborne	+ 79.4	− .2	+ 79.6	Oktibbeha	− 4.7	− .1	− 4.6
Clarke	− 46.0	− 69.1	+ 23.1				
Clay	+ 2.8	+ 11.2	− 8.4	Panola	+ 1.4	...	+ 1.4
Coahoma	− 4.9	− .2	− 4.7	Pearl River	− 93.7	− 83.1	− 10.6
Copiah	+ 15.3	− 64.6	+ 79.9	Perry	+ 14.3	+ 12.9	+ 1.4
Covington	− 15.1	− 18.5	+ 3.4	Pike	+ 28.9	+ 19.9	+ 9.0
				Pontotoc	+ 29.2	+ 13.7	+ 15.5
De Soto	− 11.3	+ .9	− 12.2	Prentiss	+ 31.6	+ 13.2	+ 18.4
Forrest	− 53.3	− 53.5	+ .2	Quitman	− 28.0	...	− 28.0
Franklin	+ 97.5	+122.6	− 25.1				
				Rankin	+ 81.3	+ 50.4	+ 30.9
George	+ 7.8	+ 18.8	− 11.0				
Greene	+ 46.3	+ 39.3	+ 7.0	Scott	+ 53.6	+ 19.6	+ 34.0
Grenada	+ 52.0	+ 44.6	+ 7.4	Sharkey	− 17.9	...	− 17.9
				Simpson	− 19.1	− 22.1	+ 3.0
Hancock	− 36.0	+ 19.3	− 55.3	Smith	+ 107.3	+ 81.6	+ 25.7
Harrison	− .4	− 13.8	+ 13.4	Stone	− 35.7	− 34.3	− 1.4
Hinds	+ 42.5	+ 10.3	+ 32.2	Sunflower	− 1.2	+ 2.7	− 3.9
Holmes	− 17.2	− 1.6	− 15.6				
Humphreys	− 8.0	...	− 8.0	Tallahatchie	+ 7.3	+ 24.6	− 17.3
				Tate	+ 10.3	...	+ 10.3
Issaquena	+ .1	...	+ .1	Tippah	+ 19.7	+ 5.7	+ 14.0
Itawamba	+ 58.2	+ 23.7	+ 34.5	Tishomingo	+ 42.9	+ 15.7	+ 27.2
				Tunica	− 28.5	...	− 28.5
Jackson	+ 13.0	+ 9.9	+ 3.1				
Jasper	− 105.3	− 72.8	− 32.5	Union	+ 60.6	+ 26.5	+ 34.1
Jefferson	+ 27.1	+ 9.3	+ 17.8				
Jefferson Davis	− 23.0	− 12.1	− 10.9	Walthall	+ 25.7	+ 27.8	− 2.1
Jones	− 85.7	− 73.9	− 11.8	Warren	+ 89.7	+ 4.4	+ 85.3
				Washington	+ 1.1	...	+ 1.1
Kemper	+ 15.9	− 15.4	+ 31.3	Wayne	+ 70.4	+ 64.1	+ 6.3
				Webster	+ 3.6	+ 6.3	− 2.7
Lafayette	+ 19.5	+ 14.8	+ 4.7	Wilkinson	+ 38.0	+ 14.6	+ 23.4
Lamar	− 47.3	− 28.5	− 18.8	Winston	+ 70.5	+ 67.5	+ 3.0
Lauderdale	+ 68.5	+ 58.3	+ 10.2				
Lawrence	+ 24.9	+ 10.9	+ 14.0	Yalobusha	+ 51.3	+ 35.9	+ 15.4
Leake	+ 21.7	− 10.2	+ 31.9	Yazoo	+ 46.5	...	+ 46.5
Lee	− .3	...	− .3				
Leflore	+ 11.7	...	+ 11.7				
Lincoln	+ 54.0	+ 57.0	− 3.0	All counties	+1,031.1	+620.8	+410.8

Table 15.—*Sawtimber volume on commercial forest land by species and county, Mississippi, 1973*

County	All species	Softwood	Hardwood	County	All species	Softwood	Hardwood
	— — *Million board feet* — —				— — *Million board feet* — —		
Adams	254.5	89.5	165.0	Lowndes	270.4	192.0	78.4
Alcorn	185.7	106.5	79.2				
Amite	1,292.0	987.7	304.3	Madison	549.1	216.4	332.7
Attala	948.0	689.1	258.9	Marion	572.8	440.0	132.8
				Marshall	346.8	100.5	246.3
Benton	586.7	146.2	440.5	Monroe	507.9	247.9	260.0
Bolivar	286.5	...	286.5	Montgomery	363.5	120.6	242.9
Calhoun	481.3	265.2	216.1	Neshoba	950.5	661.7	288.8
Carroll	323.3	40.1	283.2	Newton	661.9	459.3	202.6
Chickasaw	123.6	77.5	46.1	Noxubee	783.3	620.0	163.3
Choctaw	297.4	250.6	46.8				
Claiborne	400.2	85.1	315.1	Oktibbeha	297.7	175.3	122.4
Clarke	718.2	325.1	393.1				
Clay	347.1	142.4	204.7	Panola	94.4	...	94.4
Coahoma	178.6	14.9	163.7	Pearl River	435.9	354.3	81.6
Copiah	1,105.5	745.5	360.0	Perry	1,301.9	1,044.0	257.9
Covington	437.8	215.0	222.8	Pike	477.0	340.5	136.5
				Pontotoc	368.4	197.5	170.9
De Soto	97.5	16.1	81.4	Prentiss	285.9	159.5	126.4
Forrest	352.4	315.8	36.6	Quitman	20.3	...	20.3
Franklin	2,412.0	2,067.3	344.7				
				Rankin	1,122.8	653.3	469.5
George	687.3	568.8	118.5				
Greene	986.7	873.7	113.0	Scott	1,169.3	586.4	582.9
Grenada	412.8	265.0	147.8	Sharkey	351.3	...	351.3
				Simpson	525.5	395.7	129.8
Hancock	109.0	44.3	64.7	Smith	1,669.3	1,056.6	612.7
Harrison	558.5	498.3	60.2	Stone	605.9	473.8	132.1
Hinds	262.1	60.4	201.7	Sunflower	220.3	77.3	143.0
Holmes	256.6	69.7	186.9				
Humphreys	124.1	...	124.1	Tallahatchie	164.7	...	164.7
				Tate	203.6	...	203.6
Issaquena	504.5	...	504.5	Tippah	378.0	170.6	207.4
Itawamba	457.3	202.7	254.6	Tishomingo	407.2	163.1	244.1
				Tunica	89.4	...	89.4
Jackson	1,060.4	680.5	379.9				
Jasper	878.4	747.3	131.1	Union	217.5	52.1	165.4
Jefferson	1,036.1	744.5	291.6				
Jefferson Davis	315.5	287.8	27.7	Walthall	684.8	557.3	127.5
Jones	810.9	662.4	148.5	Warren	1,140.4	55.2	1,085.2
				Washington	92.0	...	92.0
Kemper	1,113.4	955.7	157.7	Wayne	1,704.1	1,332.9	371.2
				Webster	427.6	197.5	230.1
Lafayette	447.3	338.9	108.4	Wilkinson	2,144.4	1,680.7	463.7
Lamar	258.8	210.4	48.4	Winston	1,196.3	693.3	503.0
Lauderdale	1,201.1	650.6	550.5				
Lawrence	846.4	538.9	307.5	Yalobusha	487.8	223.5	264.3
Leake	1,028.9	437.9	591.0	Yazoo	909.9	...	909.9
Lee	69.9	...	69.9				
Leflore	180.4	...	180.4				
Lincoln	991.4	796.8	194.6	All counties	49,625.9	29,913.0	19,712.9

18

Table 16.—*Net change in sawtimber volume between 1967 and 1973, by species group and county, Mississippi*

County	All species	Softwood	Hardwood	County	All species	Softwood	Hardwood
	— — — *Million board feet* — ——				— — — *Million board feet* — ——		
Adams	− 477.4	− 401.1	− 76.3	Lowndes	+ 102.5	+ 91.7	+ 10.8
Alcorn	+ 8.1	+ 23.3	− 15.2				
Amite	+ 320.4	+ 222.4	+ 98.0	Madison	+ 224.1	+ 105.5	+ 118.6
Attala	+ 295.6	+ 140.0	+ 155.6	Marion	+ 48.3	− 8.8	+ 57.1
				Marshall	+ 111.1	+ 25.2	+ 85.9
Benton	+ 113.4	+ 50.1	+ 63.3	Monroe	+ 108.6	+ 93.3	+ 15.3
Bolivar	+ 26.2	− 12.8	+ 39.0	Montgomery	− 40.3	− 31.3	− 9.0
Calhoun	+ 200.5	+ 115.1	+ 85.4	Neshoba	+ 232.8	+ 83.9	+ 148.9
Carroll	+ 42.8	+ 19.4	+ 23.4	Newton	+ 265.9	+ 320.4	− 54.5
Chickasaw	− 65.3	− 54.8	− 10.5	Noxubee	+ 144.1	+ 190.5	− 46.4
Choctaw	− 26.3	+ 39.6	− 65.9				
Claiborne	− 13.7	− 24.9	+ 11.2	Oktibbeha	+ 46.8	+ 7.8	+ 39.0
Clarke	− 349.6	− 325.7	− 23.9				
Clay	+ 76.2	+ 93.5	− 17.3	Panola	− .9	...	· .9
Coahoma	+ 66.7	+ 1.0	+ 65.7	Pearl River	− 356.8	− 333.7	− 23.1
Copiah	− 91.1	− 169.4	+ 78.3	Perry	+ 104.3	+ 102.7	+ 1.6
Covington	− 80.4	− 83.9	+ 3.5	Pike	+ 162.7	+ 145.6	+ 17.1
				Pontotoc	+ 210.6	+ 134.9	+ 75.7
De Soto	− 11.7	+ 5.2	− 16.9	Prentiss	+ 152.5	+ 86.8	+ 65.7
Forrest	− 260.1	− 265.8	+ 5.7	Quitman	− 59.0		59.0
Franklin	+ 752.9	+ 644.6	+ 108.3				
				Rankin	+ 311.9	+ 156.3	+ 155.6
George	+ 106.9	+ 108.1	− 1.2				
Greene	+ 167.8	+ 91.9	+ 75.9	Scott	+ 493.3	+ 150.3	+ 343.0
Grenada	+ 274.9	+ 225.0	+ 49.9	Sharkey	− 50.5	...	− 50.5
				Simpson	− 21.1	− 83.3	+ 62.2
Hancock	− 79.8	− 52.1	− 27.7	Smith	+ 454.5	+ 326.2	+ 128.3
Harrison	− 451.6	− 472.4	+ 20.8	Stone	− 55.3	− 89.4	+ 34.1
Hinds	+ 204.4	+ 2.7	+ 201.7	Sunflower	+ 21.2	+ 26.0	− 4.8
Holmes	+ 5.1	+ 10.2	− 5.1				
Humphreys	+ 16.5	...	+ 16.5	Tallahatchie	− 30.8	− 14.7	− 16.1
				Tate	+ 97.8	...	+ 97.8
Issaquena	− 40.0	...	− 40.0	Tippah	+ 149.6	+ 77.6	+ 72.0
Itawamba	+ 260.0	+ 150.6	+ 109.4	Tishomingo	+ 137.6	+ 46.9	+ 90.7
				Tunica	− 71.5	...	− 71.5
Jackson	+ 92.9	+ 142.5	− 49.6				
Jasper	− 65.7	+ 27.3	− 93.0	Union	+ 111.8	+ 38.6	+ 73.2
Jefferson	+ 149.2	+ 42.7	+ 106.5				
Jefferson Davis	− 59.8	+ 4.5	− 64.3	Walthall	+ 137.0	+ 184.8	− 47.8
Jones	− 324.4	− 328.5	+ 4.1	Warren	+ 391.7	+ 21.0	+ 370.7
				Washington	− 25.4	...	− 25.4
Kemper	+ 89.3	+ 48.8	+ 40.5	Wayne	+ 208.0	+ 175.6	+ 32.4
				Webster	+ 125.9	+ 87.5	+ 38.4
Lafayette	+ 37.2	+ 37.9	− 40.7	Wilkinson	+ 382.4	+ 289.3	+ 93.1
Lamar	− 221.3	− 202.2	− 19.1	Winston	+ 628.5	+ 408.3	+ 220.2
Lauderdale	+ 295.3	− 2.2	+ 297.5				
Lawrence	+ 118.5	+ 29.5	+ 89.0				
Leake	+ 121.3	− 52.0	+ 173.3	Yalobusha	+ 120.6	+ 45.1	+ 75.5
Lee	− 8.4	...	− 8.4	Yazoo	+ 86.5	...	+ 86.5
Leflore	+ 57.9	...	+ 57.9				
Lincoln	+ 320.9	+ 277.5	+ 43.4	All counties	+ 6,655.3	+ 2,966.2	+ 3,689.1

19

Van Hooser, D.D.

    1973. Midcycle evaluation of Mississippi timber resources. South. For. Exp. Stn., New Orleans, La. 19 p. (USDA For. Serv. Resour. Bull. SO-44)

Between 1967 and 1972 forest acreage in Mississippi decreased by 1 percent, but softwood volume increased by 10 percent and hardwood by 6 percent. More than 0.5 billion cubic feet of roundwood were harvested from the State's forests in 1972.

Additional keywords: Forest acreage, timber growth, timber cut, forest industries.

Oklahoma Forest Industries, 1972

Daniel F. Bertelson

Southern Forest Experiment Station
New Orleans, Louisiana
Forest Service, U. S. Department of Agriculture

1973

ahoma Forest
ustries, 1972

l F. Bertelson

Southern Forest Experiment Station
Forest Service, U. S. Department of Agriculture

in cooperation with .

Oklahoma Forestry Division
of
State Department of Agriculture

1973

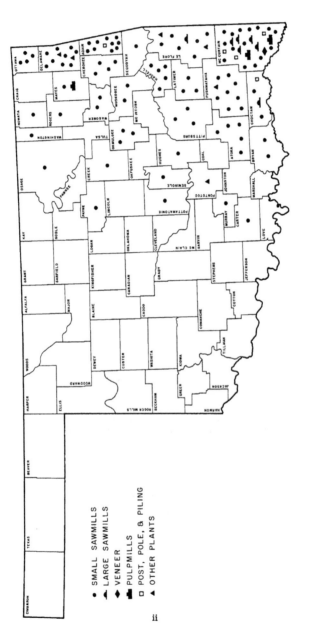

SMALL SAWMILLS

LARGE SAWMILLS

VENEER

PULPMILLS

POST, POLE, & PILING

OTHER PLANTS

Primary wood-using plants in Oklahoma, 1972

ii

Oklahoma Forest Industries, 1972

Daniel F. Bertelson

Oklahoma forests supplied more than 64 million cubic feet of roundwood to forest industries in 1972. Pine made up over three-fourths of the total. In terms of volume harvested, saw logs were the leading product, with pulpwood second (fig. 1). The two combined accounted for 79 percent of the roundwood produced. Veneer logs added 11 percent and posts made up more than half the remainder. A total of 118 wood-using plants were in operation.

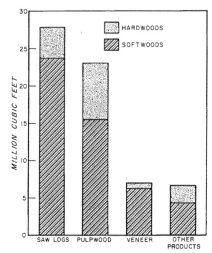

Figure 1.—*Output of industrial roundwood in Oklahoma, by product, 1972.*

More than 99 percent of the softwood came from a five-county region in the southeast corner of the State. Hardwood output was concentrated in the eastern half of the State, but some counties in the west also contributed. McCurtain County, in the extreme southeast, has the most wood-using plants. It also had the largest wood harvest—a total of 44 million feet, or more than two-thirds of the State total.

These are among the major findings of a new canvass of all primary forest industries in Oklahoma. Previous surveys—in 1955 and 1965—covered only forest industries in 17 eastern counties. In 1972, personnel of the Forestry Division of the Oklahoma State Department of Agriculture visited all primary wood-using plants; the canvass was made under supervision of Roger L. Davis. Data were compiled and analyzed by the Forest Resources Research Unit of the Southern Forest Experiment Station.

This report tabulates total production and shows softwood and hardwood output by county. It also lists names and addresses of all primary forest industries; plant locations are mapped on page ii.

SAW LOGS

Oklahoma produced 169 million board feet of saw logs in 1972. This was 43 percent of the total roundwood harvested. Softwoods, exclusively pine, made up 85 percent of the saw-log volume. Oaks and the gums accounted for more than half of the hardwood.

Of the 103 sawmills in operation, seven were large mills that cut a total of 166 million board feet during the year. They processed 83 percent of the lumber manufactured in Oklahoma; more than 99 percent of their output was softwood. The other 96 sawmills were classed as small, in that they individually cut less than 3 million board feet annually. In total, they processed 33 million board feet, of which 81 percent was hardwood. Production of individual mills ranged from 113 million board feet for the largest to 1,300 board feet for a part-time operation.

Oklahoma imported 34 million board feet of saw logs in 1972, and exported 4 million board feet to surrounding States, chiefly Arkansas. At least 20 percent of the saw logs cut within the State were transported over county lines before being sawn into lumber.

PULPWOOD

The 285,654 cords of roundwood cut in 1972 accounted for 36 percent of the State's timber harvest. This volume was more than triple that in 1971 and more than nine times the harvest a decade ago (fig. 2).

In 1962, Oklahoma had two pulpmills with a daily capability of 140 tons. In 1972, there were three mills with a capacity of 2,270 tons. The largest mill, able to pulp 1,600 tons daily, began operation in 1971 but did not reach full production until 1972.

Two mills, including the new one, are in McCurtain County, and in 1972 more than three-fourths of the round pulpwood cut in the State came from this county. In fact, McCurtain's production for this year ranked second in the entire South. The harvest in southeastern counties will be further stimulated by opening of a new mill in Texarkana, Texas, and by expansion of a mill in Ashdown, Arkansas.

Hardwoods comprised most of the roundwood cut in 1972, but now softwoods—all pine—comprise two-thirds of the harvest.

In addition to the roundwood, the equivalent of 184,000 cords of Oklahoma plant byproducts was chipped for pulp.

OTHER PRODUCTS

The veneer log harvest in Oklahoma totaled 42 million board feet, accounting for 11 percent of the State's production. Oklahoma has one veneer plant, which manufactures southern pine plywood. All hardwood veneer logs are sent to mills in other States. The main hardwood veneer species is pecan, but some cottonwood, black walnut, elm, and hackberry logs are also shipped.

Oklahoma produced almost 5.8 million pine posts in 1972, together with 196,000 poles and piling. These roundwood products made up about 7 percent of the timber harvest. The remaining 3 percent went into charcoal wood, handle stock, and excelsior.

PLANT RESIDUES

In converting roundwood into primary products, Oklahoma forest industries generated 23 million cubic feet of residues. Of this volume, 16.3 million was in coarse items such as slabs, edgings, cull pieces, and other material suitable for conversion into pulp chips. The rest consisted of finer particles such as sawdust and shavings. Of the total, 88 percent was converted to useful byproducts.

Pulp chips are the most profitable byproduct, and Oklahoma industries used 85 percent of

Figure 2.—
Pulpwood production in Oklahoma, 1962-1972.

2

their coarse residues for this purpose. Addition of a small quantity of fines brought total use for pulp to 15 million cubic feet. Since the unused coarse residues are largely scattered among small sawmills, it will be difficult to increase the percentage of recovery greatly.

Five million cubic feet, chiefly fines, were put to such miscellaneous purposes as charcoal, animal bedding, and soil mulch. Another 500,-000 cubic feet were burned for domestic and industrial fuel. The remaining 3 million cubic feet were mostly fine particles with no market.

Over 273,000 tons of bark were accumulated by Oklahoma wood-using plants in 1972. More than three-fourths was utilized, chiefly as industrial fuel. Small amounts went into charcoal, domestic fuel, animal bedding, and soil mulch.

Table 1. *Volume of industrial roundwood, 1972*

Product	Standard units	Volume in standard units			Roundwood volume		
		All species	Softwood	Hardwood	All species	Softwood	Hardwood
					- - - - M cu.ft.- - - -		
Saw logs	M bd.ft.[1]	169,249	143,630	25,619	27,898	23,627	4,271
Veneer logs	M bd.ft.[1]	42,155	37,877	4,278	6,949	6,231	718
Pulpwood	Std. cords	285,654	190,791	94,863	23,043	15,454	7,589
Poles and piling	M pieces	196	196	...	762	762	...
Posts	M pieces	5,774	5,774	...	3,568	3,568	...
Misc. products[2]	M cu.ft.	2,202	...	2,202	2,202	...	2,202
Total					64,422	49,642	14,780

[1]International 1/4-inch rule.
[2]Includes chemical wood, handlestock, and excelsior.

Table 2. *Industrial roundwood by species, 1972*

Species group	Saw logs	Veneer logs	Pulpwood	Poles and piling	Posts	Miscellaneous products
	- - - M bd.ft.[1]- - -		Std. cords	- - M pieces- -		M cu.ft.
Softwood:						
Pines	143,630	37,877	190,791	196	5,774	...
Total						
Hardwood:						
Black and tupelo gums	362	...	[2] 18,336	...	...	...
Sweetgum	1,200	...	[3] ...	...	...	48
Red oaks	8,435	...	29,788	...	...	623
White oaks	3,485	...	...	...	...	1,181
Other hardwoods	12,137	4,278	46,739	...	...	350
Total						
All species	169,249	42,155	285,654	196	5,774	2,202

[1]International 1/4-inch rule.
[2]Black and tupelo combined with sweetgum.
[3]Red and white oaks combined.

4

Table 3. *Residues produced by primary wood-using plants, 1972*

Type of industry[1]	All species			Softwood			Hardwood		
	Total	Fine[2]	Coarse[3]	Total	Fine[2]	Coarse[3]	Total	Fine[2]	Coarse[3]
	- - - - - - - - - - - - - - - - M cu. ft. - - - - - - - - - - - - - - -								
Lumber and veneer	22,675	6,542	16,133	21,074	5,853	15,221	1,601	689	912
Piling, poles, and posts	41	25	16	41	25	16	...	...	...
Miscellaneous products	431	303	128	431	303	128	...	...	...
All products	23,147	6,870	16,277	21,546	6,181	15,365	1,601	689	912

[1]Excludes woodpulp industry.
[2]Fine residues includes sawdust, screenings, and other material generally too small for chipping.
[3]Coarse residues include slabs, edgings, trimmings, and other material generally suitable for chipping.

Table 4. *Volume of primary plant byproducts, 1972[1]*

Type of use	All species	Softwood	Hardwood
	- - - - - M cu.ft. - - - - -		
Fuel[2]	526	411	115
Fiber[3]	14,895	14,791	104
Other[4]	4,890	4,647	243
Total	20,311	19,849	462

[1]Excludes woodpulp industry.
[2]Includes all residues used as fuel by industrial plants and domestic fuel either sold or given away.
[3]Includes all residues used in manufacture of fiber products, such as pulp or hardboard.
[4]Includes residues used as livestock bedding, mulch, and specialty items.

Table 5. *Movement of industrial roundwood, by product, 1972*

Product	Unit	Out of State receipts	Logged and remained in State	Logged and shipped out of State	Total receipts	Total production
		- - - - - - - - - - Standard units - - - - - - - - - -				
Saw logs	M bd.ft.[1]	33,891	164,899	4,350	198,790	169,249
Pulpwood	Std. cords	239,709	201,986	83,668	441,695	285,654
Poles and piling	M pieces	3	42	154	45	196
Posts	M pieces	260	3,598	2,176	3,858	5,774
Miscellaneous products[2]	M cu.ft.	803	8,356	795	9,159	9,151

[1]International 1/4-inch rule.
[2]Includes veneer, chemical wood, handlestock, and excelsior.

Table 6. *Sawlog production by county, 1972*

County	All species	Softwood	Hardwood	County	All species	Softwood	Hardwood
		- - - - M bd.ft.[1] - - - -				- - - - M bd.ft.[1] - - - -	
Adair	444	3	441	Murray	1	...	1
Atoka	1,156	174	982	Muskogee	166	...	166
Beaver	158	...	158	Nowata	960	...	960
Bryan	503	...	503				
				Okfuskee	303	...	303
Carter	1	...	1	Okmulgee	170	...	170
Cherokee	333	29	304	Osage	2,098	...	2,098
Choctaw	3,622	1,939	1,683	Ottawa	1,107	...	1,107
Coal	64	...	64				
Craig	1,086	...	1,086	Payne	367	...	367
Creek	579	...	579	Pittsburg	652	21	631
				Pontotoc	62	...	62
Delaware	1,679	4	1,675	Pottawatomie	3	...	3
				Pushmataha	19,164	16,499	2,665
Garvin	1	...	1				
				Rogers	290	...	290
Haskell	304	35	269				
Hughes	79	...	79	Seminole	1	...	1
				Sequoyah	395	...	395
Johnston	67	...	67				
				Tulsa	288	...	288
Latimer	894	524	370				
Le Flore	11,330	10,298	1,032	Wagoner	297	...	297
				Washington	1,334	...	1,334
McCurtain	119,009	114,104	4,905				
McIntosh	271	...	271				
Mayes	11	...	11	All counties	169,249	143,630	25,619

[1] International 1/4-inch rule.

Table 7. *Sawlog movement, 1972*

County[1]	Logged and remained in county	Outgoing shipments	Incoming shipments	Total log receipts
		- - - - - - - *M bd.ft.*[2] - - - - - - -		
Adair	304	140	484	788
Atoka	575	581	276	851
Cherokee	103	230	...	103
Choctaw	1,301	2,321	6,010	7,311
Delaware	257	1,422	43	300
Haskell	146	158	227	373
Latimer	155	739	...	155
Le Flore	7,138	4,192	792	7,930
McCurtain	116,402	2,606	46,681	163,083
Okmulgee	126	44	1,185	1,311
Ottawa	1,096	11	3,644	4,740
Pittsburg	122	530	3	125
Pushmataha	3,206	15,959	623	3,829
All other counties	4,068	5,316	3,823	7,891
All counties	134,999	34,249	63,791	198,790

[1]Counties with less than three plants are omitted.
[2]International 1/4-inch rule.

7

Table 8. *Round pulpwood production, 1972*

County[1]	All species	Softwood	Hardwood
	- - - Standard cords - - -		
Alfalfa	1,148		1,148
Beckham	2,455	...	2,455
Blaine	3,045	...	3,045
Caddo	303	...	303
Carter	971	...	971
Choctaw	2,752	1,866	886
Creek	4,147	...	4,147
Custer	1,876		1,876
Ellis	1,709	...	1,709
Haskell	2,057	200	1,857
Hughes	2,016	...	2,016
Jefferson	261	...	261
Kiowa	847		847
Le Flore	9,158	2,614	6,544
Lincoln	4,393	...	4,393
Love	185	...	185
McCurtain	215,241	165,168	50,073
Okfuskee	990	...	990
Oklahoma	869	...	869
Okmulgee	126	...	126
Pittsburg	2,188	...	2,188
Pontotoc	45	...	45
Pushmataha	28,872	20,943	7,929
All counties	285,654	190,791	94,863

[1]Counties with no pulpwood production are omitted.

Table 9. *Veneer-log production by county, 1972*

County[1]	All species
	M bd.ft.[2]
Adair	21
Atoka	283
Bryan	288
Choctaw	949
Coal	28
Craig	53
Delaware	76
Hughes	281
Le Flore	377
McCurtain	33,281
Nowata	30
Ottawa	62
Pontotoc	294
Pushmataha	5,685
Seminole	447
All counties	42,155

[1]Counties with negligible output are omitted.
[2]International 1/4-inch rule.

Table 10. *Pole and piling production by county, 1972*

County[1]	All species (softwood)
	M pieces
Choctaw	12
Latimer	2
Le Flore	30
McCurtain	125
Pushmata	27
All counties	196

[1] Counties with negligible output are omitted.

Table 11. *Commercial post production by county, 1972*

County[1]	All species (softwood)
	M pieces
Choctaw	755
Latimer	378
Le Flore	1,332
McCurtain	2,191
Pittsburg	1,118
All counties	5,774

[1] Counties with negligible output are omitted.

Table 12. *Output of miscellaneous products by county, 1972*

County[1]	All species (hardwood)
	M cu.ft.
Delaware	689
Latimer	276
Le Flore	1,196
Pontotoc	25
Pushmataha	16
All counties	2,202

[1] Counties with negligible output are omitted.

9

Table 13. *Industrial roundwood production by county, 1972*

County	All species	Softwood	Hardwood	County	All species	Softwood	Hardwood
	- - - *M cubic feet* - - -				- - - -*M cubic feet*- - -		
Adair	78	1	77	Lincoln	351	...	351
Alfalfa	92	...	92	Love	15	...	15
Atoka	240	29	211				
				McCurtain	44,291	39,319	4,972
Beaver	26		26	McIntosh	45	...	45
Beckham	196	...	196	Mayes	2		2
Blaine	244	...	244	Muskogee	28		28
Bryan	132	...	132				
				Nowata	165	...	165
Caddo	24	...	24				
Carter	78	...	78	Okfuskee	130	...	130
Cherokee	56	5	51	Oklahoma	70		70
Choctaw	1,493	982	511	Okmulgee	38		38
Coal	15	...	15	Osage	350	...	350
Craig	190	...	190	Ottawa	195	...	195
Creek	428	...	428				
Custer	150	...	150	Payne	61	...	61
				Pittsburg	284	4	280
Delaware	982	1	981	Pontotoc	88	...	88
				Pushmataha	7,238	6,044	1,194
Ellis	137	...	137				
				Rogers	48	...	48
Haskell	215	22	193				
Hughes	222	...	222	Seminole	75		75
				Sequoyah	66	...	66
Jefferson	21		21	Tulsa	48	...	48
Johnston	11	...	11				
				Wagoner	49	...	49
Kiowa	68		68	Washington	222	...	222
Latimer	666	328	338				
Le Flore	4,799	2,907	1,892	All counties	64,422	49,642	14,780

10

Table 14. *Plant byproducts by county, 1972*

County[1]	All species		Softwood		Hardwood	
	Fine	Coarse	Fine	Coarse	Fine	Coarse
	- - - - - - - M cubic feet - - - - - - -					
Atoka	23	21	...	...	23	21
Cherokee	7	12	...	1	7	11
Choctaw	10	770	2	759	8	11
Delaware	4	14	...	1	4	13
Haskell	...	31	...	2	...	29
Latimer	...	9	...	4		5
Le Flore	336	719	336	676	...	43
McCurtain	4,573	13,687	4,474	13,594	99	93
All other counties	92	3	...	...	92	3
All counties	5,045	15,266	4,812	15,037	233	229

[1]Omitted counties have either negligible volume or less than three plants.

Table 15. *Unused plant residues by county, 1972*

County[1]	All species		Softwood		Hardwood	
	Fine	Coarse	Fine	Coarse	Fine	Coarse
	- - - - - - - -M cubic feet - - - - - - - -					
Atoka	37	60	14	19	23	41
Cherokee	...	1	...	...	...	1
Choctaw	686	197	629	123	57	74
Delaware	16	16	...	...	16	16
Haskell	26	10	3	3	23	
Latimer	10	8	6	6	4	2
Le Flore	144	173	59	97	85	76
McCurtain	902	428	658	80	244	348
All other counties	4	118	...	...	4	118
All counties	1,825	1,011	1,369	328	456	683

[1]Omitted counties have either negligible volume or less than three plants.

Table 16. *Bark used by county, 1972*

County	All species	Softwood	Hardwood
	- - - - - Tons - - - - -		
Delaware	108	2	106
Le Flore	4,115	4,101	14
McCurtain	63,017	63,017	...
Other[1]	148,496	121,699	26,797
All counties	215,736	188,819	26,917

[1] Includes all pulpwood bark and all bark from counties with less than 3 plants.

Table 17. *Bark unused by county, 1972*

County	All species	Softwood	Hardwood
	- - - - - Tons - - - - -		
Atoka	887	163	724
Cherokee	118	1	117
Choctaw	22,995	21,955	1,040
Delaware	227	...	227
Haskell	406	40	366
Latimer	140	68	72
Le Flore	2,310	878	1,432
McCurtain	21,490	16,066	5,424
Other[1]	9,205	6,406	2,799
All counties	57,778	45,577	12,201

[1] Includes all pulpwood bark and all bark from counties with less than 3 plants.

Table 18. *Large sawmills[1]*

County	Firm	Plant	
		Location	Address [2]
Choctaw	Fry Forest Products[3]	Hugo	Box 458
Le Flore	Burnett Lumber Co[3]	Heavener	Box 158
McCurtain	T.L. Clouse Sawmill[3]	Broken Bow	Rt. 1, Box 1820
	Peebles Lumber Co.[3]	Idabel	Box 708
	Reynolds-Wilson Lumber Co.[3]	Idabel	Box F
	Thomason Lumber Co.[3]	Broken Bow	Box 804
	Weyerhaeuser Co.[3]	Wright City	Box 269

[1] Output of 3 million board feet or more.
[2] Office address specified when different from plant location.
[3] Residues chipped and sold to pulpmills.

Table 19. *Small sawmills*[1]

County	Firm	Plant	
		Location	Address[2]
Adair	George Brown Sawmill	Stilwell	Rt. 2
	E.J. Davis Sawmill	Stilwell	Rt. 2
	Hadlow-Campbell Sawmill	Stilwell	Rt. 2
	Joe Morton Sawmill	Stilwell	Rt. 2
	Odell Parker Sawmill	Stilwell	Rt. 2
	Reese Tie Co.	Stilwell	Box 467
	Sherman Sanders Sawmill	Westville	Rt. 2
	Fred Shephard Sawmill	Stilwell	Rt. 2
	Daniel Vaughn	Christie	Rt. 3, Stilwell
	Henry Vaughn Sawmill	Christie	Rt. 2, Westville
Atoka	C. & W. Co., Atoka Mill	Farris	Rt. 2, Antlers
	Goff's Sawmill	Lane	Rt. 1
	Monroe Isom Sawmill	Daisy	Star Rt.
	J. & J. Lumber Co.	Lane	Rt. 1
	Smith Sawmill	Tushka	Rt. 5, Atoka
Bryan	Gray's Sawmill	Durant	Rt. 1
	Summers Sawmill	Caddo	Box 403
Carter	Joe Walker	Gene Autry	
Cherokee	Horn Sawmill	Moody	Box 215B, Tahlequah
	Johnson Sawmill	Welling	Rt. 1
	Raymond Reck Sawmill	Eidon	Rt. 3, Tahlequah
	Webster Sawmill	Tahlequah	Rt. 2
Choctaw	Chapel Sawmill	Sawyer	Star Rt.
	Willis Bros. Lumber & Tie Co.	Boswell	Box 433, DeQueen,Ark.
Creek	Gordon Vanbrunt Sawmill	Stroud	1421 Woodland Dr., Prague
Delaware	Anderson Sawmill	Leach	Star Rt.
	Barns Sawmill	Jay	Rt. 1
	Blevins Sawmill	Jay	Rt. 1
	Gatewood Sawmill	Kansas	Rt. 4, Siloam Springs, Ark.
	I.L. Harmon	Jay	Rt. 1, Box 128
	Johnson Sawmill	Topsy	Star Rt., Spavinaw
	I.D. McCrary Sawmill	Twin Oaks	Rt. 1, Colcord
	Tyer Sawmill	Kansas	Rt. 4, Siloam Springs, Ark.
	Woods Sawmill	Leach	Locust Grove

13

Table 19. *Small sawmills*[1] (Continued)

County	Firm	Plant	
		Location	Address[2]
Haskell	Levi Bray Sawmill	Enterprise	Rt. 4, Stigler
	Ford Sawmill	Lequire	Rt. 1, McCurtain
	Floyd Lane Sawmill	McCurtain	
	Harvey Nunn Sawmill	McCurtain	Rt. 1
	Williams Lumber Co.	McCurtain	Box 209
Hughes	Wetumka Hardwood Mill	Wetumka	516 S. Canadian
Latimer	Cook Sawmill	Red Oak	Panola
	Joe Luna Sawmill	Red Oak	Star Rt.
	Moody Sawmill	Red Oak	Star Rt.
Le Flore	Sam Bennett Sawmill	Wister	Rt. 1, Box 193
	Noel Bethel Sawmill	Wister	Rt. 1
	Garner Lumber Co.	Wister	Box 206
	Montgomery Sawmill	Heavener	Star Rt.
	Ollar Sawmill	Howe	Rt. 1, Box 78
	L.G. Thornburg Sawmill	Honobia	Box 141, Wister
McCurtain	O.J. Allen	Oak Hill	Rt. 2, Box 180 Broken Bow
	G.D. Brewer Sawmill[3]	Eagletown	Rt. 1, DeQueen,Ark.
	Covington Sawmill	Broken Bow	Box 345
	Davis Bros. Sawmill	Eagletown	Star Rt.
	Hamil Sawmill	Garvin	Rt. 2, Haworth
	Willy Hill Sawmill	Haworth	Box 111
	Honeywell Sawmill	Valliant	Star Rt.
	Huffman Wood Preserving,Inc.[3]	Broken Bow	Drawer A
	Jess Jenkens Tie Mill	America	Rt. 1, Haworth
	Lowell Morphew Sawmill	Eagletown	Rt. 3, Gillham,Ark.
	Porton Tie Mill	Moon	Rt. 2, Idabel
	Smith Lumber Co.	Valliant	Star Rt.
	Sullivan-Miller Tie Mill	Tom	Rt. 1
	Tunnell Bros. Tie Mill	America	Rt. 1, Arkinda,Ark.
	Ralph Webb Sawmill	Watson	Star Rt.
Mayes	L.D. Nutter Sawmill	Iron Post	Star Rt. S.;Locust Grove
Murray	Ralph Thomasson, Jr.	Davis	Rt. 1
Muskogee	Marion Parker	Webbers Falls	Rt. 2
	Leon Thompson Sawmill	Ft. Gibson	Rt. 1
Nowata	C. & H. Lumber Co.	Nowata	Box 461

Table 19. *Small sawmills*[1] (Continued)

| County | Firm | Plant | |
		Location	Address[2]
Okmulgee	Beaver Handle Mill	Dewar	Box 347
	Millwork Supply	Morris	Box K
	Whitlock Sawmill	Henryetta	Rt. 3, Box 46
Osage	Bowers Lumber Co.	Fairfax	Box 523
Ottawa	Anderson Sawmill	Afton	Box 210
	Bennett Lumber Co.	Wyandotte	Rt. 1, Miami
	Burleson Sawmill	Wyandotte	Rt. 1, Seneca,Mo.
	Prater and Son	Wyandotte	Rt. 1, Box 364,Seneca, Mo.
Payne	John Bingerman	Yale	Rt. 1
Pittsburg	Bill Johnston	Indianola	Rt. 1
	Pedigo Sawmill	Bache	Rt. 4, Box 610, McAlester
	Vaughn Sawmill	Hartshorne	Rt. 1, Mt. Vernon, Texas
Pottawatomie	Jess Currie	Tecumseh	
Pushmataha	Ray Belcher Sawmill	Stanley	Box 597, Antlers
	Birchfield Lumber Co.[3]	Antlers	Rt. 2
	C & W Lumber Co., Pushmataha Mill	Antlers	Rt. 2
	Dunham Tie Mill	Antlers	Rt. 1
	U.S. Heath Sawmill	Finley	Box 166
	Henslee Lumber Sales	Antlers	Box 516
	Andrew Jackson Tie Mill	Antlers	Rt. 2
	A.L. Jackson Jr. Lumber Mill	Nashoba	Star Rt., Snow
Rogers	Brasier Sawmill	Claremore	Rt. 2
Seminole	Melvin Mullins	Sasaskwa	Rt. 1, Konawa
Sequoyah	Johnson & Johnson Sawmill	Sallisaw	411 W. Creek St.
Wagoner	Ed Gilbert Sawmill	Coweta	
	Leonard Holloway Sawmill	Wagoner	410 N. Gertrude
Washington	Kenneth Gougler	Talala	Rt. 1

[1]Output of less than 3 million board feet.
[2]Office address specified when different from plant location.
[3]Residues chipped and sold to pulpmills.

15

Table 20. *Wood pulpmills*

County	Firm	Location
McCurtain	Weyerhaeuser Co., Craig Plant	Broken Bow
	Weyerhaeuser Co., Valliant Operation	Valliant
Mayes	Georgia-Pacific, Gypsum Division	Pryor

Table 21. *Veneer plant*

County	Firm	Plant Location	Address
McCurtain	Weyerhaeuser Co.[1]	Wright City	Box 269

[1]Residues chipped and sold to pulpmills.

Table 22. *Post, pole, and piling plants*

County	Firm	Plant Location	Address[1]
Adair	Reese Tie Co.	Stilwell	Box 467
Choctaw	Fry Forest Products Division	Hugo	Box 458
McCurtain	Huffman Wood Preserving, Inc.	Broken Bow	Drawer A
	Mixon Bros. Wood Preserving Co.	Idabel	Box 307
	Stouter Lumber Co.	Valliant	Box 307

[1]Office address specified when different from plant location.

Table 23. *Miscellaneous plants*

County	Firm	Plant Location	Address[1]
Delaware	Beaver Handle Co.[2]	Spavinaw	Star Rt.
	Cherokee Forest Industries[3]	Bull Hollow	Rt. 2, Jay
Le Flore	Heavener Charcoal Co.[3]	Heavener	Box 146
	Taliaina Charcoal Co.[3]	Talihina	Rt. 1
Pontotoc	Shur-Plug Co.[4]	Oil Center	Box 853,Ada
Pushmataha	Clayton Charcoal Co.[3]	Clayton	Rt. A, Box 23-1A

[1]Office address specified when different from plant location.
[2] Handlestock.
[3] Charcoal.
[4] Excelsior.

16

Bertelson, Daniel F.

   1973. Oklahoma forest industries, 1972. South. For.
       Exp. Stn., New Orleans, La. 16 p. (USDA
       For. Serv. Resour. Bull. SO-45)

Oklahoma forests supplied more than 64 million cubic feet
of roundwood to forest industries in 1972. Saw logs and
pulpwood were the major products, accounting for 79 percent of the harvest. A total of 118 primary wood-using
plants were in operation.

Lightning Source UK Ltd.
Milton Keynes UK
UKHW011816281118
333023UK00010B/688/P